THE COMPLETE POEMS

THE COMPLETE POEMS

WILLIAM EMPSON

Edited with Introduction and Notes by
JOHN HAFFENDEN

ALLEN LANE
THE PENGUIN PRESS

ALLEN LANE
THE PENGUIN PRESS

Published by the Penguin Group
Penguin Books Ltd, 27 Wrights Lane, London w8 5TZ, England
Penguin Putnam Inc., 375 Hudson Street, New York, New York 10014, USA
Penguin Books Australia Ltd, Ringwood, Victoria, Australia
Penguin Books Canada Ltd, 10 Alcorn Avenue, Toronto, Ontario, Canada M4V 3B2
Penguin Books (NZ) Ltd, Private Bag 102902, NSMC, Auckland, New Zealand

Penguin Books Ltd, Registered Offices: Harmondsworth, Middlesex, England

First published 2000
10 9 8 7 6 5 4 3 2 1

Set in 10/13.5 pt PostScript Adobe Sabon
Typeset by Rowland Phototypesetting Ltd, Bury St Edmunds, Suffolk
Printed in Great Britain by The Bath Press, Bath

A CIP catalogue record for this book is available from the British Library

ISBN 0-713-99287-5

CONTENTS

ABBREVIATIONS

A	*Argufying: Essays on Literature and Culture* (London, 1987)
CP	*Collected Poems* (London, 1955)
CP 1949	*The Collected Poems of William Empson* (New York, 1949)
DNB	*Dictionary of National Biography* (London, 1917–22)
E in G	*Empson in Granta* (Tunbridge Wells, 1993)
Gill	Roma Gill (ed.), *William Empson: The Man and His Work* (London, 1974)
GS	*The Gathering Storm* (London, 1940)
Harvard	*Morris Gray Poetry Reading* (Harvard University, 1973)
Listen	*William Empson Reading Selected Poems* (Hull, 1959)
Morelli	Angelo Morelli, *La Poesia di William Empson* (Catania, 1959)
Norris	Christopher Norris, *William Empson and the Philosophy of Literary Criticism* (London, 1978)
OED	*Oxford English Dictionary*
P	*Poems* (London, 1935)
P 1934	*Poems* (Tokyo, 1934)
Pastoral	*Some Versions of Pastoral* (London, 1935; 1966)
PL	John Milton, *Paradise Lost*
RB	*The Royal Beasts and Other Works* (London, 1986)
Ricks	Christopher Ricks, 'Empson's Poetry', in Gill
SCW	*The Structure of Complex Words* (London, 1951; 3rd edn., 1977)
ST	*Seven Types of Ambiguity* (1930; 3rd edn., 1953)
TGA	Philip and Averil Gardner, *The God Approached* (London, 1978)
Thurley	Geoffrey Thurley, *The Ironic Harvest* (London, 1974)
Ulysses	James Joyce, *Ulysses* (1922), ed. Jeri Johnson (Oxford, 1993)
Wain	John Wain, *Professing Poetry* (London, 1977)
WE	William Empson

Willis   J. H. Willis, Jr., 'The Poetry of William Empson' (Columbia University, New York, 1967)

For full bibliographical information, see Bibliography. Where possible, the Penguin edition is cited.

INTRODUCTION

And, if I publish a volume of verse with notes longer than the text, as I want to do, will that be a prose work or a verse one? I ask out of curiosity, you understand . . .
                              – William Empson in a letter to his publisher, *c.* 1930

I can always offer some verses if that's any good.
                              – letter to Michael Roberts, 7 December 1932

The first or only reason for writing verse is to clear your own mind and fix your own feelings, and for this purpose it would be stupid to borrow from people, and for this purpose you 'wanted' to be as concentrated as possible. Mr Eliot said somewhere that a poet ought to practice his art at least once a week, and some years ago I was able to ask the oracle whether he thought this really necessary, a question on which much seemed to hang. After brooding and avoiding traffic for a while he answered with the full weight of his impressiveness, and I am sure without irony, that he had been thinking of someone else when he wrote that, and in such a case as my own the great effort of the poet must be to write as little as possible.   – 'A London Letter', *Poetry* 49 (January 1937)

A profound enough criticism could extract an entire cultural history from a simple lyric.   – 'The Verbal Analysis', *Kenyon Review* 12 (1950)

. . . dark texts need notes
       – John Donne, 'To the Countess of Bedford' ('You have refined me'), l. 11

William Empson became known to the literary world as the precocious author of *Seven Types of Ambiguity* (1930), which he began drafting in his fourth year as an undergraduate (his final year, as things turned out) and published at the age of twenty-four. But he had started as a playwright and poet some time before he ever wrote a serious word of criticism. Indeed, in 1929 his chief ambition was to publish a volume of poetry.

As his publisher arranged things, however, his first collection of poems appeared only in 1935, nearly six years after he was made to quit Cambridge.

He had been publishing poems in Cambridge periodicals, especially in the *Cambridge Review* and in *Experiment* (a progressive literary magazine which he co-edited) since June 1927, and his prominence as a poet received its national annunciation with the appearance of *Cambridge Poetry 1929*, published by Leonard and Virginia Woolf at the Hogarth Press. A sampler of pieces by twenty-three Cambridge undergraduates, the Hogarth Press volume gathered together work by Julian Bell, Ronald Bottrall, Richard Eberhart, John Lehmann, Michael Redgrave, James Reeves, Hugh Sykes Davies, Basil Wright and, not forgetting the only woman to be represented in the anthology, E. E. Phare – later better known as the literary scholar Elsie Duncan-Jones. In terms of proportional representation, the three student editors of the volume – Christopher 'Kit' Saltmarshe, John Davenport, Basil Wright – recognized that Empson and T. H. White deserved the largest share, with six poems each. Accordingly, of Empson's fairly modest published output – just twenty poems by the end of 1928 – they generously reprinted nearly a third: 'Part of Mandevil's Travels', 'To an Old Lady', 'Villanelle', 'Letter' (later called 'Letter II'), 'Legal Fiction' and 'Arachne'.

Empson was singled out for praise in a review by F. R. Leavis:

He is an original poet who has studied the right poets (the right ones for him) in the right way. His poems have a tough intellectual content (his interest in the ideas and the sciences, and his way of using his erudition, remind us of Donne – safely), and they evince an intense preoccupation with technique. These characteristics result sometimes in what seems to me an unprofitable obscurity, in faults like those common in the Metaphysicals . . . But Mr Empson commands respect. Three of his poems, *To an Old Lady*, *Villanelle*, and *Arachne*, raise no doubts at all in me: there is a compelling drive behind them.[1]

Three years later, in the 'Epilogue' to his influential *New Bearings in English Poetry* (1932), Leavis was to place Empson's 'remarkable' poems in the choice tradition of John Donne and T. S. Eliot:

Mr Empson's poetry is quite unlike Mr Eliot's, but without the creative stir and the reorientation produced by Mr Eliot it would not have been written . . . he has clearly learnt a great deal from Donne. And his debt to Donne is at the same time a debt to Mr Eliot . . . Mr Empson's importance is that he is a very intelligent man with an intense interest, not only in emotions and words, but also in ideas and the sciences, and that he has acquired enough mastery of technique to write poetry in which all this is apparent . . .

But it will not do to let this reference to Donne imply a misleading account of Mr Empson. He is very original: not only his ideas but his attitude towards them and his treatment of them are modern. The wit for which his poetry is remarkable is modern, and highly characteristic . . . all Mr Empson's poems are worth attention. He is often difficult, and sometimes, I think, unjustifiably so; but his verse always has a rich and strongly characteristic life, for he is as intensely interested in his technique as in his ideas.[2]

Perhaps that encomium does not really say all that much; in truth, it says just one thing two or three times: that Empson was strong on both ideas and technique (though Leavis presents no analytical detail to show quite what he meant). Yet Leavis says it with warm conviction; and the Leavis *imprimatur* was worth having in 1932, even though *New Bearings* goes on to give many more pages of enthusiastic description to the work of Ronald Bottrall. (In 1950, Leavis would assert that both Empson and Bottrall had failed 'to develop, or to develop satisfactorily'.)[3] But there is no doubt that Leavis felt sincerely enthusiastic for Empson's poetry in the early years, and acknowledged its brilliant originality – whatever the influences the young poet had absorbed. He began to cite Empson's poetry in his classes.[4] He was just as enthusiastic – at the beginning of the 1930s – about Empson's prose (*Seven Types of Ambiguity*), which he saluted on a number of occasions – as in 'Criticism of the Year' (1931), where he praised the volume as 'the most important critical book of the year . . . one of the most important . . . in the language; written by a first-class mind'.[5] In a 1931 letter outlining his then prospective book *New Bearings* to Ian Parsons (Empson's friend and publisher at Chatto & Windus), Leavis choicely wound up with congratulations for publishing Empson's 'magnificent' book and with the candid hope that his own volume would presently be listed alongside it: 'It's a book that I confess (I'm afraid this is not modest) I should like to be in company with.'[6]

In 1929 the buzz of interest in Empson's poetry extended beyond the school of English at Cambridge. Even Ludwig Wittgenstein, who had returned that autumn, was tipped off about Empson – or had perhaps met him, there seems to be no way of knowing for sure – and was eager to learn about his poetry. In a later year Leavis was to tell a story that seems to have been meant to emphasize what he called 'something like an antipathy of temperament' between himself and Wittgenstein (whose interest in English literature 'had remained rudimentary,' Leavis alleged). Yet this anecdote assuredly redounds to the credit both of Wittgenstein and of Empson:

He said to me once (it must have been soon after his return to Cambridge): 'Do you know a man called Empson?' I replied: 'No, but I've just come on him in *Cambridge Poetry 1929*, which I've reviewed for *The Cambridge Review*.' 'Is he any good?' 'It's surprising,' I said, 'but there are six poems of his in the book, and they are all poems [*sic*] and very distinctive.' 'What are they like?' asked Wittgenstein. I replied that there was little point in my describing them, since he didn't know enough about English poetry. 'If you like them,' he said, 'you can describe them.' So I started: 'You know Donne?' No, he didn't know Donne. I had been going to say that Empson, I had heard, had come up from Winchester with an award in mathematics and for his Second Part had gone over to English [Empson had in fact taken Part II of the mathematical Tripos before going over to English] and, working for the Tripos, had read closely Donne's *Songs and Sonnets*, which was a set text. Baulked, I made a few lame observations about the nature of the conceit, and gave up. 'I should like to see his poems,' said Wittgenstein. 'You can,' I answered; 'I'll bring you the book.' 'I'll come round to yours,' he said. He did soon after, and went to the point at once: 'Where's that anthology? Read me his best poem.' The book was handy; opening it, I said, with 'Legal Fictions' ['Legal Fiction'] before my eyes: 'I don't know whether this is his best poem, but it will do.' When I had read it, Wittgenstein said, 'Explain it!' So I began to do so, taking the first line first. 'Oh! I understand that,' he interrupted, and, looking over my arm at the text, 'But what does this mean?' He pointed two or three lines on. At the third or fourth interruption of the same kind I shut the book, and said, 'I'm not playing.' 'It's perfectly plain that you don't understand the poem in the least,' he said. 'Give me the book.' I complied, and sure enough, without any difficulty, he went through the poem, explaining the analogical structure that I should have explained myself, if he had allowed me.[7]

If Leavis momentarily collapsed when Wittgenstein put him through his critical paces, there is a further fine irony underlying the fact that Wittgenstein could so readily appreciate Empson's poetry. Earlier, probably in 1926, Empson had reflected on the apathetic contemporary response to what he called 'the closing tautology of Wittgenstein [in his *Tractatus Logico-Philosophicus*]; "Whereof one cannot speak, thereof one must remain silent." The detachment of that phrase from its context is the weakness of our generation. Could not Romeo be written? Were the Songs and Sonets what cannot be said? What philosophy cannot state, art lays open. But philosophy has only just found out that it cannot state, all that we have no art to lay open.'[8] Those words perhaps mark the moment at which Empson determined to write poetry. Imaginative literature has to encompass more than the philosophers dream of expounding; a complex art must reach the parts that conceptual thought falls short of. In that sense, Empson's poetry stands for an attempt to meet the challenge of Wittgenstein's aphorism, the philosopher's ruling on the limits of language. (Three years later, Empson was to quote Wittgenstein in 'This Last Pain'.)

As for the repute Empson enjoyed among his contemporaries, Richard Eberhart, who would remember Empson as 'brisk, quick-moving, florid', may have been somewhat sentimental when he eulogized Empson's poetry in 1944; but this bouquet still says a great deal for the state of Empson's standing in 1929:

In Cambridge everybody talked about Empson's poetry. His poems challenged the mind, seemed to defy the understanding; they amused and they enchanted; and even then they afforded a kind of parlor game, whiling away lively hours of puzzlement at many a dinner party. The shock and impact of this new kind of poetry were so considerable that people at that time had no way to measure its contemporary or timeless value. They were amazed by it. Eliot was already enthroned. The 'Oxford Group' [W. H. Auden and his Oxford contemporaries] had not yet got fully under way. And Cambridge was buzzing with activity.[9]

To be sure, Eberhart was not cheering the poems merely with the benefit of hindsight: in the early 1930s he had very enthusiastically corresponded with I. A. Richards on the subject of Empson's most exacting – least enticing? – poem, 'Bacchus'.[10] Other contemporaries have borne witness to the astonishment of Empson's poetry: Jacob Bronowski, John Davenport, Humphrey Jennings, John Marks, E. E. Phare, Kathleen Raine, Kit Salt-marshe, Hugh Sykes Davies, Edward M. Wilson, Basil Wright.

The year 1929 also saw Empson's first solo appearance. *Letter IV*, which was written by May and published that autumn by W. Heffer &

Sons of Cambridge, was the first in a series of booklets – 'single, hitherto unpublished poems by Cambridge poets of established reputation' – called *Songs for Sixpence*, edited by Bronowski and J. M. Reeves.[11] The print run was a generous 1,000 copies; and while it is not known how many were sold, a quantity were definitely pulped in the 1930s. But Empson may well have felt relieved that the poem attracted so little attention at the time, for he presently became dissatisfied with it and decided to reissue it only in 1949, in revised form, for the American edition of *Collected Poems*.

Empson had gone up to Magdalene College with a scholarship to study mathematics, and he gained a First in Part 1 of the Mathematical Tripos in 1926 (this achievement, it has to be said, was not in the least exceptional: the majority of mathematicians got Firsts at this initial stage); and he was one of a mathematical threesome to receive a college prize: 'books to the amount of £2.12s.6d'.[12] All the same, during his second year Empson committed more and more of his energies to literature, including the writing of his own poetry, where he exerted vast intellectual initiative, though the process did not involve any wholesale transference of interest from the sciences to the arts.

He broke surface first as a playwright. On 4 March 1926, he wrote in his journal: 'I have had in mind, for a week or so . . . the idea of a play'; but that entry goes on, disappointingly, 'I shall take the easier step of describing it here' – though it does include a full outline of the play he would never write.[13] He essayed several dramatic pieces, and one of the unfinished efforts features lengthy passages of dull blank verse, but he brought only a single short play to a satisfactory completion. *Three Stories*, a one-act melodrama topped and tailed in verse, was performed on 5 February 1927 in a season of 'Nursery' productions at the Amateur Dramatic Company. It was part of a triple bill, though only one of the other plays was an original piece: *Dragons: A Symbolic Play in Three Scenes* was by Basil Wright – the future film director, Governor of the British Film Institute and President of the International Association of Documentary Film Producers – who acted alongside Humphrey Jennings personating 'A Man in a Bowler Hat'. But *Dragons* was not much liked, so *Granta* was happy to report:

Mr Empson of Magdalene's play, *Three Stories*, was quite another thing. He had achieved an almost complete mastery of his Oedipus complex, and used it for very intelligent purposes. A theme of the rebellion of an idealist young man led from excellent Shavian comedy to plain, honest melodrama, and was framed within romantic scenes in heroic couplets and contrasted with a scientific disquisition fathered on to Dracula. It sounds very complicated, but, if we interpreted it rightly, it amounted to something like this: that the ethical problems of life differ from the scientific problems only if one conceives them romantically, and even then, the apparent romanticism achieved, they become scientific again. The last line of the play, in which the hero, having slain his business-like ogre, is compelled to proclaim himself a 'managing young man', we thought a triumph.[14]

A witty skit, *Three Stories* (which is now available in the post-humous *The Royal Beasts and Other Works*) delighted a young and like-minded audience, and it was salted with enough social criticism to satisfy a deep need in Empson's carelessly (consistently) rebellious nature. As *Granta* opined with pomp: 'It was pleasant to find a new dramatist experimenting with a complicated technique, with one, too, which seems admirably suited for the production of a modern play; and perhaps still more so to find him at the same time not unskilful of dialogue and repartée, to keep the audience attentive and bemused.' It also gave Empson an opportunity to besport himself in public, and it marked the début of a Winchester contemporary, Parsons, who took the part of the young ideal-ist, Gerald. The *Cambridge Review* observed: 'Mr Empson gave a very competent performance as the novelist in his own play. Mr I. M. Parsons shows distinct promise as a juvenile.'[15] *Granta* wholly agreed: '*Three Stories* also pleased us, because it proved to the world the merits of Mr I. M. Parsons as an actor' – though it omitted (perhaps tellingly?) to offer any opinion of Empson's turn on the boards.

It was probably as a direct result of writing and acting in his own play that Empson felt ready and willing to review theatre and cinema for both *Granta* and the *Cambridge Review*: starting with the movies in 1927, he was reviewing both by 1928–9. In addition, for the session 1927–8, when he was still in his third year as a student of mathematics, he was the 'Skipper' (or literary editor) of *Granta*. His output was quite remarkable, a tribute to his powers of assimilation and quick-witted responsiveness. James Jensen has provided this helpful précis:

The bulk of Empson's contributions to *Granta* consists of about sixty book reviews of widely varying interest and length – only a few run to much more than five

hundred words and a good many are only one or two sentences long. In addition
... there are about fifteen movie and drama reviews, also uneven in character,
but occasionally quite provocative, plus some clowning and riddling material of
no particular consequence. Though books of literary or esthetic value predominate
among those he reviewed, they by no means constitute a monopoly; the list includes
such titles as *British Farmers in Denmark*, *Sex Relations without Marriage*, and
ABC of Adler's Psychology. Indeed, extended examples of close verbal analysis,
at least in the serious way we now think of it, would be an absurd anomaly in the
hearty, gamesome pages of *Granta*. The atmosphere of the magazine is highly
precocious but unstable, wavering between formidable gravity and witty or impu-
dent lightheartedness which does not always escape silliness, nor always try to.
Yet nearly all Empson's reviews exhibit an air of alert knowledgeableness, an easy
habituation to the critical context . . .'[16]

(The total of Empson's book reviews is now reckoned to be seventy.)[17]

The character of the criticism that swiftly emerged, culminating in
Seven Types of Ambiguity, was by no means an accidental achievement,
for Empson had set out what amounted to a programme even during his
second year as an undergraduate. The goal of the new criticism, as he
formulated it in his review of Forster's *Aspects of the Novel* in October
1927, was to make an 'attempt, successful or not, to include all possible
attitudes, to turn upon a given situation every tool, however irrelevant
or disconnected, of the contemporary mind'.[18] In due course, the same
manifesto would apply in all respects to his own criticism and poetry: for
Empson, those tools included the lessons of Marx, J. G. Frazer and Freud.

Empson may be said to have come of age as a critic within six
months of drafting that ambitious and intoxicating brief, with a review
of *Blue Trousers*, the classic novel by Lady Murasaki (in a translation by
Arthur Waley). The rich comedy of the fiction, and its 'architectural
qualities', excited him to rehearse its success with a virtuoso critical
performance: it is by far the fullest book review he wrote at Cambridge,
a cascade of ideas and insights. The piece is fully Empsonian, and is worth
quoting at some length, from the helter-skelter inventory of the second
paragraph (which is a single 300-word sentence) right to the end:

The critic, in giving way to boundless superlatives, might seem to be led astray by
accidental qualities; by the romantic fantasy gratification in a hero of matchless
beauty, charm which (we are told) had never been seen in the world before, rich

with imperial scents (the privilege of his house), master of palaces four hundred yards square, of vast gardens adorned with forgotten cunning, and pathways of finely powdered jade, of numberless concubines, each of whom, when going on a journey as unostentatiously as possible, takes twenty coaches (and the number of outriders is extremely small), of uncounted mysterious and guilty secrets, such as the paternity of the Emperor, and of endless details of polite versifying; by the Wordsworthian air of simple truth, with which all this Vathek detail is carried off, and without which, even from so courtly an authoress, it would be too crude to please; by the curiosity continually excited as to what exactly the customs were, and how they worked, the shock of being reminded that these witty and cultivated women were entirely secluded, and the difficulty of finding out, for instance, Genji's methods of governing, or the nature of the Labour troubles so often hinted at; by the mingled sense of our civilization's inferiority in these extremes of delicacy, and of the practical Westerners' superiority to so 'quaint' and flower-chattering a people, from which we are startled back into fantasy identification with Genji when (filling an awkward pause) he embarks on a discourse about plum-blossom or novel-writing, or the limitations of their social love-poetry, making criticisms that seem so naturally one's own; indeed, by the modernity of the conversation of all the characters; one is continually thinking 'Waley *must* have made that up,' and then finding it woven incidentally into the next paragraph.

It may be such factors as these, superimposed on the original novel, that make it such a continual delight to read, and so liable to be rated too highly. But there are in this volume three or four comedies of situation; between Genji, his new child wife, and his chief concubine (what gross farce it sounds); about Yugiri, the faithful lover, now in domestication; and about the marrying off of Tamakatsura, who was prevented by a sad accident from entering the Emperor's household; in each of these one is dizzy with the subtlety of the writing, with each clause, each placidly given detail, there is a new twist to the dialogue, a different construction is put upon the relations of these always charming people. There is nothing exotic about it, it is what the western novel has done continually, but it is done supremely here.[19]

James Jensen has perceptively remarked:

Perhaps the only reason this is not an even more obvious example of Empsonian analysis is that it is concerned not with the so-called 'accidental qualities' of particular words and phrases in lyric poetry but with these qualities as they are produced by the broader structural components of the novel – setting, characterization, tone. Nonetheless, the basic technique is sufficiently recognizable: within the unity of a single sentence [the first paragraph quoted above] he lists five main sources of the novel's appeal (romantic gratification, Wordsworthian tone, cultural exoticism, tension between superiority and inferiority, sophisticated dialogue), amassing under each source varied but illustrative specimens of response designed to reproduce in concentrated form something of the actual sentient texture of the entire novel.[20]

To borrow Empson's own words from another context, he looks at the novel from enough points of view to make one feel that something in the real world is being considered.

And yet probably the most astonishing thing of all is that Empson had not even started officially to read English literature when he wrote that piece in 1928: he was just a week away from tackling Part II of the Mathematical Tripos (for which the legendary Frank Ramsey, brother of the future Archbishop of Canterbury, was one of his examiners). Perhaps it is not surprising that he got to be only Senior Optime (Upper Second), and not a Wrangler (First).[21] There was no prize that time round.

The next academic session, 1928–9, turned out to be a splendidly busy one for him, the start of a brilliant career. Magdalene allowed him to stay on for a second degree despite the fact that his final result in Maths had fallen short of stardom.[22] His fame as a poet, and Richards's reports of his amazing work on literary ambiguity, must have reassured the Governing Body that they had done well to let him proceed with his studies. He also busied himself with numerous other activities; among them, he found time in March 1929 to take the title role in a three-night run of *The Tragedy of Tragedies: or the Life and Death of Tom Thumb the Great*, by Henry Fielding; this was the first production (with Empson sporting a 'creation of sack-cloth' by no less an artist than Humphrey Jennings) of a group called the Mummers, which was founded by the gangling young Alistair Cooke (the future journalist and world-renowned broadcaster) as the first mixed ('co-ed') dramatic society at Cambridge. *Granta* remarked with a suitably indulgent double edge that *Tom Thumb* 'is a burlesque directed against the heroic tragedies popular in [Fielding's] time. The whole cast recognized the burlesque, Mr Empson particularly its direction. Only those who know Mr Empson, or share his particular sense of the quaint, could enjoy his acting; but his interpretation was by far the most intelligent.'[23]

Despite such distractions, he carried off a 'special distinction' in Part I of the English Tripos (it was an accolade also attained that year by Muriel Bradbrook, future Mistress of Girton College). Not only did Empson win a Magdalene College prize for English, he was unanimously elected on 15 June to a Charles Kingsley Bye-Fellowship, with an emolument of £150, for the year 1929–30.[24] On 20 June he formally subscribed himself, in age-old Latin formula, to the 'sodality' of the college.

Just seven weeks later, however, he was effectively 'sent down' by the Fellows who had just appointed him a junior fellow.[25] The entry in *College Orders and Memoranda 1907–1946* reads: 'It was resolved that William Empson be deprived of his Bye-Fellowship and that his name be at once removed from the College Books.'[26] That stark sentence was signed by A. B. Ramsay (Master) and A. S. Ramsey (President), and then by the seven Fellows in attendance: V. S. Vernon-Jones (Senior Tutor), Talbot Peel, Stephen Gaselee, F. R. Salter, Francis H. H. Clark (Dean), F. McD. F. Turner and F. R. F. Scott (Junior Tutor). The only other official record of Empson's catastrophe is that written up in the Minutes of the Governing Body over two months later, on 7 October, by A. S. Ramsey: 'After an adjournment to the following day and as a result of certain investigations it was resolved nem. con. that Mr. W. Empson's Bye-Fellowship should cease forthwith and his name be removed from the College Books.' Two current Fellows of the College, Richard Luckett and Ronald Hyam, who have pieced together a candid account of the whole débâcle, observe: 'It should be noted that the decision to deprive him of his Fellowship was only "resolved": that is to say, it was *not* an agreed and unanimous decision.'[27] Empson was to have no further direct dealings with Magdalene until the college elected Professor Sir William Empson (as he had become) to an Honorary Fellowship exactly fifty years later, in 1979.

It now seems most strange, as the King of France said of Cordelia, that he who even but now was their best object, the argument of their praise, should commit a thing so monstrous to dismantle so many folds of favour. Precisely what happened that July 1929 has become the stuff of legend, with as many versions as there were gossips to embroider them. But certain facts are patent. Empson had been lodging for a time in a college hostel called Kingsley House, in Chesterton Road, where he seems to have carried on in a free-and-easy, not to say licentious, way; he came and went just as it suited him, and – allegedly – he had even introduced a woman into his room and made love to her there. Upon his election as junior fellow, he was assigned rooms in Magdalene College proper; but even as his bags were about to be carried across the road, a college servant found that Empson had contraceptives in his possession. Empson had been disastrously careless. And yet his inadvertence might not have been particularly damaging in itself except for the fact that the servant gossiped about it to other servants, who in turn noised the news about town. Since a public scandal appeared to be imminent, the Master (who was to take up the high office of Vice-Chancellor the following year) decided to convene an extraordinary meeting of the Governing Body in order to put it down. But the Governing Body, so far from dealing out a token punishment and a deft hushing-up, decided in its collective wisdom to exact the most severe penalty available to it – both to deprive Empson of his Bye-Fellowship and to remove his name from the College books (as the University Statutes empowered it to do, since sexual misconduct was deemed to be a University offence). Even his tutorial file was forthwith destroyed, so that as far as Magdalene was concerned, it should be as if he had never passed their way; they could not rescind his University degree, but in all other respects he was to become a non-person.[28] This ruthless decision meant too that he could no longer reside within the town bounds.

Empson's mock-heroic response to being thrown out of Cambridge was to pen some verses entitled 'Warning to undergraduates', putting to good use the octosyllabic couplets of Samuel Butler's burlesque *Hudibras*. Written within a few weeks of the fell event itself, but first published only after his death, it is testimony to Empson's buoyant generosity of spirit that he could so quickly translate a painfully humiliating setback into a form of 'smilingness' (to borrow Byron's word).

Quite coincidentally, in the very month (June 1929) when he gained his degree, Empson wrote from Magdalene College to offer a collection of 'about twenty poems' for consideration by Parsons, who had recently joined the publishing house of Chatto & Windus. As far as Empson was concerned, his poetry had top priority – for almost as an afterthought he posed the tentative question: 'I was thinking of offering a grammatico-critical essay to the Hogarth called the Seven Types of Ambiguity: you don't do small essays (15,000 words) do you?'[29] It was the first outside news of a study that would presently become a major advance in literary criticism. By the beginning of July he discovered – to his own apparent surprise but to no one's regret – 'Ambiguity is growing on my hands . . .'[30]

In a postcard sent on 2 July, he confidently projected: 'Shall let you have Ambiguity in six weeks or so from now.' In the event, the bulk of the book was delivered to Chatto & Windus by the end of the year, with the remainder following by April 1930. Parsons felt hesitant about the poems – 'it is rather difficult to make a decision on so little work'[31] – but asked to see them in any case; he received the packet on 14 June, along with this modest and beguiling message: 'Most of them you have seen already. There are twenty-three of them. I doubt if I have turned out enough even now (dear me; I mean turned out of the collection, of course, not "output" in a professional sense) (though that would be true too); I should be glad of your advice.' Parsons felt eager to take the critical book ('Your self-generatory style – if I may call it! – seems to me just suited to this kind of analysis'),[32] but not yet the poems; so that towards the end of July he wrote again: 'I am so glad to hear that Ambiguity is progressing so swiftly and satisfactorily, and I am already very anxious to discover your seven varieties . . . Meanwhile I am sending you back with this the MS of the poems you sent us originally.'[33]

Seven Types of Ambiguity was accepted for publication on 13 April 1930 (with an advance of £25, and royalty terms that are magnificent by today's standards: 15% on the first 6,000 copies sold, 20% thereafter); and Parsons duly took an informal lien on the poems: if the criticism performed well, it might help to float the poetry. But subscription sales of Seven Types amounted to only 146 copies by late in 1930, which did not augur well.[34] (Incidentally, so far from sitting back, anxiously or excitedly, to await the reception of his first book, Empson promptly moved on to some of the work that would be collected in his second volume, Some Versions of Pastoral, in 1935: he was teasing out Alice in Wonderland, for instance, by that autumn, as a letter from Parsons of 7 November 1930 indicates: 'Meanwhile I hope you are progressing with "Alice".' Empson's essay 'Alice in Wonderland: The Child as Swain' eventually appeared in Pastoral, 1935.) The reviews of Seven Types were nevertheless resplendent; a new critical star had assuredly arrived, and Leavis once again hailed him in the Cambridge Review: 'His book is the work of a mind that is fully alive in this age, and such a book has a very unusual importance.' Furthermore, remembering how much the poems had fascinated him eighteen months before, Leavis closed with this helpful prompt: 'And, immediately, there is that book of poems which he has given us a right to demand.'[35] Seven Types of Ambiguity brought Empson international fame,

but it did not immediately sell well. It was not until February 1933 that
Parsons asked again about the poems,[36] but being a loyal friend he spoke
of them once more on 24 May 1934: 'What about your essays? . . . And
how about poems?' In the meantime, Empson's reputation was helped by
appearances in other publications, including the much-discussed antho-
logy *New Signatures*, edited by Michael Roberts (1932), which reprinted
five of his poems ('This Last Pain', 'Letter', 'Note on Local Flora', 'Camping
Out' and 'Invitation to Juno').[37]

    Poems, a collection of thirty poems with notes, bound in crimson
cloth and priced at 6s., appeared in an edition of 1,000 copies in May
1935 – just a year after Dylan Thomas's début volume, *18 Poems*. (Empson
received an advance on royalties of £10.) The title-page was decorated
with a hatched drawing of a feathered hat of fashion especially designed
by Parsons's wife, the artist Trekkie Ritchie[38] – who would appear to have
taken inspiration from the single prose poem in the collection, 'Poem
about a Ball in the Nineteenth Century', which opens: 'Feather, feather,
if it was a feather, feathers for fair'. (Six hundred copies were sold by
1940, and the remaining warehouse stock was destroyed by German
bombing raids in 1940 and 1941.)[39] The volume received extensive critical
coverage, much of it favourable, though some of the reviewers felt per-
plexed by the density of the verse, and by the allusive obscurity. It was
really the young Empson's book: even though he was nearly thirty by the
time *Poems* came out, the majority of the works were the product of his
early twenties. Twenty of the poems had been published before 1930
(sixteen date from 1927 and 1928), though the book did contain most of
those that Empson had composed in the early 1930s, including the sceptical
and stoical 'This Last Pain', the deistic 'Doctrinal Point', and his wonderful
declaration of largesse, 'Homage to the British Museum'. (Nine others
published by 1935, including 'Letter IV' and 'Travel Note' – subsequently
retitled 'Four Legs, Two Legs, Three Legs' – were not included.)

    However, almost a year in advance of Empson's first British volume,
fourteen of the early poems were bound in a marbled cover for private
circulation, likewise with the bare title *Poems* (1934), by The Fox &
Daffodil Press, at Kinuta-mura, near Tokyo (where Empson was a univer-
sity teacher from 1931 to 1934). For the poems included in this rare
collection, see Appendix 7. A note written in Japanese and signed by
'Members of the Fox and Daffodil Press' – Tamotsu Sone, Yoshitaka

Sakai and Tsuneo Kitamura (who were presumably among Empson's students at the Tokyo Bunrika Daigaku) – translates as follows:

This collection of poems was printed with the author's approval on the limitation of 100 copies, so as to be distributed among his acquaintances and pupils. Mr Empson will return to England before long, and we shall be very happy if this small volume becomes a good memento of his sojourn in Japan. We are deeply indebted to Mr Shinobu, head of the Kairyudo Publishing Company, for this publication.

In 1936, he received the double accolade of representation in two crucial anthologies: W. B. Yeats selected 'Arachne' for inclusion in *The Oxford Book of Modern Verse*, and Michael Roberts chose no fewer than six poems for *The Faber Book of Modern Verse*.

But Empson had moved on as a poet. Even while teaching in Japan, which he found had a 'clogging effect' on his poetry, he wrote in response to an appreciative letter from his friend Sylvia Townsend Warner, 'It is very pleasant, but not very invigorating, to have you write so generously about my verses: they were mostly done at Cambridge, and aren't like what I want to do now'[40] – albeit that from 1933 to 1939 he would return again and again to the enormous task of constructing his epic-in-little about drink and divinity, the powers of alcohol and the horrors of politics: 'Bacchus'. After three years in London, where he made his way as a freelance writer, and a further two years (1937–9) in China, where he taught with the exiled Peking University in extremely difficult wartime conditions, he came home with sufficient poems – they covered an enormous range of subjects from metaphysics to melancholy, from social climbing to political satire, and from love to loss – for a second volume to be called *The Gathering Storm* (which beat Sir Winston Churchill to that pregnant title).[41]

Having first proposed this book in March 1940 to Chatto & Windus, where Parsons was willing to take it on, Empson presently opted to assign it to Faber & Faber, in particular because T. S. Eliot had expressed admiration for his verse. *The Gathering Storm*, bound in a hue of charcoal and wrapped in a jacket of matt black with lettering blocked out in white, was published on 19 September 1940, in an edition of 1,000 copies at 6s. Eliot's blurb for the jacket of *The Gathering Storm* – though unattributed, there can really be no doubt that it is by Eliot – regaled the reader with this paradoxical praise:

No poet of the younger generation has achieved reputation on a smaller output of verse than William Empson. His first volume made him known as the most brilliantly obscure of modern poets. This, his second volume, should not only increase the admiration of his admirers but bring him a larger public. For there is a remarkable development towards clarity and simplicity, and the expression, at times, of intense feeling.[42]

Nearly 400 copies were sold within the first year, but it took until the close of 1950 for the printing to be quite exhausted.[43] Since it had not proved possible to place *Poems* with an American publisher, Empson trusted (as Parsons later reported) that Eliot's influence in America 'would result in a combined American edition of both books'. In a letter of 1939 to John Hayward, Eliot had exuberantly compared Empson to the poets who made up what literary history has come to think of as the 'Auden generation': 'damned if I don't think Bill has more brain power, as well as more resistance to the ills that flesh is heir to (Shakespeare, as quoted by Mr Sollory) than the rest of 'em poets', adding in a postscript: 'If Empson's poems have not been published in America, Harcourt Brace ought to get a lien on them.'[44]

But during and immediately after the war there were hiccups in the furtherance of the mission to find an American publisher. 'Is there even now a chance of a combined edition of my verse in America?' Empson urged Eliot in February 1946. 'Kathleen Raine tells me that the British Council (in its devious processes) needs an existing text of my verse if it is to be advertised. I am aware that Kathleen's dilemma would not strike an American publisher offhand as a bull point, but I said I would pass it on; and on my own side I think I could reasonably ask not to be out of print for an indefinite future. You on your side might say that without one seriously good new poem you wouldn't consider negotiating a combined edition – or what actually would you say?'[45] In 1946, the Dial Press, New York, agreed to publish a volume combining *Poems* (1935) and *The Gathering Storm*;[46] but a year later, in October 1947, they reported to Faber & Faber that they would be unable to publish the volume for a further two years, and so offered to release the poems. Similarly, James Laughlin IV, publisher of New Directions, who was doing rather well with sales of an American edition of *Seven Types* (1947), hesitated about issuing a selection of the poems.[47] ('I am all for having New Directions do the poems,' Empson was to write on 21 November 1947.) Frustrated by the lack of progress, Empson chose to vent his annoyance directly to Eliot, whom he unjustly blamed for the situation in the USA.[48] In reply, Eliot sought to rebuke Empson, in a letter of 29 April 1948, for sending him 'the most insulting letter which I have ever received' – Empson had written it on 1 April (he appears not to have noticed the date, but in any case he was not fooling) – and proceeded to set the record straight. There had never been any failure of commitment on the part of Faber & Faber, Eliot returned: on the contrary, positive and accountable steps had been taken in the interests of Empson's work.[49] Nonetheless, Empson's ill-judged charge had rallied Eliot: on 8 April, Eliot wrote to Allen Tate: 'And until I can get William Empson's poems published in New York I am not so much interested in anyone else.'[50] By 12 July 1948, when Empson was teaching summer school at Kenyon College, Gambier, Ohio (on leave from his university in China), Empson himself was happy to report to Parsons: 'Allen Tate is lecturing here and has written to an American publisher telling them to do my collected verse . . .'[51] And then Eliot too wrote to Tate, just two weeks later: 'If this reaches you before the summer school has broken up please tell Empson that we have now a firm offer for his poems from Harcourt, Brace and Co. which is what I always wanted, and I hope they may be able to bring the book out early next year.'[52] *The Collected Poems of William Empson* was duly published by Harcourt, Brace on 24 March 1949, in an edition of 2,000 copies.[53] (It brought together the full contents of the British volumes, *Poems* and *The Gathering Storm*, with the addition of 'Letter IV', 'Let it go', 'Thanks for a Wedding Present' and 'Sonnet'.)

Despite running into that sticky patch in their relations, Empson and Eliot remained on good terms; and Eliot never faltered in his goodwill towards Empson's poetry. When the Faber edition of *The Gathering Storm* went out of print in January 1951, it was Eliot who took the initiative in writing to Chatto's to suggest a collected edition (that is, to follow Harcourt Brace's step in putting the two earlier books of poetry into one): 'I think it would be a great pity if Empson's poems ceased to be available,' Eliot exhorted.[54]

The British edition of *Collected Poems* (price 10/6d) was published by Chatto & Windus on 29 September 1955, in an edition of 2,430 copies.

(This edition added to the tally of Empson's collected poetry two later works: a translation of a 'bit' of a Chinese ballad made in China in 1951, 'Chinese Ballad', and the script of a masque for Queen Elizabeth II's visit to Sheffield University in 1954, 'The Birth of Steel'.) Apparently the post-war appetite for Empson's work so far exceeded expectations that Parsons would report to him by January the next year: 'I'm glad to say the book is selling extremely well, nearly 1800 copies already, and orders coming in steadily. I hope you're pleased with the reviews.'[55] (Maybe the publishers should not have been so surprised: Empson's most recent collection of essays, *The Structure of Complex Words*, published in July 1951, had sold 1,350 copies within the first six weeks.) A second impression of the poems (1,250 copies) was issued in 1956, a third (1,000) in 1962; a fourth followed in 1969, a sixth in 1977.[56] In the USA (where a Meridian paperback of *Seven Types*, issued in 1954, had sold between 7,000 and 8,000 copies by October 1959), Harcourt Brace brought out *Collected Poems* in a small-format Harvest paperback, with a print-run of 8,000 copies, in February 1961.[57] In the UK, the volume eventually appeared in paperback under the imprint of the revived Hogarth Press, soon after Empson's death in 1984. The poet and biographer Andrew Motion, during a period as poetry editor at Chatto's, had taken good pains to put Empson's work back into print.

In England, the first person to seek to act on the idea of publishing a paperbound edition had been Charles Monteith, who approached Chatto & Windus in July 1972 with the request that Faber & Faber (where Monteith was then poetry editor) be permitted to issue such a paperback. Exactly a week later, his bid was turned down: Chatto had plans to issue a paperback of their own in due course.[58] It is not at all clear that Faber's attractive offer was ever conveyed to Empson, since he never held himself aloof from the necessity to promote his work in the market-place and would have seen the advantage of being reissued in Faber's outstanding paperback list: he had written to his own publisher in 1954, for example, 'I see the Poetry Book Club has now been started, and am hoping that proofs for my Collected Verse will be coming along soon.'[59] Later, in autumn 1960, he consented to be nominated for the Chair of Poetry at Oxford – 'Auden told me to apply, and is busying himself,' he informed Parsons[60] – though he deferentially withdrew his candidature just as soon as he learned that Robert Graves had also agreed to stand. 'I shall always remember the proposal and wish I had seen it in action,' Empson wrote.[61]

Finally, mention must be made of another kind of publication in which he was reluctantly caught up: the recording of his spoken performance as poet. 'My kind of verse is meant to be read rather than heard,' he stated in 1959, 'and anything which further discouraged printing of such-like stuff would seem to me bad.'[62] He was referring to what he had considered the wretched task of recording his poems for a disc that was to be issued for sale in 1961 – *William Empson Reading Selected Poems* (*Listen* LPV3), produced by George Hartley at the Marvell Press in Hull.[63] The prospect of having his poems evaluated in terms of his personal performance was an unnerving thing to Empson, an essentially shy man who was all too aware that no reader could ever hope to convey, and no listener catch (especially not without simultaneously looking over the words on the page), the compounded meanings of his poetry.[64] He had done a number of broadcasts on the radio in earlier years, notably during his period of service as BBC Chinese Editor during the war, but he had no experience of reciting his poems over the air. Yet one of the first engagements he undertook after returning from his second stint in the Far East (1947–52) was to read his poems, with introduction and commentary, for the BBC Third Programme. *The Poems of William Empson*, produced by Peter Duval Smith, went out on 15 December 1952. It was a splendid show, as polished as could be, but one of the most noticeable features about it is that Empson seems to put on two voices, one for the poetry and the other for the crisply executed prose. Few listeners would have thought to attribute this curious (and only marginally distracting) behaviour – or trick – to the effect of alcohol, but that is precisely how Empson tried to explain the matter in a draft of a letter to a listener who had commented on the oral peculiarities of the production:

I too hated the poetry-reading voice, and refused even to hear the records played through to test them, let alone hear the whole thing on the air (the verse and the prose were recorded at separate sittings, with the difference of sound mechanically exaggerated). One of my friends, whose judgement I respect, felt the same; but otherwise people of very varying tastes really seemed to like it. The producer was keen to get the verse reading lush, and lushed me up for it on rum and Guinness mixed; not that I blame him, I too thought that was probably the best method. It was certainly better than the trial version sober.

My first conviction is that the reader should throw himself into the verse, and not do it with 'reserved' English 'good taste'; that kind of falsity you will at least agree I avoided. I thought what I did was simply 'ham', like a provincial Shakespeare actor a hundred years ago, not a bad thing. What I chiefly wanted to get rid of, from the first version, was a 'snooty' effect, which the producer called 'proprietary' – 'you talk as if you didn't want them to know what it means'. I am not clear what class issue you raise by 'Fortnum and Mason'; it suggests trying to sound genteel, whereas my wife says she and some other people thought I sounded as if I was trying to sound low class. I wasn't conscious of either, but to make one's voice a bit less classy isn't a bad thing in itself; in Yorkshire, where I come from, to throw in a bit more dialect on suitable occasions is a recognized form of politeness for many people, not at all condescending. What is chiefly needed, for this kind of verse, is a style of speaking which allows you to emphasize a number of words close together, and this can't be done in classy colloquial English, where it is a positive mannerism to suggest that you are in an inner circle by being deliciously unstressed.

No doubt these problems wouldn't arise if I had a bit more competence at reading . . .

Explanations or extenuations apart, the effect is riveting. Naomi Lewis would justly respond in a contemporary review:

This was a most deliberate and exact performance; yet I have rarely been stirred to so lively an interest by a group of contemporary poems read by its author. Mr Empson keeps for his verse a special and indescribable voice – a metaphysical voice, it might be correct to call it – which is not in the least like the one he uses for his commentary. Yet, if this results in him presenting his love poems in the sardonic tones of a seventeenth-century New England elder directing the trial of a witch, certainly not a word is lost, and for some time after, one loses the taste for any other sort of verse delivery; the ordinary voice seems insipid, less than positive.[65]

In 1959, when he undertook to record his poems for the *Listen* label, he offered every kind of excuse to explain why he deplored his own reading – even (or perhaps especially) the fact that the 'unpuncturable' young producer had managed to put him in a bad mood:

He made me give him two meals and hung around till he could take the night train back to Hessle, refusing to remain in London to edit the disc next day. I was so cross with him that I read the first side in a frightfully snooty voice, murdering the poetry, which I thought I had learned not to do. However I insisted on doing again three poems which it was positively bad taste to have read facetiously, and I daresay the effect will work out tolerably various in tone. He had allowed only just enough time, and much of the reading seemed to me painful to hear played back. But I expect it will do no great harm.[66]

(Empson had a patrician voice, with a slightly sardonic timbre, which there could be no disguising.[67]) Hartley's enterprise was so bravely 'amateurish' that only 100 copies of the first pressing were released, in March 1961, with the consequence that the record instantly became a collector's item. Copies are indeed rare.[68]

John Wain, who knew Empson and whose article 'Ambiguous Gifts: Notes on the Poetry of William Empson, in *Penguin New Writing* (1950), had deftly set the terms for the post-war popularity and influence of Empson's work, was in a strong position to evaluate the nature of the performance; he reviewed it for the *Observer*:

It is more restrained than his performances in a public hall. When Empson reads to a large audience, he allows himself a very wide range of sheer volume, shouting some passages like a Neapolitan stevedore, laryngitically croaking others. When reading to a handful of people in someone's sitting-room after dinner, he adopts a much quieter style, and it is this quiet style that is to be heard here. Not that there are no variations; they are particularly noticeable where there is an abrupt change of subject-matter from poem to poem. For instance, the beautifully tender and gentle 'To an Old Lady' is followed immediately by the most boisterous 'Camping Out': the first describes a stately human ruin, the second the antics of fiercely alive young lovers; the poet's voice takes on an altogether different tone, though the curious angularity of rhythm, so attractive to some and so off-putting to others, is equally present in both.

Buy this record. It is like a gulp of rough, red wine after an evening of sweet, bottled cider-substitute.[69]

(According to Empson himself, when he was introduced to Wain in the 1950s, he hailed him, 'Hello, young man, I'm told you imitate me.' Wain replied, 'Imitate you? Why, I invented you!' – a reply which Empson said 'quite won my heart'. He must have been pleased to be treated to such a display of wit and nerve instead of sycophancy or embarrassment – but his response illustrates his generosity too.)

Even less partisan listeners testified to the force of Empson's readings. John Crowe Ransom, who heard a performance in 1948, reported that Empson's reading of 'Bacchus' carried 'the blazing beauty of fireworks'.[70] Alan Brownjohn has written of the 'considerable impression' Empson made upon him with a reading at the Poetry Society in Oxford in 1953:

At that time his extraordinary reciting voice, which thinned to a hardly less remarkable whisper in his last years, was undiminished in volume: a loud sort of high-pitched drone, or boom, which would sweep down suddenly on the well-known lines and fling them away with a seeming disdain for his own highly-wrought ambiguities. It was a performance of unmistakable power. Empson *meant* his love poems, and charged their recital with surprising passion. For more than one undergraduate listener it was clear on that evening that there might be a modern metaphysical poetry in which wit and emotional intensity balanced and assisted each other.[71]

Likewise, Peter Porter testified:

I heard William Empson read his poems in public on several occasions in the Fifties and Sixties, and recall his performances with the keenest pleasure as among the most exciting poetry readings I have been to. They were also (and I don't want to add to the legend of his eccentricity) most unusual. At later readings, he tended rather like a disc jockey in Tennessee to outweigh the poems (the discs he was playing, so to speak) with linking talk, but there was never any doubt of the emotional commitment of his performances. When he read 'Missing Dates', all elements of over-familiarity and parody fell away; the Movement might never have been. And he charged 'Bacchus' with the emotion of a Shakespearean tragedian at the height of his power: the most difficult poem in the world became a brazenly baroque speech of farewell by a burnt-out over-reacher. I am quite used to poets pulling out all the stops – Empson's readings were something else again. They reinforced a conviction I built up as I got to know his poetry better: that it is among the most deeply felt as well as the most grandly imagined verse put before the public this century.[72]

Just so: for all his reputation as the modern metaphysician, as the poet of witty riddling (or arid intellectualism – mentally fidgeting and scarcely truly feeling – as adverse critics would suggest), what mattered as much as anything to Empson himself was that his poetry was the vehicle of powerful emotion. 'The first or only reason for writing verse', he wrote in 1937, 'is to clear your own mind or fix your own feelings.'[73] In some books he is put down as 'the poet's poet'; yet even his admirers among the poets, whether elders or contemporaries (in addition to Eliot, they ranged from Auden, Edith Sitwell and John Betjeman to Roy Campbell and Dylan Thomas), tended to salute him principally for his intellectual capacities – as did his mentor I. A. Richards. Robert Lowell wrote to Empson in 1958: 'it can't be denied that almost no praise would be too high for your poems. You have the stamina of Donne, yet a far more useful and empirical knowledge of modern science and English metrics. I think you are the most intelligent poet writing in our language and perhaps the best. I put you with Hardy and Graves and Auden and Philip Larkin.'[74] Elsewhere, Lowell hailed him as 'the king of the critics', and spoke with tremendous enthusiasm of the 'intellect' in his poetry, though he also wrote on one occasion, 'Empson's best poems, half a dozen or more, though intellectual are forthright' – presumably implying by the conditional that forthrightness is really the better part of poetry.[75] However, even if Lowell finally came to think of Empson-the-poet as more icon than inspiration, there is little doubt that much of Lowell's own early poetry, in the 1940s, took fire from Empson's.[76] John Berryman, who also revelled in Empson-the-critic, noted with a manner that looks like surprise on the flyleaf of his copy of *Collected Poems* (1949): 'a poetry matter-of-fact, alert, spare; & yet *elegant*', which was similarly a warm tribute to the character of the poetry.[77] Stephen Spender on one occasion wrote to Empson, 'you might not realize what gratitude and admiration I feel not just for your poetry but for the person I feel present in it';[78] and his friend Louis MacNeice put on record his opinion that 'surprisingly', Empson 'is generally a humane and quite often a moving poet'.[79] However, as far as Empson himself was concerned, Alan Brownjohn and Peter Porter would have been *dans le vrai*: the essence of his metaphysical poetry was emotional intensity. He was to speak of this main matter in 1956, in an amicable letter to A. Alvarez. The shock of the candid declaration, the controlled pain, in the final sentence is enough to inspire pity and terror (it is notable too how at the end of the sentence Empson has the manners to mitigate any embarrassment that his declaration might cause Alvarez):

You hinted in the pub after I had read my poems that I was playing to the gallery; which rather amused me, because I suspected you were disillusioned at not finding them esoteric enough. They weren't meant to be at all esoteric. They came from more isolation and suffering than is suited to public performance, but that is well known to be true of most performances, including clowns'.[80]

Empson was alert to the fact that a number of poets in the 1950s (to varying degrees) – most especially Wain and Alvarez – took his work as a model, emulating what they considered to be (as the critic Anthony Hartley was to remark in a review) the non-conformist, cool, scientific and analytical cast of his poems, the distrust of rhetoric and sentiment, and the attempt to convey complicated states of thought and moral meaning.[81] They also admired his skills as a technician: the fact, for example, that he had brought the terza rima and villanelle, as well as ottava rima and rime royal, to such a high level of accomplishment in contemporary English poetry. Since Empson recognized that the poetry of his admirers was borrowing or mimicking the accidentals but not the driving emotion of his work – the 'isolation and suffering' – he was to observe in a BBC broadcast on 'Literary Opinion' in 1954:

Recently the magazine *Encounter* had a joke poem, with very funny notes, meaning that Empson is a bad influence on young poets. Do you know, I rather often said this myself to young poets, both in England and America, who have kindly shown me their stuff. It seems to me that Empson's own poetry, though it comes from a rather limited and narrow talent anyhow, isn't nearly as narrow as what turns up when somebody imitates it; that does feel very narrow, and I wouldn't be sensible if I didn't agree.[82]

What some readers had not discerned beneath the stimulating (and exacting) metaphorical diversity, the heady tropes and the syntactical density of his poems was the fact that – for all the Eliotic appearance of the poetic materials (and some of the mannerisms) – Empson had entered the lists of poetry with a challenge to the dominant modernist mode or 'tradition' set up by Eliot. He would explain in 1974:

Most of the poets who were starting to write around 1930 hoped to learn methods and techniques from the French Symbolists and the seventeenth-century English Metaphysicals; but Mallarmé would consider it vulgar to argue, if ever confronted with argufying in poetry, whereas Donne did it all the time. The young Eliot was large-minded and courageous, I still think, to write so much (in his prose) recommending Donne, a poet so very remote from his own practice, and I suppose he was merely being charitable or reassuring to his disciples when he told them they needn't actually bother about the arguments.

I imitated Donne only, which made me appear pointlessly gawky or half undressed; but I still think that the two methods cannot be combined – you cannot write both like Mallarmé and like Donne at the same time, or anyway not energetically enough.[83]

Though he later acknowledged that 'argufying' was 'perhaps a tiresomely playful word', nevertheless he believed it served to convey the idea that poetry can properly and powerfully represent 'the kind of arguing we do in ordinary life . . . a not specially dignified sort of arguing'.[84] At any rate, the term validly differentiated his own kind of poetry – conducting a debate, urging a position, driven by the imperative of reason – against the Symbolist–Imagist axis: the modernist doctrine of writing in pictures, of commending the visual above the conceptual, image over verb.

In the 1952 BBC broadcast, Empson began:

First of all I want to say something about the whole idea of my sort of poetry – why anybody should want it. There was a general movement in the 1920s for the revival of what is called Metaphysical Poetry, mainly the style of John Donne, and mine I think was more direct imitation than anybody else's. This kind of poetry works by what are called 'conceits', following out a comparison ruthlessly or carrying an argument to an absurd extreme, without paying any attention to the demands of 'romantic' poetry, that the theme has to be exalted by the stock suggestions of the 'images' presented, or the words used, so that a general poetical tone is somehow in the atmosphere. I think many people found my verse difficult, when it first came out between the two wars, merely because they did not realize they were expected to hold on to the argument so firmly and with such indifference to other kinds of poetical effect.

However when I talk in this placid way about the technique it must seem a bit pointless. There is no reason after all why anyone should like the result. The object of the style, in my mind and I believe in Donne's mind, is to convey a mental state of great tension, in which conflicting impulses have no longer any barriers between them and therefore the strangeness of the world is felt very acutely.

In the typescript there followed a notable sentence, specifically adverting to Graves's early theory of poetry as therapeutic, which was omitted from the programme as broadcast: 'Some theories of poetry maintain that poetry ought first to state a conflict and then resolve it, but this kind of poetry seems to thrive on *un*-resolved and direct conflict, which is only resolved if at all by giving this sense of the strangeness of the world.' It is perhaps in that gap between conflict and closure that both the strength and the difficulty of Empson's poetry lie, since the intricate problem does not always yield up the limpid solution. The poet Craig Raine has correctly adjudged, 'Eliot's obscurity is radically different in kind from that of Donne whose only real follower in recent times has been William Empson'; all the same, Raine goes on to complain, Empson's poetry suffers from a problem to which he applies the term 'the undistributed middle . . . – the reader doesn't get it'.[85] But that may well come down to the same thing: it is the creative paradox of Empson's poetry that the poet's struggle with an 'unresolved conflict' can seem to the reader like an 'undistributed middle'. If Empson knew the answers, it is certain to say, he would not have written the riddles. However, even if it is sometimes the case, as Raine would argue, that local obscurities of lexis, allusion or syntax get in the way of full comprehension, there is no question but that Empson himself insisted upon the importance of structure. Robin Skelton, reporting on a personal chat, wrote in 1956: 'William Empson has said that in writing poetry he is looking for manipulatable wholes.'[86] While one might beg leave to doubt whether the term 'manipulatable' was Empson's own, the point is still well made.

The other persistent difficulty of Empson's poetry, or perhaps principally of the early poetry, is that the areas of learned reference he embraced or negotiated lay far outside the normal order for most poets. Between the 1920s and the early 1930s, the imaginative issues of his poetry were stirred by the human implications of modern science – not just astrophysics ('The World's End', 'Camping Out', 'Letter I', 'Earth has Shrunk in the Wash'), but equally biology ('Invitation to Juno'), botany ('Value is in Activity' and 'China'), chemistry ('Villanelle', 'Bacchus', 'Missing Dates'), entomology ('The Ants'), geometry ('Letter V'), evolutionism ('Plenum and Vacuum'), anthropology ('Homage to the British Museum'), theories of time ('Dissatisfaction with Metaphysics'); the list could go on. A poet abreast of his age, he devoured the literature of the new science. In a letter to a Chinese acquaintance written in 1947 (at a time when he had virtually stopped writing his poetry), he looked back with wonder:

The point where I most disagree with you is about science. I should have thought that the present age had very little to boast about in any form of imaginative work except the scientific one, and it is obvious that a physicist like Einstein or Eddington [Sir Arthur Eddington, Plumian Professor of Astronomy in the University of Cambridge] is making superb uses of the imagination. A critic who cuts himself off from the only fertile part of the contemporary mind is I think unlikely to understand what good work feels like when it is new, and as far as my own work is concerned anyway I am sure I have always found the world-picture of the scientists much more stimulating and useable than that of any 'literary influence'. In any case it seems to me trivial to say that scientific thought isn't real thought; it only suggests a quarrel between different faculties in a university about which should get more money and better buildings. For that matter all the good philosophy in the last fifty years has been influenced very strongly by modern physics, so by your own account poetry ought to be influenced too, but only as the lady's-maid who is not given the clothes till the fashion for them is out of date.[87]

But this is not to say that his poems are *about* science; as Lewis Wolpert has remarked: 'Camping Out' is not really about astrophysics.[88] The peculiar strength of Empson's poetry derives from the scope and ingenuity of his analogizing imagination. Monroe K. Spears, who has written on the subject of 'Cosmology and the Writer', states that 'The World's End' 'is one of the few successful poems about Relativity, contrasting its cosmos with the Miltonic and with extravagant Romantic imagery', which is fair enough. Yet 'The World's End' is the only poem by Empson in which the science is both topic and trope, both tenor and vehicle. Spears also suggests: ' "To an Old Lady" may well be the only good poem based on astronomy (more or less modern in this case), and specifically on the possibility of space flight to another inhabited planet of the solar system (it would have to be specifically Mars).'[89] But that reflection goes to show that Spears is not quite keeping his mind on the poem: whereas Empson is majestically figurative, positing his mother as out of this world, spiritually and socially at a far remove, Spears takes a literal view – albeit that he covers himself with the phrase 'based on'. But Mum is not a metaphor. (T. R. Henn, who incidentally had been one of Empson's examiners for the English Tripos in 1929, in an article on 'Science and Poetry' in 1961, specifically and mistakenly identified the 'old lady' as the moon.[90]) As for space flight, the real point is the very idea of it; and in many of Empson's works the idea of it is integrity and independence: it represents a bid for freedom from authority and institutionalism. The important question that Empson confronts in his poetry is this: is the imagination equal to the challenge, the moral imposition, of the new science?

Empson's apprehension of the place of the sciences in the modern world charged his poetry (according to his friend Kathleen Raine) with distressing questions about the way in which man tries 'to impose order on fields of knowledge and experience so contradictory as to threaten the mind that contains them with disorder – the compulsion, as Empson writes, to "learn a style from a despair" '.[91] The imagination he brought to the late 1920s 'had to adjust itself to a new scientific world-view at once alarming and inspiring,' Raine recalled. Feeling that any enormous shifts in scientific knowledge of the physical world radically challenge received ethics, Empson treated the conflict in a spirit of painful perplexity. Like E. M. Forster when he worried that 'the post-war world of the '20s would not add up into sense',[92] he took to his troubled heart the contradictions of his age. He wrote in an early article, for instance,

The scientific view of truth . . . is that the mind, otherwise passive, collects propositions about the external world; the application of scientific ideas to poetry is interesting because it reduces that idea of truth . . . to a self contradiction.
    And yet one must not accept such a contradiction as final . . .[93]

It is precisely for that reason that he disparaged the simple-mindedness of anyone who presumed to make up a synthesis out of radically opposed accounts of the world. His impatience with facile thinking is evident, for instance, in a review of C. E. Playne's *The Pre-War Mind in Britain* (1928): 'She has the "scientific" mind; she is fond, for instance, of repeating two opposite things earnestly, in the hope of implying a synthesis which combines them . . .'[94] He made just the same protest in another early review (1927): 'It is a fallacy that men of great abilities can produce what Mr Eliot calls a "synthesis" simply by explaining their mental habits; they must do it by producing a work of art.'[95] That distinction between 'mental habits' and imaginative creativity he knew to be vital for his own poetry; it is small wonder that he later felt exasperated by certain critics who judged his own metaphysical poetry to be over-intellectualized. The big issue, in poetry as in life, was that science does not readily or necessarily accommodate itself to human culture, ideas or ethical structures: 'life involves maintaining oneself between contradictions that can't be solved by analysis', as he famously said in his notes to 'Bacchus'.

If several of the early poems address vexed moral issues in terms of scientific lore, Empson also claimed that in his later poetry – the poems first collected in *The Gathering Storm* – he was just as much of a political poet. His overtly political poetry can be seen to begin as early as the satirical 'Part of Mandevil's Travels' in 1928. He is a political poet both in the general sense – his range of subjects encompasses the nature of aggression and warfare, dreams and despair, courage and fear, duty and desire, communication, and death – and in the particular sense, since he writes with deep commitment of national endurance and survival ('China') and of his faith in the political and spiritual destiny of the Chinese peoples he has learned to respect ('Autumn on Nan-Yueh').

Empson never made very high claims for his poetry – he once called it 'too specialized'[96] – but his best poems (he remarked in an interview) are 'complicated in the way that life really is'.[97] As Geoffrey Hill has written, Empson's poetry and his *Seven Types* are 'essentially pragmatic'; and Hill pinpointed this connection: 'Empson's interest in both poetry and criticism is fixated on the perennial problems of conduct and belief.'[98] John Fuller has also maintained: 'Empson *is* in fact a poet of vision, where the only true vision is a question of discovering what man's position in the world really is.'[99]

Text

The basis for this edition is *Collected Poems* (1955; corrected impression, 1956), which incorporated *Poems* (1935), *The Gathering Storm*, 'Letter IV', 'Let it go', 'Thanks for a Wedding Present', 'Sonnet', 'Chinese Ballad' and 'The Birth of Steel'. Since Empson had more than one opportunity to revise or repair the copy of that final collection (as he thought it), there are relatively few contentious problems with the text. Equally, however, Empson would suffer mistakes to creep into each new edition: he told Chatto & Windus in October 1951, for example:

As to the verse, I have done a page of corrections of the Harcourt Brace [edition], and suggest that you post it to them after using it yourself. I am sorry to be such a nuisance about correcting proofs, but my eye regularly slides over mistakes when I am reading my own stuff (in the H. B. case I never saw proofs at all anyway). I have an idea that there are some other mistakes which I told them but can't now find, though I have looked carefully ... The American mistakes are extras.[100]

All the same, he did not take very kindly to being advised to correct his often complicated syntax – 'I asked [John] Hayward to tell me of misprints, and he sent me a list of my bad grammar, which I have firmly ignored,' he wrote in 1956[101] – so an editor is bound to tread lightly when amending this text.

The poems have been collated with all printings, including periodical appearances and the 1977 Chatto & Windus impression, which caught a few errors in the 1955 printing.[102] Poems are arranged in chronological order, so far as it can be determined from all internal and external evidence (diaries and letters, and stylistic indications, as well as – in most cases – dates of first publication). Substantial variants of wording in published versions are recorded in the Notes – together with selected accidentals, including punctuation where it might affect meaning. A few autograph drafts of some of the early poems survive in the Empson Papers at the Houghton Library, but they have not yet been collated or given reference numbers, and so cannot be located in order of composition; however, some of the more interesting variants are cited in the Notes (though in a sequence which does not stand for a progressive order). Unless otherwise indicated, all quotations in the Notes derive from documents in the Empson Papers, Houghton Library, Harvard University.

Six poems which Empson published in Cambridge periodicals between May 1928 and November 1929 but which he never reprinted (we cannot know if he judged them to be inferior to other early poems, for he may have overlooked them) – 'Une Brioche pour Cerbère', 'New World Bistres', 'Laus Melpomines', 'Insomnia', 'Essay' and 'UFA Nightmare' – are included in this edition. But two pieces which are obviously slighter are placed in an appendix: a fragment beginning 'Moaning inadequately' (first published in *The Royal Beasts*), and a squib with an august title, 'Newly Discovered War Poems', which filled out a page of light verse in *Granta*.

At an uncertain date between 1929 and 1931, Empson submitted versions of some of his early poems – including 'Earth has Shrunk in the Wash', 'Homage to the British Museum' ('Hymn to the B. M.'), 'Letter I' (then called 'Letter II'), 'Letter III', 'Note on Local Flora' and 'This Last Pain' (both of which were as yet untitled) – for possible use in an anthology of contemporary verse that Brian Howard (who is now best known as the original of Anthony Blanche in Evelyn Waugh's *Brideshead Revisited*) proposed to edit. Howard duly notified Empson that his contribution had been accepted, but sent him no word at all when the project subsequently fell through. In a number of letters to George Rylands (a friend of Howard's), Empson attempted to chase Howard for further information about the fate of his poems – principally because, as he told Rylands in an undated letter from Tokyo: 'I can't remember whether there really were any I haven't kept copies of . . . If you see him, or hear of his address, I should be grateful if you would try to make him disgorge them. There is no hurry about it, except that I suppose the probability of his losing them varies as the time.' Empson never did recover them, and in due course he clearly forgot which poems he had submitted. I have traced to the School Library of Eton College the sheaf of typescript that Howard had so carelessly kept; it included the only copies of three poems which were never published in Empson's lifetime: 'I remember to have wept', 'To Charlotte Haldane' and 'The Extasie' (first published in the *London Review of Books*, 17 August 1989).

Looking to the beginning of his career as poet, we do not know exactly when Empson started writing, nor how many poems he wrote in the years before the period of his high productivity at Cambridge in the late 1920s – let alone which ones. But at least we know he was attempting verse at the latest by 29 June 1920, when he was thirteen, because that was the date on which he jotted the first poem in the present volume, the verses beginning 'Mother, saying Anne good night', into the autograph book of a preparatory school contemporary, J. A. Simson. In the autumn of that year he moved on to Winchester College, where we know that he wrote a number of poems; though it is not at all certain that any of them have survived. Charles Madge, who knew Empson in the 1930s (when Madge was married for a while to Kathleen Raine), reported in 1956 in a review of *Collected Poems* his belief that some of the early poems in the volume had been written while Empson was still a schoolboy at Winchester. In turn, Martin Dodsworth, in 1963, relayed Madge's putative information with the cautionary comment: 'While this is quite possible, it must be said that there is no evidence for it one way or the other.'[103] Six years later, Empson remarked to a newspaper journalist: 'Dodsworth got his facts wrong in his article in *the Review*. I wrote none of the *Collected Poems* at Winchester. I was cheek by jowl with [John] Sparrow there who was editing the *Devotions* [by John Donne] at the time, but I didn't dream of writing anything remotely like that. I definitely was not bitten by Donne until Cambridge and it became clear I wanted to write argumentative poetry.'[104] Further testimony comes in the form of a letter from Empson to J. H. Willis, Jr., who put the direct question in 1964. 'I had written some poems before going to Cambridge,' Empson at last conceded, 'but feel sure that I destroyed them all.'[105] Those two statements, five years apart, are by no means contradictory, since the latter simply declares that he had indeed written some poems before 1925, while the former says equally frankly that none of the pre-Cambridge poems were included in *Collected Poems*. Still, two lines of Empson's schoolboy output have survived for the delectation of posterity. It seems that in an attempt to rag the histrionic lessons in Divinity given by Dr Montague Rendall ('Monty'), the showy Headmaster of Winchester, Empson once designed a little cardboard puppet show of the story of Jonah, which he rendered in verses of his own. This couplet was held in mind for more than sixty years by the eminent agricultural economist Dr Colin Clark:

> Useful gourd to shelter my head
> Without this gourd I would soon be dead.

Clark acted as the barker, attracting audiences to watch Empson's performance.[106]

Sad to say, the only other verses which could be by Empson are those published as 'Four Epigrams' (see Appendix 5) in the *Wykehamist* (27 May 1925); but – to put the case a bit more warmly – it is possible that Empson did write them. On the other hand, it has to be admitted that the attribution was in a later year denied by his college contemporary, Ian Parsons; effectively denied too by a number of his other contemporaries – John Sparrow, Sir William Hayter, Lord Wilberforce – all of whom told Sir Jeremy Morse in 1989 that they did not think of him as a poet at Winchester. 'He was my junior prefect in Sixth that year, and I think, though of course one can't be sure at this remote time, that I should have known if he was sending poems to the Wykehamist,' wrote Hayter.[107] However, since one of the 'epigrams' was printed with the curiously doubtful title, 'Decoration (?)' – and the little poem in question really does read like the early Empson (compare 'Part of Mandevil's Travels' or 'Letter II'), though with a touch of William Carlos Williams about it – might we be justified in the suspicion that perhaps Empson did not offer them for publication, but that they were appropriated and put into print without his permission – albeit the editor had some difficulty in making out Empson's handwriting? Intriguing thoughts aside, it is notable that the epigram 'Night' makes use of an unusual kenning with reference to the stars, 'many-fingered' (presumably after the classical epithet for the dawn, 'rosy-fingered'), which Empson was to use in 'Letter II' – 'Crossing and doubling, many-fingered, hounded, / Those desperate stars' (ll. 17–18). Similarly, 'Dogma' opens with an allusion to Jesus Christ's walking on the water (John 6: 19; Matthew 14: 25) which features also in line 22 of 'Bacchus'. And finally, is it purely by coincidence that 'Decoration (?)' is a meditation on the set of a toy theatre?

Since Empson's death, a number of poems have come to light among the papers left in his study, all of which help to give us a better sense of the chronology of his career as poet – and to determine when he stopped writing poetry. Written between the late 1920s and the late 1940s, they include 'Warning to undergraduates', his wounded and yet witty response to being ejected from Magdalene College, and a frankly autobiographical exercise which fitly closes the 'Letter' series of poems: 'Letter VI' was written to commemorate the marriage of his Cambridge friend Desmond Lee on 23 March 1935. Other efforts unpublished by Empson include lengthy portions (amounting to about forty pages) of an untitled and incomplete play, mostly in prose but with some verse, about the strange internecine intrigues of a King and Queen, their Son and his dying brother, which do not warrant publication in a collected edition of the poems. However, to satisfy the reader's curiosity in the unknown quantity, here is a sample of the verse:

Q. Dear boy, you will listen to me. Something's happened.
   You aren't going to be difficult, and talk, are you?
   It's only, you see, I'm anxious about your brother.
   The doctor didn't seem to hold out hope.
   No, he may get better, it isn't certain at all.
   If you have to be king you will behave yourself,
   You won't say pert silly things, and talk,
   You aren't going to come clattering into our sorrow,

And have to be coaxed, and given answers to?
You are too young, aren't you, you do so, it would be out of place,
We don't want to listen to you now, you can't
Not be hushed by much older and wiser mourning.
If it comes to the worst, we can rely on you,
You are going to be good, and try and be helpful, aren't you
And take an intelligent interest in being king.
S. You needn't worry, mother, once I'm caught
I shall be interested. I shall have intrigues.
I shall go poking about with counsellors.
This will be a menace to the state, and so will that.
Of course I shall be a perfectly good fussy king.
I shall be so wise, so proud, so farseeing,
Work so hard, be such a ghastly nuisance,
I shall be killed, young, pleased with myself.
What did you think? Did you take me for any stronger?

(A further passage is quoted in the note to lines 5–6 of 'Rebuke for a dropped brick'.)

At the tail end of his career, Empson was to delight in telling Ricks, in January 1975: 'It occurs to me that I have just been composing some poetry, which you might like to hear about.' This supposedly new composition consisted of a handful of lines for Kyd's *The Spanish Tragedy* which he felt were required in order to prove his long-held belief that the play had been severely censored in early productions. 'It would be a hit produced with that tiny addition. O.K.,' he waggishly proclaimed.[108] He would repeat the trick a year later for Marlowe's *Doctor Faustus*, for which he made up an equally passable 10-line passage (though neither piece belongs to his own style as poet).[109]

But to come more exactly to the end of his work in poetry, he was to tell Christopher Norris and David Wilson in an interview: 'I wrote several [poems] in Peking under the communists but I don't think I printed any ... I don't feel I'm cut off from it. I might hope to get back.'[110] Certainly, the villanelle in this volume beginning 'The ages change' was written 'under the communists' in the sense that it dates from the late 1940s, though it probably predates the actual inauguration of the People's Republic of China on 1 October 1949. Furthermore, Philip Hobsbaum, who worked on a doctorate under Empson's supervision between 1959 and 1962, has reported: 'He always said he was writing but that the poems were no good because he wasn't old enough. Writing poetry was like taking baths, he said: necessary only for the young and the old. Middle-aged gents exempt . . . Well, middle-aged or not, Empson always maintained that he was writing and said that it was lyrical stuff like the verse of Swinburne. He used to talk a good deal about "the singing line" and said that was what was missing from a lot of modern poetry.'[111] If some of the poems written 'under the communists' were lost or thrown away, only one further poem has been preserved which fits the terms of reference as recounted by Hobsbaum; Empson almost certainly began to draft it at the time of the advent of the Chinese Communists in the later part of 1948, and it is even possible that he continued to work on it as late as the 1950s and 1960s. It is assuredly a homage to Swinburne since it borrows and brilliantly sustains the form and style of Swinburne's 'Dolores'; and, running to 200 lines (in 25 stanzas), it is also the second longest poem he ever wrote. But above all it is a homage to his wife. Some sense of the subject-matter of 'The Wife is Praised' may be derived from a letter that Empson wrote to his friend Tambimuttu (1915–83, Ceylonese poet, editor of *Poetry London*, 1939–47) in March 1948: 'Don't you think it is time someone wrote a long didactic poem in terza rima telling people what to do in bed? Verse about the world situation was all right in the thirties but does seem now to strike rather a chill. A new battle for freedom to print highminded advice about sex would strike something a bit warmer, wouldn't it?'[112] (Evidently, in the event, Swinburne's formal scheme turned out to be more accommodating than terza rima.) Unfortunately, however, Empson's executors have decided that this poem may not be published at this time: they take the view that it is an unfinished 'private' poem; that it is not of the same quality as the published poetry; that Empson could have published it during his lifetime if he had so wished; and that its posthumous publication would not enhance his reputation. For my part, I consider it a wonderfully accomplished, ingenious and witty manifesto; and I believe it complements and contextualizes many other writings by Empson, most notably his essays on James Joyce. I think it appropriate also to extend to it an observation that Empson himself made in a review of the uncollected verse of a fellow poet he greatly admired: 'Even in the minor works of Dylan Thomas, a glittering or searching detail is always liable to crop up; besides, his major poems are hard to plumb, but the ideas get repeated, so that a weaker but simpler use of one of them may turn out a great help.'[113] Empson felt wholly averse to keeping any literary remains 'under wraps' (as he put it in the same review); and he further claimed in a related context, 'I stubbornly won't hide anything.'[114] Notwithstanding, it must be said that his Estate has been faced with a genuine dilemma (since Empson did not apparently try to publish the poem, and did not leave testamentary directions about it) and has acted in good faith.

Annotation

Empson was all in favour of good bibliography and textual criticism; avid for annotation. He was positively insistent upon its being done, and done thoroughly. John Livingston Lowes's revelatory enquiry into Coleridge's sources, *The Road to Xanadu* (1927), was one of his favourite critical texts of the 1920s; by the 1930s he was anatomizing with considerable sympathy Richard Bentley's notorious edition, *Milton's Paradise Lost* (1732), for an essay ('Milton and Bentley') to be included in *Some Versions of Pastoral*; and even at the end of his career at Sheffield University he worked long and hard on a controversial redaction of Coleridge's 'The Rime of the Ancient Mariner' for his edition of *Coleridge's Verse: A Selection* (co-edited with David Pirie, 1972). After Empson was ejected from Magdalene College, Julian Trevelyan, in his role as secretary of the free-thinking discussion group known as the Heretics, invited him – perhaps as a gesture of defiance to authority – to return to Cambridge in order to give a paper on a subject of his choice. Empson responded, after very little hesitation:

It now occurs to me that I could read a paper . . . about whether poems ought to be annotated, whether it is important, and why it is hard. If you want a bright caption I suggest 'Sphinx, or the future of exegesis'; and I can do that as soon as you want it. If it is too short for a paper (it is too long for a life) I could give examples from the Bentley edition of Milton, and the answers to Bentley, which I have been getting very excited about (not because any of them are any good, of course, but they raise the crucial questions, and the answers by contemporaries are sometimes illuminating).

Myself, of course, I am in favour of being chatty and explaining everything, but that is undergraduate of me. Once you begin to parley with the reasons for the impossibility of explanations you are whirled o'er the backside of the world far off.[115]

This must have been written in the autumn of 1929, and it was almost certainly at that time that he put together an engaging essay on the subject, posthumously published as 'Obscurity and Annotation', which urges the proposition that authors really ought to write notes on their own poetry.

Poets, on the face of it, have either got to be easier or to write their own notes; readers have either got to take more trouble over reading or cease to regard notes as pretentious and a sign of bad poetry . . .

Certainly some notes may be pedantic, and some impertinent, but the idea that all are likely to be (that one should look harshly on them at first sight) is unwise at all times, and particularly unwise just now. For it seems important that both parties should try to be tolerant on the matter; there is a genuine crux about notes giving information because the notion of general knowledge has changed . . . It really ought to be possible to write simple, goodhumoured, illuminating and long notes to one's own poems without annoying the reader. I quite see that no one has yet written notes to his own poems without looking a fool, but as knowledge becomes increasingly various it will eventually have to be done.[116]

From the very beginning, even when he first offered to Chatto & Windus his collection of 'about twenty poems', with the inducement (or perhaps it was meant as an apology) that few of them would occupy more than a single page of text, he added:

On the other hand I should want to print very full notes; at least as long as the text itself; explaining not only particular references, paraphrasing particularly condensed grammar, and so on, but the point of a poem as a whole, and making any critical remarks that seemed interesting. And I should apologize for notes on such a scale, and say it was more of an impertinence to expect people to puzzle out my verses than to explain them at the end, and I should avoid the Eliot air of intellectual snobbery.[117]

Although a number of Eliot's notes to *The Waste Land*, written in July 1922, were (as Grover Smith has argued) clearly meant for serious purposes[118] – and such crucial notes might seem even to be tendentious, formulating a critical reading of the meaning of Tiresias (l. 218), for example, and of Saint Augustine and the Buddha (l. 309), which students and other readers have been only too grateful to rehearse down the years – others have an air of arch learning or starchy antiquarianism.[119] Eliot came to think so too: in 'The Frontiers of Criticism' (1956) he spoke with regret of 'the remarkable exposition of bogus scholarship' he had found it necessary to compose to meet the commercial expediency of bulking out the poem as a book: and he now felt 'penitent' because his notes had 'stimulated the wrong kind of interest'.[120]

Empson aimed from the start to go in for honest dealing with his readers, a kind of contract: he wanted his readers to have full access to the means and materials of his poetry. Though tricky, his poems were not intended to be tricksy: the poet did not propose to keep any cards up his sleeve. At best, a note was to serve as a function of the poem, and at the least it should be complementary – as well as showing that the poet desired to be positively communicative. The note should act as a 'prose bridge', as Empson put it in a 'Note on Notes' (in *The Gathering Storm*), included below in Appendix 1. (W. H. Auden, in contrast, was to speak of the prose acting as 'an ironic contrast' to the poetry in a work such as *The Orators*, which is again quite different from Empson's approach: Auden thought to give his prose a mode of operation *within* the work rather than as a commentary upon it.)[121] Empson wrote to Parsons in 1929: 'When I am not actually faced with explaining them I feel notes aren't wanted; but I think people would be more easily tempted to read verse if there was plenty of critical writing thrown in, demanding less concentration of attention, and with more literary-critical magazine or novel-reading interest – I know *I* should. And there is a rather portentous air about compact verses without notes, like a seduction without conversation.'[122]

Empson's beguiling position, adopted as early as 1929 (ten years before John Crowe Ransom finally named the new criticism New Criticism), is at odds with what literary historians like to think of as the rule of the Modernist–New Critical aesthetic, the doctrine of semantic autonomy and organic form, which invalidates the author as someone who might originate and critically shape the meaning of a poem. If it is the special nature of many postmodernist texts to be self-commenting, so transgressing the sacred boundary between 'work' and 'commentary', as Steven Connor suggests, Empson was a postmodernist – in that sense only – *avant la lettre*: before anyone thought to pass the law.[123] Naturally,

Empson had much to say over the years in favour of intentionalism, and I have discussed his views at length in the Introduction to *Argufying* (1987); suffice it to say here that he was always insistent, with respect to his own work, that he really desired to mediate between the poetry and his readers. In a letter to his publisher enclosing a list of errata to the American edition of *Collected Poems*, he decided to add a note on the poem 'Flighting for Duck', for one sensible (and so perhaps critically presumptuous) reason: 'The only point of writing a note on this simple and not very good poem is that some reviewer expressed bafflement, and I want to be consistent in trying to remove all trivial grounds for bafflement.'[124]

Reviewers have from time to time expressed outrage at Empson's notes, which they reckon to be either a pre-emptive strike, highjacking the reader's prerogative, or else merely impertinent. In one particular case, the notes were scorned as a bardic betrayal. Basil de Selincourt declared in the *Observer* in 1940: 'Mr Empson gives the game away when he explains that the pleasure we have to expect from modern poetry is the pleasure of the cross-word puzzle. So the happiest reader is the man of practised shrewdness, the man with a flair for every squirrel's cache.'[125] It is an index of Empson's sincerity in this matter that he responded with sheer anger.

Sir,

I confess I am irritated at being treated as a cheat who has by an accident exposed himself. I do not see that this misunderstanding could come from anything but a great and habitual greed for misunderstanding on such points. You are a cheat. I am not.

Yours very sincerely

W. Empson

I open this paper to try to explain the point at issue, because you are unlikely to see it. I do not mind being told that my poetry is bad. It probably is. The question of honour arises when I am told that I am a *cheat* who has 'given the game away'. I do not know how much effort it would take to make you understand that this was dirty talk on your part, but it was dirty talk.[126]

Certainly, as it might appear with hindsight, Empson had done himself few favours by appealing to the reader, in his 'Note on Notes' in *The Gathering Storm*, in terms of the 'crossword puzzle' interest of his kind of poetry (though he had immediately added: 'At the same time, of course, any decent poetry has got more than puzzle interest in it'). Nonetheless, Selincourt's accusation that Empson was thereby a fraud, betraying the Romantic tradition of the mystique of poetry, undoubtedly took unfair advantage of Empson's 'puzzle' metaphor, which was offered as an encouragingly domestic analogy rather than as the nub of his poetry – or the knack of how to read it.

One reasonable (albeit also appropriately riddling) way to look at the notes was provided by Hilary Corke in a review of *Collected Poems* (1955) which indirectly serves to answer Selincourt's complaint:

[Empson] is a critic of great distinction, and one whose poems are as much criticisms of his criticism as his criticisms are in another sense poems about his poems. Indeed, this poet's 'unit of creation' is not the poem alone, but the poem *plus* the note upon it . . . What remains in the mind is not 'a poem' in the old sense (a memorable and musical sequence of language), but an intellectual structure that, something like a sculptural 'mobile', shifts its parts this way and that. The conservative are free to prefer the older sort of poem, but not to condemn Mr Empson's sort for not being what it does not set out to be.[127]

Although Stanley Sultan has argued that Eliot's 'Notes' are really the notes *of*, and not *on*, *The Waste Land*, that useful distinction would be better applied – in the way Corke suggested – to Empson's 'Notes'.[128] His volumes of poetry are, in the best sense, double-voiced.

In a published response to a questionnaire in 1976, Empson was to observe among other matters: 'The deep intention may often be a thing the author himself is doubtful about . . . Obviously you need to think about his "biography", his formative experiences and relation to his public. Why ever not? . . . A real subject may be almost hidden behind a protective cover subject.'[129] The chance to come directly at Empson's sources and personal references, allusions and intertexts, affords us the opportunity also to evaluate the important relation between the poems and the various glosses, large and little, that he supplied to his readers from time to time. In my Notes to the poems in this volume, therefore, following Empson's own glosses on each poem, which are reproduced (in bold) from *Collected Poems* (1955), I have included later observations by Empson, taken from interviews, readings and broadcasts, in the belief that all points of information, even including those by the poet himself, may validly help to establish individual critical interpretations. Empson was given to remarking, for example, that the real subject of a number of his early poems was 'boy being afraid of girl'; and perhaps only a close reckoning with the play of his allusiveness and intertextuality can enable us to comprehend the full scope of that casual observation.

The project to make such interpretative possibilities available to the reader is wholly in accord with Empson's hopes, and his own critical practices. Philip Larkin was to write to Empson's son Jacob, not long after Empson's death: 'although I much admired and respected Empson's verse I frankly could make little of it and had to be content with a sort of dog-like devotion'.[130] Empson himself was conscious that readers found his verse difficult, and was anxious to help. Eight months before he died, when preparations were in hand for the Hogarth Press reissue of *Collected Poems*, he offered to provide additional glosses in the hope of giving his audience a better purchase on the poems. (Eliot, in contrast, declared that he would much prefer to 'abolish' the notes to *The Waste Land*.)[131] So Empson was most disappointed to be told that the publishers did not wish to reset the volume, because of the cost involved:

When I am invited to read some of the poems I always talk a bit about each poem before reading it, giving the circumstances and what not, and would not expect them to swallow the naked text. I offered to write down a shortened version of this, preferably on the opposing page, but was assured that the plan would be impossibly expensive. I hope it may yet be done later on, perhaps soon after I am dead . . .[132]

I hope that the present edition goes some way to meet his wish.

Notes

1 F. R. Leavis, 'Cambridge Poetry', *Cambridge Review* 50 (1 March 1929), 318. I. A. Richards sounded the same cautiously Romantic caveat: 'We may value this adroitness in emotional logic variously, but we cannot deny it. And enough sensibility may be suspected beneath the startling compression of his verses to carry him some distance if he should later find a direction in which to travel. He may be merely bottling a contemporary atmosphere – but he may have an explosive mixture of his own' ('Cambridge Poetry', *Granta* 38 (8 March 1929), 359).

2 F. R. Leavis, *New Bearings in English Poetry* (London: Chatto & Windus, 1932; reissued with 'Retrospect 1950', 1950; Harmondsworth: Penguin, 1963), pp. 159–61.

3 Leavis, *New Bearings*, p. 183. In the 1930s Empson would likewise do a good deal to promote Bottrall's work; as he related in a letter to Bottrall dated 26 January [1937]: 'I have taken Crooked Eclipses to Ian Parsons, who said he hadn't understood or "got on with" your earlier stuff and that he doubted whether he would like this, but would try. I think it would do Chatto's good to have an author. Eliot was very regretful to me about refusing it and suggested Hamish Miles if Chatto refuse. There is a lot of good stuff in it, I thought' (Humanities Research Center, University of Texas at Austin).

In 1952, when Bottrall consulted him about a volume to be entitled *The Palisades*, Empson remarked:

I feel in this volume too that the expressions of despair don't really go all round your character, and that the attempts to put a bit of hope into the last lines of a poem (as in *Prometheus*) tend to feel, though rational a bit strained.

However I have not much leg to complain on when I have myself stopped trying to write verse; your question in *Dead Ends* 'What is the poet to say?' seems pretty searching. (19 October 1952)

4 Randall Pope, letter to E. E. Phare, 3 December 1929: 'The Empson cultus is ubiquitous. Public readings of his poems are given, as you probably know. Leavis mentions him in every lecture. Some poem of his is to be found in nearly everyone's rooms; even in the possession of people who would not dream of reading the work of an ordinary poet' (courtesy of E. E. Duncan-Jones).

5 F. R. Leavis, 'Criticism of the Year', *Bookman* 81 (December 1931), 180.

6 F. R. Leavis, letter to Ian Parsons, 12 August 1931 (Reading). By 1943 Leavis had moderated his praise of *ST*:

A useful exercise for the moderately seasoned student would be to go through W. Empson's *Seven Types of Ambiguity*, or parts of it, discriminating between the profitable and the unprofitable, the valid and the vicious. Empson's extremely mixed and uneven book, offering as it does a good deal of valuable stimulus, serves the better as a warning – a warning against temptation that the analyst whose practice is to be a discipline must resist. It abounds in instances of ingenuity that has taken the bit between its teeth. (*Education and the University: A Sketch for an 'English School'* (London: Chatto & Windus, 1943; 2nd edn., 1949: Cambridge University Press, 1979), p. 71)

7 F. R. Leavis, *The Critic as Anti-Philosopher*, ed. G. Singh (London: Chatto & Windus, 1982), pp. 144–5.

8 WE, undated notebook. Throughout this volume, quotations from Empson

('WE') for which no source is specified refer to unpublished documents in the Empson Papers at the Houghton Library, Harvard University.

9 Richard Eberhart, 'Empson's Poetry', *Accent* 4:4 (Summer 1944); reprinted in *On Poetry and Poets* (Urbana: University of Illinois Press, 1979), pp. 117–18.

10 The Eberhart–Richards correspondence is in the Richards Papers, Old Library, Magdalene College, Cambridge (courtesy of Dr Richard Luckett, Pepys Librarian).

11 Only six pamphlets were eventually issued in the series: the others were by Bell, White, Davenport, Redgrave and Bronowski.

12 *Cambridge University Reporter*, 11 August 1926, p. 1357.

13 For details, see John Haffenden, 'Introduction', in *RB*, p. 70 note 7.

14 'Birth at the A. D. C.', *Granta* 36 (11 February 1927), 238.

15 Guy Naylor, 'A. D. C. Nursery Productions', *Cambridge Review* 48 (1927), 250–51.

16 James Jensen, 'Some Ambiguous Preliminaries: Empson in *The Granta*', *Criticism* 8 (Fall 1966), 350.

17 See Christopher Ricks, 'Empson's *Granta*' [1], *Granta* (Easter Term, 1978).

18 'Forster-Mother', *Granta* (28 October 1927), 61; reprinted in *E in G*, pp. 21–2.

19 'Baby Austin', *Granta* (11 May 1928), 419; *E in G*, pp. 54–5.

20 Jensen, 'Some Ambiguous Preliminaries', p. 360.

21 *Cambridge University Reporter*, 16 June 1928, p. 1134.

22 The Minutes of a meeting of the Governing Body of Magdalene College held on 16 May 1928 record: 'It was agreed that if Mr Empson made application to come into residence for a fourth year continuation of his scholarship should be conditional on his obtaining a first class in the tripos and subsequently taking another Tripos.'

23 A. R. P., 'The Moke from his stall', *Granta* 38 (19 April 1929), 378.

24 *College Orders and Memoranda 1907–1946*, p. 208 (Old Library, Magdalene College).

25 'William Empson was effectually "sent down" in the summer of 1931 [*read* 1929] when his bye fellowship at Magdalene was withheld' (M. C. Bradbrook, 'Lowry's Cambridge', in *Malcolm Lowry: Eighty Years On*, ed. Sue Vice (Basingstoke: Macmillan Press, 1989), pp. 139–40).

26 *College Orders and Memoranda 1907–1946*, p. 210.

27 R. Luckett and R. Hyam, 'Empson and the Engines of Love: The Governing Body Decision of 1929', *Magdalene College Magazine and Record*, n.s. 35 (1990–91), 33–8.

28 The sole item that seems to have escaped the purge is a small card recording the simple details of his scholarships and prizes, terms kept, and dates and results of examinations (Old Library, Magdalene College). See also a letter from Malcolm Lowry in 1940, in Sherrill E. Grace (ed.), *Sursum Corda! The Collected Letters*

of Malcolm Lowry, Vol. 1: *1926–1946* (London: Jonathan Cape, 1995), p. 282; and Anthony Powell, *Journals 1982–1986* (London: Heinemann, 1995), p. 263.

29 WE, letter to Ian Parsons, undated, received 6 June 1929. The source of my account of the correspondence between Empson and Parsons is the archive of Chatto & Windus, which is now located in the Library of the University of Reading.

30 WE, letter to Parsons, received 2 July 1929.

31 Parsons, letter to WE, 6 June 1929. 'Before putting you to the trouble of preparing elaborate notes, etc.,' Parsons added, 'would it not be best for you to send us a typescript of the twenty odd poems, without any notes, which you intend to include.'

32 Parsons, letter to WE, 13 April 1930.

33 Parsons, letter to WE, 24 July 1929.

34 Parsons, letter to WE, 7 November 1930.

35 F. R. Leavis, 'Intelligence and Sensibility', *Cambridge Review* (16 January 1931), 187.

36 Parsons acknowledged that Leavis's praise of the work had done much to promote Empson's interests: ' "Ambiguity" has now established a certain reputation (the Leavis propagand [*sic*] it steadily), though only among the elect, and it might be a good plan to follow up with some poetry pretty soon. How do you feel? . . . It would be nice, anyway, to have a book of your poems on the stocks' (20 February 1933).

37 *New Signatures* (published in February 1932 by Hogarth Press) also blazoned work by eight other poets, including Auden, Bell, C. Day-Lewis, William Plomer and Stephen Spender. Michael Roberts tried in his preface (or, better, manifesto) to promulgate the idea of a new generation or group whose work burned with revolutionary ardour; yet, albeit that Auden, Day-Lewis and Spender were assuredly political, there was really less unanimity of purpose in the collection than Roberts sought to proclaim. Notwithstanding, it was a signal achievement, as J. H. Willis, Jr., has observed: 'The poems in *New Signatures* vigorously announced the arrival of a second generation of modernist poets on the Hogarth list. The press was once more, if briefly, on the leading edge of modern poetry, a position not enjoyed since the Woolfs had hand printed Eliot's *Waste Land* in 1923' (*Leonard and Virginia Woolf as Publishers: The Hogarth Press, 1917–41* (Charlottesville and London: University Press of Virginia, 1992), p. 200).

38 See obituary of Trekkie Parsons (1902–95) by Janet Adam Smith in the *Independent* (29 July 1995); and *The Times* (2 August 1995).

39 By way of contrast, Auden's first volume, *Poems* (1930), also initially 1,000 copies, had sold more than 6,500 in the decade; *Look, Stranger!* (1936) sold out an initial printing of 2,350 copies within two months – but his sales were quite exceptional in the 1930s.

40 WE, letter to Sylvia Townsend Warner, 4 June 1932 (Reading).

41 The volume was dedicated to the memory of Phyllis Chroustchoff, who had

been Empson's friend since his Bloomsbury days in the early 1930s and who had committed suicide in March 1938 (see note to ll. 73–92 of 'Bacchus').

42 Mrs Valerie Eliot kindly informs me (19 September 1996) that she too feels 'pretty sure' the blurb was written by Eliot. The poet and critic Delmore Schwartz, who seems to have twigged for himself the authorship, had taken mischievous delight in writing to Tate in 1941: 'I was reading something the Old Possum had written about Empson's poetry (if that's what it is) and came upon the enchanting phrase, "(Empson's poetry is) brilliantly obscure." In English A, Section 17 [at Harvard University, where Schwartz was teaching with John Berryman], any Freshman who tried that would be failed. The best I could do with the thing was to think that Eliot must have been thinking of a torchlight procession through a cave' (27 January 1941, in *Letters of Delmore Schwartz*, ed. Robert Phillips (Princeton, New Jersey: Ontario Review Press, 1984), p. 107). But Schwartz dismally failed in any case to appreciate Empson's poetry; he wrote to James Laughlin: 'Mudge [Evelyn Leigh Mudge (1879–1962)] is an intelligent poet but boring, like Empson' (*Delmore Schwartz and James Laughlin: Selected Letters*, ed. Robert Phillips (New York and London: W. W. Norton & Co., 1993), p. 132).

43 Information in a letter of 11 February 1966 from Charles Monteith, Faber & Faber Ltd., to J. H. Willis, Jr., cited in Willis, p. 271. By contrast, Auden's *Another Time* (also published by Faber in the UK in 1940), enjoyed print runs which added up in the first seven years to 4,870 copies in the UK and 1,500 copies in the USA. Of *New Year Letter* (1941), Faber printed 4,000 copies in the first five years; Random House printed 2,000 copies of its edition (entitled *The Double Man*), which sold out by 1943 (information from Nicholas Jenkins, 'A Critical Edition of W. H. Auden's *The Double Man*', unpub. Ph.D. thesis, Oxford University, 1996).

44 Quoted in John Hayward, letter to Frank V. Morley ('Tarantula's Special News Service, Letter V', October 1939), King's College Library, Cambridge (JDH/FVM/13).

45 WE, letter to T. S. Eliot, 11 February 1946 (Faber & Faber).

46 Sidney G. Phillips, Dial Press Inc., letters to Chatto & Windus, 18 November 1946, 29 October 1947 (Reading).

47 Parsons, letter to WE, 18 August 1948. New Directions sold 4,169 copies of *ST* between 1947 and October 1954.

48 On 1 April 1948 Empson sent Eliot the following charges, which contained a mass of misapprehensions:

I am extremely annoyed with you for mucking up the chance of an American edition of my verse. I have heard recently from Laughlin that he won't publish me till he has finished publishing Vernon Watkins, and he advises me not to wait. He suggests that I should try Allen Tate at *Henry Holt* or a small publisher *Harry Duncan*, The Cummington Press, Mass. I gave The Gathering Storm to Faber's seven years ago or more (after Chatto's had accepted it) on the definite understanding that you would try to get me an American edition, and so far as I can learn you have positively hampered that ambition so far as you have done anything about it at all. I could well understand your no longer taking any interest in publishing, but if that is all why should you twice prevent Laughlin from printing my verse? Well then, I have to go to America this June for six weeks' lecturing (if they give me a visa), and shall I try to do something about the suggested publishers myself? It would be better if you would take a hand, but if you are not interested in the matter please at least tell me so. (Faber & Faber; courtesy of Mrs Valerie Eliot)

49 Eliot, letter to WE, 29 April 1948 (Houghton Library).
50 Eliot, letter to Allen Tate, 8 April 1948 (Record 24); Princeton University Library.
51 WE, letter to Parsons, 12 July 1948.
52 Eliot, letter to Tate, 26 July 1948 (Record 24); Princeton University Library. Parsons confirmed the bid in a letter to Empson, 13 August 1948:

[Peter] Du Sautoy of Faber's rang me up yesterday to say that when T.S.E. was in America recently he was able to interest Harcourt Brace in your collected Poems (this was after Laughlin had said he couldn't do them yet awhile), and I agreed that Faber's should go ahead and see if they could clinch the deal. I hope it goes through, though I must say these Americans puzzle me – Brace gives up AMBIGUITY because he couldn't sell it and Laughlin takes it on and does extremely well with it; then the next minute Laughlin gets cold feet about the Poems and Brace decides to take them on!

53 According to a letter (17 February 1965) to Willis from Margaret Marshall, Harcourt, Brace and World, Inc., a large portion of this edition was eventually sold, though it probably did not pay for itself (quoted in Willis, p. 400). Lucy Pascocello, Rights and Permissions Manager, Harcourt, Brace & Co., wrote to me (20 October 1995) that the firm's 'Records Retention center was unable to locate any correspondence or information for COLLECTED POEMS or SEVEN TYPES OF AMBIGUITY', so presumably all production files have been destroyed.
54 Eliot, letter to Parsons, 24 January 1951 (Reading). Faber & Faber released their rights to *The Gathering Storm* on 26 September.
55 Parsons, letter to WE, 4 January 1956.
56 Norah Smallwood, Chatto & Windus, letter to Willis, 11 February 1966; cited in Willis, pp. 271–2.
57 Catherine McCarthy, Harcourt, Brace and Co., letter to Peter du Sautoy, Faber & Faber, 5 August 1959 (Reading).
58 Charles Monteith, letter to Smallwood, 14 July 1972; Smallwood to Monteith, 20 July 1972 (Reading). Monteith is famous as the editor who recognized the worth of William Golding's *Lord of the Flies* when several other publishers had turned it down; his catches in the 1960s included Seamus Heaney.

59 WE, letter to Parsons, undated letter [March 1954].

60 WE to Parsons, 6 December 1960.

61 Ibid. On 19 November he had written to Parsons:

Things are about back to where they were when I spoke to you about putting in for the Oxford Professorship, and you expressed a benevolent interest. Afterwards I was told that the election would be next autumn, and then Oxford refused to let a Cambridge man stand; but now they have thrown it open to all comers and the election is next February. I take it the Milton book [*Milton's God*, 1961] won't be out by then, which is probably just as well.

Helen Gardner and Edith [*read* Enid] Starkie are both putting in, and either would make the first Oxford female professor; I am told that sentiments of chivalry are very likely to win the day. Eliot has refused to stand, but I gather that talent-scouts are peering into distant valleys.

I have been getting almost chronic teachers' stomach-ache recently, and would be rather relieved to lose; but as a sport it seems quite entertaining. Let me know if you have any tips for wooing the electorate.

62 WE to Parsons, 14 May 1959.

63 See George Hartley, 'The Domestic School of Publishing', *Guardian*, 20 October 1961; *Selected Letters of Philip Larkin, 1940–1985*, ed. Anthony Thwaite (London: Faber & Faber, 1992), pp. xxvii–xxviii.

64 'The disc-editor in the suburbs of Hull has revived,' Empson wished to reassure Parsons on 29 November 1959, 'and I sent him about 1,200 words for the sleeve of my poems, trying to do notes suitable for hearers with no text (wasting time again I fear); none of it comes straight from the notes in your text.' (His sleeve-notes are reproduced in the Notes.)

65 Naomi Lewis, 'Radio Notes', *New Statesman*, 10 January 1953. John Hayward reported to I. A. Richards on 26 December 1952: 'Bill . . . has done some broadcasting, including an absorbingly interesting & entertaining albeit somewhat eccentric (in a British manner) reading of his own poems. He seemed to me to ruin some & to illuminate others by his declamatory style' (I. A. Richards Collection, Box 46, Old Library, Magdalene College, Cambridge). On another occasion, 'C. W.', in a review of *The Poet Speaks*, no. 7, ed. Peter Orr (Argo RG 517) – a miscellany of poets recorded in association with the British Council and the Poetry Room in the Lamont Library of Harvard University – would dismiss as 'professorial dustiness' Empson's reading of 'Legal Fiction' and 'To an Old Lady' (*Records and Recording*, April 1967).

66 WE to Parsons, 21 April 1959. In 1961, when the disc was eventually issued, Empson commented to Parsons: 'though the reviews struck me as very bad, several people have told me that they liked the record. It came out unproduced, as it was, and if you like that it is O.K. Not bad as a prestige object, somehow, is my impression, but very little good otherwise' (20 November 1961).

67 G. S. Fraser characterizes Empson's mode of utterance in *The Modern Writer and His World* (rev. edn., Harmondsworth: Penguin, 1964, p. 316), basing his observations on close acquaintance: 'everything that he writes, both in prose and in verse, has the run of his speaking voice, an odd, sad, snarly voice, rising now and again to a very high pitch, the Cambridge voice of the late 1920s. This voice, pouncing and drawling, is natural to him and it is an excellent instrument for expressing anger, scorn, and melancholy despair.'

68 'The first pressing was of 100 copies only and was out of pressing by 4th June,' Hartley wrote to Chatto's on 26 November 1961. 'We issued a new pressing at the beginning of this month' (Reading). In December he sent a royalty cheque for £15.

69 John Wain, 'A Gulp of Rough Red Wine', *Observer Weekend Review*, 19 February 1961, p. 26. Compare Julian Trevelyan's account of readings at Cambridge, when Empson was in his twenties: 'By far the most brilliant member of the *Experiment* group was William Empson whom we all, to some degree, worshipped. He rolled his great eyes round and round as he read his poems, looking like the mythical dog with eyes like saucers in Anderson's *Tinderbox* ... He read them in a low drone, accenting suddenly unexpected words to bring out some hidden cross meaning' (*Indigo Days* (London: MacGibbon & Kee, 1957), p. 16).

70 John Crowe Ransom, in 'Coping with the Flood' (anonymous review of *CP 1949*), *Time* 53 (18 April 1949), 44.

71 Alan Brownjohn, 'A Preference for Poetry: Oxford Undergraduate Writing of the Early 1950s', *Yearbook of English Studies* 17 (1987), p. 73.

72 Peter Porter, 'Those Stay Most Haunting' (review of *TGA*), *New Statesman* 96 (22 & 29 December 1978), 880.

73 'A London Letter', *Poetry*, 49 (January 1937), 222.

74 Robert Lowell, letter to WE, 29 January 1958 (Houghton Library). John Betjeman, reviewing *CP* in the *Daily Telegraph* (18 November 1955), remarked: 'William Empson's "Collected Poems" are few and difficult, and to me reluctantly fascinating. I turn to them again and again.' Roy Campbell, in 'William Empson: Contemporary English Poet and Scholar' (an undated article produced during the war by the Central Office of Information and circulated in agreement with the British Council (S.6547)), offered these generous personal remarks:

In the notes you meet Mr Empson himself, and that is a charming experience. You meet a man with a radiant human curiosity and an erudition about non-academical things which counterbalances the very learned scholar who is also inherent in Empson. Little chips and splinters of personal experience and reminiscence fit into the main outlines of his more impersonal and philosophic utterance. You feel that the annotator is intensely human, although the poet may be completely impersonal. But the annotator certainly breaks the ice in introducing you personally to the poet. Empson's poetry is full of doom and disillusion, but for all that there is an uncommon witty gaiety about it . . . In listening to Empson's conversation one gets a key to the amazingly mathematical construction which underlies his poetry, for although his conversation sparkles with all the incidental brilliancies which are the delight of all convivial company, one is even more struck by the architectural design of his reasoning and the control which he exerts over the most abstruse and complicated matters.

75 Ian Hamilton, 'A Conversation with Robert Lowell', *Review* 26 (Summer 1971); reprinted in *Robert Lowell: Interviews and Memoirs*, ed. Jeffrey Meyers (Ann Arbor: The University of Michigan Press, 1988), p. 154. Philip Booth, 'Summers in Castine: Contact Prints, 1955–1965', *Salmagundi* 37 (Spring 1977); reprinted in *Robert Lowell*, ed. Meyers, p. 196. Lowell, 'Digressions from Larkin's 20th-Century Verse', *Encounter* 40:5 (May 1973), 68.

When Ricks approached Lowell to see if he would contribute to the Empson *festschrift* (*William Empson: The Man and His Work*, ed. Roma Gill, 1974), Lowell replied (16 January 1973):

Doing something on William has long defeated me, I'm afraid. No poem comes; a considered critical essay is beyond my uncritical talents; I can't somehow catch hold of him briefly in a paragraph or two. My kind of judgment edged out of reminiscence would be impertinent in a festschrift. I've been through this with my old friend Allen Tate, and finally did nothing. William is one of the few (only?) people I read every scrap of and am never disappointed. I don't want to disappoint by promising a piece I won't write. (courtesy of Christopher Ricks)

76 Robert Fitzgerald speaks of Empson's influence on Lowell's *Lord Weary's Castle* (1946), in 'The Things of the Eye', *Poetry* 132 (May 1978), reprinted in *Robert Lowell: Interviews and Memoirs*, ed. Meyers, p. 225.
77 Berryman's copy in Special Collections, Wilson Library, University of Minnesota. Berryman and Lowell's contemporary Randall Jarrell was to write: 'I have not written about the hard or dry or "classical" tendencies of some modern verse – what Empson and Marianne Moore have in common, for instance . . .' ('The End of the Line', *Nation*, 21 February 1942; reprinted in *Kipling, Auden & Co.: Essays and Reviews 1935–1964* (New York: Farrar, Straus & Giroux, 1980), p. 83).
78 Stephen Spender, letter to WE, 22 June 1961 (Houghton Library).
79 Louis MacNeice, entry for Empson in *The Concise Encyclopedia of English and American Poets and Poetry*, ed. Stephen Spender and Donald Hall (London: Hutchinson & Co., 1963), p. 128. MacNeice concluded with the remark, 'And of his generation he is probably unique in that he has not a trace of self-pity.'
80 WE, letter to A. Alvarez, 29 August 1956 (courtesy of A. Alvarez). Alvarez was to write the following year, in 'A Style from a Despair: William Empson': 'the poetry is an outcome of a peculiarly strong and sensitive feeling for the intellectual

tone of the time. Empson seems to create less out of personal situations than out of an emotional response to something he has already known with his wits, intellectually . . . It is as a stylist of poetry and ideas that, I think, Empson is most important' (*Twentieth Century* 161 (April 1957), 346). Fraser was astute to note of Empson's verse: 'There is a sense of an intricate, witty, and deliberately puzzling form being imposed on a massive and almost unbearable personal unhappiness' (*Contemporary Poets*, ed. James Vinson (London and Basingstoke: Macmillan Press, 1970; 3rd edn., 1980), p. 439). Likewise Graham Hough, in an obituary article on Empson: 'It is often the case that what comes across to most readers as an intricate intellectual puzzle was experienced as a painful knot of feeling' (*London Review of Books*, 21 June–4 July 1984, p. 17). Compare David Perkins's remarks:

Intricate, ironically poised, sardonic, and disintoxicated, Empson's poems appealed because of their intellectual excitement, complexity, and honest bleakness . . .

Yet strong emotion was present. If his style was witty and 'metaphysical' in some ways, his hurt was Hardy's. He accused God for not existing and man for his mortality . . . We may be tempted to justify Empson's style by New Critical considerations, but the state of mind and the psychological struggle embodied in his poems are what fascinates and holds us. (*A History of Modern Poetry: Modernism and After* (Cambridge: Harvard University Press, 1987), pp. 100–101)

81 See Anthony Hartley, 'Poets of the Fifties', *Spectator* 193 (27 August 1954), 260–61.

82 Empson, 'Literary Opinion' (broadcast 20 October 1954). The villanelle-parody was Patric Dickinson's 'At the Villa Nelle', which concludes: 'That the young have taken Empson for a master / One cannot but regard as a disaster' (*Encounter* 3:1 (July 1954), 63). An article entitled 'Double Target', in *The Times Literary Supplement* (10 September 1954), remarked: 'Poets of smaller stature than Mr Eliot or Mr Pound, poets in some ways much more "traditionalist" like Mr Empson or Mr Graves, today provide young poets with more practical working models than the two great experimental masters.' In a letter to *TLS* (1 October 1954), Graves took exception to that observation: 'Let us . . . hope that your reviewer does not envisage Mr Empson and myself as respectively the Waller and Denham of a new Augustan age.' Anthony Thwaite disputed the notion of undue indebtedness in a letter, 'Young Writers', *Encounter* 2:5 (May 1954), 67–8. For an example of direct (and acknowledged) influence, see Wain's 'The Marksman'. Other parodies of Empson include Dylan Thomas's incomplete villanelle, written in 1940, 'Request to Leda: Homage to William Empson', *Horizon* 6:31 (July 1942), 6; D. J. Enright, 'Underneath the Arches', *Essays in Criticism* (October 1956); Richard Kell, 'Empsonium', *London Magazine* 6:10 (October 1959), 55–6; L. E. Sissman, 'Just a Whack at Empson', *the Review* (June 1963), 75; and

Anthony Burgess, *Enderby Outside* (1968; Harmondsworth, Middlesex: Penguin, 1995), pp. 350–51. See also Babette Deutsch, 'Just a Smack at Empson's Epigoni', *Poetry London–New York* 1:3 (Winter 1957), 47. Fraser, in his introduction to *Poetry Now: An Anthology* (London: Faber & Faber, 1956, p. 23), remarked that Empson's epigoni found in him 'a mind of the first order . . . exercising an ironic control over an inner core of passion'. Edwin Muir, in a review of Fraser's collection (*Observer*, 14 October 1956), disputed Fraser's claim with this tribute: 'The passion in Mr Empson's poetry is uncomfortably real, almost raw (*Slowly the poison the whole blood-stream fills*), and the control is difficult. He moves us by the spectacle of a shocking struggle for control. In his followers the control is almost complete; the passion is stifled before it has a chance to be born.' In a review of the anthologies *The Chatto Book of Modern Poetry*, ed. C. Day Lewis and John Lehmann (London: Chatto & Windus, 1956), and *New Lines*, ed. Robert Conquest (London: Macmillan, 1956), Ian Gregor concluded: 'In the austere Pantheon of the new poets two prominent niches are occupied by George Orwell and Mr Empson. The hatred of theoretical systems of the one and the tense verbal exactness of the other have blended to influence a body of poetry which is notably different from that of recent decades' (*Tablet*, 10 November 1956).

    Aspects of Empson's poetry had an influence too on certain poems by Auden, most notably 'Time will say nothing but I told you so' (1940; entitled 'Villanelle' on first publication in 1941); 'Sometimes we see astonishingly clearly' (1949); and 'All that which lies outside our sort of why' (1956): see John Fuller, *W. H. Auden: A Commentary* (London: Faber & Faber, 1998), pp. 400, 409, 467. Sylvia Plath also took lessons from Empson, in her juvenilia of the early 1950s, in poems such as 'To Eva Descending the Stair: A Villanelle': see *Collected Poems*, ed. Ted Hughes (London: Faber & Faber, 1981), p. 303.

83 WE, in *Contemporary Poets*, ed. Vinson, p. 438.

84 WE, 'Argufying in Poetry', *Listener*, 22 August 1963, p. 277; reprinted in *A*, p. 167. In a later year (? 1984) he would put it to his editor in another way, pseudo-dyspeptically: 'Nowadays it is usual for a poet to present himself as a lost bunnyrabbit' (draft letter to Andrew Motion).

85 Craig Raine, *Haydn and the Valve Trumpet* (London and Boston: Faber & Faber, 1990), pp. 122, 192.

86 Robin Skelton, *The Poetic Pattern* (London: Routledge & Kegan Paul, 1956), p. 32. Joseph E. Duncan likewise highlighted the importance to Empson of 'the need for a complex intellectual structure to shape and direct the poem's emotional force' (*The Revival of Metaphysical Poetry: The History of a Style, 1800 to the Present* (Minneapolis: University of Minnesota Press, 1959), p. 196).

87 WE, letter to Qien Xuexi, 7 September 1947 (courtesy of Qien Xuexi). 'The advances of science in our time, though very likely to cause disaster,' Empson was to argue in the 1970s, 'have been so magnificent that I could not wish to have been born earlier; and I estimate that most of the poets worth study who were in

fact born earlier would have felt so if they were alive now' ('*The Ancient Mariner*: An Answer to Robert Penn Warren', in *The Strengths of Shakespeare's Shrew*, ed. John Haffenden (Sheffield: Sheffield Academic Press, 1996), p. 146).

88 Lewis Wolpert in conversation with Haffenden, 23 September 1996; also Wolpert, 'Let There be Enlightenment' (review of *The Faber Book of Science*, ed. John Carey), *Sunday Times Book Review*, 17 September 1995, p. 4.

89 Monroe K. Spears, 'Cosmology and the Writer', *Hudson Review* 47:1 (Spring 1994), 37.

90 T. R. Henn, 'Science and Poetry', *Nature* (5 August 1961), pp. 534–9.

91 Kathleen Raine, 'And Learn a Style from a Despair', *New Statesman & Nation* 50 (5 November 1955).

92 E. M. Forster, *The Hill of Devi and Other Writings*, ed. Elizabeth Heine (London: Edward Arnold, 1983), p. 71.

93 Review of Elizabeth Holmes, *Aspects of Elizabethan Imagery*, in *Criterion*, 9:37 (July 1930), p. 770; reprinted in *Strengths of Shakespeare's Shrew*, p. 68.

94 'Playne but Worthy', *Granta*, 27 April 1928, p. 376; *E in G*, p. 51.

95 'More Barren Leaves' (review of *Proper Studies*, by Aldous Huxley), *Granta*, 18 November 1927, p. 123; *E in G*, p. 28.

96 'William Empson in conversation with Christopher Ricks', *the Review* nos. 6 and 7 (June 1963), 33; see Appendix 2 below.

97 Empson in interview with Christopher Norris and David Wilson (typescript copy kindly supplied by Christopher Norris).

98 Geoffrey Hill, 'A Dream of Reason', *Essays in Criticism* 14:1 (1964), 92, 100.

99 John Fuller, 'An Edifice of Meaning', *Encounter* 45:5 (November 1974), 76. Willis, in an examination of Empson's vocabulary and word usage (in the canon as it stood in 1967), noted that there are seven words used more than thirty times in the poetry: *all* (71 times), *make* (47), *one* (44), *man* (37), *earth* (34), *end* (34), *know* (31): 'Generalizing from such a count, it can be said that Empson's most frequently used words agree with the predominant theme of the poems – a humanistic emphasis upon man's dilemma on earth between the many (all) and the one, his struggles to make, act, or know in a world which causes any such action or knowledge to be difficult if not impossible.' The variety of Empson's other usages leads Willis to this conclusion: 'In spite of his frequently enunciated despair, it is apparent that Empson's practice is to use words expressive of positive action, change, expansion, variety, and multiplicity. He shows his humanistic concerns by concentrating on man's observing, ratiocinative faculties . . . The preponderant terms . . . are essentially optimistic' (Willis, pp. 416–18).

100 WE, letter to Parsons, 12 October 1951. In another, undated letter [1956], listing a few emendations, he casually – alarmingly (or amazingly, if you prefer) – remarked: 'Here are the misprints I can find; I feel sure there were some more, but as I remember they were harmless, in that one could guess what was meant.'

101 WE, letter to Parsons, 9 October 1956.

102 The Hogarth Press edition of 1984, though it included a new short prefatory note by Empson written in 1983, was otherwise a direct reprint of the 1977 edition.

103 Charles Madge, 'Empson Agonistes', *Listen* 2:1 (Summer 1956), 19–22. Julian Trevelyan repeated the idea in *Indigo Days*, p. 16. Martin Dodsworth, 'Empson at Cambridge', *the Review* nos. 6 and 7 (June 1963), 3–13.

104 John Horder, 'William Empson, Straight', *Guardian*, 12 August 1969.

105 WE, letter to Willis, 18 June 1964; quoted in Willis.

106 Colin Clark, letter to Haffenden, 12 August 1985.

107 Sir William Hayter, letter to Sir Jeremy Morse, 20 July 1989, and Douglas Jay, letter to Morse, 19 May 1989 (courtesy of Sir Jeremy Morse); Morse, letter to Haffenden, 3 February 1990.

108 WE, letter to Ricks, 19 January 1975 (courtesy of Christopher Ricks); quoted in *Essays on Renaissance Literature*, vol. II: *The Drama*, ed. J. Haffenden (Cambridge: Cambridge University Press, 1994), pp. 58–9.

109 See Christopher Ricks, '*Doctor Faustus* and Hell on Earth', *Essays in Criticism* 35:2 (April 1985); reprinted in *Essays in Appreciation* (Oxford: Clarendon Press, 1996), p. 102.

110 See n. 97 above.

111 Philip Hobsbaum, letter to Haffenden, 27 June 1985.

112 WE, letter to Tambimuttu, 12 March 1948 (Houghton Library). Empson was consistent in opposing censorship and suppression, and in upholding the right to challenge received morality; he was to write to Christopher Ricks on 19 January 1975: 'It is a very good thing for a poet, one might say the ideal, to be saying something which is considered very shocking at the time.'

113 'Some More Dylan Thomas', *Listener* (28 October 1971); reprinted in *A*, p. 408.

114 Draft of 'Mr Empson and the Fire Sermon', *Essays in Criticism* 6:4 (October 1956), 481–2.

115 WE, undated letter [1929–30] to Trevelyan (courtesy of the late Julian Trevelyan, whose papers are now in the Wren Library of Trinity College, Cambridge).

116 *A*, pp. 70–87.

117 WE, undated letter to Parsons, received 6 June 1929.

118 Grover Smith, *The Waste Land* (London: George Allen & Unwin, 1983), p. 81 (Unwin Critical Library). See also Jo Ellen Green Kaiser, 'Disciplining *The Waste Land*, or How to Lead Critics into Temptation', *Twentieth Century Literature* 44:1 (Spring 1998), pp. 82–99.

119 In 1929, Empson took this view:

When Mr Eliot writes notes to *The Waste Land* so as to imply 'well, if you haven't read such and such a play by Middleton, you had better go and do it at once' – the schoolmaster's tone is an anachronism, it belongs to a time when knowledge could be treated as a unified field. An odd reference does not even show that the writer is learned on a subject; it may merely be a piece of information that had stuck in his head, and become useful as a metaphor. Everybody's reading is miscellaneous and scrappy, like his. ('Obscurity and Annotation', *A*, p. 71)

120 Eliot, *On Poetry and Poets* (London, 1957), pp. 109–10. The publication history of *The Waste Land* is now known to be more complicated than Eliot liked to maintain: see Lawrence Rainey, 'The Price of Modernism: Publishing *The Waste Land*', in *T. S. Eliot: The Modernist in History*, ed. Ronald Bush (Cambridge: Cambridge University Press, 1991), pp. 91–133.
121 Quoted from a reported lecture by Auden, 'The Future of English Poetic Drama' (1938), in W. H. Auden and Christopher Isherwood, *Plays and Other Dramatic Writings by W. H. Auden, 1928–1938*, ed. Edward Mendelson (London, 1989), p. 521.
122 WE, undated letter to Parsons, received on 14 June 1929. He would make use of the same joke in 'Obscurity and Annotation', *A*, p. 72.
123 Steven Connor, *Postmodernist Culture: An Introduction to Theories of the Contemporary* (Oxford: Basil Blackwell, 1989), p. 99.
124 Undated letter to Parsons (Reading).
125 Basil de Selincourt, 'Poetic Black-Out', *Observer*, 6 October 1940, p. 3.
126 WE, undated and unsent letter [October 1940] to Selincourt. However, he was not above melodramatizing the critical reception of his work. In the *Morning Post* (9 July 1935), a fairly appreciative short notice of *Poems* (which incidentally remarked, 'he is a better poet than Miss [Marianne] Moore') closed with the observation: 'Mr Empson, it may be added, has very courteously provided notes to smooth away the difficulties and explain the allusions in his verse.' Empson detected an irony or sarcasm which an impartial reader might not have; he told Michael Roberts in an undated letter: 'I had a rather nice review in the Morning Post, saying that I was courteous but a coward' (Berg Collection, New York Public Library). That is not to say that Empson could not tolerate criticism; to illustrate the contrast, this is how he was to write to Hayward on 16 December 1940:

Of course I wouldn't resent your criticism, very glad to get any. But I am alarmed to hear you found the poems too obscure; if you, then anyone. The idea that they might be 'intended' for some special kind of mind or might be willing to make *some* 'concessions' doesn't come into my picture at all; one is much too busy trying to get the poem right to start imagining audiences. And this though the whole labour is to make the thing quite *clear*. (courtesy of Eric Homberger)

127 Hilary Corke, 'Riding a Hare', *Listener*, 54:1388 (6 October 1955), 565.
128 S. Sultan, *Ulysses, The Waste Land, and Modernism* (Port Washington, N.Y.:

1977), p. 41; cited in Smith, *The Waste Land*, p. 80. J. H. Willis, Jr., notes: 'Never providing exact documentation, Empson's notes, while explanatory, are often self-contained. Contrapuntal in effect, usually providing another dimension to the poem, they expand the meaning, or add the pleasures of prose to poetry' (*William Empson* (New York and London: Columbia University Press, 1969), pp. 28–9). Jean-Jacques Lecercle has some interesting things to say about the 'strangeness' of Empson's notes, in 'William Empson's Cosmicomics' (*William Empson: The Critical Achievement*, ed. Christopher Norris and Nigel Mapp (Cambridge: Cambridge University Press, 1993), pp. 269–93):

Empson's notes are not at all like Eliot's. They do not indicate sources but provide explanations in the etymological sense of unfolding of meaning. Besides, we do need them. They often provide meaning which is so close to Wittgenstein's 'private language' (that notorious impossibility) that we could hardly have expected to recover it . . . There is a teasing aspect to the notes: more information is proffered than we could reasonably have expected, and yet some of the information we did expect – at times, most of it – is withdrawn. Nor is this, of course, a criticism of Empson: complete explanation would reduce the reader's effort towards understanding to nothing, insufferably constrain his or her freedom of interpretation, and make the act of reading somewhat boring. (pp. 273–4)

129 'On Criticism', *Agenda* 14:3 (Autumn 1976), 24. Empson was completely sanguine about the critic's business of enquiring into unconscious mechanisms. When W. K. Wimsatt, Jr., in his famous essay on 'The Intentional Fallacy', questioned whether it would be a legitimate critical proceeding to ask Eliot if he had Donne or Marvell in mind when writing *The Waste Land*, Empson wrote in the margin of the copy he had to hand: 'the poet may mean more than he knew – easily may not want to tell. No reason for not asking' (Wimsatt, *The Verbal Icon: Studies in the Meaning of Poetry* (Lexington: University of Kentucky Press, 1954), p. 18). When Wimsatt objected (p. 17), 'And Eliot himself, in his notes, has justified his poetic practice in terms of intention', Empson responded: 'how could he not?' And against Wimsatt's famous remark (p. 3), 'The poem is not the critic's own and not the author's (it is detached from the author at birth and goes about the world beyond his power to intend about it or control it)', Empson commented with exasperation: 'But both author and critic are part of the world.'
130 Philip Larkin, letter to Jacob Empson, 15 May 1984 (courtesy of Jacob Empson).
131 Eliot, letter to Bonamy Dobrée, 14 November 1957 (Special Collections, Brotherton Library, University of Leeds).
132 WE, letter to Harwood, 14 August 1983.

ACKNOWLEDGEMENTS

William Empson loved crossword puzzles; so much so that he relished not only solving the clues themselves but reading *through* the clues to the character of the compilers. 'Crosswords, oh yes,' he once remarked. 'Well, the chaps at *The Times* seem to be Roman Catholics these days, and there are a whole lot of estate agents at the *Telegraph*. Rather curious, that' (John Horder, 'William Empson, Straight', *Guardian*, 12 August 1969). The last words he ever spoke to me, as I was being invited by a nurse firmly to leave his hospital room at the end of a visiting hour, were: 'Aren't you going to help me with the crossword?' He looked as though he really wanted a positive answer. In truth, I feel I have been helping with the crossword – or perhaps the jigsaw – ever since.

I have incurred many debts while putting together this edition. The task began in 1982, but it was only at the close of the 1980s, when I was appointed a British Academy Research Reader, that I was able to make consistent progress with this and other Empsonian undertakings. First, therefore, I owe an enormous debt of gratitude to the British Academy.

The project was given a further (and decisive) boost when I was elected a Visiting Fellow Commoner at Trinity College, Cambridge, for a few months in 1995–6; and it is with great pleasure that I thank the Master and Fellows for that privilege. I am grateful to Sir Michael and Lady Atiyah for their cordial welcome, and to the Fellows for giving so freely of their knowledge and counsel, and for their good cheer. I would like to mention in particular my friend and ally Dr Eric Griffiths (who valiantly put me up to be a VFC and then sensibly left me to get on with it), Professor W. Sidney Allen, Professor Horace Barlow, Professor Anne Barton, Professor John Davidson, Christopher Decker, Dr Nicholas Denyer, H. J. Easterling, Professor Kevin Gray, Dr A. Boyd Hilton, Dr Neil Hopkinson, Sean Hughes, Professor Sir Andrew Huxley, Dr David McKitterick, the late Jeremy Maule, Professor Sir James Mirrlees, Dr Chris Morley, Professor Robert Neild, Dr H. Osborn, Professor Roger Paulin, Dr Adrian Poole, Dr Matthew Reynolds, Dr James Robinson,

Professor Sir Martin Roth, A. P. Simm (Junior Bursar), Dr Alan Weeds and Dr G. P. Winter. Laura Pieters Cordy (Fellows' Computer Room) was unstinting with her organizational advice and labours.

I am extremely grateful also to the Leverhulme Foundation for awarding me a Fellowship towards my research in Cambridge in 1995.

My gratitude is due also to the staff of the Houghton Library at Harvard University, especially Leslie Morris (Curator of Manuscripts); Rodney G. Dennis (former Curator), who has an infectious zest for Empson's poetry; and Elizabeth A. Falsey, for her generosity and helpfulness – a true friend. They are great facilitators.

I am indebted to many other individuals who have generously helped me in various capacities: C. P. Adams, A. Alvarez, Robert J. Bertholf (Curator, The Poetry/Rare Books Collection, State University of New York at Buffalo), Andrew Best, S. F. Bolt, Michael Bott (Reading University Library), the late Muriel Bradbrook, Peter Cheeseman, Igor Chroustchoff, Colin Clark, A. A. Cole (Consultant Archivist, Unilever, London), Alistair Cooke, Clive W. Cornell (W. Heffer & Sons Ltd.), C. Cruickshank (Archivist, Faber & Faber Ltd.), Lawrence Danson, the late Hugh Sykes Davies, Norman Davies (General Dental Council), Colin Davis, Alec Daykin, E. E. Duncan-Jones, Ellen S. Dunlap (former Research Librarian, Harry Ransom Humanities Research Center, University of Texas at Austin), Simon Duval Smith, Richard Eberhart, Valerie Eliot, Charles Empson, Jacob Empson, Mogador Empson, the late Lady (Monica) Empson, D. J. Enright, Rachel Falconer, Elizabeth Fallaize, Valerie Flint, John Fuller, Helen Gardner (Society of Authors), Stephen Garrett, Margaret Garrod (Archive Manager, The History of Advertising Trust), Roma Gill, Michael Halls, Claire Harman, the late Sir Rupert Hart-Davis, Stratis Haviaras, David Hawkes, the late Sir William Hayter, Cathy Henderson (Research Librarian, Harry Ransom Humanities Research Center, University of Texas at Austin), Philip Hobsbaum, Theodore Hofmann, Eric Homberger, Alan Howe, Allegra Huston, Yukio Irie, Soji Iwasaki, Tom Jaine, Nicholas Jenkins, Jin Yue Lin, John Henry (David) Jones, Ryuichi Kajiki, J. L. S. Keesing (Scientific Liaison Officer, Royal Botanic Gardens, Kew), Richard J. Kelly, Gilbert Kennedy, Mary Kent (Consumer Relations Officer, Elida Gibbs), the late Sir Desmond Lee, Lady Lee, E. S. Leedham-Green (Cambridge University Library), Li Fu-ning, Richard Luckett (Pepys Librarian), Ian MacKillop, the late Eric Mackerness, Brian Marsden, M. C. Meredith (School Librarian, Eton College), Ivor H. Mills, Ray Monk, Sir Jeremy

Morse, Andrew Motion, Christopher Norris, Kazuo Ogawa, Timothy O'Sullivan, A. E. B. Owen (former Keeper of Manuscripts, Cambridge University Library), Barbara Ozieblo, Lucy Pascocello (Rights and Permissions Manager, Harcourt, Brace & Co.), Chris Petter (University Archivist and Head of Special Collections, University of Victoria, Victoria, B.C., Canada), David Pirie, Jean F. Preston (Curator of Manuscripts, Princeton University Library), Kate Price, Qien Xuexi, Eleanor L. Rands (Senior Assistant Editor, *Oxford English Dictionary*), Stefenie Reiter (Marketing Manager, Ciro Pearls Ltd., London), the late Dorothea Richards, Sachiyo Fujita Round, the late George Rylands, Catherine Jane Sharrock, Chris Sheppard (Special Collections, Brotherton Library, University of Leeds), Ann Silver (Physiological Society Publications Consultant), J. A. Simson, the late Norah Smallwood (Chatto & Windus), Anthony Smith, the late Janet Adam Smith, the late John Sparrow, Alice Stewart, Sun Yu-mei, the late Lola Szladits (Curator of the Berg Collection, New York Public Library), Lee Taylor (Library/Information Service, National Sound Archive, British Library), Anthony Thwaite, Shigehiko Toyama, the late Julian Trevelyan, Robert Vas Dias, Sue Vice, Robert Viscusi, the late John Wain, William Wain, Wang Zuo-liang, Marina Warner, Saffron Whithead (*Physiological Society Magazine*), the late J. M. Whittaker, J. H. Willis, Jr., C. Anne Wilson, David Wilson, Lewis Wolpert, the late Basil Wright, Yang Hsien-yi, the late Yang Zhouhan, Shoichiro Yasuda, Jack Zipes, Michael Zolk and Dr Anna Zytkow. I want to extend thanks also to my colleague Derek Roper for his constant willingness to suggest solutions to the posers I have e-mailed to him.

My indebtedness to many brave predecessors, editors and critics, is obvious on every page of this volume; but I should like to acknowledge in particular my sense of deep obligation to J. H. Willis, Jr., for his pioneering Ph.D. dissertation, 'The Poetry of William Empson', and to Philip and Averil Gardner for *The God Approached: A Commentary on the Poems of William Empson*.

Extracts from unpublished letters by T. S. Eliot are reproduced by kind permission of Mrs Valerie Eliot; an extract from an unpublished letter by Philip Larkin, by permission of Anthony Thwaite.

Hetta, Lady Empson, gave me her wholesale faith and support; I am sad that she did not live to see this volume brought to a completion. My thanks go also to my agent Peter Robinson; and to Paul Keegan, who has been a model editor in commissioning the project and withholding harassment. Professor Christopher Ricks, General Editor of the Penguin English Poets, has been generous with his energy, his hospitality and his care; I owe much to his loving comprehension of Empson's work. Lindeth Vasey has been an exemplary copy-editor, patient beyond measure with my stubbornness and stupidity, all errors in this volume remain my responsibility.

TABLE OF DATES

1906   *27 September* William Empson born at Yokefleet Hall, Howden, near Goole, Yorkshire; youngest child of Arthur Reginald Empson (landowner and squire) and his wife Laura Micklethwait; his siblings: John ('Jack', born 1891), Arthur (1892), Charles (1898) and Maria Eleanor Katharine ('Molly') (1902).

1914   *16 May* Death of Jack, a lieutenant in the Royal Flying Corps, in an aeroplane crash.
Enrols at a preparatory school, Praetoria House School, near Folkestone, Kent, where mathematics becomes his forte.

1916   *15 March* Death of his father, aged 63.

1920   Writes first known poem, 'Mother, saying Anne good night', by 29 June, aged 13.
Wins an entrance scholarship to Winchester College; specializes in mathematics and science; falls under 'the drug of Swinburne'.

1924   *December* Wins Milner Scholarship to Magdalene College, Cambridge.

1925   Wins English literature prize at Winchester, where the second master writes of him: 'He has a distinctly enterprising intellect, but must remember that his opinions on the big questions of life can still be only tentative and experimental.' Comes second (*proxime accessit*) to the future Labour MP Richard Crossman in a competition for the Warden and Fellows' Prize for an English Essay (John Sparrow, future Warden of All Souls College, Oxford, is third).
October Goes up to Cambridge, where his tutor for mathematics is A. S. Ramsey, father of the mathematical prodigy Frank Ramsey and the future Archbishop of Canterbury, Michael Ramsey. Joins humanist discussion society, The Heretics.

1926   *February–March* T. S. Eliot delivers Clark Lectures, 'The Metaphysical Poets of the Seventeenth Century', at Trinity College, Cambridge. Although Empson does not attend all the lectures, he takes part in informal conversations with Eliot. In a later year he will write in tribute to Eliot, 'I feel, like most other verse writers of my generation, that I do not know for certain how much of my own mind he invented, let alone how much of it is a reaction against him or indeed a consequence of misreading him. He has a very penetrating influence, perhaps not unlike an east wind.' Participates in debates at the Union.

12 June Publishes his first literary notice in *Granta*.

June Gains First class Part I of the Mathematical Tripos; awarded college prize.

1927   *5 February* Acts in a production at the Cambridge ADC of his one-act play, *Three Stories*.

Begins reviewing film and theatre, as well as books, for *Granta* and *Cambridge Review*; becomes 'Skipper' (literary editor) of *Granta*.

June Publishes first poem at Cambridge, 'Poem about a Ball in the Nineteenth Century'.

1928   *June* Senior Optime (Upper Second) in Part II of the Mathematical Tripos: a disappointing result.

October Registers for the English Tripos; tutored by I. A. Richards at Magdalene College; attends Richards's lectures on 'Practical Criticism'. Begins work towards *Seven Types of Ambiguity*. Becomes president of The Heretics.

November Launches avant-garde magazine, *Experiment*, co-edited with Jacob Bronowski, Humphrey Jennings and Hugh Sykes Davies (seven issues, the last in May 1931).

1929   *20 January* Gives a talk at Cambridge on ambiguity in literature.

February Publishes 'Ambiguity in Shakespeare: Sonnet XVI' in *Experiment* (included in *Seven Types of Ambiguity*).

March Takes title role in *The Tragedy of Tragedies: or the Life and Death of Tom Thumb the Great* by Henry Fielding, in a production by the Cambridge Mummers.

June Gains First class with 'special distinction' in Part I of English Tripos; awarded a Magdalene College prize; elected to a Charles Kingsley Bye-Fellowship for 1929–30.

July Discovered by college servant to be in possession of contraceptives; the Governing Body of Magdalene College deprives Empson of his Bye-Fellowship and removes his name from the college books. He moves to 65 Marchmont Street, London, where he lives as a freelance writer for the next two years; is cultivated by literary figures including T. S. Eliot, Virginia Woolf, Harold Monro and Sylvia Townsend Warner.

November Letter IV published by W. Heffer & Sons, Cambridge.

Six poems feature in *Cambridge Poetry 1929*, published by Leonard and Virginia Woolf at the Hogarth Press.

Publishes 'Some Notes on Mr Eliot' (a further preview of *Seven Types*) in *Experiment*.

1930   *November Seven Types of Ambiguity* published in London.

1931   *29 August* Begins three-year contract as a professor of English at Tokyo University of Literature and Science (Bunrika Daigaku); teaches also at Tokyo Imperial University.

Seven Types published by Harcourt, Brace & Company, New York.

1932   *February* Five poems are included in anthology, *New Signatures*, published by the Hogarth Press.

1934   *Poems*, in an edition of 100 copies, privately printed by The Fox & Daffodil Press, Kinuta-mura, near Tokyo.

8 July Returns to London, where he spends the next three years as a freelance writer.

1935   *May Poems* published in London.

October Some Versions of Pastoral published.

Publishes translations into Basic English of two works by J. B. S. Haldane, *The Outlook of Science* and *Science and Well-Being*.

Gains MA, University of Cambridge.

1936   W. B. Yeats includes a poem in the *Oxford Book of Modern Verse*; Michael Roberts picks six for *The Faber Book of Modern Verse*.

1937   *August* Takes up appointment at National Peking University, arriving just as the Japanese invade; journeys through China with I. A. Richards and his wife; works with the exiled Peking universities – amalgamated as the Temporary University (*Chang-sha lin-shih ta-hsueh*).

1937–8   At Nan-Yueh, Hunan Province; journeys to Hong Kong.

1938–9   Continues university teaching with the National Southwest Associated University (*Hsi-na lien-ho ta-hsueh* [*Xinan Lianhe Daxue*]), in remote exile, in the town of Mengtzu and then in Kunming, the capital of Yunnan province, near the Indo-China (Vietnam) border.

1939   *Autumn* Returns to England by way of the USA, where he broadcasts on Basic English in Boston.

1940   *28 January* Arrives back in England.

       26 June Joins the Monitoring Service of the BBC at Wood Norton Hall, near Evesham in Worcestershire, working as a sub-editor.

       September The Gathering Storm published in London.

1941   Transfers to the BBC Overseas Service in London; becomes a Talks Assistant and then Chinese Editor, organizing talks to China and propaganda programmes for the Home Service; for two years, works alongside George Orwell.

       2 December Marries Hester Henrietta Crouse ('Hetta'), a South African artist, at St Stephen's Church, Hampstead, London.

1942   *9 November* Birth of first son, William Hendrik Mogador.

1944   *30 September* Birth of second son, Jacob Arthur Calais.

1947–52   Teaches at National Peking University, his post being subsidized by the British Council; witnesses the civil war and the six-week siege of Peking late in 1948 and then the Communist takeover and the inauguration of the People's Republic of China, including the beginnings of reform and 'thought control'.

1948   *July–August* Teaches summer school at Kenyon College, Gambier, Ohio, on leave from Peking.

1949   *24 March The Collected Poems of William Empson* published in New York.

1950   Further summer school visit to Kenyon College.

1951   *July The Structure of Complex Words* published in London.

1952   *Summer* Returns with family to England.

       15 December The Poems of William Empson broadcast by BBC.

1953   *October* Takes up Chair of English Literature at the University of Sheffield, where he works for the next eighteen years (1971).

1954   *May* Gresham Professor in Rhetoric, Gresham College, London, lecturing on 'The last Plays of Shakespeare and their Relation to the Elizabethan Theatre'.

       June–July Fellow of the School of Letters, Indiana University, Bloomington, Indiana.

       27 October The Birth of Steel: A Light Masque performed for Queen Elizabeth II at the University of Sheffield.

1955   *29 September Collected Poems* published in London.

1959   *William Empson Reading Selected Poems* (*Listen* LPV 3) recorded.

1961 *February The Collected Poems of William Empson* (New York) issued in paperback.
Milton's God published in London.
William Empson Reading Selected Poems issued.

1964 *Autumn* Visiting Professor, English Department, University of Ghana, Legon, Accra, Ghana.

1968 Hon. D. Litt., University of East Anglia, Norwich.
Ingram Merrill Foundation Award.
June–August Visiting Professor, Department of English, State University of New York at Buffalo.

1971 Hon. D. Litt., University of Bristol.

1972 *January–February* Gives Waynflete Lectures on 'The Editorial Choice of the Text of a Poem', at Magdalen College, Oxford.
Publishes *Coleridge's Verse: A Selection* (with David B. Pirie).

1973 Visiting Professor, York University, Toronto.

1974 *Lent Term* Delivers Clark Lectures at Trinity College, Cambridge, on 'The Progress of Criticism'.
Hon. D. Litt., University of Sheffield.
Honorary member of the American Academy of Arts and Letters/ The National Institute of Arts and Letters.

1974–5 Visiting Professor of English, Pennsylvania State University.

1976 *Autumn* Visiting Professor, Department of English, University of Delaware, Newark, Delaware.
Fellow of the British Academy.
Honorary Fellow of the Modern Language Association of America.

1977 *10 June* Hon. Litt. D., University of Cambridge.

1979 Knighted in New Year Honours for 'services to English literature'.
Elected Honorary Fellow, Magdalene College, Cambridge.

1982 *January–April* Visiting Professor, University of Miami, Florida.

1984 *15 April* Dies in London.
Collected Poems reissued; *Using Biography* published.

1986 *The Royal Beasts and Other Works* and *Essays on Shakespeare* published.

1987 *Argufying: Essays on Literature and Culture* and *Faustus and the Censor: The English Faust-book and Marlowe's 'Doctor Faustus'* published.

1993 *Essays on Renaissance Literature*, Vol. 1: *Donne and the New Philosophy*.

BIBLIOGRAPHY

Works by Empson

Books and Uncollected Items

Cambridge Poetry 1929, ed. Christopher Saltmarshe, John Davenport and Basil Wright (Hogarth Living Poets, no. 8) (London: Leonard and Virginia Woolf at the Hogarth Press, 1929)

Letter IV (*Songs for Sixpence*, no. 1) (Cambridge: W. Heffer & Sons, 1929)

Seven Types of Ambiguity (London: Chatto & Windus, 1930; 2nd edn., rev., 1947; 3rd edn., rev., 1953)

Poems (Kinuta-mura, Tokyo: The Fox & Daffodil Press, 1934)

Poems (London: Chatto & Windus, 1935)

Some Versions of Pastoral (London: Chatto & Windus, 1935; paperback issue with 'Preface to Peregrine Edition', Harmondsworth: Penguin, 1966; reissue of 1935 edn. with 'Preface to 1974 Edition', London: Chatto & Windus, 1974)

'A London Letter', *Poetry* 49 (January 1937), 219–20

The Gathering Storm (London: Faber & Faber, 1940)

The Collected Poems of William Empson (New York: Harcourt, Brace, 1949; corrected paperback edn., New York: Harvest Books, 1961)

The Structure of Complex Words (London: Chatto & Windus, 1951; 2nd edn., 1952; 3rd edn., 1977)

'The Birth of Steel: A Light Masque', *Sheffield University Gazette Jubilee Number* no. 21 (November 1954), 5–7

'Yes and No', *Essays in Criticism* 5:1 (January 1955), 89–90

Collected Poems (London: Chatto & Windus, 1955; corrected impression, 1956)

'Mr Empson and the Fire Sermon', *Essays in Criticism* 6:4 (October 1956), 481–2

Milton's God (London: Chatto & Windus, 1961, rev. 1965; rev. edn. with additional material, Cambridge: Cambridge University Press, 1981)

Coleridge's Verse: A Selection, ed. with David B. Pirie (London: Faber & Faber, 1972); reissued as *Selected Poems* (Manchester: Carcarnet Press [Fyfield Books], 1989)

'On Criticism', *Agenda* 14:3 (1976), 3–44

Using Biography (London: Chatto & Windus, 1984)

'Empson on Tennyson', *Tennyson Research Bulletin* 4:3 (November 1984), 107–9

Essays on Shakespeare, ed. David Pirie (Cambridge: Cambridge University Press, 1986)

The Royal Beasts and Other Works, ed. J. Haffenden (London: Chatto & Windus, 1986; Iowa City: University of Iowa Press, 1988)

Argufying: Essays on Literature and Culture, ed. J. Haffenden (London: Chatto & Windus, 1987; Iowa City: University of Iowa Press, 1987)

Faustus and the Censor: The English Faust-book and Marlowe's 'Doctor Faustus', ed. John Henry Jones (Oxford: Basil Blackwell, 1987)

Empson in Granta (Tunbridge Wells, Kent: The Foundling Press, 1993)

Essays on Renaissance Literature, ed. J. Haffenden (Cambridge: Cambridge University Press), Vol. 1: *Donne and the New Philosophy* (1993); Vol. 2: *The Drama* (1994)

The Strengths of Shakespeare's Shrew: Essays, Memoirs and Reviews, ed. J. Haffenden (Sheffield: Sheffield Academic Press, 1996)

Recordings

Album of Twentieth Century Poetry in English (Library of Congress record PLII)

The Ambiguity of William Empson, BBC Radio 3 (22 October 1977), produced by David Perry (National Sound Archive, British Library: T1726W)

The Caedmon Treasury of Modern Poets Reading Their Own Poetry (New York: Caedmon, 1957) (CDL 52006)

Contemporary Poets Reading Their Own Poems, British Council (National Sound Archive, British Library: 10226 WR)

Morris Gray Poetry Reading, introduced by Anthony Hecht, Harvard University, 13 April 1973, Woodberry Poetry Room, Lamont Library, Harvard University (PR 6009.M7 A6x 1973)

The Poems of William Empson, ed. Peter Duval Smith, BBC Third Programme, 15 December 1952 (Recording no. DLO 19754/A)

The Poet Speaks, no. 7, ed. Peter Orr, British Council/Poetry Room in the Lamont Library of Harvard University (Argo RG 517)

Poetry at the Mermaid, 23 July 1961 (National Sound Archive, British Library: 360R)

Selections from Collected Poems, 7 November 1960, Woodberry Poetry Room, Lamont Library, Harvard University (PR 6009.M7 A6x 1960)

William Empson Reading His Poems at Kenyon College, Gambier, Ohio, on November 7, 1948 (Library of Congress Recorded Poetry and Literature: LCCN 94-838721/R)

William Empson Reading Selected Poems (Hull: Marvell Press: *Listen* LPV 3, 1961)

Musical Setting

Robin Holloway's cycle *Three Poems by William Empson* ('Villanelle', 'Missing Dates' and 'Let it go'), composed in 1965, was first performed – under the auspices of the Society for the Promotion of New Music, as part of a concert at the Purcell Room, London, on 25 April 1973 – by the London Contemporary Chamber Players under Elgar Howarth, and sung by Rosanne Creffield. The concert was reviewed by Max Loppert, *Financial Times* (26 April 1973) and by 'A. E. P.', *Daily Telegraph* (26 April 1973).

Reference

Alexander, Harriet Semmes, *American and British Poetry: a Guide to the Criticism, 1925–1978* (Manchester: Manchester University Press, 1984)

— *American and British Poetry: A Guide to the Criticism 1979–1990* (Athens, Ohio: Ohio University Press/Swallow Press, 1996)

Day, Frank, *Sir William Empson: An Annotated Bibliography* (New York and London: Garland Publishing, 1984)

Fraser, G. S., 'William Empson', in *Contemporary Poets*, ed. James Vinson (London and Basingstoke: Macmillan Press, 1970; 3rd edn., London and Basingstoke: Macmillan Press, and New York: St Martin's Press, 1980), pp. 437–9

Johnson, Michael L., 'William Empson: A Chronological Bibliography', *Bulletin of Bibliography and Magazine Notes* 29:4 (December 1972), 134–9

Kunitz, Stanley (ed.), *Twentieth Century Authors: First Supplement* (New York: H. W. Wilson Co., 1955), pp. 307–8

Lowbridge, Peter, 'An Empson Bibliography', *the Review* nos. 6 & 7 (June 1963), 63–73

McMillan, Peter, 'William Empson', in *British Poets, 1914–1945* (*Dictionary of Literary Biography*, Vol. 20), ed. Donald E. Stanford (Detroit, Mich.: Gale Research, 1983), pp. 126–31

MacNeice, Louis, 'William Empson', in *The Concise Encyclopedia of English and American Poets and Poetry*, ed. Stephen Spender and Donald Hall (London: Hutchinson, 1963), pp. 127–8

Megaw, Moira, 'An Empson Bibliography', in Gill, pp. 213–44

Meller, Horst, 'William Empson', in *Englische Dichter der Moderne: Ihr Leben und Werk*, ed. Rudolf Sühnel and Dieter Riesner (Berlin: Erich Schmidt, 1971), pp. 474–88

Wain, John, 'William Empson', *Dictionary of National Biography: 1981– 1985* (Oxford: Oxford University Press, 1990), pp. 130–31

Wood, Michael, 'William Empson', in *Reference Guide to English Literature*, 2nd edn., ed. D. L. Kirkpatrick (Chicago and London: St James Press, 1991), pp. 540–42

Books and Monographs on Empson

Constable, John (ed.), *Critical Essays on William Empson* (Aldershot, Hants.: Scolar Press, 1993)

Fry, Paul H., *William Empson: Prophet Against Sacrifice* (London and New York: Routledge, 1991)

Gardner, Philip and Averil, *The God Approached: A Commentary on the Poems of William Empson* (London: Chatto & Windus, 1978)

Gill, Roma (ed.), *William Empson: The Man and His Work* (London: Routledge & Kegan Paul, 1974)

[Havely, Cicely], *William Empson and F. R. Leavis* (Arts: A Third Level Course: Twentieth Century Poetry, Units 18 and 19) (Milton Keynes: Open University Press, 1976)

Meller, Horst, *Das Gedicht als Einübung: Zum Dichtungsverständnis William Empsons* (Heidelberg: Carl Winter Universitätsverlag, 1974)

Morelli, Angelo, *La Poesia di William Empson* (Catania: Niccolò Giannotta, 1959)

Norris, Christopher, *William Empson and the Philosophy of Literary Criticism* (London: Athlone Press, 1978); with postscript by WE

— and Nigel Mapp (eds.), *William Empson: The Critical Achievement* (Cambridge: Cambridge University Press, 1993)

Will, R. G., 'The Poetry of William Empson – an analysis based on Wittgenstein's views of language and meaning' (unpub. Ph.D. dissertation, University of the Western Cape, South Africa, 1987)

'William Empson Special Number', *the Review* nos. 6 & 7 (June 1963)

Willis, Jr., John Howard, 'The Poetry of William Empson' (unpub. Ph.D. dissertation, Columbia University, New York, 1967; digest in *Dissertation Abstracts*, XXVIII (1967), item 2271 A)

— *William Empson* (Columbia Essays on Modern Writers, no. 39) (New York and London: Columbia University Press, 1969)

Articles, Poems and Reviews

Alvarez, A., 'A Style from a Despair: William Empson', *The Twentieth Century* 161 (April 1957), 344–53; reprinted in *The Shaping Spirit: Studies in Modern English and American Poets* (London: Chatto & Windus, 1958), pub. in the USA as *Stewards of Excellence* (New York: Charles Scribner's Sons, 1958)

Anon., 'Ambiguous Gifts' (on Empson special number of *the Review*), *The Times Literary Supplement* (16 August 1963), p. 625.

Anon., 'Birth at the A. D. C.' (on *Three Stories*), *Granta* 36: 807 (1927), 238

Anon., 'Coping with the Flood' (*CP 1949*), *Time* 53 (18 April 1949), 44

Anon., review of *GS*, *Listener* 25 (6 February 1941), 204, 207

Anon., 'In the Movement', *Spectator* 193: 6588 (1 October 1954), 399–400

Anon., 'One At a Time' (review of *Letter IV*), *Cambridge Review* 50 (29 November 1929), 159–61

Anon., 'Poets of the Year: Voices of the Free Spirit' (*GS*), *The Times Literary Supplement* (7 December 1940), p. xxii

Anon., 'Puzzles in Verse: The Cult of Ambiguity' (*GS*), *The Times Literary Supplement* (12 October 1940), p. 522

Auden, W. H., 'A Toast (To Professor William Empson on the occasion of his retirement in 1971)', *Epistle to a Godson* (London: Faber & Faber, 1972)

Barrows, Herbert, 'William Empson – Poet of Wit' (*CP 1949*), *New York Times Book Review* (27 March 1949), p. 5

Batchelor, J. B., review of Gill, *Modern Language Review* 70:2 (April 1975), 411–14

Bateson, F. W., 'Auden's (and Empson's) Heirs', *Essays in Criticism* 7 (January 1957), 76–80 (see Hayman below for reply)

Beaver, Harold, 'Tilting at Windbags' (Norris), *New Statesman* 96 (11 August 1978), 185–6

Bergonzi, Bernard, 'A Note on William Empson' (*CP*), *Stand* no. 11 (Winter–Spring 1956), 26–7

Bernhart, Walter, review of *Das Gedicht als Einübung*, by H. Meller, *Germanisch-romanische Monatsschrift* (Heidelberg: Carl Winter Universitätsverlag) 28:2 (1978), 254–7

Berry, Francis, 'William Empson' (poem), in Gill, pp. 208–12

Blackburn, Thomas, *The Price of an Eye* (New York: William Morrow, 1961)

Bonnerot, Louis, review of *P*, *Revue Anglo-Américaine* 13 (1935–6), 256–7

Bottrall, Ronald, 'William Empson' (poem), in Gill, pp. 49–51

Bradbrook, M. C., 'The Ambiguity of William Empson', in Gill, pp. 2–12

— 'Lowry's Cambridge', in *Malcolm Lowry: Eighty Years On*, ed. Sue Vice (Basingstoke, Hants.: Macmillan Press, 1989), pp. 125–46

— 'Minor prophecies' (*RB*), *Guardian* (14 November 1986), p. 9

— 'Sir William Empson (1906–1984): A Memoir', *Kenyon Review*, n.s. 7:4 (Fall 1985); reprinted as 'Sir William Empson (1906–84)', in *Shakespeare in His Context: The Constellated Globe* (Hemel Hempstead, Herts.: Harvester Wheatsheaf, 1989)

Breitkreuz, Hartmut, 'Empson's "The Beautiful Train"', *Explicator* 31:2 (October 1972), item 9

— 'William Empsons *The Beautiful Train*', *Archiv für das Studium der neueren Sprachen und Literaturen* 209 (August 1972), pp. 119–22

Bronowski, Jacob, 'The Imaginative Mind in Science', in *The Visionary Eye: Essays in the Arts, Literature, and Science* (Cambridge, Mass.: MIT Press, 1978)

— 'Poetry at the Universities', *Cambridge Review* 50 (30 November 1928), 169–70

— 'Recollections of Humphrey Jennings', *Twentieth Century* 165 (January 1959), 45–50

Brooks, Cleanth, and Robert Penn Warren, *Understanding Poetry* (New York: Henry Holt, 1938; 1951, 1958)

Brownjohn, Alan, 'Accurately Penned' (*CP*), *Departure* (Oxford) 3:9 (Spring 1956), 20–21

— 'A Preference for Poetry: Oxford Undergraduate Writing of the Early 1950s', *Yearbook of English Studies* 17 (1987), 62–74

Carey, John, 'Burnt-out Case' (*RB*), *Sunday Times* (30 November 1986), p. 53

Clarke, Austin, 'The Cryptic Key' (*CP*), *Irish Times* (5 November 1955), p. 6

Combecher, Hans, 'William Empson: Legal Fiction', *Deutung englischer Gedichte*, 1 (Frankfurt, 1965), pp. 111–14

Conquest, Robert (ed.), *New Lines* (London: Macmillan, 1956)

Cooke, Fletcher, '*Poems*, by Empson', *Granta* 45 (9 October 1935), 17

Corke, Hilary, 'Riding a Hare' (*CP*), *Listener* 54:1388 (6 October 1955), 565

Culler, Jonathan, 'A Critic Against the Christians', *The Times Literary Supplement* (23 November 1984), pp. 1327–8

Cunningham, Valentine, *British Writers of the Thirties* (Oxford: Oxford University Press, 1988)

D., J. L., 'Songs for Sixpence' (review of *Letter IV*), *Granta* 39 (1929), 378

Daiches, David, review of *CP 1949*, *New York Herald Tribune Weekly Book Review* (22 May 1949), p. 3

Danby, John F., 'William Empson', *Critical Quarterly* 1 (Summer 1959), 99–104

Das, B., 'A Note on the Poetry of William Empson', *Literary Criterion* (Mysore) 6:4 (Summer 1965), 11–18

Davidson, Eugene, 'Poets' Shelf' (*CP 1949*), *Yale Review* 28:4 (June 1949), 723–4

Davie, Donald, 'Hanging Judgment' (on Empson special number of *the Review*), *Guardian* (12 July 1963), p. 7

— review of *William Empson Reading Selected Poems*, *Spectator* 206 (1961), 40

[Davies], Hugh Sykes, 'Hommage' (parody-poem), *Cambridge Review* 50 (1 November 1929), 74

Deutsch, Babette, *Poetry Handbook: A Dictionary of Terms* (New York: Funk and Wagnalls, 1957)

— *Poetry in Our Time* (New York: Columbia University Press, 1952; 1956)

Deveson, Tom, 'Duels with God' (*RB*), *The Times Educational Supplement* (19 December 1986), p. 17

Dodsworth, Martin, 'Empson at Cambridge', *the Review* nos. 6 & 7 (June 1963), 3–13

— 'Empson of Yokefleet', *Sewanee Review* 93:3 (Summer 1985), 428–34

Donoghue, Denis, 'Reading a Poem: Empson's "Arachne"', *Studies: An Irish Quarterly Review* 45 (Summer 1956), 219–26; revised in *England, Their England* (Berkeley and Los Angeles: University of California Press, 1989), pp. 299–305

— 'Some Versions of Empson' (Gill), *The Times Literary Supplement* (7 June 1974), pp. 597–8

Drew, Elizabeth, *Poetry: A Modern Guide to Its Understanding and Enjoyment* (New York: W. W. Norton & Co., 1959), pp. 138–40

— with John L. Sweeney, *Directions in Modern Poetry* (New York: W. W. Norton, 1940; reprinted New York: Gordian Press, 1967), pp. 81–83, 204–7

Duncan, Joseph E., 'William Empson', in *The Revival of Metaphysical Poetry: The History of a Style, 1800 to the Present* (Minneapolis: University of Minnesota Press, 1959; New York: Octagon Books, 1969), pp. 196–202

Durrell, Lawrence, *A Key to Modern Poetry* (London: Peter Nevill, and Norman: University of Oklahoma Press, 1952)

Eagleton, Terry, 'The Critic as Clown', in *Against the Grain: Essays 1975–1985* (London: Verso, 1986), pp. 149–65

Eberhart, Richard, 'Empson's Poetry', *Accent: A Quarterly of New Literature* 4:4 (Summer 1944), 195–207; reprinted in *On Poetry and Poets* (Urbana: University of Illinois Press, 1979), pp. 111–25

— 'A Whack at Empson' (poem), *New England Review* 1:1 (1978), 47–8

Engle, Paul, and Joseph Langland (eds.), *The Poet's Choice* (New York: Dell, 1962) (includes 'Bacchus', with comment by Empson)

Enright, D. J., 'Literature and/or Belief: A Progress Report', *Essays in Criticism* 6:1 (January 1956), 60–69

— ' "The Son of Spiders" ' (*CP*), *Month* 8 (March 1956), 176–8

Evans, Ifor, 'Volumes of Verse' (*CP*), *Birmingham Post: Christmas Book Supplement* (22 November 1955), p. 9

Every, George, review of *P*, *Criterion* 15:58 (October 1935), 144–5

Falck, Colin, 'This Deep Blankness', *the Review* nos. 6 & 7 (June 1963), 49–61

Farmer, A. J., review of *CP*, *Études Anglaises* 9:4 (October–December 1956), 358–60

Fenton, James, 'Ars Poetica 36: Difficult Form', *Independent on Sunday* (23 September 1990), p. 31

Fitts, Dudley, 'Poetry Chronicle' (*CP 1949*), *Partisan Review* 16:4 (April 1949), 432–6

Fitzgerald, Robert, ' "Bejeweled, The Great Sun" ' (*CP 1949*), *New Republic* 120:17 (25 April 1949), 22–3

Forrest-Thomson, Veronica, 'Rational Artifice: Some Remarks on the Poetry of William Empson', *Yearbook of English Studies* 4 (1974), 225–38; reprinted in *Poetic Artifice: A Theory of Twentieth-Century Poetry* (Manchester: Manchester University Press, 1978)

Fowler, Roger, review of Gill, *Language and Style* 10:1 (1977), 66–70

Fraser, G. S., 'The Man within the Name: William Empson as Poet, Critic, and Friend', in Gill, pp. 52–75

— *The Modern Writer and His World* (London: Derek Verschoyle, 1953; New York: Criterion, 1955; rev. edn. Harmondsworth: Penguin, 1964)

— ' "Not Wrongly Moved . . ." ' (*CP*), *The Times Literary Supplement* (7 October 1955); reprinted in *Vision and Rhetoric: Studies in*

Modern Poetry (London: Faber & Faber, 1959; New York: Barnes and Noble, 1960), pp. 193–201

— 'On the Interpretation of the Difficult Poem', in *Interpretations: Essays on Twelve English Poems*, ed. John Wain (London: Routledge & Kegan Paul, 1955), pp. 211–37

— *Poetry Now: An Anthology* (London: Faber & Faber, 1956), pp. 23–5

— 'The Western Mind' (*GS*), *Poetry* (London) 1:5 (March–April 1941), 151–3

Friar, Kimon, and John Malcolm Brinnin, *Modern Poetry: American and British* (New York: Appleton-Century-Crofts, 1951)

Fukuhara, Rintaro, 'Mr William Empson in Japan', in Gill, pp. 21–33

Fuller, John, 'An Edifice of Meaning' (Gill), *Encounter* 45:5 (November 1974), 75–9

— 'Empson's Tone', *the Review* nos. 6 & 7 (June 1963), 21–5

Fuller, Roy, 'Too High-Flown a Genius?' (*TGA*, Norris), *Encounter* 53 (July 1979), 41–8

Gardner, Philip, '"Meaning" in the Poetry of William Empson', *The Humanities Association Review/La Revue de l'Association des Humanités* (Kingston, Ontario, Canada) 18:1 (Spring 1967), 75–86

Go, Kenji, '"Argufying" in Empson's "Aubade"', *Studies in English Literature* (Tokyo), English Number 1994, pp. 31–45

Grigson, Geoffrey, 'A Letter from England', *Poetry* (Chicago) 49 (November 1936), 101–3

— 'Correspondence', *Poetry* (Chicago) 50 (May 1937), 115–16

Gross, Harvey, *Sound and Form in Modern Poetry* (Ann Arbor: University of Michigan, 1964)

Gross, John, 'The furry Wurroos' (*RB*), *Observer*, 16 November 1986

Grubb, Frederick, *A Vision of Reality: A Study of Liberalism in Twentieth-Century Verse* (London: Chatto & Windus, 1965), pp. 128–34

Gunn, Thom, review of *CP*, *London Magazine* 3:2 (February 1956), 70–75

— 'Correspondence' (rejoinder to K. Raine's response to his review of *CP*), *London Magazine* 3:4 (April 1956), 64–5

Haffenden, John, 'The Importance of Empson: The Poems', *Essays in Criticism* 35:1 (January 1985), 1–24

— 'Introduction', in *A*, pp. 1–63

— 'Introduction', in *RB*, pp. 7–77

Hamilton, Anne, *The Seven Principles of Poetry* (Boston: Writer, Inc., 1940)

Hamilton, Ian, 'A girl can't go on laughing all the time', *the Review* nos. 6 & 7 (June 1963), 36–42; reprinted in *A Poetry Chronicle* (London: Faber & Faber, 1973)

— 'The Learning of Strangeness' (*RB*), *The Times Literary Supplement* (14 November 1986), p. 1272

Hardy, Barbara, 'William Empson and *Seven Types of Ambiguity*', *Sewanee Review* 90:3 (Summer 1982), 430–39

Hartley, Anthony, 'Empson and Auden', *Spectator* 195 (9 December 1955), 815–16

— 'Poets of the Fifties', *Spectator* 193 (27 August 1954), 260–61

Hawkes, Terence, 'Take me to your Leda', *Shakespeare Survey* 40 (1988), 21–32; reprinted in *Meaning by Shakespeare* (London and New York: Routledge, 1992)

Hawthorn, J. M., 'Commitment in the Poetry of William Empson', *Trivium* 4 (May 1969), 21–30

— *Identity and Relationship: A Contribution to Marxist Theory of Literary Criticism* (London: Lawrence & Wishart, 1973), pp. 87–90

Hayman, Ronald, reply to Bateson's 'Auden's (and Empson's) Heirs', *Essays in Criticism* 7 (1957), 465–8 (with Bateson's response, pp. 468–70)

Hayward, John, 'Teasing Tricks – & True Poetry' (*CP*), *Sunday Times* (16 October 1955), p. 4

Hedges, William L., 'The Empson Treatment', *Accent* 17 (Winter 1957), 231–41

Henn, T. R., 'Science and Poetry', *Nature* 191 (5 August 1961), 534–9

Hill, Geoffrey, 'A Dream of Reason' (on Empson special number of *the Review*), *Essays in Criticism* 14:1 (1964), 91–101

Hobsbaum, Philip, review of *CP*, *Delta* (Cambridge) 8 (Spring 1956), 31–7

Holloway, John, 'The Two Languages', *London Magazine* 6 (November 1959), 16

Homberger, Eric, *The Art of the Real: Poetry in England and America since 1939* (London: J. M. Dent & Sons and Totowa, NJ: Rowman and Littlefield, 1972)

Horder, John, 'William Empson, Straight' (profile), *Guardian* (12 August 1969), p. 6

Hough, Graham, 'Graham Hough Thinks about William Empson and His Work' (obituary essay), *London Review of Books* (21 June–4 July 1984), pp. 16–17

Hughes, Richard, 'New Poetry' (*P*), *Spectator* 155 (9 August 1935), 233

Humphries, Rolfe, 'Verse Chronicle' (*CP 1949*), *Nation* 168 (2 April 1949), 396

Hyman, Stanley Edgar, *The Armed Vision: A Study in the Methods of Modern Literary Criticism* (New York: Knopf, 1948)

Izzo, Carlo, *Poesia Inglese Contemporanea da Thomas Hardy agli Apocalittici* (Parma: Ugo Guanda, 1950)

James, Trevor, 'On My Head Be It' (*GS*), *Life and Letters To-Day* 27 (December 1940), 204–9

Jensen, James, 'Some Ambiguous Preliminaries: Empson in *The Granta*', *Criticism* 8 (Fall 1966), 349–61

Jerome, Judson, *Poetry: Premeditated Art* (Boston: Houghton Mifflin Company, 1968), pp. 51–3

Johnson, Michael L., 'From Hardy to Empson: The Swerve of the Modern', *South Atlantic Review* 50:1 (January 1985), 47–58

Kell, Richard, 'Empsonium' (parody), *London Magazine* 6:10 (October 1959), 55–6

Kenner, Hugh, 'The Son of Spiders' (*CP 1949*), *Poetry* (Chicago) 76:3 (June 1950), 150–55

Kent, Christopher, 'Through the looking-glass' (*CP*), *Tablet* 206 (22 October 1955), 394–5

Kermode, Frank, 'On a Chinese Mountain' (*RB*), *London Review of Books* (20 November 1986), pp. 8–10; reprinted in *An Appetite for Poetry* (London: William Collins Sons and Cambridge: Harvard University Press, 1989)

Kinsella, Thomas, 'Two aspects of a modern poet' (*CP*), *The Irish Press* 26 (28 January 1956), 4

Krautz, Joachim, 'Imagery and Sexual Connotations in William Empson's *Aubade*', *Zeitschrift für Anglistik und Amerikanistik* 42:3 (1994), 235–42

Leavis, F. R., 'Cambridge Poetry', *Cambridge Review* 50 (1 March 1929), 317–18

— 'Education and the University: (III) Literary Studies', *Scrutiny* 9 (March 1941), 310

— 'English Letter', *Poetry* (Chicago) 46 (August 1935), 274–8

— *New Bearings in English Poetry* (London: Chatto & Windus, 1932); reissued with 'Retrospect 1950' (London: Chatto & Windus; New York: George Stewart, 1950; Harmondsworth, Middlesex: Penguin, 1963)

Lecercle, Jean-Jacques, 'William Empson's Cosmicomics', in Norris and Mapp (eds.), *William Empson*, pp. 269–93

Lehmann, John, 'The Road to East Coker' (*GS*), *Tribune* (18 October 1940), pp. 16–17

Lerner, Lawrence, 'A Silly Impulsive Eagle' (*RB*), *Spectator* 257 (1986), 35

Levi, Peter, 'Hot gin and peppermint' (*RB*), *Independent* (4 December 1986), p. 13

Lewis, Naomi, 'Sir Oracle' (*CP*), *Observer* (30 October 1955), p. 12

Lindop, Grevel, 'Poetry in the 1930s and 1940s', in *The Penguin History of Literature*, Vol. 7: *The Twentieth Century*, ed. Martin Dodsworth (Harmondsworth: Penguin, 1994), pp. 285–8

Linneman, S. S. N. D., M. Rose Ann, 'Donne as Catalyst in the Poetry of Elinor Wylie, Wallace Stevens, Herbert Read, and William Empson', *Xavier University Studies* 1 (1962), 264–72

Longland, J. L., 'Two Cambridge Magazines' (on *Experiment* no. 3), *Cambridge Review* 50 (5 June 1929), 538–9

Lowell, Robert, 'Digressions from Larkin's 20th-Century Verse', *Encounter* 40:5 (May 1973), 66–8

Lucas, John, 'William Empson: An Appreciation', *Poetry Review* 74:2 (June 1984), 21–2

Luckett, R., and R. Hyam, 'Empson and the Engines of Love: The Governing Body Decision of 1929', *Magdalene College Magazine and Record*, n.s. 35 (1990–91), 33–40

McElroy, Walter, 'Poetry Transatlantic' (*CP 1949*), *Hudson Review* 2:2 (Summer 1949), 300–11

MacKillop, Ian, 'Empson in Granta', *Cambridge Review* 117 (May 1996), 72–4

— *F. R. Leavis: A Life in Criticism* (Harmondsworth: Allen Lane, 1995)

MacNeice, Louis, 'Mr Empson as a Poet', *New Verse* no. 16 (August–September 1935), 17–18

— *Modern Poetry* (London, 1938)

Madge, Charles, 'Empson Agonistes' (*CP*), *Listen: A Review of Poetry and Criticism* 2:1 (Summer 1956), 19–22

Martin, Loveday, 'The Poetry of William Empson' (*CP*), *Contemporary Review* 189 (March 1956), 179

Mason, H. A., 'William Empson's Verse' (*P*), *Scrutiny* 4:3 (December 1935), 302–4

Maxwell-Mahon, W. D., 'The Divided Glancer: A Comment on William Empson', *English Studies in Africa* (Johannesburg) 11:1 (March 1968), 35–41

—— 'The Early Poetry of Empson', *Unisa English Studies* (University of South Africa) 10:1 (1972), 12–22

—— 'William Empson: The Development of an Idiom', *Unisa English Studies* 8:1 (March 1970), 24–6

Megaw, Moira, 'Empson Approached' (*TGA*), *Essays in Criticism* 31:1 (1981), 73–81

Meller, Horst, 'William Empson: *This Last Pain*', in *Zeitgenössische Englische Dichtung*, I: *Lyrik*, ed. H. Meller (Frankfurt, 1966), pp. 80–88

—— 'William Empsons *Arachne*: Eine Interpretation', *Archiv für das Studium der neueren Sprachen und Literaturen* 201 (August 1964), 185–90

Mellers, W. H., 'Cats in Air-Pumps (Or Poets in 1940)' (*GS*), *Scrutiny* 9:3 (December 1940), 289–300

Meyer, Gerard Previn, 'Ingenuous Ingenuity' (*CP* 1949), *Saturday Review of Literature* 32:12 (19 March 1949), 18–19

Mills, Ivor, 'Empson's Missing Dates' (a letter), *Physiological Society Magazine* no. 26 (Spring 1997), 13

Morrison, Blake, *The Movement: English Poetry and Fiction of the 1950s* (Oxford: Oxford University Press, 1980)

Muir, Edwin, 'Neat, Muted and Despondent' (*Poetry Now*, ed. G. S. Fraser), *Observer* (14 October 1956), p. 17

Naylor, Guy, 'A. D. C. Nursery Productions' (*Three Stories*), *Cambridge Review* 48 (1927), 250–51

Oakes, Philip, 'New Poetry' (*CP*), *Truth* 155 (2 December 1955), 1513

Ogawa, Kazuo, *English Poetry: Its Appreciation and Analysis* (Tokyo: Kenkyusha, 1978)

Okada, Sumie, *Western Writers in Japan* (Basingstoke, Hants.: Macmillan Press, 1999)

Ormerod, David, 'Empson's "Invitation to Juno"', *Explicator* 25:2 (October 1966), item 13

Otten, Kurt, 'William Empson: "This Last Pain" ', in *Die Modern Englische Lyrik: Interpretationen*, ed. Horst Oppel (Berlin: Erich Schmidt Verlag, 1967), pp. 185–92

Perkins, David, *A History of Modern Poetry: Modernism and After* (Cambridge and London: Harvard University Press, 1987)

Pfister, Manfred, 'Die Villanelle in der englischen Moderne: Joyce, Empson, Dylan Thomas', *Archiv für das Studium der neueren Sprachen und Literaturen* 219 (1982), 296–308

Pinsker, Sanford, 'Finite but Unbounded: The Poetic World of William Empson', *University of Windsor Review* (Ontario) 3:1 (Fall 1967), 88–96

Porter, Peter, 'Those Stay Most Haunting' (*TGA*), *New Statesman* 96 (22 & 29 December 1978), 880–81

Press, John, *The Chequer'd Shade: Reflections on Obscurity in Poetry* (London: Oxford University Press, 1963)

Pritchard, R. E., 'Milton's Satan and Empson's Old Lady', *Notes & Queries* 34 (232):1 (March 1987), 59–60

Pritchard, William H., 'The Old Buffer – The Royal Beasts and Other Works', *American Scholar* 58 (Autumn 1989), 592–7

Raine, Kathleen, 'And Learn a Style from a Despair' (*CP*), *New Statesman & Nation* 50 (5 November 1955), 580–82

— 'Correspondence' (reply to Gunn's review of *CP*), *London Magazine* 3:3 (March 1956), 66–7

— *Defending Ancient Springs* (London: Oxford University Press, 1967)

— 'Extracts from Unpublished Memoirs', in Gill, pp. 13–20; revised for *The Land Unknown* (see below)

— 'Four Poets', *New Statesman & Nation* 20 (29 December 1940), 686–7

— *The Land Unknown* (London: Hamish Hamilton, and New York: George Braziller, 1975)

Ransom, John Crowe, *The New Criticism* (Norfolk, Conn.: New Directions, 1941)

Richards, I. A., 'Cambridge Poetry' (review of *Cambridge Poetry 1929*), *Granta* 38 (8 March 1929), 359

— 'Empson's "Poems" ' (*P*), *Cambridge Review* 57 (14 February 1936), 253

— ' "How Does a Poem Know When It Is Finished?" ', in *Parts and Wholes: The Hayden Colloquium on Scientific Method and Concept*, ed. Daniel Lerner (New York: Free Press of Glencoe, and London:

Macmillan Press, 1963), pp. 163–74; reprinted in *Poetries and Sciences* (London: Routledge & Kegan Paul, 1970), pp. 105–21

— *How to Read a Page: A Course in Effective Reading with an Introduction to a Hundred Great Words* (New York: W. W. Norton, 1942; London: Kegan Paul, Trench, Trubner & Co., 1943), pp.79–81

— 'Semantic Frontiersman', in Gill, pp. 98–108

— 'William Empson', *Furioso: A Special Note*, 12 January 1940 (unpaginated supplement to *Furioso* 1:3 (Spring 1940))

Ricks, Christopher, 'Criticism at the Present Time: Two Notes', 2. 'William Empson and "the loony hooters" ', *Essays in Appreciation* (Oxford: Clarendon Press, 1996), pp. 341–53

— '*Doctor Faustus* and Hell on Earth', *Essays in Criticism* 35:2 (April 1985), 1–18; reprinted in *Essays in Appreciation* (Oxford: Clarendon Press, 1996)

— 'Empson's *Granta*' [1], *Granta* (Easter Term, 1978), [4–7]

— 'Empson's *Granta*, Part 2', *Granta* ('May Week' issue, June 1978), 25–6

— 'Empson's Poetry', in Gill, pp. 145–207; revised in *The Force of Poetry* (Oxford: Clarendon Press, 1984)

— 'William Empson, 1906–1984', *Proceedings of the British Academy* 71 (1985), 539–54

— 'William Empson in Conversation with Christopher Ricks', *the Review* nos. 6 & 7 (1963), pp. 26–35

Ridler, Anne, 'Passion into thought' (*CP*), *Manchester Guardian* (4 November 1955), p. 4

Roberts, Michael, 'Aspects of English Poetry: 1932–37', *Poetry* (Chicago) 49 (January 1937), 210–17

— 'A Metaphysical Poet' (*P*), *London Mercury* 32:190 (August 1935), 387–9

— (ed.), *New Country: Prose and Poetry by the Authors of New Signatures* (London: Hogarth Press, 1933)

— (ed.), *New Signatures* (London: Hogarth Press, 1932)

Rodway, A. E., 'The Structure of Complex Verse' (*CP*), *Essays in Criticism* 6:2 (April 1956), 232–40

Rogers, Byron, 'Man of Words' (interview), *Star* (Sheffield) (31 March 1967), p. 4

Rossetti, Geoffrey W., 'One at a Time' (on *Songs for Sixpence*), *Cambridge Review* 50 (29 November 1929), 159–60

Ryle, John, 'Flaming Heart of Darkness', *Guardian Friday Review* (7 June 1996), p. 3

Sainsbury, Ian, 'An "old fogey" Retires' (interview), *Morning Telegraph* (Sheffield) (20 July 1971), p. 6

Sale, Roger, 'The Achievement of William Empson', *Hudson Review* 19:3 (Autumn 1966), 369–90; reprinted in *Modern Heroism: Essays on D. H. Lawrence, William Empson, and J. R. R. Tolkien* (Berkeley and Los Angeles: University of California Press, 1973) (Empson's response is in *Hudson Review* 20:4 (Winter 1967), 534–8)

Sassoon, Siegfried, 'What Hope for Poetry?' (*P*), *Harper's Bazaar* (December 1935), pp. 23, 88

Schutz, Fred C., 'Apiarian Imagery in Empson's "To an Old Lady"', *Notes on Contemporary Literature* 4:2 (1974), 5–7

Selincourt, Basil de, 'Poetic Black-out' (*GS*), *Observer* (6 October 1940), p. 3

Simpson, David, 'The Collected Poems of William Empson', *Arrows* no. 65 (Jubilee Edition, 1955), 26–7

Singer, Burns, 'In Stars or in Ourselves?' (*CP*), *Encounter* 6:1 (January 1956), 82–6

Sissman, L. E., 'Just a Whack at Empson' (parody-poem), *the Review* nos. 6 and 7 (June 1963), 75

Sitwell, Edith, 'Four New Poets' (*P*), *London Mercury* 33 (February 1936), 383–90

— and Robert Herring, 'A Correspondence on the Young English Poets', *Life and Letters To-day* (December 1935), pp. 16–24

Skelton, Robin, *The Poetic Pattern* (London: Routledge & Kegan Paul, 1956)

Sparrow, John, *Sense and Poetry* (New Haven, Conn.: Yale University Press, 1934)

Spears, Monroe K., 'Cosmology and the Writer', *Hudson Review* 47:1 (Spring 1994), 29–45

Spector, Robert Donald, 'Form and Content in Empson's "Missing Dates"', *Modern Language Notes* 74 (April 1959), 310–11

Spender, Stephen, *Poetry Since 1939* (London: Longman for the British Council, 1946)

— 'The Year's Poetry, 1940' (*GS*), *Horizon* 3:14 (February 1941), 142–3

Stock, A. G., '*New Signatures* in Retrospect', in Gill, pp. 126–44

Strickland, Geoffrey, 'The Poetry of William Empson', *Mandrake* 2:9 (1953), 245–55

Swaab, Peter, '"Quite, Quite Hairy, All Over": Empson and the Royal Beasts' (*RB*), *Cambridge Review* 108:2299 (December 1987), 165–70

Symons, Julian, 'Recent Poetry' (*GS*), *New English Weekly* 18:13 (16 January 1941), 150

— review of *CP*, *Punch* 229:6010 (9 November 1955), 557–8

Taylor, Geoffrey, 'New Verse' (*CP*), *Time and Tide* 36:46 (12 November 1955), 1470, 1472

Taylor, Paul, 'The King of Ambiguity', *Independent*, Section II: *Arts* (25 July 1994), p. 19

Thomas, Dylan, 'Request to Leda: Homage to William Empson' (parody-poem), *Horizon* 6:31 (July 1942), 6

Thompson, Mark, '"On the borderland": Empson first and last', *Edinburgh Review* no. 85 (1991), 101–38

Thurley, Geoffrey, '"Partial fires": Empson's poetry', in *The Ironic Harvest: English Poetry in the Twentieth Century* (London: Edward Arnold and New York: St Martin's Press, 1974), pp. 38–53

Thwaite, Anthony, *Contemporary English Poetry: An Introduction* (Philadelphia, Penn.: Dufour, 1961)

— *Essays on Contemporary British Poetry* (Tokyo: Kenkyusha, 1957)

Tindall, William York, *Forces in Modern British Literature: 1885–1946* (New York: Alfred A. Knopf, 1947)

Tolley, A. T., *The Poetry of the Thirties* (London: Gollancz, 1975)

Tomlinson, Charles, 'Poetry Today', in *The Pelican Guide to English Literature*, Vol. VII: *The Modern Age*, ed. Boris Ford (Harmondsworth: Penguin, 1961; 2nd edn., rev., 1964), pp. 465–6

Touster, Saul, 'Empson's "Legal Fiction"', *the Review* nos. 6 & 7 (June 1963), 45–8

Trevelyan, Julian, *Indigo Days* (London: MacGibbon & Kee, 1957)

Troy, William, 'Poetry and "The Non-Euclidean Predicament"' (*CP 1949*), *Poetry* (Chicago) 74:4 (July 1949), 234–6

Vickery, John B., 'On First Reading Empson's "Letter II": Notes on Poem as Structure', *Journal of Contemporary Literature and Aesthetics* 4:1–2 (1981), 17–26

Vidan, Ivo, 'General Studies: The Royal Beasts and Other Works', *Journal of Modern Literature* 16:2–3 (Fall 1989), 340

Wain, John, 'Ambiguous Gifts: Notes on the Poetry of William Empson', *Penguin New Writing*, no. 40, ed. John Lehmann (Harmondsworth:

Penguin, 1950), pp. 116–28; reprinted as 'Ambiguous Gifts: The Poetry of William Empson', in *Preliminary Essays* (London: Macmillan, 1957), pp. 169–80

— 'Eighth Type of Ambiguity' (poem), in Conquest, pp. 90–91

— 'The Poetic Mind of William Empson', *New Lugano Review* 8–9 (1976), 95–114, 118; reprinted as 'The Poetry of William Empson', in *Professing Poetry*, pp. 284–332 (see next entry)

— *Professing Poetry* (London: Macmillan, 1977; New York: Viking, 1978)

— 'What worries Wuzzoo' (*RB*), *Sunday Telegraph* (16 November 1986)

Waller, John, 'The Butcher, The Baker, The Candlestick Maker' (*GS*), *Poetry Review* 32 (January–February 1941), 25–6 (with reply by Marguerite Wykeham, pp. 119–20)

Wanning, Andrews, 'Neither Cassandra nor Comrade' (*GS*), *Furioso: A Magazine of Poetry* 1:4 (Summer 1941), 53–4

Watson, George, 'Prophet Against God: William Empson (1906–84)', *Hudson Review* 49:1 (Spring 1996), 1–12

Wellek, René, review of Norris, *Modern Language Review* 75:1 (January 1980), 182–5

Wharton, Gordon, 'Head and Heart' (*CP*), *Books and Bookmen* 1:2 (November 1955), 38–9

Wilbur, Richard, 'Seven Poets' (*CP 1949*), *Sewanee Review* 58:1 (January–March 1950), 130–34

Wood, Michael, 'Incomparable Empson' (Gill), *New York Review of Books* (23 January 1975), pp. 30–33

Wood, Neal, *Communism and British Intellectuals* (London: Victor Gollancz and New York: Columbia University Press, 1959)

THE COMPLETE POEMS

The Fire Sermon

*Everything, Bhikkhus, is on fire. What everything, Bhikkhus, is
on fire? The eye is on fire, the visible is on fire, the knowledge of
the visible is on fire, the contact with the visible is on fire, the
feeling which arises from the contact with the visible is on fire,*
₅ *be it pleasure, be it pain, be it neither pleasure nor pain. By what
fire is it kindled? By the fire of lust, by the fire of hate by the fire
of delusion it is kindled, by birth age death pain lamentation
sorrow grief despair it is kindled, thus I say. The ear . . . say. The
nose . . . say. The tongue . . . say. The body . . . say. The mind*
₁₀ *. . . say.*

*Knowing this, Bhikkhus, the wise man, following the Aryan
path, learned in the law, becomes weary of the eye, he becomes
weary of the visible, he becomes weary of the knowledge of the
visible, he becomes weary of the contact of the visible, he*
₁₅ *becomes weary of the feeling which arises from the
contact of the visible, be it pleasure, be it pain, be it neither
pleasure nor pain. He becomes weary of the ear . . . pain. He
becomes weary of the nose . . . pain. He becomes weary of the
tongue . . . pain. He becomes weary of the body . . . pain. He*
₂₀ *becomes weary of the mind . . . pain.*

*When he is weary of these things, he becomes empty of desire.
When he is empty of desire, he becomes free. When he is free he
knows that he is free, that rebirth is at an end, that virtue is
accomplished, that duty is done, and that there is no more*
₂₅ *returning to this world; thus he knows.*

Mother, saying Anne good night,
Feared the dark would cause her fright.
'Four angels guard you,' low she said,
'One at the foot and one at the head –'

5 'Mother – quick – the pillow!! – There!!!
Missed that angel, skimmed his hair.
Never mind, we'll get the next.
Ooh! but angels make me vexed!!'

Mother, shocked, gasped feebly 'Anne!!!'
10 (A pillow disabled the water-can.)
Said Anne, 'I won't have things in white
Chant prayers about my bed all night.'

Song of the amateur psychologist

It is a deep-rooted
far stirring in strong shadow kingdoms
and ripens among
the slow rustle
5   of that midnight orchard
whose woven branches are
soft, plump or stretching, are too small
to dream of, myriad,
intercellular;
10   in timid contact
of whose slow rhythmic fingers
are woven the proud worlds.

Cathedral caverns
in not glinting limestone
15   water there changing always
the fretted hollow curves;
high vaulted arches
of the uncharted cellars,
and, it is a discovery,
20   too large for a short stride
too steep, there pass
downwards beneath them
these narrow and stone stairs.

But now rest yourself a moment, and lean
25   on the great pillars, feel
how in darkness they hum softly
holding the lit palace
and hearing riot in the halls.

Men come here often
30   with lanterns carefully,
looking over their shoulders
and feeling it something of an expedition

to choose just the one vintage
that is called for.
35   Also on great occasions
they unbrick old archways
and there lie guarded
the rich tawny
secret potions;
40   they that were buried
in an autumn
long past; are ruby,
are precious, aged
now, potent, secure.

45   Strike a light before we go on;
we need, rather, the same assurance
and yellow courage of your candle.
Guard him well however do not let him
peer from your fist too rashly at the groining
50   there is a strong and cold wind up the stairs.

Let us descend now
but carefully, they are high steps
and steep, for walking.
After a dozen of them
55   there is an even darkness
that has waited so long
it is not a light thing to disturb,
and they go on down
beyond that, it is not easy
60   to imagine what we might see
if we were holding a light house in our hands.
Might there not be – might there not –
the unchained
the insane perspective
65   the no end
and your cry recoiling –

ah, I can quite imagine you saying it, with an air of apocalyptic
and desperate capability, sincerity, security almost –

'The low roof goes
down, the stairs
arriving proudly
at no final pinpoint
go straight down
only, down always.'

Two centos

i

At Algezir,[1] and will in overplus,[2]
Their herdsmen,[3] well content to think thee page,[4] divided.[3]
Tell Isabel the queen, I looked not[5] thus
Leander, Mr Ekenhead and I did.[6]

ii

5   of them that are overcome with. Woe[1]
stay me with flagons,[2] civilly delight.[3]
So lovers contracts, images of those,[4]
so be I equalled with,[5] as dark as night.[6]

Do thy worst, blind Cupid,[7] dark amid the blaze of.[8] Woe
10   to the crown of pride,[1] and Phineus prophets old,[5]
did cry To-whoo To-whoo, and the sun did shine so[9]
(the lords and owners of,[10] poor Toms-a)[11] cold.

i
1. Chaucer Prologue l. 57.
2. Shakespeare Sonnet no. cxxxv.
3. Genesis, chapter 13.
4. Donne Elegy xvi.
5. Marlowe Ed II.
6. Don Juan, canto 2, stanza 105.

ii
1. Isaiah. xxviii.1.
2. Song of Solomon. ii.5.
3. Pope. Arbuthnot. 313.
4. Donne. Songs and Sonets. Womans constancy.
5. Paradise Lost. iii.34.
6. Shakespeare Sonet cxlvii.
7. Lear. Act iv scene 6.
8. Sams. Ag. 80.
9. Wordsworth. Idiot Boy.
10. Shakespeare Sonnet xciv.
11. Lear. Act iv scene 1.

Two songs from a libretto

i

You advise me coldly then to accept whatever
Drifts from the casual turning of the day;
Not to order an assured heart; never
To look down the coherent vestige of my way;

5   Secure in my bars, only, to let all pass;
Hear now my marriage, now my funeral bell;
Sure of a safe continuance of darkness,
Of remaining, in my heart, inviolable.

ii

Simply we do not know what are the turnings
10   Expound our poising of obscure desires,
What Minotaur in irritable matched burnings
Yearns and shall gore her intricate my fires.

Simply that no despair known of knowing
Inn continent compact continuable
15   Would mine the minor rapture of her going
Would leave me liefless but not despicable.

Simply I shall not answer for what answer
She may on her return return, or helms
Or masters the same tortured dancer.
20   Simply the mechanism overwhelms.

The Ants

We tunnel through your noonday out to you.
We carry our tube's narrow darkness there
Where, nostrum-plastered, with prepared air,
With old men running and trains whining through

5   We ants may tap your aphids for your dew.
You may not wish their sucking or our care;
Our all-but freedom, too, your branch must bear,
High as roots' depth in earth, all earth to view.

No, by too much this station the air nears.
10   How small a chink lets in how dire a foe.
What though the garden in one glance appears?

Winter will come and all her leaves will go.
We do not know what skeleton endures.
Carry at least her parasites below.

Value is in Activity

Celestial sphere, an acid green canvas hollow,
His circus that exhibits him, the juggler
Tosses, an apple that four others follow,
Nor heeds, not eating it, the central smuggler.

5   Nor heeds if the core be brown with maggots' raven,
Dwarf seeds unnavelled a last frost has scolded,
Mites that their high narrow echoing cavern
Invites forward, or with close brown pips, green folded.

Some beetles (the tupped females can worm out)
10   Massed in their halls of knowingly chewed splinter
Eat faster than the treasured fungi sprout
And stave off suffocation until winter.

Invitation to Juno

Lucretius could not credit centaurs;
Such bicycle he deemed asynchronous.
'Man superannuates the horse;
Horse pulses will not gear with ours.'

5   Johnson could see no bicycle would go;
'You bear yourself, and the machine as well.'
Gennets for germans sprang not from Othello,
Ixion rides upon a single wheel.

Courage. Weren't strips of heart culture seen
10 Of late mating two periodicities?
Did not once the adroit Darwin
Graft annual upon perennial trees?

The World's End

'Fly with me then to all's and the world's end
And plumb for safety down the gaps of stars;
Let the last gulf or topless cliff befriend,
What tyrant there our variance debars?'

5   Alas, how hope for freedom, no bars bind;
Space is like earth, rounded, a padded cell;
Plumb the stars' depth, your lead bumps you behind;
Blind Satan's voice rattled the whole of Hell.

On cushioned air what is such metal worth
10   To pierce to the gulf that lies so snugly curled?
Each tangent plain touches one top of earth,
Each point in one direction ends the world.

Apple of knowledge and forgetful mere
From Tantalus too differential bend.
15   The shadow clings. The world's end is here.
This place's curvature precludes its end.

Plenum and Vacuum

Delicate goose-step of penned scorpions
Patrols its weal under glass-cautered bubble;
Postpones, fire-cinct, their suicide defiance,
Pierced carapace stung in mid vault of bell.

5   From infant screams the eyes' blood-gorged veins
Called ringed orbiculars to guard their balls;
These stays squeeze yet eyes no relief ensanguines,
These frowns, sphincter, void-centred, burst wrinkled hold-alls.

Matter includes what must matter enclose,
10   Its consequent space, the glass firmament's air-holes.
Heaven's but an attribute of her seven rainbows.
It is Styx coerces and not Hell controls.

Une Brioche pour Cerbère

Tom nods. No senior angels see or grapple.
Tom enters Eden, nodding, the back way.
Borrows from Adam, and then eats, the Apple.
'Thank you so much for a delightful stay.'

5   If it works, it works. Nod to the man at the door.
Nor heed what gulfs, how much of earth between.
If radio light, from the last sphere before
Outer dark, reflects you, you are seen.

So can the poles look in each other's eyes.
10   Within that charmed last vacuate of air
Who is my neighbour, and who safe from spies?
Earth sees me nod. No, nothing to declare.

Porter, report not my heart contraband.
Of you, you primitive culture, stored flame,
15   I scoptophile, friend by short cut, had planned
To view the rites, no high priest first to tame.

My dear, my earth, how offer me your halls?
Grant me your Eden, I see Eden Station,
Whence stationed gauge you whose full scale appalls
20   And all whose porters would ask explanation?

Rolling the Lawn

You can't beat English lawns. Our final hope
Is flat despair. Each morning therefore ere
I greet the office, through the weekday air,
Holding the Holy Roller at the slope
5   (The English fetish, not the Texas Pope)
Hither and thither on my toes with care
I roll ours flatter and flatter. Long, in prayer,
I grub for daisies at whose roots I grope.

Roll not the abdominal wall; the walls of Troy
10   Lead, since a plumb-line ordered, could destroy.
Roll rather, where no mole dare sap, the lawn,
And ne'er his tumuli shall tomb your brawn.
World, roll yourself; and bear your roller, soul,
As martyrs gridirons, when God calls the roll.

Dissatisfaction with Metaphysics

High over Mecca Allah's prophet's corpse
(The empty focus opposite the sun)
Receives homage, centre of the universe.
How smooth his epicycles round him run,
Whose hearth is cold, and all his wives undone.

Two mirrors with Infinity to dine
Drink him below the table when they please.
Adam and Eve breed still their dotted line,
Repeated incest, a plain series.
Their trick is all philosophers' disease.

New safe straight lines are finite though unbounded,
Old epicycles numberless in vain.
Then deeper than e'er plummet, plummet sounded,
Then corpses flew, when God flooded the plain.
He promised Noah not to flood again.

Poem about a Ball in the Nineteenth Century

Feather, feather, if it was a feather, feathers for fair, or to be fair,
aroused. Round to be airy, feather, if it was airy, very, aviary,
fairy, peacock, and to be well surrounded. Well-aired, amoving,
to peacock, cared-for, share dancing inner to be among aware.
5   Peacock around, peacock to care for dancing, an air, fairing, will
he become, to stare. Peacock around, rounded, to turn the
wearer, turning in air, peacock and I declare, to wear for
dancing, to be among, to have become preferred. Peacock, a
feather, there, found together, grounded, to bearer share turned
10   for dancing, among them peacock a feather feather, dancing and
to declare for turning, turning a feather as it were for dancing,
turning for dancing, dancing being begun turning together,
together to be become, barely a feather being, beware, being a
peacock only on the stair, staring at, only a peacock to be
15   coming, fairly becoming for a peacock, be fair together being
around in air, peacock to be becoming lastly, peacock around to
be become together, peacock a very peacock to be there.

    Moving and to make one the pair, to wear for asking of all
there, wearing and to be one for wearing, to one by moving of
20   all there.

    Reproof, recovered, solitaire.

    Grounded and being well surrounded, so feathered that if a
peacock sounded, rounded and with an air for wearing, aloof
and grounded to beware.

25   Aloof, overt, to stare.

    Will he be there, can he be there, be there?

    Being a feathered peacock.

    Only a feathered peacock on the stair.

Address to a tennis-player

Gracious are you still unaltered, halted, untired no larger, Peter,
still lively competent 'So long' and so long after, laughter and
after all no, thou art Peter, upon this rock I build.

(Oh petering out no, unhaltered but very rocky, very trying,
flying the Blue Peter, beaten why, on the rocks, crying, an
old crock, cracking up breaking up, even trying making up, oh
never mind, a mind made up.)

Peter Pan, Scarborough Rock. I crack up Peter.

Unbeaten, beaten gold, a gold repeater, unhand me, minute
hand, cold clock that rocks the cradle, lifeline crack
rocket racquet, planned stand caught first-court grand stand,
unbeaten, racks the world. Knock, it stays unaltered, all rock,
sweeter to pay Paul meeter to run amok, to shock St Paul's dean
and chapeetre, sheet-iron attraction, ossi-assuefaction, petri- or
putri-, Peter a better faction, knock knock it shall remain
unlocked, third not the clock stopped, rocked, dropped, cock
cocked amidden promptly crew to tears, grew to dears, beautied
but grouted ears, pouted about his peers, boudoired abounded,
powdered or peerless, reappears.

Biers, a rock of peat as, bares bears purr peering to his
burrs. Bar star, starring poor staring Peter; thus far no, burthen
rock-girt, further; three-crowned, weeping, a triple crowing;
bitter to butter, goes out, to fair well, Simple to Simon Peter; a
rock for bread, a roc's egg for a pie. I Am That is it I Lord, give
them Peter, they dare, he bears, scarlet, Herod's purple, not
Christ, Pall's. Speech mitre Peter, key and lock bewray thee, he
carrying, Iscariot, can they deny Peter, mock wearing
Christopher renamed. Pie rock bun spy Lord, Peter face-owner
hungry, tossed Pan-cake arse-end, Peter across ascending, upside
scream cream down, once rot, hot cross buns.

New World Bistres

The darkest is near dawn, we are almost butter.
The churning is fixed now; we have 'gone to sleep'
In body, and become a living pat;
It is then that the arm churning it aches most
5   And dares least pause against the ceaseless turning.
I am sure he will soon stumble upon the gift,
Maypole his membranes, Ciro be his eyes,
A secret order, assumptive distillation;
Fitting together it will be won and seem nothing,
10   Mild artifact, false pearl, corpse margarine.
    Oh socketed too deep, oh more than tears,
Than any faint unhurrying resurrection,
That even rain, manna (the manner born,
The man born of the manor, and that bourne
15   No traveller returns. Turn Athanasius,
Turn Cardinal Bourne. The Palace, Washing Day.
Lux and her cherub, here is a myth handy).
Those glacial, dried soap film, shaken packets,
That rain of hushing elixir-centred sequins,
20   Falling through space, gracious, a feather swaying.
    Rising, triumphant, hooter, whine, mosquito,
The separator, pausing by violent movement
Stands at the even not skimming of stood cream.
Moss can be grown on tops. Gyroscopes
25   Holed with grim jewels set in resounding brass
Rector and tractor of earth's vertiges,
Claw, widely patented, pierce, sinking,
Armoured resentience their lead fathom line.

Sea Voyage

Re-plyed, extorted, oft transposed and fleeting,
Tune from plucked cotton, the cat's-cradle pattern
Dances round fingers that would scratch in meeting
And dures and fosters their abandoned kitten.
Drawn taut, this flickering of wit would freeze,
And grave, knot-diamond, its filigrees.

Pillowed on gulfs between exiguous bobbins
The Son of Spiders, crucified to lace,
Suspends a red rag to a thousand dobbins
And sails so powered to a better place.
All his gained ports, thought's inter-reached trapeze,
Map-sail, transport him towards Hercules,

Earth-bound. Blue-sea-bound, the crisp silver foam,
Forbad be crystal, a lace eringo,
Flaps from the haunch seven petticoats at home,
Wards, silk, in ocean overskirt, her rainbow.
Sand-rope, the sodden goblet of the seas
Holds, concentrate, her liquid pedigrees.
We sum in port her banquet of degrees.

High Dive

A cry, a greenish hollow undulation
Echoes slapping across the enclosed bathing-pool.
It is irrotational; one potential function
(Hollow, the cry of hounds) will give the rule.

5   Holding it then, I Sanctus brood thereover,
Inform *in posse* the tank's triple infinite
(So handy for co-ordinates), chauffeur
The girdered sky, and need not dive in it;

Stand, wolf-chased Phoebus, ϕ infinite-reined,
10   Aton of maggots of reflected girder
(Steeds that on Jonah a grim start have gained),
And need not keep the moment, nor yet murder.

Crashing and gay, musical and shocking, ·
They (green for hares) however, tear me down,
15   Rut or retract, by gulf or rocks. Menacing,
Assuring, their tin reverberant town

'Thicker than water' (cleaned out before solid),
Agglutinate, whose wounds raw air composes,
Shall clot (already has forewarned with olive
20   These doves undriven that coo, Ark neuroses),

Unless, in act, to turbulence, discerning
His shade, not image, on smashed glass disbanded,
One, curve and pause, conscious of strain of turning
Only (muscle on bone, the rein cone now handed)

25   Unchart the second, the obstetric, chooses,
Leaves isle equation by not frozen ford,
And, to break scent, under foamed new phusis
Dives to receive in memory reward.

Fall to them, Lucifer, Sun's Son. Splash high
30   Jezebel. Throw her down. They feast, I flee
Her poised tired head and eye
Whose skull pike-high mirrors and waits for me.

Leave outer concrete for the termite city
Where scab to bullet and strong brick has grown;
35   Plunge, and in vortex that destroys it, puppy,
Drink deep the imaged solid of the bone.

To an Old Lady

Ripeness is all; her in her cooling planet
Revere; do not presume to think her wasted.
Project her no projectile, plan nor man it;
Gods cool in turn, by the sun long outlasted.

5   Our earth alone given no name of god
Gives, too, no hold for such a leap to aid her;
Landing, you break some palace and seem odd;
Bees sting their need, the keeper's queen invader.

No, to your telescope; spy out the land;
10   Watch while her ritual is still to see,
Still stand her temples emptying in the sand
Whose waves o'erthrew their crumbled tracery;

Still stand uncalled-on her soul's appanage;
Much social detail whose successor fades,
15   Wit used to run a house and to play Bridge,
And tragic fervour, to dismiss her maids.

Years her precession do not throw from gear.
She reads a compass certain of her pole;
Confident, finds no confines on her sphere,
20   Whose failing crops are in her sole control.

Stars how much further from me fill my night.
Strange that she too should be inaccessible,
Who shares my sun. He curtains her from sight,
And but in darkness is she visible.

Part of Mandevil's Travels

CHAPTER 87: '*Of the faith and belyfe of Prester John, but he hath not all the full beliefe as we have.*'

Done into Verse, with Comment

'I feel half an Englishman already'
KING AMANULLAH after firing off a torpedo

Mandevil's river of dry jewels grows
Day-cycled, deathly, and iron-fruited trees;
From Paradise it runs to Pantoroze
And with great waves into the gravely seas.

5   (Olympe, and Paradise Terrestre the same
    Whence, bent to improve, King Alleluiah came
    High (Higher, in fact, as Milton boasted) hurled
    Clings to the cold slates of the Roof of the World.)

Spears pierce its desert basin, the long dawn:
10   Tower, noon, all cliquant, dock-side cranes, sag-fruited:
    And, sand-born weight, brief by waste sand upborne,
    Leave, gulfed, ere night, the bare plain, deeper rooted.

    (Herr Trinkler, there of late, reports of these,
    A million acres of dead poplar trees.
15   Well may new pit-heads to wise A appeal;
    Our desolation is of harsher steel.)

Antred, of malachite, its boulders thunder:
Involve their cataracts, one known weekend:
Then, deep, a labyrinth of landslides, under
20   The gravely sea, and seen no more, descend.

(It is cracked mud the motor service dints;
Five clays, diluvian, covered some chipped flints.
Tour well the slag-heaps, royalty, we own
The arid sowing, the tumultuous stone.)

25   Fish of another fashion the dry sea
Ride: can blast through eddies, and sail on:
Can rend the hunters whose nets drag the scree:
Are full good savour: are for Prester John.

(Paradise, like Bohemia, has no coast;
30   Of bombs and bowlers it has power to boast,
But mail-dark fish, spawned in grit-silted grotto,
Adam comes here for; and recites my motto.)

Laus Melpomines

Ah! God, they mock me, all the deaths that be,
They come no nearer than to spit at me.
My groans that miss the mortal shapes of tears
Sound as the sounding sorrows of the sea.

5   Is this the darkest morning of a dawn?
These gawds the rainbow by which God has sworn?
Are these the echoes of an art shall be
That writhe around me as I rage forlorn?

Ah! Death, discern me, and with healing hands
10 Cool the cracked critic that contentious stands.
How long must hungry harbingers of years
Howl all about me in revolting bands?

How long must yet the senseless snake of sneers
Resound and bellow on the path of peers,
15 And still the sole sad Sisyphus of style
Roll on my reins the very rock of tears?

I know the laboured number of their plays,
Have counted all their countless matinées,
And every morning that the afternoon
20 Treads in its wake, leaves me less heart to praise.

The Extasie

Walking together in the muddy lane
The shallow pauses in her conversation
Were deep, like puddles, as the blue sky;
So thin a film separated our firmaments.

5   We who are strong stand on our own feet.
You misunderstand me. We stand on the reflections of our feet.
Unsupported, we do not know whether to fall upwards or
     downwards,
Nor when the water will come through our shoes.

Camping Out

And now she cleans her teeth into the lake:
Gives it (God's grace) for her own bounty's sake
What morning's pale and the crisp mist debars:
Its glass of the divine (that will could break)
Restores, beyond nature: or lets Heaven take
(Itself being dimmed) her pattern, who half awake
Milks between rocks a straddled sky of stars.

Soap tension the star pattern magnifies.
Smoothly Madonna through-assumes the skies
Whose vaults are opened to achieve the Lord.
No, it is we soaring explore galaxies,
Our bullet boat light's speed by thousands flies.
Who moves so among stars their frame unties;
See where they blur, and die, and are outsoared.

Insomnia

Satan when ultimate chaos he would fly
battered at random by hot dry wet cold
(Probably nor Probability
his view the total cauldron of a sky
5   Milton nor Brownian hesitance foretold)
One purposed whirlwind helpless whole hours could hold.

From Bottomless Pit's bottom originally
who durst his sail-broad vans unfold
thence till (God's help the rival gust came by)
10   Hell seemed as Heaven undistinguished high
through pudding still unstirred of Anarch old
had sunk yet, down for ever, by one blast controlled.

So to the naked chaos that am I,
potion whose cooling boat grates crystal shoaled
15   gears on a mixed bank allotropically
untempered patchwork to the naked eye,
one hour the snow's one pattern, and I bold,
gale knew its point all night, though nine through compass
    rolled.

Though large charged carpet units insulately
20   alone processed, each from the former's mould,
each further angle could new shades supply,
roads every earlier opposite to tie
in single type Hell's very warders scrolled,
Nine intersterile species nightmare's full Nine were foaled.

Letter I

You were amused to find you too could fear
'The eternal silence of the infinite spaces,'
That net-work without fish, that mere
Extended idleness, those pointless places
5   Who, being possibilized to bear faces,
Yours and the light from it, up-buoyed,
Even of the galaxies are void.

I approve, myself, dark spaces between stars;
All privacy's their gift; they carry glances
10 Through gulfs; and as for messages (thus Mars'
Renown for wisdom their wise tact enhances,
Hanged on the thread of radio advances)
For messages, they are a wise go-between,
And say what they think common-sense has seen.

15 Only, have we space, common-sense in common,
A tribe whose life-blood is our sacrament,
Physics or metaphysics for your showman,
For my physician in this banishment?
Too non-Euclidean predicament.
20 Where is that darkness that gives light its place?
Or where such darkness as would hide your face?

Our jovial sun, if he avoids exploding
(These times are critical), will cease to grin,
Will lose your circumambient foreboding;
25 Loose the full radiance his mass can win
While packed with mass holds all that radiance in;
Flame far too hot not to seem utter cold
And hide a tumult never to be told.

Letter II

Searching the cave gallery of your face
My torch meets fresco after fresco ravishes
Rebegets me; it crumbles each; no trace
Stays to remind me what each heaven lavishes.

5   How judge their triumph, these primeval stocks,
When to the sketchbook nought but this remains,
A gleam where jellyfish have died on rocks,
Bare canvas that the golden frame disdains?

Glancing, walk on; there are portraits yet, untried,
10   Unbleached; the process, do not hope to change.
Let us mark in general terms their wealth, how wide
Their sense of character, their styles, their range.

Only walk on; the greater part have gone;
Whom lust, nor cash, nor habit join, are cold;
15   The sands are shifting as you walk; walk on,
The new is an emptier darkness than the old.

Crossing and doubling, many-fingered, hounded,
Those desperate stars, those worms dying in flower
Ashed paper holds, nose-sailing, search their bounded
20   Darkness for a last acre to devour.

Villanelle

It is the pain, it is the pain, endures.
Your chemic beauty burned my muscles through.
Poise of my hands reminded me of yours.

What later purge from this deep toxin cures?
5   What kindness now could the old salve renew?
It is the pain, it is the pain, endures.

The infection slept (custom or change inures)
And when pain's secondary phase was due
Poise of my hands reminded me of yours.

10   How safe I felt, whom memory assures,
Rich that your grace safely by heart I knew.
It is the pain, it is the pain, endures.

My stare drank deep beauty that still allures.
My heart pumps yet the poison draught of you.
15   Poise of my hands reminded me of yours.

You are still kind whom the same shape immures.
Kind and beyond adieu. We miss our cue.
It is the pain, it is the pain, endures.
Poise of my hands reminded me of yours.

Arachne

Twixt devil and deep sea, man hacks his caves;
Birth, death; one, many; what is true, and seems;
Earth's vast hot iron, cold space's empty waves:

King spider, walks the velvet roof of streams:
5   Must bird and fish, must god and beast avoid:
Dance, like nine angels, on pin-point extremes.

His gleaming bubble between void and void,
Tribe-membrane, that by mutual tension stands,
Earth's surface film, is at a breath destroyed.

10   Bubbles gleam brightest with least depth of lands
But two is least can with full tension strain,
Two molecules; one, and the film disbands.

We two suffice. But oh beware, whose vain
Hydroptic soap my meagre water saves.
15   Male spiders must not be too early slain.

The Scales

The proper scale would pat you on the head
But Alice showed her pup Ulysses' bough
Well from behind a thistle, wise with dread;

And though your gulf-sprung mountains I allow
(Snow-puppy curves, rose-solemn dado band)
Charming for nurse, I am not nurse just now.

Why pat or stride them, when the train will land
Me high, through climbing tunnels, at your side,
And careful fingers meet through castle sand.

Claim slyly rather that the tunnels hide
Solomon's gems, white vistas, preserved kings,
By jackal sandhole to your air flung wide.

Say (she suspects) to sea Nile only brings
Delta and indecision, who instead
Far back up country does enormous things.

Essay

Let Rome in Tiber melt, and the wide arch
Of the ranged empire fall.

The wide arch of free stones that did not fall
(High through gravity, unmoved, unmortared)
Budded to Bows of Promise in small skies
Of many Norman recessed painted porches;
5   Jerked into Gothic as it cracked; melted
Only to flow towards heaven into spires.
    The cream-bowl of that arch (reflected sky)
One must observe by ski-ing its crisp flakes
And needs dynamics to approve its calm.
10   The roar of wind freezing your ears, the hiss
Of ploughed snow, only, insisting speed,
You watch the unchanged tarpaulin of white surface
(Sail in the wind, or sheet when stairs are burning)
And the huge valley and more distant dado
15   Move not the calm perspective of their Bonzo,
Maintain the nursery of their cart-horse curves.
Or you may skim (ten times that scale) in buses
The vast and hollow English skulls of cloud-banks,
(I have not done so) or compute the sun's
20   Intolerable curve (he rides straight as yet)
And let him not aim merely at Hercules.
    These casual remarks would only claim
Such legacies arrive at least inverted;
The larger the estates, the more diffuse;
25   The more admired, the more extraordinary,
The more as the third son, on milk-white palfrey,
Taking your bailiff as your Sancho Panza,
(To find your fortune somewhere in the next village)
You set off with no hope of riding round.

Legal Fiction

Law makes long spokes of the short stakes of men.
Your well fenced out real estate of mind
No high flat of the nomad citizen
Looks over, or train leaves behind.

5   Your rights extend under and above your claim
Without bound; you own land in Heaven and Hell;
Your part of earth's surface and mass the same,
Of all cosmos' volume, and all stars as well.

Your rights reach down where all owners meet, in Hell's
10   Pointed exclusive conclave, at earth's centre
(Your spun farm's root still on that axis dwells);
And up, through galaxies, a growing sector.

You are nomad yet; the lighthouse beam you own
Flashes, like Lucifer, through the firmament.
15   Earth's axis varies; your dark central cone
Wavers, a candle's shadow, at the end.

Sleeping out in a College Cloister

Stevenson says they wake at two o'clock
Who lie with Earth, when the birds wake, and sigh;
Turn over, as does she, once in the night;
Breathe and consider what this quiet is,
5   Conscious of sleep a moment, and the stars.
But it's about then one stamped on someone
And chose an animate basis for one's mattress,
It must be later you look round and notice
The ground plan has been narrowed and moved up;
10   How much more foliage appears by starlight;
That Hall shelters at night under the trees.
   Earth at a decent distance is the Globe
(One has seen them smaller); within a hundred miles
She's *terra firma*, you look down to her.
15   There is a nightmare period between
(As if it were a thing you had to swallow)
When it engulfs the sky, and remains alien,
When the full size of the thing coming upon you
Rapes the mind, and will not be unimagined.
20   The creepiness of Cambridge scenery,
In the same way, consists in having trees,
And never, from any view-point, looking 'wooded' –
What was once virgin forest, in safe hands.
   But here the opposite disorder charms;
25   What was planned as airy and wide open space,
Grown cramped, seem stifled here under traditions,
(Traditor), their chosen proportions lost;
Here jungle re-engulfs palace and campus;
The '*high* hall garden' of Lawn-Tennyson
30   (This is the uncomfortable view of night)
Drowned under flounces and bell-calm of trees.

Earth has Shrunk in the Wash

They pass too fast. Ships, and there's time for sighing;
Express and motor, Doug can jump between.
Only dry earth now asteroid her flying
Mates, if they miss her, must flick past unseen;

5   Or striking breasts that once the air defended
(Bubble of rainbow straddling between twilights,
Mother-of-pearl that with earth's oyster ended)
They crash and burrow and spill all through skylights.

There, airless now, from the bare sun take cancer,
10   Curve spines as earth and gravitation wane,
Starve on the mirror images of plants, or
Miss diabeatic down odd carbon chain.

One daily tortures the poor Christ anew
(On every planet moderately true)
15   But has much more to do,
And can so much entail here,
Daily brings rabbits to a new Australia,
New unforeseen, new cataclysmic failure,

And cannot tell. He who all answers brings
20   May (ever in the great taskmaster's eye)
Dowser be of his candle as of springs,
And pump the valley with the tunnel dry.

I remember to have wept with a sense of the unnecessary.
'Do you think me so ungenerous that I need to be deceived about
    this?
Do you think me such a fool that these tactics will deceive me?'
Now, on the contrary, I shall speak with reverence of liars.

5   What you must save for is the Golden Bowl,
Cast anthropoid, beaten to delicacy;
One depends for that, though hollow, upon industrialism,
Upon milkwhite metal, upon furnaces all night.
Having got the thing one may fill it when required, at leisure,
10   From any river, from the common tap;
Those cloud-pipes being frozen, with marine tears;
And there will always be flowers to stick into it in the
    springtime.

Lies would be more serious if one could lie about the matter in
    hand;
But it is an impertinence to think oneself so penetrating.
15   What people tell you by lies is how they would deal with this if it
    was true,
What they would like to make you think about this,
How they lie when they are lying about this,
The fact that they think this worth repeating or inventing,
Or the fact that they will endeavour to make this true,
20   And, whether the external circumstances are favourable to them
    or not,
These are important truths, and you have been told them.

People who feel that lies make life intolerable,
That it is madness to attempt living, since people are liars,
Are like people who look at the handbook before the picture,
25   Are like people who wish the words of a poem to have a single
    meaning,
Are unable to feel safe unless they are irrelevantly informed.

Lies are the discipline of knowing that people are not you.
It is licentious not to lie to a friend.
The belief in truth leads to many untrue beliefs.
30   It leads to the belief that a series of earnest statements make a
      poem.

If one could speak the whole truth about lies one would be
      contradicting oneself.

Do you think me so ungenerous that I need to be deceived about
      this?
Do you think me such a fool that these tactics will deceive me?

To Charlotte Haldane

(who asked for a poem on her birthday).

A task of terror. I must first dissent
From all the frankness that such themes intend,
And all who blame and who commend.

What insolence and what abandonment
To claim at large that one has known a friend,
And, knowing, could in thought amend;

That all her value, in such knowing pent,
One dare show her, and say no more was meant,
'Madame, l'addition', on one paper penned.

And would I sum you to your end,
Even to reign, myself, God at your judgement,
And so assure you what he best can send?

Flighting for Duck

Egyptian banks, an avenue of clay,
Define the drain between constructed marshes
(Two silted lakes, silver and brown, with grass,
Without background, far from hills, at evening).
Its pomp makes a high road between their sheets
(Mud shoals, a new alluvium, dabbled water,
Shallow, and specked with thistles, not yet mastered)
At the subdued triumph of whose end
Two transept banks, the castle guard, meet it,
Screening the deeper water they surround
With even line of low but commanding pinetrees
Dark but distinguished as a row of peacocks.
The darker silhouette is where a barn
Straddling two banks over a lesser channel
Stands pillared upon treetrunks like a guildhall
Empty, mudheaped, through which the alluvial scheme
Flows temporary as the modern world.
The mud's tough glue is drying our still feet.
A mild but powerful flow moves through the flats
Laden with soil to feed the further warping.

'What was that drumming in the sky? What cry
Squawked from the rustled rushes a reply?
Was it near? Are they coming?
Could you hear?' Sound travels a good way by night;
That farm dog barking's half a mile away.
But when the swarms gathering for food repay us
This hint of anti-aircraft is disarmed
And as the fleets at a shot reascend
The eye orders their unreachable chaos
(The stars are moving like these duck, but slower,
Sublime, their tails absurd, their voices harsh)
And analyses into groups the crowds.
Two surfaces of birds, higher and lower,
Rise up and cross each other and distend

35 As one flight to the river turns, alarmed.
They are out of shot, and like the turning clouds
From meditative cigarettes amuse,
Manure in smoke over the fructuant marsh,
Curled vapour, incense from the cult of Ouse.

40 Bang. Bang. Two duck blur 'mid the social crew;
For man created, to man's larder due.
With plump or splash on the new-nurtured field
To Reason's arm they proper homage yield.
'The well-taught dogs wait but the voice to run,
45 Eager, and conscious of the murd'ring gun.'

Starlit, mistcircled, one whole pearl embrowned,
An even dusked silver of earth and sky
Held me, dazzled with cobwebs, staring round.

The black band of my hat leapt to my eye.
50 Alone in sight not coloured like the ground
It lit, like a struck match, everything by.

Letter III

Re-edify me, moon, give me again
My undetailed order, the designer's sketches.
Strong from your beams I can sustain the sun's
That discompose me to disparate pain.
Your vast reflection from that altar runs
But 'o'er the dark her silver mantle' stretches;
Boxed, therefore, in your cedar, my cigarette
Kept moist, and with borrowed fragrance, may do yet.

My pleasure in the simile thins.
The moon's softness makes deep velvet of shadows;
Only lightning beats it for the lace of Gothic
On parties waiting for romance of ruins.
No lunacy, no re-imagined flick
The full relief your restoration glows.
On my each face you a full sky unfurl;
You heal the blind into a round of pearl.

'When sleepless lovers, just at twelve, awake'
(God made such light, before sun or focus, shine)
I, nightmare past, in sane day take no harm,
(Passed too the cold bitter pallor of day-break),
And diffused shadowless daylight of your calm
Empties its heaven into my square garish sky-sign.
These then your crowns: offspring of Heaven first-born,
Earth's *terra firma*, the Hell-Gate of Horn.

Rebuke for a dropped brick

Vulture, to eat his heart, staked down,
Known suicide's, Prometheus', Jove-hated
And still at cross-roads; to have shown renown
Twisted, and leave him fumigated

5   Whose heart draped for a sleeve, beaten purple,
Gold leaf, a laurel and a covering,
Fretted buttressed ball made, ant-like, of church bell,
Contains pulp Nessus of not knowing.

Myth

Young Theseus makes a mission of his doom
And strides from narrow to more narrow room.
His hand, a flame on the sand powder-train,
Hisses, well certain that the clue will find,
5   And crumbles it behind,
The Minotaur to gain.

No victim yet could the sand rope renew.
At least he holds a secondary clue.
He, least surprised, has this escape devised:
10   Wind he the spinster's wool, his sail unfolds
Where Ariadne holds
Her cobweb, ill-advised.

UFA Nightmare

Gramophony. Telephony. Photophony.
The mighty handles and persensate dials
That rule my liner multi-implicate
Ring round, Stonehenge, a wide cold concrete room.
5   (I run the row from A to O, and so
– To and fro; periscope, radio –
We know which way we go.)
    'If we can reach the point
Before the tide, there is another style.
10   I shall checkmate, given the whole board;
Juggling the very tittles in the air
Shall counterblast the dreadnought machiner.'
    (Scamper, scamper, scamper.
Huge elbows tumble toward chaos.
15   Lurch, sag, and hesitation on the dials.)
    A tiny figure, seated in the engine,
    Weevil clicking in a hollow oak,
    Pedals, parched with the fear of solitude.

Warning to undergraduates

My friends who have not yet gone down
From that strange cackling little town,
Attend, before you burn your boats,
To these few simple College Notes.

5   Lock up whatever it appears
Might give a celibate Ideas.
You'd best import your own stout box;
They keep the keys of College locks
(Not that they wish, especially, to;
10   It is their duty, and they do).

Remember what a porter's for;
He hears *ad portam*, at the door;
He carries (*portat*) as he ought
(Dons love a Latin pun, with port)
15   All tales and all exciting letters
Straight to the councils of his betters[1]
(Not that he wishes so to thrill;
But it's his duty, and he will).

Remember that a bedder's dreams
20   Are very active on such themes.
Don't let her fancies loose one minute
(Take most care when there's nothing in it).
'Don't clear the table, please, today,
Till we have started for the play.'
25   – She'll know what *that* means, right away.

Remember, though it's wise to chat,
She's getting 'evidence' from that.
Which, kept the necessary years,
At last will tickle the right ears.

30   Remember nobody will *say*
When talk is getting under way.
A perfect freedom they allow,
Eagerly hoping for a row.

Which, when it comes, I hope you'll try
35   To counter with a working lie.
Without deceiving, this endears.
They have been practising for years.

But oh, whatever game you play
(Here is the moral of my lay)
40   *Never* believe the words they say
To make you give yourself away.

For oh, to such too careless men
What awful things will happen then.
See where the chaste good dons in rows
45   (A squinting, lily-like repose)
Have heard more tattle than one knows.
See where the Majesty of Cambridge towers;
Gives orders far beyond its powers;
Wields the unwieldy keys of Hell,
50   And shoos you from the town as well.
See, peeping, anxious, and discreet,
And listening for each other's feet,
Your various *kinderhearted* judges;
They hope you will not bear them grudges.
55   Their friendship is now much enhanced.
You must not think they're not advanced.[2]
Their minds are desperately broad;
They sat in terror on the festive Board
And damned you hardly of their own accord.
60   It is not *them* you must abuse.
And have you any further news?

Oh do be warned by what will happen there,
And go to Bedford or to Leicester Square.

Or would you please those who control your ends
Follow where their high patronage commends,
And stick to what you learned at school, my friends.

Notes

1. Do not suppose these facts are wrong;
   I learn in suffering what I teach in song.

2. The noblest art's the art to blot,
   Just there I've blotted a whole lot.

This Last Pain

This last pain for the damned the Fathers found:
'They knew the bliss with which they were not crowned.'
   Such, but on earth, let me foretell,
   Is all, of heaven or of hell.

5   Man, as the prying housemaid of the soul,
May know her happiness by eye to hole:
   He's safe; the key is lost; he knows
   Door will not open, nor hole close.

'What is conceivable can happen too,'
10   Said Wittgenstein, who had not dreamt of you;
   But wisely; if we worked it long
   We should forget where it was wrong.

Those thorns are crowns which, woven into knots,
Crackle under and soon boil fool's pots;
15   And no man's watching, wise and long,
   Would ever stare them into song.

Thorns burn to a consistent ash, like man;
A splendid cleanser for the frying-pan:
   And those who leap from pan to fire
20   Should this brave opposite admire.

All those large dreams by which men long live well
Are magic-lanterned on the smoke of hell;
   This then is real, I have implied,
   A painted, small, transparent slide.

25   These the inventive can hand-paint at leisure,
Or most emporia would stock our measure;
   And feasting in their dappled shade
   We should forget how they were made.

Feign then what's by a decent tact believed
30 And act that state is only so conceived,
       And build an edifice of form
       For house where phantoms may keep warm.

Imagine, then, by miracle, with me,
(Ambiguous gifts, as what gods give must be)
35   What could not possibly be there,
       And learn a style from a despair.

Description of a View

Well boiled in acid and then laid on glass
(A labelled strip) the specimen of building,
Though concrete, was not sure what size it was,
And was so large as to compare with nothing.
5   High to a low and vulnerable sky
It rose, and could have scraped it if it chose;
But, plain, and firm, and cleanly, like stretched string,
It would not think of doing such a thing;
On trust, it did not try.
10   My eye walked up the ladder of its windows.

Stretched in the crane's long pencil of a stalk
(Whose dry but tough metal brown of grass
Flowered its salted down on this tall chalk)
Sole as the bridge Milton gave Death to pass
15   The beam of Justice as in doubt for ever
Hung like a Zeppelin over London river.
Its lifted sealine impiously threatened deluge,
Fixed, like a level rainbow, to the sky;

Whose blue glittered with a frosted silver
20   Like palace walls in Grimm papered with needles,
The sands all shining in its larger concrete,
A dome compact of all but visible stars.

Homage to the British Museum

There is a Supreme God in the ethnological section;
A hollow toad shape, faced with a blank shield.
He needs his belly to include the Pantheon,
Which is inserted through a hole behind.
At the navel, at the points formally stressed, at the organs of
    sense,
Lice glue themselves, dolls, local deities,
His smooth wood creeps with all the creeds of the world.

Attending there let us absorb the cultures of nations
And dissolve into our judgement all their codes.
Then, being clogged with a natural hesitation
(People are continually asking one the way out),
Let us stand here and admit that we have no road.
Being everything, let us admit that is to be something,
Or give ourselves the benefit of the doubt;
Let us offer our pinch of dust all to this God,
And grant his reign over the entire building.

Note on Local Flora

There is a tree native in Turkestan,
Or further east towards the Tree of Heaven,
Whose hard cold cones, not being wards to time,
Will leave their mother only for good cause;
5   Will ripen only in a forest fire;
Wait, to be fathered as was Bacchus once,
Through men's long lives, that image of time's end.
I knew the Phoenix was a vegetable.
So Semele desired her deity
10   As this in Kew thirsts for the Red Dawn.

Letter IV

Hatched in a rasping darkness of dry sand
　　The child cicada some brave root discovers:
Sucks with dumb mouth while his long climb is planned
　　That high must tunnel through the dust that smothers:
5　　　　Parturient with urine from this lover
Coheres from chaos, only to evade,
An ordered Nature his own waste has made,
And builds his mortared Babel from the incumbent shade.

On my unpointed Atlantic where bergs float
10　　In endless cold: its scream of gulls: the claw,
A Roman feather at the back of the throat,
　　Wave-shutter, hanging, flapping, nape and jaw;
　　　　You lay your sunbeam and a part can soar
As tear-clouds, safe beneath their maker, move
15　In air-ships' gross security, rove and prove
The virgin's fertile lands, Spain-stolen, treasure-trove.

The highest in his bowels (God had come)
　　Israel, determined to digest, had striven;
'I will not let thee go,' told Helium,
20　　The unvalenced self-enclosing air of Heaven.
　　　　These risings have more earth-born gas as leaven,
Cheaper, less 'bitter in the belly,' free
If rain to make but little in the sea
Or if on fire to make too fierce an empyry.

25　Therefore, my dear, though you can have it all
　　As giving goes, the car more safe would ride
Slung on star-netting of a larger ball
　　　　Putting its eggs in wicker-work skywide:
　　　　Stars less monogamously deified:
30　Who not by light, merely by being far,
Make real Rotational Phenomena,
Prove that I satellite and you true centre are.

Who, being fixed and far, calm and surprise:
Being no further, shutter and enclose
35 A rounded universe: who name the size,
Imply the creature that can count their rows.
Your sun alone yielding its beauty glows
In growth upon the planet. They are song
Or call the tune to make the dancing throng
40 Free only as they aloof compose it and are strong.

Doctrinal Point

The god approached dissolves into the air.

Magnolias, for instance, when in bud,
Are right in doing anything they can think of;
Free by predestination in the blood,
5   Saved by their own sap, shed for themselves,
Their texture can impose their architecture;
Their sapient matter is always already informed.

Whether they burgeon, massed wax flames, or flare
Plump spaced-out saints, in their gross prime, at prayer,
10   Or leave the sooted branches bare
To sag at tip from a sole blossom there
They know no act that will not make them fair.

Professor Eddington with the same insolence
Called all physics one tautology;
15   If you describe things with the right tensors
All law becomes the fact that they can be described with them;
This is the Assumption of the description.
The duality of choice becomes the singularity of existence;
The effort of virtue the unconsciousness of foreknowledge.

20   That over-all that Solomon should wear
Gives these no cope who cannot know of care.
They have no gap to spare that they should share
The rare calyx we stare at in despair.
They have no other that they should compare.
25   Their arch of promise the wide Heaviside layer
They rise above a vault into the air.

Letter V

Not locus if you will but envelope,
Paths of light not atoms of good form;
Such tangent praise, less crashing, not less warm,
May gain more intimacy for less hope.

5   Not the enclosed letter, then, the spirited air,
The detached marble, not the discovered face;
I can love so for truth, as still for grace,
Your humility that will not hear or care.

You are a metaphor and they are lies
10 Or there true least where their knot chance unfurls;
You are the grit only of those glanced pearls
That not for me shall melt back to small eyes.

Wide-grasping glass in which to gaze alone
Your curve bars even fancy at its gates;
15 You are the map only of the divine states
You, made, nor known, nor knowing in, make known.

Yet if I love you but as Cause unknown
Cause has at least the Form that has been shown,
Or love what you imply but to exclude
20 That vacuum has your edge, your attitude.

Duality too has its Principal.
These lines you grant me may invert to points;
Or paired, poor grazing misses, at your joints,
Cross you on painless arrows to the wall.

Letter VI: a marriage

Rejoice where possible all hares of March
And any daffodils not forced at this date.
I too attempt an epithalamion
Never to be thrust on your unwilling notice
5   Still less before the public, annotated.
    Life's not more strange than this traditional theme.

Terrified by the purity of your dry beauty
Dry tough and fresh as the grass on chalk downs –
The metaphor now seems stale to me only because
10 It drove me younger to as empty a love –
I have not dared mention to you even the ideal
Version of love sent neatly in typescript
Not altered before publication
And drowned on meeting in my interminable yattering
    conversation.
15   My life's more weak than this traditional theme.

Envisioning however the same beauty in taxiboys
And failing to recognize in one case
What with drink and the infantilism of the Japanese type
The fact that it had not yet attained puberty
20 I was most rightly (because of another case
Where the jealousy of the driver seemed the chief factor)
– Not indeed technically, named only in vernacular newspapers,
And who knows who knows –
Deported from that virtuous and aesthetic country;
25   Life being as strange as this traditional theme.

I remember only once bathing in the sight of your eyes
Paying some attention to this bloodless series
– One would think to the first – the grey eyes open

Large milky lit fastened steadily on me
30 Not knowing what to think of what might come next
Supposing I was ever to stop haranguing the tea party;
    There is a social weight on the traditional theme.

It seemed to me impossible to admit that such a signal
(Of which I was certain, which you would now certainly deny)
35 So dissolving and so noble, had been even recognized,
Still less, having sent them to their owner out of a clownish
        honesty,
To make sensual capital out of writings
Of a sort so much lectured on
As to be practised with decency only for clinical purposes.
40   Life is allied to this traditional theme.

Nor am I sure I did not imagine a comparison
– I was at least hushed and ashamed by those perhaps
        misinterpreted eyes –
To the eyes I was to see not long after on my mother,
Thank God not since as yet, cool, liquid, larger than possible,
45 Expecting ill-treatment, inquiring, a young girl's,
When after inducing a goodnatured virgin to seduce me
In a morass of mutual misunderstandings, I was kicked out
From a settled job, and hoped I had escaped from you.
    But life was as strange as this traditional theme.

50 One of these poems at least occurred, long after being written.
In the next bed to you in a pub in Vienna
I watched the moon shadow of the window upright
Walk clear across neck and face, in perhaps half an hour,
Continually illuminating new beauties,
55 Placing in you one minute after another everything
I know of admirable in the history of man.
    There is not much more in this traditional theme.

I as in one instant felt during that time
By a trick with time I have known otherwise
60 Only in the absurd race of an ill-designed chemistry examination

Where the quarters struck consecutively; but that I won;
Perhaps inversely too in the still photograph
Of shooting a snipe, already behind me, before I knew I had
    tried
– I am trying to remember triumphs –
65   What else but this is the traditional theme?

Maintained one exhausting ecstasy
Interrupted only at moments by a nuisance
A foam of self-consciousness and delight, through which I now
    know that this occurred.
As the shadow passed to your hair, leaving only truth, I spoke.
70 You woke and understood this at once. A porcine
Expression of complacent pleasure
Rounded with a fine clang my series
Before you turned over and hid the face under the bedclothes.
    One could fit this into the traditional theme.

Bacchus

The laughing god born of a startling answer
  (Cymbal of clash in the divided glancer
  Forcing from heaven's the force of earth's desire)
Capped a retort to sublime earth by fire
5 And starred round within man its salt and glitter
    (Round goblet, but for star- or whirled- map fitter?
    Earth lost in him is still but earth fulfilled),
Troubled the water till the spirit 'stilled
And flowered round tears-of-wine round the dimmed flask
10   (The roundest ones crack least under this task;
    It is the delicate glass stands heat, better than stone.
    This is the vessel could have stood alone
    Were it not fitted both to earth and sky),
Which trickled to a sea, though wit was dry,
15 Making a brew thicker than blood, being brine,
Being the mother water which was first made blood,
All living blood, and whatever blood makes wine.

The god arkitect whose coping with the Flood
Groyned the white stallion arches of the main
20   (And miner deeps that in the dome of the brain
    Take Iris' arches' pupillage and Word)
Walked on the bucking water like a bird
And, guard, went round its rampart and its ball
    (Columbus' egg sat on earth's garden wall
25   And held the equitation of his bar;
    Waves beat his bounds until he foamed a star
    And mapped with fire the skyline that he ploughed),
Trod and divined the inwheeling serene cloud,
    (And who knows if Narcissus dumb and bent –)
30 Shed and fermented to a firmament
    (– May use his pool as mirror for the skies?)
Blind Hera's revelation peacock eyes
    (Before-and-behind

Trophies the golden throne
35   May still be planted on;
   Incestuous Chaos will breed permanent).
Helled to earth's centre Ixion at the wheel
   (He boxed the compassing of his appeal.
   Her centaur, born thence, schooled
40   This hero, the paunched beaker, ether-cooled)
Still makes go round the whirled fooled clouded wheal.

The god who fled down with a standard yard
   (Surveying with that reed which was his guard
   He showed to John the new Jerusalem.
45   It was a sugar-cane containing rum,
   And hence the fire on which these works depend)
Taught and quivered strung upon the bend
An outmost crystal a recumbent flame
   (He drinks all cups the tyrant could acclaim;
50   He still is dumb, illimitably wined;
   Burns still his nose and liver for mankind . . .)
It is an ether, such an agony.
In the thin choking air of Caucasus
He under operation lies for ever
55 Smelling the chlorine in the chloroform.
The plains around him flood with the destroyers
Pasturing the stallions in the standing corn.

The herm whose length measured degrees of heat
   (Small lar that sunned itself in Mercury
60   And perked one word there that made space ends meet)
Fluttered his snake too lightly into see
   (Most fertile thief, and journal to inquire)
The mortal Eden forming, and the fire.
A smash resounding in its constancy.
65 This burst the planet Bacchus in the sky.
Thence dry lone asteroids took heart to be.
So soon the amalgam with mercury
This plumbing: given with it free, the house
Not built with hands: the silver crucible,

70 Butt-armed: the sovereigns: eats into flaked sloughs.
Paste for the backs of mirrors, there he lies;
Leper scales fall always from his eyes.

She whom the god had snatched into a cloud
Came up my stair and called to me across
75 The gulf she floated over of despair.
Came roaring up as through triumphal arches
Called I should warm my hands on her gold cope
Called her despair the coping of her fire.

The god in making fire from her despair
80 Cast from the parabola of falling arches
An arch that cast his focus to the skyline
    Cold focus burning from the other's fire
    Arachne sailing her own rope of cloud
    A Tracer photon with a rocket's life-line
85 And purged his path with a thin fan of fire

Round steel behind the lights of the god's car

A wheel of fire that span her head across
Borne soaring forward through a crowd of cloud
Robed in fire round as heaven's cope
90 The god had lit up her despair to fire
Fire behind grates of a part of her despair
And rang like bells the vaults and the dark arches.

Your Teeth are Ivory Towers

There are some critics say our verse is bad
Because Piaget's babies had the same affection,
Proved by interview. These young were mad,

They spoke not to Piaget but to themselves. Protection
5   Indeed may safely grow less frank; a Ba
Cordial in more than one direction

Can speak well to itself and yet please Pa.
So too Escape Verse has grown mortal sin.
This gives just one advantage; a moral Ha

10   Can now be retorted in kind. Panoplied in
Virtuous indignation, gnawing his bone,
A man like Leavis plans an Escape. To begin

With brickbats as your basis of the known
Is to lose ground, and these ones were compiled
15   From a larger building: The safety valve alone

Knows the worst truth about the engine; only the child
Has not yet been misled. You say you hate
Your valve or child? You may be wise or mild.

The claim is that no final judge can state
20   The truth between you; there is no such man.
This leads to anarchy; we must deliberate.

We could once carry anarchy, when we ran
Christ and the magnificent milord
As rival pets; the thing is, if we still can

25   Lacking either. Or take Faust, who could afford
'All things that move between the quiet poles'
To be made his own. He had them all on board.

The poles define the surface and it rolls
Between their warring virtues; the spry arts
30   Can keep a steady hold on the controls

By seeming to evade. But if it parts
Into uncommunicable spacetimes, few
Will hint or ogle, when the stoutest heart's

Best direct yell will never reach; though you
35   Look through the very corners of your eyes
Still you will find no star behind the blue;

This gives no scope for trickwork. He who tries
Talk must always plot and then sustain,
Talk to himself until the star replies,

40   Or in despair that it could speak again
Assume what answers any wits have found
In evening dress on rafts upon the main,
Not therefore uneventful or soon drowned.

Aubade

Hours before dawn we were woken by the quake.
My house was on a cliff. The thing could take
Bookloads off shelves, break bottles in a row.
Then the long pause and then the bigger shake.
It seemed the best thing to be up and go.

And far too large for my feet to step by.
I hoped that various buildings were brought low.
The heart of standing is you cannot fly.

It seemed quite safe till she got up and dressed.
The guarded tourist makes the guide the test.
Then I said The Garden? Laughing she said No.
Taxi for her and for me healthy rest.
It seemed the best thing to be up and go.

The language problem but you have to try.
Some solid ground for lying could she show?
The heart of standing is you cannot fly.

None of these deaths were her point at all.
The thing was that being woken he would bawl
And finding her not in earshot he would know.
I tried saying Half an Hour to pay this call.
It seemed the best thing to be up and go.

I slept, and blank as that I would yet lie.
Till you have seen what a threat holds below,
The heart of standing is you cannot fly.

Tell me again about Europe and her pains,
Who's tortured by the drought, who by the rains.
Glut me with floods where only the swine can row
Who cuts his throat and let him count his gains.
It seemed the best thing to be up and go.

30 A bedshift flight to a Far Eastern sky.
Only the same war on a stronger toe.
The heart of standing is you cannot fly.

Tell me more quickly what I lost by this,
Or tell me with less drama what they miss
35 Who call no die a god for a good throw,
Who say after two aliens had one kiss
It seemed the best thing to be up and go.

But as to risings, I can tell you why.
It is on contradiction that they grow.
40 It seemed the best thing to be up and go.
Up was the heartening and the strong reply.
The heart of standing is we cannot fly.

The Fool

Describe the Fool who knows
All but his foes.
Wading through tears striding the covered sneers
And against tide, he goes.

5   Delighting in the freedom of those bounds
Your scorn and even your reason are his aid.
It is an absolute health that will not heal his wounds.
Wisdom's the charger mounts him above shade,

Hanged by suspense and eternally delayed.
10   'Your eyes are corpse-worms;
Your lips poison-flowers.'
They become stars, the eyes he thus transforms.
All the lips' whispers are cool summer showers.

C. HATAKEYAMA [*Trans. W. E.*]

The Shadow

It caught my eye, my shadow, as it ran,
My bad luck, and it had a plan.
Clearly new friends for play
Were what it wanted, since it went away.
5   I had often giggled when
It dug lines in my forehead,
Or stole oil from my hair to dye its gown.
Feeling it drive its needle through my heart
I had often laughed and enjoyed licking the blood.
10   You want to please your pets. I began
To fear it was disgusted, since it ran;

Unprepared on laughing to hear rise
Tenfolded echoes, scattering mimicries,
Come from the hills and fields and the far skies.

C. HATAKEYAMA [*Trans. W. E.*]

The Small Bird to the Big

Fly up and away, large hawk,
To the eternal day of the abyss,
Belittling the night about the mountains.
Your eyes that are our terror
5   Are well employed about the secrets of the moon
Or the larger betrayals of the noon-day.
Do not stay just above
So that I must hide shuddering under inadequate twigs.
Sail through the dry smoke of volcanoes
10   Or the damp clouds if they will better encourage your feathers.
Then shall I weep with joy seeing your splendour,
Forget my cowardice, forget my weakness,
Feel the whole sunlight fall upon my tears.
I shall believe you a key to Paradise.
15   I shall believe you the chief light upon this dark grey world.

C. HATAKEYAMA [*Trans. W. E.*]

Four Legs, Two Legs, Three Legs

Delphic and Theban and Corinthian,
Three lines, by the odd chance, met at a point,
The delta zero, the case trivial.

A young man's cross-road but a shady one.
5   Killing a mistaken black cat in the dark
He had no other metaphysical trait.

God walks in a mysterious way
Neither delighteth he in any man's legs.

The wrecked girl, still raddled with Napoleon's paint,
10   Nose eaten by a less clear conqueror,
Still orientated to the average dawn,
Behind, Sahara, before, Nile and man
A toy abandoned, sure, after so many,
That the next sun will take her for a walk,
15   Still lifts a touching dog's face eager for a sign.

Not one for generalizing his solutions
Oedipus placed the riddle with a name.
Another triumph for the commonplace.
While too much to pretend she fell and burst
20   It is a comfort that the Sphinx took such an answer.

Reflection from Rochester

'But wretched Man is still in arms for Fear.'

'From fear to fear, successively betrayed' –
By making risks to give a cause for fear
(Feeling safe with causes, and from birth afraid),

By climbing higher not to look down, by mere
5   Destruction of the accustomed because strange
(Too complex a loved system, or too clear),

By needing change but not too great a change
And therefore a new fear – man has achieved
All the advantage of a wider range,

10   Successfully has the first fear deceived,
Thought the wheels run on sleepers. This is not
The law of nature it has been believed.

Increasing power (it has increased a lot)
Embarrasses 'attempted suicides',
15   Narrows their margin. Policies that got

'Virility from war' get much besides;
The mind, as well in mining as in gas
War's parallel, now less easily decides

On a good root-confusion to amass
20   Much safety from irrelevant despair.
Mere change in numbers made the process crass.

We now turn blank eyes for a pattern there
Where first the race of armament was made;
Where a less involute compulsion played.
25   'For hunger or for love they bite and tear.'

Courage means Running

Fearful 'had the root of the matter', bringing
Him things to fear, and he read well that ran;
Muchafraid went over the river singing

Though none knew what she sang. Usual for a man
Of Bunyan's courage to respect fear. It is the two
Most exquisite surfaces of knowledge can

Get clap (the other is the eye). Steadily you
Should clean your teeth, for your own weapon's near
Your own throat always. No purpose, view,

Or song but's weak if without the ballast of fear.
We fail to hang on those firm times that met
And knew a fear because when simply here

It does not suggest its transformation. Yet
To escape emotion (a common hope) and attain
Cold truth is essentially to get

Out by a rival emotion fear. We gain
Truth, to put it sanely, by gift of pleasure
And courage, but, since pleasure knits with pain,

Both presume fear. To take fear as the measure
May be a measure of self-respect. Indeed
As the operative clue in seeking treasure

Is normally trivial and the urgent creed
To balance enough possibles; as both bard
And hack must blur or peg lest you misread;

As to be hurt is petty, and to be hard
Stupidity; as the economists raise
Bafflement to a boast we all take as guard;

As the wise patience of England is a gaze
Over the drop, and 'high' policy means clinging;
30 There is not much else that we dare to praise.

Ignorance of Death

Then there is this civilizing love of death, by which
Even music and painting tell you what else to love.
Buddhists and Christians contrive to agree about death

Making death their ideal basis for different ideals.
5   The Communists however disapprove of death
Except when practical. The people who dig up

Corpses and rape them are I understand not reported.
The Freudians regard the death-wish as fundamental,
Though 'the clamour of life' proceeds from its rival 'Eros'.

10   Whether you are to admire a given case for making less clamour
Is not their story. Liberal hopefulness
Regards death as a mere border to an improving picture.

Because we have neither hereditary nor direct knowledge of
        death
It is the trigger of the literary man's biggest gun
15   And we are happy to equate it to any conceived calm.

Heaven me, when a man is ready to die about something
Other than himself, and is in fact ready because of that,
Not because of himself, that is something clear about himself.

Otherwise I feel very blank upon this topic,
20   And think that though important, and proper for anyone to
        bring up,
It is one that most people should be prepared to be blank upon.

Missing Dates

Slowly the poison the whole blood stream fills.
It is not the effort nor the failure tires.
The waste remains, the waste remains and kills.

It is not your system or clear sight that mills
5 Down small to the consequence a life requires;
Slowly the poison the whole blood stream fills.

They bled an old dog dry yet the exchange rills
Of young dog blood gave but a month's desires;
The waste remains, the waste remains and kills.

10 It is the Chinese tombs and the slag hills
Usurp the soil, and not the soil retires.
Slowly the poison the whole blood stream fills.

Not to have fire is to be a skin that shrills.
The complete fire is death. From partial fires
15 The waste remains, the waste remains and kills.

It is the poems you have lost, the ills
From missing dates, at which the heart expires.
Slowly the poison the whole blood stream fills.
The waste remains, the waste remains and kills.

Success

I have mislaid the torment and the fear.
You should be praised for taking them away.
Those that doubt drugs, let them doubt which was here.

Well are they doubted for they turn out dear.
5 I feed on flatness and am last to leave.
Verse likes despair. Blame it upon the beer
I have mislaid the torment and the fear.

All losses haunt us. It was a reprieve
Made Dostoevsky talk out queer and clear.

10 Those stay most haunting that most soon deceive

And turn out no loss of the various Zoo
The public spirits or the private play.
Praised once for having taken these away
What is it else then such a thing can do?

15 Lose is Find with great marsh lights like you.
Those that doubt drugs, let them doubt which was here
When this leaves the green afterlight of day.
Nor they nor I know what we shall believe.
You should be praised for taking them away.

Just a Smack at Auden

Waiting for the end, boys, waiting for the end.
What is there to be or do?
What's become of me or you?
Are we kind or are we true?
Sitting two and two, boys, waiting for the end.

Shall I build a tower, boys, knowing it will rend
Crack upon the hour, boys, waiting for the end?
Shall I pluck a flower, boys, shall I save or spend?
All turns sour, boys, waiting for the end.

Shall I send a wire, boys? Where is there to send?
All are under fire, boys, waiting for the end.
Shall I turn a sire, boys? Shall I choose a friend?
The fat is in the pyre, boys, waiting for the end.

Shall I make it clear, boys, for all to apprehend,
Those that will not hear, boys, waiting for the end,
Knowing it is near, boys, trying to pretend,
Sitting in cold fear, boys, waiting for the end?

Shall we send a cable, boys, accurately penned,
Knowing we are able, boys, waiting for the end,
Via the Tower of Babel, boys? Christ will not ascend.
He's hiding in his stable, boys, waiting for the end.

Shall we blow a bubble, boys, glittering to distend,
Hiding from our trouble, boys, waiting for the end?
When you build on rubble, boys, Nature will append
Double and re-double, boys, waiting for the end.

Shall we make a tale, boys, that things are sure to mend,
Playing bluff and hale, boys, waiting for the end?
It will be born stale, boys, stinking to offend,
Dying ere it fail, boys, waiting for the end.

30   Shall we all go wild, boys, waste and make them lend,
Playing at the child, boys, waiting for the end?
It has all been filed, boys, history has a trend,
Each of us enisled boys, waiting for the end.

What was said by Marx, boys, what did he perpend?
35   No good being sparks, boys, waiting for the end.
Treason of the clerks, boys, curtains that descend,
Lights becoming darks, boys, waiting for the end.

Waiting for the end, boys, waiting for the end.
Not a chance of blend, boys, things have got to tend.
40   Think of those who vend, boys, think of how we wend,
Waiting for the end, boys, waiting for the end.

The Beautiful Train

(A Japanese one, in Manchuria,
from Siberia southwards, September 1937)

Argentina in one swing of the bell skirt,
Without visible steps, shivering in her power,
Could shunt a call passing from wing to wing.

Laughing the last art to syncopate
Or counterpoint all dances in their turns,
Arbours and balconies and room and shade,
It lopes for home;
And I a twister love what I abhor,

So firm, so burdened, on such light gay feet.

Manchouli

I find it normal, passing these great frontiers,
That you scan the crowds in rags eagerly each side
With awe; that the nations seem real; that their ambitions
Having such achieved variety within one type, seem sane;
5   I find it normal;
So too to extract false comfort from that word.

Reflection from Anita Loos

No man is sure he does not need to climb.
It is not human to feel safely placed.
'A girl can't go on laughing all the time.'

Wrecked by their games and jeering at their prime
There are who can, but who can praise their taste?
No man is sure he does not need to climb.

Love rules the world but is it rude, or slime?
All nasty things are sure to be disgraced.
A girl can't go on laughing all the time.

Christ stinks of torture who was caught in lime.
No star he aimed at is entirely waste.
No man is sure he does not need to climb.

It is too weak to speak of right and crime.
Gentlemen prefer bound feet and the wasp waist.
A girl can't go on laughing all the time.

It gives a million gambits for a mime
On which a social system can be based:
No man is sure he does not need to climb,
A girl can't go on laughing all the time.

The Teasers

Not but they die, the teasers and the dreams,
Not but they die,
                  and tell the careful flood
To give them what they clamour for and why.

You could not fancy where they rip to blood,
You could not fancy
                  nor that mud
I have heard speak that will not cake or dry.

Our claims to act appear so small to these,
Our claims to act
                  colder lunacies
That cheat the love, the moment, the small fact.

Make no escape because they flash and die,
Make no escape
                  build up your love,
Leave what you die for and be safe to die.

Not but they die, the terrors and the dreams,
Not but they die. In the long run the sane man
Comes out best. He is dead too. The themes

Of despair and triumph so far always outran
Rumination in writing. The short view
Could be so long it saw where it began.

But what reflections are much gain to you.
Not to imagine is a thing to claim.
Remember what you once wanted to do

And will want to have done when the time came,
Then you need seldom feel and short sight
Is the magnifying glass able for the flame.

Advice

Not busting now before the fish away
I would not make such murders of my teens.
I made no purpose of the first of May.
Crash is a cloth but poisons are all greens.

5   The lovely grass is brown is dry is grey.

The useful sheep feed safely on that shade
Yet rushing on the green one if soon stabbed
Can then go munching on unburst

Nor ask a policy to drown a smell.

10   The great and good, more murderously scabbed,
No dug-out on whose lawns could spoil no game,
Cosy in bath-chairs and not known to shame
(G. P. came late) looked wiser than we stayed.

Their long experience who all were first
15   Would disadvise you to say Now is Hell
Knowing worst not known to who can still say Worst.

Anecdote from Talk

John Watson was a tin-mine man
   An expert of his kind.
He worked up country in Malaya
   On whisky, not resigned,
   On whisky but not blind.

He told a friend he felt like death,
   And what you say's repeated.
The manager says 'I just sent for him
   With "Here's ten dollars, beat it

For Christ's sake to Singapore.
   I'm glad to pay the fare.
Just think of the nuisance, man, for me,
   If you pass out here."

Next day John Watson tapped the door
   With "Right, take my gun.
You've changed my mind, I mean to live."
   "I'll keep any gun.
   But I'll keep no madman."'

'This is the funny part,' the manager says,
   'He was shot just the same.
Of course I had to pass him to a dickey job.
   Just the natives, no-one to blame.
   But it was quick how it came.
   Three weeks.'

China

The dragon hatched a cockatrice
    (Cheese crumbles and not many mites repair)
There is a Nature about this
    (The spring and rawness tantalize the air)

5   Most proud of being most at ease
    (The sea is the most solid ground)
Where comfort is on hands and knees
    (The nations perch about around)

Red hills bleed naked into screes
10   (The classics are a single school –)
The few large trees are holy trees
    (– They teach the nations how to rule)

They will not teach the Japanese
    (They rule by music and by rites)
15   They are as like them as two peas
    (All nations are untidy sights)

The serious music strains to squeeze
    (The angel coolies sing like us –)
Duties, and literature, and fees
20   (– to lift an under-roaded bus)

The paddy-fields are wings of bees
    (The Great Wall as a dragon crawls –)
To one who flies or one who sees
    (– the twisted contour of their walls)

25   A liver fluke of sheep agrees
    Most rightly proud of her complacencies
With snail so well they make one piece
    Most wrecked and longest of all histories.

Autumn on Nan-Yüeh

(With the exiled universities of Peking)

The soul remembering its loneliness
Shudders in many cradles . . .
. . . soldier, honest wife by turns,
Cradle within cradle, and all in flight, and all
Deformed because there is no deformity
But saves us from a dream.   W. B. YEATS

If flight's as general as this
   And every movement starts a wing
('Turn but a stone,' the poet found
   Winged angels crawling that could sting),
5 Eagles by hypothesis
   And always taking a new fling,
Scorners eternal of the ground
   And all the rocks where one could cling,
We obviously give a miss
10   To earth and all that kind of thing,
And cart our Paradise around
   Or all that footless birds can bring.

I have flown here, part of the way,
   Being air-minded where I must
15 (The Victorian train supplies a bed;
   Without it, where I could, I bussed),
But here for quite a time I stay
   Acquiring moss and so forth – rust,
And it is true I flew, I fled,
20   I ran about on hope, on trust,
I felt I had escaped from They
   Who sat on pedestals and fussed.
But is it true one ought to dread
   This timid flap, that shirk, that lust?
25 We do not fly when we are clay.
   We hope to fly when we are dust.

The holy mountain where I live
   Has got some bearing on the Yeats.
Sacred to Buddha, and a god
30   Itself, it straddles the two fates;
And has deformities to give
   You dreams by all its paths and gates.
They may be dreamless. It is odd
   To hear them yell out jokes and hates
35 And pass the pilgrims through a sieve,
   Brought there in baskets or in crates.
The pilgrims fly because they plod.
   The topmost abbot has passed Greats.

'The soul remembering' is just
40   What we professors have to do.
(The souls aren't lonely now; this room
   Beds four and as I write holds two.
They shudder at the winter's thrust
   In cradles that encourage 'flu.)
45 The abandoned libraries entomb
   What all the lectures still go through,
And men get curiously non-plussed
   Searching the memory for a clue.
The proper Pegasi to groom
50   Are those your mind is willing to.
Let textual variants be discussed;
   We teach a poem as it grew.

Remembering prose is quite a trouble
   But of Mrs Woolf one tatter
55 Many years have failed to smother.
   As a piece of classroom patter
It would not repay me double.
   Empire-builder reads the yatter
In one monthly, then another:
60   'Thank God I left' (this is my smatter)

'That pernicious hubble-bubble
   If only to hear baboons chatter
And coolies beat their wives.' A brother
   I feel and it is me I flatter.

65 They say the witches thought they flew
   Because some drug made them feel queer.
There is exorbitance enough
   And a large broomstick in plain beer.
As for the Tiger Bone, the brew
70   With roses we can still get here,
The village brand is coarse and rough,
   And the hot water far from clear.
It makes a grog. It is not true
   That only an appalling fear
75 Would drive a man to drink the stuff.
   Besides, you do not drink to steer
Far out away into the blue.
   The chaps use drink for getting near.

Verse has been lectured to a treat
80   Against Escape and being blah.
It struck me trying not to fly
   Let them escape a bit too far.
It is an aeronautic feat
   Called soaring, makes you quite a star
85 (The Queen and Alice did) to try
   And keep yourself just where you are.
But who was bold enough to meet
   Exactly who on Phoebus' car
Slung on a Blimp to be a spy
90   I ask before I cry Hurrah?

I pushed the Yeats up to the top
   Feeling it master of a flow
Of personal chat that would not end
   Without one root from which to grow.

95   That excellent poet's organ stop
      Has very wisely let us go
Just scolding all. He does not send
      Any advice so far below.
But yet this Dream, that's such a flop,
100   As all the latest people know,
He makes no leak we ought to mend
      Or gas-escape that should not blow,
But what they fly from, whence they drop,
      The truth that they forsake for show.

105 Besides, I do not really like
      The verses about 'Up the Boys',
The revolutionary romp,
      The hearty uproar that deploys
A sit-down literary strike;
110   The other curly-headed toy's
The superrealistic comp.
      By a good student who enjoys
A nightmare handy as a bike.
      You find a cluster of them cloys.
115 But all conventions have their pomp
      And all styles can come down to noise.

Indeed I finally agree
      You do in practice have to say
This crude talk about Escape
120   Cannot be theorized away.
Yeats is adroit enough to see
      His old word Dream must now leave play
For dreams in quite another shape,
      And Freud, and that his word can stay.
125 That force and breadth of mind all we
      Can't hope for, whether bleak or gay;
We put his soundings down on tape
      And mark where others went astray.
So dreams it may be right to flee,
130   And as to fleeing, that we may.

So far I seem to have forgot
   About the men who really soar.
We think about them quite a bit;
   Elsewhere there's reason to think more.
135 With Ministers upon the spot
   (Driven a long way from the War)
And training camps, the place is fit
   For bombs. The railway was the chore
Next town. The thing is, they can not
140   Take aim. Two hundred on one floor
Were wedding guests cleverly hit
   Seven times and none left to deplore.

Politics are what verse should
   Not fly from, or it goes all wrong.
145 I feel the force of that all right,
   And had I speeches they were song.
But really, does it do much good
   To put in verse however strong
The welter of a doubt at night
150   At home, in which I too belong?
The heat-mists that my vision hood
   Shudder precisely with the throng.
England I think an eagle flight
   May come too late, may take too long.
155 What would I teach it? Where it could
   The place has answered like a gong.

What are these things I do not face,
   The reasons for entire despair,
Trenching the map into the lines
160   That prove no building can be square?
Not nationalism nor yet race
   Poisons the mind, poisons the air,
Excuses, consequences, signs,
   But not the large thing that is there.

165 Real enough to keep a place
    Like this from owning its new heir;
But economics are divines,
    They have the floor, they have the flair. . . .

Revolt and mercy fired no sparks
170   In the Red argument at all;
Only what all of us desire,
    That the whole system should not stall.
The real impressiveness of Marx
    Lay in combining a high call
175 With what seemed proof that certain fire
    Attended all who joined with Saul.
Stalin amended his remarks
    By saying that they would not fall
But must be trod into the mire
180   (And till his baby state could crawl
It must not venture on such larks).
    This let them back against a wall.

The tedious triumphs of the mind
    Are more required than some suppose
185 To make a destiny absurd
    And dung a desert for a rose.
It seems unpleasantly refined
    To put things off till someone knows.
Economists have got the bird
190   And dignity and high repose.
One asked me twenty years to find
    The thread to where the monster grows.
But we wait upon the word
    They may too late or not disclose.

195 'This passive style might pass perhaps
    Squatting in England with the beer.
But if that's all you think of, what
    In God's name are you doing here?

If economics sent the Japs
200   They have the rudder that will steer;
Pretence of sympathy is not
      So rare it pays you for a tear.
Hark at these Germans, hopeful chaps,
      Who mean to split the country dear.'
205   It is more hopeful on the spot.
      The 'News', the conferences that leer,
The creeping fog, the civil traps,
      These are what force you into fear.

Besides, you aren't quite good for nowt
210   Or clinging wholly as a burr
Replacing men who must get out,
      Nor is it shameful to aver
A vague desire to be about
      Where the important things occur . . .
215   And no desire at all to tout
      About how blood strokes down my fur –
We have a Pandarus school of trout
      That hangs round battles just to purr –
The Golden Bough, you needn't doubt,
220   'Are crucifixions what they were?' . . .

. . .

I said I wouldn't fly again
      For quite a bit. I did not know.
Even in breathing tempest-tossed,
      Scattering to winnow and to sow,
225   With convolutions for a brain,
      Man moves, and we have got to go.
Claiming no heavy personal cost
      I feel the poem would be slow
Furtively finished on the plain.
230   We have had the autumn here. But oh

That lovely balcony is lost
    Just as the mountains take the snow.
The soldiers will come here and train.
    The streams will chatter as they flow.

Let it go

It is this deep blankness is the real thing strange.
    The more things happen to you the more you can't
        Tell or remember even what they were.

The contradictions cover such a range.
5   The talk would talk and go so far aslant.
        You don't want madhouse and the whole thing there.

Thanks for a Wedding Present

[It was a compass on a necklace with the poem:

Magnetic Powers cannot harm your House
Since Beauty, Wit and Love its walls de-Gauss.
And if, when nights are dark, your feet should stray
By chance or instinct to the Load of Hay
With me drink deep and on th' uncharted track
Let my Magnetic Power guide you back.]

She bears your gift as one safe to return
   From longer journeys asking braver fuel
      Than a poor needle losing itself an hour

Within a *Load of Hay* needs heart to learn.
   She wears the birth of physics as a jewel
      And of the maritime empires as a flower.

Sonnet

Not wrongly moved by this dismaying scene
   The thinkers like the nations getting caught
   Joined in the organizing that they fought
To scorch all earth of all but one machine.

5   It can be swung, is what these hopers mean,
   For all the loony hooters can be bought
   On the small ball. It can then all be taught
And reconverted to be kind and clean.

A more heartening fact about the cultures of man
10   Is their appalling stubbornness. The sea
Is always calm ten fathoms down. The gigan-

  -tic anthropological circus riotously
Holds open all its booths. The pygmy plan
   Is one note each and the tune goes out free.

The ages change, and they impose their rules.
It would not do much good to miss the bus.
We must endure, and stand between two fools.

Two colonies of Europe now form schools
5 Holding absolute power, both of them fatuous.
The ages change, and they impose their rules.

One claims the State is naked between ghouls
The other makes it total Octopus.
We must endure, and stand between two fools.

10 A says No Bath not Superheated Steam. B cools
This off by Only Solid Ice. For us
The ages change, and they impose their rules.

Both base their pride upon ill-gotten tools
And boast their history an Exodus.
15 We must endure, and stand between two fools.

There is world and time; the Fates have got large spools;
There need not only Europe make a fuss.
The ages change, and they impose their rules.
We must endure, and stand between two fools.

Chinese Ballad

Now he has seen the girl Hsiang-Hsiang,
    Now back to the guerrilla band;
And she goes with him down the vale
    And pauses at the strand.

5   The mud is yellow, deep, and thick,
    And their feet stick, where the stream turns.
'Make me two models out of this,
    That clutches as it yearns.

'Make one of me and one of you,
10   And both shall be alive.
Were there no magic in the dolls
    The children could not thrive.

'When you have made them smash them back:
    They yet shall live again.
15 Again make dolls of you and me
    But mix them grain by grain.

'So your flesh shall be part of mine
    And part of mine be yours.
Brother and sister we shall be
20   Whose unity endures.

'Always the sister doll will cry,
    Made in these careful ways,
Cry on and on, Come back to me,
    Come back, in a few days.'

The Birth of Steel: A Light Masque

[By William Empson, with additions (printed here between
asterisks) by the producer Peter Cheeseman and the stage
manager Alan Curtis.]

*After an orchestral introduction the curtain of the Inner Stage,
which is decorated with Alchemical symbols, rises revealing a
Gothic chamber bathed in a dull red light. There is a furnace in
the centre; in front of it two of the Alchemist's minions, dressed*
5 *in blue smocks, lean together back to back like playing cards,
fast asleep. A third minion poses gazing at the distance.*
    *There is a sharp fanfare, and the Alchemist, bearded and
dressed in a long purple robe, hurries forward. He bows low,
and addresses Her Majesty the Queen very seriously.*

ALCHEMIST:
10 Your Majesty, my name is Smith,
The lordliest name to conjure with;
Iron all my family made. I'll now display
A stronger metal, a more brilliant way.
*My alchemy its light on iron turns;
15 With phlogiston my great alembic burns,
Though unsuccessful yet, with Paracelsus' aid
Today my minions hope to forge a stronger blade.

He pauses, and comes forward, as mystic music begins to play.

For Zarathustra spake to me last night
20 In hour of Ashtaroth, by burning light
Of Erebus . . .

*There is a drum roll, he pulls from his gown a great sparkling
stone, and, holding it up cries . . .*

Hic Petrus
25 In Chalybem Ferrum Transmutabit.

*A sharp fanfare is played. Then mystic music steals in again
quietly, as he speaks, burning with enthusiasm.*

This long-sought stone provides the key you seek,
'Twill change your brittle iron to nobler steel
30   For ancient seekers missed the way of truth,

The Alchemist's minion sees the sign he was expecting; during
the rest of the Alchemist's speech he wakens the other two, they
look for themselves, and he, the watcher, moves cautiously down
to the Alchemist to tell him . . .

35   Seeking to gild their leaden crucibles.
But I, with deeper learning, know that wealth
On Steel, not fickle gold, must founded be;
And this existent stone, their bootless dream
To real profit turns, and does not seem
40   To . . .

The minion taps him on the shoulder.

MINION:
Master, two black pigeons on yon oak!
Now let it out! Now let it smoke!*

There is a great turmoil of music from the orchestra, the
45   *inquisitive crowd bustle in, the Alchemist signals to his minions,*
and they move a heavy anvil out of the chamber and sit on it.
The watcher fetches tongs and grips the furnace door, the
Alchemist approaches it, and recoils as a blast of hot air and
smoke comes out of the furnace. The crowd yell with laughter.
50   *The Alchemist stiffens.*

ALCHEMIST:
Ignore the mockery of the hoi polloi;
All genius they hope, vainly, to annoy.

The crowd laugh again, the Alchemist signals to the two minions
sitting on the anvil; they fetch hammers and lean on them,
55   *snoozing. A solemn chorale is sung in alchemical Latin, while the*
Alchemist and the other minion describe a large Magic Circle
with a whitewash brush and a bucket.

*Ut ferrum transmutarent veniunt
Cum ferro in ignem exspectant
60   Ut ferrum transmutarent veniunt
Cum ferro in ignem sperant.*

*The circle completed, the orchestra play forging music, the
minion opens the furnace door, draws out the sword and places
it on the anvil. The crowd gather round but move away sharply
65   as the hammers hit the sword. As the music ends the sword is
lifted up and brought forward. The Alchemist looks at it.*

ALCHEMIST:
The time has come to try my new-forged blade;

*He advances to touch the sword with the magic stone, but as he
does so, the Devil appears. The crowd recoil with gasp of horror,
70   but the Alchemist draws himself up defiantly.*

ALCHEMIST:
Upon this anvil let it be assayed.

*The minion raises the sword high above the anvil and brings it
down heavily. The Devil raises his arms: the sword smashes. The
crowd laugh, the Devil jumps up and down with glee.*

ALCHEMIST:
75   It has failed. It has failed.

*The minions gather round him miserably, downstage. One has
brought the Alchemist's Book. They crouch on the floor,
desperately thumbing through it for a solution. The orchestra
play a mournful 'Blues'. The crowd watch, with almost
80   sympathetic curiosity. The Alchemist raises his head sadly to Her
Majesty the Queen.*

ALCHEMIST:
I appeal!
It is essential that I conquer steel.

*The xylophone plays a cheerful little tune. The Alchemist looks
85   in the book. He sees something. He is excited, he mumbles*

Minerva, Minerva *(He stands)* Minerva descend! Only Minerva
     now
Can save all strength, whether for sword or plough.

The orchestra begins, quietly, a dignified march, gradually
building up to a great climax. The Alchemist arranges the crowd
90   *and his minions await in respectful order the Goddess's descent.*
Suddenly they raise their arms and sing –

Hail to Minerva. Hail to Minerva.
Hail, Hail . . . . . .

The Goddess appears, descending in a golden chair decorated
95   *with the symbol of Wisdom, an Owl. The chair reaches the*
ground, Minerva stands, the Alchemist, his minions and the
Crowd fall to their knees and hide their heads in fear and
wonder. There is a fanfare of trumpets. The Goddess makes a
respectful curtsey to H. M. the Queen.

MINERVA:
100   Royalty, I am yourself. As you would wish
I now create Sheffield.

She fetches from her chair four white lab. coats and a silver box.
She distributes the coats to the minions and finally to the
Alchemist.

105   *Be you the watcher of the governing dial
And you the pourer of the chemical phial:
You with a slide rule I invest
To calculate, design, and test.*
(The Alchemist approaches) This poor fish
110   I turn into a steel technician,

She turns upstage and makes a great gesture at the chamber.

And every worker to a real magician.

There is a clash of cymbals, and the appearance of the chamber
alters to that of a modern factory showing an electric arc furnace
115   *with its two great electrodes and lit in a bright green light. Music*
indicating frenzied activity is played, and the three minions, now

dressed in shimmering white lab. coats, open the silver box, take
out a slide rule, a rack of test tubes and a clock, and begin to
slide, shake and wind them with alarming speed. Minerva has
120 *gone back to her chair and returns with a glossy book under her*
arm. She sees their frenzied activity and stills it, and the
orchestra, with a gesture –

MINERVA:
But not too fast! It is now time to look
With patience on my future serious book.

125 *She places the new book on top of the old one. The Alchemist*
peers at it, and then reads, while his minions calculate and pour
the contents of the test tubes into one large one.

ALCHEMIST:
*Massive, pearly glistening lustre,
Structure undulatingly lamellar, slaty,

130 *(The crowd gape, open-mouthed: they are impressed)*

In colour greenish grey to near leek green;
Slightly translucent, soft, and unctuous:
Difficultly frangible, and dense
Three times as water;

135 *(He turns over a page)*

Dodecahedral structure, with slip planes
In three oblique directions; atomic spacing
One point three six eight four ANGSTROMS.*

Frenzied music is played again, two minions take the fat test tube
140 *up to the furnace while one sets the alarm clock. A minion at the*
furnace waits by a lever and looks at the Alchemist, who looks at
Minerva. Minerva nods, the Alchemist signals to the minion with
the clock and the minion with the lever. The lever is pulled
down, the clock is started . . . . .

145 *Suddenly the alarm rings, the crowd start back and a minion*
stops the alarm. The minions at the furnace draw out the steel
and take it to a drop hammer. A triumphant trumpet rises out of
the forging music, and the two minions confidently cake-walk

downstage to the Alchemist, one displaying a glittering sword in
150 *his hands. Suddenly the music changes, and the devil's tune is*
heard; the crowd gasp, the devil leaps in, and saunters forward.
But Minerva, seeing him advancing to the sword, waves him off
the stage, and the devil, vanquished, screams through the crowd.
Minerva comes forward; the rest watch her –

MINERVA:
155 Majesty, as you know, we spirits are
Diffused, not distant in a star.
The real magician is two groups of men;
The hand has worked with the mind; but then
Each has got both. We need not puzzle how
160 They made it work if they can do it now.

She moves up to her chair, all turning to watch her, and as she
slowly ascends, the chorus sing –

MEN:
Puddling iron, casting iron,
Is the work of this environ;
165 And it suits the British Lion
PUDDLING IRON

WOMEN:
Blending steel, rolling steel
That's the way to get a meal;
And we're right ahead of the field
170 BLENDING STEEL

The Alchemist and his assistants move off in slow procession
with the sword held high.

MEN:
Puddling iron, casting iron,
Send the sparks up to Orion,
175 Give the Goddess more to fly on
CASTING IRON

The crowd move slowly out.

MEN AND WOMEN:
Puddling iron, blending steel;
Turn the fire on – to anneal
180   What you feel – about the siren
    BLENDING STEEL
      PUDDLING IRON
        ROLLING STEEL.

The stage is empty, and a drop curtain, with a design
185   *representing modern industry, descends.*

(i) *Poems* (1935)

There is a feeling, often justified, that it is annoying when an author writes his own notes, so I shall give a note about these notes. It is impertinent to expect hard work from the reader merely because you have failed to show what you were comparing to what, and though to write notes on such a point is a confession of failure it seems an inoffensive one. A claim is implied that the poem is worth publishing though the author knows it is imperfect, but this has a chance of being true. Also there is no longer a reasonably small field which may be taken as general knowledge. It is impertinent to suggest that the reader ought to possess already any odd bit of information one may have picked up in a field where one is oneself ignorant; such a point may be explained in a note without trouble to anybody; and it does not require much fortitude to endure seeing what you already know in a note. Notes are annoying when they are attempts to woo admiration for the poem or the poet, but that I hope I can avoid. Of course there are queerer forces at work; to write notes at all is to risk making a fool of yourself, and the better poems tend to require fewer notes. But it seems to me that there has been an unfortunate suggestion of writing for a clique about a good deal of recent poetry, and that very much of it might be avoided by a mere willingness to explain incidental difficulties.

(ii) *The Gathering Storm* (1940)

[Epigraph]
Like cats in air-pumps, to subsist we strive
On joys too thin to keep the soul alive.

[Dedication]
In memory of PHYLLIS CHROUSTCHOFF

[Prefatory Note]
A remark about the order had best be made at once, in case a reader begin at the beginning. The poems are roughly in the order of their writing, as they were in my other collection (*Poems*: published by Chatto & Windus in 1935), and the first verse of the first poem here (*Bacchus*) has already been published as the last poem in that. However though *Bacchus* was planned and begun in Japan in 1933 the middle parts of it only got finished in China in 1939, so by the time rule it might as well be put at the end of the book. I put it first because it is in a style I felt I ought to get out of, and I end the book with a somewhat prattling long poem ['Autumn on Nan-Yüeh'] written under refugee conditions in Hunan; the idea is that there is a change in the style of the poems, whether good or bad, connected with the steady approach of war which we were conscious of during those years.

Note on Notes
These notes may well look absurdly pretentious, and they start off with the most extreme example ['Bacchus']. Some of the later ones are more like travel notes, and anyway I think many people (like myself) prefer to read poetry mixed with prose; it gives you more to go by; the conventions of poetry have been getting far off from normal life, so that to have a prose bridge makes reading poetry seem more natural. No doubt the notes are partly needed through my incompetence in writing; they had better have been worked into the text. I do the best I can. But partly they are meant to be like answers to a crossword puzzle; a sort of puzzle interest is part of the pleasure that you are meant to get from the verse, and that I get myself when I go back to it. It is clear that you try to guess the puzzle before you turn to the answer; but you aren't offended with the newspaper for publishing the whole answer, even when you had guessed it. There would be no point in publishing a puzzle in a newspaper, if it were admittedly so simple that there was no need to publish the answer. And the comparison is not quite a random one; the fashion for obscure poetry, as a recent development, came in at about the same time as the fashion for crossword puzzles; and it seems to me that this revival of interest in

poetry, an old and natural thing, has got a bad name merely by failing to know itself and refusing to publish the answers.

Aldous Huxley has written very well about snob interest in poetry, 'that delicious thing old Uncle Virgil said, you remember'; and as most people would, he treats puzzle interest as a branch of this. They are both good things, but I will not have my puzzle called their snob. There is no longer the field of 'general knowledge' that old Uncle Virgil used to be in, because there are now more interesting things to know than anybody (or any poet) knows. There is no longer therefore a justification for snob treatment of them; nobody any longer can say, even as a joke, 'what I don't know isn't knowledge'. We are left with puzzle interest, and this though it has most of the virtues of the old snob interest has a distinguishing feature; it is not offended by seeing the answers in notes.

At the same time, of course, any decent poetry has got more than puzzle interest in it, and the motives behind making the puzzle are themselves very mixed. It is always part of the claim of the puzzle in poetry that this is the best way to say something. Clearly interest in mere puzzle can be bad for a writer (and marks of an obscure moral worry about whether there was too much puzzle interest going on are I am afraid a disfiguring feature of my small output here). What we had before us to write about, in the years when these poems were written, was chiefly the gathering storm of the present war; and so far as I can feel I had anything to say about that I would want to get it said somehow, even if only in a note.

Empson reverted to the note from *Poems* (1935) in *Collected Poems* (1949) and in *Collected Poems* (1955).
For note on the dedication, see note to l. 73 of 'Bacchus'.

(iii) *William Empson Reading Selected Poems* (1961)

I have tried to make these notes do what I have felt to be needed, or have simply been asked, when invited to give a reading of the poems. Notes are bound to be rather hit-or-miss, different people wanting different things, but may at least show that the author wants to be intelligible.

(iv) *Collected Poems* (1984)

[Prefatory Note]

The frontispiece was taken in Gambier, Ohio at the Kenyon Summer School to which I was flown from Peking; the date was 1948–49. The other man is Charles Coffin, a patient and understanding listener, as the picture shows. We would be discussing a seventeenth-century poet; I do not think I ever discussed my own poetry like that. But it takes the eye most of the way back to the character who wrote the poems; snapshots of the old professor are off the point.

When I. A. Richards saw the villanelle beginning 'Slowly the poison . . .' ['Missing Dates'] he said it was the best comic poem I had done so far; and I must have betrayed my surprise, because he added, not to hurt my feelings, that of course it was *deep* humour. I was not hurt but relieved; denouncing the universe has never seemed to me a sensible thing for a poem to do, and I had feared that my villanelle might be tainted with that pomposity. Much of the verse here is about the strangeness of the world, in which we are often tripped up and made helpless, and the first thing to do in that situation is to understand it. In such a case, it is usual for some to laugh and others not. I was feeling very earnest when I was snapped, though the effect is comical; and this makes it seem a suitable lead-in for the poems.

RICKS: I think the obvious first question for anybody who likes and believes your poems as much as I do is why there haven't been many of them lately.

EMPSON: Well, it wasn't a rule. I just found in Peking I was writing some and it struck me they were bad, I didn't want to print them. I hope that when I'm made to retire, I'll be able to start writing again. If you look at the collected edition of a nineteenth-century poet, you'll find that the middle bit is frightfully bad – he begins well and he often gets alright again at the end, but all that long middle bit you might just as well leave out, I think. When I found I didn't want to print, I said O.K., I'll leave it alone. The motives which made me want to write had I suppose largely disappeared. I didn't feel I had to do it, anyway. I think many people actually feel they've got to go on, because it's the only way they can support their wife and children or something, and it very often happens with poets that they have this haunting feeling that they are given magical powers which are suddenly taken away from them. Well, they'd very much better stop writing poetry and do something else, I think.

RICKS: What do you think are the motives that will re-appear when you retire? What will be different then?

EMPSON: Well, merely that you wouldn't feel so distracted by practical things that have to be done. The capacity to reflect about life can re-appear. The old often do feel more sympathetic to the young than the middle-aged because the middle-aged have got to earn the money, after all.

RICKS: Have you kept copies of the poems you haven't printed?

EMPSON: I haven't destroyed the copies; they may be lying about.

RICKS: Because a friend of mine has found out about this play [*Three Stories*] which made you very famous at Cambridge.

EMPSON: That I'm sure was destroyed. It wasn't very good anyway. But I tried quite a lot to write plays. The failed plays were lying around in quite a quantity for some time. I don't know whether they're still in a drawer, so to speak. Turning out the drawers will be an occupation for my old age, except that I shall have to find some means of earning money for my wife and children. The retirement is awfully important in the modern academic world; it keeps them much more sane to think that at the age of sixty-five all this is going to stop. I'll have to be purged and renewed.

RICKS: One thing struck me about your long-playing record: the way in which you left out 'Arachne', although everybody has kept on about it. I've always felt that 'Arachne' presents your interest in life's contradictions more crudely and unsympathetically than some of the other poems. What do you think about that poem?

EMPSON: I left it out because I'd come to think that it was in rather bad taste. It's boy being afraid of girl, as usual, but it's boy being too rude to girl. I thought it had rather a nasty feeling, that's why I left it out.

RICKS: Do you read all the things about yourself? Have you read *La Poesia di William Empson*, by Morelli? It's the only book on your poems.

EMPSON: No. I've agreed to have a selection translated into Italian. It's very odd, that. The Italians are very energetic, of course. There's a translation of *Seven Types of Ambiguity* appearing in Italian now [*Sette tipi di ambiguità*, trans. Giorgio Melchiori (Turin: Einaudi, 1965)]. I had a long correspondence with the author, who pointed out a great deal of nonsense in it. It was rather a severe correspondence. I scolded him back for not understanding the high bogs and the mountains, but he wiped my eye a good deal.

RICKS: A similar thing from the record was that you played down both 'This Last Pain' and 'The Teasers', though these are the poems which I think the people who have written well about you, like Wain and Fraser and Alvarez, offer a lot of space to. What exactly is your disagreement with the current view of these? Ought I to remind you of your note on 'This Last Pain'?

EMPSON: Somebody told me it was like Oscar Wilde saying that you ought to wear a mask and then you'll grow into your mask. This seemed to me positively embarrassing. I didn't want to be like Oscar Wilde in this business of being affected, and I couldn't see why it was different. I felt uneasy about it. I do feel it's writing, as it were, to a theory without my being quite sure what the theory comes to, or what it means or something. I felt rather doubtful whether it meant anything very sensible. I do think it's pretty. I like it for the singing line quality. But it seemed to me I was writing up a subject which I hadn't thought through. That was why I felt shy about it.

RICKS: At the end there is very good formulation of your general thing about not rushing to these hateful available extremes by which we either know what we're doing and then we burn people, or we don't know what we're doing and then we're indifferent when people are shot. I thought it got over that difficulty. It's a poem which is always in mind, as explaining to people how one can behave without believing in these awful absolutes and on the other hand without not believing in them.

EMPSON: Yes, you express it very sympathetically. I feel that kind of thing quite seriously. I'm sure that's O.K. But then when I'm suddenly told it's exactly like Oscar Wilde, being affected and so on, and . . . though a most worthy man and very able, kind and helpful and so on, the thought of behaving like Oscar Wilde does get under my skin. It means being affected all the time. That's not what I'd want it to say. So, in a sense, I've never come to terms with the poem again somehow.

RICKS: What about 'The Teasers', then?

EMPSON: Well, I wrote a lot more of it, and it started grousing and grumbling about the conditions of the modern world, and then I thought this is disagreeable, I don't like what I'm saying, and so I cut it down to rags so that it doesn't make sense, you can't find out what it's about. Of course, these powerful minds in the business of criticism, they're fascinated by something that doesn't make sense; but they can't make out what was in the cut verses because it was something quite irrelevant.

RICKS: You think it's all not true, what they say about it?

EMPSON: When dear old George Fraser says it was all against being horrified by women when they're menstruating, and offering my person to all the women in the world and so forth, I was much shocked. I don't entertain these shocking sentiments at all, do you see? Absolutely nothing to do with what was in my mind; I wouldn't even have thought it was in George's mind. No, I'm afraid that the business of guessing what it means when there isn't enough evidence to tell the answer is one we've all trained ourselves in. I just cut out the bits I thought were in bad taste and it didn't leave enough to make any sense really. That's what happened to 'The Teasers'. But a beautiful metrical invention, I do say. I wish I'd been able to go on with it because it sings so; but that was what happened, I could only give this cut version.

RICKS: Are there any ways in which you feel that people have misconstrued or been positively unhelpful?

EMPSON: I don't quite think that. When I was young, Dr Leavis praised me very much; although I do insist I was getting published already. The idea that I've never repaid him properly is, it seems to me, unnecessary. But still, he praised my first volume and then, when the second one came out, he swung away and said it was a failure of nerve, it showed that Empson had become too cowardly to write good poetry. Twenty years later you'll find this copied out exactly by the Leavis disciples. Well, he was quite right, I think, to feel that he'd overpraised Empson before – that was what was really going on in his mind, perhaps. But the idea that Empson lost his nerve with the second volume has always seemed to me very unreasonable. The first book, you see, is about the young man feeling frightened, frightened of women, frightened of jobs, frightened of everything, not knowing what he could possibly do. The second book is all about politics, saying we're going to have this second world war and we mustn't get too frightened about it. Well, dear me, if you call the first brave and the second cowardly it seems to me that you haven't the faintest idea of what the poems are about. And so I do get irritated when I see these disciples of Dr Leavis still repeating that the second volume showed a failure of nerve. You may say it's a failure of nerve to stop writing altogether, but I don't know that I think that. It wasn't a failure of nerve to write *The Gathering Storm*: I still say that.

RICKS: I think it's poems like 'Aubade' and 'Reflection from Rochester' which run most in my mind, but it's true that they are very much harder to talk about, aren't they? We know where we are with all that Donne/ Metaphysical line, we talk about your calm and your poise and so on, whereas the late ones are pretty difficult to criticize.

EMPSON: Well, they were meant to be plain good sense, what everyone was feeling about the occasion; they're meant to be very much about the political situation. 'Aubade' is about the sexual situation. When I was in Japan, from 1931 to 1934, it was usual for the old hand in the English colony to warn the young man: don't you go and marry a Japanese because we're going to be at war with Japan within ten years; you'll have awful trouble if you marry a Japanese, and this is what the poem is about. But, of course, the critic – as it is so far away and so long ago – simply doesn't know that's what it's about.

RICKS: Yes, but it does get difficult all the same. At the end of 'Aubade' I can see what it's about, but I'd find it very difficult to translate into French.

EMPSON: Well, I suppose it chiefly meant that you can't get away from this world war if it's going to happen, and that it isn't any use thinking you can go to the South Sea Islands – lots of people got awfully caught by thinking they could get right away to the South Sea Islands – the very centre of the more important parts of the war. London was a good deal quieter. It just says 'All right, we can't marry, we must expect to separate.' But it's the last verse you're thinking of. I just thought there ought to be more in it to claim the puzzle was larger. It's kind of passive endurance. We have to put up with it, we can't avoid this situation of history. It's pretty flat, I should have thought. I can tell you why people make revolutions: they feel a conflict and they don't know what they expect, and they make a revolution merely because they get so irritated. It seemed the best thing in this case to leave the house; and I would leave Japan after my three years. It seems sensible to do something about it, whereas in fact you can do nothing about it, so eventually the country will have to resist. Surely that's enough for it to mean, isn't it? Owing to your beautiful sympathy and your expecting it to be good, you thought it meant something wiser.

RICKS: Why I think it's so good is that the two refrains are quite incompatible in the first two-thirds of the poem. Now, at the end, they start to swap over in a curious sort of way, and start to merge into quite a different attitude: it seems to me that it's about on the one hand, the tragic principle of integrity and dignity and so on, and also about a comic principle, of decency and comfort. Why I think it's so good – 'it seemed the best thing to be up and go' – is because it doesn't – as everyone now thinks – insist that looking after oneself, or not going mad, is terribly ignoble. The danger of the tragic principle is of one kind of soulishness by which this other principle comes to be thought of as mere expediency.

EMPSON: You get a good deal of Chadbandism now, that's quite true, yes. If I was moralizing now, like most middle-aged men in most periods, I would moralize in rather a low-minded way. That's a good reason for not writing poetry at my time of life. I sympathize with what you say. But after all, if you're saying that the conflict is between 'the heart of standing is you cannot fly' and 'it seemed the best thing to be up and go' – if you are an Englishman with the right attachments living in Japan, you could leave Japan and go back to England, where you might resist the forces of evil, the invader. Surely that would do if you want an absolutely flat solution of the two refrains. One is to go away from Japan and the other is to stay in England.

RICKS: Yes, I agree it makes very good literal sense, and I think it's a good story. But I also meant that it insisted that there are two principles and that they are both, in certain circumstances, equally desirable and as good as each other. It's like your note in *Essays in Criticism* about saints: that some people object to saints on the grounds that there is another moral principle which is not saintly at all; it's not that saints have the moral principles and that other people are rather desperately expedient – it does seem to me that the poem widens out to be about this kind of thing. All these things that Hugh Kenner doesn't like about you: when he quotes your remark about life not being a matter of understanding things but of maintaining one's defences and equilibrium, and living as well as one can, and that not only maiden aunts have to do that – he thinks that's very like a cockroach, and disagreeable.

EMPSON: I'm glad I haven't read Hugh Kenner.

RICKS: So you picked upon him as an adversary by the merest chance in *Milton's God*?

EMPSON: No. He wrote wickedly about other matters. If he wrote wickedly about me it is pure accident.

RICKS: But, of course, he's terribly clever. He's very good on Alice, and how important Alice is for you.

EMPSON: Well, when I say he's wicked, what I mean is I disagree with his fundamental attitude. He's more neo-Christian than any other neo-Christian, I think. A very able man, but with a mistaken hold of wrong principles. But what he said about my poetry was very incidental to that. But I'm delighted with your thinking of the two refrains of 'Aubade' corresponding to the two legs which we must all stand on – one of them heroism and the other reasonable good sense; it never occurred to me. Of course, they're meant to be a slight contrast. But I never piled so much dignity on to the story.

RICKS: I think 'Let it go' is good because, where everybody else is saying it's our duty to go mad, and be Christ, and take the whole burden of the world on our shoulders, and so on – what you say is that it's our duty not to go mad, but, on the contrary, rather quietly to try and make things better.

EMPSON: There I think your kind heart is putting too much into it. I'm saying what lots of people would have said in prose. I just happened to put it into six rhyming lines.

RICKS: But it's very difficult to put the case for not going mad in a way that doesn't sound just complacent and uncaring. It's a very eerie poem, isn't it? That 'whole thing there' at the end is like a maniac on the Tube, fixing one with his eye and threatening these terrible things. You think it's a cheerful poem, do you?

EMPSON: I certainly don't want to present myself as the wise old Toby: I'm as liable to go mad as the next man. I'd certainly insist that it's rather lucky I preserved my sanity. I don't deny that the prospects of horror are always fairly large.

RICKS: What do you feel about the influence you're supposed to have had on the poets of the fifties?

EMPSON: Well, honestly, I don't like much of it. But it's largely because I'm an old buffer: the point has been reached where it is unusual for new poetry to seem very good to me. I haven't liked it very much; but I haven't liked any poetry, whether it's supposed to be imitating me or not. This seems a fairly irrelevant angle, but the fact is that I don't react very readily to any modern poetry. I was hearing a young poet give a reading of his work, and he was explaining afterwards how much he hated all the other ones his age. He was talking about one of these and I said 'He has a singing line, hasn't he?' Meaning, as I thought, that he had the root of the matter in him. This chap pounced and said 'That's it, you've got it! Just a writer of lyrics!' He thought that if it sounds pretty that means you're bad. Well, I thought he hadn't got the root of the matter in him. Milton could say 'God damn you to hell' and make it a singing line, but these people think it's got to sound ugly or they aren't sincere. I think it's Samuel Butler who describes a wallpaper of the Victorian period, with flowers on it, and he says that some bees came in and they went to every one of the flowers all the way down and then they went to every one of the flowers all the way up and they tested every one of these right across the area, and they never realized that *none* of the flowers had any honey.

RICKS: Do you ever feel it's strange how much of your taste is really very traditional? You actually praised a bit of Swinburne at one point, didn't you?

EMPSON: Well, about Swinburne, if we're going off on to that. I think he only wrote well when – well, there are a few good things about revolutionary politics which cheered him up – but normally he only wrote well about his appalling ideas about sex, which is all about one side torturing the other. Very remote from my own ambitions in bed, but somehow it was what he wrote well about. When he is writing about that, he isn't vague, he isn't any of the things that T. S. Eliot said he was. Of course, later in life, when he became settled down, he'd got nothing to write about. He did exactly what Mr Eliot says about him. But when he's writing well, in the first poems and ballads, he isn't any of these things at all. I think Mr Eliot just didn't like the subject, very rightly, and said it was all about nothing, whereas it was about this slightly appalling thing. Fiddling while he burned Rome is so unlike what everyone else thinks of Nero burning Rome as being like:

> When with flame all around him aspirant
> Stood flushed as a harp-player stands
> The implacable beautiful tyrant
> Rose-crowned having death in his hands.

The rest of the verse becomes so ludicrous that you can't read it aloud without laughing. But that bit is what most of the Romantics had been aiming at, finally getting into focus. I think that, though madly queer and morally most undesirable, it is frightfully good poetry. I myself have never been able to imitate it. But I think that most poets have been affected by things they can't do. Coming back to my kind of poetry, I think it's a specialized kind. I began to feel that I was beginning to parody myself, that it was too narrow. That was why I thought it was bad, in a way. I certainly don't think that the only good kind of poetry is like mine: I think mine is too specialized.

RICKS: But yours is actually like lots of different things, isn't it? It seems to me in some ways dangerous that it was first praised in terms of Donne and the Metaphysicals, because it's obvious now that there's an increasing dissatisfaction with Donne and the Metaphysicals.

EMPSON: I still think he's wonderful. I think he meant something: I think he was attacking Christianity in his love poems. This has gone completely out, it's completely out of fashion to believe that. In fact, you're most earnestly told you mustn't. But this movement of fashion is all nonsense: it needs to be removed. Once you realize the love poems are defiant, you think they're good and courageous again. As long as you think they are only fribbles by a man who fully accepted the Church and State he was quarrelling with, you think it's in very bad taste. Of course it seems in very bad taste if you think it's all nonsense. So I think this misunderstanding of Donne is the result of the entirely mistaken criticism which was led by T. S. Eliot, in a book called *A Garland for John Donne*, which was, in fact, the kiss of death, the crown of thorns. When I was starting writing there was a lot being written – by Robert Graves as much as anybody – about how poetry ought to be about a conflict: it needn't resolve a conflict (on the whole, a Victorian opinion – 'In Memoriam' was to solve the problem about whether you live for ever or not), but he thought the poem ought to be about a conflict which is raging in the mind of the writer but hasn't been solved. He should write about the things that really worry him, in fact worry him to the point of madness. The poem is a kind of clinical object, done to prevent him from going mad. It is therefore not addressed to any public, but it is useless to him unless it is in fact clear and readable, because he has to – as it were – address it to the audience within himself. It isn't expressed unless it's a thing which somebody else can read, so if it's obscure it actually fails in this therapeutic function, it isn't saving his sanity. But nevertheless he doesn't write it for any group or – he doesn't even write it for Laura Riding. This really was the principle I was going on.

RICKS: Then why are so many of them obscure? Some of your early ones are very hard to understand, aren't they?

EMPSON: Well, all this was when I settled into it. When I started doing it, I thought it would be very nice to write beautiful things like the poet Donne. I would sit by the fire trying to think of an interesting puzzle. Although, as a matter of fact, most of them turned out to be love poems about boy being too afraid of girl to tell her anything, the simple desire to think of something rather like Donne was the basic impulse. But I think my few good ones are all on the basis of expressing an unresolved conflict. It does seem to me a very good formula which applies to a lot of kinds of poetry. I think it's completely out of fashion, isn't it? Nobody says that now. In a way, you see, as you approach middle age, though in fact you're a seething pit of scorpions, you don't recognize them in that form. You're getting things tidy: 'Can I get the boy to college?' and things like that are what you are thinking about. So it doesn't appear to you in this direct way, as an unresolved conflict which you need to express in a poem. You often do feel it again when you're old, when you're seriously old, when you've been forced to retire and the pressure of making actual decisions in the world is no longer what you ought to be thinking about. The idea that you write old and young fits in with the idea of poetry as the expression of an unresolved conflict.

RICKS: But one reason why I think *The Gathering Storm* is so good is because in a way it is about practical things. It seems to me that your poems are very concerned to put what can be said for the other side: 'Courage means Running' is, as you say, about what can be said for Munich. In this you anticipate the sort of things that A. J. P. Taylor has said about it. 'Reflection from Rochester' explains how, although we hate it, we go on with the arms race.

EMPSON: Well, everybody has to think about these things, really. As a matter of fact, everybody who reads the newspapers is thinking about these things. This degree of wisdom is not at all out of the way. It isn't what poets usually write about, that's all. Most poetry today is in the Imagist tradition, and it simply isn't the fashion in poetry to understand things; people understand these things in prose perfectly well. I accept your praise with great comfort and satisfaction; I agree that the whole tendency of modern criticism has been not to encourage people to be as sensible as they would be if they had to deal with the matter really, in prose. But the more we praise the good sense of Empson, the more I feel how clever I've been, how right I was to stop writing. If I'd gone on it would have got appallingly boring. It's only because I stopped in time that you still think it's poetry.

APPENDIX 3 *On Stopping Poetry: an extract from a letter to Christopher Ricks*

Apartment 514, 1000A Plaza Drive, State College, Pennsylvania
19 January 1975

My dear Christopher,
[. . .] I haven't the book here, but I think you credited me ['Empson's Poetry', in *William Empson*, ed. Gill] with strong family feelings, and said I stopped writing poetry because I married. There was much else which was a positive comfort to have said, but I had already thought it a gap, a limitation in your mind that you cannot imagine a man taking a real interest in public affairs. I hope I have a normal amount of domestic piety and affection, and I wish now that I had more children – I respect you for having so many. But I dropped all my literary interests, even reviewing, because I got absorbed in the war; I thought the defeat of Hitler so important that I could do nothing else (it was a time of great happiness, looking back, and anyway considerable pleasure, but I have just a steady trickle of mental productiveness, and it was then all directed into propaganda). I still think the war was quite important enough for that, and a good deal of my previous poetry had been concerned to say so; it could not be called a betrayal of my deeper interests. I remember being scolded briefly by a journalist in a pub near the BBC, on his way out, near the end of the war, because I had dropped all my literary work so completely – 'just left us cold', he said, assuming there was nothing else I was good at really; I was startled by an attack from such an unexpected quarter. Nursing myself back into literary work after the war was rather a business, closely connected with trying to get a complete cure from a stomach ulcer; I first, for about a year, wrote an essay on Buddhist sculpture before 1000 AD, which got lost afterwards. This got me ready to resume my profession as teacher of English Literature, without throwing me into it rawly. Then, when I got to China, carrying about lots of unfinished disordered bits of paper of course I found I had lost the whole chapter on Metaphor (I was writing *Complex Words*) and was surprised to find that,

going slowly, I could recover it from memory. There was a real gap, and an urgent practical need to get over it; but there was no such need to start writing poetry again, and the theme which all the modern poets I admired had been working on, which I had been working on too, had been blown out like a candle.

I suppose I look ridiculous when I claim to have been a political poet too, like Auden and Spender and all those geared-up propaganda boys in Oxford (whereas I was in Cambridge); and it is true that I never learned the technique so was never considered a political poet. But my second volume of verse *The Gathering Storm* means by the title just what Winston Churchill did when he stole it, the gradual sinister confusing approach to the Second World War. Of course the title was chosen after writing the poems, during the early years of the war, but nearly all the poems really are considering this prospect, with which I had been fairly closely confronted, in China, Japan, Indochina and Korea. Well then, after the war had been won, I was in the same cleft stick as my brother poets, and I am inclined to congratulate myself upon stopping writing.

It is a very good thing for a poet, one might say the ideal, to be saying something which is considered very shocking at the time, so bad that he is on the verge of being persecuted for this none the less popular doctrine, and then ten years later everybody in his society agrees with him, so that even Tories emit a grudging assent. There is bound to be a slight difficulty for his later output; he cannot merely continue to demand what has already been granted (more socialism at home, the Popular Front abroad). But surely it was not essential to appear in a white sheet of shame, denouncing themselves for having said what everyone now agreed to (only Louis MacNeice kept out of this, I think, and obviously at severe nervous cost). However, most poets have to go on earning the only way they know how, whereas I could escape into another profession. I only met my wife because Hitler attacked Russia, because that made her feel free to do propaganda against him in Afrikaans; we met at the BBC Liars' School for training propagandists; and she was determined to go to China because everybody except the Foreign Office knew it was going Communist. The domestic pressures upon me were the most strongly political ones.

Oh well. Thanks all the same.

Reading this over, I see it is too glib, and some other process was probably at work earlier to make the poetry I hammered out strike me as unfit for publication. My war started in 1937, when I refugeed with the Chinese universities, and I went on writing criticism there, also the Anita Loos poem, which I now think bad.

W. E.

A topic sentence and then the rest of the poem an expansion, simultaneously literal and figurative. We need a diagram which we can easily draw for ourselves.

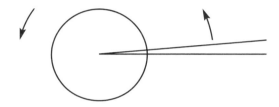

short stakes: Both the stakes the prospector drives in to mark the boundaries of his claim (l. 5) and the posts of the fence that keeps cattle (say) in and trespassers out of the spun farm (l. 11). Rights in this land include everything under and above (l. 5).

They are *stakes*, too, in the sense in which a landowner is said to have a *stake* in the country. He has invested money, time and toil in his property; he has something *at stake*.

spokes: Because the earth rotates. (I am being thus explicit because in several classrooms I have met readers of high credentials who did not take this in.)

real estate of mind: The figurative meaning is being underlined: this is a state of mind and more, a set of mental acquisitions and developments, as much as it is a plot of earth. As such, its privacy is important.

No high flat: (however much of a skyscraper penthouse apartment it may be) can command this. Its heights and its depths are quite beyond any such survey. Though the poem itself may seem to be attempting something of the sort, the fourth verse reaffirms what this fourth line has asserted and adds indications as to why this is so, which are no small part of the completing movement.

nomad citizen: In contrast to the farmer (cultivating his garden). The fourth verse 'comforts' this farmer, who may feel rather tied by his holding. He does a lot of travelling inevitably if his property is sweeping illimitably about in this fashion. It is a disturbing sort of comfort however: Lucifer is 'fallen from heaven' (Isaiah, 14:12) and the self itself is shadowed by itself, hidden from whatever light it may produce.

you own land in Heaven and Hell: Both the conventional Heaven (and Dante's Inferno) *and* all that they betoken. Line 7 perhaps illustrates another sense of 'unfinished' from that with which we are concerned: it seems to be in a rough, stop-gap, kind of state but line 9 picks up again with

where all owners meet, in Hell's / pointed exclusive conclave: A conclave is a locked-up place; specifically, the cardinals electing a pope. Behind the geometrical authority of the center (as determining the course of any circumference) there may be 'the grand consult' of Milton's fallen Fiends as well as the uncomfortable communality of this joint possession – a high price, indeed a confiscatory price, to pay for being an owner.

APPENDIX 5 *Winchester Verses?*

These epigrams were published anonymously in *The Wykehamist* no. 660 (27 May 1925). It is not possible to establish whether or not Empson was their author, but they date from his very last month at Winchester College, when he was eighteen years of age, and are the only poems published during his time at the school which attain a real sophistication, as verse and as pastiche. (For further discussion, see the section on 'Text' in the Introduction, pp. xlii–xliii.)

Dogma

Walking upon the water that is death,
The groundless tumble of obscene decay,
I stand a moment; though I fall away
In that same thought, that very catch of breath,
5   I stand; it is the earth that vanisheth.

Night

In toilsome dance, disorderly array,
I see them posturing the night away;
I see them stand; then, to abrupt guitars
They many-fingered turn; they're stiff, the stars.

Instruction

Along the benches with decree sublime
His hollow mumble paralyses time;
His ponderous sentences roll word for word
In triple phalanx, in assault assured.

5 An age we wait, till he strolls back to write
The same upon the wall, the same recite,
Slowly, inevitably; oh my Lord,
Alas, alas that I am half so bored.

Decoration (?)

Flat staring yellow daisies, brown at centre;
Deep leaves; stiff-curving, grey-green stalks, like string,
Upon a warm, grey, cardboard, wall-paper, background;
Paradise – represented in a toy theatre.

Notes

Dogma
1 *Walking upon the water*: Jesus Christ walked on the water. Cf. 'Bacchus', l. 22 and note.
5 *the earth that vanisheth*: 'I lift mine eyes to see: earth vanisheth', l. 1, by Christina Rossetti, *Verses* (1893).

Night
1 *disorderly array*: 'Anon a company of horse and foot, / Advancing in disorderly array, / Came up the vale' (Robert Southey, *Roderick, The Last of the Goths*, Book XIV: 'The Rescue').
4 *many-fingered*: see note to l. 17 of 'Letter II'.

Instruction
1 *decree sublime*: 'Shall Wisdom's voice / From out the bosom of these troubled times / Repeat the dictates of her calmer mind, / And shall the venerable halls ye fill / Refuse to echo the sublime decree?' (Wordsworth, *The Excursion*, Book IX, ll. 400–404).

APPENDIX 6 *A Fragment and a Squib*

Fragment[1]

Moaning inadequately
and without sufficient despair
several town councillors
were there.

5   Desperate ladders, mid bison, weeps
green green, unstable, a flame,
round, sweet, the tulip-face too certain
oh centred viewed enclosed.

The shift, the fine fault in flint,
10   fine packed and central grit, troglodyte
in the great parting centred.

Two teeth not meeting

The just irregular crystal,
needles not quite, the glanced sliding lances,
15   dual piercing, a reach-me-down, on edge.

Newly Discovered War Poems[2]

The sappers dug through Archie yesterday.
There he was buried slap in the way of the mine.
And – Oh, my God!
Scrunch.
5   Trickle, trickle, trickle.
   Archie used to say

One day was like another day
His love for play on any day was gay.
He threw a many yesterdays away.
He had a better stomach, as a sapper, than I have.
Where is this bullet?
Give it me: mud, mud, mud.
Mud, oh, my God! Oh, my God! mud.
Oh, my mud!
Ping.

Notes

1 First published in *RB*.
2 First published in *Granta* (2 November 1928).

APPENDIX 7 *Publication of Empson's Poems*

Table of contents of the early volumes, 1934–40

Poems (Tokyo, 1934)

Part of Mandevil's Travels
To an Old Lady
Villanelle
Letter [Letter II]
Legal Fiction
Arachne
Letter [Letter I]
Poem [The Scales]
This Last Pain
Note on Local Flora
Camping Out
Invitation to Juno
Homage to the British Museum
Bacchus (stanza 1)

Poems (London, 1935)

The Ants
Value is in Activity
Invitation to Juno
The World's End
Plenum and Vacuum
Rolling the Lawn
Dissatisfaction with Metaphysics
Poem about a Ball in the Nineteenth Century
Sea Voyage

High Dive
To an Old Lady
Part of Mandevil's Travels
Camping Out
Letter I
Letter II
Villanelle
Arachne
The Scales
Legal Fiction
Sleeping Out in College Cloister
Earth has Shrunk in the Wash
Flighting for Duck
Letter III
This Last Pain
Description of a View
Homage to the British Museum
Note on Local Flora
Doctrinal Point
Letter V
Bacchus (stanza 1)

The Gathering Storm (London, 1940)

Bacchus (complete)
Your Teeth are Ivory Towers
Aubade
The Fool
The Shadow
The Small Bird to the Big
Four legs, three legs, two legs
Reflection from Rochester
Courage means Running
Ignorance of Death
Missing Dates
Success
Just a Smack at Auden

The Beautiful Train
Manchouli
Reflection from Anita Loos
The Teasers
Advice
Anecdote from Talk
China
Autumn on Nan-Yueh

Collected Poems

The Collected Poems of William Empson (New York, 1949)

Combined contents of *Poems* (1935) and *The Gathering Storm* (1940), with an alteration to one title, 'Four Legs, Three Legs, Two Legs', and with these four additional poems:
Letter IV
Let it go
Thanks for a Wedding Present
Sonnet

Collected Poems (London, 1955, 1956, 1984)

Contents as *The Collected Poems of William Empson* (1949), plus two further pieces:
Chinese Ballad
The Birth of Steel

Posthumous poems

The Royal Beasts and Other Works (1986)

(i) First appearances of the following poems:
'Mother, saying Anne good night'
Song of the amateur psychologist

Two centos
Address to a tennis-player
Two fragments
Two songs from a libretto
Rebuke for a dropped brick
Myth
Warning to undergraduates
Letter VI: a marriage
'The ages change, and they impose their rules'
'Not but they die, the terrors and the dreams'

(ii) The following poems reprinted from early periodical appearances:
Une Brioche pour Cerbère
New World Bistres
Laus Melpomines
Insomnia
Essay
UFA Nightmare

(ii) In the *London Review of Books* (17 August 1989):
'I remember to have wept'
To Charlotte Haldane
The Extasie

NOTES

For items included in the Bibliography (pp. lxxvi–xciv), abbreviated information is given below. All quotations from Empson are in bold.

The Fire Sermon

The 'Fire Sermon' features in the first part of the *Maha-Vagga* (the 'Great' or 'Greater' Division) of the *Vinaya-Pitaka*; that is, the third of the five books of the Pali *Tipitaka* – the oldest collection of the canonical literature, a Middle Indic version of the Buddha's teaching as first preserved through oral transmission by the early Hinayana schools and written down long afterwards in Ceylon. (There are no surviving written documents about early Buddhism dating from the time of the Buddha's life, 563–483 BC.)

The best-known version – to which T. S. Eliot refers in his notes to *The Waste Land* – is the late-nineteenth-century translation by Henry Clarke Warren in *Buddhism in Translations* (Harvard Oriental Series III (Cambridge, Mass., 1896), pp. 351–3), and is reproduced below to afford a basis for evaluation. WE positioned his synthesized translation in place of a dedication or epigraph both in *P* and in *CP*, leaving readers to assume that it was a motto or a statement of faith; that at the least it spoke to the themes or philosophy of the poetry itself. Yet WE later denied that it was his gospel; so what is its significance in relation to his own work? In the Warren translation:

All things, O priests, are on fire. And what, O priests, are all these things which are on fire?

The eye, O priests, is on fire; forms are on fire; eye-consciousness is on fire; impressions received by the eye are on fire; and whatever sensation, pleasant, unpleasant or indifferent, originates in dependence on impressions received by the eye, that also is on fire.

And with what are these on fire?

With the fire of passion, say I, with the fire of hatred, with the fire of infatuation; with birth, old age, death, sorrow, lamentation, misery, grief and despair are they on fire.

The ear is on fire; sounds are on fire; . . . the nose is on fire; odours are on fire; . . . the tongue is on fire; tastes are on fire; . . . the body is on fire; things tangible are on fire; . . . the mind is on fire; ideas are on fire; . . . mind-consciousness is on fire; impressions received by the mind are on fire; and whatever sensation, pleasant, unpleasant or indifferent, originates in dependence on impressions received by the mind, that also is on fire.

And with what are these on fire?

With the fire of passion, say I, with the fire of hatred, with the fire of infatuation; with birth, old age, death, sorrow, lamentation, misery, grief and despair are they on fire.

Perceiving this, O priests, the learned and noble disciple conceives an aversion for the eye, conceives an aversion for forms, conceives an aversion for eye-consciousness, conceives an aversion for the impressions received by the eye; and whatever sensation, pleasant, unpleasant or indifferent, originates in dependance on impressions received by the eye, for that also he conceives an aversion. Conceives an aversion for the ear, conceives an aversion for sounds, . . . conceives an aversion for the nose, conceives an aversion for odours, . . . conceives an aversion for the tongue, conceives an aversion for tastes, . . . conceives an aversion for the body, conceives an aversion for things tangible, . . . conceives an aversion for the mind, conceives an aversion for ideas, conceives an aversion for mind-consciousness, conceives an aversion for the impressions received by the mind; and whatever sensation, pleasant, unpleasant or indifferent, originates in dependence on impressions received by the mind, for this also he conceives an aversion. And in conceiving this aversion, he becomes divested of passion, and by the absence of passion he becomes free, and when he is free he becomes aware that he is free; and he knows that rebirth is exhausted, that he has lived the holy life, that he has done what it behooved him to do, and that he is no more for this world.

The other notable translation available to WE is by T. W. Rhys Davids and Hermann Oldenberg, in *The Sacred Books of the East*, ed. F. Max Müller, Vol. XIII: *Vinaya Texts*, Part 1 (Oxford, 1881), pp. 134–5. Surprisingly, Sir Charles Eliot, whom WE admired, gave only a brief and not altogether helpful extract in his authoritative *Hinduism and Buddhism*, Vol. I (London, 1921), p. 147, although Eliot's great work was 'the book I learned from', WE later said (*Milton's God*, p. 239). Ananda Coomaraswamy, in *Buddhism and the Gospel of Buddhism* (London, 1928), pp. 42–3, provided a 'summary' or condensed version of the Warren translation.

Faced with such a powerful piece of preaching, certain reviewers of *CP* (and later commentators) suggested that WE had espoused Buddhism. In 'A Style from a Despair: William Empson' (1957), for example, A. Alvarez observed that 'the later poems seem to be less personal discoveries than expansions of the passage from the Fire Sermon which Empson has put at the front of *Collected Poems*'. Likewise Graham Hough, in an obituary article (1984), remarked: 'A number of the poems (and this is too rarely noticed) are, as it were, footnotes to the Buddhist Fire Sermon that serves as epigraph to the whole volume.' On the other hand, A. E. Rodway noted (1956) that at a poetry reading at Nottingham University, WE denied that the 'Fire Sermon' had especial significance for him; it was there in the book, he was reported to have said (no doubt by way of steering clear of elaborate explanations), 'because I liked it'. But Rodway was having none of such bluff: 'Somebody's leg was being pulled,' he ribbed WE.

WE, with his liking for a public quarrel, promptly replied:

Though grateful to Mr Rodway for his appreciative review of my Collected Poems, I feel I ought to answer his query about the version of the Fire Sermon put at the start. I thought I made an earnest and patient effort to explain myself at the poetry-reading he mentions, but with the quaint rigour of the modern young he presumes I was trying to cheat – 'somebody's leg was being pulled'.

Like many others about thirty years ago, I looked up the Fire Sermon (recorded in Ceylon as one of the first sermons of the Buddha, given soon after he had decided that it was just possible to make himself understood) because of Mr Eliot's *Waste Land*. With all the repetitions it takes about ten minutes, and the experience is rather like having a steam-roller go over you;* but I had to select details from three or four translations before I could get a version which would bear so much repeating. Afterwards, while in the East, I came to admire Buddhism a good deal more; I have written a book about the statues ['The Faces of Buddha'], which has been lost, after a lot of travel in pursuit of them. So it did not seem to me odd, for an omnibus volume, to reprint this version of the Fire Sermon from the start of my first book of poetry; somebody might even find it convenient.

I was shocked, at the reading mentioned by Mr Rodway, to gather from some questions that my book might be used to support the current religious revival, and I said that, if a son of mine wanted to become a Buddhist monk, I would beg him not to. This felt to me very unlike pulling anybody's leg, however low-minded it might appear to neo-Christians. Of course I think Buddhism much better than Christianity, because it managed to get away from the neolithic craving to gloat over human sacrifice; but even so I feel that it should be applied cautiously, like the new wonder-drugs.

The Fire Sermon itself is unlike most of Buddhism, and leaves Christianity far behind, in maintaining that all existence as such, even in the highest heaven, is inherently evil. Such is the great interest of it; but I think this all-embracing hatred commonly attracts only bad characters; and, to do Mr Eliot justice, I do not think that it is explicitly stated in his devotional verse. There is a fine article by George Orwell on Gandhi, saying what a nice clean smell Gandhi left behind him, but also saying that common men do not (as the religious like to presume) simply fail to become saints; when they understand the issue, they often feel it would be morally wrong to become a saint – especially as not loving one person more than another.† I am glad Mr Rodway recognized that my verse sometimes tries to bring out

*Cf. Eliot's remark in his Clark Lectures of 1926: 'On one side the conceit is merely the development in poetry of an expository device known to preachers from the earliest times, the extended, detailed, interminable simile. The Buddha used it in the Fire Sermon and elsewhere . . .' (*The Varieties of Metaphysical Poetry*, ed. Ronald Schuchard (London, 1993), p. 130).

†George Orwell, 'Reflections on Gandhi', *Partisan Review*, January 1949; reprinted in *The Penguin Essays of George Orwell* (Harmondsworth, Middlesex, 1984), pp. 465–72.

these very sharp contrasts between one and another of our accepted moral beliefs; it is much pleasanter than being thought a Parnassian fribble, as for example by Mr Enright in your previous number.* But, all the same, when I mention fire in my verse I mean it to have the usual confused background of ideas, not (as Mr Rodway thinks) the specific and raging dogma of the Fire Sermon. I can be sure of this because, though I probably never thought about the Fire Sermon when writing or revising, I had already decided that I thought its doctrine wrong, though fascinating and in a way intelligible. You might say that it is present as one extreme of the range of human thought, because the poetry often tries to take the position 'what I am saying is admitted to be true, though people look at it in so many different ways'; but even so it is pretty remote, and not appealed to. ('Mr Empson and the Fire Sermon', pp. 481–2)

WE felt anxious to quell this notion, that he might have been proselytizing for Buddhism, and thus took equal pains to reply to a student periodical at the University of Sheffield. David Simpson, in an appreciative notice (1955) of *CP*, erred just a little in suggesting, 'in the preface to his new book', Professor Empson had 'taken for his text the Heraclitean notion that fire, being in constant motion, is therefore present in all forms of life, because life itself is in constant motion'.

WE duly fired back this witty and informative essay (originally, no doubt, submitted as a letter) which appeared under the title 'Everything, beggars, is on fire':

Arrows of last year carried a generous review of my Collected Poems, which, however, said I had 'taken as my text' *The Fire Sermon* of the Buddha. I feel I ought to try to clear this up, as I am also having to do in the Oxford *Essays in Criticism* [the reply to Rodway above]. I realize now that it was rather asking for misunderstanding to put the thing first, as authors generally mean that seriously, but I meant hardly more than I admired the famous object and thought I had made, by picking words from various learned translations, an English version suitable for reciting in full – a rather unnerving experience if you do all the repetitions.

It is said to be one of the earliest sermons of the Buddha, and carries the unearthliness of his system as far as is conceivable. One should realize that it denounces not only all existence on earth but all existence recognizable as such, even in the highest heaven. A man may naturally pause before agreeing that he believes all that. To be sure, the coolness of Buddhism towards Heaven, and towards the supernatural in general, is one of its most attractive features. On one occasion when the Buddha was preaching, the magic of his words became too much for him and he rose forty feet into the air, but he shouted down to the audience begging them to pay no attention; it would be over in a moment, and wasn't of the smallest interest compared to what he was saying. Any lecturer can sympathize with this

---

* 'Is the poetry of William Empson – to consider this type of writing at its best – much more than a sophisticated witticism, an ingenious joke? It is clear enough (and this is a sign of some virtue) that the poet is playing about, that he does not believe in what he is saying even while he is engaged in saying it' (Enright, 'Literature and/or Belief', p. 62).

point of view. Also we are told there was a minor god who became interested in philosophy, and one of his questions was so difficult that he was referred up and up in the hierarchy (it is always thought of as like a Government Department) till he was asking it of the Supreme God, who was rather embarrassed but quite plucky about this, so he waved his hand and the clouds gradually rolled back till at last, infinitely far below, the divine eyes could pick out the Buddha, crosslegged under a bo-tree. 'I can tell you who knows the answer,' said the Supreme God; 'it's That Man, down there.' The basic position, of course, is that Buddhists believe in abandoning selfhood, sometimes interpreted as merging oneself into the Absolute or the impersonal Godhead. If you are good but rather a busybody you are liable to be reborn as a god yourself, which may hold up getting to Nirvana indefinitely; just as over here a too virtuous scholar is liable to be made to do administration.

When I was first confronted with the idea that I had advertised myself as a Buddhist I said that, if a son of mine wanted to become a Buddhist monk, I would beg him not to; this is so, but I would not want to speak of the condition with great horror. When I was refugeeing with the Peking universities at Kunming (on the Burma Road) in 1939 there was an English Buddhist in an entirely genuine and severe monastery across the lake, who could sometimes be induced to boat over for a vegetarian dinner. He was keen to get a monk's passport, but I believe he left that monastery before the yearly three weeks of marathon, or almost incessant, meditation, with bangs on the head if you were found dozing at the squatting-post. He turned up at the War Office a few years later as an Intelligence Officer; I forget whether we sat on committees together about the Far East, with me representing the BBC Far Eastern Division, but I remember him in his uniform very well; I heard he was considered the only man they had had there who continued throughout his military career to think it wicked to kill even the lice on his body. Not that it was very surprising; a number of people felt they disapproved of Hitler enough to allow of stretching one or two points.

Buddhism deserves respect; for one thing, though not only, as an extreme; it needs to be remembered when one tries to survey what the human mind could think about a subject. But I naturally would not want to present myself as a believer by mistake. (*A*, pp. 599–600)

WE's extensive and complex responsiveness to Buddhism developed for both negative and positive reasons, in part out of certain fundamental quarrels with I. A. Richards and T. S. Eliot. The point of departure was Richards's so-called 'Theory of Value'. 'Nothing less than our whole sense of man's history and destiny is involved in our final decision as to value,' Richards had written in 1924 – a claim which WE heeded throughout his career. 'To set up as a critic is to set up as a judge of values . . . For the arts are an appraisal of existence,' Richards added in a ringing challenge (*Principles of Literary Criticism* (London, 1924; 1967), pp. 230, 46). Richards's Benthamite theory of value was concerned with 'the effort to attain maximum satisfaction through coherent systematization' – 'the systematization of impulses' (pp. 42, 38). Positive impulses he termed 'appetencies', and anything which worked to satisfy such impulses must be regarded as good or valuable. The full and ordered life necessarily maximized its varied satisfactions and minimized suppression and sacrifice. Given such a goal, the individual's accession to a life replete with self-realization and self-knowledge, poetry must take up the role of religion for the modern world. Poetry's intrinsic, vital and self-justifying function is to engender 'the best life . . . that in which as much as possible of our possible personality is engaged' (p. 229). Poetry fulfils itself in creating mental and moral health. In *The Foundations of Aesthetics* (written in collaboration with C. K. Ogden and James Wood (London, 1922), pp. 75, 91), Richards had taken the term 'synaesthesis' to stand for the state of equilibrium and harmony so engendered. Equilibrium 'brings into play all our faculties . . . Through no other experience can the full richness and complexity of our environment be realized. The ultimate value of equilibrium is that it is better to be fully than partially alive.'

According to the Theory of Value, poetry – which Richards later extolled as 'the supreme organ of the mind's self-ordering growth' (*Speculative Instruments* (London, 1955), p. 9) – can 'save' us: it will replace religion by relegating any magical view of the world and enthroning a fundamental secularism. He arrived at this doctrine by way of insisting upon what he considered a key distinction: between the language employed for enunciating true beliefs (scientific verities) and the language of poetry, which comprises 'pseudo-statements'. The latter are 'not necessarily false,' he explained, but 'merely a form of words whose scientific truth or falsity is irrelevant to the purpose in hand' (*Science and Poetry*, 1926; reprinted as *Poetries and Sciences* (London, 1970), p. 6on). Accordingly, his argument reaches the point of maximum resistance to organized religion:

Countless pseudo-statements – about God, about the universe, about human nature, the relations of mind to mind, about the soul, its rank and destiny – pseudo-statements which are pivotal points in the organization of the mind, vital to its well-being, have suddenly become, for sincere, honest and informed minds, impossible to believe as for centuries they have been believed . . .

This is the contemporary situation. The remedy . . . is to cut our pseudo-statements free from that kind of belief which is appropriate to verified statements. So released they will be changed, of course, but they can still be the main instrument by which we order our attitudes to one another and to the world. (*Poetries and Sciences*, pp. 60–61)

T. S. Eliot disparaged such secular salvationism as a revival of Matthew Arnold's views on literature and dogma: 'it is like saying that the wallpaper will save us when the walls have crumbled'. But Eliot conceded earlier in the same review of *Science and Poetry* that the theory

is probably quite true. Nevertheless is it only one aspect; it is a psychological theory of value, but we must also have a moral theory of value. The two are incompatible, but both must be held, and that is just the problem. If I believe, as I do believe, that the chief distinction of man is to glorify God and enjoy Him for ever, Mr Richards's theory of value is inadequate: my advantage is that I can believe my own and his too, whereas he is limited to his own. ('Literature, Science, and Dogma', *Dial* 32 (March 1927), 243, 241)

Not surprisingly, WE found himself baffled by Eliot's claim that he could readily accommodate both his own faith in the transcendent truths of the Christian religion and a doctrine of value which served to profane it. WE accordingly sought to strengthen the foundations of Richards's Theory of Value, which he believed he could best do by challenging it. If it makes any sort of claim to universal validity, WE felt, Richards's argument for a humanistic standard of valuation must be capable of accounting for other cultures. When Richards adjudged, for example, that traditional statements about God and destiny should properly be reduced to the status of pseudo-statements, he had clearly fixed his sights on the Christian conception of Heaven. But he was every bit as resistant to any manifestation of religion: he rejected the notion that *synaesthesis* or equilibrium could possibly stand for 'Nirvana, Ecstasy, Sublimation or At-oneness with Nature' (*Foundations of Aesthetics*, p. 75).*

In an essay pointedly entitled in the plural, 'Theories of Value' (Appendix 1 of *SCW*), WE would seek to question, publicly and sympathetically, what amounted to the wholesale anti-religiosity of Richards's position. Since WE was teaching in Japan when he started working towards 'Theories of Value', he found it both convenient and stimulating to submit Richards's theory to the best local test, the Buddhist religion. The early Buddhist 'assertion' that 'all existence is suffering,' he remarks, is nowadays construed by some scholars as being susceptible to the interpretation that the concept of Nirvana stands for 'a re-absorption into the Absolute' (which was exactly the quasi-pantheistic alternative to the Christian Godhead for which WE would argue from the late 1940s on):

This brings it [Buddhism] into line with a mystical strain in all the great religions, one which has usually been at loggerheads with the offer of Heaven; and there I think we find the great historical antagonist of anything like the Richards Theory of Value – that is, of any self-fulfilment theory. It is opposed to any such theory not because it is pessimistic but because it does not believe in the individual. I cannot pretend that I have any capacity to act as a go-between in this quarrel ... if the Theory of Value merely recommends the satisfaction of the human creature, whatever makes it really satisfied, Professor Richards need not be as secure against the religions as he intended to be. What satisfied the most impulses might turn out to be the same as what was to the glory of God or even as what tended to Nirvana. (*SCW*, pp. 424–5)

*Cf. John Paul Russo, *I. A. Richards: His Life and Work* (London, 1989), pp. 196–7.

The Buddha had insisted: 'The foolish man conceives the idea of "self", the wise man sees there is no ground on which to build the idea of "self" ... All therefore is but evil ...' (Max Müller, *Selections from Buddha* (Boston, 1886), p. 35); and the Sanskrit term *Nirvana* (the Pali is *Nibbana*) derives from the root *va* ('blow') and the prefix *nir* (meaning 'out' or 'off') – *Nibbana* refers precisely to *dying out* as of a fire* – but such terms of extinction refer not to a soul or to the individual, which do not exist in Buddhism, but to passions such as craving: *tanha*.

Applying such reflections in a brief introduction to an edition of Eliot's *Selected Essays* (Tokyo: Kinseido, 1933), WE paradoxically pointed out that what Eliot claimed for Christianity was true also for Buddhism. Eliot's '**stress on society and tradition rather than the individual is likely to be welcome in Japan, but in the Far East it is not an argument for Christianity but for Buddhism**'. (Incidentally, WE declared too his own belief that Eliot and the Buddhists were '**certainly right**' about the unimportance of personality (*A*, p. 569).) Buddhism must be respected not only because the West has to realize that it holds no prerogatives in the truths of metaphysics or ethics, but because Buddhism may be the one sustainable and evolving faith: '**The race of man ... is now pooling its traditions. Either Mr Eliot's support of Christianity from tradition is a claim that the truth is national or racial or otherwise accidental, or the True Orthodoxy must not limit itself to the traditions of Christianity ... And if there is any sort of practical issue between the two, it is worth pointing out that Buddhism is the last of the great religions that can be conceived as changing itself in the future "so as to be believable"** ' (*A*, pp. 568–9).

There is no doubt that in the 1930s, particularly in the period leading up to the first appearance of 'Fire Sermon', WE was concerned to proclaim the powerful attractions of Buddhism. This inclination reached its zenith in 1933, when WE drafted a talk on the tortured subject of death wishes. 'Death and Its Desires', its posthumous published title, opens with a recital of the 'Fire Sermon' following this declaration: '**It is a supreme example of the beauty of at any rate one sort of death wish when in an almost pure form, and it will make discussion look very flimsy.**' Certain '**logical puzzles,**' he goes on, '**need I think to be stressed in praising Buddhism; the worship of death here goes both with a plan for a better life and a fundamental doubt about the nature of death when attained**'; furthermore, '**the special Buddhist version of a death wish I think needs isolating. It is that no sort of temporal life whatever can satisfy the human spirit, and therefore that we must work for an existence outside time on whatever terms ... The point I want to make about this version of a death wish is that I doubt whether any process of analysis could show it to be wrong**' (*A*, pp. 535, 537).

---

*According to Sangharakshita, the 'Pali equivalent *nibbana* is made up of the negative particle *ni* and *vana* meaning selfish desire or craving' (*A Survey of Buddhism: its doctrines and methods through the ages* (Glasgow, 1957; 6th edn., 1987), p. 26).

The intensity of his fascination with Buddhism into the 1940s cannot be overestimated: he spent long periods in the Far East undertaking arduous travels in search of Buddhist icons so that he could write up a descriptive and theoretical, illustrated monograph, which was subsequently lost by a careless friend – it may well have run to more than 30,000 words – entitled 'The Faces of Buddha' (he would later consider it his favourite of his own works); and then in 1942, while otherwise stretched by his work for the Far Eastern Department of the BBC, he would write the outline of a ballet, *The Elephant and the Birds*, based on the story of the Buddha in his incarnation as an elephant – a subject taken from the *Jataka*, the Pali canon of tales of the Buddha's former births (see *RB*).

Among the papers WE left at his death are some handwritten pages, evidently dating from the early 1930s, which compare the Buddha's teaching and the European view of individual self-fulfilment; and since these possibly constituted a draft version of his introduction to 'The Faces of Buddha', it is worthwhile quoting at length:

The Buddha was not an isolated and discontented philosopher like Schopenhauer in his hotel, but the leader of an exceptionally successful religious movement in touch and in sympathy with popular ideas. On many points his assertions called forth discussion and contradiction but when he said that all existence involves suffering no one disputed the dictum: no one talked of the pleasures of life or used those arguments which come so copiously to the healthy-minded modern essayist when he devotes a page or two to disproving pessimism. On this point the views and temperament of the Buddha were clearly those of educated India. (The existence of this conviction and temperament in a large body of intellectual men is as important as the belief in the value of life and the love of activity for its own sake which is common among Europeans. Both tempers must be taken into account by every theory which is not merely personal but endeavours to ascertain what the human race think and feel about existence.)

The sombre and meditative cast of Indian thought is not due to physical degeneration or a depressing climate. Many authors speak as if the Hindus lived in a damp relaxing heat in which physical and moral stamina alike decay. I myself think that as to climate India is preferable to Europe. The Burmese are among the most cheerful people in the world and the Japanese among the most vigorous, and the latter are at least as much Buddhists as Europeans are Christians. It might be plausibly maintained that Europeans' love of activity is mainly due to the intolerable climate and uncomfortable institutions of the continent, which involve a continual struggle with the weather and continual discussion forbidding any calm and contemplative view of things. The Indian being less troubled by these evils is able to judge what is the value of life in itself, as an experience for the individual not as part of a universal struggle, which is the common view of seriously minded Europeans, though as to this struggle they have but hazy ideas as to the antagonists, the cause and the result.

The Buddhist doctrine does not mean that life is something trifling and unimportant, to be lived anyhow. On the contrary, birth as a human being is an opportunity of inestimable value, He who is so born has at least a chance of hearing the truth and acquiring merit. 'Hard is it to be born as a man, hard to come to hear the true law', and when the chance comes, the good fortune of the being who has attained the human form and the actual issues which depend on his using it rightly are dwelt on with an earnestness not surpassed by Christian homiletics.

. . . The temper which prompts the Buddha's utterances is not that of Ecclesiastes – the melancholy of satiety which, having enjoyed all, finds that all is vanity – but rather the regretful verdict of one who while sympathizing with the nobler passions – love ambition the quest of knowledge – is forced to pronounce them unsatisfactory. The human mind craves after something which is permanent, something of which it can say This is mine. It longs to be something or to produce something which is not transitory and which has an absolute value in and for itself. But neither in this world nor in any other world are such states or actions possible. Only in Nirvana do we find a state which rises above the transitory because it rises above desire . . . When Christian writers attempt to describe the joys of a heaven which is eternally satisfying they have usually to fall back on negative phrases such as Eye hath not seen nor ear heard.

The European view of life differs from the Asiatic chiefly in attributing a value to actions in themselves and in not being disturbed by the fact that their results are impermanent. It is, in fact, the theoretical side of the will to live, which can find expression in a treatise on metaphysics as well as in an act of procreation. An Englishman according to his capacity and mental culture is satisfied with some such rule of existence as having a good time, or playing the game, or doing his duty, or working for some cause. The majority of intelligent men are prepared to devote their lives to the service of the British Empire: the fact that it must pass away as certainly as the Empire of Babylon does not disturb them and is hardly ever present to their minds . . . [I]t [the Buddhist view of life] says it is a fine thing to be a man and have the power of helping others; that the best life is that which is entirely unselfish and a continual sacrifice. But looking at existence as a whole, and accepting the theory that the happiest and best life is a life of self-sacrifice, it declines to consider as satisfactory a world in which this principle holds good (the ideal of continual activity that makes the world better . . . implies a background of evil).

In sum, even while seeking to buttress Richards's Theory of Value, WE also found himself extolling the Buddhist doctrine that 'no sort of temporal life can satisfy the human spirit'. No one could have been more alive to the strangeness of this paradox than WE himself. And yet it goes very far to justify his decision to place 'The Fire Sermon' at the forefront of his poetry, in accord with the common theme of the poems (as he so memorably expressed it in his notes to 'Bacchus') that '**life involves maintaining oneself between contradictions that can't be solved by analysis**'. He evidently regarded Buddhism as a *tertium quid* (a third something) between Richards's humanist argument for self-fulfilment through poetry and the ghastly god of the Christians who was appeased by the sacrifice of his son and who will mark one down for heaven or hell.

More than forty years after WE first promoted his version of 'The Fire Sermon', John Wain (an admirer of his work) was to enquire, sympathetically but firmly, into WE's reasons for continuing to give it pride of place in *CP*: 'To keep this flag at the mast-head across twenty years must surely indicate something; but, no, we find Empson a year later [in his reply to Rodway's review] casually washing his hands of it . . . So the Fire Sermon is important enough to Empson's poetry to put up in front, and given a new lease there after twenty years, while being "**pretty remote, and not appealed to**". Is this, one wonders, a procedure Empson would expect from the poets about whom he writes such brilliant criticism? . . . Empson might continue for years to draw some kind of strength from the Fire Sermon (even if he "**probably never thought about**" it), by treating it as one of the stakes that supported a clothes-line' (reprinted in 'The Poetry of William Empson', *Professing Poetry*, pp. 325–7).

WE, in a personal response to Wain, took the opportunity to concede, perhaps for the first time:

About the Fire Sermon. I suppose I should not have put it at the front. The book contains several translations, made without knowing the language concerned but with fuss about accuracy and nearly all good I think. There is no other recitable translation of this, and a reader of the *Waste Land* needs one. I feel I failed to get enough attention for it. However, I suppose I was guilty of religiosity a little, hinting perhaps 'We all feel that life is inadequate for us' . . . That the practical test of a religion must be whether it makes people better I agree, and I agree that the Fire Sermon probably wouldn't. That it has a quieter kind of merit all the same is a paradox often found in literature.

However, among his ultimate misgivings about Buddhism, in addition to his crucial conviction as a rationalist that the way of self-negation was finally not for him, WE identified what he called a '**political fault**' in its system: '**that it does little to make people feel in practical life the reality of the brotherhood of man**' ('Death and Its Desires', *A*, p. 544). Later, he was moved to proselytize for a quasi-pantheistic view of the big metaphysical question; as he would put it in 1964, specifically with eager reference to Aldous Huxley's *The Perennial Philosophy* (1948): '**His answer is that one should stop believing in this all-executive Father, but accept an impersonal "Divine Ground", as in Hinduism and in the mystics of all other religions; thus becoming morally free to recognize that the world contains wonderful things as well as horrible things**' (*A*, p. 617). Nevertheless, he retained for the rest of his life a high regard for the Buddhist teaching, not least because it represented in the scheme of things a perhaps unanswerable challenge to the Christian faith.

In a draft of the letter published (in 1956) in the Sheffield University students' periodical *Arrows*, WE made his position still more understandable and urgent:

If one of my sons when he is older wants to become a monk I shall cry and beg him on my knees not to do it;* obviously this wouldn't change his mind, but I do hope that my saying it now can remove one of the confusions in your mind. I did not mean to recommend being a monk. Secondly, I did not myself write the Fire Sermon, as your critic seems to suggest; I can safely promise I will never do anything so rough till I die. It is the most staggeringly terrible thing ever said by the Buddha. It not only says, do you see, that all life on earth is bad, but that life in any conceivable heaven would be equally bad, on the same metaphysical grounds. This of course smashes straight through Christianity. But I do not believe myself that life on earth is nothing but suffering (and this is the fundamental position of the Buddha) let alone what may go on in all the heavens. You may well say then that I simply oughtn't to have put the Fire Sermon at the beginning of my poems.

The truth is, though it sounds silly, that I printed my version of the Fire Sermon because it is the only one that can actually be recited in the English language in full. You must realize that this apparently short bit of text, if you put in all the repetitions, takes more than a quarter of an hour, and to sit and listen to it is a pretty appalling experience. The English language can do almost anything, and with a little pushing you can make it do just enough to imitate the fierceness of the original, or at least to get something which can be repeated all these times without sounding bad. But nobody else had done it; T. S. Eliot, who I understand actually learned Sanskrit, had told literary characters that they ought to know about the Fire Sermon, and I looked the subject up, and I suppose I collated at least five different translations before I settled on what I consider the actor's text. I usually do what I am told to, and I first printed it, long ago now, because my friends told me that there really ought to be a usable text of the Fire Sermon printed in the English language. I go on printing it in the Collected Edition because I stubbornly won't hide anything.

Well yes, this I hope sounds clear enough, but it sounds like an excuse, meaning please it is only an accident I printed the Fire Sermon. That would be quite untrue; I have been employed for ten years in China and Japan, and my nose has been rubbed very firmly in the Buddha. When I think what to say next, I rather suspect that any further gab about it would only be rather trivial; but it is the case that, though it is only an accident that I have the Fire Sermon to start my Collected Poems (rather an impudent accident, you may say, but never mind; many good translators have only known their own language), still I seriously want it there, and would have made a row if for some technical reason I couldn't have it.† The Europeans have got to realize that Asia really exists; that is really why I feel sure I ought to keep that bit in. My state of mind seems to be that of the grandfather T. H.

*In 1933, WE had expressed himself much less vehemently: 'I would be sorry to hear of one of my friends becoming either a Buddhist or Christian monk, though I would expect him to be less hurt in bringing his mind to accept being a Buddhist one' ('Mr Eliot and the East', *A*, p. 569).

†When T. S. Eliot was arranging for the US publication of *CP 1949*, WE wrote to him: 'I should like to have the Fire Sermon on the flyleaf as in the Chatto edition [of *P*]' (2 December 1946). It had not been included in *GS*.

Huxley, not that of Aldous Huxley, though he has made a very fine anthology of the mystics right across Europe and Asia in *The Perennial Philosophy*.

Well, I suppose this only expresses a confused state of mind, but I would always want to remove any accidental confusion. (Empson Papers)

For comparison, the warmth – the zeal – of his period as Buddhist 'fellow-traveller' can be appreciated from the style of a talk he wrote in 1939, while visiting Richards in Massachusetts, on his way home from China. Drafted as a radio broadcast for a Boston station (WRUL), with a view to illustrating the powers of Basic English, he took for its title the single, provocative word 'Life'. Since every culture necessarily values life by its estimate of the meaning of death, WE felt bound to bring up Buddhism as the most heartening rival to Christianity – and it is noticeable how on this topic his tone heightens with enthusiasm, and his rhythm mimes 'The Fire Sermon' itself:

This is the teaching that went across all the east of Asia and by only touching a country made it strong. It seemed beautiful, it seemed safe, it seemed a new way of living and a good one and it gave fruit to millions of men. And this is what it said, and it said, 'Death, there is no other possible good thing but death,' and it said that very clearly. The facts about the behaviour of men are very much stranger than they seem to us. And so it is important to say . . . that almost all the effects of the Fire Sermon were good effects. For example, hundreds of thousands of men have been burned while still living in the name of Jesus, and probably no man has been so burned in the name of Buddha. But the Buddha said things that gave much more reason for burning, much more hate of common living, much more poison, if you are looking at the simple words, than the words of Christ. But in fact they did no damage. As a question of history, where these words came they did good. (Empson Papers)

1 *Bhikkhus*: *bhikku* (Pali), generally translated as 'monk', comes from a verbal root meaning 'to beg'; originally, a mendicant follower of the Buddha.

11–12 *the Aryan path*: historically, *Aryan* (Vedic *arian*) designates the ancient people who invaded or settled in Iran and northern India at about the time of the collapse of the Indus civilization (*c.* 1600 BC); they spoke an early form of Sanskrit called 'Vedic' – the name being taken from the earliest Indian texts, the *Veda* (the Aryan religion is Vedism, which gradually spread into the region of the Ganges River Valley; and Hinduism evolved from the syncretism of Aryan and indigenous non-Aryan elements). In late Sanskrit, *arya* means 'noble, of good family'. Still later, 'Aryan' was used to embrace the so-called Indo-European family of languages. See *Encyclopaedia of Buddhism*, ed. G. P. Malalasekera (Ceylon, 1966), Vol. 2, pp. 105–6.

Perhaps the majority of translators of the Fire Sermon have avoided using 'Aryan' – not always or necessarily for political reasons but because of its appalling historical and etymological obscurity. Where WE chooses an exact, simple formula,

Rhys Davids and Oldenberg refer more awkwardly, albeit correctly, to 'a disciple learned (in the scriptures), walking in the Noble Path'; and Coomaraswamy opts for deceptive thrift: 'a true disciple'.

Fully aware in 1935 of the policy of 'Aryanization' being pursued by the Nazi régime in Germany, WE evidently felt that was another reason for recovering the historical meaning of the term. In 'Ballet of the Far East' (1937) he would observe: '**The man who made the supreme expression of the Far Eastern view of God and man was the Buddha, and he was an Aryan, the same race as ourselves; in fact it was he, not Herr Hitler, who first used this adjective as a term of general praise, rather as we use "noble"** ' (*A*, pp. 577–8).

'Mother, saying Anne good night'

WE's first surviving poem, written by 29 June 1920, aged 13 (see Introduction, p. xli); first published in *RB*. The text is taken from the autograph book of J. A. Simson.

3–4 '*Four angels . . . one at the head* –': parodying a once-popular nursery charm: 'Matthew, Mark, Luke, and John, / Bless the bed that I lay on; / Four corners to my bed, / Four angels round my head, / One at head and one at feet, / And two to keep my soul asleep!' (recorded by James Orchard Halliwell-Phillips, in *Popular Rhymes and Nursery Tales* (London, 1849), pp. 210–11).

Song of the amateur psychologist

Written in 1926; first published in *RB*.

Directly after writing out a fair copy in a notebook, WE commented: '**It is good rousing stuff, I still think.**' In 1965 he was to recall: '**One of my earliest memories is of clutching a candle in my shaking hand and climbing over heaps of coal as I wound up the thread left by my sister across the vasty and labyrinthine cellars of Yokefleet Hall** [the family home near Goole in Yorkshire]' ('The Variants for the Byzantium Poems', *Using Biography*, p. 182). The same memory may lie at the back of the portrayal of a 'Young Theseus' in the more mature 'Myth' (see below).

Cf. WE's remarks in 'Alice in Wonderland: The Child as Swain' (hereafter 'Alice: Child as Swain'): '**To make the dream-story from which *Wonderland* was elaborated seem Freudian one has only to tell it. A fall through a deep hole into the secrets of Mother Earth produces a new enclosed soul wondering who it is, what will be its position in the world and how it can get out**' (*Pastoral*, p. 216).

Mark Thompson (' "On the borderland" ') remarks that the poem 'comes straight out of [Eliot's] "The Hollow Men" (1925). The narrator speaks from a staircase . . . that locus of decisions in Eliot's "La Figlia che piange" and later in "Ash-Wednesday".'

6 *whose . . . are*: WE noted against this line in his fair copy: '**Braincell Pseudopodia.**'
9 *intercellular*: 'situated between or among cells' (*OED*).
16 *fretted hollow curves*: cf. 'Rebuke for a dropped brick', l. 7.
17 *high vaulted arches*: cf. 'Bacchus', l. 92.
49 *groining*: cf. 'Bacchus', l. 19.

Two centos

First published in *RB*.

Two songs from a libretto

These lyrics date from about October 1927; first published in *RB*.

    Although too little of the libretto survives to give a clear idea of its intended plot, one may infer that WE meant somehow to combine literary satire with a tale about a young girl May being pressed into a loveless marriage by her ignorant and wickedly venal aunts. Both begun and apparently abandoned just as Empson turned twenty-one, it follows up the romantic melodrama of his play *Three Stories* (see *RB*).

    In one draft passage two aunts try to persuade the girl to take heed of a promising match:

Aunt (1) **You'll hardly if ever**
   (2)   **You'll never discover**
   (1) **So handsome rich clever**
   (2)   **A more worthy lover**

to which the girl replies:

      Search for him out some worthy lass
      Ere my affection cow him.
  (1) **So must the Spring name dawns in vain,**
      And pullulent, uncurling,
      Leave you sequestered, cold inane
      Pale tendrils curling?

(2) Girl, have you never turned to see,
 Nor caught your breath in turning?
 Have you no sighing after tea
 For sharp romance's burning?

 . . .

(1) Ah you may waive the more convulsive passions,
 So to be sober, elegant, endears
 One who can see your heart and feel your fashions
 And know the intimate sympathy of years.

Another passage begins with May asking about the extract from F. H. Bradley's *Appearance and Reality* quoted by Eliot in his note to l. 411 of *The Waste Land*:

 What did Professor Bradley say whom
 T. S. Eliot quotes?
 (1) Surely but only in the notes
 (2) Why, should I have read *all* the notes?
 Girl. His notes are *part* of what he quotes
 (2) These modern writers get my goats
 (1) The girl is overstrung and dotes
 (2) Come, let's be daring, burn our boats,
 Have you the notes here?
 Read out the notes dear.
 (*The note is intoned.*)
 (2) Well, if that isn't bonny.

Aunt (1) presently remarks:

 Since so far May this remarkable Law
 And the world at large seem to have got together
 Let them get on together a bit *more*.

to which the first song above is the girl's response; it is followed by these lines:

 (2) May do try and make a good impression
 Johnny is coming and will take possession.
 (1) Be plain and unsilly like us
 He says he don't mind if he does.

16 *liefless*: *lief* (now obsolete) is normally an adjective for 'beloved' or 'dear', though also used in a quasi-substantive sense: (*OED*) 'a beloved, a dear one; a friend, sweetheart, mistress; occas. a wife'.

The Ants

First published, as 'Sonnet', *Cambridge Review* 49 (27 April 1928), 369.

CP: **The ants build mud galleries into trees to protect the green-fly they get sugar from, and keep them warm in the nest during winter.**

For *Listen* WE noted: '**It is a love-poem with the author afraid of the woman.**'
    In an undated letter to John Wain (who had sympathetically discussed the poem in Wain, pp. 284–90), WE ventured:

The Ants was the first poem I thought worth keeping, and copies the assumption of Eliot that city life is very bad, not needing war to make it so. Large-scale disaster is expected but not of any specific kind. However it fits war very well. I forget the circumstances of writing it completely, and had done when writing the notes for the sleeve, so you may be right. It would be written during my first two years at Cambridge, but why I dont know. I expect the sexual situation was bad.

    Earlier, however, in a letter to J. A. Stephens, who had sent WE an essay on his work, WE offered this more substantial gloss (28 October 1957):

The ants' tunnels are compared to the London Underground, which has advertisements for patent medicines on the walls and a special ventilation system. It is true that the trains roar rather than 'whine' [l. 4] when passing through, but I might claim that they whine when heard from further off. The subject of *nears* [l. 9] could equally well be *station* or *air*, since AB = BA, but the tube station we have now reached is too close to the dangerous surface of the planet. Surely the pity is felt quite as much for men as for ants. It is meant to be a love-poem; the woman's mind and sympathies are the open air, and seem unmeritable, even if safe to reach, so that the lover is like city workers in their tube.

    To W. D. Maxwell-Mahon, WE wrote on 6 November 1967:

In *The Ants* . . . it occurred to me that the queer habits of these ants were like an unsatisfactory love-affair with a person revered but not understood (to which as a student I was sadly prone). I described the ants, making the parallel as far as I could see it, but I did not feel I had to invent a human story in detail to fit it, at all points. The onset of neurotic (uncaused) fear seemed to me a probable result, worth making the start of the sestet [l. 9]. But I definitely did not mean to say [as Maxwell-Mahon had] that 'the self-conscious mind breeds thoughts from neuroses'. This would seem to me very gorblimey, very pretentious, partly because I doubt if it makes sense. You take for granted that it must be a Symbolist poem, but my poems are never that.

Part of the inspiration came from *The Life of the White Ant*, by Maurice Maeterlinck (London, 1927), which WE reviewed for *Granta*, 4 November 1927:

M. Maeterlinck has taken upon himself one of the artist's new, important and honourable functions, that of digesting the discoveries of the scientist into an emotionally available form. It is his business to enrich our possible satisfactions with those of the creatures of this elaborate civilization. He has told us with authority many strange facts, and pointed out where others were lacking, but the work itself calls for a more desperate effort of imagination. It is no use, for instance, wondering whether it mustn't be horrid for the poor creatures to eat each other's dung, when in the workers the whole process of digestion is inverted; or whether it must not be very sad to be blind, when they are so perfectly sure of their world and can communicate with such nicety. The life of a termite, as he interprets it, is one of vivid but unrelieved horror; capable creatures of wide initiative do not usually think of themselves like that. It is hard to suppose a termite would agree. (*E in G*, pp. 23–4)

Cf. WE's analysis of the 'honey-bees' in *Henry V*, I.ii.187–204 (*ST*, pp. 138–9).
　　See also Morelli, pp. 69–72; Willis, pp. 95–9; Thurley, pp. 41–2; Ricks, pp. 183–4, Wain, pp. 294–90; *TGA*, pp. 39–41.

1 *tunnel*: cf. 'The Scales', l. 8, 'Earth has Shrunk in the Wash', l. 22, and 'Letter IV', l. 4.
3 *nostrum-plastered*: in respect of ant-life (the white ant described by Maeterlinck, *The Life of the White Ant*, is a termite by another name), the phrase refers both to the viscous substance with which the insects build their nests and galleries, and to the fungus gardens that they grow in the formicary to feed their young (cf. stanza 3 of 'Value is in Activity').
3 *with prepared air*: see WE's comments to Stephens above; also W. M. Wheeler, *Social Life Among the Insects* (London, 1923), p. 272: 'The nests of some fungus-growing termites are provided with chimney-like structures, communicating with large tubular cavities which have been interpreted by Escherich as a system of ventilating shafts . . . [with] a careful regulation of temperature and humidity.'
5 *We ants . . . your dew*: Maeterlinck notes (p. 142) that 'the *Lasius Flavus*, our little brown ant, has real stables underground in which herds of aphides are kept; these give forth a sugary moisture that the ant goes and milks just as we milk our cows and goats'. WE must also have read Auguste Forel's *The Social World of the Ants Compared with That of Man*, trans. by C. K. Ogden and published in February 1928 (London and New York), which observes: 'It seems strange that excrement should be so nourishing, but it is a fact that the excrement of aphids and coccids, and probably also that of other ant-cattle, is very sweet and is eliminated in the form of honey-dew.' Forel notes that Pierre Huber, who was the first to discover this, in *Recherches sur les moeurs des fourmis indigènes* (Geneva,

1810), 'observed that when the ants are keeping these aphids, they tap them with their antennae, one after the other, in a friendly manner' (p. 494).

5 aphids] aphides *1928*, *CP 1949* (Maeterlinck's spelling)

6 *their sucking or our care*: Wheeler (*Social Life Among the Insects*, p. 178) remarks that Phytophthora, i.e. plant-lice [especially aphids], scale-insects, mealy bugs, etc., 'pierce the integument of the plants with their slender, pointed mouth-parts and imbibe the juices . . .' See also Forel, *Social World of the Ants*, p. 493.

7 *your branch must bear*: Wheeler notes: 'Termites may build either in the ground or on the trunks or branches of trees' (*Social Life Among the Insects*, p. 262).

8 *High . . . all earth to view*: cf. Milton's account of how God the Almighty Father looked down from 'the pure empyrean where he sits . . . His own works and their works at once to view' (*PL*, III.57, 59). Given 'air' (l. 9), cf. too Edna St Vincent Millay's sonnet 'Mindful of you the sodden earth in spring', l. 12: 'Of a bird's wings too high in air to view, – ' (*Collected Poems* (New York, 1956), p. 563).

8 *as roots' depth*: Wheeler notes a number of species of ants 'devote themselves to pasturing their cattle on the roots' (*Social Life Among the Insects*, p. 179).

10 *How small a chink lets in how dire a foe*: cf. Samson's complaint: 'What boots it at one gate to make defence, / And at another to let in the foe / Effeminately vanquished?' (Milton, *Samson Agonistes*, ll. 560–62); and *PL*, IV.371–3: 'this high seat your Heaven / Ill fenced for Heaven to keep out such a foe / As now is entered'.

11 *What though the garden in one glance appears*: cf. WE's observation, in 'Alice: Child as Swain': '**Alice peering through the hole into the garden may be wanting a return to the womb as well as an escape from it; she is fond, we are told, of taking both sides of an argument when talking to herself, and the whole book balances between the luscious nonsense-world of fantasy, and the ironic nonsense-world of fact**' (*Pastoral*, pp. 216–17). In *Alice's Adventures in Wonderland* (1865) the big Alice, having fallen down a rabbit-hole, found herself (ch. I) in a place of barred doors; but she managed to open one – 'and found that it led into a small passage, not much larger than a rat-hole: she knelt down and looked along the passage into the loveliest garden you ever saw.' Likewise in ch. II, we are told: 'Poor Alice! It was as much as she could do, lying down on one side, to look through into the garden with one eye; but to get through was more hopeless than ever: she sat down and began to cry again.'

Value is in Activity

First published, as 'Inhabitants', *Cambridge Review* 49 (6 June 1928), 507.

CP: **The beetles live underground (inside the globe of the earth) and are only compared to the creatures that may be in the apple; hence to the juggler.**

The periodical version included an epigraph, quoted in Greek, from Aristotle's *Nichomachean Ethics* (I.7, 1098ᵃ16), which defines the motto that WE used for his title: human good is achieved through 'activity of soul in accordance with excellence or virtue'. Cf. WE's remarks in a review of John Laird, *An Enquiry into Moral Notions*: '**whether or not the values open to us are measurable, we cannot measure them, and it is of much value merely to stand up between the forces to which we are exposed**' (*Spectator*, 29 November 1935, p. 912).

For *Listen* WE noted: '**The apple and the Big Top and the earth are simply compared.**'

In response to J. A. Stephens, WE offered:

I was thinking [in l. 1] of an actual circus tent painted green, as I remember, but anyhow it is compared to the surface of the earth, which is predominantly green. So is the apple, being still young [l. 3]; it is also sour ('acid', hence no hyphen for *acid-green*). How can you say the interior is unmolested if it may have maggots or mites? Late frosts [l. 6] are very dangerous to the fruit-harvest, and there is meant to be a comparison to a man's character which has been warped by being bullied when a child.

See also Dodsworth, 'Empson at Cambridge', pp. 8–11; Morelli, pp. 72–5; Willis, pp. 99–104; Ricks, pp. 184–6; Wain, pp. 294–6; *TGA*, pp. 42–4.

1 an] the *1928*
6 Dwarf seeds unnavelled a last frost] With dwarfed unnavelling the first sun *1928*
7 Mites that] With mites *1928*
9 beetles] beetles, *1928*
9 *tupped*: fucked (or impregnated); see Iago's scurrilous proclamation in *Othello*, I.i.88–9: 'Even now, now, very now, an old black ram / Is tupping your white ewe.'
10–11 *halls of . . . treasured fungi*: Wheeler tells how the huge nests of the fungus-growing termites (or 'white ants')

contain a number of large, spherical chambers surrounding the royal cell and connected with it and with one another by galleries. In each chamber there are one or more fungus gardens . . . [These] are really the nurseries of the termitarium and are full of just-hatched young, which crop the food-bodies like so many little snow-white sheep. Neither the workers nor the soldiers feed on the fungus, but the king and queen and other reproductive forms receive the same food as the young. (*Social Life Among the Insects*, pp. 270–71)

See also J. B. S. Haldane, *Possible Worlds* (London, 1927), p. 66.
10 *knowingly chewed splinter*: 'The concentrated nests . . . consist either of earth or woody material or of both . . . Both the soil and the wood may be swallowed by the workers and after mixture with secretions, either regurgitated or passed

through the intestine and used as building material, or particles of soil or wood may be merely bitten off and agglutinated with saliva' (Wheeler, *Social Life Among the Insects*, p. 261: see notes on 'The Ants').

11 sprout] sprout, *1928*

Invitation to Juno

First published in *Cambridge Review* 49 (4 May 1928), 387; reprinted in *New Signatures* (1932).

CP: Dr Johnson said it, somewhere in Boswell. Iago threatened Brabantio about gennets. Ixion rides on one wheel because he failed in an attempt at mixed marriage with Juno which would have produced demigods, two-wheeled because inheriting two life-periods.

The periodical printing of this seduction poem included two additional stanzas, the first after the present second stanza, the other at the end:

> Hybrids, at least, have been extremely sterile.
> I know, of that cross, no recorded female.
> And can we, my dear, smile
> At mule or hinny our estates entail?
> . . .
> Your triple brass, my trimorphic money
> (No clean-run Stock) in such a Cross enskied
> Shall breed that three-fold Trinity
> Saint Athanasius thrice denied.

Willis (p. 108) comments: 'This last stanza, blessedly eliminated from the final version of "Invitation", is a confusing and unpleasant conglomeration of commerce, heresy, betrayal, torture, theology, astronomy, genetics, and sex.' A *hinny* is the offspring of a she-ass by a stallion; as Darwin remarked in *The Origin of Species* (1859), 'Both the mule and the hinny resemble more closely the ass than the horse' (cited in *OED*). Willis further notes (p. 107): 'One problem here is the girl's "triple brass". An alloy sometimes made from copper, tin, and zinc, this three-in-one brass implies the Trinity as well as boldness and impudence (compare Horace's "aes triplex" in the *Odes*, 1.3.9).' *Trimorphic* means (*OED*) 'having, or existing in, three forms: *spec.* a. *Bot.* Having flowers with pistils and stamens of three different relative lengths'; Darwin treats trimorphism in ch. IX, 'Hybridism', of *The Origin of Species*. For St Athanasius on the Trinity, see 'New World Bistres', note on l. 15.

For a student, Kazuo Ogawa, in Tokyo in the early 1930s, WE wrote these notes:

The root idea of the poem is more sensual than it seems. The poet is suffering from some bodily weakness, and so, 'his pulses did not gear with hers'; they were 'asynchronous'.

The poet is an Ixion, and his mistress, a Juno. The poet is inviting (hence the title of the poem 'Invitation to Juno') her to another trial following Darwin's experiment in botany.

'Courage' may mean: (1) have courage to 'credit' *i.e.* believe my tact, (2) have courage to be seduced again.

(quoted by Ogawa, in English, in a Japanese commentary on 'Invitation to Juno', in the periodical *Eigo-seinen*, July 1939; collected in his *English Poetry*, p. 30)

Writing to J. A. Stephens (28 October 1957), WE observed:

This again [like 'The Ants'] was meant as primarily a love-poem – 'You wouldn't love me, being a superior nature – even if you could'; I agree that it is bad, because it fails to have enough point [to] it at the end.

I cut a last verse because I felt shy about [*MS missing*].

See Izzo, *Poesia Inglese*, p. 575; Morelli, pp. 28–32; Ormerod, 'Empson's "Invitation to Juno" '; Willis, pp. 104–9; Ricks, p. 184; *TGA*, pp. 44–6.

1–4 *Lucretius . . . ours*: 'centaurs' (l. 1) because of their relation to the myth of Ixion and Juno (Hera). A mortal king, Ixion was thwarted in his desire for an affair with Juno, the divine wife of Jupiter (Zeus), when Jupiter sent him a clever little creation of 'virtual reality' in the place of his wife: this cloud in Juno's likeness, impregnated by Ixion, brought forth the outcast Centaurus, who in turn sired the centaurs on the mares of Magnesia. Jupiter punished Ixion by fixing him to a burning wheel – not a 'bicycle' (l. 2) but a unicycle (cf. 'Bacchus', ll. 37–41). The rationalist Lucretius dismisses the possible existence of the centaur in *De Rerum Naturae*, V.878–924 (Loeb edn., pp. 402–5).

But *there never were*, nor ever can be, Centaurs – *creatures with a double nature*, combining organs of different origin in a single body so that there may be a balance of power between attributes drawn from two distinct sources. This can be inferred by the dullest wit from these facts. First, a horse reaches its vigorous prime in about three years, a boy far from it . . . Then, when the horse's limbs are flagging and his mettle is fading, then is the very time when the boy is crowned with the flower of youth . . . You need not suppose, therefore, that there can ever be a Centaur, compounded of man and draught-horse, or . . . any other such monstrous hybrid between species whose bodies are obviously incompatible . . . [E]ach species develops according to its own kind, and they all guard their specific characters in obedience to the laws of nature (Lucretius, *On the Nature of the Universe*, trans. R. E. Latham (Harmondsworth, 1951), pp. 198–9)

5–6 *Johnson . . . machine as well*: 'Mr Fergusson, the self-taught philosopher, told him of a new-invented machine which went without horses: a man who sat in it turned a handle, which worked a spring that drove it forward. "Then, Sir, (said Johnson,) what is gained is, the man has his choice whether he will move himself alone, or himself and the machine too"' (Boswell, *Life of Johnson*, ed. R. W. Chapman (1904); new edn., ed. J. D. Fleeman (Oxford, 1953), p. 420).

5 would] could *1928*

6 'You . . . well.'] You . . . well *1928*

7 *Gennets for germans*] "Gennets for germans" *1928*

7 *Gennets for germans sprang not from Othello*: 'Because we come to do you service and you think we are ruffians, you'll have your daughter covered with a Barbary horse; you'll have your nephews neigh to you; you'll have coursers for cousins and gennets for germans' (*Othello*, I.i.109–14). A 'gennet' (French *genet*) is a small Spanish horse; 'german' means close kin, as in cousin.

8 Ixion] And Ixion *1928, 1932, CP 1949*

8 *Ixion rides upon a single wheel*: WE's punning use of the verb 'rides' – which might suggest that Ixion is an active agent, whereas it is his especial punishment in Hell to be strapped to an eternally-revolving wheel for his hubris – might be licensed by Virgil's equally ambiguous construction, *Ixionii uento rota constitit orbis* (*Georgics*, IV.484), where '*rota . . . orbis*' translates literally as 'the wheel of his [Ixion's] turning'. As R. A. B. Mynors suggests (P. Vergili Maronis, *Opera* (Oxford, 1969)), *orbis rotae* would seem the proper expression for Ixion's fate; and Ovid has *Ixionis orbis* (*Metamorphoses*, X.42). Cf. 'Bacchus', l. 37. (Cf. too 'Ixion' by Robert Browning; see C. R. Tracy, 'Browning's Heresies', *Studies in Philology* 33 (1936), 624.)

9–10 *strips of heart culture . . . two periodicities*: WE, in notes written to Stephens, observes: '*Heart culture* **meant tiny pieces of tissue from a heart being grown separately on jelly supplied with chemicals – the scientific report stuck in my head because choosing heart tissue seemed "poetical".**' As the embryonic heart develops *in utero* (or, experimentally, in tissue culture *in vitro*), the various individual cardiac muscle cells exhibit spontaneous (myogenic) activity and beat with a characteristic individual rate. As development proceeds and the cells touch one another, gap junctions are formed between them and the cells become organized into a network (syncytium): they then adopt a common rate.

11 Did not once the adroit] Could not Professor Charles *1928, 1932, P 1934*; Did not at one time even *CP 1949*

Philip Hobsbaum writes: 'In one of our discussions [A.] Alvarez and I queried his revision of a line in his "Invitation to Juno". He had changed "Could not Professor Charles Darwin" to "Could not at one time even Darwin", which we thought weak. Empson objected that Darwin had not been a professor, but agreed that the line was weak. I see that in *Collected Poems* [1955] . . . it now reads "Did not once the adroit Darwin", which is even worse' ('Some Recollections', in a letter to Haffenden, 6 May 1985).

11–12 *Did not . . . / Graft annual upon perennial trees*: WE admitted to J. A. Stephens in his letter of 28 October 1957: **'Darwin I think mentioned the grafting in the *Origin*, but I have never looked up the reference.'** (He probably meant that he had never stopped to check the reference; he had certainly read *The Origin of Species*.) In ch. IX, 'Hybridism', Darwin remarks: 'Great diversity in the size of two plants . . . one being evergreen and the other deciduous . . . do not always prevent the two grafting together . . . although there is a clear and great difference between the mere adhesion of grafted stocks, and the union of the male and female elements in the act of reproduction, yet . . . there is a rude degree of parallelism in the results of grafting and of crossing distinct species' (*The Works of Charles Darwin*, ed. Paul H. Barrett and R. B. Freeman, Vol. 16: *The Origin of Species, 1876* (London, 1988), pp. 256–7).

The World's End

First published, as 'Relativity', *Cambridge Review* 49 (11 May 1928), 406.
The periodical printing included a second verse (dropped in *P*):

> 'Live there, your back freezing to all's wall,
> Or brinked by chasm that all chasms bounds;
> There, with two times at choice, all plots forestall,
> Or, no time backing you, what force surrounds?'

WE had obviously intended to embed within the first line a further pun on Shakespeare's title *All's Well that Ends Well*, but the joke is already, and more deftly, incorporated in the first line of the poem.

WE noted for *Listen*: **'The finite but unbounded universe, popularized by Eddington (I wrote this in about 1928), makes flight seem useless for the lovers.'**

'When a physicist refers to curvature of space he at once falls under suspicion of talking metaphysics,' wrote Sir Arthur Eddington in the 1930s. 'Yet space is a prominent feature of the physical world; and measurement of space – lengths, distances, volumes – is part of the normal occupation of a physicist' (*The Expanding Universe* (Harmondsworth, 1940), p. 35). Unlike the physicist, WE responded to relativity theory with a metaphysical poetry of awe and alarm, for the dreadful correlative of the curvature of space (agreed by Albert Einstein and Willem de Sitter) is 'closed space': in the famous phrase, the universe was found to be 'finite but unbounded' (p. 40). The latest research, as Eddington put it with remarkably calm clarity, tended to suggest 'that the curvature actually leads to a complete bending round and closing up of space, so that it becomes a domain of finite extent' (p. 39).

See Morelli, pp. 86–90; *TGA*, pp. 47–9. Willis (pp. 109–14) notes: 'In addition to Eddington and Einstein, Empson clearly had Marvell's "The Definition of Love" in mind when writing "The World's End" ' (p. 110).

1–3 with me . . . cliff befriend] **to the world's end, dear, / Plumb space through stars. / Let final chasm, topless cliff, appear** *1928*

4 *What tyrant . . . variance debars*: *variance* means, among other things, difference, divergence, discrepancy, as well as quarrel, disagreement, contention or falling-out; so the sense of the rhetorical question posed in stanza 1 is: 'Can we not escape from the supreme authority – call it "God" – of this world, and assert our independence in a separate planet?' WE built upon this idea in 'Double Plots' (drafted in the early 1930s), where he cited Donne's sonnet 'I am a little world made cunningly', and commented – with particular reference to Donne's mixed exultation at the discovery, 'beyond that heaven which was most high', of 'new sphears' and 'new lands': **'The idea that you can get right away to America, that human affairs are not organized round one certainly right authority (e.g. the Pope) is directly compared to the new idea that there are other worlds like this one, so that the inhabitants of each can live in their own way'** (*Pastoral*, p. 65). Yet the following stanzas of WE's poem supply a grim response to the cry for freedom: you can't buck the system.

6–7 *Space is like earth . . . / Plumb the stars' depth, your lead bumps you behind*: 'There is nothing beyond and yet there is no boundary . . . History never repeats itself. But in the space dimensions we should, if we went on, ultimately come back to the starting point . . . A ray of light from the sun would . . . take about 1,000 million years to go round the world; and after the journey the rays would converge again at the starting point . . .' (Eddington, *Space Time and Gravitation* (Cambridge, 1920), pp. 159–61). Accordingly, in a sense – with respect to the title of the poem – the world never ends. Cf. 'Dissatisfaction with Metaphysics', l. 11, and 'To an Old Lady', l. 19. With regard to 'lead': **'I can't see that there is any ambiguity on *lead*'** (typed letter to Maxwell-Mahon, 21 August 1973).

8 *Blind Satan's voice rattled the whole of Hell*: WE noted in *CP*: **'blind like his author Milton. "He called so loud that all the hollow deep / Of Hell resounded." '** (*PL*, I.314–15.) *Rattled* in the sense of upset or annoyed, but also because Satan is in a cage to which God holds the key, so that Satan's shout simply rattles the bars – and yet, most chillingly of all, there are 'no bars' (l. 5): the metaphor of imprisonment runs through 'padded cell' (l. 6), to 'metal . . . pierce' (ll. 9–10). (The prison described by the modern scientific gospel may well be literally 'padded' and 'cushioned' (l. 9), and yet it is awfully like Jeremy Bentham's conception of a panopticon in which a single guard can keep an eye on all prisoners at all times:

it is 'rounded' (l. 6), and based on the concept of 'curvature' (l. 16); life is a prison.)
9–10 cushioned air . . . the gulf that] air, on cushions, what's a file worth / To pierce that chasm *1928*

11–12 *Each tangent plain . . . / Each point . . . the world*: *TGA* (p. 48) comments: 'since tangents can be drawn to touch a curve at any point, no single point on the curve can be designated the "top"; thus any or none may be . . . Any point, in any direction, is the "end" of this relative world, and any act of "pointing" likewise.'

13–14 *Apple of knowledge . . . / From Tantalus*: as a punishment for his moot crimes, Tantalus was subjected to an ingenious punishment (*Odyssey* XI.582–93): standing up to his neck in water, with fruit trees teasingly above him, he was forced to suffer from unassuageable thirst and hunger, because the water withdrew from him whenever he stooped to drink and the fruit wafted out of his reach whenever he attempted to pluck it. WE likens his predicament to the span of human time between the Garden of Eden and the final, unblessed oblivion. *Forgetful mere* is a circumlocution for the water of Lethe, since *Lethe* itself derives from the Greek for forgetfulness, and *mere* means merely lake – in the way that Spenser uses the phrase 'Lethe lake' (*The Shepheardes Calender*, 'March', l. 23). Cf. WE's observation, in 'Alice: Child as Swain': **'I said that the sea of tears she swims in was the amniotic fluid, which is much too simple. You may take it as Lethe in which the souls were bathed before re-birth (and it is their own tears; they forget, as we forget our childhood, through the repression of pain) or as the "solution" of an intellectual contradiction through Intuition and a return to the Unconscious'** (*Pastoral*, p. 217).

14 *differential*: WE noted in *CP*: **'they follow his movements exactly, as if calculated like the differential coefficients used in forming this view of the world.'** *Differential* relates to infinitesimal differences (as in differential calculus).

15 The shadow clings. The world's] The world's *1928*

16 *precludes*: WE noted in *CP*: ' "stops from happening" and "already shuts". End in space but blurred onto end in time conceived as eventual justice – "what there is of it occurs here".'

Plenum and Vacuum

First published in *P*, though very likely written by 1928–30.

CP: The scorpions kill themselves when put under glass and frightened with fire; Darwin tried this, but I forget whether it was true or not. *Weal:* the scar of a burn, made as the glass was, the ground still under control of their commonwealth, the circle of the glass rim and the gain of death. 'The veins produced eye muscles to guard the eyeballs from screams.' The screaming-fit is supposed to be abandoned by civilized people, so that the machinery of facial expression depends on a central reality no longer present. *Ensanguines:* makes bloody or hopeful. Matter *includes* space on relativity theory, in a logical not spatial sense, because from a given distribution of matter you might calculate the space-time in which it seems to move freely. The line is not meant to be read as anapaests. Then the space not in our space-time, which we cannot enter, is thought of as glass with the universe as a bubble in it. 'Noviens Styx interfusa coercet'; not Hell but its surrounding hatred is real and a cause of action. The thought supposed to be common to the examples is that the object has become empty so that one is left with an unescapable system of things each nothing in itself.

See Morelli, pp. 75–81; Willis, pp. 114–17; *TGA*, pp. 49–53.

1–4 *Delicate goose-step of penned scorpions ... stung in mid vault of bell*: notwithstanding WE's note about Darwin placing scorpions in a ring of fire, Darwin describes only cannibalism in scorpions, in *Journal of Researches into the Natural History & Geology of the Countries Visited During the Voyage Round the World of H.M.S. 'Beagle'* (1890). In *Life of Johnson* (WE's more likely source), Boswell recounts how he told Johnson, in 1768:

that I had several times, when in Italy, seen the experiment of placing a scorpion within a circle of burning coals; that it ran round and round in extreme pain; and finding no way to escape, retired to the centre, and like a true Stoick philosopher, darted its sting into its head, and thus at once freed itself from its woes. '*This must end 'em.*' I said, this was a curious fact, as it shewed deliberate suicide in a reptile. Johnson would not admit the fact. He said, Maupertuis was of opinion that it does not kill itself, but dies of the heat; that it gets to the centre of the circle, as the coolest place; that its turning its tail in upon its head is merely a convulsion, and that it does not sting itself. He said he would be satisfied if the great anatomist Morgagni, after dissecting a scorpion on which the experiment had been tried, should certify that its sting had penetrated its head. (ed. Fleeman, pp. 392–3)

Johnson was right to express scepticism, it seems: J. Henri Fabre (whom WE may have read and misremembered) did try this, only to discover that this torment had the effect of inducing in the frenzied creature a deceptive 'swoon', a 'paralysing spasm', from which it would surprisingly recover after a lapse of time (*The Glow-Worm and Other Beetles*, trans. Alexander Teixeira de Mattos (London, 1919), p. 407).

In his letter to Maxwell-Mahon (21 August 1973), WE noted:

the comparisons to insects are not meant to make you think 'we are better class than insects, and ought to have better class treatment'; I could never understand why Boswell felt 'sadly humbled' when he saw a monkey, and still expect that he was only pretending. What is clear is that the insects have an even worse time than we do, even more deeply sunk in the flypaper.

The scorpions of course actually did have small flames put all round the glass bowl in which they were enclosed . . . The verse you quote [ll. 1–4] struck me as very good; I had forgotten it, because the poem is no use for reading aloud.

Pinsker (pp. 93–4) suggests that 'the "scorpions" are connected with masculinity fears which manifest themselves in the "infant screams" and the "ringed orbiculars" . . . which "guard their balls" '.

2 *Patrols its weal under glass-cautered bubble*: cf. the closing stanza of George Herbert, 'The Sacrifice': 'But now I die, now all is finishèd. / My woe, man's weal; and now I bow my head . . .' (ll. 249–50). WE analysed those lines in the first edition of *ST*: '**The force of *but* is that their wickedness will go on; "My side will be pierced but I shall not feel it." To gauge his attitude towards this fact, one must consider . . . that *weal*, which claims here to mean prosperity, carries some trace of its other meaning at that time, not a scar but a pustule (as in "Commonweal" it is the social order, good and bad, which is identified with the tribe's relation to its totem)'** (p. 289). Cf. 'Letter I', l. 16, to appreciate the force of WE's sense of the ramifying implications of *weal/wheal*; and 'Bacchus', l. 41. *Glass-cautered* is a nonce-term (*cauterized* means burned or seared with a hot iron or caustic; a *cauter* is a branding-iron), so *glass-cautered bubble* may suggest a blood blister produced by the process of hot 'cupping' – which would in turn suggest that 'bubble' represents the lifeblood of the globe itself. Accordingly, for 'bubble', cf. 'Arachne', ll. 7–9, and 'Earth has Shrunk in the Wash', l. 6.

3 *fire-cinct*: girt or encircled with fire.

5–8 *From infant screams the eyes' blood-gorged veins . . . wrinkled hold-alls*: Darwin discusses the contraction of the orbiculars, the sphincters or muscles which enclose the eye (the noun *orbicular* is used by him), during the infant's fit of screaming, in *The Expression of the Emotions in Man and Animals* (1872) (*Works of Charles Darwin*, ed. Barrett and Freeman, vol. 23 (London, 1989), pp. 119–33). The burden of WE's stanza, on the redundancy of an archaic reflex, is conveyed in this summary by Darwin: 'When infants scream loudly from hunger or pain, the circulation is affected, and the eyes tend to become gorged with blood: consequently the muscles surrounding the eyes are strongly contracted as a protection' (p. 351). (See *ST*, p. 49 for WE's comments on the fact that facial muscles, designed for crude purposes, are used to convey '**fine shades of "expression"** '.)

7 *These stays squeeze . . . ensanguines*: as *TGA* notes, *stays* here appears to be a pun: 'reliable "defences" or painful corsets' (p. 51). According to Milton, the blood shed by Satan when smitten by Michael's sword 'flowed / Sanguine, such as celestial spirits may bleed' (*PL*, VI.332–3). The sense of WE's line is that in modernity and in modern man the contraction of the orbicular muscles no longer affords much literal relief to blood-gorged eyes (see note above). Just as the scorpion appears not to fight its fate but just to kill itself, so modern man goes through the motions of genuine feeling, because of being imprinted with atavistic habit, but he (or she)

no longer genuinely feels enough to scream against the horror of the cosmos.
8–10 *void-centred . . . / Matter includes . . . firmament's air-holes*: cf. Eddington, in
The Nature of the Physical World (Cambridge, 1928): 'In 1911 Rutherford intro-
duced the greatest change in our idea of matter since the time of Democritus . . . the
most arresting change is not the rearrangement of space and time by Einstein but
the dissolution of all that we regard as most solid into tiny specks floating in a void.
That gives an abrupt jar to those who think that things are more or less what they
seem.' If the corpuscular theory of matter is exploded into the vacuum of quantum
theory, WE argues, mankind's contractual conscience with respect to sin and punish-
ment may well be no more than an ethical agreement projected upon a literal
unreality. If we now know that the universe is more or less vacuous – apropos the
poem title – we might conclude that all of our myths of divinity and redemption
('Heaven', l. 11), as well as our ethical constraints ('Hell', l. 12), are assuredly nothing
but metaphysical conceptions or else empty notions.
12 *It is Styx coerces and not Hell controls*: an allusion to *noviens Styx interfusa
coercet*, which Virgil uses twice: 'Styx holds fast with his ninefold circles' (*Georgics*,
IV.480; *Aeneid*, VI.439). The verb *coercere* means to restrain within bounds,
confine, shut up; WE takes the apparent modern sense of the Latin, from which
it is only indirectly derived. Virgil's reference to the magic of the 'ninefold stream'
of Styx was mediated for WE by a favourite text, *From Religion to Philosophy:
A Study in the Origins of Western Speculation* (London, 1912), by F. M. Cornford,
who quotes from the *Georgics* (p. 24 note 2). Cornford refers the powerful meaning
of the river Styx to the fifteenth book of the *Iliad*, where Hera swears by 'Earth
and the broad Heaven above and the dripping water of Styx, which is the greatest
and most dreadful Oath for the blessed Gods': 'the Gods swear by the two
great primary divisions of the universe, Earth and Heaven, and by Styx'. Its full
significance is explained in Hesiod's *Theogony* when one of the Olympians is
convicted of perjury and lying, and is subjected to the paralysing coldness of this
ancient river which 'traverses that desolate place where are the sources and limits
of the Earth and Tartarus, of the Sea and of the starry Heaven'. As a result, Styx,
as Cornford explains, is pictured as a barrier (since *Horkos*, Oath, was originally
equivalent to *herkos*, fence). WE therefore suggests that we are controlled not by
the sanctity of active principle but by the fear of painful sanction. We may well
think Hell a fable, and yet the power of taboo holds sway as what Cornford calls
'the negative, forbidding aspect of Power' (pp. 23–5).

Une Brioche pour Cerbère

First published in *Cambridge Review* 49 (4 May 1928), 388.
    The fourth stanza is omitted from an autograph MS (fair copy), which
begins:

To show the career in the womb of wit
Partly I use the method I expound,
Partly give birth to the heads of it,
Last count the feet, and try to soothe the sound.

TITLE: a brioche is a pastry shaped in a half-globe; it can also mean a blunder. Cerberus is the grotesque dog of Hades, sometimes depicted with three heads and a mane or tail of snakes, or fifty heads, as Hesiod has it (*Theogony* 311). Whereas Heracles penetrated to the underworld to overcome Cerberus (*Iliad*, VIII.367), WE's Tom distracts the dog with a bun and so slips back into Eden; cf. the surreptitious way Satan entered Eden in *Paradise Lost*.

10 *vacuate*: emptiness, vacuum.

15 *scoptophile*: voyeur, sexually stimulated by looking at the sexual activity of others. Charles Rycroft points out: 'The spelling "scoptophilia" dates from a mistake made by Freud's first translators' (*A Critical Dictionary of Psychoanalysis* (London, 1968), p. 148). See S. Freud, 'Psychogenic Visual Disturbance according to Psycho-Analytical Conceptions' (1910), trans. by E. Colburn Mayne, in *Collected Papers*, ed. Joan Rivière (London, 1924), vol. II, pp. 105–12. WE similarly used the term vis-à-vis Shakespeare's attitude to 'Mr W. H.' as manifested in Sonnet 81, wherein the poet's **'partly scoptophile desire to see him settled in love has by now been with a painful irony thwarted or over-satisfied . . .'** (*ST*, p. 75).

Rolling the Lawn

First published in *Cambridge Review* 49 (4 May 1928), 388.

CP: *Our . . . despair*: said by Belial in Milton ('in act more graceful and humane'). There was some advertisement urging us to roll the abdominal wall and thus improve our health.

TGA (p. 53) comments on the 'technical insouciance' of the form employed here: 'the head of a Miltonic sonnet joined to a tail of three Augustan couplets'.

See also Morelli, pp. 34–8; Willis, pp. 118–19; Thurley, pp. 42–3; Meller, 'Auf der Suche nach poetischer Identität: *Rolling the Lawn*', in *Das Gedicht*, pp. 179–91; *TGA*, pp. 53–5.

1 *beat*: punning: 'excel, do better than' or 'hit, pound, thrash' (English lawns must be flat, immaculate, unfeatured, unabused).

1–2 *Our final hope / Is flat despair*: Belial, in *PL*, offers a desperate counsel to the fallen angels; since nothing can avail them against the 'omnipotent decree' of God, the best thing they can do is to provoke him into annihilating them: 'Thus repulsed, our final hope / Is flat despair: we must exasperate / The almighty victor to spend all his rage, / And that must end us, that must be our cure' (II.142–5). Cf. 'Courage means Running', l. 28 (in its emended version in *CP* 1956); and 'Success', l. 5.

flat: the Miltonic sense, as quoted, means 'absolute'; but WE also exploits the literal, and punning, sense: to an Englishman, the goodly ordering of Nature is next to godliness.

4–5 *the Holy Roller at the slope / (The English fetish, not the Texas Pope)*: in the cult of horticulture, the emblem or 'fetish' of the devoted gardener is the roller (it merits nothing less than capitalization). But this sovereign gardening aid is not to be confused with a zanily energetic religious group in the USA, whose members 'roll' about when in possession of the Holy Spirit. Eric Partridge defined Holy Rollers as 'Roman Catholics, since ca. 1920' (*A Dictionary of Slang and Unconventional Usage*, Vol. II: *The Supplement*, 7th edn., London, 1970): WE was aware of this meaning, as shown by his reference to 'Pope': he rejoiced in a confusion of Christian sectarians.

5 fetish] symbol *1928*

7 prayer,] prayer *1928*

9 not the] not th' *1928*

9–10 *the walls of Troy / Lead, since a plumb-line ordered, could destroy*: the plumb-lines used to build the walls of Troy are not in Homer (*Iliad*, XXI.441–57), but are mentioned, twice in the *Troades* of Euripides, where VI.814 refers literally to 'stone-workings produced by the rule' (the Greek word is *kanon* > Eng. canon, which may suggest 'ordered'). Thus, it is better to mind your garden than to erect a citadel, which might be laid waste by the wrong work of human hands (bullets), as lead in another form (plumb-line) enables it to be built well in the first place.

13 World, roll yourself; and bear your roller] Deathless, roll on, fair world; bear rollers *1928*

13 *World, roll yourself*: in view of the early variant 'roll on, fair world', cf. W. S. Gilbert's exhortation 'To the Terrestrial Globe': 'Roll on, thou ball, roll on! / Through pathless realms of space / Roll on! / What though I'm in a sorry mess? / What though I cannot meet my bills? . . . ./ Roll on!' (*The Bab Ballads* (London, 1898), pp. 539–40). Just a few weeks before publishing his poem, WE had been alerted to the ballad by Sir Arthur E. Shipley, in his account of the aquatic organisms known as the *Volvocineae* (*Hunting under the Microscope* (London, 1928), p. 85), and in a review of Shipley's book, WE complained: '**He brings to bear on this material a cultural background in the form of small jokes, harmless, complacent, and out of place, that is sharply detached from the rest of the text; the more romantic or impressive organisms have a quotation from W. S. Gilbert**' ('Man and Superman', *Granta* (27 January 1928); in *E in G*, p. 36).

14 *martyrs gridirons*: legend tells of two martyrs – St Laurence of Rome and St Vincent of Saragossa, proto-Martyr of Spain – who were roasted on gridirons; they are invariably represented with the emblem of a gridiron. The badge of an

Englishman's devotion to the works and days of God's world is the garden roller: it is just as good as a gridiron to get you into heaven.

Dissatisfaction with Metaphysics

First published, as 'Disillusion with Metaphysics', in *Experiment* 1 (November 1928), 48.

CP: There was a myth that no element would receive Mahomet's body, so that it hung between them and would appear self-subsisting. The earth's orbit being an ellipse has two foci with the sun at one of them; one might have a complicated theory, entirely wrong, making the other focus the important one. I failed to make a pun on *focus* and its original sense *hearth*. Two mirrors have any number of reflections (the self-conscious mind); a dotted line is used for 'and so on'. The mind makes a system by inbreeding from a few fixed ideas. Prospero's book of magical knowledge was buried deeper than ever plummet sounded, and the depths of knowledge which had previously been sounded became deepest during the disaster of the Flood.

In his letter of 21 August 1973, Empson told Maxwell-Mahon: 'Dissatisfaction with M is meant to be a quite jolly little poem, as you realize, but it is trying to laugh off the fright of being caught on the flypaper. People will only interpret things in a way which is grist to their mill, and so the effects of any action are quite incalculable; however, the advance of science may produce more safety if more caution. This need not be treated as very deep.'

Willis (pp. 119–23) remarks that the poem is in 'a unique and experimental stanzaic form ... The three cinquaines of fairly regular iambic pentameter verse recall the beginnings of rime royal and Spenserian stanzas, but neither one nor the other, these stanzas have a truncated effect – a sense of incomplete development. Without the closing completeness of the rime royal's final couplets, Empson's stanza is open ended, "a plain series"' (p. 120). See also Meller, 'Warnung vor den Fallstricken der Philosophen: *Dissatisfaction with Metaphysics*', in *Das Gedicht*, pp. 201–7; *TGA*, pp. 55–8.

1–3 *High over Mecca Allah's prophet's corpse* ... *centre of the universe*: the legend that the coffin of the Prophet Mahomet was made to levitate by means of some perfidious trickery was a widespread piece of anti-Islamic propaganda:

his companions (such as consulted with him, and concealed his falsness and treachery) ... judging that the disdaine of *Mahomet* would be their discredit, and his fall their soyle and shame, they fetch him againe, they chest him in an iron coffin (saith *Sabellicus* and *Nauclerus*) they bring him unto the famous Temple of Mecha (in which citie he was borne) with great solemnitie, as if he had never been scared upon the dunghill with swine: they convey to the roofe of the Temple mightie Loadstones, they lift up the iron coffin, where the Loadstones according to their nature draw to them the iron, and hold it up, and there hangs *Mahomet* on high. (Henry Smith, *Gods Arrow Against Atheists* (London, 1605), p. 52)

Samuel Butler took it as a standing joke that a boy's kite might be taken for a celestial wonder as it, 'in the *Aery region* yet, / Hangs like the Body of *Mahomet*' (*Hudibras*, ed. John Wilders [II.iii] (Oxford, 1967), p. 165). By the nineteenth century, the myth was admitted to have been a Christian fabrication. WE's most likely source was Washington Irving's *Mahomet and His Successors* (1849; ed. Henry A. Pochmann and E. N. Feltskog (Madison, Wis., 1970)), which allowed: 'The marvellous tale, so long considered veritable, that the coffin of Mahomet remained suspended in the air without any support . . . is proved to be an idle fiction' (p. 191). With regard to the Prophet Mahomet receiving 'homage', it is an Islamic myth that Mahomet ascended to heaven, and that Mecca is the navel of the universe – the place where heavenly power and bliss directly touch the earth. WE's phrasing berates ancient Islamic lore as the stuff of defunct and dissatisfying metaphysics.

For '(The empty focus opposite the sun)', Sir William Muir observed, in *The Mohammedan Controversy* (Edinburgh, 1887), p. 49: 'It is certainly a novel idea to speak of Mohammed or his Coran under the simile of the moon; his own people style him the sun, and our Saviour the moon, and they would laugh to scorn any mention of their Prophet's "*borrowed* light" melting into that of the Gospel.' For 'focus', compare 'Letter III', l. 18 and note.

1 corpse] corpse, *1928*

2–5 *sun . . . run . . . undone*: cf. Herbert's 'The Sacrifice' – 'Arise, arise, they come. Look how they run. / Alas! what haste they make to be undone! / How with their lanterns do they seek the sun!' (ll. 33–5) – which WE quoted at the start of an early essay, 'An Early Romantic: Henry Vaughan' (1929; *A*, pp. 260–63); WE noted that Vaughan imitates Herbert, albeit less successfully, in his 'Ascension-day': 'They pass as at the last great day, and run / In their white robes to seek the risen Sun'.

4 his] the *1928*

4 *epicycles*: as *TGA* (p. 56) points out, 'epicycle' has 'two astronomical meanings: one the geocentric path of a planet . . . the other a small circle which has its centre on the circumference of another . . .' Assuming the Prophet to be the fixed centre of the cosmos (just as the earth was believed to be the hub of the Ptolemaic system of astronomy), the greater and lesser planets would ride their epicycles in correspondence with his central position. Raphael tells Adam about the vanity of those astronomical speculators who 'build, unbuild, contrive / To save appearances, how gird the sphere / With centric and eccentric scribbled o'er, / Cycle and epicycle, orb in orb' (*PL*, VIII.81–4). See also note on l. 12 below.

5 *all his wives undone*:

The number of his wives is uncertain. Abulfeda, who writes with more caution than other of the Arabic historians, limits it to fifteen, though some make it as much as twenty-five . . . The plea alleged for his indulging in a greater number of wives than he permitted to his followers, was a desire to beget a race of prophets for his people. If such indeed were his desire, it was disappointed. Of all his children, Fatima the wife of Ali alone survived him, and she died within a short time after his death. Of her descendants, none excepting her eldest son Hassan ever sat on the throne of the Caliphs. (Irving, *Mahomet and His Successors*, p. 193)

6 *Two mirrors with Infinity*: WE felt vexed by discussions of the physics and metaphysics of time; here, specifically, with the concept of infinite regression. In the *Cambridge Review* (25 May 1928), 446–7), he reviewed J. W. Dunne's philosophical study *An Experiment with Time* (London, 1927) in terms which bear directly upon this stanza:

Mr Dunne starts from, and his theory is a courageous attempt to deal with, the fact that the simple idea of time leads to an infinite regression. Time is thought of as a measured line like a ruler, with the present moment moving along it; this idea demands a second time, for the present moment to move along the first time with; and in the same way there must be a third time moving the present moment along the second, and so on. That is true and important. But it does not mean that all those times 'are really there', or that it would mean very much if they were; all it comes to is that the idea of time as a dimension is one thing, and the peculiar properties of our attention another. For that matter, no finite series of time-dimensions will make the least difference to the problem, so that the 'absolute time' which solves it cannot be analogous to a limit. In fact, Mr Dunne simply drops the problem; his infinite series is introduced to explain why it is that our consciousness is fixed to a moving present moment, and the conclusion reached is that it is not: we only live in the present moment out of habit.

To this infinite series of times is attached an infinite series of observers. This again is an important idea and one must admire the intrepid Mr Dunne for trying to deal with it . . .

A conscious observer, it is quite true, is one who observes that he observes, and observes that he observes that he observes. This is a second infinite series. But Mr Dunne suddenly equates the two, and says that the second man, who is certain that the first is certain, lives in the second space, so that he has the first time dimension laid open to him, and a fixed rate of movement only along the second. It is this second man who pops out when the first man is asleep (so that he is not busy being certain about him) and is able to look into the future. This second man is the same fellow, too, I suppose, as the one that makes 'A and "A implies B"' *imply* B, he is the relation between substance and relation, and your second reflection when you stand between two mirrors. 'It all fits in.' But I don't believe all these men are *concerned* to be real people, let alone *being* real people, let alone all being the same real person. I cannot see why, even supposing the second time dimension to exist in the same sense as the first one, it should keep an observer at all; what I take to be the proof that he exists begins 'Now, the points in O'O'' are being . . . observed from O' to O'' by whatever is our ultimate observer.' That is a plain assumption that there is such a thing, apart from the humble creature in three dimensions. (O' and O'', of course, are 'in' four.)

The lid is put on the story by the Absolute Observer, who is as real as any of them. He simply comes at the end of the infinite series, and presumably decides how fast time shall go. He is a soul, has free will, with power, I should hope, to give Absolution and immortality along an infinite number of time-dimensions. This is a full-blown myth, practically at the chapel stage. It would be tiresome of me to point out that series, if we must use the mathematical analogy, are sometimes divergent, sometimes oscillating, and that, interesting as it would be to have some sort of critique to deal with infinite regressions, Mr Dunne has made no attempt to supply one.

See also WE's comments (*ST*, p. 43) on the 'two main scales' on which the human mind measures time; likewise the observation that the infinities of mathematics 'may be a convenient fiction or a product of definition' (p. 128).

Given WE's comment that 'two mirrors' represent 'the self-conscious mind' (in *CP* above), see also, in 'Alice: Child as Swain': '*Wonderland* is a dream, but the *Looking-Glass* is self-consciousness' (*Pastoral*, p. 206); and his observation that the 'praise of the child in the Alices' depends in part on the idea 'that you can only understand people or even things by having such a life in yourself to be their mirror' (p. 221).

Among WE's unpublished papers are the following lines which pertain to the preoccupations of this poem:

> You need to know (since space, if not time, repeats)
> That all the company in the two mirrors
> Move like a chorus, you being in step with the rest of it;
> Move like your shadow (you being, like Dracula
> And Butler's Cavaliers, no dial by moonlight);
> That all the Antipodes are still White;
> That their no- (unknown) minds and this part-mind,
> By the nature of God, by the whim of Leibnitz,
> Still ethereally correspond between fronts;
> Or if time repeats too
> That you stride all the Platonic years without faltering.

(Dracula could not cast a shadow. For Butler on the 'Cavaliers, no dial by moonlight', see *Hudibras*, III.ii.175–6 – '*True as a Dyal to the Sun, / Although it be not shin'd upon*' – though WE, through a Coleridgean conflation, combined that passage with this earlier one describing a certain invention of the Conjurer: 'He made an instrument to know / If the Moon shine at full, or no, / That would as soon as e're she shon, streit / Whether 'twere Day or Night demonstrate' (II.iii.261–4).)

8–10 *Adam and Eve . . . series . . . all philosophers' disease*: according to biblical myth, all humans descend directly from Adam and Eve: this is a simple fiction which calls for no further metaphysical explanation. Dunne, in *An Experiment with Time*, defines a 'series' as 'a collection of individually distinguishable items arranged, or considered as arranged, in a sequence determined by some sort of ascertainable law. The members of the series – the individually distinguishable items – are called its *"Terms"*.' Thus, the 'terms' in the Bible are each and every human being in direct line of descent – 'a plain series'. And yet, again according to Dunne, philosophers would rightly be sceptical of a serial explanation, and

> would proceed, without a moment's delay, to an exhaustive and systematic examination of the character of the apparent series, in order to ascertain (*a*) what were the true serial elements in the case, and (*b*) whether the serialism were or were not the sort of thing that might prove of importance. For, of course, it might turn out to be an entirely negligible affair. But, to people [i.e. philosophers] who have devoted their lives to the search for a simple explanation of the universe, the idea that one of their approximate fundamentals – next door, indeed, to the sought-for nothingness – might prove to be of a serial character would be bound to appear a supposition to be avoided at almost any cost.

WE's 'all philosophers' disease', which pokes fun at Dunne's quest for a sophisticated metaphysics, suggests that philosophers at once make up a plague of fictions *and* are made to feel radically uncomfortable ('dis-eased') by something as 'plain' and simple as a 'dotted line'.

In an unpublished essay (dating from early 1935), which again bears directly upon this poem, WE wrote of Dunne's complicated theory of temporal perception:

> Most of the puzzles of philosophy can . . . be stated as infinite regresses. There must be a relation between substance and relation, the free self-conscious mind must be able to choose to choose to choose, and to know that it knows, and so on. They are not all alike, but each is a way of showing that a puzzle exists, and each is obviously a fiction after the first few terms. The central fallacy of Mr Dunne's position, one to which the human mind is deeply attached, is that if you can fit together several things that you know are fictions the result will be real. The same real man in this theory, constructed from corresponding units of different series, chooses to choose, knows that he knows, and lives for ever in the second time-dimension.
>
> When we set out to know a sequence of events we think of them as laid out, waiting to be known, in a spacelike time-order; we do not think of the process of knowing as laid out too, but as carried on always in the present moment. So it is plausible to fit the two regresses together; to say that the mind, when it knows that it knows, is knowing in the second time, that moves the present moment along the spacelike time . . . But if this were so, any mind, whenever it was self-conscious, would be independent of the spacelike time . . .

Like the exploded myths appertaining to the Prophet Mahomet, the poem argues, the philosophers' fictions purporting to explain time are still not equal to our reality: hence the 'dissatisfaction' of the poem's title.

11 New safe straight lines are finite though unbounded,] But modern lines are finite, though unbounded; *1928*

11 *New safe . . . unbounded*: see note for ll. 6–7 of 'The World's End'.

12 *Old epicycles numberless in vain*: 'to save the phenomena,' as the Schoolmen used to say (to make natural phenomena fit in with Ptolemaic learning), astronomers postulated a number of epicycles to explain the eccentric motions of the planets. Even Copernicus needed as many as thirty-four extra circles – the forced marriage of fact and *a priori* fiction. See note on l. 4 above.

13 *deeper than e'er plummet, plummet sounded*: the magus Prospero declares (*The Tempest*, V.i.50–51, 54–7): 'But this rough magic / I here abjure; . . . / . . . I'll break my staff, / Bury it certain fathoms in the earth, / And deeper than did ever plummet sound / I'll drown my book.'

14 *Then corpses flew, when God flooded the plain*: the witty paradox of this reference to the Flood (Genesis 6:9–9:17) echoes Marvell's conceit of the river in flood in stanza 60 of 'Upon Appleton House' (e.g. ll. 477–8: 'How Boats can over bridges sail; / And Fishes do the Stables scale').

15 *He promised Noah not to flood again*: Genesis (8:21, 9:14–16) refers to God's covenant – signalled by the rainbow – 'never to destroy / The earth again by flood,' as Milton put it (*PL*, XI.892–3). Cf. 'Laus Melpomines', l. 6; and 'Earth has Shrunk in the Wash', l. 6.

Poem about a Ball in the Nineteenth Century

First published poem at Cambridge, in *Magdalene College Magazine* no. 8 (June 1927), 111. 'The College takes some satisfaction,' an editorial was to report nearly sixty years on, 'from the fact that the definitive text of Empson's *Poem about a Ball* (1927) is still to be found printed correctly only in our pages' (*Magdalene College Magazine and Record*, n.s. no. 30, 1985–6). Reprinted in *Experiment* no. 7 (Spring 1931), 59.

CP: There is a case for hating this sort of poetry and calling it meaningless; I had better explain, to protect myself, that no other poem in the book disregards meaning in the sense that this one does. At the same time it is meant to be direct description.

The first sentence is supposed to be said softly and doubtfully, getting to normal tone on the last word. The main idea is the clash between pride in the clothes etc. and moral contempt for it. *Air*: an atmosphere, a tune, a grand manner. The last line might look back on the ball long after, reminded by the furnishings.

For *Listen* WE observed: 'A bit of romantic description imitating Gertrude Stein.'

WE's contemporary (perhaps ambiguous?) admiration for Gertrude Stein is conveyed in this passage from *ST*: 'It is possible that there are some writers who write very largely with this sense of a language as such, so that their effects would be almost out of reach of analysis . . . Miss Gertrude Stein . . . implores the passing tribute of a sigh' (p. 25).

His later opinion of Stein figures in 'Proletarian Literature':

To produce pure proletarian art the artist must be at one with the worker; this is impossible, not for political reasons, but because the artist never is at one with any public. The grandest attempt at escape from this is provided by Gertrude Stein, who claims to be a direct expression of the Zeitgeist (the present stage of the dialectic process) and therefore to need no other relation to a public of any kind. She has in fact a very definite relation to her public, and I should call her work a version of child-cult, which is a version of pastoral; this does not by any means make it bad. (*Pastoral*, p. 19)

In an unscripted reading at an Oxford University summer school, probably in the 1960s, WE remarked that this prose poem was meant to be 'teasing and romantic . . . and many a heart is broken after the ball'. The couple in the poem end up 'blaming each other for doing what they are all doing – that is, trying to be sexually attractive to one another' (tape recording courtesy of Roma Gill).

Just five months before WE published his poem, T. S. Eliot lamented in the *Nation and Athenaeum* (27 January 1927, p. 595): 'There is something precisely *ominous* about Miss Stein . . . Moreover, her work is not improving, it is not amusing, it is not interesting, it is not good for one's mind. But its rhythms have a peculiar hypnotic power not met with before. It has a kinship with the saxophone. If this is of the future, then the future is, as it very likely is, of the barbarians. But this is the future in which we ought not to be interested.' Furthermore, in the very month the poem appeared, Laura Riding published in the experimental journal *transition* no. 3 (June 1927) a thoroughgoing indictment of Stein's methods: Stein 'uses language automatically to record pure, ultimate obviousness'; the design that her words make 'is literally abstract and mathematical because they [her words] are etymologically transparent and commonplace, mechanical but not eccentric . . .' She creates an 'atmosphere of continuousness . . . by an intense and unflagging repetitiousness and by an artificially assumed and regulated child-mentality . . .' Stein's words 'contain no references, no meanings, no caricatures, no jokes, no despairs' (pp. 160–61, 163–4). Whether or not WE read Riding's piece that June, he certainly did read it in the (slightly modified) version in *A Survey of Modernist Poetry*, by Riding and Robert Graves (London, 1927), pp. 274–87.

Of Stein's own work, WE may have read *Three Lives* (London, 1915), *The Making of Americans* (Paris, 1925) and *Geography and Plays* (Boston, 1922).

But then again he might have read only a few recent manifestations, notably including 'An Elucidation', which appeared in *transition* no. 1 (April 1927, pp. 64–78), and to cite its briefest and most famous sample, from 'First Example':

Suppose, to suppose, suppose a rose is a rose is a rose is a rose.

    To suppose, we suppose that there arose here and there that here and there there arose an instance of knowing that there are here and there that there are there that they will prepare, that they do care to come again. Are they to come again.

WE is known to have avoided most lectures during his years at Cambridge, but it is probable that curiosity drove him to hear Stein, who in Spring 1926 delivered her famous – and famously, stupefyingly reiterative – lecture entitled 'Composition as Explanation'; however, even if he did not actually go to it, he took pains to read it when it appeared later that year from the Hogarth Press. (Some months later, he would occasionally deploy in his own work one of the key words from her lecture, 'equilibration'. WE made use of both of Stein's forms, 'equilibration' and 'equilibrating', in reviews published in *Granta* (6 May and 14 October 1927); e.g. conflating the influence of Richards's *Science and Poetry* and Stein's *Composition as Explanation* when so writing off a film: '**half-baked, it gave you half-heartedly whatever you looked for; an equilibration of magical attitudes, or a tiresome sentimental film**' (*E in G*, p. 67).)

    The Hogarth Press edition of *Composition as Explanation* included a few poems – 'Preciosilla', 'A Saint in Seven', 'Sitwell Edith Sitwell' and 'Jean Cocteau' – which Stein had also read at her lecture. Therefore, WE was exposed to enough of the early work to feel sufficiently beguiled to trade on her tricks. 'Preciosilla', for example, closes:

Please be please be get, please get wet, wet naturally, naturally in weather. Could it be fire more firier. Could it be so in ate struck. Could it be gold up, gold up stringing, in it while while which is hanging, hanging in dingling, dingling in pinning, not so. Not so dots large dressed dots, big sizes, less laced, less laced diamonds, diamonds white, diamonds bright, diamonds in the in the light, diamonds light diamonds door diamonds hanging to be four, two four, all before, this bean, lessly, all most, a best, willow, vest, a green guest, guest, go go go go go go go. Go go. Not guessed. Go go.

    Toasted susie is my ice-cream.

WE's 'poem' accords with the prescription that Stein insists upon in an essay 'Portraits and Repetition': 'In doing a portrait of any one, the repetition consists in knowing that that one is a kind of a one, that the things he does have been done by others like him that the things he says have been said by others like him.' But, she goes on: 'a portrait of him saying and hearing what he says and hears while he is saying and hearing it there is then in so doing neither memory nor repetition'; further, 'I tried to include colour and movement' – specifically, that is to say, in *Tender Buttons* (1914). On the other hand, Stein professed: 'I was of course not interested in emotion', because 'I was creating in my writing by simply looking.' As far as she was concerned, words had to make do without association or descriptive mimesis.

However, WE did not confine himself to her modernist, nominalist, non-representational criteria. While he certainly makes use of several of Stein's favourite devices or tics, including phrasal repetition and permutation, parataxis, syntactic parallelism, synecdoche and a seeming indeterminacy, everything in his poem is apt to the occasion, its social and emotional energies, and its rhythms – the head-spinning ball, the beat of the music, the breathlessness, the vanity, the velleity, the vulnerability of the female speaker; the anxious insistence on centrality, on being the belle and on captivating that certain single male – 'together to be become' – without whom a woman is not one in society. Equally, though WE's general arrangement seems like so many of Stein's in being oblique, riddling and non-specific, and pulsing from phrase to phrase to the point of neurasthenia, his poem engages and conjures with more puns, jokes, pertinent surprises and knowing ambiguities than Stein's work customarily entertains – 'to be fair, aroused', 'pea-cock and I declare', 'to bearer share', 'fairly becoming for a peacock' – principally because he is concerned to tell a story, to convey a hectic, unfocused and only partly rationalized experience: that of a girl who is rebuffed at the ball and whose equivocal consolation is to mock herself in retrospect – or is it the man she mocks? – as 'only a feathered peacock'. As *TGA* notes (p. 59): 'the last three lines, with their lovely resolution on to a fading iambic pentameter, have an air of nostalgia'. Every element, phrase and rhythm in WE's tribute to Stein's example is apt to the occasion and the emotion; it is intelligent and coherent; and it is teasingly intelligible.

Willis (pp. 123–7) suggests that this poem 'seems to echo some of Hopkins' – particularly the last lines of 'The Leaden Echo and the Golden Echo': 'So be beginning, be beginning to despair. / . . . / Be beginning to despair, to despair, / Despair, despair, despair, despair.' See also Maxwell-Mahon, 'The Early Poetry of Empson', pp. 12–14; Morelli, pp. 38–40; *TGA*, pp. 58–60; Lecercle, 'William Empson's Cosmicomics', pp. 283–4.

1 *Feather, feather*: by a possibly irrelevant coincidence, these words are used in *Through the Looking Glass* (1871), when, in the face of Alice's sad efforts to row with knitting needles, the sheep gives the right order: ' "Feather! Feather!" the Sheep cried again, taking more needles. "You'll be catching a crab directly" ' (Chapter V). WE casually noted, in 'Alice: Child as Swain': '**Everyone recognizes . . . the rowing, the academic old sheep, and the way it laughs scornfully when Alice doesn't know the technical slang of rowing**' (*Pastoral*, p. 230).
13 **together to be**] together to *CP 1949, CP*

21 *solitaire*: probably used as adjective and substantive: (a) solitary; (b) a person who lives in seclusion or solitude, perhaps after suffering a mortifying rebuff (at the ball). Also a card game, to be played in solitude.

Address to a tennis-player

First published in *RB*.

    This prose poem, an association-exercise on the gospel story of St Peter (his call, his denial, his death), probably dates from the period of WE's first published poem, 'Poem about a Ball in the Nineteenth Century' (June 1927); like that poem (**There is a good case for hating this sort of poetry and calling it meaningless,**' WE wrote in his note), it is clearly influenced by the work of Gertrude Stein – and perhaps also by the experimentalism of the 'Sirens' chapter of James Joyce's *Ulysses*.

3 *thou art Peter, upon this rock I build*: 'And I say also unto thee, That thou art Peter, and upon this rock I will build my church; and the gates of hell shall not prevail against it' (Matt. 16: 18).

4 *unhaltered*: a 'halter' is some form of restraint, such as the halter for a horse; but it may also mean a noose for hanging a criminal. Accordingly, *unhaltered* here means 'unfettered, unhampered; free of a halter'.

10–12 *rocks the cradle . . . racks the world*: parodies the refrain – 'For the hand that rocks the cradle / Is the hand that rules the world' – of the popular lyric 'What Rules the World', by the American lawyer and verse-writer William Ross Wallace (*c*. 1819–81). (See Ralph L. Woods, *A Treasury of the Familiar* (Chicago, 1945), pp. 326–7.) Joyce alludes to the song in the 'Sirens' chapter of *Ulysses*. Cf. Hopkins's protest to Despair in his sonnet 'Carrion Comfort', ll. 5–6: 'O thou terrible, why wouldst thou rude on me / Thy wring-world right foot rock?'

12 *Knock*: 'Ask, and it shall be given you; seek, and ye shall find; knock, and it shall be opened unto you' (Matt. 7: 7).

13 *sweeter to pay Paul*: from the proverbial saying 'to rob (or borrow from) Peter to pay Paul'.

14–15 *ossi-assuefaction, petri- or putri-*: 'ossifaction' is 'the formation of bone; the process of becoming or changing into bone' (*OED*); 'assuefaction' means 'the action or process of accustoming; the fact of becoming, or state of being, accustomed or used to a thing; use, habituation' (*OED*) (Stephen Dedalus remarks in the 'Oxen of the Sun' chapter of Joyce's *Ulysses*: 'Assuefaction minorates atrocities'); 'petrifaction' means the same as petrification, that is, 'conversion into stone or stony substance' (*OED*), and 'putrifaction', a state of rottenness; the decaying of organic matter.

15–16 *knock knock it shall remain unlocked*: after the death of Jesus, Peter is clapped into prison, but an angel comes and leads him out to freedom; then Peter goes to the house of Mary, mother of John: 'And as Peter knocked at the door of the gate, a damsel came to hearken, named Rhoda. And when she knew Peter's voice, she opened not the gate for gladness, but ran in, and told how Peter stood before the gate. And they said unto her, Thou art mad. But she constantly affirmed that it was even so. Then said they, It is his angel. But Peter continued knocking: and when they had opened the door, and saw him, they were astonished' (Acts 12: 13–16).

17 *amidden*: a nonce-word punning on *amid* ('in the middle of') and *midden* (dunghill or cesspit).

18 *grouted*: past participle of transitive verb *to grout*, meaning 'to fill up or finish with "grout" or liquid mortar; to cement' (*OED*).

20 *Biers . . . bears*: cf. Shakespeare's Sonnet 12, ll. 7–8: 'summer's green all girded up in sheaves / Borne on the bier with white and bristly beard . . .'

22 *weeping, a triple crowing*: 'Jesus said unto him, Verily I say unto thee, That this night, before the cock crow, thou shalt deny me thrice . . . And Peter remembered the word of Jesus, which said unto him, Before the cock crow, thou shalt deny me thrice. And he went out, and wept bitterly' (Matt. 26: 34, 75). Peter became the first Pope, and the Pope's mitre consists of three crowns.

23 *Simple to Simon Peter*: Simple Simon stars in the eponymous advertising jingle, dating from 1764: 'Simple Simon met a pieman / Going to the fair: / Says Simple Simon to the pieman, / "Let me taste your ware."' The name Peter derives from the Greek for 'stone' (whence Christ's invocation of his apostle Simon in Matt. 4: 17–19), and see note for Peter as 'rock', above. St Matthew's gospel uses the formula 'Simon who is called Peter'; and the combination 'Simon Peter' figures often in the gospels.

24 *a roc's egg*: the 'roc', or 'rukh', is an enormous mythical bird, reported in Marco Polo's account of Madagascar; now best known from the *Arabian Nights*, in which Sinbad the Sailor finds one.

24 *I Am That is it I Lord*: conflates God's answer to Moses in Exod. 3: 14 – 'I AM THAT I AM: and he said, Thus shalt thou say unto the children of Israel, I AM hath sent me unto you' – with Matt. 26: 25: 'Then Judas, which betrayed him, answered and said, Master, is it I? He said unto him, Thou hast said.' It is likely too that this phrasing parodies the Sanskrit *tat tvam asi* ('That art thou'), which refers to the universal immanence of the transcendent spiritual Ground of all existence.

25-6 *scarlet, Herod's purple, not Christ, Pall's*: Herod Antipas, governor of Galilee during the period of Christ's ministry, and in that sense responsible for the crucifixion, would have worn the purple (Latin *purpureus*) garment befitting his rank. WE would also have been keen to include the adjectival sense of *purple*, 'Of this colour as being the hue of mourning . . . or of penitence' (*OED* 1c); and, in view of the gospel report that Christ's body was drained of blood before the moment of his death, the phrase 'scarlet . . . not Christ' may also include the sense, 'Used *poet.* to describe the colour of blood. (Properly said of the crimson venous blood, the colour of arterial blood being scarlet.) Hence, Bloody, blood-stained' (*OED* 1d). Matt. 27: 28 also records, 'And they stripped him [Jesus], and put on him a scarlet robe' (cf. Mark 15: 17, and John 19: 2, which specify 'purple').

For 'purple . . . Pall's', cf. the carol 'As Joseph was a-walking': 'He neither shall be clothed / In purple nor in pall, / But all in fair linen / As were babies all.' The *pall* (Lat. *pallium*) is an ecclesiastical vestment worn by the Pope, the archbishops and some bishops in the Roman Catholic Church; but, since the syntax allows the term to be connected back to 'Herod's purple', *Pall* may also refer to the 'purple', a fine or rich cloth worn as a robe or mantle by a person of high rank. Finally, a pun gives the verb *palls*: 'becomes satiated or cloyed' or else 'pale, dim, faint'.

26 *Peter, key and lock*: 'And I will give unto thee the keys of the kingdom of heaven: and whatsoever thou shalt bind on earth shall be bound in heaven: and whatsoever thou shalt loose on earth shall be loosed in heaven' (Matt. 16: 19).

26 *bewray*: 'And after a while came unto him they that stood by, and said to Peter, Surely thou also art one of them; for thy speech bewrayeth thee' (Matt. 26: 73). 'Bewray' means expose, reveal, make known, betray.

26-8 *he carrying . . . mock wearing Christopher renamed*: conflates the biblical story (Matt. 27: 31–2) of how, after Jesus is scourged, crowned with thorns and mocked, the soldiers compel Simon of Cyrene to carry his cross, with the legend that St Christopher hoisted Christ upon his shoulders and carried him across a river – which is why he bears the Greek name *Christophorus* or 'Christ-bearer'.

27 *Iscariot*: second name of the Apostle who betrayed Jesus.

28 *face-owner*: see Shakespeare's Sonnet 94 ('They that have pow'r to hurt . . .'), ll. 7–8: 'They are the lords and owners of their faces, / Others but stewards of their excellence.' This sonnet is analysed in detail in chapter 3, 'They That Have Power: Twist of Heroic-Pastoral Ideas in Shakespeare into an Ironical Acceptance of Aristocracy', of *Pastoral*. Cf. 'Two centos', Part ii, l. 12.

29-30 *arse-end, Peter across ascending, upside . . . down*: Eusebius, citing Origen, related that Peter was crucified head downwards, at his own request (see the painting of *The Martyrdom of St Peter*, by Caravaggio): the martyrdom is thought to have taken place in the reign of Nero, during the persecution of AD 64.

30 *hot cross buns*: buns trimmed with a cross, commonly eaten (hot) on Good Friday, the day that memorializes Christ's crucifixion.

New World Bistres

First published in *Cambridge Review* 49 (6 June 1928), 492.

TITLE: 'bistre' (adj.) is a blackish-brown colour (or artist's medium), often referred to as 'soot brown' because it is derived from wood soot. WE has perhaps made the word into a pluralized noun by analogy with 'the blues' (being in the dumps): everything in this poem is restlessly turning in the mind, from the butter churn to the washing tub and the gyroscopes.

2-3 *we have 'gone to sleep' / In body, and become a living pat*: 'we are laid asleep / In body, and become a living soul' (William Wordsworth, 'Lines Composed a Few Miles above Tintern Abbey' (1798), ll. 45-6).

7 *Ciro be his eyes*: see Ariel's song apropos the fate of Ferdinand's father Alonso in consequence of his supposed death by drowning: 'Full fathom five thy father lies, / Of his bones are coral made; / Those are pearls that were his eyes . . .' (*The Tempest*, I.ii.399-401). 'Ciro' specifically refers to the artificial pearls manufactured by Ciro Pearls Ltd., which were extensively advertised in the 1920s in periodicals such as the *Sketch* and the *Tatler* See also note on l. 10.

8 *assumptive*: characterized by assumption; appropriative, taken for granted, assumptious, arrogant, making undue claims.

10 *pearl . . . margarine*: 'margarine' is the legal name for any imitation butter; originally applied to the glyceride of 'margaric acid', the fatty substance found in certain animal and vegetable oils, the term derives from Greek *márgaron*: pearl, referring to the pearly lustre of the crystals of the acid.

11 *too deep, oh more than tears*: 'To me the meanest flower that blows can give / Thoughts that do often lie too deep for tears' (Wordsworth, 'Ode: Intimations of Immortality from Recollections of Early Childhood' (1807), ll. 202-3).

12-13 *faint unhurrying resurrection . . . manna*: cf. Ezra Pound, 'Hugh Selwyn Mauberley (Life and Contacts)' (1920), ll. 350-53: 'Amid the precipitation, down-float / Of insubstantial manna, / Lifting the faint susurrus / Of his subjective hosannah.'

'Manna' is 'the substance miraculously supplied as food to the Children of Israel during their progress through the Wilderness. (See *Exodus* xvi)' (*OED*). Among other possible meanings, 'manna' is used for the secretions of certain species of eucalyptus and the common larch. However, given 'tears' (l. 11), WE is presumably referring also to 'manna in tears', for which the *OED* cites (1853): '*Manna in tears* is a pure kind, in bright and roundish white grains.' Further, given the preceding reference to 'distillation' (l. 8) and the subsequent association with the grains of soap powder (l. 19), the connotations clearly extend to *OED* 5: 'In early *Chemistry*: A white powder', for which it cites (1706): '*Chymical Manna*, a Substance distill'd from Precipitate, whiter than Snow.'

13 *the manner born*: 'And to my mind, though I am native here / And to the manner born, it is a custom / More honoured in the breach than the observance' (*Hamlet*, I.iv.16–18).

14 *The man born of the manor*: the son and heir of a country mansion (the chief house of a landed estate), with seignorial rights.

14–15 *bourne / No traveller returns*: 'But that the dread of something after death, / The undiscovered country from whose bourn / No traveller returns, puzzles the will, / And makes us rather bear those ills we have' (*Hamlet*, III.i.80–83).

15 *Athanasius*: reaffirmed the centrality to canon law of the doctrine of the Trinity. Jesus Christ must be held to enjoy equal ontological status with God the Father (*homoousios*: that is, 'consubstantial' or 'of the same being'), Athanasius argued, because the Son, or Logos, could not be the Redeemer unless he were not a subordinate but one with God the Father. Arius the Alexandrian, who had persuasively argued that the Son was a divine intermediate being, was condemned at the Council of Nicaea in AD 325. See R. P. C. Hanson, *The Search for the Christian Doctrine of God: The Arian Controversy 318–381* (Edinburgh, 1988); M. Wiles, 'The Philosophy in Christianity: Arius and Athanasius', in *The Philosophy in Christianity*, ed. G. Vesey (Cambridge, 1989), pp. 41–52.

One of WE's most deeply rooted convictions, enunciated at length and with passion in *Milton's God*, was his contempt for Christianity, which he tagged the '**torture-worship**'. In particular, he scorned the doctrine of the Trinity: '**The doctrine of the Trinity is necessary, or the Father appears too evil in his "satisfaction" at the crucifixion of his Son. But to present Jesus as one with the Father only turns him into a hypocrite; when he prays for his enemies to be forgiven, he knows under his other title he will take revenge.**' He even believed his father agreed:

The Creed of St Athanasius (my mother told me as a boy that my father threatened the Vicar to walk out if it was read, but unfortunately happened to be asleep when the occasion arose) amounts to saying that the Father and the Son both are and are not identical, and that you will go to Hell unless you believe both . . . It is hard to call up the identity of Father and Son at such points, and envisage God as driving a hard bargain with himself before he agrees to torture himself to death out of love for mankind . . . Only if this God had a craving to torture his Son could the Son bargain with him about it. In return for those three hours of ecstasy, the Father would give up the pleasure of torturing for all eternity a small proportion of mankind; though such a tiny proportion, it has usually been agreed, that his eternal pleasure can scarcely be diminished. (*Milton's God*, p. 246)

Just so, WE wrote to John Wain in 1977: '**When I said that one can't discuss whether a man believes in the Trinity, I gave the reason: that it is a set of verbal contradictions (in Athanasius at least), so that he can only inure his mind to accepting them.**'

16 *Cardinal Bourne*: Francis Alphonsus Bourne (1861–1935) was appointed in 1903, at the youthful age of 42 (he had been made a bishop in his mid-thirties), to the archiepiscopal see of Westminster, which he occupied for over thirty-one years.

17 *Lux and her cherub*: 'Lux', the trade name for soap flakes, suggests ' "light" (Latin *lux*) and "luxury" ' (*Dictionary of Trade Name Origins*). Lux was said to be particularly good for washing delicate fabrics, and the packaging often featured a child ('cherub'). An advertisement (in the 1920s) read: 'The beautiful flakes are whisked into a cream-like lather. You simply toss the filmy "Lux" diamonds into hot water!' See ll. 18–20.

19 *elixir-centred*: 'elixir', as used in alchemy, refers to 'a preparation by the use of which it was hoped to change the baser metals into gold. Occas. = "the philosopher's stone" ' (*OED*). More generally, the term can mean an essence, tincture or quintessence.

22 *separator*: a cream separator is a device for separating cream from milk.

25 *resounding brass*: Virgil's Salmoneus, in the *Aeneid*, had sought to imitate thunder by galloping his horses over brass (*ære*); Dryden translates thus: 'Ambitious Fool, with horny Hoofs to pass / O're hollow Arches, of resounding brass; / To rival Thunder, in its rapid Course: / And imitate inimitable Force' ('The Sixth Book of the Æneis', ll. 796–99, *The Works of John Dryden*, vol. V, ed. William Frost (Berkeley, Los Angeles and London, 1987), p. 555). Cf. 1 Cor. 13: 1: 'If I speak with the tongues of men and of angels, but have not love, I am become sounding brass, or a clanging cymbal.'

26 *Rector*: ruler or governor; God is known as the 'supreme Rector of the Universe'.

26 *vertiges*: French for 'vertigo', so WE must mean to refer to the giddiness, the disordered whirling, of the turning world; although, given 'tractor' in the same line, he may also be catching the sense of the obsolete *vertilage*, which refers to the preparation of ground for seed.

28 *resentience*: 'resentient' (obsolete) means 'that which causes a change of feeling'; *OED* refers the word only to Vaughan's 'The Timber', l. 27: 'Or what *resentient* can work more within, / Than true remorse, when with past sins at strife?' WE may have read this usage as adjectival and coined a better noun.

Sea Voyage

First published, as 'Sea-Voyage', in *Cambridge Review* 50 (16 November 1928), 131, without the final line (19). It had a headnote by WE which it is nevertheless bafflingly difficult to apply to the poem: '**Verses 1 and 2: a new idea, at first elaborate and exciting in itself, should become with practice a simple unit, an indivisible tool. Verse 3: it should hold itself ready to be re-analysed.**'

CP: The first and third verses are supposed to describe the sea-cat's claws, and cat's cradles are foam tumbling and sliding back. *Replyed:* bent back, like a sharp answer. *Dures:* hardens the product and lasts long in itself. *Abandoned* by the wave its parent, and a wicked little thing anyway. *Taut:* the lines of string in the game would make a knot, the water ice, the salt a crystal. The second verse tries to connect the triumphs of man with the forms of the original sea. Ezekiel was called the Son of Man; it might mean 'any hero acting for, representative of, mankind'. Man himself in the tortures of his spirituality becomes the red rag that he can hold out, as in making a bull charge, to catch the power of the seahorses. Pillows and bobbins are used in making lace, like the lace of the foam; also like webs, making man the ingenious spider – some spiders fly on a thread overseas. The sail that gets up a thousand horse-power is the map of tracks of his voyages, lace because so full of holes; the trapeze is made of the parallel tracks to and from a place. All his experience adds to his power, and the earth sails (according to some astronomers) towards the constellation of Hercules – not towards a higher god; his origins are still inherent in him, as his achievements are already inherent in the sea. The flower *eringo* (I was wrong in thinking the stress on the first and third syllables) made a frothed-up Elizabethan aphrodisiac; the sea can only hint by its movement at the powers inherent in it, like a girl not allowed to try out her powers in company but dressing at home. To develop its salts into crystals is taken to be a first stage in developing its powers; which need to be kept in their place, so that it is like the devil kept quiet by being set to make ropes of sand. Viewed as one cup of drink the sea is held in by the sands round it from which one could make a glass goblet. The banquet (soup, fish, meat) follows the order of the evolution of species.

For *Listen* WE noted: ' "Sea Voyage" feels the energies of the world to be mysteriously rich; and soup-fish-meat follows the order of the evolution of species.'

With respect to WE's observation that the first and third verses are meant to describe a 'sea-cat's claws', the designation *sea-cat* embraces various fishes including the great weever (*Trachinus draco*) – which, according to Willis (p. 130), 'makes a fine pun for a producer of filigrees and lace'; the wolf-fish (*Anarrhichas lupus*); a type of shark (*Scyllium catulus*); and even the thrillingly named *Chimæra monstrosa*. However, *TGA* (p. 60) may well be correct in observing that the original version of that note (in *P*) made much better sense, with a dash after 'sea' and not a hyphenated 'sea-cat's' followed by a comma: 'The first and third verses are supposed to describe the sea – cat's claws and cat's cradles are foam tumbling and sliding back.'

Willis (pp. 127–34) notes:

Empson's stanzaic pattern is that of six iambic pentameter lines [a number are feminine rhymes and hence hendecasyllabic] rhymed ababcc, with the exception of the additional seventh line in the third stanza. This stanza was employed by Matthew Arnold in his 'Mycerinus', and, with an Alexandrine for a last line, it was one of Oscar Wilde's favorite forms. As Enid Hamer points out, it has been most successfully employed in poems of a 'reflective or elegiac cast' [*The Metres of English Poetry* (London and New York, 1930), p. 168] . . . Miss Hamer remarks that the form looks like a shortened ottava rima. How appropriate it is, then, that Empson's voyage, a shorter affair, echoes stanzaically the great ottava rima of Yeats's 'Sailing to Byzantium'.

See also Morelli, pp. 97–102; *TGA*, pp. 60–64.

1 *Re-plyed, extorted*: since 'reply' derives from Old French *replier*, to fold again, turn back, to reply, it can sustain the aggressive connotation that WE asks of it here (one obsolete definition of the word extends to the sense of *retorting upon* one). 'To extort' stems from Lat. *extorquere*, to twist out, tear away; applied to the use of force or other intimidation used to wrest or extract something – information or money – from a resistant person.

2 Tune . . . cotton] (Tune . . . cotton) *1928*

2 *cat's-cradle*: 'a children's game in which two players alternately take from each other's fingers an intertwined cord so as always to produce a symmetrical figure' (*OED*).

4 dures . . . abandoned] lasting . . . disownered *1928*

4 *dures*: archaic, from Latin *durare*, to harden, endure, sustain.

5–6 *Drawn taut . . . filigrees*: the intricate web of the cat's-cradle constructed round the fingers, or the ball of stuff at which the cat snatches with its claws (ll. 1–4), if compacted or hardened or frozen solid, would resemble – being as it were a 'knot-diamond' – the engraved ball that is the networked map of the globe (in stanza 2): it would appear to be striated (filigreed).

5–6 this flickering of wit would freeze, / And grave, knot-diamond, its] **the flickered crystal, wit to these, / Dures, diamond, to grave that's** *1928*

7 *Pillowed on gulfs between exiguous bobbins*: one possible sense of this and the following lines is that man is dreaming (asleep on lace-embroidered pillows) of maritime explorations across the globe: the map in his head is criss-crossed with multiple sailing routes (ll. 11–12); if taken more literally, l. 7 may connote the vulnerably spindly masts of a ship above the *gulfs* of the ocean: the sails may be seen as both 'lace' and a 'red rag'. 'Exiguous' means: 'Scanty in measure or number; extremely small, diminutive, minute' (*OED*). For 'gulfs', cf. 'Letter I', ll. 9–10.

8 *Son of Spiders*: in the Old Testament, the prophet Ezekiel is continually addressed as 'Son of man', though the phrase is also used simply to signify a human being – 'a man'; in the New Testament, Jesus frequently uses the title of himself, with reference to his ultimate triumph as Redeemer and Judge. 'Son of God' also was a messianic title, signifying a status as redeemer. (Cf. also 'Arachne', l. 4.) Also includes the idea that man has trenched the globe with innumerable lines of navigation, so that the map resembles a spider's web.

9 *a red rag to a thousand dobbins*: the cliché 'a red rag to a bull' refers to reflex anger, a predictable incitement; 'dobbins' are usually jaded and unexcitable horses, worn out with long toil.

12 *towards Hercules*: WE remarked in a footnote in 1928: '**The solar system, I understand, is moving towards that constellation.**' Sir William Herschel (1738–1822) determined in 1783 that the solar system was heading towards a point in the constellation Hercules; though often later questioned, his findings are now known to be close to modern estimates which have shifted the solar 'apex' to the neighbouring constellation Lyra; the solar velocity thitherward is only about 12 miles a second. Leopold Bloom, urinating under the night sky, meditates upon 'our system plunging towards the constellation of Hercules' (*Ulysses*). Cf. 'Essay', l. 21.

13 *Blue-sea-bound . . . foam*: the initial notion is of the foam of the sea breaking from the ship – a flashing white fluidity – which is subsequently compared, in ll. 15–16, to a woman's petticoats or furbelows.

14 *eringo*: a candied root of the Sea Holly (*Eryngium maritimum*), supposedly used as an aphrodisiac. Sir John Falstaff famously hails Mistress Ford: 'Let the sky rain potatoes; let it thunder to the tune of Green Sleeves, hail kissing-comfits, and snow eringoes . . . I will shelter me here' (*Merry Wives of Windsor*, V.v.20). Dryden's translation of Juvenal's sixth satire (ll. 418–19) mocks those 'Who lewdly Dancing at a Midnight-Ball, / For hot Eringoes, and Fat Oysters call'.

17 Sand-rope] Sand rope *1928*

17 *Sand-rope*: 'to make a rope of sand' is proverbial for a futile or superfluous activity. Cf. Herbert, 'The Collar', ll. 21–4: 'forsake thy cage, / Thy rope of sands, / Which pettie thoughts have made, and made to thee / Good cable, to enforce and draw'. Thomas Adams argued (*c*. 1625), 'Sand is not fit, one would thinke, to binde an unruly beast, they call it *Irritum laborum*, proverbially, a rope of sand: yet is this the cordage and ligature to shackle the roaring monster' (James L. Hedges, 'Thomas Adams, Robert Burton, and Herbert's "The Collar"', *Seventeenth Century Notes* 31 (1973), 47–8). Cf. 'Myth', l. 7.

18 her] its *1928*

19 port] toast *P*

19 *port*: in *ST* (p. 134), WE drew attention to Pope's use of the pun in *The Dunciad*, IV.201–2 – 'Where Bentley late tempestuous wont to sport / In troubled waters, but now sleeps in port' – with this commentary: '**The pun is sustained into an allegory by the rest of the couplet;** *tempestuous* **and** *sport* **are satirical in much the same way as the last word. But here, I grant, we have a simply funny pun; its parts are united by derivation indeed, but too accidentally to give dignity; it jumps out of its setting, yapping, and bites the Master in the ankles.**' Cf. *SCW*, p. 54.

High Dive

First published in *P*, though possibly written some years earlier (?1928).

CP: You can give a single mathematical expression for all the movements of the water (so contemplate it all in one act, like God) but this may become impossible either through its getting more movement or less, from its becoming solid or from the splash and eddy made by the diver. These are compared to the two ways down from the diving-board, solid and airy, one of which the man must take; hence to the idea that one must go from the godlike state of contemplation even when attained either into action which cannot wholly foresee its consequences or into a fixed condition, due to fear, which does not give real knowledge and leads to neurosis. A wolf tried to eat the sun in Northern mythology during eclipses. φ is a usual symbol for this potential function, Aton the heretical Egyptian sun-god with hands at the ends of its rays; both are connected with the horse chariot of the classical sun-god. The maggots are the rippling reflections that show the movement of the water and suggest cantering horses. Hare-hunters wore green coats. *Thicker than water* as blood is in the proverb; I am using F. M. Cornford's theory that the order behind the 'physical' world was originally thought of as the life-blood of the tribe, so that it changes when that does (there is a fear of society in the feeling that you must take the dive once you have gone up). That is why the water of the tank, taken in contemplation as the universe, is called φύσις* and agglutinate and liable to clog. A termite city actually uses dung for its concrete, but a scab suggests creatures shapeless if you remove their shells. The puppy was carrying a bone over a bridge and dived after the reflection and lost the bone.

For *Listen* WE noted: 'One would be ashamed to walk down; the proper thing is to take a decisive action whose results are incalculable. The mathematical terms recall that you couldn't work out the splash.'

Forrest-Thomson, in 'Rational Artifice', gives a clear-headed account of the nature of the complexity of WE's poetry, with specific reference to the first two stanzas of this poem:

The diver above the pool can see it in three ways and these correspond to three different kinds of assumed extra-linguistic reality. The ordinary description [ll. 1–2] speaks for itself: the water's movement is presented as it would appear to a man who inhabits the world of everyday experience. The movement is then described [ll. 3–4] as it would appear in a

---

*In a marginal note on the page proofs for *CP*, where the word had been given as 'phusis', WE remarked: '*Phusis* in Greek letters, if you would; or it isn't obviously the same word as "physics".'

mathematical formulation . . . [T]he bathing-pool is like the world viewed from inside a closed system of conceptual relations . . . because the third vision of the pool [ll. 5–6] equates it with God's view of the creation . . . The poet, in so far as he identifies himself with these viewpoints, is released from any commitment to action; this is made clear in the last lines of the second stanza. The tank's triple infinite . . . contains all the possibilities of movement but any actual movement on the part of the diver would destroy the water's stable condition and hence its potential character, along with the accuracy of the mathematical description. (pp. 232–3)

See also Morelli, pp. 102–3; Willis, pp. 134–9; Ricks, pp. 186–8; *TGA*, pp. 64–70.

3 *irrotational*: in dynamics, when each part of the fluid has no rotation about its own axis. WE characterizes the water in the swimming-pool as being preternaturally undisturbed: a stationary block of liquid.

4 *Hollow, the cry of hounds*: this famous exclamation for calling hounds to a hunt introduces the running metaphor that the speaker of the poem is a kind of Actaeon being hunted down by huntsmen and their hounds (ll. 9, 11, 14, etc.). The only way he can throw the hounds off the scent is to dive into the pool: the leap of ultimate risk will be at once a bound for freedom.

4 *the rule*: ' **"The rule" set by the required Phi tells you the movements of the waves in the swimmingtank for all future time, but when the water becomes turbulent no such wave-function can be provided**' (WE's letter to Maxwell-Mahon, 6 November 1967).

5 *I Sanctus brood*: like God (whose 'Spirit . . . moved upon the face of the waters': Gen. 1: 2) or Christ (*Sanctus*, the Holy One), the speaker, omniscient and anxious, contemplates the world of water. See also *PL* I. 17, 19–21.

6 *Inform in posse . . . triple infinite*: as a God, he has no need to immerse himself in the element he has created: he comprehends it in its full potential. Cf. Sir Thomas Browne's observation in *Religio Medici*: 'In the seed of a Plant to the eyes of God, and to the understanding of man, there exist, though in an invisible way, the perfect leaves, flowers, and fruits thereof: (for things that are *in posse* to the sense, are actually existent to the understanding). Thus God beholds all things, who contemplates as fully his workes in their Epitome, as in their full volume . . .' (*The Works of Sir Thomas Browne*, ed. Geoffrey Keynes (London, 1928; 1964), vol. 1, p. 62). Forrest-Thomson observes, 'Mathematically the expression is "triple" because it describes the water's movement in terms of the three axes of the system of Cartesian co-ordinates, just as it is "infinite" because a potential function takes no account of boundaries. Theologically "triple" suggests . . . the Trinity, just as "God" suggests infinity' ('Rational Artifice', p. 233).

7–8 *chauffeur / The girdered sky*: the pool itself is housed in the controlled environment of a cantilevered building. As a sun god – he is *Phoebus* in l. 9 – he controls or drives (chauffeurs) the horses of the sun; and evidently, in that case, there is an implied pun on *chauffeur/chauffer*: to heat or chafe.

9 *wolf-chased Phoebus, φ*: Phoebus is the Greek sun-god; the wolf that consumed the sun in Norse mythology is Fenrir. The first two letters of *Phoebus* make the Greek φ, the symbol for the potential function in the calculus of wave theory.

10 *Aton*: poised on the diving-board, the high-diver assumes a commanding posture with arms extended (looking like Leonardo da Vinci's drawing of the proportions of the human figure). In Egyptian religion, Aton or Aten was one of the names of the sun: the solar disk being represented with many rays each ending in a hand, and with some of the hands holding ankh-signs (symbolizing the giving of life). In the fourteenth century BC, Amenhotep (Amenophis) IV established the cult of Aten as a monotheistic religion: the king set himself up as an incarnation of the divinity and even changed his name to *Akh-en-aten* ('Glorious-Spirit-of-Aten'). On 4 November 1927 WE had reviewed in *Granta* a well-informed historical fiction by Dmitri Merezhkosvky, *Akhnaton: King of Egypt*, trans. Natalie A. Duddington (London and Toronto, 1927): 'This is an exciting and touching historical novel with a most interesting subject. The subject is irritatingly misunderstood, the book creeps with cheap historical allusions dragged in edgeways ... There is no evidence for his having these cosmic shames and horrors' (*E in G*, p. 25). Arthur Weigall – whose work WE also reviewed – proposed the facilely syncretistic view that Akhnaton 'had promulgated a doctrine which was in its outward aspect a worship of that invisible and formless Power, named the Aton, made apparent to mankind in the life-giving energy of sunlight, but which, in its inner meaning, was simply a belief in one God, all-powerful, all-loving, the tender Father of every living creature, by whom all things had their being' (*Flights into Antiquity* (London, 1928), p. 248). WE's review (*Granta*, 27 April 1928, 375–6) scoffed at the very notion of an orderly progression culminating in Christianity: '**Mr Weigall's is the pert little Wellsian outlook**' (*E in G*, p. 47).

10 *maggots . . . girder*: the reflections of the girders of the roof ripple like maggots on the surface of the pool; the metaphor of maggots (prompted by the writhing of the light) suggests that to launch oneself into the waters (sea) of life is a deathly risk; also, that life is lived astride the grave.

11 *Steeds that on Jonah . . . gained*: when Jonah was commanded by God to preach repentance to Nineveh, he took flight on a ship; but when a storm arose, Jonah was identified as the one against whom God was wrathful and cast into the sea. However, 'a great fish' (putatively a whale) swallowed him and after three days vomited him onto dry land – whereupon he resolved to do better by God's will. WE's line is ambiguous, suggesting both that the horses of the sea (the bloodthirsty hunters) are gaining ground in pursuit of Jonah and – more shockingly – that they are already tearing him apart. Once again, the risky leap into life is figured in terms of fear. (Some exegetes see Jonah as an avatar of Christ; compare Matt. 12: 40.)

11 gained),] gained) *P*, *CP 1949*, *CP*. WP wrote to Parsons on 29 May 1956: '11, 17, 20. commas at the ends of lines after gained), solid), and neuroses). It merely makes the grammar a bit clearer' (Reading).

14 *They (green for hares)*: Forrest-Thomson remarks on 'the comparison of the diver to a hare pursued by hunters in green coats (chlorinated water). These hunters stand for the assumption of a fixed society . . . Development from physical fact – the chlorinated water is green – to imaginative identification – the green of the hare-hunters' coats – to thematic implication – the individual is pursued – presents us with a contrast between the individual and society' ('Rational Artifice', pp. 233–4).

15 *Rut or retract*: 'rut' can mean, in accord with the secondary motif of being pursued by a hunt, 'to cut or pierce with a weapon', and 'to fling, cast or throw', which would suggest that the hunt has topped the diving tower and is then to be imagined as hurling the diver to his death. Equally, 'to rut' can mean 'to be under the influence of sexual excitement', which – in accordance with the Actaeon–Diana myth – would signify the fear of woman; so the phrase might hint at male anxiety with regard to *vagina dentata*.

16 *reverberant town*: whether reverberating or merely resonant, the teeming city (town) life is disparaged as hollow and worthless.

17 *'Thicker than water'*: *blood is thicker than water* is recorded in John Ray's collection of proverbs (1672).

18 *Agglutinate*: in terms of bacteriology, agglutination refers to the coalescence or clumping of bacteria or red blood-corpuscles. See Haldane's observations on the question of why blood transfusions, even those between close relatives, have on occasion proved harmful or fatal: 'very often the red corpuscles of the injected blood are treated in the same way as bacteria to which a man is immune. They are first rendered sticky, or "agglutinated", and then broken up, by substances found in the blood serum of the recipient' ('Blood Transfusion', *Possible Worlds*, p. 87). On Haldane, see note to 'To Charlotte Haldane'. But *agglutinate* (ppl. a.) can also mean 'glued' or 'cemented together', so the suggestion in WE's phrasing could be that any society is united by ties of blood – yet those bonds can prove to be deadly.

19–20 *forewarned with olive . . . Ark neuroses*: *TGA* (p. 67) glosses: ' "The Ark" colloquially represents antediluvian attitudes, and such "Ark neuroses" are exemplified in doves, imagined staying indoors vacuously cooing to themselves, neither forced out, nor tempted out by the promise of the olive branch.'

24 *the rein cone now handed*: according to *TGA* (p. 68), this 'rather artificial phrase' is 'a kind of diagram in which the cone shape formed by Phoebus' spread-out reins assumes the hands of Aton and narrows into the diver's extended arms'.

25 *obstetric*: relates to midwifery, the art of the *accoucheur*. Cf. Pope, *The Dunciad*, IV.394: 'And Douglas lend his soft, obstetric hand'.

27 *phusis*: according to Cornford, the primitive mentality represented the vehicle of kinship – the *sympathetic continuum* – as a subtle and mobile form of matter, both animate and divine, derived not from the natural parent but from the totem-ancestor: a homogeneous substance which is Soul and God, the substrate of all things and the source of their growth. Nature (*physis*) is thus 'a soul-substance, a supersensible and yet material thing . . . This supersensible extended substance was . . . from the first and always, not a natural object; although it was called "Nature," it was really metaphysical – a representation . . .' (*From Religion to Philosophy*, pp. 86–7, 124–43). Cf. 'Letter I', ll. 16–17.

29 *Fall to them, Lucifer, Sun's Son*: 'How art thou fallen from heaven, O Lucifer, son of the morning! . . . For thou hast said in thine heart, I will ascend into heaven, I will exalt my throne above the stars of God . . . I will ascend above the heights of the clouds; I will be like the most High' (Isa. 14: 12–14). Helel, son of Shahar, a king of Babylon, chose to foresee himself as enthroned in heaven, on an equality with the supreme godhead; he was brought low for his presumption. In the Latin Bible, the name Helel ben Sahar ('Shining one, son of dawn') was given as 'Lucifer' ('light-bearer'), meaning the morning star (Lucifer or Venus); but patristic writers tended to link the phrase with Luke 10: 18 (where Jesus says, 'I beheld Satan as lightning fall from heaven') and Rev. 9: 1 ('I saw a star fall from heaven unto earth . . .'), so that Lucifer becomes a common name for Satan. In the following lines, WE links the fate of Helel (Lucifer) with that of Jezebel (see next note): both presumed upon godhead, both were laid low. Cf. WE's contention in *Pastoral* that in Milton's 'On the Morning of Christ's Nativity' the figure of Christ '**counts as the sun, but in** *Paradise Regained* **(i. 294) he becomes Our Morning Star, who is Lucifer, who is Satan; the doubt about the symbolism fits Milton's secret parallel between the two**' (p. 149). Cf. Joyce, *Ulysses*, p. 50: 'All-bright he falls, proud lightning of the intellect, Lucifer . . .'

29–32 *Splash high | Jezebel . . . waits for me*: Jezebel, wife of Ahab, king of Israel in the ninth century BC, combated the worship of God in favour of Baal-worship. The prophet Elijah the Tishbite foretold her doom with the words, 'The dogs shall eat Jezebel by the wall of Jezreel' (1 Kings 21: 23). In the words WE draws on directly: 'And when Jehu was come to Jezreel, Jezebel heard of it; and she painted her face, and tired her head, and looked out at a window . . . And he [Jehu] lifted up his face to the window, and said, Who is on my side? who? And there looked out to him two or three eunuchs. And he said, Throw her down. So they threw her down: and some of her blood was sprinkled on the wall, and on the horses: and he trode her under foot. And when he was come in, he did eat and drink, and said, Go, see now this cursed woman, and bury her: for she is a king's daughter. And they went to bury her: but they found no more of her than the skull, and the feet, and the palms of her hands' (2 Kings 9: 30, 32–5). (WE exploits the double meaning of 'tired': 'exhausted, satiated' and 'attired, adorned'.) WE sees Lucifer and Jezebel as in a sense his prototypes: they defied God even as he chooses to express contempt for the Christian God, and both were brought down. Perhaps the hounds that are represented as hunting down the high diver are the hounds of heaven.

35 *Plunge, and in vortex*: Forrest-Thomson notes 'the plain physical fact that by turning in order to dive the man creates a vortex, first in air, then in water' ('Rational Artifice', p. 233).

To an Old Lady

First published in *Cambridge Review* 49 (20 April 1928), 347; reprinted in *Cambridge Poetry* 1929 and in *transition* nos. 19-20 (June 1930), 137.

CP: **First three words from** *King Lear.* **Our earth without a god's name such as the other planets have is compared to some body of people (absurd to say 'the present generation') without fundamental beliefs as a basis for action. When a hive needs a new queen and the keeper puts one in the bees sometimes kill her.** *Her precession* **is some customary movement of the planet, meant to suggest the dignity of 'procession'. The unconfined surface of her sphere is like the universe in being finite but unbounded, but I failed to get that into the line.**

In *The Ambiguity of William Empson*, WE informally explained further that his mother:

most unfortunately read [this poem]. I thought she was never going to but it appeared in a student magazine. She was scolding me because I wouldn't take my civil service examinations. She said I was wasting my life, what did I think I was going to do being a poet, and so on. Then the while denouncing my activities she paused, always willing to be fair, and said, 'I will say, that poem about your Granny, William, now that showed decent feeling.' And I was greatly relieved by her saying this; I thought the situation was very embarrassing. She thought it was about her own mother, who actually was being rather a handful at the time, you see, and I meant it about her. This cleared the matter up very much. And indeed, you see, all these things are meant to be general. It proves the poem was true – that she thought it was about her mother, who really didn't play bridge, otherwise it might have been real. The idea is that we – our ideas in common are so many, we agree on so many points – we somehow can't talk to each other, and why it is that, it seems mysterious. And the bang at the end saying she is only seen in the darkness is, what it really means is, you don't find out how reliable she is until you're in real trouble. Which I didn't know at the time I wrote it.

T. R. Henn, in 'Science and Poetry', lamented what he supposed to be the fact that few contemporary poets had 'attempted any kind of "liaison of vocabulary" between science and poetry'; poets were failing as mediators: 'on the whole it seems as if modern poets distrust technological achievements; as in William Empson's "To an Old Lady" (which is the Moon)' (p. 535). WE felt annoyed by the imputation that he shied away from science, as well as by the flat misunderstanding of his poem (Alan Bold, in the *Cambridge Book of English Verse, 1939–1975*, made the same mistake), and so drafted this letter to Henn on 21 August 1961:

The old lady was my mother, and I was saying that though we were so completely in the same tradition, or were planets of the same sun, we had no contact and only recognized each other in times of trouble, when no longer self-enclosed in the confidence of our tradition ('but in darkness is she visible'). As the moon can be seen in the daytime, the lady cannot be compared to it, and she is said in the first line to be compared to a planet. When I said it would be better not to do space-travel to her I was thinking only of the personal situation – that to try to explain such feelings would cause embarrassment. I did not mean that I disapproved of space-travel, and I think I do not deserve to be accused of meaning such a silly thing.

I have been trying to write a piece about Donne, showing that the metaphors from astronomy meant a great deal to him in personal terms, and were felt to raise theological questions. This was commonly supposed when I was young and imitating Donne, but since then there has been a great drive to insist that he was only making silly jokes. I think this is done by people who consider it their Christian duty to exclude any heretical ideas from Donne, but the effect is to make his work seem trivial and in bad taste.

Thus I have even seen it said that, in comparing his love to a pair of compasses, Donne meant an irony against materialism – he despised his love for being like a tool. But he loved his compasses for being so elegant and for being so sensible; and the whole point of the poem is to say 'This kind of love is real.' Criticism which leaves out the whole point, I find, usually imputes nasty and trivial meanings to the author.

I am thus used to seeing the thing done to Donne, but to have it done to me, his humble imitator, seems a new extremity of unpleasantness. And yet, writing to *Nature* to complain of such a thing would seem adding to it, somehow. (Empson Papers)

See Morelli, pp. 42–6; Willis, pp. 139–44; Thurley, pp. 39–40; Ricks, pp. 179–82; *TGA*, pp. 70–74.

1 *Ripeness is all*: the quotation from *King Lear* (V.ii.10) may be meant as an unequivocal compliment to the 'old lady', but it preserves a trace from its original context (8–10), where the phrase is spoken by Edgar to a father who sees himself as ripe for little but despair and death: 'What, in ill thoughts again? Men must endure / Their going hence even as their coming hither. / Ripeness is all. Come on.'

5 *Our earth alone given no name of god*: '**Mum was not a sanctimonious woman,**

and it seemed clear to me that the Martians would not call the earth after some quite unexpected god. Still, it is true she was a Christian and I wasn't; and it might have been easier to talk to her if I had been' (his letter to Maxwell-Mahon, 21 August 1973).

7 *seem odd*: M. C. Bradbrook recalled of her contemporaries at Cambridge in the 1920s (including WE): 'We were innocently confident in our right to pronounce judgement . . . We were given to words like "report" (verb and noun) and "analysis", but "insist" – that favourite Leavisism – had not made its appearance very prominently. Our strongest term of disapprobation was "odd"' ('I. A. Richards at Cambridge', in *I. A. Richards: Essays in His Honor*, ed. Reuben Brower, Helen Vendler and John Hollander (New York, 1973), p. 71).

8 *Bees sting . . . queen invader*: Schutz explains:

A queen bee is introduced into a hive in two situations: 1) When a keeper has hived a cast of bees without a queen; 2) When, by observation, the keeper sees that a full colony has an aged queen who is not breeding well and above all is not producing (as is normal) a number of cells each season. In the first situation the keeper introduces the new queen in a paper ended box through which she eats her way, slowly acquiring the hive smell, and the workers do not kill her. In the second situation the keeper follows the same procedures and when the new queen is free in the hive the workers or drones normally turn the old queen out of the hive or kill her. So long as procedures like these are followed . . . the new queen is not killed . . . The metaphor involved is substitutional . . . but Empson's point is that if the new queen seems entirely new, an invader, she will be killed. The political and social implications of the image are therefore those of Edmund Burke: if change is a total break with the past (revolution), only chaos follows. Moral and social security follow from historical tradition: the ritual and temples (stanza three), the social detail, wit, tragic fervor (stanza four). ('Apiarian Imagery in Empson's "To an Old Lady"', p. 6)

In an undated loose-leaf journal note, the young WE scribbled:

I was so furious with mama for damping my wanting to be capable with bees (it *was* the right time of day then, he admitted later), . . . it was July, they had been a day or two in the rain already, she did not want them, though the other hive was filled only with corpses. I dressed up the incident so illuminatingly as the type of my hating her, of my not daring to show any activity, or venturing (except in letters) on sketching any methods and subjects . . . the impulse of taking the bees without her knowledge, the walking from her to swarm without giving my wish to be handy away further, the paralysis in fact . . . My mother apologizing to the old man [presumably a beekeeper] afterwards, he would never have been allowed to have come if his wife had known, said she was so sorry to have given him such trouble, after his illness, and she had told William it would be too much strain. Unconscious probably that she hadn't, thinking in fact in terms of the attitudes evoked in talking to different people, her attitude to such a situation can only be worked out and made intelligible with reference to a multitude of insincere kind answers, and never by herself presumably known. (Empson Papers)

11–12 *Still stand . . . waves o'erthrew . . . crumbled tracery*: Pritchard notes the borrowing from Milton's account of Satan's fallen army, which resembles 'scattered sedge / Afloat, when with fierce winds Orion armed / Hath vexed the Red Sea coast, whose waves o'erthrew / Busiris and his Memphian chivalry . . .' (*PL*, I.304–7): 'The association is less with the powerfully disturbing star (though that may have played its part) than with images of fallen power and desolation; the loss of authority and rule in barren sand (of lifeless planet, desert or time) suggests another memory, of Shelley's "Ozymandias" ' ('Milton's Satan and Empson's Old Lady', pp. 59–60).

13 *her soul's appanage*: 'appanage' means a territory or property (such as might be provided for the maintenance of the young children of royalty or the aristocracy), or, more loosely, a specially appropriated possession, a perquisite. WE's phrase can be construed as saluting his mother's personal, economic and territorial privileges or prerogatives.

17–18 *Years her precession . . . her pole*: OED notes that 'precession' (1) has sometimes been used in error in the sense of a 'going forward, advance, procession'; but has an extended meaning (2) that WE's usage would appear to seek to embrace: 'The action or fact of preceding in time, order, or rank; precedence.' In astronomical terms, precession is the steady motion of the rotation axis of a planet (the old lady) when it is subject to the torque (turning forces) exerted by external gravitational influences. WE, however, was unconcerned here about precise definitions; as far as he was concerned, the old lady is simply the best sort of planet, constant and true in her motion.

19 *no confines on her sphere*: Bronowski, a friend of WE's at Cambridge, remarks: 'the heart of the metaphor comes from mathematics: it is the theorem that a surface can be finite in extent and yet have no boundaries, no confines. The surface of a sphere . . . is of this kind: it is finite in extent, and yet if you or the old lady walk all over it you will never meet any boundary and will seem to be going on to infinity' ('The Imaginative Mind in Science', p. 27). Cf. 'The World's End'.

21 night.] night, *P 1934*, *P*, *CP 1949*, *CP*. 'While I am at it, there ought to be a full stop not a comma after *night* in the *Old Lady* poem, for the rhythm' ('Corrigenda', *CP*).

23 *sun*: ' "Sun" not "son" is meant; though isolated we shared a system closer than the great minds in books' (*Listen*). In his letter to Maxwell-Mahon (6 November 1967), WE added: 'I thought I said in my note that the *sun* is not explained by the poem; it meant the traditions which I shared with my mother. The whole conception of the poem of course is that relations with Mum are compared to space travel.'

23–4 *He curtains . . . but in darkness is she visible*: the primary point of reference for WE's paradox is Milton's description of the lake of hell where Satan and his angels are revealed at the opening of *PL*, I.61–7: 'A dungeon horrible, on all sides round / As one great furnace flamed, yet from those flames / No light, but rather darkness visible / Served only to discover sights of woe, / Regions of sorrow, doleful shades, where peace / And rest can never dwell, hope never comes / That comes to all . . .' However, 'curtains', together with the run of references to regal or imperial majesty in connection with the mother, suggests a secondary source, Pope's *The Dunciad*, which hails the goddess of Dullness: 'Yet, yet a moment, one dim ray of light / Indulge, dread Chaos, and eternal Night! / Of darkness visible so much be lent, / As half to show, half veil, the deep intent. / Ye pow'rs! whose mysteries restored I sing, / To whom Time bears me on his rapid wing, / Suspend a while your force inertly strong, / Then take at once the poet and the song' (IV.1–8). Moreover, the antecedent of 'He' is the sun; but 'curtains' is a slang idiom for death.

In WE's letters to Maxwell-Mahon (6 November 1967) – with reference less to hermeneutics than to personal impulse – ' "But in darkness" etc. meant that you didn't realize what a strong support she was till you were in real trouble'; and (21 August 1973): 'The bang in the last line, "but in darkness", was meant to imply: "It's only when you're in real trouble that you see the old woman at her best", and this was written before I was thrown out of Cambridge, when I thought her behaviour justified my tribute. I ought to have put this in the notes, but was shy about it.'

Part of Mandevil's Travels

First published in *Experiment* no. 1 (November 1928), pp. 38–9; then in *Cambridge Poetry 1929*.

CP: *Gravely*, the spelling of the original, means 'of gravel' but suggests graves. Milton said

> *on the snowy top*
> *Of cold Olympus rules the middle air,*
> *Their highest heaven,*

which doesn't fit; the boast was only that the Christian heaven was higher. The Roof of the World is, I believe, the Himalayas; the geography here is as dim as Mandevil's. 'Spears (first shoots of the metal trees – of man's use of metal) poke up above ground in the basin of the river during the dawn; the same spears at noon tower like cranes, and before night are engulfed and leave the plain bare; they are upheld only by sand which goes deeper than their roots.' I meant the motor service from Baghdad to Haifa, though that is far enough from where Herr Trinkler was. The *weekend* is copied from Mandevil. The *motto* is the King's remark at the beginning (as quoted in the papers).

TITLE: As the title and subtitle together indicate, the poem takes its initial inspiration from a 'part' (several chapters, not just 87) of the curious book of travels, which WE studied in Everyman's Library edition, *The Travels of Sir John Mandeville [and] The Journal of Friar Odoric* (London and New York, 1928), a reprint of the text of 1568 and 1887, with certain passages restored which the first printers omitted apparently in error. Originally published in French between 1357 and 1371, *Travels*, probably written by a Liège physician named Johains à la Barbe or else Jehan à la Barbe, recounts in extraordinary but suppositious detail the knight's exotic travels and findings from Turkey or Asia Minor through Egypt, India and the Asian plateau, and even unto Cathay. WE is particularly taken by the magical description of the paradisial kingdom of the fabulous Christian potentate known as Prester John (a king and priest – *rex et sacerdos* – whence his title 'Prester' or 'Presbyter') which is blessed with every natural bounty from fish of rare savour to gems beyond price. John Donne adverts to 'Prester Jack' in his mock-panegyric 'Upon Mr Thomas Coryat's Crudities'. Prester John's kingdom is located by some commentators in Abyssinia, but by others in the modern Afghanistan – 'the Roof of the World' – which gave WE this opportunity to juxtapose the legendary Prester John with his successor, Amir Amanullah, King of Afghanistan (see note on Motto below).

WE's spelling of the name 'Mandevil' is anomalous, but must be granted the benefit of a deliberate pun on 'man-devil', as *TGA* suggests (p. 77).

Meller provides helpful commentary in 'Politische Tagessatire als Pastiche und Puzzlespiel des *wit*: *Part of Mandevil's Travels*', in *Das Gedicht*, pp. 192–200. See also Morelli, pp. 103–4; Willis, pp. 144–9; *TGA*, pp. 74–7.

EPIGRAPH: **belyfe of] beliefe of** *1928, 1929, P 1934, P, CP 1949,* CP. WE's spelling otherwise exactly follows the Everyman edition, so a minor correction here is appropriate.

MOTTO: WE was incited to write his poem six months after King Amanullah's state visit to England in March 1928, and so creatively misremembered the immortally damning words that the king was reported to have spoken after firing off his torpedo. What WE was trying to recall was a sarcastic article 'Civilization' (by 'Y.Y.'), which pretended to imagine just how astonished the future inhabitants of Afghanistan might feel, three hundred years hence:

to read that their former monarch, when visiting England, was taken to see tanks at Lulworth Cove and bombing aeroplanes at Hendon, and was given a trip in a submarine and allowed to fire a torpedo off Spithead, but that he was never taken to see the Poet Laureate. The Afghans will conclude from this that England must have been an exceedingly warlike nation with little time or inclination to cultivate the arts of peace. It was after his trip in the submarine that King Amanullah himself exclaimed: 'I shall soon be the complete Westerner now,' assuming, no doubt, that a Western European is never so happy as when he is in a submarine. (*New Statesman*, 24 March 1928, p. 756)

1–4 *Mandevil's river . . . gravely seas*: an epitome of the major matter of chapter 87 of Mandeville's *Travels*, which records 'a great floud that cometh from Paradise, and it is full of precious stones, and no drop of water, and it runneth with great waves into the gravely sea . . .' (p. 198); and also of a terrifying magical plain in which 'grow trees that at the rising of the Son ech day begin to grow, and so grow they to midday, and beare fruit, but no man dare eate of that fruite, for it is a maner of yron, and after middaye it turneth againe to the earth, so that when the Sonne goeth downe it is nothinge seene, and so doeth it every day' (p. 199) – a periphrasis that WE renders down in l. 2. The kingdom of Prester John – 'a great Emperour of Inde' – 'is departed in yles because of great flods that come out of Paradise' (p. 195).

3 *Pantoroze*: Prester John's kingdom is 'the yle of Pantoroze'; WE's spelling 'Pantarose' may be a simple mistake, a lapse of memory.

5 *Paradise Terrestre*: 'Beyond the yles of the lande of Prester John . . . wildernesse and myrke land lasteth to Paradise terrestre, where Adam and Eve were sette' (Mandeville, *Travels*, p. 219).

6 *bent to improve, King Alleluiah*: WE's parody or travesty of the name Amanullah (*Alleluiah* or *Hallelujah* means 'Praise (ye) the Lord' = *Jah*, or *Jahweh*). Amanullah Khan came as a petitioner to the West in hopes of modernizing his country.

7 *Higher, in fact, as Milton boasted*: refers to the ancient Gods, Saturn and the other Titans, who 'on the snowy top / Of cold Olympus ruled the middle air / Their highest heaven' (*PL*, I.515–17), and who are 'Down cast and damp' to find Satan laid low in Hell (l. 523).

10 *cliquant*: 'cliquant' is not recorded by the *OED*; WE may be modifying the adjective *clinquant*, meaning 'glittering with gold or silver, or decked in false glitter or tinsel', to suggest associated meanings or puns. He may have assimilated the term from Max Beerbohm's essay 'Dandies and Dandies' (1896); cf. 'Your Teeth are Ivory Towers'.

10 *sag-fruited*: WE coins this participle by analogy with 'sag-bellied' or 'sag-bottomed'; the preternatural trees, which shoot up like 'spears' from the parched ground and are full-grown by noon, bear iron fruit that naturally sags.

13–14 *Herr Trinkler . . . dead poplar trees*: between May 1927 and September 1928 Dr Trinkler made a further exploration across the Tibetan plateau and into Chinese Turkestan. *The Times* reported the first news of his findings on 28 September 1928 (WE gave the date as 29 September, in a footnote to *1928*), p. 13: 'After the Ice Age the basin of Chinese Turkestan contained a large inland lake, which later dried up and sands accumulated on the site. Between the present cultivated area and the desert there is a large belt of dead poplar trees covering 2,000 square miles.' (The correct figure is 1,280,000 in acres; WE's 'million' is poetic licence.) Dr Trinkler gave a full account in chapter IX, 'Dead Poplar Woods', in *The Stormswept Roof of Asia* (London, 1931).

13 Trinkler] Trinckler *1928*, *1929*, P *1934*, P, CP *1949*, CP. WE paid scant attention to the spelling, but since he is referring to the actual German explorer and geologist Dr Emil Trinkler (author of *Through the Heart of Afghanistan*, trans. B. K. Featherstone (London, 1928)), there is no reason to perpetuate the error.

15–16 *Well may new pit-heads . . . harsher steel*: Amanullah's visit included an outing to the mines of the Bradford Colliery Company, and coincided with a devastating slump in the coal-mining industry: 250,000 miners were out of work. As the *Manchester Guardian Weekly* reported: 'It could not have been a pleasant plunge to take, for a pit cage is not a reassuring vehicle – dirty and ramshackle and uncomfortable. But the King took the plunge, and one is assured that down below he personally wielded a pick at the coal face' (30 March 1928, p. 248). Later that day, as the *Guardian* went on, the king 'pushed a £100 note into the hand of a Sheffield disabled soldier as he left the Sheffield town hall'. (He also gave the Lord Mayor of London £1,000 for London's poor, and then he and his Queen went on a two-and-a-half-hour shopping spree in Waring and Gillow's, Oxford Street (*The Times*, 27 March 1928).)

17 *Antred*: WE coins this participle as a direct borrowing from Shakespeare's noun 'antres' (i.e. *caves*). Othello reports (I.iii.139–42) that he wooed Desdemona with a detailed account – which, as WE knew, may owe something to Mandeville – of 'my travels' history; / Wherein of antres vast, and deserts idle, / Rough quarries, rocks and hills, whose heads touch heaven'.

17–20 *Antred . . . descend*: this stanza about the dry flood (see note for ll. 1–4, above), moving like a violent quicksand, derives from one sentence in *Travels*: 'this floud runneth three dayes in the weke so fast, & stirreth great stones of the roches with him that make muche noise, and as sone as they come into the gravely sea, they are no more sene' (pp. 198–9). Mandeville's 'muche noise' becomes WE's 'thunder' (vb.), and 'three dayes in the weke' is transformed into 'one known weekend'. Cf. Malcolm Letts: 'This is an Alexander story, but recalls the Sabbath river of Josephus, to which Mandeville refers in chapter XIV, which flowed all the days of the week except on Saturday, when it rested' (*Sir John Mandeville: The Man and his Book* (London, 1949), p. 80).

17 *malachite*: Mandeville does not mention this semi-precious ornamental stone, though it is known to have been found in ancient times. WE must have considered it an appropriately exotic stone for Prester John.

22 *Five clays, diluvian, covered some chipped flints*: Dr Trinkler reported geographical changes at the time of the Ice Age and during the huge floods that consumed Chinese Turkestan as the ice melted; it is apt that WE refers this layered landscape to the period of Noah's Flood (Genesis 6–8): successive floods, and erosions of rock into strata of clay, might well have drowned the sparse evidence of prehistoric tool-making ('chipped flints').

23–4 *Tour well . . . we own . . . tumultuous stone*: what the primeval forces of nature did to Afghanistan, the coal-mining industry has done to England: the despoliation of the landscape is similar.

25–8 *Fish . . . Prester John*: 'And al if it so be that there bee no water in the sea, yet men may finde therein right good fishe, and of another fashion & shape than is in any other seas, and also they are of full good savour' (Mandeville, *Travels*, p. 198). WE identifies such 'fish' as submarines (see note for Motto, above).

29 *Paradise, like Bohemia, has no coast*: Shakespeare, in *The Winter's Tale*, III.iii, gives Bohemia a sea-coast; why, asks WE, did Amanullah, king of a land-bound country, Afghanistan, feel such fascination with submarines and naval warfare?

31 *mail-dark*: echoes classical kennings like 'wine-dark' (as of the sea); the armoured (or 'mailed') fish in question here are the submarines constructed in dry dock.

32 *Adam*: as king of 'Paradise Terrestre' (l. 5), Amanullah is a likely Adam.

32 *recites my motto*: see note to the Motto misremembered by WE. At the time of King Amanullah's visit it was reported in a review of *Afghanistan of the Afghans*, by Sirdar Ikbal Ali Shah, and of Trinkler's *Through the Heart of Afghanistan*, that for Afghanistan

Western culture and Western ideas in general are quite another matter; they need not necessarily be accepted. The present Amir – a highly intelligent man, at present engaged in scouring Europe, and England in particular, in search of importable ideas – has recognized this distinction from the beginning. He commonly wears European clothes even in his own capital [cf. l. 30], uses a Rolls-Royce, has electric light in his palace . . . Afghanistan is an Eastern State and he intends that it shall remain an Eastern State, into which tourists and Christian or Bolshevik missionaries will not be admitted. He seeks the blessings of civilization without its drawbacks. ('Afghanistan', *New Statesman*, 31 March 1928, p. 797)

Amanullah seems to have been considerably beguiled (or corrupted) by Western ideas: on his return to Afghanistan he pressed for internal reforms including an education programme, road-building projects and emancipation of women, whereupon his opponents, led by the mullahs, obliged him to abdicate in January 1929; he presently left for permanent exile in Zurich.

When the poem was reprinted in *Cambridge Poetry 1929*, WE added a note – '**This was written when the King seemed a successful reformer, and calls for apology now**' – which suggests that it may have been meant as a panegyric and not so obviously a satire. But in 1929 WE must have felt sorry for the king.

Laus Melpomines

First published in *Granta* (16 November 1928), p. 123.

The title, the metrical and stanzaic form (rhyming aaba), and the subject-matter parody Swinburne's 'Laus Veneris' ('In Praise of Venus' – or Aphrodite), though they are also underpinned by Fitzgerald's translation of *The Rubáiyát of Omar Khayyám*. WE's rhymes on 'be', 'me' and 'sea' in the first stanza, for example, exactly rehearse the rhyme-words of Swinburne's ll. 53–6, and WE cites that stanza when discussing the fifth type of ambiguity (which 'occurs when the author is discovering his idea in the act of writing, or not holding it all in his mind at once, so that, for instance, there is a simile which applies to nothing exactly, but lies half-way between two things when the author is moving from one to the other' (*ST*, p. 184)). WE's comments are apt to this synaesthetically-challenged poem – as when he writes of 'echoes' that somehow 'writhe' (ll. 7–8), and 'harbingers' that 'Howl' (ll. 11–12). Swinburne, he observed in *ST*, 'uses . . . the fifth type for a sort of mutual comparison which . . . is not interested in either of the things compared; he merely uses the connections between them to present the reader with a wide group of his stock associations. The mixed epithets of two metaphors are combined as if in a single statement not intended to be analysed but to convey a "mood"' (p. 193). WE parodies Swinburne's fondness for unsubtle sound effects, notably alliterations. (Likewise, ll. 4 and 16 mock the besetting weakness of Dante Gabriel Rossetti's verse, as in the final line of Sonnet XXXIX, 'Sleepless Dreams', from *The House of Life*: 'And watered with the wasteful warmth of tears?') Whereas Swinburne (blasphemously) appeals, 'Ah God' (ll. 77, 149) and then 'Ah love', WE cries out 'Ah! God' and 'Ah! Death' (ll. 1, 9). WE, as the jaded theatre critic, addresses his lament to the figure of Melpomene, muse of tragedy. Part of the point was highlighted when WE remarked in *ST* upon Swinburne's 'diffused use of grammar, by which several precise conceits can be dissolved into a vagueness' (p. 32).

This parody, in the best tradition of the genre, is an act of homage to a poetic idol. Forty years on, WE was to write in a letter to *The Times Literary Supplement* (20 February 1969):

To answer Mr Singh's query (February 6): I meant the sadistic or masochistic passages in the first *Poems and Ballads* as what are frightfully good poetry though morally most undesirable. It is hard to list the best poems because they are so prone to internal collapse. For instance, the verse in *Dolores* about Nero fiddling while Rome burned:

> When, with flame all around him aspirant,
> Stood flushed as a harp-player stands,
> The implacable beautiful tyrant
> Rose-crowned, having death in his hands

this is knock-down; but the rest of the verse, saying what an enormous noise the Emperor made, a thunder of lyres louder than the fall of buildings, is absurd in an equally decisive manner.

No doubt positive virtues in Swinburne, such as readiness to take a dare, are part of what the reader admires; and I do not expect that the verses do actual harm. I was devoted to them as a schoolboy, when I was being beaten rather too often; and it was quite clear to me that this literary taste did nothing to make me enjoy being beaten. (Can the poet really have been removed from Eton because he proved that he did? What a triumph it would be!) But I cannot help regarding sadism very glumly, as the only perversion really deserving the name, and it seems important to get clear that one can appreciate the poetry without sharing the mental disease. All this, I think, has been familiar since the poems first appeared 100 years ago: I was only pointing out that our current orthodoxy has succeeded in blinding itself to quite large areas of English poetry.

Marking students does seem necessary, but marking the authors studied, as is done now with such immense self-satisfaction, feels to me odd. To the question 'Are sausages better than marmalade? Arrive at an evaluation', even the most expert chef could hardly say more than 'I prefer both, at breakfast, with the marmalade after.' Swinburne and Dylan Thomas were trying to do very different things. However, not to be too proud to join in a round game, I answer that I would mark Thomas rather above Swinburne, as I would sausages rather above marmalade; but then, I would mark Thomas pretty high.

Philip Hobsbaum, who studied with WE in 1959–62, has recalled that WE aspired to emulate Swinburne: 'He always said he was writing but that the poems were no good because he wasn't old enough. Writing poetry was like taking baths, he said: necessary only for the young and the old. Middle-aged gents exempt . . . Well, middle-aged or not, Empson always maintained that he was writing and said that it was lyrical stuff like the verse of Swinburne. He used to talk a good deal about "the singing line" and said that was what was missing from a lot of modern poetry' (letter to Haffenden, 27 June 1985).

See also WE's remark, in 'Alice: Child as Swain': '**Dodgson** [Lewis Carroll] **was fond of saying that one parodied the best poems, or anyway that parody showed no lack of admiration, but a certain bitterness is inherent in parody; if the meaning is not "This poem is absurd" it must be "In my present mood of emotional sterility the poem will not work, or I am afraid to let it work, on *me*" ' (*Pastoral*, p. 210).

1 *Ah! God, they mock me, all the deaths*: cf. the plaint of Milton's Adam: 'Why am I mocked with death, and lengthened out / To deathless pain?' (*PL*, X.774–5).
2 *spit at me*: cf. Herbert, 'The Sacrifice', l. 133: 'Behold, they spit on me' (see *ST*, p. 267).
3 *groans that miss the mortal shapes*: cf. the opening, spoken by the Attendant Spirit, of Milton's 'A Masque' ('Comus'), ll. 1–3: 'Before the starry threshold of

Jove's court / My mansion is, where those immortal shapes / Of bright aerial spirits live ensphered'; and Pope, 'Eloisa to Abelard', l. 83, where the jealous god 'bids them make mistaken mortals groan'.

4 *sounding sorrows of the sea*: cf. Milton, 'Lycidas', ll. 154–5: 'Ay me! Whilst thee the shores, and sounding seas / Wash far away, where'er thy bones are hurled'; and Swinburne, 'The Triumph of Time', l. 202: 'Full of the sound of the sorrow of years'.

6 *gawds . . . God*: the chime here parodies Swinburne's sound-effects; 'gawd' was not only the Cockney pronunciation of 'God' but also at one time rather smart; also given 'mock' (l. 1) and 'spit' (l. 2), a variant of 'gauds' (jests, scoffs).

6 *the rainbow by which God has sworn*: God's covenant with Noah in Gen. 9: 12–17. Cf. 'Essay', l. 3.

9–10 *Ah! Death, discern me . . . with healing hands / Cool . . . stands*: cf. Swinburne, 'The Garden of Proserpine' (1866), ll. 49–52: 'Pale, beyond porch and portal, / Crowned with calm leaves, she stands / Who gathers all things mortal / With cold immortal hands'. Cf. also the speech by Meleager in Swinburne's *Atalanta in Calydon* (1865): 'Lo, for their blood I die; and mine own blood / For bloodshedding of mine is mixed therewith, / That death may not discern me from my kin' (*The Poems of Algernon Charles Swinburne*, vol. IV (London, 1904), p. 329). Perhaps cf. too Rossetti's Sonnet XLI, 'Through Death to Love', l. 7: 'Our hearts discern wild images of Death'.

14 *Resound and bellow*: cf. Pope, 'The Rape of the Lock', v. 50: 'Blue Neptune storms, the bellowing deeps resound.'

15 *sole sad*: compare W. S. Blunt, *Giselda: A Society Novel in Rhymed Verse*, chapter II, l. 349: 'The sole sad gap between us'; and Eugene Lee-Hamilton, 'Peter of Portugal to Inez de Castro. (1356)' (*Imaginary Sonnets*), l. 6: 'and I the sole sad thing'.

15–16 *Sisyphus . . . / Roll . . . rock*: Sisyphus, son of Aeolus, is tormented in Hades by having eternally to roll a rock up a hill, though it will always inevitably roll down again (*Odyssey* XI.593ff.).

17–18 *I know . . . countless matinées*: cf. T. S. Eliot, 'The Love Song of J. Alfred Prufrock' (1915), ll. 49–51: 'For I have known them all already, known them all – / Have known the evenings, mornings, afternoons, / I have measured out my life with coffee spoons'.

20 *less heart*: cf. Swinburne, 'Six Years Old', l. 33: 'Had even my love less heart to love you, / A better song were ours'.

The Extasie

First published in *London Review of Books* 11:15 (17 August 1989), 21. See also headnote to 'The Scales'.

Camping Out

First published in *Experiment* no. 2 (February 1929), 15; reprinted in *New Signatures* (1932).

CP: The intention behind the oddness of the theme, however much it may fail, was not to be satirical but to show indifference to satire from outside. She gives the lake its pattern of reflected stars, now made of toothpaste, as God's grace allows man virtues that nature wouldn't; the mist and pale (pale light or boundary) of morning have made it unable to reflect real stars any longer. *Soap tension* is meant to stand for the action of surface tension between more or less concentrated soap solutions which makes the specks fly apart. *Their frame unties:* if any particle of matter got a speed greater than that of light it would have infinite mass and might be supposed to crumple up round itself the whole of space–time – 'a great enough ecstasy makes the common world unreal'.

In recording *The Poems of William Empson*, WE commented:

I shall give these poems in the order they were written in. The first I think brings out the shock quality of the technique and at the same time shows it isn't necessarily meant to be funny, or as they say 'bitter', or indeed painful in any way. The poem is called *CAMPING OUT*, and is built on the one fact that if you throw soapy spots on to the surface of water they all repel each other, they move away from each other, because soap lowers the surface tension of water and the outside water pulls them, so that they look as if you were rapidly approaching a group of stars. Camping out together makes the lovers feel especially free from settled society, as if in a space-ship, but to see the stars like this they would have to be moving faster than light, and on the Einstein Theory this would crack up the whole of space. The idea is that a great enough ecstasy can make the common world unreal. The tension in the poem, without which I admit this style is rather fatuous, you could perhaps express by saying 'This kind of affair is in one way outside society but in another way normal and necessary to it, indeed it makes it'; but there is no agony about the thing, and the more obvious tension comes from making poetry about an unusual topic, cleaning teeth.

In *Contemporary Poets Reading Their Own Poems*, WE remarked that this poem is 'carrying the conceit method very far. The basic idea . . . is that these two young lovers are camping by a lake . . . It doesn't seem disgusting to me.'

On *Harvard*, he remarked that the girl 'is cleaning her teeth, and this is regarded with exultation by the young man. The specks of the toothpaste in the lake echo the stars above, which are invisible as they are in fog [l. 3]; they copy the universe, they set a pattern for the universe. This is where it could be called metaphysical, and slightly like Donne. In the second verse . . . the specks expand, all in proportion, exactly as if you were approaching a constellation at enormous speed.'

Houghton preserves four sheets of manuscript draft: *MS1* is an early draft of the first stanza and variants of the first two lines of stanza 2; *MS2* (the first draft to provide the title) has three trial versions of stanza 1; *MS3* an advanced state of stanza 1 and variants of stanza 2; *MS4* the complete poem with minor emendations. An interesting feature of *MS1* and *MS2* is that line 1 of the poem began in the form '**She cleaned her teeth into the lake**', with '**cleaned**' being emended to '**cleans**'; the second attempt on *MS2* reads '**She cleans her teeth {with paste} into the lake**' ({} indicates a deletion), with '**Later**' and '**And now**' being tried out in the margin; '**And now**' wins the day in the third version on *MS2*. *MS1* of 'Insomnia', which was evidently written at about the same time as both 'Camping Out' and 'The Scales', includes a draft reading of ll. 1 and 7 of 'Camping Out' (see notes to 'Insomnia').

See Morelli, pp. 65–9; Willis, pp. 149–53; Thurley, pp. 47–8; Ricks, pp. 191–2; *TGA*, pp. 78–81.

The woman looks like the creator of a galaxy, and in a microcosmic way she creates a world and like a Madonna or goddess she can then plunge into the universe she has created. (WE borrows the Christian doctrine of Christ's – and Mary's – bodily assumption into Heaven: in that sense the sky would 'achieve the Lord' (l. 10), whereas WE suggests that only a spaceship could possibly shoot off from earth.) That small creation, control and penetration is then compared to doing it in the larger sphere, the universe beyond our world, which would actually be disastrous. Yet the tone is confident, because the poem is also talking about the nature of ecstatic human love, which can allow itself the boldness of whimsy. The frame of the natural world may threaten destruction if it is broken but it may yet be escaped, 'outsoared' (l. 14), in the separate world of love.

4 will] Will *1929, 1932, P 1934, CP 1949*
5 nature] Nature *MS2, MS3, MS4, 1929, 1932, P 1934, CP 1949*
7–11 *Milks . . . galaxies*: *TGA* (p. 80) remarks: 'The Greek root of the word "galaxies" links the idea of milk to that of stars.' (Galaxy derives from the Greek for 'milk'; hence the Milky Way.)
8 *Soap tension . . . magnifies*: '**The toothpaste specks as they go apart on the water look like approaching a constellation at more than the speed of light**' (*Listen*). In an early draft (*MS1*), this line reads: '**The stars move still; soap tension magnifies**'; the latter phrase was amended on the same sheet first to '**their pattern magnifies**' and then to '**Their pattern the soap's tension magnifies**'; in *MS3* the line reads both '**Her pattern the soap tension magnifies**' and '**Soap tension her star pattern magnifies**', with the latter version being carried forward to *MS4*. It was presumably at a late stage of the process of drafting that WE opted not for '**her**' but for the definite article.

Carl H. Snyder explains: 'Soap, detergents, and any other substances that accumulate at surfaces and change their properties sharply, especially by lowering the surface tension, are *surface-active agents* or, more briefly, *surfactants* . . . Even a small amount of a surface-active agent can produce dramatic effects. At a concentration of 0.1%, for example, soap lowers water's surface tension by almost 70%' (*The Extraordinary Chemistry of Ordinary Things*, 2nd edn. (New York and Chichester, 1995), pp. 324–5). See also 'Arachne', l. 14.

9 *through-assumes*: punning on the myth of the Assumption into Heaven of the Virgin Mary (which became an article of Roman Catholic doctrine nearly a quarter-century later), WE coins his verb by analogy with Donne's usage in 'To the Countess of Bedford' ('Honour is so sublime perfection'), ll. 26–7: 'that we / May in your through-shine front your heart's thoughts see'. Cf. 'Doctrinal Point', l. 17.

10 achieve] receive *Harvard*

11 galaxies,] galaxies; *1929, 1932, P 1934*

12–14 *Our bullet boat . . . outsoared*: any material object which attempted to exceed the highest possible velocity in the universe would destroy the universe. Einstein's Relativity leaves us one known absolute – 'the velocity of light is the maximum possible velocity' – as James A. Coleman elucidates: 'the material objects with which we are familiar can never even travel as fast as light, because their mass would become infinite, which means that an *infinite* amount of energy would be required to get them up there. An infinite amount of energy means *all* the energy in the universe *plus a great deal more*' (*Relativity for the Layman* (Harmondsworth, 1969), p. 62).

MS4 alone carries the rejected reading: '**Light's speed by thousands our shot boat outflies**.'

12 *bullet boat*: WE is perhaps recalling Donne's fantasia on the death of Elizabeth Drury, 'Of the Progress of the Soul: The Second Anniversary': 'Thou hast thy expansion now, and liberty; / Think that a rusty piece, discharged, is flown / In pieces, and the bullet is his own, / And freely flies' (ll. 180–83).

13 *Who moves so among stars their frame unties*: by glossing the meaning in his *CP* note in terms of '**ecstasy**', WE happily profanes the neo-Platonic teaching that mankind may attain to a knowledge of divine things only through the state of exaltation for which the Greek term is 'ecstasy' (see Plotinus, *Enneads*, VI.9–11).

WE is using 'frame' in a slightly more specialized sense than is usual: according to Einstein's theory, as Eddington explained, 'the question of a unique right frame of space does not arise. There is a frame of space *relative* to the nebular observers, others *relative* to other stars. Frames of space are relative' (*Nature of the Physical World*, p. 21).

13 unties;] unties, *1929, 1932, P 1934*

Insomnia

First published in *Cambridge Review* 50 (19 April 1929), 373.

Seven manuscript sheets (*MS1–7*) are preserved at Houghton. *MS1* has early drafts of lines 1–15; *MS2* an emended draft of lines 1–18; *MS3* two emended versions of lines 1–2; *MS4* (on which the title 'Insomnia' is deleted and an alternative title ventured further down the sheet: '**Indecision and Insomnia**') has an emended version of the first three stanzas, plus some phrases towards stanza 4; *MS5* (which also features a title in the form '**Indecision and Insomnia**') has stanzas 1 and 3 together with two versions of stanza 2; *MS6* gives two states of stanza 4; and *MS7* has the complete poem, though with two emended versions of stanza 4. To judge from the evidence of *MS1*, which includes the draft lines '**She cleaned her teeth into the lake**' and '**{And} Milked between stones {rocks} a straddled way {sky} of stars**', as well as references to '**Delta**', '**Solomon's Mines**', '**Sandcastle tunnels**', '**Australia**' and '**jackal**', this poem was drafted at about the same time as 'The Scales' and 'Camping Out'.

The technical accomplishment Willis finds a limited success: 'The six-line stanza, generally iambic, rhymed abaabb and containing two couplets (or two near rhymes), is restrictive and repetitive . . . Metric variations (the last line is an alexandrine), and the frequency of feminine endings for the a-rhymed lines, afford a slight measure of flexibility, however' (p. 260).

1–2 *Satan when ultimate chaos . . . hot dry wet cold*: Satan has been let out of hell by Sin, and is making his way through Chaos: travelling conditions are terrible, and Satan sinks into air-pockets, is tossed up again on fiery updraughts and is 'nigh foundered' in boggy patches. This primeval chaos is 'a dark / Illimitable ocean without bound, / Without dimension, where length, breadth, and highth, / And time and place are lost; where eldest Night / And Chaos, ancestors of Nature, hold / Eternal anarchy, amidst the noise / Of endless wars, and by confusion stand. / For Hot, Cold, Moist, and Dry, four champions fierce / Strive here for mastery . . .' (*PL*, II.891–9). Cf. Ovid, *Met.* I.19ff. The succession of 'hot dry wet cold' is a little version of Milton's 'verse-filling asyndetons' at II.948–50 (see *Paradise Lost*, ed. John Carey (Harlow, Essex, 1971), p. 134).

2–5 *battered at random . . . Probably nor Probability . . . Brownian hesitance foretold*: on leaving hell, WE suggests, Satan must have been subjected, when in Chaos, to the so-called Brownian movement – named after the Scottish botanist Robert Brown (1773–1858) – the random movement, the wobbling or fluctuation, of microscopic particles suspended in a liquid or gas. (See, e.g., Einstein's 1905 paper, *Investigations on the Theory of the Brownian Movement*, which WE would have studied.) The physicist Jean-Baptiste Perrin proved in 1909 that atoms and molecules are actual physical entities – as Milton seems to have intuited in the buffeting that Satan suffers in Chaos. Cf. WE's later remarks (*ST*, p. 104): 'in recent atomic physics there is a shift in progress, which tends to attach the notion of a probability to the natural object rather than to the fallibility of the human mind'; and a review of Joseph Needham, *The Sceptical Biologist* (1930):

Many scientific laws, in particular the one that energy is always diffusing itself towards a dead level, are laws of averages; not certain, but very probable for large numbers of molecules. Now in small living cells there are so few of the large molecules concerned that large variations in these laws are to be expected. Some writers have sought their freedom in this; Mr Needham points out that all the molecules are still obeying their individual laws. This attack has since the date of the essay been pushed further, and makes 'probability', once a device by which human ignorance dealt with large numbers, now an inherent property of each separate molecule; but this does not upset Mr Needham's position; the notion of an atom's probability is a mystery, and very *like* what one feels about people, but it is not its business to give freedom to the organism. (*A*, p. 529)

4 *his view the total cauldron of a sky*: Satan, cast into the 'great deep' of hell, finds 'The dismal situation waste and wild, / A dungeon horrible, on all sides round / As one great furnace flamed, yet from those flames / No light, but rather darkness visible' (*PL*, I.60–63); he experiences 'these livid flames / . . . pale and dreadful' (182–3), 'the torrid clime / . . . vaulted with fire' (297–8) and 'the cope of hell / 'Twixt upper, nether, and surrounding fires' (345–6).

5 *Milton nor Brownian hesitance foretold*: this line appears in *MS1*, *MS2* and *MS3* in the form '**No Brownian hesitance the bard foretold**'. On *MS2*, '**Milton**' is added in the left margin, so implying the (better) syntax that WE may have considered at this stage of his drafting – 'Milton no Brownian hesitance foretold'; notwithstanding, the reading '**nor**' is definite in *MS4*, *MS5* and *MS7*.

6 *One purposed whirlwind*: Milton does not say that Satan was stalled by a whirlwind: WE is probably referring to 'The strong rebuff of some tumultuous cloud' (*PL*, II.936) which checked Satan's fall through Chaos (see note to ll. 9–12). Otherwise, WE may be recalling an earlier episode where, following his account of the four rivers of hell and 'Lethe the river of oblivion', Milton adds this withering detail: 'Beyond this flood a frozen continent / Lies dark and wild, beat with perpetual storms / Of whirlwind and dire hail' (II.587–9).

7 *Bottomless Pit's bottom*: trounced for their rebellion against God, such is the fate of the rebel angels: 'headlong themselves they threw / Down from the verge of heaven, eternal wrath / Burnt after them to the bottomless pit' (*PL*, VI.864–6). All the same, Erebus, or hell, is given a 'lowest bottom' (II.882).

8 *his sail-broad vans*: Satan, in order to raise himself from the abasement of hell, tries to spread his wings – 'his sail-broad vans' (*PL*, II.927).

9–12 *God's help the rival gust . . . had sunk yet, down for ever, by one blast controlled*: Satan's fluttering 'pennons' were in danger of proving useless as a means of upholding him, 'had not by ill chance / The strong rebuff of some tumultuous cloud / Instinct with fire and nitre hurried him / As many miles aloft' (II.935–8). 'God's help' is WE's gloss on Milton's account.

10 *Heaven undistinguished high*: cf. *PL*, II.1047–8: 'heaven . . . / . . . undetermined square or round'.

11 *pudding still unstirred*: see ll. 1–2 and note. *MS3* and *MS5* refer to this state as 'unshuffled pudding' and 'ill-stirred', and *MS4* as a 'pack unshuffled'. Cf. WE's commentary on *The Dunciad*, 'Where, in nice balance, truth with gold she weighs, / And solid pudding against empty praise' (I.53–4), in *ST*, p. 153, which includes the remark, 'it is gay and generous of Pope to have so much sympathy with *pudding*'.

11 *Anarch old*: Chaos (*PL*, II.988). *MS1* refers to Anarchy as 'megalo-Anarch'.

19–21 *carpet units . . . new shades supply*: *MS5* includes the annotation: 'the same materials repeated of carpet → new balance of colour scheme in new angle'. An unfinished essay on carpets and the commixtures of their colours, which almost certainly dates from the late 1920s, illustrates WE's appreciation of aesthetics and optical effects:

Pleasure in Persian carpets depends on odd incidental factors in your habits of vision. Before you are trained to appreciate them they look better if you are tired, whereas pictures are just the other way; and personally, being shortsighted, I find I get not merely a better but an entirely new colour-scheme by looking at them without glasses. Indeed one might recommend the use of blurring-glasses to estimate a carpet quickly: you see then harmonies of colour which only long acquaintance allow[s] to grow on you. When possible it is nearly as good (unless your eyes are very strong) to look at it from a fair distance. One reason may be that different colours are intended to work, not only by contrast and correspondence as in an ordinary colour-scheme, but also by an effort of the eye which conceives neighbouring colours as mixed, so as to give richer colours . . .

Where this effect does not visibly take place, so that you see much the same colours after blurring as before, it is still often possible to get a pleasanter first impression of the carpet; the forms seem simple, well proportioned, and strong enough alone to carry the colours; you are not puzzled by the arabesques. This I think is because many of the carpets make their effect by a sharp contrast, in tone, between form and colour, whereas European art has usually tried to harmonize them . . .

Another great source of subtlety in colour is the change of shade as you see (especially the reds) at different angles. A large carpet hanging right up the wall may give a continuous scale of such colour changes, so that the eye may pick out (as in looking at a flower) as many shades as it chooses. Often there are two or three shades on the way up which allow the scheme to harmonize, and the whole pattern seems to re-form itself with a set of colours that the eye extends far beyond the region where they can occur . . .

That the eye can make such a maze or stew of colours into an orderly design is very remarkable: a great deal of the work of creation must be thrown into the appreciator.

22 *roads . . . tie*: a marginal note, in *MS4*, seems to be relevant here: '**difference between cynical** [?, perhaps "**original**"] **opposites fades, and** S[atan]'**s children build the bridge**'; the reference is to *Paradise Lost*, II.1024–30: 'Sin and Death amain / Following his track, such was the will of heaven, / Paved after him a broad and beaten way / Over the dark abyss, whose boiling gulf / Tamely endured a bridge of wondrous length / From hell continued reaching the utmost orb / Of this frail world . . .'

24 *Nine . . . Nine were foaled*: the rebel angels fall through the 'wild anarchy' of Chaos for a period of nine days (*PL*, VI.871), and then lie stupefied in hell for a further nine days (I.50). Edgar, in the guise of Poor Tom, sings: 'Swithin footed thrice the wold, / A met the night mare and her nine foal, / Bid her alight / And her troth plight, / And aroint thee, witch, aroint thee!' (*King Lear*, III.iv.113–17). For Virgil, the underworld is immured by the ninefold Styx (*Aeneid*, VI.439); and Milton's Satan knows that a 'huge convex of fire, / . . . immures us round / Ninefold' (*PL*, II.434–6). For 'intersterile', *MS4* gives the rejected readings '**mutually sterile**' and '**incommensurate**'.

Letter I

First published – minus final stanza – in *Experiment* no. 1 (November 1928), 4; and reprinted, as 'Letter', in *New Signatures* (1932), and *P 1934*. In *The Year's Poetry 1935*, it had acquired stanza 4.

Manuscript evidence suggests that the culminating stanza was drafted at much the same time as the poem 'Doctrinal Point' (1935): see the notes to that poem. Only one manuscript page survives: an advanced draft of stanza 4. A typescript of the earlier, three-stanza version – with the title 'Letter ii' – was sent to Brian Howard for possible inclusion in a projected anthology (now in the School Library, Eton College, which is here abbreviated *Eton*); see also M. J. Lancaster, *Brian Howard* (London, 1968).

CP: **The network without fish is empty space which you could measure, lay an imaginary net of co-ordinates over, opposed in verse 3 to the condition when two stars are not connected by space at all; these are compared to two people without ideas or society in common, hence with no 'physics' between them in what F. M. Cornford said was the primitive sense of the word. Lacking a common lifeblood shared from one totem (showman because tragic hero) they are connected by no idea whose name is derived from 'physics'. A big enough and concentrated enough star would, I understand, separate itself out from our space altogether. Verse 4 describes a similar failure of communication which may in the end happen to the sun;** *your circumambient foreboding* **is 'the empty space round him which connects us to him and which you fear.' The** *thread* **was meant to be 'the unlikely chance** that we ever learn to talk to them by radio and thus find out that they are not wise'.

The full series of 'Letter' poems, including 'Letter VI: a marriage' (which was not published during WE's lifetime), was addressed to his Cambridge friend and contemporary Desmond Lee (1908–93), a tall and striking-looking man, who took Firsts in both parts of the Classical Tripos. Lee was one of Wittgenstein's favourite pupils during his second period at Cambridge (from 1929). Lee was for some years a university lecturer in Classics, and then Headmaster of Winchester (1954–68). He married Elizabeth Crockenden in 1935 (see notes to 'Letter VI: a marriage'). According to Lee's own account, this series of poems began when Lee quoted to WE Pascal's famous remark (ll. 1–2), only to learn that WE profoundly disagreed with it. As soon as WE completed each of the 'Letters', he would send Lee a typescript (with the exception, presumably, of 'Letter VI', which he may have kept more tactfully to himself). Though WE obviously felt homoerotic attraction, there was apparently no overt declaration, and Lee, while clearly not unaware, simply refused to acknowledge the poems: he would not meet WE on such terms. He was to write, in his unpublished typescript 'Autobiographical Notes, started in 1984': 'I do not think anyone has known that I was the addressee, nor do I think it is of great consequence. The last letter was accompanied by a note saying he would not "bother me" with any more . . . Retrospectively I think I probably felt that they [the poems, to which Lee did not respond] would introduce an intensity into our relations which was not appropriate in day-to-day affairs.' Lee struck out the last clause (from 'which'), and substituted by hand: 'and which neither of us wanted'. (Courtesy of the late Sir Desmond Lee.) WE, in his interview with Ricks, refers to the subject of many of his early love-poems in terms of '**boy being afraid of girl**'; but in the case of the 'Letter' series (and perhaps only in these poems) 'girl' stands for 'boy'.

See also Morelli, pp. 46–57; Willis, pp. 153–9; *TGA*, pp. 81–6.

2 *The eternal silence of the infinite spaces*: reference to Pascal's resonant (albeit contextually impersonal) declaration, 'Le silence éternel de ces espaces infinis m'effraie' (*Pensées* (1670; trans. 1688), III.206): 'The eternal silence of these infinite spaces [the heavens] terrifies me.' Apropos Pascal's observation, WE incidentally remarked, in a handwritten note from the 1930s: '**English won't take two successive adjective-nouns.**' (Pascal's arresting words are quoted by Haldane in the opening essay, 'On Scales', of *Possible Worlds*, p. 1; WE's review of the volume, entitled 'Almost', appeared in *Granta*, 27 January 1928; *E in G*, pp. 34–5.)

3 *net-work without fish*: 'The system of the stars is floating in an ocean – not merely an ocean of space, not merely an ocean of ether, but an ocean that is so far material that one atom or thereabouts occurs in each cubic inch. It is a placid ocean' (A. S. Eddington, *Stars and Atoms* (Oxford, 1927), p. 67). In *Nature of the Physical World*, which appeared in the month when WE first published this poem, Eddington reiterated: 'space is *like* a network of distances . . . a self-supporting system of linkage which can be contemplated without reference to extraneous linkages' (pp. 81–2).

3–4 *that mere / Extended idleness, those pointless places*: WE attributes to his interlocutor the observation that the aether or interspace is non-material and hence unlocatable, allowing a pun on 'pointless' (*not to be pointed at* as well as *purposeless*). Eddington confirms this unnervingly necessitous state of affairs: 'There is . . . no reason to transfer to this vague background of aether the properties of a material ocean . . . In particular there is no reason to suppose that it can partition out space in a definite way, as a material ocean would do . . . There need not be anything corresponding to permanent identity in the constituent portions of aether; we cannot lay our finger at one spot and say "this piece of aether was a few seconds ago over there"'' (Eddington, *Space Time and Gravitation*, p. 40). Eddington also points out: 'The physical world is not to be analysed into isolated particles of matter or electricity with featureless interspace. We have to attribute as much character to the interspace as to the particles . . . We postulate aether to bear the characters of the interspace as we postulate matter or electricity to bear the characters of the particles . . .' (*Nature of the Physical World*, pp. 32–3).

5 *Who*: TGA protests (p. 82): ' ''who'' . . . seems merely perverse'. Correct grammar would seem to require 'which'.

5 possibilized] *Year's Poetry 1935, CP 1956*; **possibilised** *Eton*; **possiblized** *P, CP*. WE wrote to Parsons (29 May 1956), sending emendations to *CP* for *CP 1956*: '**insert "i", "possibilized". I am not sure about the rule, but it needs to be pronounced like that.**'

5 *possibilized to bear faces*: cf. Stephen Dedalus's Aristotelian observation, in 'Oxen of the Sun': 'But, gramercy, what of those Godpossibled souls that we nightly impossibilise, which is the sin against the Holy Ghost, Very God, Lord and Giver of Life?' (*Ulysses*). See also note to ll. 3–4 above, especially the ruling that we postulate ('possibilize') an aether to bear the characters of the interspace. In using the ugly verb 'possibilize' WE may have had in mind Coleridge's invention of '*credibilizing* power' – the power that facilitates the famous 'willing suspension of disbelief' (*Lectures and Notes on Shakspere, and other English Poets*, ed. T. Ashe (London, 1893), p. 349).

5 faces,] **faces** *1928, 1932*

6 and] **or** *Listen*

6–7 Yours . . . are] **(Pascal's or such as yours) up-buoyed / Are even of universes** *Eton, 1928, 1932, P 1934* (*Eton* has 'your's')

6 *up-buoyed*: OED cites an instance of the verb 'up-buoy' from 1652 (prefix 'up-', III.4.b). WE may be recalling Coleridge's usage in 'The Visit of the Gods' (?1799), which hails the 'Immortals', the 'Divinities', not singly but *en masse*, who will carry the poet up and away to the heavens: 'with your wings of upbuoyance / Bear aloft to your homes, to your banquets of joyance' (ll. 13–14).

7 *void*: contradicting the terrifying anxiety attributed to the auditor in this poem, Eddington insisted: 'We must rid our minds of the idea that the word space in science has anything to do with *void* . . . the physicist does not conceive of space as void. Where it is empty of all else there is still the aether' (*Nature of the Physical World*, p. 137).

10–11 *Mars' / Renown for wisdom*: the compliment makes little sense in mythical terms; Minerva is goddess of wisdom, and Mars, variously god of war and agriculture, is widely regarded as a buffoon. WE must have had in mind the popular notion that the planet Mars is home to intelligent beings at an advanced state of civilization. In 1877 the astronomer Giovanni Schiaparelli had identified on the surface of Mars strangely etched lines which he characterized as *canali*; and in H. G. Wells's *The War of the Worlds* (1898), horrid aggressive Martians invade earth (and are defeated only by some bacteria).

12 *Hanged on the thread*: puns on the cliché 'hanging by a thread'; but the use of the participial form also suggests an allusion to the Authorized Version of Acts 5: 30: 'The God of our fathers raised up Jesus, whom ye slew and hanged on a tree.' Cf. 'Description of a View', ll. 15–16 and note.

14 *what they think common-sense has seen*: Eddington is adamant that whenever we express commonsense about location in space, we are in fact exploiting '*sense* knowledge' (*Nature of the Physical World*, p. 17).

15 *Only, have we space*: 'Whether the sentence . . . is interrogatory, as the final question mark indicates . . . , or whether it is hortatory . . . , the problem it states is the familiar one Marvell struggles over with his coy mistress . . . Clearly, what is needed is a proper amount of distance, the dark space which surrounds and displays to advantage a light-reflecting planet or its lunar satellite' (Willis, p. 157).

16–18 *A tribe whose life-blood is our sacrament*: Cornford, discussing primitive beliefs about the nature of the world, notes that 'the human group and the departments of Nature surrounding it were unified in one solid fabric of *moirai* – one comprehensive system of custom and taboo'. A group in the totemic stage derives its solidarity neither from family relationships nor even from blood-kinship, but from its peculiar relation to its particular totem. 'The word *totem* itself is said to mean simply "tribe"; and this fact marks that the totem . . . *is* the social group . . . The members of a totem-clan normally believe themselves to be descended from a totem-ancestor . . . By virtue of this descent they are of one blood . . .' Group-kinship embraces both 'continuity of the blood' and 'identity of function', Cornford further explains. 'Both aspects are covered by the conception of "nature" (*physis*)' (*From Religion to Philosophy*, pp. 55, 57, 87).

In loose-leaf notes from 1931–4, WE wrote: ' "**The tribe**" (**Cornford**) is only a primitive alternative [to godhead] because a man needs God most when he sees fit to defy his tribe.'

He comments further in 'Double Plots' in *Pastoral*:

The connexion between pantheism and deification is perhaps best approached by a speculative route. F. M. Cornford developed a theory in *From Religion to Philosophy* that the primitive Greeks invented Nature by throwing out onto the universe the idea of a common life-blood; the living force that made natural events follow reasonable laws, and in particular made the crops grow, was identified with the blood which made the members of the tribe into a unity and which they shared with their totem. So the physicist is well connected by derivation to the physician, the 'leech' who lets blood. However this may have been in primitive Greece it was a natural fancy for a Christian; the Logos had been formulated as the underlying Reason of the universe and was also the Christ who had saved man by shedding his blood and sharing it in the Communion. (pp. 67–8)

17 *Physics or metaphysics*: primitive religion assumed a fusion of Nature (external nature as revealed through the senses) and the supernatural, so allaying our troubling modern split between physics and metaphysics: 'The "Nature" of which the first philosophers tell us with confident dogmatism is from the first a metaphysical entity; not merely a natural element, but an element endowed with supernatural life and powers, *a substance which is also Soul and God*.' *Physis* and Soul are homogeneous, a living 'soul-substance' or else 'a material continuum charged with vital force': 'a supersensible, metaphysical entity, or in other words a representation, which . . . is of mythical origin.' Accordingly, ' "Soul" and *physis* are not merely analogous, but identical. The two conceptions – Soul, and ultimate matter – are as yet fused in one' (Cornford, *From Religion to Philosophy*, pp. 123, 129, 131). See also 'High Dive', l. 27 and note.

17 *showman*: primitive totem, or else perhaps the Christ (see note to ll. 16–18 above).

19 *non-Euclidean predicament*: the four-dimensional world of space–time is curved, or warped, in non-Euclidean geometry: 'The terms "curved space" and "non-Euclidean space" are used practically synonymously' (Eddington, *Nature of the Physical World*, p. 157).

20 *Where is that darkness that gives light its place*: 'A feature of the relativity theory which seems to have aroused special interest among philosophers is the absoluteness of the velocity of light . . . the peculiarity of a velocity of 299,796 kilometres a second is that it coincides with the grain of the world . . . But it is much more than that; it is the speed at which the mass of matter becomes infinite, lengths contract to zero, clocks stand still' (Eddington, *Nature of the Physical World*, pp. 54–5). WE noted in a review: 'any serious attempt at establishing a relativity turns out to establish an absolute; in the case of Einstein the velocity of light' ('A Doctrine of Aesthetics' (1949); *A*, p. 212).

20 light its] light in its *Year's Poetry 1935*

22–3 *jovial sun, if he avoids exploding . . . will cease to grin*: WE remarked, for *Listen*: ' "**Sun**" again [as in 'To an Old Lady']; **enough mass would make it close up space–time round itself, which is compared to a neurotic collapse. Most of these love-poems praise love for preventing madness.**' Jupiter, chief deity of the Roman state (Greek *Zeus*), takes his name from *Djovis-pater*, the root *div* meaning 'to shine' (the etymology is preserved in the phrase *sub Jove*: 'under the open sky'); astrologically, the natal planet Jupiter bestows (or radiates) joy, mirthfulness and conviviality. Yet WE's conditional clause refers to a terrifying adumbration by Haldane: 'Stars occasionally burst, expanding enormously, giving out a vast amount of heat, and then dying down again. No one knows why this occurs, but it does seem to happen to stars not at all unlike the sun. If it happened to the sun, the earth would stand as much chance of survival as a butterfly in a furnace' ('The Last Judgment', *Possible Worlds*, p. 290).

24 *circumambient*: encompassing, like the space circumfusing the earth. Cf. Coleridge, 'Limbo' (1817–18), l. 34: 'Whose circumambience doth these ghosts enthrall'.

25–6 *Loose the full radiance . . . radiance in*: 'Astronomical evidence seems to leave practically no doubt that in the so-called *white dwarf* stars the density of matter far transcends anything of which we have terrestrial experience; in the Companion of Sirius, for example, the density is about a ton to the cubic inch' (Eddington, *Nature of the Physical World*, p. 203). Eddington discusses the 'Contraction Hypothesis' in *Stars and Atoms* (1927), pp. 94–8, and radiation of mass, pp. 113–21. The poem was written ten years before scientists produced equations for the nuclear processes of the sun, but it was known that the sun was 'packed with mass' – some 2,000 quadrillion tons of energy – and that 'the heat emitted by the sun each year has a mass of 120 billion tons' (*Stars and Atoms*, p. 98).

The sole surviving manuscript draft of this stanza incorporates an interesting variant of l. 25, '**Shall flame that radiance his whole mass can win**'.

26 that] his *MS, Listen*

27–8 *Flame far too hot . . . never to be told*: clinches the argument by drawing attention to the fact that the poet's passion is not unlike the energy of the sun. He seeks to turn the lover's attention away from her terrors and towards his own fear of expressing love. The fate of the sun could well be that of the Companion of Sirius, with massive energy (cf. ll. 25–6 and note) but no radiation. Such an extraordinary star 'may be in an awkward predicament – it will be losing heat continually *but will not have enough energy to cool down . . .*,' observes Eddington. 'The final fate of the white dwarf is to become at the same time the hottest and the coldest matter in the universe . . . Because the star is intensely hot it has enough energy to cool down if it wants to; because it is so intensely cold it has stopped radiating and no longer wants to grow any colder' (*Stars and Atoms*, pp. 124,

127). WE frames that astonishing paradox in a witty conceit; it is a version of wishing not to keep blowing hot and cold but to fulfil his love.

Letter II

First published, as 'Letter', in *Cambridge Review* 49 (6 June 1928), 485; reprinted in *Cambridge Poetry 1929*.

CP: 'Which ravishes and re-begets me. The torch crumbles each fresco.' *Stocks:* the early race that made the pictures. 'The greater part of the frescoes has gone. Those whom neither lust nor . . .' are compared to the fresco situation since they forget. The shifting sand is meant to imply that the cave may fall in and bury the explorer. They have a ground in common only so long as there is something new to find out about each other.

For *Listen* WE wrote: 'But here the young couple are merely curious about each other, therefore lose interest in whatever they think they have found out; a nagging process.'

In his letter to Maxwell-Mahon (6 November 1967), WE conceded: 'I daresay the language is rather too violent for the subject, another unsatisfactory student love affair, but they seemed to me upsetting enough at the time.'

In *The Ambiguity of William Empson*, WE commented:

Now I want to read one or two of these early poems which are mostly love poems, very much boy is afraid of girl – finding difficulties – finding that everything ties you up. Life is such that it is almost impossible to move, this Kafka sentiment knocking about a great deal. And this kind of point is of course needed to explain what is there, otherwise it would be a fairly empty puzzle, I think. And *Letter II* has to be described I think as making too much fuss, the young people are inquisitive about each other, they want to know about each other and after they've found out it's no longer interesting. And so they are going to be left feeling depressed at the end, and you may say this is nothing to make so much fuss about – but I don't know, these things do feel painful to young people at the time after all. The comparison is to Lascaux and so on – you are discovering the caves left by pre-historic man and as you let the light in they are destroyed, they are no longer interesting, and that goes on until the last verse . . . , if you crumple up paper and light it, the sparks moving about in the paper are like stars looking about for something more to burn. The emptiness becomes much larger and of course the acres are very small areas where they might find a bit more to burn.

Here WE in 1977 referred the central metaphor to the great caves at Lascaux in the Dordogne; and yet they were not discovered until 1939. However, he did possess a copy (now in the Houghton Library, Harvard) of a guidebook by the explorer and prehistorian, the Abbé Henri Breuil (1877–1961), *Les Peintures et Gravures pariétales de la Caverne de Niaux (Ariège)* (Toulouse: Imprimerie Edouard Privat, n.d.), which would indicate that he might have visited Niaux in southern France, and maybe other caves in the Pyrenees (notably Altamira), perhaps in Summer 1927. In Summer 1953, he was to take his wife and children for a camping holiday in the Dordogne.

The syntax and plurisignification are discussed by Vickery in 'On First Reading Empson's "Letter II"'. See also Willis, pp. 159–64; Ricks, pp. 193–5; *TGA*, pp. 86–9.

2–3 *ravishes / Rebegets*: presumably WE is echoing Donne's plaint, in 'A Nocturnal upon S. Lucy's Day, being the shortest day', ll. 17–18, of having been annihilated by love: 'He ruined me, and I am re-begot / Of absence, darkness, death; things which are not.'

4 each] their *Listen*

6 remains,] remains *CP 1949*

8 that the golden] the gold *1928, 1929, CP 1949*. While correcting the page proofs for *CP*, WE jotted at the foot of the page: '**I no longer see what the point was in throwing away the rhythm unnecessarily there**' (Reading). His revised version, though regularizing the metre, does away with an original ambiguity which allowed that (i) primitive art is a lily that needs no gilding (a reading which implies that 'When' in l. 6 is to be treated as a subordinate conjunction governing the clauses of both 6–7 and 8), and (ii) the embellished picture-frame would scorn to set off primeval pictures. This metaphor is developed in references in ll. 2, 6, 8 and 9.

11 terms their] terms, what *1928, 1929*

17 *Crossing and doubling*: as well as functioning as descriptive epithets (the line adds up to a compounded modifier governing 'stars' in the following line), these present participles allow for a pun on *double-crossing* which accords with the sense of persecution and flight conveyed by 'hounded' and 'desperate'.

17 *many-fingered*: recalling the classical epithet for the dawn, 'rosy-fingered', this governs 'stars' in the following line. The kenning, which incorporates a pun on 'light-fingered', is not original to WE, though he may have been unaware of previous instances. Mostly, the phrase has been employed literally to describe foliage, as by F. W. Faber in 'The Mourner's Dream' ('many-fingered cedars'), or else other buds and sprouts: R. W. Buchanan speaks of the 'silent many-fingered grass' in 'The Swallows'; though F. H. French makes use of the image as an insinuating trope in 'The Battle of the Marne' ('It is the race creates our soul / By touches many-fingered'). But cf. George MacDonald, 'Summer' (*A Threefold Cord*), ll. 1–2: 'Summer, sweet Summer, many-fingered Summer! / We hold thee very dear, as well we may'.

18 *worms dying in flower*: '**The phrase "worms dying in flower"** . . . **is an attempt**

at describing the final movement of the sparks when you burn a crumpled piece of paper (please light one and watch it); I had no idea of recalling what previous poets had said about glow-worms etc. . . .' (WE letter to Maxwell-Mahon, 6 November 1967). However, WE must also be recalling the Son's declaration to the Father that he will presently drive the rebel angels down to an immutable hell – 'To their prepared ill mansion . . . / To chains of darkness, and the undying worm' (*PL*, VI.738–9). The phrase may also contain a nod to Blake's lyric 'The Sick Rose' ('O Rose, thou art sick, / The invisible worm . . .').

19 *Ashed paper*: torch-light, literally burning paper.

19–20 *bounded / Darkness*: God the Son boasts that although he suffers himself to be sacrificed, he will rise again victorious, vanquishing death: 'I through the ample air in triumph high / Shall lead hell captive maugre hell, and show / The powers of darkness bound . . .' (*PL*, III.254–6). (Cf. also *PL*, III.538–9; and Colossians 1: 13: 'power of darkness'.)

Villanelle

First published in *Cambridge Review* 50 (26 October 1928), 52; reprinted in *Cambridge Poetry 1929* and in *Recent Poetry* (1933).

On *Poetry at the Mermaid* (1961), WE observed that the villanelle was an old Italian form revived by James Joyce in *A Portrait of the Artist* (it is not clear that WE thought Joyce's poem – for we now know it was Joyce's own poem, written long before it came to be quoted in the novel – to be either ludicrous or ironic, as some commentators now argue). But the best latterday practitioner of the villanelle as a form was W. H. Auden who, in *The Sea and the Mirror* (1944), 'wiped the eye of everybody who tries to revive the villanelle. Miranda speaks a perfect villanelle. Miranda is panting . . . [and] what she speaks is a perfect villanelle. He's a wonderful technician.' In contrast to such excellence, WE said, 'My villanelle is very stiff; but it's like a tombstone – it's meant to be stiff.'

See Willis, pp. 165–73 and *TGA*, pp. 90–92.

1 *It is the pain, it is the pain, endures*: echoes Othello, who refers self-tormentingly to what he considers the necessity of killing Desdemona as a just retribution for her seeming infidelity: 'It is the cause, it is the cause, my soul. / Let me not name it to you, you chaste stars. / It is the cause . . .' (*Othello*, V.ii.1–3). In *ST* WE had commented on Othello's phrasing:

The stress may be on *it* or on *cause* . . . This favours Dr Johnson's meaning: 'It is not the act of murder that horrifies me here; it is the cause of it.' But regarding the stress as on *it* (an actor should stress both) we are made to wonder what *it* was that was *causing* the tempest in his mind; and are given only the 'irrelevant' statement that it was the *cause*. If it is necessary to find one word for what was in his mind, I should myself plump for *blood*; but it is no use assuming, for the ease of mind of the *chaste stars* of criticism, that one cause can be assigned, and one thing it is the cause of. There is no primary meaning for lack of information, and the secondary meaning, therefore, holds the focus of consciousness, that we are listening to a mind withdrawn upon itself, and baffled by its own agonies. (p. 217)

In *SCW* (p. 82), WE was to analyse the changes of meaning and connotation in 'pain', finding links between 'pain', 'pine' and 'peine' – as in the torture of *peine forte et dure*. (See also Babette Deutsch, *Poetry in Our Time* (New York, 1957), p. 213.)
2 *chemic*: an archaic adjective which presumably echoes Donne's substantive usage in 'Love's Alchemy', when lamenting the inconstancy of love: 'And as no chemic yet the elixir got, / But glorifies his pregnant pot, / If by the way to him befall / Some odoriferous thing, or medicinal, / So, lovers dream a rich and long delight, / But get a winter-seeming summer's night' (ll. 7–12).
3 *Poise of my hands*: cf. Edward Dowden, 'Leonardo's "Monna Lisa"', ll. 6–8: 'Tangle the sense no more lest I should hate / Thy delicate tyranny, the inviolate / Poise of thy folded hands'. Perhaps cf. too WE's comments on a collection of stories by William Fryer Harvey, *The Beast with Five Fingers and Other Tales* (London, 1928): '**The name story** [which was later made into a film starring Peter Lorre] **is about a blind man who concentrated all his sensitivity on his hand, so that it begins to do automatic writing, acquires an Ur-soul, and finally outlives him**' (*Granta*, 1 June 1928; *E in G*, p. 61).
11 *your grace safely by heart I knew*: 'grace' puns on the senses of (i) charm, attractiveness, and (ii) prayer said before or after a meal.
14 *My heart pumps yet the poison draught of you*: cf. Shakespeare's Sonnet 118, l. 14: 'Drugs poison him that so fell sick of you'; he too mentions 'purge' (l. 4). Both 'poison' and 'purge' suggest an antitoxin. WE uses the disease conceit again in 'Missing Dates' and 'Advice'.
16 *immures*: literally, walls in, surrounds with a wall; figuratively, excludes, shuts off or secludes *from*.

Arachne

First published in *Cambridge Review* 49 (6 June 1928), 490; reprinted in *Cambridge Poetry 1929* and *Recent Poetry* (1933).
    This poem is WE's first achievement in a form he favoured, terza rima; the others are 'The Scales', 'Your Teeth are Ivory Towers', 'Reflection from Rochester' and 'Courage means Running'.

CP: **The caves of cavemen are thought of as by the sea to escape the savage creatures inland. 'Man lives between the contradictory absolutes of philosophy,** the one and the many, etc. As king spider man walks delicately between two elements, avoiding the enemies which live in both. Man must dance, etc. Human society is placed in this matter like individual men, the atoms who make up its bubble.' The spider's legs push down the unbroken surface of the water like a soft carpet, which brings in the surface-tension idea. The bubble surface is called land, the thin fertile surface of the earth, because the bubble is the globe of the world. The water saves the soap because the soap alone couldn't make a bubble. Arachne was a queen spider and disastrously proud.

For his senior colleague Rintaro Fukuhara, at *Tokyo* Bunrika *Daigaku* (Tokyo University of Literature and Science) in 1933 or 1934, WE scribbled marginal glosses to the poem in his copy of *Recent Poetry* (p. 50). That page, with WE's holograph annotations, was photographically reproduced by Fukuhara on the front page of the Japanese journal *Rising Generation* 71:10 (15 August 1934); and then set in a slightly confused and confusing tabular form which melds certain discrete parts of WE's garnish of glosses for the sake of convenience (though keyed to the text by line numbers), in the memoir 'Mr William Empson in Japan' (p. 24). Below I separate out the glosses so as to tie them more exactly to the relevant passages; they are identified by the abbreviation *1933*.

See Meller, 'William Empsons *Arachne*' and 'Metaphysische Liebeslyrik im Denkraum neuester *New Philosophy*: Zum *Arachne*-Gedicht', in *Das Gedicht*, pp. 208–22; Donoghue, 'Reading a Poem: Empson's "Arachne" '; Willis, pp. 173–81; Maxwell-Mahon, 'Early Poetry of Empson', pp. 14–15; Ricks, pp. 195–7; Wain, pp. 296–8; *TGA*, pp. 92–5.

Arachne makes a further showing in 'Bacchus', l. 83.

1 *Twixt devil and deep sea*: proverbial, meaning to find oneself between two difficulties that are equally dangerous (as between Scylla and Charybdis): *OED* 'devil', 22b.

1–6 *man hacks . . . pin-point extremes*: 'primitive cavemen on the shore between sea and wild animals in the forest[.] Man can only live on surfaces, between opposites each of which would destroy him' *1933*.

2 *one, many*: 'The supreme example of the problem of the One and the Many was given by the Logos who was an individual man' (*Pastoral*, p. 81).

3 *Earth's vast hot iron*: the innermost core of the earth is solid iron crystal.

3 *waves*:] waves. *1928, 1929*

4–5 *King spider . . . god and beast avoid*: Haldane remarked upon the moral of the water surface: 'There is a force which is as formidable to an insect as gravitation to a mammal. This is surface tension . . . An insect going for a drink is in as great danger as a man leaning over a precipice in search of food. If it once falls into the grip of the surface tension of the water – that is to say, gets wet – it is likely to remain so until it drowns. A few insects, such as water-beetles, contrive to be unwettable, the majority keep well away from their drink by means of a long proboscis' ('On Being the Right Size', *Possible Worlds*, pp. 19–20; Empson's Basic English version of that passage is in *The Outlook of Science*, p. 48). Willis (p. 179) compares WE's arachnid with Pope's well-balanced spider in *Essay on Man*, 'Epistle I', ll. 217–18. Cf. also 'Sea Voyage', l. 8.

4 streams:] streams; *1928*, *1929*

5 *Must bird and fish, must god and beast*: cf. Pope's invocation of the Divine dispensation, in *Essay on Man*, Epistle I.237–41: 'Vast Chain of Being, which from God began, / Natures ethereal, human, angel, man, / Beast, bird, fish, insect, what no eye can see, / No glass can reach! from Infinite to thee, / From thee to nothing.'

5 avoid:] avoid; *1928*, *1929*

6 *Dance, like nine angels, on pin-point extremes*: the quodlibet 'How many angels can dance on the point of a pin (or needle)?', used to snub pedantry or pettifogging, is attributed to various medieval theologians: see especially Sir Gurney Benham, who finds evidence to pin it to Aquinas (*Benham's Book of Quotations* (London, 1948), 493a). In post-canonical and apocalyptic writings, the angels are ranked in various orders; the best-known hierarchy of nine orders is that popularized by Dionysius the Pseudo-Areopagite (*c.* early fifth century), in chapter 15 of his *De coelesti hierarchia* (*On the Celestial Hierarchy*).

8 *Tribe-membrane . . . stands*:

membrane – surface of living tissue; life dependant on surface reactions (like osmosis making sap rise)

tribe – taken as a unity made by mutual tensions – one part removed society would break up helplessly – hence like a membrane and like a bubble *1933*

For an account of WE's use of Cornford's theory of the significance of *phusis* in primitive tribal society, see notes on 'High Dive', l. 27, and 'Letter I', ll. 16–18, 17. Cf. ll. 8–9 to 'Camping Out', l. 8.

10 *Bubbles gleam . . . depth of lands*: 'shallow soil which makes rapid growth of some plants[:] the bubble has already been compared to the earth. The colour effects from interference of light come when it is two molecules thick' *1933*. Soap bubbles may iridesce because of the differing thicknesses of the film. For bubbles, cf. 'Plenum and Vacuum', l. 2, and 'Earth has Shrunk in the Wash', l. 6.

11–12 *But two . . . / Two molecules*: according to Haldane in 'On Scales', the scientists 'Gorter and Grendel, and Flicke and Morse, have shown by quite independent methods that the oily film surrounding a red blood corpuscle is just two molecules thick' (*Possible Worlds*, p. 6). The reference in l. 14 to 'Hydroptic soap' must actually suggest a change of metaphorical tack – or else the logic fails – for to manage the effect of soap and water, one needs a vast array of molecules. Perhaps WE is suggesting that what soap is to water at the molecular level, so woman is to man at the emotional level: the combination of man and woman is the basic building block of society, just as molecules of water and soap must come together to form bubbles. See note to ll. 13–14. Again, cf. 'Camping Out', l. 8.

13–14 *We two suffice . . . water saves*: '**The two molecules of thickness then compared to the sexual pair as basis of society. Bubble = soap and water. [T]he woman is then called soap and the man water[;] soap alone couldn't make a bubble**' *1933*.

14 *Hydroptic*: hydropic, dropsical; Donne uses the word both figuratively in his letters (when referring to himself as afflicted by 'an hydroptique immoderate desire of humane learning and languages'), and literally – this is WE's likeliest point of reference, given the context of a withdrawal, withholding or retention of moisture – in 'A Nocturnal upon S. Lucy's Day', ll. 5–6: 'The world's whole sap is sunk: / The general balm th'hydroptic earth hath drunk'.

15 *Male spiders . . . early slain*: '**The jump from woman as soap molecule to woman as female spider (bigger than male and eats it after fertilizing) depends on the soap molecule being bigger than the water one. This rather weak jump makes the end too personal beside the rest**' *1933*. Darwin, confronted with the evidence of the extreme inequality of size between the sexes of the spiders, the cautious little male and the big, coy, cannibalistic female, seems to have favoured the explanation that male spiders – in order to cope with females who favour mating and feeding in one fell go – gradually adapted into a diminutive race, 'until at last they would dwindle to the smallest possible size compatible with the exercise of the generative functions' (*Works of Charles Darwin*, ed. Barrett and Freeman, Vol. 22: *The Descent of Man, and Selection in relation to Sex*, Part Two (London, 1989), pp. 282–3).

The Scales

Probably written in 1929; first published, with the blank title 'Poem', in *Experiment* no. 6 (October 1930), p. 12; reprinted, as 'Poem', in *New Signatures* (1932) and *P 1934*.

CP: **Alice in Wonderland, Ulysses appearing to Nausicaa, and the jackal sandhole through which the heroes escaped in Rider Haggard's** *King Solomon's Mines. At your side* **means on the mountains compared to her, first seeming on toy scale then full size; the** *castle* **is a toy sand-castle, and the tunnels on either scale stand for difficulties of communication; then the Nile takes on the tunnel symbolism as being for long unknown up country.**

For *Listen* WE noted: '*Scales* – in the sense of the first estimate of size which decides what kind of tool to use; an excuse to a woman for not showing enough love.'

Four pages of manuscript draft are preserved at Houghton. *MS1* has rough drafts of ll. 1–9; *MS2* is a good draft, with minor emendations, of ll. 1–6. *MS3* is a fair draft of the full poem, with minor changes (including this interesting deleted reading of the opening phrase: '**With proper scale I'd pat**'). *MS4* has the complete poem, with minimal variant readings including the opening phrase as: '**The proper style would pat you on the head**'. *MS3* has a draft of the poem 'The Extasie'. *MS1* also includes at the head of the sheet the following notations: '**mountains turn pink | railway tunnel | sand | delta. | Nile fertile behind | dado, nurse | King S's mines. | jackal**'. *MS1* of 'Insomnia', which was evidently written at about the same time as 'The Scales' (as well as 'Camping Out'), includes these notes: '**Delta | Solomon's Mines | Sandcastle tunnels | Australia | jackal**'.

Willis's exposition of the poem (pp. 181–7) includes the remark that a 'Freudian interpretation of the passage, involving trains, tunnels, height, curves, and fingers, seems possible since Empson's note clearly equates the girl and the mountain or castle' (p. 185); furthermore: 'As a supplication to a coy or prudish mistress the poem would take its place with "Invitation [to Juno]", and "Letter I". If the reader protests against a sexual reading, he may decide "Scales" is another examination of the problem of epistemology or metaphysics . . . But whether or not the knowledge sought is intellectual or carnal, the proper scale in life or love is essential to the undertaking' (p. 187). See also Morelli, pp. 81–5; Ricks, pp. 197–9; *TGA*, pp. 95–9.

1 *proper scale*: cf. Haldane's essay 'On Scales', in *Possible Worlds*, and 'Sleeping out in a College Cloister', ll. 12–14 and note.

1 *pat you on the head*: the obvious primary sense relates to the patronizing mode of offering congratulations – as to a child; but cf. also 'The World's End', l. 7.

2 *Alice showed her pup Ulysses' bough*: in chapter 4 of *Alice's Adventures in Wonderland*, the shrunken Alice, fearful of an 'enormous' galumphing puppy, takes shelter behind a thistle and diverts the barking beast by throwing a stick for it; when the 'pup' seems to be quite worn out, she makes her escape. ' "And yet what a dear little puppy it was!" said Alice . . . "I should have liked teaching it tricks very much, if – if only I'd been the right size to do it!' WE conflates Alice's stick with the branch that Odysseus puts to use on the sandy beach to shield (or 'protect') his nakedness from the gaze of Nausicaa: 'the goodly Odysseus came forth from beneath the bushes, and with his stout hand he broke from the thick wood a leafy branch, that he might hold it about him and hide therewith his nakedness' (*The Odyssey*, VI.127–9, trans. A. T. Murray (1919), vol. I, p. 215).

5–6 *dado . . . nurse*: much on WE's mind during his final year at Cambridge; not long before writing this poem (it is reasonable to assume), he had protested, in a review of *As You Like It*:

I can explain my feelings so little about this I must just say what they were; I was terribly depressed . . . Why is it that seeing Shakespeare . . . at the Festival Theatre is like hearing your love-letters read out in a divorce court: you feel keenly your own past lack of judgment, and it might all have been written by Sir James Barrie?

Partly because the guts are taken out . . . one ought to feel it was *brave* of them all to romp like that; Nature was not really kindly, and Nurse not in reserve. The effect of the (extremely beautiful) black and white settings . . . was firstly to give me a real shock of terror at the idea of camping out without any conveniences in all that snow, and then to make me think of it all as happening on a nursery dado or in an aquarium. (*Granta* (16 November 1928); *E in G*, p. 86)

See also 'Essay', l. 14 and note.
8 *tunnels*: cf. 'The Ants', l. 1, 'Earth has Shrunk in the Wash', l. 22, and 'Letter IV', l. 4.
10–12 *the tunnels hide . . . jackal sandhole*: in chapter XVI of Rider Haggard's *King Solomon's Mines* (1886), Quartermain and his companions penetrate to the place of death of the 'white forms' of the petrified kings of Kukuanaland: 'They were human forms indeed, or rather had been human forms; now they were *stalactites* . . . preserved for ever by the silicious fluid . . . wrapped in a shroud of ice-like spar, through which the features could be dimly made out . . .' (*King Solomon's Mines*, ed. Dennis Butts (Oxford, 1989), p. 268). Solomon's treasure – diamonds, gold, ivory – lies in the next chamber, where the adventurers are trapped by the evil Gagool and so doomed to die of asphyxiation until they discover a jackal hole at the end of a tunnel (pp. 297–8).
14 *Delta*: the triangular tract of alluvial land at the mouth of the Nile, so named by Herodotus because of its resemblance to a triangle, i.e. the form of the Greek letter; cf. 'Four Legs, Two Legs, Three Legs', l. 3.

Essay

First published in *Magdalene College Magazine* no. 61 (June 1929), 79. The text in this edition incorporates two emendations (ll. 21–22) that Empson wrote by hand on a copy of the poem torn from a copy of the magazine (the original readings cited as *Magazine*), in the Empson Papers.

The 'Essay' from which this poem – the last WE published while an undergraduate – takes its title is likely to have been the following piece, which may have been written as part of the emergent *Seven Types*. June 1929 was to be his last month at the university: see 'Warning to undergraduates'. We can only speculate about why WE did not publish this short essay: perhaps he lost it among his papers during his removal to London; perhaps he could not find a fit place for it in his scheme of literary ambiguities; or perhaps he was better pleased with the way this poem took up the idea of the arch, even though he would later omit it from his collected poems:

The Latin word from which our word *arch* was derived meant a bent bow, a static order maintained by the exercise of force; it then came to mean an arch in architecture, an arrangement by which unmortared stones would stand together up in the air; from both these it suggested human society, in which free men of their own choice are held together in an order which places them higher than they could stand alone, indeed places them in a way that might seem against their nature. In so far as they make a bridge the idea is of the state poised over the chaos of nature, in so far as they make a roof the idea is of the state as a protection for the speaker, without which he could not live, but with which, thinking of himself as an individual, he is not at the moment identifying himself (he is not part of the arch but underneath it). I suppose the grandest single flash of poetry from this association was Antony's

> Let Rome in Tyber melt, and the wide Arch
> Of the raing'd Empire fall. Heere is my space (*A & C.*, I.i.35–36)

The grandeur of Rome is associated with the arches of its remaining buildings; Rome is particularly associated with the idea of freedom and order from arches; and the word *raing'd* suggests the orderly placing of the stones. Then the *raing'd empire* is thought of as a single *arch*, stretching over the whole world, like the canopy of heaven; the impossibility of the thing is godlike; *Empire* is connected with 'Empyrean'; and it is the Rome that Antony abandons which keeps the sky from falling. Further the arch is over the Tiber; the pax Romana is balanced over a rush to destruction, as the arch of heaven is over the abyss; the arch here also becomes the rainbow, the sign of God's promise that the earth should never be drowned again, nor Rome melt in Tiber; hence the overtone of blasphemy. *Raing'd* means widespread, in order, fitting together, fitting one above another (in a hierarchy) and drawn up like an army prepared for war; the next phrase, that the person of Cleopatra was his space (Donne uses the same notion) implies that the Roman social order corresponds to the order made by God when he created space itself out of chaos; Antony does not even want three dimensions if they mean the possibility of separation. The idea behind Shakespeare's political writing, it has been well said, is 'an everpresent sense of the breaking of the flood-gates'; the whole force of this is invoked by Antony, and disastrously made nothing by comparison with Cleopatra.

> no man is the lord of anything
> Though in and of him there be much consisting
> Till he communicate his parts to others:
> Nor doth he of himself know them for aught
> Till he behold them form'd in the applause
> Where they're extended; who, like an arch, reverberate

The voice again, or like a gate of steel
Fronting the sun, receives and renders back
His figure and his heat.   [*Troilus and Cressida*, III.iii. 10–18]

This version explains the idea of the arch almost too clearly and objectively to make good poetry; Shakespeare was well aware what he was doing with it. The next simile is interesting as it brings in the sun as symbol of the god-like hero, of Achilles; it is not only ordinary men, it is the very heroes of tragedies themselves, who need to be at peace with the social order (though one would no more expect them to need this than the sun to need reflecting).

Antony's line contrasts the arch of society with the love of one woman, and the metaphor elsewhere shows some inclination to spread onto both cases. Brachiano, trying to win back the White Devil, says

> Be thou at peace with me, let all the world
> Threaten the cannon.
> *Flamineo.*   Mark his penitence.
> Best natures do commit the grossest faults,
> When they're given o'er to jealousy, as best wine,
> Dying, makes strongest vinegar. I'll tell you
> The sea's more rough and raging than calm rivers
> But not so sweet nor wholesome. A quiet woman
> Is a still water under a great bridge;
> A man may shoot her safely.   [*The White Devil*, IV.ii. 169–77]

The arch of the bridge, in these lovely lines, seems a bitter metaphor for the vagina, rather as a harlot was called a 'road'. (He is advising them not to be great and dignified but kind and cautious; and his suicidal contempt of the advice shows through his expression of it.)

I suspect that there is a trace of this idea in two Shakespearean passages, where the idea of unfaithfulness is connected with the contrast between earth and the arch of heaven: *Cymbeline* I.vi.30 and *Troilus* V.ii.140.

Clearly when the symbol from the Latin arch has reached this degree of elaboration it has a great deal to do with the Greek one; the social order is connected by a pun with the ruler of the society. This is useful for poetry because it unites opposite ideas already closely connected; the king and the people he represents, the tribe and the totem which is at once a visible object and its life-blood, the arch and the key-stone without which it falls to the ground.

As a matter of the history of an English word, it seems to be true that *arch* took on this wealth of association from a sort of pun between the Latin and Greek forms, with various allied Gothonic forms to give body. But as the complex is useful, so the pun is natural; the original Greek, meaning both a principal and a principle, with the idea of *arch*aic, of tradition, thrown in, itself contains it; and Latin combines the *arcus* of archers, also *arca* meaning a (curved) roofed box or ark (the outside structure rather than the fact of containing something), with *arx* which is the chief of the fortifications.

It is from this complex of ideas, too, that references to the arches of brows take their importance: this arch guards the window of the soul and the seat of the problem is consciousness; the chief means of knowledge by and of the owner; it is compared to the arch of buildings, the social order, and the order of the universe, a thing it is nearly always useful for a poet to do.

3 *Bows of Promise*: God's covenant with Noah, sealed with a rainbow, in Gen. 9: 12–17. Cf. 'Laus Melpomines', l. 6, and 'Doctrinal Point', l. 25.

4–6 *Norman . . . / Jerked into Gothic . . . into spires*: Norman architecture, which flourished in England 1066–*c*.1150, is a developed form of the Romanesque school, as evidenced in many of the great churches of England including Winchester, Worcester, Gloucester, Bury St Edmunds, Norwich and Ely. Ornamentation often takes geometric forms such as the chevron or zigzag, stars and cables. WE's lines offer an epitome of the development of English ecclesiastical architecture from the Norman invasion, through Early English and Decorated, and so culminating in the vertiginous vaults of the Perpendicular period (1377–1546). Cf. 'Letter III', l. 11.

14 *dado*: 'any lining, painting or papering of the lower part of an interior wall, of a different material or colour from that of the upper part' (*OED*). WE may have passed his youngest years in a nursery with a picturesque dado showing a landscape, or else he favoured the idea of a beautiful distant prospect as being nature's dado. Cf. 'The Scales', l. 5 and note.

15 *Bonzo*: 'the figure of a comically-shaped puppy which came into vogue through a series of drawings by G. E. Studdy (the first of which appeared in *The Sketch* 8 Nov. 1922), and is used in various forms, as toys, etc.' (*OED*).

21 let him not aim] leave him not aimed *Magazine*

21 *at Hercules*: see 'Sea Voyage', note to l. 12.

22 casual] critical *Magazine*

26 *palfrey*: saddle-horse (traditionally or poetically ridden by a damsel).

27 *Sancho Panza*: the rustic who acts as Don Quixote's servant in Cervantes' *Don Quixote de la Mancha* (1605). See WE's later reflections on Cervantes' use of heroic and pastoral:

One cause of the range of *Don Quixote*, the skyline beyond skyline of its irony, is that though mock-heroic it is straight pastoral; only at the second level, rather as the heroic becomes genuine, does the pastoral become mock . . . the two conventions are alike, so that the book puzzles us between them; we cannot think one fatuous and not the other . . . This makes the satire seem more important by making his heroism less unreal, as do the cautiously implied comparisons of him to Christ, which make him the fool who becomes the judge. ('The Beggar's Opera', *Pastoral*, pp. 161–2)

Legal Fiction

First published in *Cambridge Review* 50 (30 November 1928), 171; reprinted in *Cambridge Poetry 1929*.

This poem explores the pragmatic, moral and eschatological ramifications of private property rights in land, taking its inspiration from the medieval Latin maxim *Cuius est solum, eius est usque ad coelum et ad inferos*: the owner of the soil has a prima facie ownership of everything reaching up to the heavens and down to the depths of the earth. It has always been a legal fiction.

On the recording *The Poems of William Empson* (1952), WE remarked that 'Legal Fiction'

has been quite well liked and used in anthologies, which I rather boast of because it is an almost pure case of the formula, that is, it carries an argument to absurdity and uses that to express a conflict of judgement. The law that ownership of land extends above and below ground is made to seem fantastic, but not because it is considered as trivial nor yet as simply wrong; so far from that, because it is so normal to the human mind; and by the way the phrase 'real estate of mind', in the poem [l. 2], is meant to be a pun combining 'state of mind' with 'real estate'. The argument is not meant to come down on either side; the case in favour of the independent peasant and the landed proprietor is I think there all right. There is a doubt in the grammar whether these characters meet in Hell or only the bits of land they own meet in Hell (which was pointed out to me by my farming brother) but that only carries the thing further. The last lines actually get their point from going outside the legal argument, because the *end* suggested is the death of all mortal creatures as well as the geometrical end of the cone driven through the earth; but that is considered fair in metaphysical poetry, and Donne himself often does it.

On an untidily handwritten page of notes (his prompt-script for a poetry reading at the launch of an unidentified anthology), WE observed further: 'Next I want to give you my political poem, which turned out useful. The Chinese Communist students felt it to show that my heart was in the right place. It is called LF, and the fiction is that if you own land outright you own a cone from the centre of the earth to the stars. Of course when peasants were fighting big landowners [in China after the Communist takeover in 1949] both of them thought of land like this. The poem only says that the belief though strange is deeply rooted' (Empson Papers).

For *Listen* he noted, 'As this has been found all right by both Chinese Communist students and American stratosphere lawyers I can claim it doesn't need explaining.'

Furthermore, in a reading of his poetry at an Oxford University summer school (of unknown date, in the 1960s), WE remarked that this was 'just a piece of political poetry', and went on to describe himself as

the son of a Yorkshire landowner who actually did, as he grew older, get more and more puzzled by the belief that some wicked coal mine was sending tunnels under his land . . . It was extraordinarily difficult to prove that anyone was mining under his land, and so claim royalties; and it occupied his mind a good deal. As for owning the air above, this really did happen when I was still a child. General Pitt-Rivers, a great archaeologist, who had a large estate in Wiltshire, shot down – just before the First World War – a government aeroplane with his elephant gun. He killed the pilot, of course, and was tried for murder at Winchester Assizes and was let off on the grounds that the man was trespassing. So the law had to be altered. (tape recording courtesy of Roma Gill)

The circumstantial detail of the anecdote is so vivid as to make it sound authentic, but no such incident has been identified: it was probably a piece of schoolboy folklore that WE picked up at Winchester. See Kevin Gray, 'Property in thin air', *Cambridge Law Journal* 50: 2 (July 1991), pp. 252–307.

On *Harvard*, where WE opened his remarks by referring to this as 'a slight poem, in a way', he observed: 'In those days, in the London *New Statesman*, a left-wing weekly magazine, you had a lady called "Sagittarius", who wrote exactly this kind of thing: she wrote witty comparisons in tidy rhyming verse which drove home the socialist policies of the magazine. Why is this not a poem by Sagittarius? I think it's rather hard to say. I do think – though her work was perfectly all right – this breathes a larger air: I would claim that, but I don't know how I could prove it to you.' He rejoiced in the memory that the poem had earned the approval of his Chinese communist students in the early 1950s; furthermore: 'I was approached by a group of American international lawyers who were doing a brochure about space travel, and they paid me five dollars – five dollars only, I regret to say – to print this poem at the top of their immensely glossy brochure . . . not of course because they thought it was beautiful but because they thought it was funny. The point of this brochure was to do with flying in the stratosphere . . . Well now, the number of poems which satisfy both American international lawyers and Chinese communist students is not very large.'

See Morelli, pp. 115–17; Drew, with Sweeney, *Directions in Modern Poetry*, pp. 204–7; Richards, ' "How Does a Poem Know When It Is Finished?" ', in *Poetries and Sciences*, pp. 115–18 (see Appendix 4 for an extract); Touster, 'Empson's "Legal Fiction" '; Willis, pp. 187–94; *TGA*, pp. 99–103; Hawkes, 'Take me to your Leda', in *Meaning by Shakespeare*.

The poem was parodied by WE's friend Hugh Sykes Davies (later a Fellow of St John's College, Cambridge), in topical verses (*Cambridge Review* 51 (1 November 1929), 74) which express indignation at WE's fate (see 'Warning to undergraduates'):

Hommage

(St Augustine confesses that, when a youth, he stole pears from an orchard)

Your well fenced out real estate of mind
Proves sorry legal fiction, Fancy's blind.
Tongue's incubus, friend's-anger's-longer check
Still sits upon, not lets depict thy wreck.
No high-flat of the nomad citizen
Looked over here, or plunder-orchard boys
But from within some scullion-denizen
Slops, petty theft, or rancour most, enjoys?
For householders will then be prey for thieves
When magistrate the stolen goods receives.

TITLE: '*Legal fiction* is used colloquially as a facetious euphemism for an untruth' (J. E. S. Simon, 'English Idioms from the Law', *Law Quarterly Review* 76 (April 1960), 304); 'an assertion accepted as true (though probably fictitious) to achieve a useful purpose, esp. in legal matters' (*The Oxford Encyclopedic English Dictionary*, ed. Joyce M. Hawkins and Robert Allen (Oxford, 1991)). Given that this poem functions in part as a wry elegy for his father, it is likely that WE had in mind Stephen Dedalus's observation, in 'Scylla and Charybdis': 'Paternity may be a legal fiction' (*Ulysses*).

7 part of] **part is of** *1929* (presumably a printing error)

9 *owners*: in his commentary at Oxford, WE remarked that his brother Arthur, who owned and farmed the family estates in Yorkshire, once wrote to say there ought to be an apostrophe to this word (meaning that the lands of all owners meet at the centre); but WE sent back a missive, '**rather triumphantly, to say they would have to settle that amongst themselves.**'

10 *exclusive conclave*: Satan and his peers are given to hold their council, an 'infernal court', at the 'high capital' Pandaemonium: 'The great seraphic lords and cherubim / In close recess and secret conclave sat' (*PL*, I.794–95).

13 *the lighthouse beam you own*: cf. Mrs Ramsey's crepuscular meditations, in Virginia Woolf, *To the Lighthouse* (London, 1927). WE wrote about Mrs Ramsey's epiphany, in 'Virginia Woolf' (1931):

The Lighthouse becomes a symbol of energies at the basis of human life, which support and exclude the understanding. Mrs Ramsey sets herself going like the lighthouse to sustain her party, and it is for this reason that the pulse is like a flame. Or one may say that the Lighthouse has at times been the symbol of reason and male power of setting large-scale things in order (for it is in sight of the Lighthouse that Mr Bankes and Mr Tansley go and talk politics on the terrace after dinner, as if they had gone on to the bridge of the ship to take their bearings), and it is then with a sort of feminist triumph that it becomes a symbol of Mrs Ramsey. (*A*, p. 444)

14 *Lucifer*: Lucifer, or Satan, may also be Hesperus, the morning star, which is associated with death in the *Aeneid*: see Daniel Gillis, *Eros and Death in the 'Aeneid'* (Rome, 1983), pp. 62–3. Otherwise, Milton's Satan is likened to 'a comet' at *PL*, II.708.

15 *your dark central cone*: cf. Mrs Ramsey's reference to 'a wedge of darkness' (*To the Lighthouse*); and A. E. Housman's use of a similar conceit, describing not a sectioned earth but the shadow of the orbiting earth which he sees as a dunce's cap, in *Last Poems* (1922), XXXVI (to which he later gave the parable-title 'Revolution'), ll. 6–8: 'Safe to the Indies has the earth conveyed / The vast and moon-eclipsing cone of night, / Her towering foolscap of eternal shade.'

16 *Wavers, a candle's shadow, at the end*: the last line, WE remarked on *Contemporary Poets Reading Their Own Poems*, 'throws the conceit away': it has to do with 'the death of the owner as well as the geometrical centre'. On *Harvard*, he enlarged: ' "at the end", of course, means you can't take it with you: it envisages the man's death as well as the geometrical point of the end of the cone. But this I think you are allowed to do; at least, Donne frequently does it in his poems. The pretence of the comparison is kept up rigidly until the last line, where it can be thrown away as a bang, so I felt that I was imitating quite exactly there.' Cf. Alice's nervousness, after she has fallen deep into the earth, and having drunk from the bottle labelled 'DRINK ME', about her shrinking size – ' "for it might end, you know, . . . in my going out altogether, like a candle. I wonder what I should be like then?" And she tried to fancy what the flame of a candle looks like after the candle is blown out, for she could not remember ever having seen such a thing' (*Alice in Wonderland*, ch. I). Cf. also 'Earth has Shrunk in the Wash', l. 21.

Sleeping out in a College Cloister

First published, as 'Sleeping Out in the Cloister', *Magdalene College Magazine* no. 60 (March 1929), 46 (cited as *1929*); reprinted in *Venture* no. 6 (June 1930), 265; and, as 'Sleeping Out in College Cloister', in *P*.

In the same issue of the college magazine, probably by coincidence, appeared Part II of a pastiche of eighteenth-century verse by Francis Turner, a Fellow in Classics at Magdalene, called 'Dies Academica', memorializing the custom for students to sleep out in fine weather in the little 'cloister' or colonnade of the Pepys Building (which enjoys a short prospect across Second Court to the College Hall, l. 11):

But see, the *Cloister* suffers wondrous Change,
Where *Scholars* strew their simple Beds and range
Their errant Sheets upon a stony Floor,
Which, like some fleeting Hospital in War,
Grants unaccustom'd Shelter. Here, the Stars
Most visibly process, the balmy Airs
Unhamper'd pass. Romantic Dormitory,
Most happy End of our Day's History,
Thee *Somnus* claims, nor him can we detain,
Whom first we sang, when *Phoebus* trimm'd his Flame
At earliest Dawn. *Pickett* his Journey goes,
Dark Harbinger of Dark, official Close
Of this our Day; he banishes the Light,
And leaves the tranquil Court to careful *Night* . . . (ll. 246–59)

However, the reference to Tennyson in l. 29 may suggest that WE had also enjoyed the experience of sleeping out in the much grander cloister of Neville's Court at Trinity College (Tennyson's college) – where the Hall fills one width of an oblong and where the trees of the 'Backs', by the River Cam, can be perceived rustling through wrought-iron screens beneath the Wren Library, at the west side.

There are two surviving manuscript drafts of the poem: *MS1* has minor variants of the first 11 lines; *MS2* is an advanced draft of the first 25 lines.

CP: *Traditor:* betrayer. 'High hall garden' comes in *Maud* and seems meant to suggest the long tradition visible in the height of the trees.

See Willis, pp. 194–8; Thurley, pp. 44–6; *TGA*, pp. 103–7.

TITLE: **out in a College**] Out under the *MS1*
1–5 *Stevenson says . . . and the stars*:

. . . there is one stirring hour unknown to those who dwell in houses, when a wakeful influence goes abroad over the sleeping hemisphere . . .

At what inaudible summons, at what gentle touch of Nature, are all these sleepers thus recalled in the same hour to life? . . . Even shepherds and old country-folk . . . have not a guess as to the means or purpose of this nightly resurrection. Towards two in the morning they declare the thing takes place; and neither know nor inquire further. And at least it is a pleasant incident . . . We have a moment to look upon the stars, and there is a special pleasure for some minds in the reflection that we share the impulse with all outdoor creatures in our neighbourhood. (Robert Louis Stevenson, *Travels with a Donkey in the Cevennes* (1879), ed. Emma Letley (Oxford, 1992), pp. 186–7)

12–14 *Earth at a decent distance is the Globe . . . / She's terra firma*: cf. Satan's initial perception of the earth as he alights on it (*PL*, III.422–3): 'a globe far off / It seemed, now seems a boundless continent . . .'

Cf. too Haldane's discussion of the unimaginability of the parsec – the eighteen billion miles which is the unit of measure used for interstellar distances in modern astronomy – 'the earth's orbit from a parsec away would . . . look as large as a halfpenny at six thousand yards' distance . . . But although we are at home on this particular scale, of 1000 kilometres or about six hundred miles to a centimetre, as regards the earth, the average person has not yet grasped the fact that on the same scale the sun is a mile off and as large as a church' ('On Scales', *Possible Worlds*, pp. 2–3). In his review of Haldane's volume, WE noted:

Did you know that, with the scale of a map of the world, you can magnify only once downwards, before space ceases to be spacelike, and only four times upwards, before it all closes round you, and there is no more room for you at the inn? Mr Haldane does that right at the beginning of the book, to get you properly brow-beaten; he even magnifies five times, simply out of bravado, to show there is nothing left; it quite visibly makes him feel stronger, it has the cosiness of all good cosmos-myths, and one can easily know everything about a world so handy. (*E in G*, pp. 34–5)

16 were] was *1929*

19 *Rapes the mind, and will not be unimagined*: Willis notes, 'The negative of an opposite means a positive; therefore the line reads "will (or must) be imagined". An unstressed negative like this one, however, may imply the negative after all, as Empson explains in *Ambiguity* (pp. 205–14). Such a "disorder in the action of the negative" suggests the reading "will (or can) be unimagined"; that is, it can be negated. Rhetorically, Empson has startled the reader with a violent verb and immediately put him at ease with an ironic understatement. He employs an ambiguity of the seventh type in the process' (p. 196).

25 space,] *CP 1956*; space *CP*. WE instructed Parsons on 29 May 1956: '**comma after** *space*'.

26 seem] seems *1929, P*. As John Hayward pointed out in a letter to WE (21 May 1956), this verb, governed by a single noun, should properly read 'seems' – as in *1929* and *P* – and 'their' (l. 27) should read 'its' (unless the antecedent of 'their' is 'traditions'). But WE was unwilling to make such changes to the final text.

26–7 *traditions, / (Traditor)*: as WE notes, 'traditor' means betrayer, traitor (post-Augustinian Latin); he must therefore have been aware that 'tradition' and 'traditor' derive from the selfsame Latin root, *tradere*: 'to hand over, to hand on, to deliver, hence to betray'; see Eric Partridge, *Origins: A Short Etymological Dictionary of Modern English*, 4th edn. (London, 1966), p. 733; *OED*, 'traditor' and 'traitor'.

28–9 *Here jungle . . . "high hall-garden" of Lawn-Tennyson*: the speaker of Tennyson's 'Maud' (1855) complains a number of times about Maud in her 'high Hall-garden', as at l. 112 and especially in the lyric XII, ll. 412, 436. WE's emphasis on '*high*' heightens the speaker's sneering posture towards the world of expansive privilege represented by 'Hall', which Nature is smothering. (Cf. 'Courage means Running', l. 29.) The jejune joke on the name and title of Alfred, Lord Tennyson, is taken from Joyce's *Ulysses*, wherein, towards the end of 'Proteus', Stephen Dedalus toys with a footling recollection of Tennyson's 'The May Queen': 'Of all the glad new year, mother, the rum tum tiddledy tum. Lawn Tennyson, gentleman poet'; the joke is repeated – 'Lawn Tennyson, gentleman poet' – in 'Scylla and Charybdis'.

28 *campus*: strictly speaking, an open space or field, not a designation for a university (the modern usage, begun in the USA, had not yet caught on in England).

Earth has Shrunk in the Wash

First published in *Experiment* no. 2 (February 1929), 45. A typescript version, differing in a few minor particulars, was sent to Brian Howard for inclusion in a proposed anthology (School Library, Eton College, here abbreviated as *Eton*).

CP: 'Earth has Shrunk in the Wash': thus becoming an asteroid without enough gravitational force to keep its atmosphere. (Civilized refinement cutting one off from other people and scientific discovery making a strange world in which man has dangerous powers.) Douglas Fairbanks jumped from motor to express in some film, but they were going in the same direction. *Take, curve, starve, miss* are imperatives. Under the new conditions man is exposed to the dangerous rays of the sun, once cut off by the air, not made to stand up straight by the tensions of a normal life, and only able to get such food as there might be on another planet, which we couldn't digest. A planet where the food-molecules were mirror images of ours (right hand for left hand glove) would play this trick. I understand that in diabetes your digestion breaks up sugars so that at each stage the molecules have an odd number of carbon atoms, whereas you can only digest those with an even number; you thus *miss* the *beat*; the new food is supposed to have this effect as well. *Dowser* is a pun on putting out a light and smelling out water.

For *Listen* Empson epitomized the poem: 'Space-travel compared to neurotic isolation and the dangers of the increase of power.'
See Willis, pp. 198–203; *TGA*, pp. 107–11.

1 *They pass too fast*: cf. Eddington's account, derived from Sir James Jeans, of the way in which 'a configuration resembling the solar system would only be formed if at a certain stage of condensation an unusual accident occurred. According to

Jeans the accident was the close approach of another star casually pursuing its way through space. This star must have passed within a distance not far outside the orbit of Neptune; it must not have passed too rapidly, but have slowly overtaken or been overtaken by the sun' (*Nature of the Physical World*, p. 177). Asteroids, on the other hand, as Jeans himself suggested, are likely to be the broken fragments of a primeval planet which had been caught inside such a danger-zone (*The Universe Around Us* (Cambridge, 1929; 1944), pp. 253, 256).

2 *Express and motor . . . between*: WE must have had in mind the heroic stunts of Douglas Fairbanks, in the role of Pete Prindle, in *His Picture in the Papers* (1916). Alistair Cooke remarked: 'Most of the 1916 stories were conventional comedy-melodrama decorated by acrobatics. In *His Picture in the Papers*, the movie audience was offered . . . a leap from a train' (*Douglas Fairbanks: The Making of a Screen Character*, Film Library series no. 2 (New York, 1940, p. 16).

3 *asteroid*: the numerous minute planetary bodies revolving round the sun between the orbits of Mars and Jupiter, also known as 'planetoids' or 'minor planets'. WE foreshadows the end of the earth: a withering world that is depleted of its atmosphere (ll. 9–10), and so reduced to the status of asteroid.

4 unseen;] unseen. *Experiment*

6–7 *Bubble of rainbow . . . earth's oyster ended*: the 'rainbow' refers to the unavailing frailty of God's covenant with man in Gen. 9: 12–16. In terms of the cinema, it is exhilarating to see a stuntman leap through a skylight; but WE is also representing the earth's atmosphere as a nacreous bubble that has terrifyingly, catastrophically, burst: cf. 'Plenum and Vacuum', l. 2, and 'Arachne', ll. 7–9.

6 between twilights,] the twilights, *Experiment*; the twilight; *Eton*

8 crash] splash *Eton*

11 *Starve on the mirror images of plants*: 'One of the most characteristic things about an enzyme is its specificity,' wrote Haldane. 'The enzyme which digests cane sugar will not touch milk sugar or malt sugar, and conversely. Enzymes have been compared to keys which will only open certain locks . . . We can often make the mirror images of these molecules, and we then find that the corresponding enzymes will only attack them slowly if at all. On going through the looking-glass, Alice would have found her digestive enzymes of no more use on the looking-glass sugars than her Yale key on the looking-glass locks' ('Enzymes', *Possible Worlds*, pp. 46–7.) In 'The Last Judgment', Haldane describes a similar scenario for the end of the world: 'The organisms found on Venus were built of molecules which were mostly mirror images of those found in terrestrial bodies. Except as sources of fat they were therefore useless for food, and some of them were a serious menace' (*Possible Worlds*, pp. 303–4).

12 diabeatic] (dia)beat(ic) *Experiment*; dia(beat)ic *Eton*. All these forms deliberately misspell 'diabetic'; WE's original segmentation was intended to stress a pun on the idea of 'missing the beat'.

13–14 *One daily tortures . . . moderately true*: this problem had also vexed Dante in *Paradiso* XIX: that of God's justice towards the virtuous heathen who has not heard of Christ's Redemption and so has never been able to profess the Christian faith that is required for salvation. WE was later to focus on the issue in his analysis of Donne's poetry, in 'Donne the Space Man' (1957):

In our time no less than in Donne's, to believe that there are rational creatures on other planets is very hard to reconcile with the belief that salvation is only through Christ . . . One might suppose, to preserve God's justice, that Christ repeats his sacrifice in all worlds . . . but this already denies uniqueness to Jesus, and must in some thorough way qualify the identity of the man with the divine person . . . The young Donne, to judge from his poems, believed that every planet could have its Incarnation, and believed this with delight, because it automatically liberated an independent conscience from any earthly religious authority. (*Essays on Renaissance Literature*, Vol. I: *Donne and the New Philosophy*, pp. 79, 81)

The tortured Christ figures again in 'Reflection from Anita Loos', ll. 10–11. See also Fry, *William Empson*, pp. 135, 166–7.

14 On] on *Experiment*

17 *Daily brings rabbits . . . Australia*: the European rabbit (*Oryctolagus cuniculus*) was introduced into Australia in 1859, and within twenty years expanded to enormous numbers, causing soil erosion and threatening native plants and animals.

19 *And cannot tell. He who all answers brings*: 'He', being 'in the great taskmaster's eye' (l. 20), must be meddlesome humanity: specifically, the well-meaning scientists who took rabbits to Australia and 'cannot tell' (reckon up) what further ecological disasters they may be preparing. There is a contradiction between 'cannot tell' and 'all answers brings'.

20 *ever in the great taskmaster's eye*: from the final line of Milton's Sonnet VII, written to mark the passing of his twenty-third year ('How soon hath time the subtle thief of youth'), and expressing his wish that in the future he will still incline to God's service. The quotation helps the irony of l. 19 by suggesting that the scientists share Milton's confidence (though he modestly remarks, 'if I have grace to use it so'). WE was in his twenty-third year when writing this poem.

20 the] his *Eton*

21 *his candle as of springs*: the scientist seeks out the sources of life but may end by extinguishing it altogether. Cf. 'Legal Fiction', l. 16.

22 *tunnel*: cf. 'The Ants', l. 1, 'The Scales', l. 8, and 'Letter IV', l. 4.

'I remember to have wept'

First published in *London Review of Books* 11:15 (17 August 1989), 21.

5 *the* Golden Bowl: the primary reference is to Ecc. 12: 5–8, that we should at all times remember death and the Creator: 'because man goeth to his long home, and the mourners go about the streets: Or ever the silver cord be loosed, or the golden bowl be broken, or the pitcher be broken at the fountain, or the wheel broken at the cistern. Then shall the dust return to the earth as it was: and the spirit shall return unto God who gave it. Vanity of vanities, saith the preacher; all is vanity.' (See also Zech. 4: 2.) Commentators believe the golden bowl hanging by a silver cord represents an image of life itself, which is extinguished when the cord is severed, and the bowl (which is sometimes taken to be the head or brain) consequently crushed on impact with the earth. Cf. 'Bacchus', ll. 69–70 and WE's note.

However, given that WE's poem is about lies, untruths and the exigencies of deception, this reference may extend to the golden bowl of Henry James's last novel (1904), in which a gilded crystal bowl with a significant flaw is emblematic of the affair between the prince, Amerigo, and Charlotte Stant, who together betray both the prince's wife, Maggie Verver, and Maggie's father, Adam (who marries Charlotte) – albeit that WE's description does not tally with James's: 'a drinking-vessel larger than a common cup, yet not of exorbitant size, and formed, to appearance, either of old fine gold or of some material once richly gilt . . .' (Harmondsworth, 1966, p. 104). WE was no great admirer of James, and disliked his later style, but he had read *The Golden Bowl* with interest; in responding to an article, 'The Ververs', by Joseph J. Firebaugh (*Essays in Criticism* 4:4 (1954), 400–410), he observed:

I agree with everything in the article about *The Golden Bowl*, except its interpretation of the results. Henry James I think was morally a very confused man, and anyhow it seems impossible to deny that his attitude to sexual passion was confused. Even though his mind insisted (as the article rightly showed) on building up a sickeningly horrible case against both father and daughter Verver, still he was telling himself he was doing what his father would have wanted, that is, showing how the good cool rich Americans can subdue the savagery of the wicked Europeans . . . James does not show any sign of thinking himself such a startling moral innovator as he would have to be before telling himself he meant what your critic very properly regards as the only sensible meaning the book could have. ('Yes and No')

6 *anthropoid*: used of humans and apes.

To Charlotte Haldane

Probably written in 1929; first published in *London Review of Books* 11:15 (17 August 1989), 21.

While studying at Magdalene College, WE was one of the young intellectuals, including Michael Redgrave, Hugh Sykes Davies, Malcolm Lowry, John Davenport and Kathleen Raine, who would meet at Roebuck House, the rambling, comfortable home (in Old Chesterton) of J. B. S. Haldane (1892–1964), Reader in Biochemistry at Cambridge, and his wife Charlotte (1894–1969), a journalist and novelist. Dark-haired and pretty, and a firm-minded feminist, Charlotte liked to cultivate writers, philosophers and aesthetes. Her husband called her gatherings 'Chatty's addled salon', and 'detested' the crew who danced attendance on her. It would later be suggested that WE had an affair with her, but this is unlikely. However, WE admired her quite well enough to respond with teasing gallantry when she asked him to write a poem on her birthday. 'To Charlotte Haldane' is written in terza rima, as if by Dante to a new Beatrice; the poet transposes his inability to offer satisfactory praise into a beautifully speechless paean.

WE relished the opportunity to get out of Magdalene and pass the time at Charlotte Haldane's open house. But he had a further motive: his deep admiration for Haldane's work in genetics, and for the compelling clarity of his essays in scientific popularization. (*Possible Worlds* became one of WE's cardinal texts; and in 1935 he would translate into Basic English two of Haldane's monographs, *The Outlook of Science* and *Science and Well-Being*.) It was worth braving the gruffness of the formidable Professor 'Jack' Haldane, with his balding block of a head and penetrating eyes, to catch a few words. In a memoir sketched for a BBC programme soon after Haldane's death, WE recalled:

He was an all-round learned man, a scientist who as an undergraduate had done well at Greats, and as well as this classical and philosophical education was always liable to quote from Hindu or Icelandic epics or what not. This of course made him exciting to talk to, and people are rather fond of saying, when such a man dies, that there can never be another one, because the field of knowledge has become too big. I expect they will go on cropping up. Such a man does not really know everything, and isn't tempted to pretend he does; he has looked up information on a variety of subjects, always sticking to the point of view which made him curious about that subject to start with. You may say, he has his own picture, and knows where everything fits in. There is nothing in the growth of modern knowledge to make that impossible any longer, I think. It is just that few people try, because the pressure makes them specialize from their schooldays, and many experts are liable to attack anyone who climbs the hedge into their field. It also takes a bit of self-confidence, naturally, and it seems to take considerable bodily strength, though I am not sure why. Haldane remarks in one of the essays that, when he was getting back to work after the First

World War [he had served in France and Iraq], he found he had acquired a craving for bodily exercise, which he hadn't time for; so he fought this as if it were a drug habit, and found after six months that he was able to go on with his reading without interruption . . . When I was an undergraduate in Cambridge, and he was Professor of Genetics there, his wife Charlotte was a generous hostess for the children [the undergraduates] and he would talk to us for short periods, or join the swimming at the end of the garden. I think this gave me the right angle on the rudeness which was perhaps his most famous trait. It was mainly a refusal to be bored, hurrying the discussion on to where it would get interesting; he quite expected to be answered back, and had no presumption that a child's ideas would be wrong – plainly, he was curious to know what we did think, perhaps as part of a social inquiry, but at that age one will put up with a lot for being taken seriously at all. One was willing enough to talk back, though secretly glad it was soon over. His obvious courage, and the presumption that his opinions would challenge orthodoxy, were always present; a brotherly gruffness was the only suitable tone. This was not unusual in the twenties; I remember a speaker at the Heretics, who was being heckled by a student, and the student was observed to blench and feel that his line of objection had better stop, and the man stroked his patriarchal beard and said: 'Continue, young man; do not be imposed upon by these white hairs.' Probably his opinions were dull enough [at this point, WE cut: 'I expect he came from a Garden City]; they have left no impression on my mind. But then, I am very bad at remembering conversation, and have found that if I appear to succeed I am only inventing; all I can say is that, when you are told Haldane was rude in talk, you should remember he had lived on, like so many of us, into a smaller-minded age. (Draft typescript in Empson Papers; the edited version in 'Portrait of J. B. S. Haldane' (*Listener* 78 (2 November 1967), 565–8) makes nonsense of part of the transcription.)

WE once retailed a curious compliment from Lowry; it sounds so extravagant, we may hope it is authentic: 'He said (we were both students at Cambridge, and I rather think we and others were swimming . . . at the bottom of J. B. S. Haldane's garden) that he would already have killed himself if he had not got my poetry to read. I thought this was just the way to talk, and felt pretty sure that nobody had said it to T. S. Eliot. But it did not lead to any greater intimacy; very likely through my fault' (Tony Kilgallon, *Lowry* (Erin, Ontario, 1973), p. 19).

After Magdalene College expelled WE, it was Charlotte Haldane who, when he carried his woes to Roebuck House, clarified the situation. Naturally, he was upset, he told her, especially as he had a book to write. When she asked him if he had any money, he answered, 'Only about £200 a year.' That was enough, she maintained: he should get himself a cheap room in London and write his book.

Flighting for Duck

First published in *Magdalene College Magazine* no. 59 (December 1928), 19–20.

CP: A *warping* is land where alluvial mud is being laid down from tidal river water, by a drainage scheme, for two or three years, to make it more fertile and less low-lying; maybe this word is only used in the part of Yorkshire where I was brought up. *Flighting* is trying to shoot the wild duck that come in to feed on marsh land around twilight. Quotation from a 'sporting print'.

The first printing featured many phrases, and even complete lines, which were later revised: it included the following passage, rhyming abbaabba, as it were two quatrains constituting the octet of a sonnet, before the final six lines (which are, and were originally set as, two tercets – that is, the sestet of the sonnet – rhyming aba bab):

> When a white owl was all would glimmer through,
> Flapping about and settling; when the green
> Sheen, echo of sunset, all had been,
> And left uncertain silver (If they flew
> Flop by your head, what was there time to do?);
> When the punt splashing and far words between
> Meant hunt for corpses, like themselves unseen,
> I walked the bank, the lines dimmed from view.

Writing in 1951, WE began by describing the compacted poetry he favoured for himself – 'a fairly narrow kind' – and then moved on to argue that 'Flighting for Duck' was nonetheless an exception to his rule:

There seems no point in struggling with the verse form unless it is using its powers of concentration, and to make it do this requires I think a state of tension or conflict in the writer, usually a painful one. If the poetry is sincere, I feel, you are writing it to find your own balance, even to cure yourself. This sort of poetry cannot worry much about the convenience of the reader, because it has more pressing business in hand; but it aims of course at being a real 'expression', an externalization of the conflict into public terms, otherwise it would not work for the writer ... The shooting poem here does not fit the theory or attitude I have tried to describe. The magazine of my college at Cambridge asked me for a poem, and as this seemed a gentlemanly public I thought they would like a poem about shooting, so I turned one out. It might be said that the result is a better poem than the ones I take more seriously, but this wouldn't be a refutation of my position; I am not trying to describe the conditions for any sort of good poem but the sort I should want to write and have generally tried to write.

This poem is about shooting on my brother's land, where I was brought up, in Yorkshire. We call it *flighting* when you wait round the marshes in the evening for the ducks to come and settle there to feed; they come at dusk and you go on as long as you can see. This country lies on the river Ouse, which joins the Humber estuary a mile further down, and the marshes are human products made for the purpose of *warping*, that is, enriching the soil with the river mud; you let the tides in on the selected fields for one or two years and then drain them again. All the land is under the hightide-level like coastal Holland, and indeed was drained by Dutch engineers in the seventeenth century, who are among my ancestors. The *Egyptian* diggings are of course the great drains, which may be up to forty feet deep and a mile or two long, ending with a lock gate at the river bank which shuts automatically as the tide comes in unless you are warping. I believe there has been no warping done there since the one I was writing about, but it will have to be done again some time if the value of the land is to be kept up; the effects only last for about a generation. (*Modern Poetry*, ed. Friar and Brinnin, pp. 498–9)

The family estate at Yokefleet Hall near Goole in Yorkshire was founded on mud; and one of the special features of the farmlands by the Ouse which delighted WE's father was the process of using mud to make the meadows, which then made money. The Blacktoft warping drain, which is probably the one that WE is describing in the poem, is three miles long and was built in 1825 – at the direction of his great-grandfather, the Rev. John Empson (1787–1861).

WE's father was enchanted by this Marvellian metamorphosis of the sour flats first into a shooter's heaven and then into ripe fields; so much so that on 13 May 1894, aged 41, he composed this poem:

Warping

He stood and watched the weary waste
   Disdainful geese flew screeching o'er
Not e'en an ass would stoop to graze
   The weeds and thistles that it bore.

The rushing river pours; leaving behind
   The wealth of many tides. Wild duck and snipe
Plover and curlew feed. Salmon and eels
   Abound. Deep through the mud the sportsman wades.

Ah! Now he sees a different scene
Fair waving corn and scented bean
Rich mustard and potato fields
The fruitful soil ungrudging yields.

Those verses hung by the stairs at Yokefleet Hall; and WE shared the old man's affection for the louring, luscious landscape. As an undergraduate, he reviewed *British Farmers in Denmark*: '**I know parts of Yorkshire that have actually gone back to swamp because the farmers couldn't agree to keep the banks mended**' ('Out of Joint', *Granta* (17 February 1928); *E in G*, pp. 40–41). But it was not just good husbandry that concerned him: he admitted he was a '**sentimentalist**'. The opening lines of 'Flighting for Duck' have no rival in WE's poetry for their rapt, exact description of a natural scene. But whether he wrote this poem as a tribute to his father, it is not possible to say: while reflecting his father's feelings for the locale, WE is more taken with details of engineering than with anything sheerly picturesque.

See Willis, pp. 203–8; *TGA*, pp. 111–16.

2 **the drain between constructed**] a channel lying between *1928*
4 **Without background**] Grandiose *1928*
10 **Screening . . . surround**] – We glimpse . . . surround – *1928*
11 **line**] file *1928*
13–17 **The . . . world.**] (The . . . world.) *1928*
14 **Straddling . . . channel**] Straddles . . . channel, *1928*
15 **Stands pillared upon treetrunks**] Stands, pillared on strong tree-trunks, *1928*
18 **The mud's tough glue is drying our still feet.**] And now, since the tide is rising, up the channel *1928*
23 **Was it near? Are they coming?**] What was that drumming? Was it near? They're coming, *1928*
25 **That farm dog barking's half a mile away.**] Did you hear the train? It's three miles to the station. / That dog that barked was half a mile away. / I hope we're not on the sky-line, by these pine-trees. *1928*
29 **The**] My *1928*
34–5 **Rise up and cross each other and distend / As one flight to the river turns, alarmed.**] Swirl and eddy as they rise alarmed, / And, curling, half to the safe river bend. *1928*
40 **Bang. Bang. Two**] Bang Bang; two *1928*
41 *For man created*: cf. Sir John Davies, 'Nosce Teipsum' (1599), l. 1661: 'For sith the World for Man created was.' (William Cowper similarly uses the phrase several times in *Adam: A Sacred Drama*.)
43 *proper homage*: cf. Byron, 'Childe Harold's Pilgrimage' (1812), II.301–2: 'Do proper homage to thine idol's eyes; / But not too humbly, or she will despise'.

44–5 *The well-taught dogs . . . / . . . murd'ring gun*: this unidentified heroic couplet was not given in quotation marks either in *1928* or in *P*. WE noted on the page proofs for *CP*: 'I took the two lines in quotation marks from the poem under an eighteenth century engraving of a shoot' (Reading).
46–8 Starlit, mistcircled . . . / An . . . silver . . . / . . . cobwebs] Star-lit, mist-circled . . . / At . . . shimmer . . . / . . . cob-webs *1928*

Letter III

First published, as 'Letter iii', in *Experiment* no. 3 (May 1929), 7. A typed version was sent to Brian Howard (in the School Library, Eton College: abbreviated as *Eton*).

CP: **Quotations from Milton and Pope. True dreams come through the gate of horn.**

For *Listen* WE commented: '**After a bad night you often get to sleep at dawn and need to go on, so the line quoted from Pope [l. 17] isn't as funny as I thought.**'
      See Willis, pp. 209–13; *TGA*, pp. 116–20.

1 *Re-edify me, moon*: this opening imperative or plea, the keyword, is a pun: hard on the heels of the religious or spiritual sense (*improve me, strengthen me, sustain me, give me backbone or moral fibre*) follows the stronger connotation of *build or construct me again* (*OED* 1). The speaker figures himself, to a degree, as a building – as an office block, topped with a 'sky-sign' or advertisement (l. 22), rather than an ancient monument or moody ruin – and from that jocular opening gambit stems a series of overt or covert references (by turns apt or arch): ll. 2, 4, 11, 12, 14, 15 and 22.
3 *beams*: a pun: wooden supports for a building *and* the smiles of the girl; see also next note.
5 *altar*: not only in the usual sense of a place of religious ceremonial, the word derives from Latin *altus*, 'high' (so any 'high place'). Here, then, the 'vast reflection' of the moon 'runs' (stems) from the 'altus', the crypto-religious 'altar', that is the sun – whose sheer rays ('beams', l. 3) assail and desiccate, destroy or burn: 'discompose . . . pain'.
5 runs] runs, *Experiment*
6 *'o'er the dark her silver mantle'*: *PL*, IV.609, where the moon illuminates the innocent (but shadowed) conjugal love of Adam and Eve.
7–8 Boxed, therefore . . . may do yet] (Boxed, darling . . . will do yet) *Experiment, Eton*

10–14 *The moon's softness . . . restoration glows*: a comparison of various kinds of light at night: lightning witnessed in ruins (such as a sacked monastery) gives a frisson by silhouetting the tracery (l. 11); social or culture-vulture 'parties' may gather to enjoy a light show at a ruined edifice; the mad (lunatics) may suffer their flashing fantasies; and anyone may revisit in imagination the flickering romance of films; but only the moon affords fully satisfactory 'glows' and 'shadows'.

11 *lace of Gothic*: refers to the flowing lines of tracery windows typical of the fully developed Gothic style of church architecture (late fourteenth century–sixteenth century). Cf. 'Essay', l. 5.

12 **On**] **Or** *Experiment*

13 *flick*: in the slang sense of a film, the word was in use in common parlance by the late 1920s (*OED*); or else a flash of lightning.

14 **restoration**] **recreation** *Experiment*

15 **unfurl;**] **unfurl.** *Experiment*

15–16 *unfurl . . . pearl*: cf. *PL*, V.1–2: 'Now Morn, her rosy steps in the eastern clime / Advancing, sowed the earth with orient pearl'; and 'Letter V', ll. 10–11.

17 '*When sleepless lovers, just at twelve, awake*': from *The Rape of the Lock*, I.16: 'And sleepless Lovers, just at Twelve, awake'.

18 **(God . . . shine)**] **– God . . . shine –** *Experiment*

18 *focus*: the Latin root signifies a hearth or fireplace. WE accommodates a range of possible meanings, including 'a centre of radiant heat' (*OED* 6b), and 'the point at which rays meet after being reflected or refracted; also, the point from which the rays appear to proceed' (*OED* 2). Cf. 'Dissatisfaction with Metaphysics', l. 12 and *CP* note.

19 **past**] **passed** *Experiment*, *Eton*

20 *the cold bitter pallor of day-break*: WE had a hatred of the dawn. Julian Trevelyan, in his autobiography *Indigo Days* (1957), describes an overnight drive with WE from London to Bolton, Lancashire (where they undertook field work for the purposes of 'Mass Observation') in 1937: 'about five in the morning, Bill became restless, and we had to stop in a café, so that he should not see the dawn that upset him strangely' (p. 83).

20 **day-break),**] **day-break)** *Experiment*

22 **heaven**] **Heaven** *Eton*

22 *sky-sign*: in a prefatory note to the second impression of *CP* (1956), WE wrote: '**A *sky-sign* was a prism displayed for advertisement, open on top, with a mirror on the back face and some writing on the front one, which was thus illuminated without expense; you never see it now.**' But it can be any advertising sign that is visible against the sky, commonly on top of a building; when electric, then 'garish'.

23–4 *your crowns . . . Horn*: the beloved embodies every blessing or gift, as if incorporating a Trinity: the essence of divine light, the solid earth giving a foundation to the poet's mortal existence and the way of true dreams: Heaven, Earth and Hell. Milton invokes the divine fountainhead, the source of light, in mystical or

neo-Platonic terms which WE arrogates to his own idolatry: 'Hail, holy Light, offspring of heaven first-born, / Or of the eternal co-eternal beam / May I express thee unblamed? . . .' (*PL* III.1–3). On *terra firma*, cf. 'Sleeping Out in a College Cloister', l. 14; and true dreams proceed out of the 'Hell-Gate of Horn': in *Odyssey* (XIX.563–5), Penelope speaks to Odysseus (as yet unaware of his true identity) of the twofold nature of dreams: 'Those dreams that pass through the gate of sawn ivory deceive men, bringing words that find no fulfilment. But those that come forth through the gate of polished horn bring true issues to pass, when any mortal sees them' (*Odyssey*, trans. Murray, II, p. 269).
23 offspring] Offspring *Experiment*

Rebuke for a dropped brick

Written in 1929, at the same time as 'Myth', which appears in a handwritten version on a typescript of this poem; first published in *RB*.

This epigrammatic, syncretistic lyric shows how one myth not only leads to another but is confused with nearly every other. For the sake of man, a philanthropic Titan steals fire from heaven, so it looks like a war between men and immortals; but another hero ends up being tortured to death by his wife – though the grammar is difficult to unpick, one strand of syntax seems to say that Prometheus' heart 'Contains pulp [of] Nessus' (ll. 5, 8). However, this complicated poem is assuredly one of those in which – as WE remarked, citing Macaulay – **'the reader must take such grammar as he can get and be thankful'** (*ST*, p. 166).

1–2 *Vulture, to eat his heart . . . Prometheus', Jove-hated*: Prometheus stole fire from Zeus (Jove) and gave it to man; as his punishment, Zeus chained Prometheus to a rock and every day sent an eagle to gnaw his liver, which continually grew back again (Hesiod, *Theog.*, 562ff., Aeschylus, *Prometheus Bound*, 7ff.). Cf. 'Bacchus', ll. 42–55.
5–6 *heart draped for a sleeve, beaten purple / Gold leaf . . . a covering*: cf. this extract from WE's unpublished and uncompleted play in which a Queen and her Son are discussing the possible murder of the brother (see Introduction, pp. xliii–xliv). The Son sardonically challenges the Queen:

> You think we had better despise ourselves for ever,
> Save our skins, not get in the way of the murder,
> There is no other urgent step at the moment,
> The rest can wait, there is time to scratch each other,
> Yes, laugh your fill, rejoice, I have been scratched,
> Let me envy you your simple pleasures.

The Queen protests:

> This is the note *you* are so fond of striking,
> This is your method, let me pay you back,
> Your way of eating at your father's heart,
> No, nothing deep, hidden in him, only
> The heart draped for a sleeve, beaten purple,
> Gold leaf, poor father, as a covering.
> Now will you know what is his mind, always?

Cf. too Gerard Manley Hopkins, 'The Windhover' (1877): 'My heart in hiding / Stirred for a bird' (ll. 7–8); WE's 'covering' and 'knowing' (ll. 6, 8) may also be compared with Hopkins's rhyming on '-ing' throughout the octet of his sonnet. While WE's phrase may incorporate the sense of 'wearing one's heart on one's sleeve', it may also refer to the Purple Heart, the American military decoration awarded for bravery in action.

'beaten . . . Gold leaf . . . fretted' (ll. 5–7): Prometheus, master-craftsman, made man from clay (Pausanius, I.16.13ff.).

6 *laurel and a covering*: laurel (or bay-tree) leaves are used as an emblem or crown of martial victory or of distinction in poetry, which might be deemed a hat or covering; though 'covering' appears also to connote the fig-leaves of Adam and Eve.

7 *Fretted*: given the reference in ll. 1–2 to Prometheus, 'fretted' may mean: (i) 'devoured, consumed, gnawed'; (ii) 'vexed, worried, distressed'; and, in juxtaposition to the architectural reference of 'buttressed', (iii) 'adorned with carving in elaborate patterns; carved or wrought into decorative patterns', as of a church (*OED*). Cf. 'Song of the amateur psychologist', l. 16.

8 *Nessus*: Heracles (Latin Hercules) and his wife Deianeira, as they approach the flooded river Evenus, encounter a centaur, Nessus (direct descendant of Ixion: see note to 'Bacchus', l. 37), who offers to bear her across. On the far side, however, the centaur attempts to rape her, and Heracles shoots him with a poisoned arrow. The dying centaur advises Deianeira to keep some of his blood since, if Heracles is tempted to stray, she has only to smear it on his clothes for him to return to her in love. But the effect is hideously different, for the garment causes Heracles such excoriating agony – his blood 'hisses and boils with the burning poison' – that he kills himself. See Ovid, *Met.*, IX.101ff.; and cf. Antony's outburst: 'The shirt of Nessus is upon me. Teach me, / Alcides [Heracles], thou mine ancestor, thy rage' (*Antony and Cleopatra*, IV.xii.43–4).

Myth

Written, along with 'Rebuke for a dropped brick', in 1929; first published in *RB*. The autograph fair copy appears on a typescript of 'Rebuke', and is followed by this abstract (see *ST*):

The seven classes of ambiguity.

1. Mere richness; (a metaphor valid from many points of view).
2. Two different meanings conveying the same point.
3. Two unconnected meanings, both wanted but not illuminating one another.
4. Irony: two apparently opposite meanings combined into a judgement.
5. Transition of meaning; (a metaphor applying halfway between two comparisons).
6. Tautology or contradiction, allowing of a variety of guesses as to its meaning.
7. Two meanings that are the opposites created by the context.

1–6 *Young Theseus . . . / The Minotaur to gain*: son of King Aegeus, Theseus volunteered to slay the Minotaur, the hybrid monster which King Minos had fastened in a labyrinth that was said to have been constructed by Daedalus. Theseus was aided by Ariadne, daughter of Minos, who fell in love with him and gave him a thread ('clue') which enabled him to retrace his path. See Ovid, *Met.*, VIII.170ff.
7 *sand rope*: see note to l. 17 of 'Sea Voyage'.
10–12 *spinster's wool, his sail unfolds / Where Ariadne holds / Her cobweb*: Theseus kept his understanding with Ariadne by sailing with her to Dia (Naxos), but then inexplicably abandoned her. Ovid has Bacchus rescue and marry her, but Plutarch reports the local legend that she was pregnant by Theseus and died in childbirth, and he also records the possibility that 'she hung herself because she was abandoned by Theseus' (*Theseus*, XX, in *Plutarch's Lives*, trans. Bernadotte Perrin (London, 1914), I, p. 41). WE seems to point to a cunning man's avoidance of commitment: the woman is duped or double-crossed. Given 'cobweb', it is likely too that WE is conflating Ariadne with Arachne: cf. his citation of 'Shakespeare's *Ariachne* (*Troilus*, V. iv), for Arachne and Ariadne, those two employers of thread' (*ST*, p. 191); see also the poem 'Arachne'.

UFA Nightmare

First published in *Experiment* no. 4 (November 1929), 28.

'UFA' stands for 'Universum Film Aktiengesellschaft', the German expressionist film production company founded in 1917. In 1927 WE had written in *Granta* an enthusiastic review of *Metropolis*, Fritz Lang's superb tale of dehumanization, set in the year 2000, which starred Brigitte Helm (1907–96) as the witch-robot Maria:

Of course everybody will see this; it is a feast I cannot review in detail. The UFA people's mastery of technical tricks, the use of angles and shadows, and, for instance, the tongue of the gong; the charm of their actors; their orchestral crowds; Brigitte Helm making two precise violent gestures and then letting well alone; the contrast between that exhilaration of the imagination one finds in their mechanical forms (not merely because they are big, by the way, great hunks of skyscraper tend to shrink in one's mind; a close-up of cams on one axle was my largest vision of the evening) and the wooden deadness of drilled workers; finally the fights and chases, and the rich gratifying of one's desire for destruction; are more than can be recommended here.

The story has been maligned, partly from its simple solution of all possible economic problems, which may or may not be provided by the English Government's adapter, partly from the difficulty, after the imaginative size, the air of Passion music, attaching to introductory machines and workers, of making the necessary change in scale. For Metropolis is the Greek city state, about as large as a mining village, and improves immensely if you keep this in mind; when you see how many babies there were to save, for instance, what had been too large for narrative point becomes intelligibly parochial. Even then, of course, the hero (no, *not* effeminate, only very delightful) was almost at once comical against the sets; the way he popped round vast acidly dignified corners, or was mocked by each of the self-opening and slamming doors; obviously, after that, we had to kill the inventor, and purge our suspicion of contrivances. (4 November 1927; *E in G*, pp. 72–3)

He did not regard the film as a forecast, as it were, of totalitarian regimentation; but he did note the conflict between the sheer beauty of industrial order and its inhumanity. Likewise, he saw the point of another UFA film, *Berlin*, a documentary by Walter Ruttmann, which he reviewed for the *Cambridge Review* (27 April 1928, p. 375):

We entered Berlin, making it the Machine Age right from the word Go, by the milk train, photographing it above, below, intimate parts of its machinery, and the view out of the carriage windows. It was a wise selection of the last, I suppose, that made one feel so exactly the excited tourist; also the music was at its best then; altogether a stirring prelude to A Day in the Life of a Great City, but we had had quite enough trains by the time we had got to the station. We got plenty more. Whenever afterwards we dallied for a moment with something charming and human like a costermonger or a stray cat we were rallied, as by a trumpet call, to look to another puffer-train, sometimes even two puffer-trains crossing, the Symbol of the Age. That was stupid because there were many much more fascinating and formally effective machines, and it would have been less banal to have been called back to them.

The producers had two intentions; this mistake brings it out quite well. They wanted to lay bare the works, the economics, the whole order of a great city; to show it opening like a flower and going through a composed cycle, to show you its functions, its explanation, its organism, to make you fall down and worship a power and glory of the world. That was put across very ably. Also they wanted to give you a personally conducted tour, to show you what *you* would see, or think yourself lucky to see, in a day in Berlin; that was why the suburban trains kept cropping up, odd things in shop windows, loose ends of dramatic incident, and picture postcards of the main streets. That was why we had that apocalyptic suicide, perhaps the most thrilling single incident the UFA technique has yet achieved; quite out of place. If the woman was made as interesting as all that, how could we go straight away and look at a bottle factory, how could she settle into our minds as part of the order of the great machine.

Desmond Flower, in a letter to the *Cambridge Review* (11 May 1928, p. 412), took issue with WE's interpretation:

The whole film seems, at least to me, to protest against mechanization, like *Metropolis* . . . The arrival by train certainly suggests excitement, but only in order that it may be dashed again by the hopeless bewilderment, and the disorganized organization of life in a city. Once he has left the station the abstract spectator, from whose point of view we look, becomes a typical Berliner, sucked into the stream of workers attending that life, which once started has to go on. If 'W. E.' will consider the chaos which results at Piccadilly Circus if one policeman leaves his place to attend to something else, perhaps he will realize why Walter Ruttmann does not allow us a pause to contemplate an isolated incident.

WE defended his analysis:

I am glad this excellent film should receive further discussion; Mr Flower is very much on the spot about it.

There is a notion now, spread by Wyndham Lewis, that one should not study a contemporary movement without 'protesting'; in his case, it is a rowdy substitute for criticism. Now, large factory cities are no doubt inconvenient in many ways, but to say that *Berlin* 'protests' against them is surely a libel; it is far more seriously engaged in elaborating their peculiar beauty. I am sure Mr Flower was fascinated and invigorated, like myself, both by the particular shots of bottle and typesetting machines, and by the sense of the whole city as a far more elaborate and (of course) not in the least 'disorganized' organism; I suppose then that while enjoying their beauty he purged his feelings, with a true Puritan 'protest', by making them the villain of the piece; his excited disapproval, in fact, made even the stray cats into evidence of mechanization; there they were, slinking; up to no good, I'll be bound.

We agree, though, that there were two conflicting elements; a description of a wicked machine city and a protest against it in favour of 'human' values (Mr Flower), or a vision of human order and an irrelevant 'human' interest in cats and suicides (me). The moral point is, of course, difficult, especially if the Future is allowed to loom so large; I am ready to admit the producers were in some degree morally on his side, but I still think the conflict was badly muddled; looking at his last sentence, my complaint is, we *were* allowed to pause, for so long that the thing fell out of its setting and demanded special treatment. ('Correspondence', *Cambridge Review* (11 May 1928), 413)

Although WE tended to think of *Metropolis* as representing the excesses of Victorian industrialism, not as a prevision of the modern totalitarian state, he noted its dark truthfulness, the frightening possibilities, it figured. This can be seen in his notice of *The Way the World is Going*, in which H. G. Wells, with his faith in rational progress, wrote off *Metropolis* as the world's silliest film. It had to be acknowledged, WE argued, that imaginatively appalling things were already at work in the world:

[H. G. Wells's] remarks are crucial as far as they go; that [*Metropolis*] was not about the future at all, but an imaginative playing in pictures with economics of about fifty years ago, was of course quite true, and one bore it in mind in watching; that it was silly could only be said by one who, whose literary generation in fact, took no interest in Art. To a generation which does, the world is odder than Mr Wells's, perhaps less strenuous and less sensible. ('Puff Puff Puff', *Granta*, 27 April 1928; *E in G*, pp. 49–50)

In a letter (5 November 1970), WE remarked: '**I wanted to write poetry with profound comparisons and** *UFA Nightmare* **was merely a thriller**' (courtesy of David Wilson).

1 *Gramophony. Telephony. Photophony*: the use of the gramophone or record-player, of a telephone and of a photophone (which conveys sound-vibrations by means of light), respectively.

3 *multi-implicate*: highly intricate, intertwined and even entangled (as of inter-linked wires and cables); certainly confusing.

4 *Stonehenge*: precisely constructed circle of colossal standing stones, probably of Neolithic date (between 2200 and 1600 BC), on Salisbury Plain, Wiltshire, aligned with the sunrise at the summer solstice so widely thought to have been a temple for sun-worship.

5 *the row from A to O*: from Alpha to Omega (from beginning to end); the phrase may also allude to Arthur Rimbaud's sonnet 'Voyelles' ('Vowels'; based on an old ABC book with coloured vowels), which opens: 'A noir, E blanc, I rouge, U vert, O bleu, voyelles, / Je dirai quelque jour vos naissances latentes.' ('A black, E white, I red, U green, O blue – I'll tell / One day, you vowels, how you come to be and whence' – *A Season in Hell and other poems*, trans. Norman Cameron (London, 1994), p. 57). WE would have read it in Arthur Symons's influential monograph, *The Symbolist Movement in Literature* (London, 1899, 1908).

11 *tittles*: given the reference to running 'the row from A to O' (l. 5), 'tittles' might refer to punctuation marks, 'a diacritic point over a letter', or specifically 'the dot over the letter *i*'; or, given the reference to 'checkmate . . . the whole board' (l. 10), to the idea of outwitting the mad scientific genius at a board-game, since it can also mean 'a pip on dice' (*OED*). It is possible too that it refers to wave-length markings on a radio or on a gramophone (ll. 6, 1).

12 *dreadnought*: dreading or fearing nothing, fearless (adj.); also the name of a British battleship, launched in 1906, which was superior in armament to all its predecessors; cf. 'liner', l. 3.

17 *Weevil clicking in a hollow oak*: cf. Andrew Marvell's account of the activities of the 'hewel', or woodpecker, in 'Upon Appleton House' (1650–52), ll. 547–50: 'But where he, tinkling with his beak, / Does find the hollow oak to speak, / That for his building he designs, / And through the tainted side he mines.' A 'weevil' is a beetle of the group *Rhyncophora*, the 'larvae of which, and sometimes the beetles themselves, are destructive by boring into . . . the bark of trees' (*OED*).

Warning to undergraduates

First published in *RB*.

Following WE's death in 1984, *Magdalene College Magazine and Record* published an obituary which included this bland and negligent sentence: 'In 1931 after election as a Bye-Fellow but before taking up his position, he was appointed to a Chair of English Literature in Tokyo and his close association with Magdalene ceased for some 45 years' ('Sir William Empson (1906–1984)', *Magdalene College Magazine and Record* 28 (1983–4), 9). Whether innocently or ingeniously, the obituary managed to get just about everything wrong, minimizing or overlooking every melodramatic particular of WE's exclusion from the college (see Introduction, pp. xxi–xxii).

As fate would have it, WE's mentor I. A. Richards was not available to ward off the disaster – he and his wife were abroad until October 1931 – and it was not until 29 September 1929 that Richards learned of it, in a letter from an undergraduate in America. Bubbling with frustration, Richards despatched a missive, at once accusing and seeking clarification, to his own old mentor, Frank Salter, Fellow in History:

Do let me know what has happened. I'm v. much concerned & feel that something v. serious must have occurred for the College to have taken such a serious & public step. I'm sorry for the College's sake which I *think* has lost one of the really big chances, & for E.['s] sake who loses his academic chance & for my own for I had been looking forward to getting some work out of him on my own linguistic stuff. I'm v. anxious to know what happened to make it impossible to hush up whatever may have arisen. I'm worried to think it must have all occurred in the Long [Vacation] when most of the Fellows would have been away. I do hope you were there. As you know I distrust very much the Master's pre-20th century Bachelor School Master's feeling, & his autocratic leanings. I do hope something unjust & unjustifiable has not occurred. I haven't any real facts & so cannot judge but at present I feel so indignant that I never want to come back. Has the Master any idea of the lives of half the young men he sees every day[?] To have made a preposterous example of our best man, without contriving some tactful way round, seems madness.

The staunch Salter replied in gratifying detail on 10 November (this letter is in the Richards collection, Magdalene College, Cambridge, and is reprinted here from *Magdalene College Magazine and Record*, n.s. no. 35 (1990–91), 33–8):

The Master announced at our afternoon meeting on St Mary M's day that certain facts had come to his notice. They were of 2 kinds: (a) that in moving WE's things from Kingsley House to College various birthcontrol mechanisms had been discovered, *and* (b) (and this is what the outside public who have heard, God knows how, something of the situation, don't seem to have heard) that he had been in the habit of having a woman in his rooms late in the evening, sometimes staying till nearly 12.00, sometimes with his door locked and that on one occasion at least (more, if I remember right) they had, when the door was *not* locked, been found by Mrs Tingey in a compromising attitude. The Master saw WE early next morning and reported to an adjourned meeting of the G. B. who thereupon resolved (not unanimously) to take away the Bye Fellowship, as they are empowered to do by Statute in case of conduct judged disgraceful, and remove his name from the books of the College. WE had not denied having used the birthcontrol gadgets but said that he had never used them actually in Kingsley House . . .

From the evidence point of view, if WE had denied everything, as he might well have done ('got them for a friend', 'got them out of curiosity' etc) I still think that the majority of the G. B. wd. have considered the case proved & acted no otherwise than they did.

What has got to be remembered is that sexual misconduct *is* a University offence & that when detected in an undergraduate, it leads almost invariably to his expulsion; as long as this is so, it is not unreasonable to expect senior members of a College to conform, or for us to find it a bit difficult to continue an offender in residence. A great deal of harm had been done in this case by the entirely unnecessary publicity which had already been given it. Mrs Tingey had in my opinion erred very greatly in not reporting the visits of the woman (as regards which she had, I think, a real grievance) *at once*, in which case [F. R. Fairfax] Scott, as WE's tutor, would have told him not to be an ass, & nothing further would have happened, or, at any rate, come to our notice. As it was, the undergraduates in Kingsley House had apparently for some time past considered it already established &, not happening to like WE, made comments whenever the woman appeared. In the next place, everyone connected with the staff, pretty well, had a good look, and no doubt a good giggle, at the birth control things. Mrs Tingey fetched her husband: when Empson's stuff was taken across to College, the porters & buttery staff also had their attention drawn to them . . . [T]hose of us who didn't agree were *forced* to go part of the way with the majority in the hopes of saving *something* and we tried to compromise on leaving Cambridge and loss of title of ByeFellow, while keeping emolument and name on the books. This would have made it possible for him to receive financial help towards literary research in London & also made it not impossible for him to get some kind of a character if he put in for the Civil Service or the like. This, however, was defeated by a large majority . . .

The Master, I ought to say, behaved quite well. He was very anxious for anything to be said for WE that cd. be said, and he did not himself take any line at all, leaving everything in the hands of the meeting, although (I suspect) quite agreeing with their decision. But he said nothing at all to influence us either way . . .

WE had little doubt that the otherwise gentle Master of Magdalene manifested a dark personal interest in hounding the culprit. To Richards, Empson relayed the devastating news in this fashion:

You wanted to be the first, I remember, to tell me I had been given a Bye-Fellowship, and I want to be the first to tell you it has been taken away again. I left some contraceptives in a drawer when my things were being moved; with criminal carelessness; I remember being no more than amused when I found they had been stolen, I didn't understand what was going on, in the way of collecting gossip and so forth, at all. As for the Body, they obeyed their own rules, poor creatures; I should like to, but cannot, feel indignation at the workings of a system with whose principles I disagree . . .

I don't know how much details would amuse you. The Master (with an air of melancholy conviction) told me that anybody who had ever touched a French letter, no matter when or why, could ever again be allowed with safety in the company of young men, because he was sure in some subtle way, however little he himself wished it, to pollute their innocence; and this in spite of the fact that his own intellectual powers would have been destroyed. As an act of grace I was allowed to poison the air of Magdalene for a day after my exposure, and this gave time for several of my judges to come and explain that I must mind and not bear a grudge, or that what they had done would be the best thing for me in the end, or that 'personally' they thought their own actions a Great Pity, or that though they were not addicted to Those Particular Vices (I wept with rage when this was said to me) I was to understand they had extremely Broad Minds.

And in a subsequent letter he responded to Richards's closer enquiries:

You ask me who made gossip; I think none was necessary. The porters told the Master they had found contraceptives, and he was very excited, and anxious to get the place purged of such things. (I think he had told them beforehand to be sure and let him know of anything they could find.) His argument to *me* was that I had caused scandal, but I think he was relying on the imagination of Mrs Tingey . . . I think it very lucky you weren't in Cambridge for the row; you would only have shocked the Master, and incurred the consequences your colleagues seemed so afraid of.

As such remarks show, he would not even try to hide or overcome his bitter dismay at the college's decision to dismiss him; but this is not to say that he was making up the sanctimonious utterances of the Master as he reported them to Richards, or indeed the humbug of certain members of the Governing Body. Other reports, albeit secondhand, pin the blame on the Master. Professor Muriel Bradbrook, whose judgement could not be dismissed as negligible or mischievous, believed that Ramsay must have dictated the decision to rescind WE's junior fellowship (interview with M. C. Bradbrook, 16 September 1992). In a published memoir she wrote too that WE 'suffered under an unusually authoritarian constitution and a Master who was Nonconformist, of a joylessness that offered a very ready target for the barbed wit of Queenie Leavis and others' ('Lowry's Cambridge', in *Malcolm Lowry: Eighty Years On*, ed. Sue Vice (London, 1989), p. 140). Independently, Michael Tanner has written that at a dinner party with Dr and Mrs F. R. Leavis in the 1960s:

Mrs Leavis did most of the talking, keeping up a remarkable flow of anecdote, and laughing a great deal, her mirth often being occasioned by remembrances of prudery and priggishness. I recall her account of how an extremely distinguished literary critic was discovered by his bedmaker to be keeping condoms in his bedside table . . . and how they were taken to the Master of his College, 'one of those innocent classics who composed Latin verses about schoolboys bathing nude', and that he had to have explained to him what the condoms were for. ('Some Recollections of the Leavises', in *The Leavises: Recollections and Impressions*, ed. Denys Thompson (Cambridge, 1984), pp. 135–6)

It is to the Master's credit that he allowed WE to speak to the Governing Body in his own defence: he did not condemn him out of hand, out of hearing. **'I'm afraid I don't know who was at the Meeting, except for the obvious people,'** WE remarked a few weeks later; **'they were hidden away in the dark rather, and I was concentrating on my little speech.'** Unfortunately, there is no record of what he said – though it is nice to imagine that he asked, as legend has it, 'Would you prefer me to go in for buggery?' But perhaps one of his essays, dating from 1954, gives us a real sense of the tact he would have tried to exercise. Cassio, Othello's fresh lieutenant, is led into a drunken affray, of which he is ashamed, and yet pride prevents him from presenting his case before his master. WE assessed Cassio's situation:

it is true Cassio could have pleaded his agony at length in person the next morning, but his unwillingness to do so seems to me ordinary decency, a mild form of the Honor doctrine which is still current. Absolute lack of pride isn't thought agreeable … The way he could get through his trouble was by firmly demanding this interview, and telling the truth coolly, and asking with concern what actual harm had been done; what goes wrong is not his excessive pride but his excessive self-abasement (nowadays he would be considered too young for the job). ('The Pride of Othello', in *The Strengths of Shakespeare's Shrew*, p. 44)

So far from pleading his agony, the ruddy-faced but impenitent WE had evidently spoken up for the cool truth as he saw it, and not for what he scorned as the 'working lie'.

TITLE: cf. Robert Graves, 'Warning to Children', published in the *New Era* 1 (1 April 1929), 545–6, and collected in *Poems 1929* (London, 1929).
1 *gone down*: graduated; go on from university.
2 *cackling*: perhaps cf. Pope, *The Dunciad* (A), I.192: 'And save the state by cackling to the Tories?'
14 *port*: cf. WE's discussion of Pope's pun on 'port', in *The Dunciad*, Book IV (*ST*, p. 134). Cf. 'Sea Voyage', l. 19.
32 *perfect freedom*: cf. Wordsworth, 'Poems dedicated to national independence and liberty', I: IV ('I grieved for Buonaparté, with a vain') (1802), ll. 10–12: 'Books, leisure, perfect freedom, and the talk / Man holds with week-day man in the hourly walk / Of the mind's business'; James Thomson, 'Weddah and Om-El-Bonain', III.174–6: 'Found perfect freedom and content, shut fast / Alive within that coffer-coffin lonely, / Which gave him issue to that chamber only'; and Tennyson, 'Oenone' (1832), l. 164: 'Commeasure perfect freedom'. The phrase refers to Horace's definition of the wise free man, in *Satires*, II.vii.83–7.
44–5 *rows … lily-like repose*: cf. Swinburne, 'Laus Veneris' (1866), ll. 87–8: 'And with short song the maidens spin and sit / Until Christ's birthnight, lily-like, arow'; and Pope, *The Dunciad* (B), II.347–8: 'Thence to the banks where rev'rend Bards repose, / They led him soft, each rev'rend Bard arose'.
61 *And have you any further news*: cf. Rupert Brooke, 'The Old Vicarage, Grantchester' (1912), l. 140: 'And is there honey still for tea?'
63 *Leicester Square*: see Christopher Ricks's note in T. S. Eliot, *Inventions of the March Hare: Poems 1909–1917* (London, 1996), pp. 200–201.
68 (note 1) *I learn in suffering what I teach in song*: cf. 'Most wretched men / Are

cradled into poetry by wrong; / They learn in suffering what they teach in song' (Shelley, 'Julian and Maddalo' (1818), ll. 544–6).

69 (note 2) *the art to blot*: 'Ev'n copious Dryden, wanted, or forgot, / The last and greatest Art, the Art to blot' (Pope, 'The First Epistle of the Second Book of Horace' (ll. 280–81), in *Imitations of Horace*).

This Last Pain

Written by 1929–30, an untitled typescript of the poem, including the present stanza 5, was sent to Brian Howard (now in the School Library, Eton College: abbreviated as *Eton*); first published (though without stanza 5) in *New Signatures*, ed. Michael Roberts (London, 1932), p. 68; reprinted in *P 1934*; published in its complete form in *P*. 'New verses are added to *Last Pain* and *Letter I*,' WE wrote in an undated letter (*c*. 1935) to John Lehmann (Harry Ransom Humanities Research Center, University of Texas at Austin).

CP: *Her*: the soul, the mistress; *he*: man, the housemaid. *But wisely*: 'it is good practical advice, because though not every ideal that can be imagined can be achieved, man can satisfy himself by pretending that he has achieved it and forgetting that he hasn't.' This touches Wittgenstein neither as philosophical argument nor as personal remark. The idea of the poem is that human nature can conceive divine states which it cannot attain; Wittgenstein is relevant only because such feelings have produced philosophies different from his. 'As the crackling of thorns under a pot, so is the laughter of a fool.' A watched pot never boils, and if it boiled would sing. The folly which has the courage to maintain careless self-deceit is compared to the mock-regal crown of thorns. By the second mention of hell I meant only Sheol, chaos. It was done somewhere by missionaries onto a pagan bonfire.

Made up of rhyming quatrains, each stanza comprises an heroic couplet followed by an answering tetrameter couplet (resembling Marvell's 'Horatian Ode' (1650) stanza, as G. S. Fraser pointed out).

On *Poems of William Empson*, the poet commented:

I shall next do a poem called *THIS LAST PAIN*, but only because the producer wanted it. Long ago a critic said it recommended Posing, a very undergraduate point of view, he said, which reminded him of Oscar Wilde. I was much struck by this, because the poem can be read like that, which had never occurred to me. The trouble with this kind of writing, indeed, though it seems so elaborately argued, is that it is always liable to topple over and mean something you hadn't wanted at all. The idea here is that the mind can imagine states which it cannot attain, in both love and religion – that is why the Fathers of the Church appear at the beginning of a love-poem – but I was also saying that the mind can partially satisfy itself by keeping up an appearance of these ideal conditions. I must say, however politely you try to phrase it, it does seem to come pretty close to recommending Posing.

By the way, Wittgenstein is brought in simply as a Positivist philosopher, technically not idealist – he was a great man – and there is a story taken for granted in one of the verses that missionaries gained an effect somewhere by showing a religious magic lantern slide on the smoke of a pagan bonfire, which I should think I was told about when I was very young.

For *Listen* he remarked gnomically: 'I always feel doubtful now in what sense this is true, a result perhaps of having picked up the idea too readily.'

Contemporary Poets Reading Their Own Poems preserves the remarks: 'Someone said I was praising lying and affectation, like Oscar Wilde ... I've always been slightly uneasy about the poem since then. If you adopt a character, so to speak, you grow into it.'

In 'William Empson in conversation with Christopher Ricks', WE elaborated:

Somebody told me it was like Oscar Wilde saying that you ought to wear a mask and then you'll grow into your mask. This seemed to me positively embarrassing. I didn't want to be like Oscar Wilde in this business of being affected, and I couldn't see why it was different. I felt uneasy about it. I do feel it's writing, as it were, to a theory without my being quite sure what the theory comes to, or what it means or something. I felt rather doubtful whether it meant anything very sensible. I do think, it's pretty. I like it for the singing line quality. But it seemed to me I was writing up a subject which I hadn't thought through. That was why I felt shy about it ... [W]hen I'm suddenly told it's exactly like Oscar Wilde, being affected and so on, and ... though a most worthy man and very able, kind and helpful and so on, the thought of behaving like Oscar Wilde does get under my skin. It means being affected all the time. That's not what I'd want it to say. So, in a sense, I've never come to terms with the poem again somehow.

According to some anonymous notes written on the flyleaf of a copy of the second impression of *CP* (1956), WE remarked at a poetry reading on 22 June 1968: 'Not a sensible way to regard life. I don't like that poem' (seen in *Ulysses* bookshop, London).

On *Harvard*, he explained:

I've always felt uneasy about this poem. I feel it's a lyrical invention, but it's merely the metre of the Ode to Cromwell by Andrew Marvell, the short couplet after the long one. But it's hard to use: I felt I'd managed to use it. This is why I like reading it out. Of course, you must remember it is a student poem. The love poems are very much boy is afraid of girl, and this poem has almost stopped saying boy is afraid of girl. It says we could make a go of it if we kept our faces straight, if we adopted the right role. It's no use telling me Oscar Wilde was an old pig – I expect he always was pretending to be something else – but among young people if you want to decide to be a doctor you have to be able to imagine whether you would like being a doctor or not; otherwise, you'll make a great mess of your life. There is a kind of truth in this doctrine that you first adopt a pretence and then it becomes real. I didn't think I was imitating Oscar Wilde, but I agree I didn't really know what I was talking about. [The poem] is not really very good, but it's true enough, as a matter of fact.

See Eberhart, 'Empson's Poetry', pp. 203–6; Morelli, pp. 90–97; Meller, 'William Empson: *This Last Pain*'; Meller, 'Ein Stil aus einer Verzweiflung: *This Last Pain*', in *Das Gedicht*, pp. 227–38; Otten, 'William Empson: "This Last Pain"'; Ricks, pp. 189–90; *TGA*, pp. 120–26; Lecercle, 'William Empson's Cosmicomics', pp. 288–93. Willis, pp. 213–24, connects the burden of the poem to Richards's differentiation, as enunciated in *Principles of Literary Criticism* (1924) and *Science and Poetry* (1926), between the scientific and the emotive uses of language, and in particular to Richards's concept of 'pseudo-statements' (cf. WE on Richards's theory, in *SCW*, pp. 423, 428–30). Johnson compares 'This Last Pain' with Thomas Hardy's 'A Plaint to Man' in 'From Hardy to Empson'.

2 *They knew . . . crowned*: St Thomas Aquinas specifies this punishment for the devils: 'Again, they are deprived of the bliss which their very nature desires' (*Summa Theologiae*, vol. 9: *Angels* (1a, 3) (London and New York, 1968), p. 294). Boethius reckoned, in *De consolatione philosophiae*, 'in omni adversitate fortunae infelicissimum est genus infortunii fuisse felicem' (*The Consolation of Philosophy* [II, iv, 4], trans. H. F. Stewart and E. K. Rand (Cambridge, Mass., 1936)); and Dante, 'Nessun maggior dolore, / Che ricordarsi del tempo felice / Nella miseria' (*Inferno* V.121–3). WE was familiar too with Mephistopheles's terrible declaration: 'Think'st thou that I, who saw the face of God / And tasted the eternal joys of heaven, / Am not tormented with ten thousand hells / In being deprived of everlasting bliss?' (Marlowe, *Dr Faustus*, I.iii.79–82), which uses in turn a quotation from St John Chrysostom (347–407): 'if one were to speak of ten thousand hells, they would be nothing compared with being excluded from the blessed vision of heaven' (*Homily in St. Matt.* xxiii.9; see John Searle, *TLS*, 15 February 1936, p. 139). Milton, in *Paradise Regained*, stipulates this especial degree of deprivation: 'the happy place / Imparts to thee no happiness, no joy, / Rather inflames thy torment, representing / Lost bliss, to thee no more communicable, / So never more in hell than when in heaven' (I.416–20); and in *PL*: 'now the thought / Both of lost happiness and lasting pain / Torments him' (I.54–6). James Joyce was to 'sermonize' in *A Portrait of the Artist as a Young Man* (1916):

Saint Thomas, the greatest doctor of the church, the angelic doctor, as he is called, says that the worst damnation consists in this, that the understanding of man is totally deprived of divine light and his affection obstinately turned away from the goodness of God . . . This, then, to be separated for ever from its greatest good, from God, and to feel the anguish of that separation, knowing full well that it is unchangeable: this is the greatest torment which the created soul is capable of bearing, *poena damni*, the pain of loss. (Harmondsworth, Middlesex, 1960, p. 128)

In some loose-leaf holograph notes dated May 1934 WE reflected on Aquinas' account of God:

Puzzled to know why reading a version of Aquinas on God was so eerie and horrible – thrilling as a fugue might be, that one would expect, but this was like reading Dracula or a Freudian case. The reason (which I don't remember seeing elsewhere) is that God there is point by point, in some points with much subtlety of observation, an extreme case of dementia praecox: only he is not mad but right: filling the heavens – a personal God could not be sane . . . God is unmoved even as outside time, has a mind perfectly simple, so there is nothing *in* it, but isn't unconscious as he might appear because he is always contemplating his own perfection. The creation of the world makes him no less perfect, because it was unnecessary and uninteresting to him, and one may see the perfection of this detachment from the fact that he chose to make it less perfect than he might have done. The torments of hell however add to its harmony, which was why he chose them – a delicately observed point: the imbecile pulls off flies' wings not from an active pleasure in cruelty but just rather than do nothing. And though one may in a sense say he has no passions he has in a perfect degree the passion of love, directly [?directed] uniformly towards himself – he feels indeed love for the creatures strictly in so far as they are like himself (if the imbecile shows any sex it is homosexual) but in an infinitely lower degree (in effect it is sexless, as without all other qualities).

3–4 *Such, but on earth . . . heaven or of hell*: echoes the ultimate lines of Emily Dickinson's lyric no. 1732, beginning 'My life closed twice before its close': 'Parting is all we know of heaven, / And all we need of hell' (ll. 7–8). WE was to remark, in 'Death and Its Desires' – drafted in 1933 – '**Probably the trouble about Emily Dickinson, an American poet and refined hermit who wrote a great number of striking metaphysical poems and became very ghoulish in later life, is that she does not get enough of this support from social ideas**' (*A*, p. 544). When approached by Penguin Books to edit for a new series a selection from a poet of his choice, WE responded on 19 December 1970:

I would like to do the one on Emily Dickinson, discussing briefly in the introduction whether she is metaphysical or mystical or why she has excited grand claims from recent critics, giving mainly the old favourites but one or two which seem to me surprising. I think her chief merit is to rely on the bone and sinew of the language itself, a phrase invented for the supposed 'line' of Wyatt, Jonson and Donne. I will have to read the book proving she was a lesbian, and will give some poems from later years about affectionate relations with women, but cannot believe I will be converted by it from regarding the major poems as (essentially) about God, Father, and distinguished clergymen, persons who excite immense feelings which one would prefer not to sustain for more than half an hour, escaping to the kitchen after that as a rule. They can be checked, if one is skilful, but I do not expect that she felt this to carry any large metaphysical doctrine. I find her a sympathetic character, in a very limited way. The remarkable thing is that, if she had not been so extravagantly feminine, all the critics would have admired the essential masculinity of her major poems. (courtesy of Penguin Books Ltd)

4 heaven . . . hell] Heaven . . . Hell *Eton*
5 *housemaid of the soul*: cf. T. S. Eliot, 'Morning at the Window' (1916), l. 3: 'damp souls of housemaids'.
5–6 soul, / May know her happiness by eye to hole:] Soul, / Knows all her happiness; he has his hole. *Eton*
8 Door will not] Not door will *Eton*
9 *What is conceivable can happen too*: '*Der Gedanke enthält die Möglichkeit der Sachlage die er denkt. Was denkbar ist, ist auch möglich*': 'The thought contains the possibility of the state of affairs which it thinks. What is thinkable is also possible' (Ludwig Wittgenstein, proposition 3.02, *Tractatus Logico-Philosophicus*, trans. by C. K. Ogden, with the assistance of F. P. Ramsey (London, 1922; 1933), pp. 42–3). One of WE's few comments in prose on Wittgenstein is: 'Of course, if you say that a statement about the existence of other people is inherently meaningless, as I take it Professor Wittgenstein would do, then all statements about value are meaningless too' (*SCW*, p. 428).
10 dreamt] dreamed *Eton*
12 where it was] the facts were *Eton*
12 wrong.] wrong: *1932*, P *1934*
13–16 *Those thorns are crowns . . . into song*: Christ's crown of thorns is satirically concatenated with the well-known proverb from Ecc. 7: 6, 'As the crackling of thorns under a pot, so is the laughter of the fool', along with the adage that watched pots never boil. As Otten observes (p. 189), the phrasing here may even embrace the literary slang 'pot-boiler'. The lines scoff at the unavailing emblems of Christianity; faiths and symbols need fundamentalist believers, but tokens of transcendence might really be nothing more than literal folly: crackling is not song.
13 are] being *1932*
14 Crackle] crackles *1932*
15–16 And no man's watching . . . / Would ever] When all your watching . . . / Would never *Eton*; Since no . . . ever *1932*
17–18 *Thorns burn . . . frying-pan*: potash is the crude potassium carbonate, K_2CO_3, created by burning plants. The name derives literally from 'pot' and 'ash'

(which is presumably the association WE carries forward from ll. 13–14). Potash makes up a very high proportion of the total alkali content of most land plants; and potash lyes can be used to make soft soaps (in compound with fatty acids and soda).

20 this brave] this their *Eton*

21 *All those large dreams by which men long live well*: cf. perhaps 'But that large grief which these enfold' (Tennyson, *In Memoriam*, V.11).

22 *magic-lanterned on the smoke of hell*: echoes two famous passages from Fitzgerald's *Rubáiyát*. (1) Stanza LXIV of the 1st edn., 1859: 'Said one – "Folks of a surly Tapster tell, / And daub his Visage with the Smoke of Hell; / They talk of some strict Testing of us – Pish! / He's a Good Fellow, and 'twill all be well." ' (The same phrasing survives in stanza XCV of the 1868 edn.) (2) Stanza LXVIII of the 1872 edn.: 'We are no other than a moving row / Of Magic Shadow-shapes that come and go / Round with this Sun-illumin'd Lantern held / In Midnight by the Master of the Show.' (The same stanza, with minimal modification, appears in the 4th edn. of 1879.) The likelihood is that WE read the *Rubáiyát* in one of the Golden Treasury editions, or the like, which would have given him both the 1859 (1st edn.) and the 1879 (4th edn.) texts. (WE was aware of the problems raised by the various versions of the *Rubáiyát*: see *ST*, p. 214.) Willis draws attention to the likely echo of Eliot's 'The Love Song of J. Alfred Prufrock': 'It is impossible to say just what I mean! / But as if a magic lantern threw the nerves in patterns on a screen' (ll. 104–5) (pp. 220–21). Cf. too the opening of Sir Philip Sidney's sonnet: 'The scourge of life, and death's extreame disgrace, / The smoke of hell, the monster called paine, / Long sham'd to be accurst in every place, / By them who of his rude resort complaine.'

As Eberhart points out, the rhythm and diction of Empson's lines recall too ll. 13–14 of Shakespeare, Sonnet 129: 'All this the world well knows, yet none knows well, / To shun the heaven that leads men to this hell' ('Empson's Poetry').

Cf. also the tenor of WE's remarks in 1957 about Donne's poetry, from 'Donne the Space Man':

When Donne, presenting himself as an unsanctified lover, implies that such couples have exactly the same right to an inherent autonomy as Christ and his church, so that religious language can be used to make claims for them, he has at least an air of meaning something much more direct and startling. All he has done, you may protest, is compare love to religion, a trope which could not have the faintest novelty . . . But he somehow manages to put the equation the other way round; instead of dignifying the individual by comparison to the public institution, he treats the institution as only a pallid imitation of the individual. All the imaginative structures which men have built to control themselves are only derived from these simple intimate basic relations. (*Essays on Renaissance Literature*, vol. I, p. 86)

22 hell] Hell *Eton*

25 can] may *Listen, Harvard*
26 most] all *1932*
26 would] will *Eton*
26 our] or *CP 1949* (probably a typo)
27–8 their . . . / We should forget how they were] its . . . / You will not think how it was *Eton*
27–8 *dappled shade . . . made*: WE is probably conjoining allusions to Hopkins's sonnet 'Pied Beauty' (1877) and to Marvell's 'The Garden' – 'Annihilating all that's made / To a green thought in a green shade' (ll. 47–8) – the latter of which he was to expound in 'Marvell's Garden' (*Pastoral*, pp. 99–119).
29–31 *Feign then . . . an edifice of form*: cf. Empson's remarks in defence of Richards:

Mr Richards said that for verbal convenience, and for the gratification of the sense that poetry is an inexplicable power, it is very proper, after realizing that beauty is not an inherent quality, to talk of it (on such occasions) as though it were . . . Surely everybody who talks about these matters nowadays has heard of the problems about verbal fictions, and the philosophy of *As if*? The prime intellectual difficulty of our age is that true beliefs may make it impossible to act rightly; that we cannot think without verbal fictions; that they must not be taken for true beliefs, and yet must be taken seriously; that it is essential to analyse beauty; essential to accept it unanalysed; essential to believe that the universe is deterministic; essential to act as if it was not. ('O Miselle Passer!' (1930); *A*, p. 198)

(See Hans Vaihinger, *The Philosophy of 'As if': A System of Theoretical, Practical and Religious Fictions of Mankind*, trans. C. K. Ogden (London, 1925).)
 Cf. too WE's remarks:

'Marina' [1930] seems to me one of Mr [T. S.] Eliot's very good poems . . . The dramatic power of his symbolism is here in full strength, and the ideas involved have almost the range of interest, the full orchestra, of the 'Waste Land'. One main reason for this is the balance maintained between otherworldliness and humanism; the essence of the poem is the vision of an order, a spiritual state, which he can conceive and cannot enter, but it is not made clear whether he conceives an order in this world to be known by a later generation (like Moses on Pisgah) or the life in heaven which is to be obtained after death (like Dante). One might at first think the second only was meant, but Marina, after all, was a real daughter; is now at sea, like himself, rather than already in the Promised Land; and is to live 'in a world of time beyond me', which can scarcely be a description of Heaven. At any rate, the humanist meaning is used at every point as a symbol of the otherworldly one; this seems the main point to insist on in a brief notice because it is the main cause of the richness of the total effect. In either case the theme is the peril and brevity of such vision. ('Recent Poetry' (1932); *A*, p. 356)

30 conceived] achieved *Eton*

33 me,] me *1932, P 1934*

34–6 *Ambiguous gifts . . . / And learn a style from a despair*: cf. WE's observations in connection with the seventh type of ambiguity, which 'occurs when the two meanings of the word, the two values of the ambiguity, are the two opposite meanings defined by the context, so that the total effect is to show a fundamental division in the writer's mind': the speaker

> satisfies two opposite impulses and, as a sort of apology, admits that they contradict, but claims that they are like the soluble contradictions, and can safely be indulged; by admitting the weakness of his thought he seems to have sterilized it, to know better already than any one who might have pointed the contradiction out; he claims the sympathy of his audience in that 'we can none of us say more than this', and gains dignity in that even from the poor material of human ignorance he can distil grace of style. One might think that contradictions of this second sort (corresponding to feeling, and not knowing one's way about the matter in hand) must always be foolish, and even if they say anything to one who understands them can quite as justifiably say the opposite to one who does not. But, indeed, human life is so much a matter of juggling with contradictory impulses (Christian-worldly, sociable-independent, and suchlike) that one is accustomed to thinking people are probably sensible if they follow first one, then the other, of two such courses; any inconsistency that it seems possible to act upon shows that they are in possession of the right number of principles, and have a fair title to humanity. (*ST*, pp. 225, 230)

34 gifts] gift *Eton*

Description of a View

First published in *Experiment* no. 6 (October 1930), 13.

CP: *Boiled in acid* as in cleaning a specimen and like the process of making concrete; *laid on glass* like the cleaned specimen because of the shop windows at the bottom. *Stretched in* is rather illogical; the stalk of the crane, hanging level over the unfinished building, the beam of a balance, the horizon, and a Zeppelin all 'stretch along'. *Impiously* because God promised not to send a Flood again and marked the promise with the rainbow; a high sealine would mean that the sea would pour in. *Down* is light brown hair on white flesh compared to the dry grass on chalk downs, compared to the rusted metal over the white building.

The building in question may have been visible from WE's lodgings at 65 Marchmont Street, near Russell Square, London, where he lived from late 1929 to July

1931; and yet 'London river' (l. 16) suggests that the building is in fact an office block, with shops at ground level, not far from the Embankment.

See Willis, pp. 224–7; *TGA*, pp. 126–9.

9 **On trust, it did not**] **It would not wish to** *Experiment*

14 **Sole**] **Lone** *Experiment*

14 *the bridge Milton gave Death to pass*: as Satan journeys from Hell across the gulf to earth, Sin and Death tag along with a kind of pontoon or causeway: 'Sin and Death amain / Following his track, such was the will of heaven, / Paved after him a broad and beaten way / Over the dark abyss' (*PL*, II.1024–7; see also X.293–305).

14 **Death**] **death** *CP 1949*

15–16 *beam . . . / Hung*: 'beam of Justice' most obviously suggests the scales of justice; perhaps too the eyebeam (cf. 'Letter III', l. 3). It may also allude to Acts 5: 30 where, in both Greek and Hebrew versions, the word 'beam' is used for 'tree' – i.e. Christ's cross. See 'Letter I', l. 12 and note; and a punning phrase in 'The Fool', l. 9.

16 *Zeppelin*: WE may be harking back to World War I, when dirigible airships carried out bombing raids over London from 1915; or, more loosely, to the R100 (which was built at Howden in Yorkshire, a few miles from the Empson home at Yokefleet, and 'which was briefly visible over the Thames on 28 January 1930' – *TGA*, pp. 128–9) or to the hydrogen-filled R101, which he had seen in its hangar and which was destroyed in a tragic accident earlier in 1930 (see also 'Letter IV', l. 15).

16 **river.**] **river;** *Experiment, CP 1949*

17 **Its**] **It** *Experiment* (presumably a typo)

17 **sealine**] **sea-mark** *Experiment*

17 *sealine*: coast-line, horizon, the line where sea and sky seem to meet (*OED*).

18–19 **sky;** / **Whose**] in *Experiment* there is no stanza break

20 *Like palace walls in Grimm*: no matching description in the Grimms' collection of tales; though Marina Warner and Jack Zipes (both of whom I have consulted) independently volunteered the possibility that WE – making use of a stretched dream image – is catching the threat in 'Little Briar Rose' (the Grimms' 'Sleeping Beauty').

20 **needles,**] **needles;** *Experiment*

21 **concrete,**] **concrete;** *Experiment*; **concrete** *CP 1949*

Homage to the British Museum

Written by 1929–30, when a typescript version, with the title 'Hymn to the B. M.', was offered to Brian Howard for possible inclusion in a proposed anthology (now in the School Library, Eton College: abbreviated as *Eton*). First published in *Poetica* (Tokyo, January 1932); reprinted in *P 1934*.

In some undated notes written for the launch of an anthology, WE noted: '**The statue it describes is of course real, but the whole section has been moved to the north of the Royal Academy. The poem is not pessimistic, because it does not say that this god rules all life, only the life of learning inside the museum.**'

At Christmas 1961 WE sent to his friend Alice Stewart a greetings card showing a full-frontal photograph of this icon, the Polynesian sea god Tangaroa. '**Not a pretty thing,**' he had to admit, '**but I once wrote a poem about it, so I am in its favour.**' (Courtesy of Dr Alice Stewart.)

See Morelli, pp. 32–4; Ricks, pp. 199–200; *TGA*, pp. 129–32; Willis, p. 229.

TITLE: **Homage to the British Museum**] **Hymn to the B. M.** *Eton*
1 ethnological section] **Ethnological Section** *Eton*
2 *faced with a blank shield*: the face of this small wooden icon (see above) takes the shape of a shield. See also note to ll. 5–7.
3 He . . . include] **It . . . contain** *Eton*
5–7 *At the navel . . . the world*: the features of the icon, its head and face (ears, nose, prissy-looking mouth and even beard), as well as other key organs of its body, are fashioned in the shape of tiny figures, as if affixed: thus it literally, organically, embodies all of the other 'dolls' or 'deities', which resemble shoots or growths. At *Harvard*, WE remarked about this icon: '**It's a remarkable effort of mind for a primitive people, I think it's very surprising.**'
7 His] **Its** *Eton*
8 absorb] **assume** *Eton*
10 hesitation] **hesitation,** *P 1934*
12 admit that] **admit** *Eton*
15 *pinch of dust*: cf. Byron, *Don Juan*, I, stanza 219: 'Let not a monument give you or me hopes, / Since not a pinch of dust remains of Cheops.' The phrase also evokes Donne's shocking remembrance of death in his Fourth Meditation: 'whats become of mans great extent and proportion, when himselfe shrinkes himselfe, and consumes himselfe to a handfull of dust; whats become of his soaring thoughts, his compassing thoughts, when himselfe brings himselfe to the ignorance, to the thoughtlessnesse of the *Grave*' (*Selected Prose*, ed. Neil Rhodes (Harmondsworth, 1987), p. 106); but WE manages simultaneously to register a hint of scepticism towards any supernal power by means of parodying the proverbial 'pinch of salt'.

However, for salutary remarks on the phrase 'pinch of dust' as it features in Donne, Tennyson, Conrad and T. S. Eliot, see Leonard Unger, 'Intertextual Eliot', in *T. S. Eliot: Essays from the 'Southern Review'*, ed. James Olney (Oxford, 1988), pp. 272–4.

15 God] god *Eton*

Note on Local Flora

First published in *Experiment* no. 5 (February 1930), 26; reprinted in *New Signatures* (1932). A typescript version – which was untitled, and therefore almost certainly predates the *Experiment* version – was sent to Brian Howard for possible inclusion in a projected anthology (now in the School Library, Eton College: here abbreviated as *Eton*).

CP: *That image:* the forest fire is like the final burning of the world.

In an undated letter to Sylvia Townsend Warner, written from Tokyo (probably in 1933), WE included this and one other poem with this comment at the foot: '**It is hard to read scribbled poems, and both these are frankly more for practice than sure they have an adequate subject. But thank you for asking for them**' (Reading).

In 1940 WE offered this expatiation upon the poem, which he winningly designated as a '**mild little epigram**':

So far as I can see, the thing only means more than what it claims to say – that is, applies to other things than this tree in Kew – by a kind of generalization: I felt that other people were *like* the tree in Kew.

There may be some obscurity of detail. The tree of course simply *is* in Kew, and my remarks about it come from a white label attached to it by the management. The Tree of Heaven is a translation of a Chinese name for a tree, one that grows normally in China, and I believe there is some kind of myth about its magical powers, so this tree is nearly magical too. Turkestan is cold, China is slow in growth and unwilling to change its way of life and (so far as Confucianism goes) rather chilly in its philosophy. One way or another the countries are supposed to fit the habits of the tree. The cones of course carry the seeds, and the tree only casts them in a forest fire, if the white label is correct. The cones, therefore, only leave their mother when there is a violent event like the fire at the end of the world mentioned I think in the Apocalypse, but anyway a stock medieval idea. The cones are not wards of time because time does not 'bring them up', help them out; they grow up when something like the end of the world happens, and that is not time but eternity. *That image* refers back to *forest fire*. Bacchus [Dionysus] was born when Jupiter [Zeus] appeared to Semele in his own nature, as she had asked him to do, and burnt her up; the forest fire acts like the father God. Then the Phoenix was also re-born in a fire, but Phoenix is the scientific name for date-palms or something like that [*phoinix* in Greek], so the Phoenix is a vegetable like the tree. The tree in Kew is unlikely to get a forest fire, which is what it needs for sexual success, but it may get one in a Red Dawn – a revolution or war in which London is so thoroughly burnt that the fire spreads to the trees in Kew.

Of course you are meant to think of corresponding human affairs, but you can choose which you like as in any other description of Nature. Continent passive people of this sort, with great powers only called out by special occasions, have got to be admired a great deal, but it seems rather an absurd kind of dignity, and also it is rather a dangerous one, because people like that positively enjoy a big smash-up. The business of not leaving your mother is made a very undignified one by Freud, and the way people like this stick to a tradition is rather the same though it seems dignified. They have a connection with Bacchus, though they would probably not be interested in drink, or would disapprove of it, in ordinary life; because they want a big sacred orgy when things smash up. They are rare and splendid creatures such as the Phoenix was supposed to be, and able like the Phoenix to live alone, but this passive power is on the one hand a dull thing, though helpful, like vegetables, and on the other hand liable to be dangerous, because human beings of this sort generally have a secret desire to make things smash up.

But this chatter on my part doesn't seem necessary to reading the poem. The facts about the tree are surely striking in themselves, and make you feel 'So life's like that, is it?' (Elizabeth Drew, with John L. Sweeney, *Directions in Modern Poetry* (New York, 1940; 1967), pp. 81–3)

Cf. WE's observation in 'Alice: Child as Swain':

Indeed about all the rationalism of Alice and her acquaintances there hangs a suggestion that these are after all questions of pure thought, academic thought whose altruism is recognized and paid for, thought meant only for the upper classes to whom the conventions are in any case natural habit; like that suggestion that the scientist is sure to be a gentleman and has plenty of space which is the fascination of Kew Gardens. (*Pastoral*, pp. 231–2)

Apropos WE's remark that the 'Tree of Heaven is a translation of a Chinese name for a tree', compare one mysterious tree in particular; Harold Acton would later remark in his precious fiction *Peonies and Ponies* (1941), which is set in Peking: 'He half-expected a phoenix to swoop down on his *wu-t'ung* tree – the only tree whereon a phoenix will deign to alight' (Harmondsworth, 1950, p. 156). But see note to l. 2.

In 1977, in response to Wain's sympathetic chapter in *Professing Poetry* (Wain talks a little about this poem on pp. 298–9), WE wrote to Wain:

Though I ought to have been thinking about war, you feel, you should protect me from being thought to have been leftist – which only a bad man would have resisted at that time.

To say that the tree 'thirsts for the Red Dawn', as the rocks in St. Paul or at least Vaughan yearn for the Second Coming, seems to me quite strong; Dinah Stock* was within her rights in saying [in *'New Signatures* in Retrospect', Gill, p. 141] it 'takes more direct notice of Leftist standpoints' and could surely have said 'not an unsympathetic one'. I never believed in the theory of I. A. R[ichards] that modern poetry should be divested of all beliefs, though I grant of course that my method was indirect. It was not meant to be aggressively dead-pan.

Likewise in 1977, on *The Ambiguity of William Empson*, he remarked:

I'd like to read a poem which is just un-rhymed – just a ten syllable line called 'Note on Local Flora'. A fussy title meaning I was living in London and this extremely strange plant was in Kew Gardens. It's one of the things you can see in London. Phoenix is the learned name for a whole group of trees, it's part of its classification; and the Red Dawn, I have to explain, means the Communist victory – everyone in my time knew what the Red Dawn was, but I find people often don't now. However it didn't mean very much, it only added to the feeling that the whole world was very strange, you understand it, it's all quite true. It was written up in Kew Gardens as part of the information under that tree. I must say I can never find it now – I don't know what's become of this tree – perhaps it's had a small fire of its own.

Thom Gunn, in an untitled review of *CP* (*London Magazine* (February 1956), 70–75), wrote about this poem:

Up to the last line this is comparatively straightforward, and perhaps this is why I find it one of Empson's best two poems . . . ; but try as I can I am not able to see what the last line means. Is 'this' simply a tree in Kew Gardens? In that case, why does it thirst for a Red Dawn, which is surely meant politically? If it refers to a person being compared to a tree, what person is it? Not Empson himself, one assumes, since he appears to have been free from the more emotional side of the political enthusiasms of the 'thirties. If not Empson, who? And if a person is being compared to a tree in Kew Gardens, surely it would be simpler to omit Kew Gardens and compare the person directly to the tree of which the description starts in the first line. If, on the other hand, a tree in Kew is simply being compared to the tree in the first line, then the political connotation of the Red Dawn is also a red herring, and extremely confusing. (p. 74)

*Amy G. Stock, whom WE first met in 1941; see also *Essays presented to Amy G. Stock, Professor of English Rajasthan University 1961–65*, ed. R. K. Paul (Jaipur: Rajasthan University Press, 1965). 'Dinah' Stock (as she was known) was '**said to have invented Jomo Kenyatta,**' WE told Ian Parsons on 30 June 1965 (Reading).

Kathleen Raine, WE's friend and Cambridge contemporary, corrected Gunn in a published response (March 1956):

Has he failed to realize that the *locale* of the poem, from the first line, is not (on the level of the imagery) either the Garden of Eden where the two trees first grew, or the Far East, the habitat of the 'tree native in Turkestan', and also of the Tree of Heaven (*ailanthus glandulosa* [*sic*]) native of Northern China; the trees are in Kew Gardens. There, a little to the West of the Temperate House, but East of the tea-rooms, by a pavilion on a raised rockery, Mr Gunn will find the Tree of Heaven, a handsome plant, resembling in its pinnate leaves and key-like seeds, the other World Tree, the Ash. The last line merely refers back to the first. The tree 'native in Turkestan' does in fact grow near the Tree of Heaven, just as Professor Empson, who so characteristically, on a visit to Kew, passed the time reading the labels, says it does. (pp. 66–7)

Gunn countered (April 1956): 'I find the suggestion that readers should know that the one tree grows to the East of the other in Kew Gardens very odd'; and he added: 'I still do not see why the tree thirsts for a *political* Red Dawn. I can see how it thirsts for its apotheosis in a mythological Red Dawn, but the political idea seems to be introduced as an afterthought, and an unconnected one' (pp. 64–5).

However, Kathleen Raine's seeming assurance with regard to the whereabouts of the relevant trees raises more problems than it resolves. Mr J. L. S. Keesing, Scientific Liaison Officer at Royal Botanic Gardens, Kew, writes: 'There is no structure at Kew which I can identify with her statement "There, a little to the West of the Temperate House, but East of the tea-rooms, by a pavilion on a raised rockery . . ." but the descriptive comments about the Tree of Heaven itself are accurate.' The Tea Rooms (Refreshment Pavilion), Mr Keesing tells me, actually lie to the south-east of the Temperate House. 'To the north of the Temperate House stands King William's Temple which is on a raised, rockery-like mound; this building was completed in 1837 and a Tree of Heaven was planted close by in the same year. This particular tree was blown down in the storm of October 1987, and actually fell across the Temple; although the tree is no longer there the Temple withstood the weight and has been restored.' (The date of the poem is relevant, for while Kew contains a considerable number of trees which occur naturally in Turkestan, other specimens have died, and tracing original locations becomes more difficult with the passage of time, partly because of changes in methods of recording and mapping.) To the south-west of the Temperate House, for example, stands the Japanese Gateway, which also stands on a mount, once occupied by a small ornamental mosque, but the mound is not at all rockery-like. Still, certain specimens do remain to bear out the burden of the poem, both literal and figurative. 'Banksias, the Australian plants which rely on bush fires for seed dispersal and germination, are grown in the Temperate House; Eucalyptus trees occur in various parts of the Gardens, and include a big old specimen near the

Ruined Archway. The main pine collections are at the south end of the Gardens, but many examples are planted elsewhere, and these do include specimens of *Pinus cembra* . . .' (letter to Haffenden, 4 December 1989).

See also Morelli, pp. 63–4; Hawthorn, *Identity and Relationship*, pp. 87–90; Ricks, pp. 200–201; *TGA*, pp. 132–6. Ryle offers some arboreally-informed reflections in 'Flaming Heart of Darkness'.

1–5 *There is a tree . . . a forest fire*: various *Pinus* species depend on fire for the dispersal of the seeds from the cones, or show extensive seed germination from the leaf litter on the ground, after bush fires. The most likely candidate is *Pinus cembra*, the Arolla Pine, which occurs naturally from Central Europe to Siberia and which has very hard cones that are stated almost never to open to release the seeds: it is generally assumed that seed liberation in this case depends either on rotting or on animal and bird damage. Another tantalizing possibility is that WE is thinking of *Metasequoia glyptostroboides* – solely because its popular Western name is Dawn Redwood (l. 10). Sad to say, however, its cones cannot be described as 'hard cold', and the tree does not depend on fire for seed distribution. (I am indebted to Mr J. L. S. Keesing for information on the trees at Kew.)

2 east] East *Warner* ('e' appears to have been overwritten to make it 'E')

2 *Tree of Heaven*: botanical name *Ailanthus altissima*; lacking any kind of cones, it has seeds with red-orange wings which are most attractive in autumn but which fall as soon as they are ripe.

5–7 *fire . . . time's end*: the Apocalyptic idea that the world will end in fire.

6–7 Wait . . . Through] And . . . Wait, through *Eton*

6 *fathered as was Bacchus once*: Bacchus (Dionysus) was son to Semele: see note to l. 9.

8 *I knew the Phoenix was a vegetable*: Sir Thomas Browne, in Book III, ch. XII ('Of the Phœnix') of *Pseudodoxia Epidemica* (1646), discusses the evidence, gleaned from Scripture and the Classics, for various possible identifications of the phoenix, and observes: 'the Palm-tree . . . is also called Phœnix; and therefore the construction will be very hard, if not applied unto some vegetable nature' (*The Works of Sir Thomas Browne*, Vol. II: *Pseudodoxia Epidemica, Bks. I–VII*, ed. Geoffrey Keynes (London, 1928; new edn., 1964), p. 194). See also Dewitt T. Starnes and Ernest William Talbert, *Classical Myth and Legend in Renaissance Dictionaries* (Chapel Hill, N. Carolina, 1955), pp. 271–75; and the entry on *Phoinix* in *Real-Encyclopädie der Classischen Altertumswissenschaft*, XX (Stuttgart, 1941), esp. columns 414–23. For the Phoenix in Milton, see *Paradise Lost*, ed. Alastair Fowler (Harlow, 1971), pp. 272–3. Cf. Marvell's 'To his Coy Mistress', ll. 11–12: 'My vegetable Love should grow / Vaster than Empires, and more slow'. WE's line may also carry an echo of the refrain of W. B. Yeats's 'His Phoenix' (1916) – 'I knew a phoenix in my youth, so let them have their day' – from *The Wild Swans at Coole* (1919).

'No-one who heard Empson read [on the disc published by *Listen*] the line "I knew the Phoenix was a vegetable", could ever find it anything but humorous – a deliberate anti-climax after the somewhat erudite mythical references earlier on' (Hawthorn, *Identity and Relationship*, p. 89).

9 *So Semele desired her deity*: a Thracian or Phrygian Earth-goddess, the tragic Semele (daughter of Cadmus) is also known as Keraunia, or 'thunder-smitten', because she was consumed by a lightning-stroke; that is, the fulminating epiphany of Zeus. A mortal woman, she consequently bore Zeus an immortal son, Dionysus ('son of Zeus'), alias Bacchus (l. 6): see, for example, Hesiod, *Theog.* 940ff. Semele's story is conveniently rehearsed by Diodorus of Sicily, Book III.64.3–6:

Zeus had become enamoured of Semele . . . but Hera, being jealous and anxious to punish the girl, . . . led her on to her ruin; for she suggested to her that it was fitting that Zeus should lie with her while having the same majesty and honour in his outward appearance as when he took Hera to his arms. Consequently Zeus, at the request of Semele that she be shown the same honours as Hera, appeared to her accompanied by thunder and lightning, but Semele, unable to endure the majesty of his grandeur, died and brought forth the babe before the appointed time. (*Diodorus of Sicily*, II, trans. C. H. Oldfather (London, 1935), p. 295)

Cf. 'Bacchus', esp. ll. 1–4; and Tennyson's 'Semele' (*c.* 1835).

Pace Gunn's complaints about the poem, it is fitting for WE to convoke Semele and the Phoenix: Milton, in 'Epitaphium Damonis' (l. 187), so designates the Phoenix: '*divina avis*'.

Letter IV

Written and dated May 1929; published on 18 November 1929 by W. Heffer & Sons Ltd., Cambridge, as the first in a series of leaflets – 'single, hitherto unpublished poems by Cambridge poets of established reputation' – called *Songs for Sixpence*, edited by Jacob Bronowski and J. M. Reeves. Printed to the left margin, without indented lines, it was issued in a sewed leaflet in reduced crown octavo (7" × 5"), with a cover design (a startling woodblock print of female nude cavorting with prickly cactus) by Raymond McGrath. The print run was a generous 1,000 copies. According to Heffer's publishing diary, WE's poem was originally to have appeared as 'Monogamy and the Next Step'; it is possible that WE himself chose to alter the title in proof. Only six pamphlets were eventually issued in the series: the others were by Julian Bell, T. H. White, John Davenport, Michael Redgrave and Jacob Bronowski. It is not known just how many copies were sold, but the warehouse stock was remaindered in February 1933 and the remaining stock pulped in April 1937. (I am grateful for details of the publication history to Clive W. Cornell, Director of W. Heffer & Sons Ltd.)

CP: I left this out of the 1935 edition because the basic feelings seemed to have nothing to do with the moral, arrived at by allegorizing Eddington; it seemed sententious. I have tinkered with it a bit since, perhaps making it tidier rather than better.

A notebook with variously emended manuscript drafts of part of the poem (I have designated the ten leaves *MS1–MS10*) survives at Houghton. *MS1* has an early draft of stanza 2; *MS2* an early draft of stanza 3; *MS3* a more developed version of stanza 2; *MS4* drafts of stanza 1; *MS5* good drafts of stanzas 2–3; *MS6* two incomplete drafts of stanza 4; *MS7* a good draft of stanza 1; *MS8–MS9* early readings of stanza 5; and *MS10* a draft of some prose notes.

In December 1929 WE gave his Cambridge friend and contemporary Edward M. Wilson (translator of the Spanish Baroque poet Luis de Góngora) a copy of the pamphlet – signed '**E.M.W. from W.E.**' – along with a loose sheet with a few glosses ('**Excuse the impertinence of these notes, which people seem to find necessary. W.E.**'), cited below as *EMW* (now in the Department of Manuscripts, Cambridge University Library). (I am indebted to Mr A. E. B. Owen, former Keeper of Manuscripts.)

On 11 April 1930, the novelist Sylvia Townsend Warner, after a dinner prepared by WE at his lodgings, recorded in her diary these notes, which refer specifically to ll. 15–24, and the final sentence to stanza 4: 'Then he explained his R. 101 to me: helium, the ur, the unassimilable gas, first used for lifting airships, afterwards nitrogen, more common, and explosive, being a mixer – so when we use love to lift the soul, it is a mixer gas, and we must be careful accordingly, love better for getting on with our fellows. He told me that gravity was framed by the influence of *all* the stars' (courtesy of Claire Harman).

In *P*, from which he omitted this poem, WE remarked in his note to 'Letter V': '**I left out the fourth, thinking it bad.**'

For *Listen*: '**The lovers form a binary stellar system, but only the rest of the universe decides how it rotates; Eddington again.**'

Later he would remark, in a letter to Maxwell-Mahon (21 August 1973): '**"Letter IV" is very much about a neurotic condition, and not I think suitable for a poetry-reading, so I haven't any experience of how it goes over.**'

See Willis, pp. 237–44 and *TGA*, pp. 136–42.

1 Hatched in a rasping] Choked in a sullen *MS4*, *MS7*, *1929*
1–8 *Hatched . . . incumbent shade*: J. H. Fabre describes how the blind larva of the cicada tunnels out of its burrow through rough soil to the open air by virtue of being swollen with urine: 'this fountain of urine is the key to the enigma. As it digs and advances the larva waters the powdery debris and converts it into a paste, which is immediately applied to the walls by the pressure of the abdomen. Aridity is followed by plasticity . . .' However, not even the piss-proud cicada, it seems,

can go on producing liquid waste without replenishing its 'bladder'; its answer is to seek out a local source of sap – a small living root. 'When its reservoir is exhausted by the conversion of dry dust into mud the miner descends to its chamber, thrusts its proboscis into the root, and drinks deep from the vat built into the wall. Its organs well filled, it re-ascends. It resumes work, damping the hard soil the better to remove it with its talons, reducing the debris to mud, in order to pack it tightly around it and obtain a free passage' (*Social Life in the Insect World*, trans. Bernard Miall (London, 1912), pp. 24–6). WE's 'lover' in l. 5 might just as well be 'mother', the source of sustenance to the 'child cicada'; but perhaps it was the rhyme-word 'smothers' in l. 4 that made him decide against it (see collation for line 5).

3 *dumb mouth . . . climb*: cf. Milton, 'Lycidas', ll. 113–15, 119: 'How well could I have spared for thee, young swain, / Enow of such as for their bellies' sake, / Creep and intrude, and climb into the fold? / . . . Blind mouths!'

3 his] the *1929*

4 *tunnel*: cf. 'The Ants', l. 1, 'The Scales', l. 8, and 'Earth has Shrunk in the Wash', l. 22.

4 dust] silt *1929*

5 urine from this lover] urine, once his lover's *1929*

6-7 *only to evade . . . made*: MS4 records this comment by WE: **'of his own waste products makes order in the chaos: understanding it by changing it (appearing to understand scientifically) only to escape from it.'** *MS4* accordingly includes the reading **'He knows an ordered Nature he has made'**.

8 *from*: **'1st verse, there might be an accent on *from* = "to get away from" and "using as his material" '** (*EMW*).

8 incumbent] eternal *MS4*, *MS7*, *1929*

8 *incumbent shade*: 'Truths, which eternity lets fall on man / With double weight, thro' these revolving spheres, / This death-deep silence, and incumbent shade: / Thoughts, such as shall revisit your last hour; / Visit uncall'd, and live when life expires' ('Night V: The Relapse', ll. 73–7, in 'The Complaint; or, Night Thoughts': *The Poetical Works of Edward Young*, ed. the Rev. John Mitford, vol. I (London, 1896), p. 80). Young exploits the phrase again in 'A Paraphrase on part of the Book of Job', ll. 77–80: 'Hath the cleft centre open'd wide to thee? / Death's inmost chambers didst thou ever see? / E'er knock at his tremendous gate, and wade / To the black portal through th'incumbent shade?' (*Poetical Works*, vol. II, p. 175). 'Incumbent' means 'pressing with weight', as the soil might press upon the cicada (or the coffin); Milton has Satan 'incumbent on the dusky air' (*PL*, I. 226).

9-10 On my . . . where bergs float / In] Into the . . . of my boat: / Its *1929*

9-16 *On my unpointed . . . treasure-trove*: WE's notebook drafts include this commentary on *MS10* (evidently written for his own sake during the process of composition): **'one moves with an ease that seems always possible, in a larger**

cooler faster world, in reach of more people . . . between the crowded, out of work, scientifically over-wrought island and the not then limited virgin corn-country (placing Elizabeth from her particular to her general . . .) and gold or jewels, treasure trove even when Spain-stolen (by or from).' 'Unpointed' is dull, featureless, pointless; unpunctuated; not fixed with mortar.

11 *Roman feather*: 'to make you vomit' (*EMW*).

13 sunbeam and a part can] breadth of sunbeam and I *1929*

15–16 *gross . . . virgin's*: 'the airship, having reached the air like the cicada, is now full of expensive people which it is taking to America' (*EMW*).

17 The] With *1929*

18–19 *Israel . . . had striven; / 'I will not let thee go'*: the title *Israel* ('God fights, God rules') was bestowed upon Jacob after his dauntless, night-long wrestling-match with an angel at Peniel, and the angel said, 'Let me go, for the day breaketh: and he [Jacob] said, I will not let thee go, except thou bless me' (Gen. 32: 26).

19 *Helium*: the second most abundant element in the universe, synthesized from hydrogen; too light to be retained by the earth's gravitational field, so all primordial helium is the product of radioactive decay. A non-flammable gas, it was used for airships until replaced by hydrogen.

20 *unvalenced*: not 'draped or fringed with a hanging or border'; but this participial adj. may also subsume connotations associated with 'valency', an obsolete term for vigour which also pertains to chemistry: 'the power or capacity of certain elements to combine with or displace a greater or less number of hydrogen (or other) atoms' (*OED²* *valency* 2).

20–21 air of Heaven. / These risings have] heaven. / We rise with a *1929*

21 *earth-born gas*: 'hydrogen, now used for airships' (*EMW*). In addition, the Giants of Greek mythology may have sprung from the blood of the mutilated Uranus, husband of Gaia (Earth): hence they were often called *Gegeneis* ('earth-born'). Cf. Donne's 'earth-born' in 'Holy Sonnet 6', l. 10.

22 *bitter in the belly*: although WE may well have taken this wording directly from the Introduction to Sir Herbert Grierson's edition of *The Poems of John Donne* (Oxford, 1929), p. xxii – 'Donne's nature had revolted, asserted its claim to life and experience. But experience is bitter as well as sweet – sweet in the mouth but bitter in the belly' – he would have known that it ultimately derives from Rev. 10: 9–10: 'And I went unto the angel, and said unto him, Give me the little book. And he said unto me, Take it, and eat it up; and it shall make thy belly bitter, but it shall be in thy mouth sweet as honey. And I took the little book out of the angel's hand, and ate it up; and it was in my mouth sweet as honey: and as soon as I had eaten it, my belly was bitter.'

23–4 If rain . . . / Or if on fire to make too fierce an] Bursting, . . . / And by its closing, scatter us from our *1929*

24 *empyry*: derives from the Greek *empyros* ('enflamed'): the empyrean, the highest heaven, sphere of fire. (Cf. Donne's use in 'Going to Bed', Elegy XIX, l. 29.)

25 *Therefore*: 'Argufying in poetry is not only mental; it also feels muscular. Saying "therefore" is like giving the reader a bang on the nose; and though it may be said that "intellectualized" poetry feels stale and unreal, a bang on the nose does not feel stale and unreal; it is just as fresh the twentieth time as it was the first; that is, if you are granted enough leisure for recovery. The word "therefore" is no more stale than the word "dawn", and has just as much imagery about it' ('Argufying in Poetry' (1963); *A*, p. 170).

25 can] may *1929, Listen*

26 would] should *MS6*

27–8 Slung on . . . / Putting] Hold the . . . / And lay *1929*

29–40 *Stars . . . strong*: WE's preparatory jottings (*MS10*) include: 'fixed-stars, not apparently giving much light, but in (special) theory of relativity (actually *owing* to their distance) = the reality of diurnal rotation, the difference between earth round sun (-woman) and sun round earth anthropo- (pre-humanist) hence self-centred. Their fixity, the imaginative relief of their presence . . .' With respect to ll. 29–32, Willis (p. 242) notes: 'Twin stars or star and satellite are produced when a star undergoes "excessive rotation", thereby breaking into two planetary bodies [see Eddington, *The Nature of the Physical World*, p. 176]. If the girl is planet, the poet is revolving satellite. If the lovers are binary stars, according to Eddington's statement, they might revolve around the same centre of gravity.'

33 *Who*: the elliptic usage of Spenser, Shakespeare, Donne and Milton. Cf. *PL*, I.49: 'Who durst defy the omnipotent to arms' – a construction on which WE commented that Milton 'sometimes uses ambiguous language to heighten the drama' (*Milton's God*, p. 37).

36–8 Imply the creature . . . *are song*] *MS9* includes this interesting variant: 'The mind abandoned from itself that goes / In a straight arrow between all the rows / And shoots itself, not nothing, at the end.' (Cf. the 'arrows' in the final line of 'Letter V'.)

36–40 Imply the creature . . . / Your sun alone yielding its beauty glows / In growth upon the planet. They are song / Or call the tune to make the dancing throng / Free only as they aloof compose it and are strong.] Receive the creature, . . . / And as your sun, by yielding beauty, glows / And moves upon the planet, they, as strong, / Resound, by being held aloof, their song, / Compose earth's nature, are his laws, consist his throng. *MS8, 1929*

39 to make] that makes *Listen*

39 *dancing throng*: although it is seemingly commonplace, WE possibly derived this phrase from the closing of James Thomson's 'Ronald and Helen', where it is used twice: ' "I went of late amid the dancing throng, / To dance with *Him* – my Love who loveth me" ' (*The Poetical Works of James Thomson*, ed. Bertram Dobell (London, 1895), vol. II, pp. 240, 242). Given 'song' (l. 38) and 'Free' and 'aloof' (l. 40), cf. too Rossetti's Sonnet L (no. II of the 'Willowwood' sequence), in *The House of Life*, ll. 1–6: 'And now Love sang: but his was such a song, / So meshed with half-remembrance hard to free, / As souls disused in death's sterility / May sing when the new birthday tarries long. / And I was made aware of a dumb throng / That stood aloof'.

Doctrinal Point

First published in *The Year's Poetry 1935*, ed. Denys Kilham Roberts, Gerald Gould and John Lehmann (London: John Lane The Bodley Head, 1935), pp. 90–91. In an undated letter to Lehmann, WE wrote: '*Doctrinal Point* hasn't appeared before. I forgot it' – which would imply that it was written some time before 1935 (Harry Ransom Humanities Research Center, University of Texas at Austin).

CP: I meant here to compare together the cope of heaven which protects the earth (a world that seems complete to those inside it, like that of the flowers), the cope of the priest-king that symbolizes the protection of heaven, the calyx that protects the growing flower, the rainbow repeating the divine promise, the Heaviside layer that keeps off ultra-violet rays (taken as 'freer' than the traditional solid cover), and vaults over tombs under the ground from which the flowers have risen. Also man was given authority over all the creatures, but this involves much toiling and spinning, as when in over-alls.

For *Listen* he noted: '*Doctrinal Point* yearns to be always sure what to do. This is arranged for you by the social world you accept, which may need to be a large and remote one.'

On *Harvard* he commented: 'It is really what they used to call Deism: it is saying that if you arrive at the point of grace, granting that you accept the concept, you will no longer require a personal god – you are, as it were, *living* like that, as the flowers are: they are untroubled. And the mystery of the conception of being in a state of grace, which is no credit to yourself, means that the problems that arise for most of humanity no longer arise. That is what is being considered – one can hardly say, *discussed* – in this poem.'

A small early notebook in the Empson Papers, evidently dating from the early 1930s, includes these remarks:

The process of knowing a person, understanding a rabbit when it screams, or gauging the character of a chicken, is so mysterious that one may very easily be understanding the attitude to life of a plant when one admires its beauty; knowing something which it too, even if without consciousness, knows – as from one living creature to another. It is very hard to see what else can be the source of so vivid a pleasure, of so delicate an impression of character, of so universal an appeal, as is found in flowers.

There are three surviving sheets of draft manuscript. *MS1* has sketches of ll. 1–4 and 12; and WE also noted on this sheet, '**poem whose subject is being puzzled**', along with the proper name '**Eddington**'. *MS2* has drafts of ll. 8–9 and 10–12, as well as (at the head of the sheet) the notation, '**X's blood in the firmament**', alluding to the A-text of Marlowe's *Dr Faustus*, scene 13, ll. 71–3: 'O I'll leap up to my God! Who pulls me down? / See, see, where Christ's blood streams in the firmament! / One drop would save my soul, half a drop: ah my Christ –'. *MS3* includes a good draft of ll. 20–26.

The poem focuses on the conflict between the prompting of mankind's consciousness, in particular our apparent need to refer our existence to an external, transcendent power, so as to find a redemption beyond ourselves, and the capacity of natural science to be self-referring or self-confirming; in the case of flowering plants, it seems, to perpetuate themselves in an unselfconscious, self-sufficient system which needs no justification. The running metaphor is an exploitation of imagery taken from Christian doctrine, especially references to the Redemption in ll. 5–9, climaxing in the representation of a blossom in the attitude of Christ on the cross (l. 11). The magnolia is solipsistic: it requires no Redeemer. Such an arrangement WE then compares to the methods and findings of modern physics, which postulates a world of abstract symbology which serves to endorse itself in a manner that, the poem argues, is not wholly dissimilar to that of the inscrutable plants. 'I should like to make it clear,' wrote Eddington in 1928, 'that the limitation of the scope of physics to pointer readings and the like is not a philosophical craze of my own but is essentially the current scientific doctrine . . . Einstein's theory . . . insists that each physical quantity should be defined as the result of certain operations of measurement and calculation . . . In science we study the linkage of pointer readings with pointer readings. The terms link together in endless cycle' (*Nature of the Physical World*, pp. 254–5, 258). In such terms, the supposedly exploratory methodology of exact science may be thought to be tautological (l. 14) – or anyway paradoxical.

The pun in the title questions (a) the *point* of Christian *doctrine*, and (b) the non-contradictory *doctrine* of modern physical science which proves itself by way of the circularity of *point*er readings. The notion of circularity is reflected in the poem to the extent that the ultimate phrase 'into the air' repeats the final phrase of the first line; the difference is that whereas l. 1 hauntingly stresses the idea that a godhead can never be realized in the conditions of mortal life, the beauty of botany is that plants are manifestly free to fulfil themselves: a god 'dissolves . . . into the air', but magnolias 'rise . . . into the air'.

A notable point of correspondence in WE's critical writings is to be found in the essay 'Double Plots', where he speaks of the prevalent desire of writers during the Renaissance '**to make the individual more independent than Christianity allowed**'. To determine the applicability to 'Doctrinal Point' of the following quotation, one needs to read *plants* for *animals*: '**The feeling for independence** peeps out in the language about animals. They are envied for not being threatened with heaven or hell, with an external last judgement; this naturally appears as a result of fear of hell, but the wider feeling, that one did not want to submit to the inquisition of a central divine authority even at best, was the necessary background of its appeal' (*Pastoral*, p. 64).

In *MS3* the final lines are followed by an extra passage about '**Charlemagne of Ballantrae**' which was further developed on another manuscript page beginning with a version of the final stanza of 'Letter I' (also 1935). Yet another version of the stanza (which never did manage to find a good permanent home) figures on a typescript page relating to 'Letter V' – though WE tried hardest of all to engineer a place for these greatly revised lines in the present poem.

> Charlemagne of Ballantrae, England's over-sleeper,
> The Beauty that has pushed so many daisies –
> Worn, hoar with springing, a cocoon your texture,
> Hedge-rows crowned round the flowered hair of paddocks,
> Puppy-rose ranked to a guard of thorn
> (Whose cold small exquisite patterns, flowering in the cold,
> Hide in its keen stretched grave-folds their flesh-warm beauty,
> Yield to its wind the scent that alone shows their passion).

('Charlemagne' could refer to a variety of apple (see Robert Hogg, *The Fruit Manual*, 5th edn. (London, 1884), p. 42), or the dog-rose, England's emblem. Not the dog-rose proper (*rosa canina*) but a smaller version of it called the downy rose (*rosa tomentosa*). The dog-rose has flowers 45–50 mm. across, the downy rose 30–40 mm.; hence 'puppy-rose', a small dog-rose (cf. 'The Scales', l. 5). The downy rose is so called because its leaflets are covered with dense down. This suggests white hair, hence old age and death. At the same time, the opening of the flower in late spring (June–July) suggests freshness and new life, so the whole thing can be an image of old age, death and resurrection. Furthermore: 'Charlemagne of Ballantrae' combines two figures each of whom embodies the same paradox. Charlemagne is one of those heroes whose return from the dead is foretold in folklore. The Master of Ballantrae was buried in the freezing earth, but came briefly to life after being dug up by the faithful Secundra in the thrilling last episode of Stevenson's novel. Charlemagne is always represented as bearded; and when the Master was exhumed it was seen that he had grown a beard while buried. (See Robert Louis Stevenson, *The Master of Ballantrae: A Winter's Tale* (1889), ch. xii.) It is whimsical to combine a French and a Scottish hero to image 'England's over-sleeper' – oversleeping perhaps because this rose (both kinds) flowers late in spring. 'Pushed so many daisies' clearly makes use of the old slang phrase for being dead, and refers to the men who have died for England's sake as represented by the rose. 'Worn': worn like a badge, and also seeming to be worn from the grey hair. 'Hoar with springing' combines the ideas of age and springtime; more simply, looking hoary as spring comes round; more fancifully, grown old with having sprung so many times. This beguiling passage is perhaps best taken in conjunction not only with 'Doctrinal Point' but also, especially for diction, with 'Note on Local Flora'.) (I am indebted to my colleague Derek Roper for his invaluable help with deciphering this riddling passage.)

See also Willis, pp. 244–7; Morelli, pp. 40–42; *TGA*, pp. 142–7.

1 The god approached dissolves into the air] **Lord God, Lord God, you should be the whole air** *MS1* (cf. Hopkins, 'The Blessed Virgin compared to the Air we Breathe' (1883), l. 122: 'O God's love, O live air').

1 *dissolves into the air*: in 'Double Plots', with specific reference to the desire to discover a freedom from 'a central divine authority', WE quotes from Marlowe Dr Faustus's famous last lines, 'All beasts are happy, / For, when they die, / Their souls are soon dissolved in elements', with the comment: '**the doubtful word** *dissolved* **allows pantheism to be still present at the end**' (*Pastoral*, p. 64). *TGA* (p. 142) suggests that this line 'may be intended as a version of a passage' in Eddington's *Nature of the Physical World*: 'Our conception of substance is only vivid so long as we do not face it. It begins to fade when we analyse it' (p. 273).

7 *Their sapient matter is always already informed*: embedding a pun on 'sap', the line may mean wise because self-sustaining (*sapientia*: discernment, taste); also, from the original sense of Latin *sapere*, literally having a taste or savour, sapid; perhaps imbued by osmosis (and so, in one sense at least, infused or 'informed'). Cf. *PL*, IX.442, IX.1018; and T. S. Eliot's use of the term in 'Mr Eliot's Sunday Morning Service' (1918), l. 2: 'The sapient sutlers of the Lord'.

The insistence upon the plants being 'always already informed' would appear to be a direct riposte to Dante's doctrinal differentiation in *Paradiso*, VII. 130–32: 'The Angels ... may be declared to be created, even as they are, in their entire being; / but the elements which thou hast named and all the things compounded of them' have by created virtue been informed. / Created was the matter which they hold, created was the informing virtue of these stars which sweep around them' (*The Paradiso of Dante Alighieri*, trans. Rev. Philip H. Wicksteed, Temple Classics (London, 1899), p. 85). WE sometime commented in handwritten notes on Canto VII (in this translation): '**Very interesting contradiction: angels are created by direct instantaneous impulse, therefore are free. But so was the prima materia, which on this view is the lowest of things, and being pure potentiality has least freedom. But freedom is precisely the potentiality to be this or that, and must be possessed in the highest degree by the lowest part of the hierarchy. This is a fundamental objection to Dante's (or Aquinas's) system.**' See also note to l. 67 of 'Bacchus'.

7 always already] **already fully** *Listen*

9 *Plump spaced-out saints, in their gross prime, at prayer*: one of the Canonical Hours of the Divine Office, Prime *is said at sunrise; but* WE *is also punning on the word in the sense of 'maturity'*.

13–14 *Professor Eddington . . . one tautology*:

a fundamental law of physics is no controlling law but a 'put-up job' as soon as we have ascertained the nature of that which is obeying it. We can measure certain forms of energy with a thermometer, momentum with a ballistic pendulum, stress with a manometer. Commonly we picture these as separate physical entities whose behaviour towards each other is controlled by a law. But now the theory is that the three instruments measure different but slightly overlapping aspects of a single physical condition, and a law connecting their measurements is of the same tautological type as a 'law' connecting measurements with a metre-rule and a foot-rule . . . (*Nature of the Physical World*, pp. 238–9)

See also, as *TGA* suggests (p. 144), Eddington in *New Pathways in Science* (Cambridge, 1935), p. 25: 'Does the external world in physics . . . really exist? . . . For my own part, any notion that I have of existing is derived from my own existence, so that my own existence is a tautological consequence of any definition that I should be willing to adopt.'

15 *tensors*: 'The progress of the relativity theory has been largely due to the development of a powerful mathematical calculus for dealing compendiously with an infinite scheme of pointer readings, and the technical term *tensor* used so largely in treatises on Einstein's theory may be translated *schedule of pointer readings*' (Eddington, *Nature of the Physical World*, p. 257).

16–17 *All law . . . the description*: Eddington remarks, with wry amusement, if not 'insolence' (l. 13): 'the mind has by its selective power fitted the processes of Nature into a frame of law of a pattern largely of its own choosing; and in the discovery of this system of law the mind may be regarded as regaining from Nature that which the mind has put into Nature' (*Nature of the Physical World*, p. 244). 'And so we see that the poetry fades out of the problem, and by the time the serious application of exact science begins we are left with only pointer readings. If then only pointer readings or their equivalents are put into the machine of scientific calculation, how can we grind out anything but pointer readings?' (ibid., p. 252).

In an unpublished typescript draft of an essay on Eddington's *The Philosophy of Physical Science* (Cambridge, 1939), WE offers observations which pertain to ll. 13–19:

Less of a success because more bare assertion; he seems too busy with his philosophy to do the science popularizing he is best at . . . These words 'subjective' and 'epistemological' get thrown about very loosely. He seems half to be saying 'daringly' that science is all 'inside the mind' and the only thing outside the mind is beautiful thoughts and holy feelings. But he has no ground for saying more than that nature turns out *more* to correspond to our concepts, when our concepts are carefully teased out under continual control from observation, than might be expected. For example Euclid seems to have claimed that his geometry was subjective and epistemological in E's sense. Starting from our native concepts about space it gets elaborate properties from them which are *also* found in space. What wouldn't occur to Euclid would be to say that the human mind *invented* space, and that this is *proved* by the fact that our native ideas about it work out all right. Even Kant only said we invented it because our ideas *don't* work out right (but lead to contradictions). It seems too much for Eddington to say that though Euclid's ideas about space were wrong, as has been proved by later experiment, still the fact that Euclid was right proves that space is an invention of the human mind.

No good making jokes for long – the extent to which a certain line of thought does seem to have been intuitively right about the universe (e.g. invention of atoms) is very striking, also the delight we rightly get from a sense [of] 'how much more right I was than I realized' (e.g. playing off Euclidean and coordinate geometry). The human mind, on certain sides only, seems to have started with an equipment remarkably well fitted for understanding the universe. But it would not occur to me in my own religious musings to say that we have invented those parts of the universe, because the only religious interest in the matter is thereby at once removed . . .

p. 104. 'We could not have this kind of a priori knowledge of laws governing an objective universe.' This seems to be the key argument. But how much knowledge could we get of a universe that went wrong on us? It seems quite conceivable that all conceivable universes exist, but that only those universes contain creatures doing science work which are fit for science work to be done in. After all it is very odd to call your first principles 'a priori' when they are the latest news. The only historical fact bearing on this point is that the human mind has again and again, after the labours of a lifetime, been able to invent principles that seem 'a priori' and that turn out to be good approximations to the truth. Let any rhetorical device be used to hammer in the fact that this is an extraordinary fact about the universe. But the answer to this Eddington sentence is surely very simple: 'It is clear from history that men would never have got so far back *prior* to the primitive ideas if they had not been encouraged by an objective universe at every stage.'

17 *Assumption*: thus capitalized, the word here cocks a snook at the Roman Catholic teaching that Mary, mother of Jesus, was assumed after death, body and soul, into heaven, but it also reflects on Eddington's account of the *a priori* principles of science: see the previous note. Cf. 'Camping Out', l. 9.

18 choice] choice thus *Year's Poetry 1935*, P

20–22 *Solomon* . . . / *Gives these no cope who cannot know of care*: Solomon ('peaceable'), son of David and Bathsheba, third king of Israel, performed the role of priest to his people: see 1 Kings 1–11. The general sense is that his mandate does not extend to the magnolias ('these'), which are unconscious and so innocent of fretful responsibility or religious faith. With 'cope' here, cf. 'Bacchus', ll. 18, 89.

In *MS 3* an additional line figures after these lines: '**Though we should tell them what they were**' – which, in WE's pronunciation, would have been a perfect rhyme with 'wear', 'care', 'air', etc. (cf. the rhymes in 'Let it go', ll. 3, 6).

20 should] could *Listen*

22 *no gap to spare that they should share*: 'they', like 'these' in l. 21, refers back to the magnolias: the phrase points to the idea of a gap between being and consciousness.

22–3 *share / The rare calyx we stare at in despair*: at the first level, 'rare calyx' signifies the pod that protects petals in the bud, the long outer perianth of the *Magnolia grandiflora*; but also, given that the Latin word *calix* means 'cup or drinking vessel', context allows that the magnolias could never join us in bowing down to the chalice of Christ's blood as raised in the Mass – which those people who don't believe in it might be considered to be '*in despair* of '.

25 *Their arch of promise the wide Heaviside layer*: lacking a religious mythology, the plants have no truck with God's covenant – the rainbow or 'arch of promise' which is the token of God's covenant with humankind (Gen. 9: 8–17); all they need is the physical vault affirmed by science, the Heaviside layer (named for the English physicist). WE remarked, on *Harvard*: '**The Heaviside layer is what keeps us safe from the long wavelengths of the sun, you understand: they [the plants] are in a sense protected.**'

25 the wide] is the warm *MS 3*

26 *They rise above a vault into the air*: free of the fear of death, and of religious sanctions, the plants simply declare their existence. As for human beings, the poem implies, we are left not with the traditional religious exhortation *Sursum corda*, nor with the miracle of the Resurrection that is negatively implied in this line, but in the sorry state of suspension described by Eddington: 'instead of standing on a firm immovable earth proudly rearing our heads towards the vault of heaven, we are hanging by our feet from a globe careering through space at a great many miles a second' (*Nature of the Physical World*, p. 247). Given 'care' in l. 21, perhaps cf. Romeo's 'Nor that is not the lark whose notes do beat / The vaulty heaven so high above our heads. / I have more care to stay than will to go' (*Romeo and Juliet*, III.v.21–3). Cf. also 'Bacchus', l. 92.

Letter V

First published in *The Year's Poetry 1934*, ed. Denys Kilham Roberts, Gerald Gould and John Lehmann (London, 1934), pp. 94–5. This poem was initially drafted in Tokyo in September 1931, as WE told Sylvia Townsend Warner in a letter of 10 October (?1932): '**I shan't write [more] verse till I leave this country, and am sending you a thing I wrote in my first month here, before the clogging effect had got to work. There ought to be some more in the middle** [i.e. after stanza 4]. **Envelope and Duality and Inversion are mainly the mathematical sort. I don't like it much**' (Reading).

There are five surviving sheets of draft manuscript (*MS1–5*), together with two typescript sheets with handwritten emendations (*TS1–2*); *MS4* is the verso of *TS2* (a sheet of A3 paper). *MS1* has variant states of ll. 9–12 (stanza 3), *MS2* drafts of ll. 1–8 (stanzas 1–2), 17–18, 21–4; *MS3* has versions of ll. 21–4 (stanza 6); *MS4* an advanced state of the whole poem. *MS5* includes a stab at ll. 17–18, in the prosaic form '**I praise you not as form but as cause**', and a draft version of some unfinished verses about '**Charlemagne of Ballantrae**' (see discussion of 'Doctrinal Point' above), as well as four further unpublished lines discussed below. *TS1*, which is dated by WE '**Tokyo Sept [19]31**'), has the whole poem, plus six additional lines following stanza 4 (see further below); so does *TS2*.

In the first printing (and in the holograph version (*MS6*) sent to Townsend Warner in ?1932), a conspicuous set of three asterisks fills a line space after stanza 4 to indicate that WE felt he had never supplied a deficiency in the poem: that is, he believed there was an unsatisfactory hiatus in the argument between stanzas 4 and 5, a failure of transitional matter. In *MS1*, for example, stanza 3 is succeeded by these curious trial lines:

> By growing on me, not by growing greater –
> Those depths in Buddhas one then sees on the waiter:
> I have loved the sea-mark of a standing negative,
> That is no place even where they can drown.
> Either a star then or a liver fluke
> But no such lamp-post as I pass by walking.

While the liver fluke eventually found its proper place in the final stanza of 'China', in a series of further drafts, holograph and typescript, WE attempted to work out this six-line verse to form a bridge between stanzas 4 and 5, beginning '**Interest on substance built this crown, / On understanding then . . .**' (other versions include '**My interest compounded you this crown**', '**My interest on your substance built your crown**', '**Interest summed your principle to a crown**' and even – in a mood, perhaps, of prosaic exasperation – '**Interest on that tireless substance named understanding**'). In *TS1*, which is embroidered with handwritten emendations, the emergent passage took this form:

> Interest on your fixity grew a crown;
> Your letting love rather as letting live;
> Your growing on one rather than growing greater –
> Those depths in Buddhas one then sees on the waiter –
> I have loved the sea-mark of a standing negative;
> That is no place even where one may drown.

– which did at least complete a pattern of rhymes.

MS5 also includes a rough draft of some rhyming verses which WE may momentarily have considered using to bridge the gap between stanzas 5 and 6, though their facetiously doggerel quality would have made them quite unsuitable for the present poem); they appear to read as follows:

If chimpanzees have hands like pianists
And rats in mazes illustrate the mind
When's every dog to find his catalyst?
Who's to convince her that she is unkind?

With considerable reluctance, WE finally abandoned his attempts to craft 'some more in the middle': on 12 May 1934 he wrote to John Lehmann, enclosing 'Letter V' (along with the first section of 'Bacchus') for possible inclusion in *The Year's Poetry 1934* (London, 1934), and adding a dejected observation: '**Both poems are incomplete but I am not likely to improve them**' (Harry Ransom Humanities Research Center, University of Texas at Austin).

CP: **A locus defines a surface by points and an envelope defines it by tangents.** *Knot chance* – where the connection of thought they make possible spreads itself into an actual meaning; pun with 'not'. *Grit* round which the pearl grew. *Your curve* is the curve of the mirror which makes it reflect a wide area, like a camera obscura, but gives the reflection an odd geometry as in non-Euclidean space, so that you can't imagine yourself inside it. 'You make me know about the states though you do not come from them, are not known there, and do not yourself know about them.' *That has been shown* by the effect of the cause, as in the argument that there must at least be a structure in the external world corresponding to that of our sense-impressions. *Imply but to exclude* repeats the idea of defining a volume by tangents all outside it. The Principle of Duality states that every proposition of a certain kind about points has a corresponding one about lines; this is supposed to show that the distinction previously drawn was unreal. Pun on Principal, chief and causer. Also 'the principle that lovers are inevitably two separate people is the rule of life, and can be made to work.' To invert lines into points is to apply the principle; the lines are in part the lines of the poem. And even without this process the tangents are arrows which though missing you may still hold you.

WE was to claim, some years later: '**I think this final *Letter* really succeeds in conveying affection, much better than the others** [i.e. the other poems in the 'Letter' sequence] **do**' (letter to Maxwell-Mahon, 6 November 1967).

See Joseph E. Duncan, *The Revival of Metaphysical Poetry* (1959), pp. 196–8, who notes: 'As the separated lovers are yet united in Donne's familiar compass conceit, Empson's lady – so unknowable and perplexingly separate – is at last known and caught through the logic of his geometry. The poem also fits into the later metaphysical tradition in suggesting the two touching spheres in Browning's "Beatrice Signorini" and the compass figure treating the epistemology of love in Hopkins' *Floris in Italy*' (p. 198). Willis (pp. 248–54) remarks: 'The poet-lover of "Letter V", like a philatelist, knows the value of the girl's envelope. "Locus" (place or address), "envelope", "good form", and "letter" in the second stanza support the postal analogy on one level. On another level, the analogies are to geometry and physics which recall the analogies of "Camping Out", and "Letter I": "locus" (system of points), "envelope" (system of planes), "paths of light" (rays and lines), "atoms of good form" (quanta or points), and "tangent".' See also *TGA*, pp. 147–51.

    F. R. Leavis appears not to have liked this poem: see note to lines 10–12 of 'Your Teeth are Ivory Towers'.

1 *envelope*: 'the locus of the ultimate intersections of consecutive curves (or surfaces) in a "family" or system of curves (or surfaces)' (*OED* 'envelope' 5).
4 *more intimacy for less hope*: '**less hope of getting to bed together, of course, what else?**' (letter to Maxwell-Mahon, 6 November 1967).
7 *I can love so for truth, as still for grace*: cf. Donne, 'The Indifferent', ll. 8–9: 'I can love her, and her, and you and you, / I can love any, so she be not true.'
7–8 I can love so for truth, as still for grace, / Your] I may praise so for truth as still for grace / The *1934*
8 humility that will not hear or] incredulous modesty that will not *MS2*
10 *their knot chance unfurls*: 'knot chance' does not appear to be simply a compound phrase (like 'knot-diamond', in 'Sea Voyage', l. 6); 'chance' is perhaps best seen as the subject, and 'their knot' the object, of the verb 'unfurls'; though *TGA* (p. 149) may be right in remarking that what is suggested is 'the way in which, in metaphor, various implications coincide, according to some hidden logic ("not chance") – implications which, it is claimed, function best when left alone'.
10–11 *unfurls; / . . . glanced pearls*: cf. 'Letter III', ll. 15–16. 'Glanced' may mean 'glimpsed', but the phrase carries a secondary suggestion of 'polished'.
12 That not for me shall] No acid now will *1934*
13–16 *Wide-grasping glass . . . make known*: '**The convex mirror distorts (like non-Euclidean geometry) but includes a wide area; "you are a means of understanding and healing though unapproachable"**' (*Listen*). Willis (p. 251) suggests that this stanza recalls John Donne's 'The Canonization', ll. 40–44: 'Who did the whole world's soul contract, and drove / Into the glasses of your eyes / (So made such mirrors, and such spies, / That they did all to you epitomize,) / Countries, towns, courts'. For 'Wide-grasping', cf. John Gay, 'A Panegyrical Epistle to Mr Thomas Snow' (1721): ll. 3–4: 'Whether thy Compter shine with sums untold, / And thy wide-grasping Hand grow black with Gold' (*The Poetical Works*, ed. G. C. Faber (Oxford, 1926), p. 177).

14 at] from *MS6, 1934*

17–18 Cause . . . Form / cause . . . form *1934*

17 unknown] Unknown *MS6*

18 Form that has been] forms of what is *MS6;* form that it has *1934*

19 exclude] exclude, *1934*

20 *attitude*: Willis (p. 252) notes, ' "Attitude", as with the "good form" of stanza one, suggests posture, mood, and deportment. It may also recall Keats's Grecian urn, that "fair attitude", that "silent form", which teases poets out of thought.'

21 *Duality too has its Principal*: the principle of duality, in projective geometry, holds that any true proposition of concepts can be transformed into equivalent concepts, dual to the first; that is, every true theorem of projective geometry has a dual form (they are mutually interchangeable) whose proof follows from that of the original theorem. The duality principle applies also in mathematical logic.

'Principal' occurs as '**Principle**' in *MS3*, *MS4*, *TS1* and *TS2* (the last being corrected by hand to '**Principal**'.

22 *These lines you grant me . . . points*: cf. Empson's discursive discussion of line 9 – 'So should the lines of life that life repair' – of Shakespeare's Sonnet XVI: '**Lines of life refers to the form of a personal appearance, in the young man himself or repeated in his descendants (as one speaks of the lines of some one's figure); time's wrinkles on that face . . .; the young man's line or lineage – his descendants; lines drawn with a pencil – a portrait; lines drawn with a pen, in writing; the lines of a poem . . .; and destiny**' (*ST*, pp. 76–7). Cf. also 'Four Legs, Two Legs, Three Legs', l. 2.

22 *invert*: an inversion in geometry is defined as 'a transformation in which for each point of a given figure is substituted another point in the same straight line from a fixed point (called the *origin* or *centre of inversion*), and so situated that the product of the distances of the two points from the centre of inversion is constant (*cyclical* or *spherical inversion*). Also extended to similar transformations involving a more complex relation of corresponding points or lines' (*OED* 'inversion' 3b); 'invert' also has the sense of a person 'whose sex instincts are inverted', i.e. reversed.

24 *Cross you on painless arrows to the wall*: for the representation of St Sebastian as a homosexual icon, see Ricks on an early poem by T. S. Eliot, 'The Love Song of St. Sebastian', in *Inventions of the March Hare* (1996), pp. 267–70.

Letter VI: a marriage

The typescript of this autobiographical poem (Empson Papers), which was first published, posthumously, in *RB*, carries the date '**23 March 1935**' – the day on which Desmond Lee, to whom WE had addressed his series of 'Letter' poems, married Elizabeth Crockenden. See headnote to 'Letter I', p. 212.

1 *hares of March*: the month when hares start to mate (though WE was fully aware too of Lewis Carroll's March Hare in *Alice's Adventures in Wonderland*, ch. VII, 'A Mad Tea-Party'). For a conjuror's hat of hares, see Ricks in T. S. Eliot, *Inventions of the March Hare*, pp. 4–9.

3 *epithalamion*: the Greek spelling of epithalamium: a nuptial song or poem.

16–24 *same beauty in taxiboys . . . that virtuous and aesthetic country*: WE had a three-year contract as a professor of English language and literature in Tokyo; but in 1934, if he had not been due to leave his post, he might well have found himself faced with the sack when he got drunk in a bar and took a taxi home, and then made a pass at the male driver. It was a deeply compromising mistake, for the taxi-driver seems to have reported the incident to the police, who in turn advised the Rector of the department that it would be better if WE left Japan. Professor Peter F. Alexander, reporting an interview with Professor Ryuichi Kajiki, has confirmed that WE 'got into serious trouble with the authorities because of his homosexual activity, and the Japanese police were involved' (*William Plomer: A Biography* (Oxford: Oxford University Press, 1989), p. 357 note 99). WE may have felt more amused than deeply abashed by the incident – he was not later reluctant to admit to **a diffused homosexual feeling**' (letter to John Hayward, 18 May 1948; King's College, Cambridge: WE/JDH/14) – and yet it was well over a year before he brought himself to tell Richards about it. '**I have told Richards, by the way, about my stupid behaviour in Japan, which I ought to have done before**,' he wrote to Sir George Sansom on 13 November 1935 (letter in Empson Papers); and it is most likely that he did so only because Richards was about to visit Japan, where he would be displeased to hear the story first at secondhand.

26,33–5 *bathing in the sight of your eyes . . . such a signal . . . recognized*: Empson never directly declared himself to Lee, but the following anecdote suggests that WE experienced spasms of jealousy, from Lee's 'Autobiographical Notes, started in 1984':

A party of us went up the river in punts. We got beyond Byron's Pool and, if I remember rightly, had lunch. And I don't think it is merely the sentimentalizing of memory to say it was a gorgeous summer day. One member of the party (there must have been six or seven of us) was a notorious pansy of the day, Malcolm Grigg. He always very much dressed the part, with broad-brimmed velour hats and the like . . . What Malcolm was wearing that day I do not remember in detail, but . . . after lunch Bill obviously got sick of his peacocking around and, with no warning, pushed him into the river on the brink of which he was unwisely standing. We fished him out quickly enough and then Bill, in a curiously characteristic gesture, stripped off his own clothes, gave them to Malcolm for the return journey, and tucked a towel round his own waist. The rest of the party were clearly unwilling to travel back with him so clad; he was a formidable character and probably slightly tight, as were we all. So the job fell to me (I thought the others were being rather pusillanimous) and the two of us returned together in one of the punts, Bill punting most of the way clad only in his towel. I do not remember the end of the journey or how Bill got back to Magdalene . . . I know that Bill behaved as perfectly as anyone could in that predicament, and that my own feelings were of amusement and a certain admiration at the way Bill carried the whole incident off. (Courtesy of the late Sir Desmond Lee)

The incident is clearly susceptible to the interpretation that, once WE had (spontaneously?) humiliated – doused – his rival, he could himself take up the ultra-masculine role ('formidable', 'punting most of the way', behaving 'perfectly') while indulging in an apparently innocent, yet most conspicuous, narcissistic display.

50–54 *One of these poems . . . occurred . . . In the next bed to you in a pub in Vienna . . . illuminating new beauties*: this anecdote seems to refer primarily to 'Letter II', which speaks of the poet as feeling ravished by lighting upon more and more facets of beauty while exploring 'the cave gallery' of the beloved's face; 'Letter III' also reflects upon a turbulent night during which the moon gave the poet strength. WE's report of the encounter in Vienna is independently corroborated by Lee's memoirs:

In 1930 I went to Germany . . . I found Bill [in Salzburg]. I can remember few details. I do not think the meeting had been pre-arranged and I do not remember how we met or where we stayed, though I remember going to a concert. I was due to go on to Vienna and to a brief visit to Wittgenstein and Bill decided to come with me, though of course he could not be included in the visit to Wittgenstein. I remember staying for a couple of nights in a small hotel near the station and having a quick look round Vienna; but then I had to leave him.

70 *porcine*: hoggish, swinish, piggish.

Bacchus

Composed over a seven-year period (1933–9), and first published in instalments, in order of publication (with original (confusing) titles): 'Bacchus' (ll. 1–17) in *New Verse* (March 1933), and reprinted in *P 1934* and *P*; 'Bacchus Two' (ll. 18–41) in *Criterion* (July 1935); 'Bacchus Four' (a misleading title, since this became the closing lines of the work – ll. 73–92 – with an extra stanza which was later dropped) in *Poetry 49* (January 1937); 'Bacchus Three' (ll. 42–57) in *Poetry* (April 1940); and 'Bacchus Four' (that is, ll. 58–72 of the final poem) in *Poetry* (February 1942). First published in full in *GS*, and reprinted in *CP 1949* and *CP*.

A typescript copy of stanza 2 was sent to Sylvia Townsend Warner (Reading).

Willis (p. 281) comments: 'The original numerical ordering of the stanzas . . . might be interpreted to mean that Empson had planned to have a four-part structure indicated by the separate titles. If this hypothesis is correct, parts one, two, and three were composed of one stanza each, while part four was composed of the remaining four stanzas . . . This theory gains support from the fact that the end of the poem published in 1937 as "Bacchus Four" was complete before the middle section (part three or "Bacchus Three").'

CP: A mythological chemical operation to distil drink is going on for the first four verses. The notion is that life involves maintaining oneself between contradictions that can't be solved by analysis; e.g. those of philosophy, which apply to all creatures, and the religious one about man being both animal and divine. Drink is taken as typical of this power because it makes you more outgoing and unself-critical, able to do it more heartily – e.g. both more witty and more sentimental. These two = the salt and water sublimed and distilled over the retort = the sea from which life arose and to which the proportions of all creatures' blood are still similar. Man is the *goblet, flask, vessel* which receives what the retort sends over. Thick glass cracks under heat from getting different expansions inside and outside, and if the flask has a flat bottom, so as to stand up alone, it cracks along the angle. Having to be round it is the same shape as a sky-map or world-map; man cannot stand alone because he is dependent both on earth and heaven. The *retort* is also the answer of Jupiter to Semele, when he appeared in his own nature, burnt her, and begot Bacchus. *Glancer:* she looked both ways and wanted heaven as real as earth. The angel at Bethesda troubled the waters when they were ready to heal you. *Thicker than water:* sea water is a stronger salt solution than blood, presumably because the sea has got saltier since we cut ourselves off from it. 'Blood is thicker than water', but blood connects us with near relations, as the phrase is used, and thus with all life. *Cymbal* – 'symbol', *whirled* – 'world'.

In the second verse a god inside the flask making the brine into drink is Noah or Neptune managing the sea. The point is to get puns for both violent disorder and building a structure – what strength or wisdom the drink gives comes through disturbing you. Noah of course has a reputation for drinking.

Cope – coping-stone and to manage, *groynes* – breakwaters, the meet of Gothic arches, the sex of the horses. The same kind of control is needed inside your head, a place also round and not well known (*miner* – 'minor'), and it requires chiefly a clarifying connection with the outside world, e.g. by the arches of the eye, whose iris (rainbow) promises safety as to Noah. The externalized Logos is a sort of promise that the outside world fits our thoughts. Christ walked on the water and the doves of Noah's ark and of the Holy Spirit before creation brooded over it; the idea is that you control the disorder of the outside world by sharing it and delighting in it. Columbus, unfortunate in life, like the Spirit called 'dove', once puzzled people about how to stand an egg on its end; the answer was to crack the shell. He is Humpty Dumpty the egg and a foam omelette because wisdom via drink requires breaking eggs, giving up static control; thus making the world go round, like a drunk's head; but he is judge as well as horsetamer –

equitation is riding and justice, *bar* is for sea horizon, drinking saloon, and law court. *Beating the bounds* could mean whipping schoolboys at places where it was important to remember boundaries of property; Humpty's wall is remembered because he fell off it. Then the cloud of vapour coming into the flask from the retort is called the cloud that Juno made Ixion mistake for herself. A cock 'treads' a hen in copulating, and treading wet mud makes a solid floor. To 'divine' something is hardly more than to guess at it, but Ixion produced a divine centaur, tutor of heroes, though he guessed wrong. Getting only the blind eyes of pride on her peacocks' tails he trampled them into stars (on the solid firmament that keeps out the water); hence like the eyes before and behind on the beasts of the Revelation they were connected with both inner and outer and could give truth. For that matter even the passive Narcissus like a dementia praecox case might be seeing the sky not himself in his pool. The error is built into a truth by a wild enough belief in it; and this process though chaotic is transferable; it can get its connection with at least a social 'outer world', because other people can be made to think the same. Thus Ixion on the wheel of torture in hell is at the tiller-wheel of the turning earth. I find the poem is giving hearty praise to people like Hitler and Mrs [Mary Baker] Eddy [founder of the Christian Science Church] in this aspect of Bacchus. *Boxing the compass* is going in all directions but also putting all space in your own box; then *compassing his appeal* is getting what he wanted. Then a settling process has to follow this; the flask is being cooled by dripping ether over it, a process only used for urgently rapid cooling; if the flask is a man he is given an anaesthetic; and the other kind of ether can be taken as the empty space the round earth cools into. As the earth was once molten its firm surface can be called *wheal* as the scar of a burn, as well as 'weal' as in commonweal.

In the third verse the fire under the retort is given by Prometheus, who escaped from heaven with the gift of fire hidden in a reed. As before, the violent thing can be punned with a measuringrod for building; Rev. xxi is where the angel measured the city of heaven with a reed. It might also be a yard of the stallions, who appear now under Tartar horsemen, laying waste the land round the Caucasus on which Prometheus is chained. In China it was felt as a major atrocity story that the Japanese had turned their horses into the ricefields, a thing apparently not done in the civil wars. We have got here to the quarrelsome stage of drink, but the god or political thinker who brings it is separate from it and can't control it.

Taught is what he did, but he is now 'taut'; Prometheus stretched helpless along the glaciers is compared to the flame clinging to the glass of the retort, and its 'quivers' are supposed to eke out a hint at the arches of the Tartar bowmen. As in Shelley [*Prometheus Unbound*] he is still helping man by keeping a secret, and drinking the cup of sacrifice (Mark x); one of the vultures at his liver may be cirrhosis and another remorse. Anyway the drink is now chiefly needed for anaesthetic. Aether meant the upper air, and he is fixed high where the air smells dry and choking, like ether. Ether and chloroform smell to me much alike though only chloroform has got chlorine in it, so I swap drugs to bring in poison gas. There is meant to be a comparison between the political case and the personal one; in a drunken quarrel a man tends to forget the cause and get angrier from an internal disunion.

For the fourth verse Mercury brought a thermometer to control the reaction by knowledge, but it burst and the mercury spoilt everything. A herm was a phallic household cult-statue, a minor version of this god, and an aberration of the planet gave the first evidence for relativity. The snakes round his staff were also used for Bacchus, as I remember, hidden under the ivy, and I connect them with the serpent that gave knowledge of good and evil; because in this verse we have reached the neurotic effects of drink; a state of overconsciousness needing continual stimulus from outside, too much of the outer world, as before there was too little. One of the asteroids is called Bacchus, but I assume this is the name of the planet they once all made together, only it burst; the bursting of the retort produces incomplete men, solitary drinkers. These men have their mettle eaten into by mercury, which attacks other metals. I forget what a silver crucible was used for in Stinks at school, but remember how fatal it was to put mercury in; we pronounced the scaly result *amalgam*, which the verse needs; the crucible had little flange arms and seemed an alchemical man via Ecclesiastes' silver cord and golden bowl. Houses are supposed to be given free with the plumbing in America; God's temple was not built with hands. I was thinking of Mandevil when I wrote 'so soon', though it would be absurd to pretend that this is part of the poem; he says that Adam was only in Eden for half an hour, 'so soon he fell'. This paste which mercury makes with metals is used for the backs of mirrors, a symbol of self-consciousness; scales fell from the eyes of blind men healed by Christ, but in this neurotic state further clarifying is no good, though the scales can go on peeling off as from lepers. We have left behind the active politicians but not the thinkers; the non-alcoholic Nietzsche seems a likely example.

After this look-round of the subject I try to present a person feeling tragic exultation in it. *Coping* is a term used about finishing brickwork, as well as for the coping-stone of an arch, and for the cope which isolates and gives divine authority to a priest; the coping of the fire in a room manages it, does not let it burn the house down.

Cast is both 'threw' and 'made a cast in metal'. The parabola is both the path of a forward fall and the shape of the reflector that throws directly forward all the light of a motorcar lamp; it has one focus at the lamp and the other at the skyline before it. Arachne who out of pride against the pride of Juno hanged herself in her own web and became a spider is here a gossamer spider, who can fly on it. A Tracer bullet lights in the air to show its path, whereas a photon though like a particle has no position till it hits; rockets were used to send ropes to save people off wrecks. The idea is that the puzzle of the Mercury section about neurotic self-consciousness (you can't know the position of a photon without destroying it) has been outfaced. Any actual car-lamp makes a fan instead of one beam; this is supposed to bring in 'his fan is in his hand, and he shall thoroughly purge his floor' and 'make straight in the desert a highway . . . every mountain shall be made low'. King Lear says he is bound upon a wheel of fire. *Span* is meant for spanned and spun. The final arches are cellars underground such as the grave.

In a preface to *GS*, WE remarked: '**I put it first** [of the poems in the volume] because it is in a style I felt I ought to get out of.'

On *The Poems of William Empson* he commented:

We are now to advance upon my great poem about drink, named 'Bacchus', which has in its small way the same kind of claim made by *Finnegans Wake* in that you can't possibly get all the points on a single hearing; in fact you need the printed page to tell you how to pick up the grammar again, after three or four lines in brackets. I printed it with notes twice the length of the poem, which it would be ridiculous to repeat here; there would be no point in broadcasting it unless I thought it could go over without them. It is not appallingly long. Four classical gods in succession are invoked for the production of alcohol, which is imagined as the chemical process of distilling. You need this of course for making whisky and so forth, but not for the much older process of making wine or beer; the classical gods had no spirits, and it has only just occurred to me that the symbolism of distillation really belongs to the modern world of industrial chemistry. However, the poem is none the worse for that; it was really meant to be about Hitler and similar victims of the enormous sense of power occasionally offered by the modern world, showing increasingly bad hangovers.

The gods in the successive paragraphs are: first, Bacchus himself setting up the apparatus, becoming both more witty and more emotional, and thus solving the contradictions of life. Then Neptune or Noah inside the flask is ruling the boiling liquid, getting power over the world because his imagination makes him able to sympathize with its disorder; he makes other people believe what he imagines; but it turns to vanity, and the cloud of vapour coming across to be cooled, in the distilling process, becomes the cloud Ixion mistook for Hera, the queen of Heaven. Then in the third verse the fire under the retort is being supplied by Prometheus, working for the public good and being tormented for it, and producing world wars. We have now got to the quarrelsome stage of drink; they forget what they are quarrelling about and get angrier out of an internal disunion. Finally Mercury brings a thermometer to control the operation by knowledge, but it bursts and the mercury spoils everything. He is the neurotic stage of drink, or the isolated theorist, and further understanding does him no good.

After this look-round of the subject I go on to a personal memory and an individual drunk, claiming all these justifications. Of course the claim of the drink is that it really does excite both new ideas and new sympathies, though at a cost.

On *Poet's Choice*, ed. Paul Engle and Joseph Langland (1962), WE related:

I am afraid I like 'Bacchus' best of my own poems, maybe as the traditional mother dotes on the imbecile. Dylan Thomas approved of it more than my other poems too. It may seem to the put-upon reader who works at it (of course it is not meant to be just Imagist) a very intellectual box of tricks, also rather put together at random; but if that were all it couldn't have been so hard to finish. I failed for years to do the central verse, about Prometheus, and then in 1939 I was invited on a little shooting trip in Northern Indo-China during the holidays. On the first evening of the drive out, after a certain amount of celebration, I fell into some pit and dislocated my arm. We were in reach of a French doctor, who gave me gas to put it back; and he said he had never seen a man coming out of gas looking so pleased. Exalted rather was what I was; I had discovered triumphantly that something *was* something else, and it was quite incidental that I had seen what to write in the poem. But I asked for a pencil as soon as I had collected myself, and still had till recently the bit of paper with

> Pasturing the stallions in the standing corn

scrawled on it with my left hand. [That bit of paper survives in the Empson Papers.]

However, though I feel that this somehow proves the poem is genuine, the idea wasn't at all hard to come by; we refugees from the Japanese were regularly hearing that they had turned their hordes [*read* horses] into the ricefields. Maybe a lot of ideas which we accept without surprise were arrived at by an illumination.

Critics have often said that my earlier poetry was tolerably close to the rhythms of the spoken language, whereas I ended in the dead rhetoric of the end-stopped ten-syllable line. But if you are trying to be vatic it is natural to be end-stopped and uncolloquial, and to say that a poem mustn't be vatic is doctrinaire; even though I have against me the strong and improbable combination of Dr Leavis and Professor Robert Graves. Even this poem, I think, can be read so that the excitement piles up; but I wouldn't deny that it is a tiresome genre, and not what a writer should go on repeating.

For *Listen* WE noted:

The stages of drink are compared to political or religious leaders; they are gods trying out the first distillation of alcohol. In the first paragraph Bacchus himself makes us both vigorous and affectionate enough to handle the contradictions of life. In the second the agitator Noah or Neptune rules the boiling liquor inside the flask; he uses any disturbance, or the very unreality of his doctrine, to make the spirit emerge. Prometheus in the third is the fire beneath it; he is the idealist revolutionary, horrified by what he produces . . . Mercury in the fourth is neurotic self-consciousness or delirium tremens; the thermometer cracks and the spilt mercury spoils the experiment. The poem then turns to an actual lady feeling what it has tried to describe.

A letter to Maxwell-Mahon (6 November 1967) includes the comment: 'I still think *Bacchus* is my best poem, because the politicians and the drunks are compared through a long process, while they get worse.'

On *Harvard*, WE remarked:

Dylan Thomas used to describe it as my good poem: he thought it was the only one that had come off. I must respect his judgement there. But it takes some sympathy to listen to. It is about drink, you understand. A mythological process of distilling spirits is going on, till nearly the end of the poem, which is historically quite wrong: in classical times they had no distillation, they had wine but not whiskey. But in the modern world one of the first great triumphs of industrial chemistry was making gin. But, considering the modern world, you naturally put the classical gods to work making gin . . . In the first verse the god of wine, Bacchus, is looking after the whole affair. In the second verse Neptune, or Noah, the sea god, is in control of the bubbling liquid, which is being boiled up so that it comes over as steam. A comparison to political affairs is going on all the time, [so] this is the agitator, or the inventor, of a new political scheme – but he acts by agitating at random. It is only by shaking to pieces the old thing that the new scheme can be brought into operation. So a boiling and bubbling at random is going on. Exciting by unreasonable means a belief in the new scheme, is the way it is established: it may become real when people believe in it. The third one [verse] is about the fire underneath, which makes the liquid bubble: it is about Prometheus, who brought fire from heaven. This is the man starting to get drunk who feels braver and stronger and wittier: he is, as it were, willing to start a new world. The second one is the political idealist, who is very unwilling to enter the world he is dealing with. Fire has been brought down from heaven and has to be applied to the world, and he falls into agony when he realizes what is going on; but, never mind, he is necessary to make the process go on. The third god is Mercury, who represents the thermometer: he is put there to control it. He is self-consciousness, do you see? The progress of the drunk leads to a nervous breakdown, a neurotic condition of some kind: neurotic self-consciousness, in a way . . . the mercury being used for the backs of mirrors. But it is simply the thermometer that explodes, and it spoils the rest of the experiment. And I then go off on to an individual in the process described. That is what happens in this poem, which I'm afraid is slightly tiresome to listen to, really, because it is so tricksy. But that is the broad intention. The human mind cannot be prevented from working like this, is what it is celebrating – though with regret, so to speak. I think it is sufficiently intelligible to sympathize with.

In a letter to Maxwell-Mahon (21 August 1973), WE commented further: 'The beliefs recommended in "Bacchus" are quite obviously not those required for the Worship of the Torture-Monster [i.e. the Christian God]. I daresay it is an unhealthy poem at bottom, but I never feel I have to warn people about that before I read it out; that aspect of it is on the surface, once the merely technical obscurity is overcome; whereas I usually do feel I ought to give a warning about "This Last Pain".'

Stanza 2, as 'Bacchus Two' (ll. 18–41), first appeared in *Criterion*; and among WE's papers is this draft of an undated letter (which was probably not despatched, at least not in this form) to T. S. Eliot: 'I am writing to offer this to the *Criterion*. The first part was published in *New Verse* (and will be in a volume [*P*] with some notes in March). I shall do some more of it if I can. It is a nice little theme, but I am afraid my air of having to be clever all the time in order to manage such solemn difficulties makes it ridiculous.'

See also Morelli, pp. 57–62; *TGA*, pp. 151–6.

1 *The laughing god ... startling answer*: Semele gave birth to Dionysus even as she was burnt by Zeus' lightning: surely a 'startling answer'. For details, see note to l. 9 of 'Note on Local Flora', and next note. Bacchus (Dionysus) is god of the vine, which begets mirth.

2 *Cymbal of clash ... the divided glancer*: the copulation of Zeus and Semele was the primordial *coup de foudre*: not only sounding like a clash of cosmic cymbals, it was a clash of the divine and the mortal. Cf. Tennyson's free-verse 'Semele' (*c.* 1835; published 1913), in which Semele speaks thus triumphantly: 'But thou, my son, who shalt be born / When I am ashes, to delight the world – / Now with measured cymbal-clash / Moving on to victory' (ll. 12–15). The 'divided glancer' is either or both Zeus and Semele, god and mortal, yearning to meld heaven and earth (looking both ways at once), and Bacchus/Dionysus himself as well: Walter F. Otto put the latter probability: 'the enigmatic god, the spirit of a dual nature and of paradox, had a human mother and, therefore, was already by his birth a native of two realms' (*Dionysus: Myth and Cult* (1933), trans. Robert B. Palmer (Bloomington and London, 1965), p. 73).

3 heaven's] Heaven's *New Verse* 1933

4 *Capped a retort*: means both to seal up the apparatus for distillation (with a stillhead) and to top a riposte. 'Retort' means both a vessel in which liquid subjected to distillation is heated and 'a sharp or incisive reply' (*OED*² *retort* sb.¹ 2a; sb.² 1), and may also be linked with 'amalgam with mercury' (see l. 67 and note), for yet a further definition of 'retort', of which WE was aware, is 'a vessel in which mercury is separated from amalgam or impurity by volatilization' (*OED*² sb.² 2).

4 *to sublime earth by fire*: the verb 'sublime' is applied in a large range of possible senses: the notion is that a human being, Semele, instigates both the distillation of wine and life on earth, since the grammatical construction admits these possibilities: that earth has been (i) subjected to the action of heat so as to convert it into a vapour, which is carried off and on cooling is deposited in a solid form, and (ii) raised to an elevated condition, transmuted into something higher, exalted, made wholly sublime. Furthermore, Semele is sometimes represented to be the Earth, and even an ancient Thracian Earth-goddess; and so Bacchus is at once earth-born and fire-born; see the prologue to Euripides, *The Bacchae*. (WE read Euripides at the latest by 1926, for in that year he wrote in a notebook, with a keen eye for religious hypocrisy: '**Very struck by a chorus in the Bacchae, in (good) translation.**

Religious fervour, how easy, how happy, is faith. Pointed out in Verrall, while they sing this, the god-priest is poisoning his political enemies inside. Immense, accurate, amusing.') Walter F. Otto speculatively remarked in 1933, 'Dionysus . . . is called "the one who is born of fire" . . . Wine, too, has a fiery nature. Some thought they might explain the myth of the fiery birth of the god from this fact. Archilochus begins his hymn to Dionysus with the words "stuck by wine's lightning bolt" ' (*Dionysus* (see note to l. 2 above), p. 146).

6 *whirled- map*: the pun on 'world-map' is self-evident. Given 'still' (l. 7), ''stilled' (l. 8) and 'Still' and 'whirled' (l. 41), cf. T. S. Eliot, 'Ash Wednesday' (1930), V.8: 'Against the Word the unstilled world still whirled'. (The text of *Collected Poems 1909–1935* (London, 1936), which WE was likely to have read, gave the line as 'Against the World the unstilled world still whirled' – an error that survived through eighteen impressions until 1961.)

7 *Earth lost in him*: the capitalized 'Him' (see collation below) suggests that Bacchus/Dionysus – true god and true man – is identified with Jesus Christ; what is lost to Jesus is gained by Bacchus.

7 him] Him *New Verse 1933*

8 *Troubled the water till the spirit 'stilled*: John tells of a pool called Bethesda where there 'lay a great multitude of impotent folk, of blind, halt, withered, waiting for the moving of the water. For an angel went down at a certain season into the pool, and troubled the water: whosoever then first after the troubling of the water stepped in was made whole of whatsoever disease he had' (John 5: 3–4). 'Spirit 'stilled' refers to the idea of spiritual faith, to the calming Spirit of God (specifically Jesus Christ), and – the elision makes the pun obvious – to the process of *di*stilling wine.

9 *tears-of-wine*: 'tears of strong wine', 'drops of liquid forming on the inner sides of a glass partly filled with strong wine' (OED^2 *tear* sb.[1]). Since Hera is usually identified with the Roman Juno, it is relevant here to note that an early (unpublished) version of a couplet, as made available to Richards in the early 1930s, included after l. 8 a version of the eventual ll. 39–40:

> (In wheeling Juno, whose feet centaur schooled
> Its hero, the paunched beaker, ether-cooled)

This version survives only because it is quoted in a typed 'protocol' – a piece of practical criticism – written by E. L. Trist, and posted to Richards (I. A. Richards Collection, Old Library, Magdalene; courtesy of Dr Richard Luckett).

9–11 *flask / (The roundest ones . . . better than stone*: the invention of glass-blowing dates from about the mid-first century BC. As WE later realized, Hellenistic protochemistry cannot be dated as far back as classical Greek texts; in a prefatory note to the second impression of *CP* (1956), he remarked: '**I forgot, by the way, that the classical gods did not know about distilling; in fact the invention of gin**

was one of the first triumphs of industrial chemistry; but that suits the poem well enough.' The first glass still was properly speaking 'late-Hellenistic', and no metal predecessor has yet been recognized.

12 could] would *P 1934*

13 fitted both to] image both of *New Verse 1933*; *P 1934*

14 wit] art *P 1934*

14 *wit was dry*: cf. an exchange between Rosaline and Biron in *Love's Labour's Lost*: 'When they are thirsty, fools would fain have drink. / *Biron*. This jest is dry to me. Gentle sweet, / Your wits makes wise things foolish' (V.ii.372–4).

15 *a brew thicker than blood, being brine*: 'We animals with backbones have a blood liquid which is almost the same as one part of sea water mixed with three parts of water without salt . . . The chemical agreement is so near that it is certainly not a question of chance . . . It is the view of some experts that in the same way as the blood liquid of present-day sea animals without backbone is almost sea water, so ours is like the sea water of a far-off time' (Haldane, 'Man as a Sea Animal', *The Inequality of Man* (London, 1932; as given in WE's Basic English version, *The Outlook of Science* (1935), p. 38).

16 which] that *P 1934*, *Listen*

17 blood . . . blood] flood . . . flood *P 1934*

17 *blood makes wine*: the miracle of changing wine into blood is the essence of the Christian communion, as an act of remembrance of Christ's sacrifice. It is a fundamental part of any ritual of a sacramental meal in which the god is devoured and incorporated within the devotee – just as the maenads (the ecstatic followers of the cult of Dionysus/Bacchus) indulged in similar wild *orgia*. Compare WE's commentary on Lucy's praise, in *The Beggar's Opera*, for the efficacy of a 'quieting draught': **'Gin alone, however, she has just pointed out, is often enough quieting in the fullest sense, and the poetic connexion between death and intoxication gives a vague rich memory of the blood of the sacrament and the apocalyptic wine of the wrath of God'** (*Pastoral*, p. 198).

18 *The god arkitect whose coping with the Flood*: Noah coped with the Flood in the manner he was told: by building an ark. He is linked with Bacchus because after the deluge receded Noah 'began to be an husbandman, and he planted a vineyard: And he drank of the wine, and was drunken' (Gen. 9: 20–21). 'Coping' means encountering or combating, as well as managing or dealing with; Noah fashioned the ribs of the ark, as a coping (covering) against the rain. But see also the following note.

19 *Groyned . . . main*: constructed groynes (breakwaters) against the sea ('main'); sea horses are suggested here, as well as waves arching like copes. Given that 'coping' (in the previous line) can also mean 'covering', 'Groyned . . . stallion arches' has the connotation of copulation (a stallion is said to 'cover' a mare in heat); see WE's comment (*ST*, p. 85) on **'the energy and beauty, the martial and aristocratic associations, of a stallion'**. Furthermore, given 'miner deeps' (l. 20), cf. Wilfred Owen, 'Strange Meeting' (1918), ll. 1–3: 'It seemed that out of battle I escaped / Down some profound dull tunnel, long since scooped / Through granites which titanic wars had groined.' Cf. too 'Song of the amateur psychologist', l. 49.

21 *Iris' arches' pupillage and Word*: Iris is goddess of the rainbow, which she personifies, mediating between heaven and earth, gods and men. As a messenger – e.g. in Euripides – she is at the beck and call of Zeus and Hera (and especially the latter: see l. 32 and note); she carries orders from on high. Her name survives in the language of the eye: hence WE's pun on '*pupil*lage', which otherwise means the condition of being a ward or minor (see the related pun on *miner* in the preceding line). The best instructions are those you receive in your nonage or youth, and assume into the inner mind (the braincase or skull is yet another form of coping). The 'Word' is the *Logos* (Gk.), a designation of Jesus Christ, the Second Person of the Trinity: 'In the beginning was the Word, and the Word was with God, and the Word was God' (John 1: 1). WE would write to Philip Hobsbaum on 2 August 1969:

The question is about

> Whose ears have heard
> The Holy Word
> Who walked among the ancient trees

and I kept telling you that this meant the Son (always good in Blake) not the Father (at this time bad). Milton in *Paradise Lost* makes the Son walk in the Garden of Eden and meet our parents just after their Fall, so that Blake certainly knew about it, though anyway it was a standard Christian interpretation of the passage in Genesis. All these professional experts, who assume that God the Father could be described as the Logos, are just ludicrously ignorant. I have found since that Kathleen Raine makes the point decisively, in her writing on Blake, and I wish I had remembered where I had got this argument from, because then you might have been convinced by her authority. Not being allowed to consider intention makes you slavish to a shocking degree, but perhaps I could have convinced you there if I had done my work better. (Courtesy of Philip Hobsbaum)

However, 'the Word' is sometimes used to refer to the Bible in general: specifically in this context, perhaps, to God's covenant with Noah in Gen. 9: 9–17.

22 *Walked on the bucking water . . . a bird*: to the astonishment of the apostles, Jesus Christ walked on the water (John 6: 19; Matt. 14: 25); Noah sent a bird to see if the Flood had receded: many birds can walk (bob) on water.

23 **And,**] **And** *Criterion 1935*

24 *Columbus' egg*: the famous lesson of the egg derives from *La Historia del mondo nuovo* (Venice, 1565) by Girolamo Benzoni, who relates that Columbus was once challenged by a Spaniard at a party:

'Mr Christopher, even if you had not found the Indies, we should not have been devoid of a man who would have attempted the same that you did, here in our own country of Spain, as it is full of great men clever in cosmography and literature.' Columbus said nothing in answer to these words, but having desired an egg to be brought to him, he placed it on the table saying: 'Gentlemen, I will lay a wager with any of you, that you will not make this egg stand up as I will, naked and without anything at all.' They all tried, and no one succeeded in making it stand up. When the egg came round to the hands of Columbus, by beating it down on the table he fixed it, having thus crushed a little of one end; wherefore all remained confused, understanding what he would have said: that after the deed is done, everybody knows how to do it . . . (*History of the New World*, trans. Rear-Admiral W. H. Smyth (London, 1857), p. 17)

WE would almost certainly have read the story, as a child, in the version by Washington Irving, *The Life and Voyages of Christopher Columbus* (1848–9). He may have been thinking here too of the Orphic legend which conceived of the primordial universe as a mystic egg: see the parody of the Orphic cosmogony in Aristophanes' *The Birds*, quoted in *Diodorus of Sicily*, I (trans. C. H. Oldfather (London, 1933), p. 89).

27 skyline] sealine *Criterion 1935*
27 that he] he had *Townsend Warner*
28 *Trod and divined*: 'Trod' both as 'walked on' and 'mated with' (like a cock with a hen); 'divine' both as 'forecasted' or 'prognosticated', and 'made divine' or 'divinized'.
28 *inwheeling*: a variant of the obsolete verb 'enwheel' – to encircle, surround – as in Cassio's salutation to Desdemona (*Othello* II.i.86–8): 'The grace of Heaven / Before, behind thee, and on every hand / Enwheel thee round!'
29–31 *Narcissus dumb and bent . . . the skies*: a beautiful youth whose vanity caused him to disdain offers of love, Narcissus spurned the Nymph Echo, whom the jealous Hera had viciously deprived of the power to initiate speech. However, since Narcissus never cared to address Echo, he might be said to be quite as *dumb* as she was. Narcissus fell in love with the image of himself that he saw while bending over a pool, and he pined away. WE gestures towards giving Narcissus some of the credit that Ovid does not afford him in *Metamorphoses* III: perhaps he was trying to make out the meaning of heaven's cope, not just mooning at himself? *Dementia praecox*, which (according to WE in his own note) Narcissus might have suffered from, is the former term for schizophrenia.
31 for] to *Harvard*
32–4 *Blind Hera's revelation . . . throne*: Hera may be said to be blind with vindictive rage at Zeus' infidelities, one of which caused her to bring about the death of Semele and the birth of Bacchus (ll. 1–4). Hera's usual symbol is the peacock; and the eyes of the peacock's tail, according to Ovid, are those of the many-eyed Argos, her watchman. These lines assimilate Hera's Olympian majesty

to the vision of St John in the post-apocalytic audience-chamber of the Christian godhead: 'and, behold, a throne was set in heaven, and one sat on the throne. And he that sat was to look upon like a jasper and a sardine stone: and there was a rainbow [see collation l. 34] round about the throne, in sight like unto an emerald . . . And before the throne there was a sea of glass like unto crystal [see l. 48]: and in the midst of the throne, and round about the throne, were four beasts full of eyes before and behind' (Rev. 4: 2–3, 6).

34 golden] rainbow *Criterion 1935*; *Townsend Warner*

36 *Incestuous Chaos . . . permanent*: according to Hesiod (*Theog.* 116), Chaos is the primeval 'gaping void'; Ovid (*Met.* I.5ff.) calls it the 'seeds' (*semina*) of all matter; in that sense, Chaos would have to breed of 'itself' – incestuously – like a yeast (Chaos indeed begot of himself Erebus and Night (Nyx) followed by Day (Hemera) and Air); so too did all the gods of the Greek pantheon. 'Breed permanent' may be understood in the sense of cloning – as of the Olympian gods, their genes replicated generation on generation; cf. 'Dissatisfaction with Metaphysics'.

36 Chaos will breed] chaos breeds as *Criterion 1935*; *Townsend Warner*

37 *Helled to earth's centre Ixion at the wheel*: if 'Hera's . . . eyes' (l. 32) are in one sense the antecedent of the verb 'Helled', then Hera hounds her rivals, notably Semele, into Hell; also, as the classic jealous wife, Hera gives her husband hell. For Ixion, see note to ll. 1–4 of 'Invitation to Juno'. 'At the wheel' suggests – misleadingly and sardonically – that Ixion is in charge of this world, as if the axle-tree spins 'under' him.

38 his] her *Harvard*

38 appeal.] appeal; *Criterion 1935*; *Townsend Warner*

39–40 *Her centaur . . . schooled / This hero*: Nephele, Hera's ethereal body-double, bore Ixion a son, Centaurus (see note to ll. 1–4 of 'Invitation to Juno'), who mated with mares and begot the tribe of centaurs: down from the waist they were horses – which do best (especially if they are of good stock) when *schooled*. His father Ixion was taught his lesson, and so 'schooled' in that sense. The lustful centaurs also indulge in alcohol abuse.

40 *paunched*: Ixion may be considered to be greedy with sexual desire, but this word also associates him with the 'hero' of the following section, Prometheus, whose fate, as decreed by Zeus, was to be *paunched* – disembowelled or eviscerated (see note to ll. 1–2 of 'Rebuke for a dropped brick').

41 *go round the whirled . . . wheal*: in addition to the senses mentioned in WE's note, the line suggests that the world is a spinning wheel or top, duped and dizzy. Moreover, to the degree that the poem is referring to victims or scapegoats, including Ixion, WE would have carried in mind the closing stanza of Herbert's 'The Sacrifice': see note to l. 2 of 'Plenum and Vacuum'. In this light, see also 'Letter I', l. 16. In a note to Philip Hobsbaum, written by hand on a typescript draft of Hobsbaum's doctoral thesis, 'Some reasons for the great variety of response to literature among modern literary critics' (Sheffield, 1968), later published as *A*

Theory of Communication (London, 1970), WE remarked about that passage in *ST:* 'I took the supposed pun on *weal*, and various other overstrained bits, out from the second edition, but I think [Rosemond] Tuve ignored that [in her *A Reading of George Herbert* (London, 1952), which aimed a good deal of criticism at WE's earlier reading of Herbert] just as you do.' (He wrote further to Hobsbaum, 'Well, I am much heartened by what you say [in *Theory of Communication*, pp. 131–4, 250], as I had come to think both I and Tuve were often in the wrong there . . . I will look out some extra bits which bear on the controversy' (letter in Special Collections, University of Victoria, Victoria, B. C., Canada).

41 wheal] weal *Criterion 1935*; *Townsend Warner*

42 *The god . . . standard yard*: Prometheus (Hesiod, *Theog.* 562ff.), who is known as the benefactor of mankind (see l. 51), stole fire from heaven and carried it down to earth concealed in a stalk of fennel (*Ferula communis*). (Originally, Prometheus is probably the type of an ancient Greek fire-god.) A 'standard yard' is a legal measure; also, it may be – pursuing the trope of alcohol – a measure (or yard) of ale; and perhaps a phallic measure: see ll. 58–9 and note below.

43–4 *Surveying with that reed . . . / He showed . . . new Jerusalem*: the angel who introduces John to the heavenly Jerusalem carries another yardstick: 'a golden reed to measure the city' (Rev. 21: 10–15). Who can say, WE suggests, whether or not all these sticks or tubes are figures for the same thing?

44 to John the new Jerusalem.] St. John the New Jerusalem; *Poetry 1940*

45–6 *sugar-cane . . . works depend*: perhaps Prometheus supplied to mankind not actual fire but the sort, like rum, that puts fire in the belly?

48 *recumbent*: perhaps the pinioned Prometheus.

49 *He drinks all cups . . . could acclaim*: powerfully confounds Jesus' words to the apostles: 'Ye shall indeed drink of the cup that I drink of' (Mark 10: 39), with Claudius's treachery in proffering a poisoned chalice to the distracted Hamlet: 'Give me drink. Hamlet, this pearl is thine. / Here's to thy health –' (V.ii.234–5). The poem supports valorous victims, notably including Ixion and Prometheus, as against every manifestation or representative of tyrannous godhead; humans deserve to best heaven.

51 *Burns still . . . for mankind*: Zeus arranged for Prometheus' liver to recover itself day by day – perhaps not unlike the liver of an alcoholic (see l. 54). Like Semele and Ixion, Prometheus is a paradigm of the sacrificial victim. Cf. 'Rebuke for a dropped brick', l. 1–2 and note. (Heracles released Prometheus by shooting the eagle. The fact that both Heracles and Dionysus are said to have got to 'Asia' in their travels serves WE's purposes at the close of this third section, especially in l. 56 where he seeks to bridge the gap between the Caucasus and China. See also note to l. 53 below.)

52 *ether, such an agony*: ether is traditionally the purer and more subtle medium of the heavens, reserved for the gods; but is now more commonly used for diethyl ether (for anaesthetic purposes) which is produced by pouring sulphuric acid upon alcohol. Human beings cannot endure either – not the 'diviner air', nor the anaesthetic agent, which can badly irritate the respiratory system ('such an agony') and often causes nausea and vomiting – not unlike a bad binge of alcohol. (Cf. 'Like a patient etherised upon a table', from Eliot's 'The Love Song of J. Alfred Prufrock' (l. 3), which may have influenced WE's phrasing.) See also note to l. 55 below.

53 *thin choking air of Caucasus*: traditionally, the place of Prometheus' punishment; Aeschylus names the place: see M. L. West's notes in his edition of Hesiod, *Theogony* (Oxford, 1966), pp. 313–15, which also gathers up the evidence for relating Prometheus to other relevant 'heroes': Ixion, Tityus, Tantalus. The evidence for a link between the travels of Dionysus, which extended as far as a lesser 'Asia' (as recounted by the god himself in *The Bacchae*), and the possibility that the region to the south of the Caucasus was the original home of the vine, is discussed in Apollodorus, *The Library*, ed. Sir James George Frazer (London, 1921), vol. I, pp. 324–5.

54 *under operation lies for ever*: 'like a patient etherised', perhaps, but just as importantly because he is subject to Zeus' cruel dealings with man.

55 *chlorine . . . chloroform*: chlorine is a poisonous greenish-yellow gas; a powerful irritant, it has a destructive effect on the respiratory system – and was the first poison gas to be used in modern warfare (at Ypres in 1915); it is produced by the electrolysis of concentrated brine (cf. l. 15). Chloroform is a clear but sweetish liquid haloform – an inhalational anaesthetic – which can cause liver damage (see ll. 51, 52).

56–7 *The plains . . . standing corn*: in his unpublished BBC radio programme 'China on the March' (1942), WE reported from his own observation in China (1937–9) that the modern Chinese is no longer fixated on Confucian tradition, he is transfixed by contingent realities: '**the Japanese turned their horses into the standing rice . . . They** [the Chinese peasants] **all knew what that meant, or at least what they thought it meant: it meant extermination; nobody could stay on the land. That was the kind of thing that made every Chinese peasant resist the invader. The bombing aeroplane is ridiculous, it might kill you, but it probably won't. But turning horses into the rice is serious: it means famine for everybody in the district next year.**' In such terms, the Japanese behave like Zeus vis-à-vis Prometheus and Ixion, and must be resisted; so must everyone who aspires to supreme power or triumphalist divinity. The verb *flood* serves to link Prometheus with Noah, for Prometheus not only predicted the Flood – Zeus' titanic attempt to kill off the human race – he showed his son Deucalion how to escape it.

58–9 *The herm whose length measured degrees of heat . . . in Mercury*: according to Jane Ellen Harrison, there is an affiliation between Dionysus, god of intoxication, and Hermes, which is 'clearly shown by the fact that in art Hermes and Dionysos appear, as they were worshipped in cultus, as herms; the symbol of both as gods of fertility is naturally the phallos. The young Dionysos . . . is not distinguishable from Hermes' (*Prolegomena to the Study of Greek Religion* (Cambridge, 1903),

p. 427). The phallus in Dionysiac processions identifies him as a god of fertility. The Romans identified Hermes with Mercury (Mercurius). A herm is represented as a pillar carved with a human head at the top and a phallus halfway up it. Mercury, a heavy silvery metallic element, makes a good thermometer. Also, though not a fire-god, Hermes is credited with inventing fire-making.

59 *lar that sunned itself*: a 'lar' is a household or ancestral god (Mercury is said to be the father of the *lares*), here a herm, which is also a thermometer that bursts from overheating: the primal force, as it were, that generates the cosmos.

60 *perked one word there that made space ends meet*: Hermes is god of eloquence, of oratory; more than the Word (see l. 21 and note), he utters the sole word – as it were, 'Be' or 'Begin' – which is the Big Bang, the origin of the universe. OED^2 (*perk* v^1 II *trans*. 2c) attributes to this line of poetry by WE the first use of this verb in the sense, 'to say or comment in a brisk, lively, or self-assertive manner'; and yet, given the context of the herm-thermometer, seeding the cosmos, its meaning ranges to include *ejaculation* in every sense. Hermes, the little god, pricks himself up, thrusts himself forward, as God. See also ll. 63–4. Since his subject is distillation, WE may also have used *perk* as an abbreviation of *percolate*. The boiling point of alcohol is 78°C, so wine must be heated with great care; WE's still is so overheated that it bursts the thermometer; and the vessel explodes.

61 *Fluttered his snake*: as herald of the gods, Hermes is represented as carrying the *kerykeion* (Latin *caduceus*), a staff on which two snakes are twined. Harrison favoured the idea that Hermes is no Olympian but the Agathos Daimon: 'We understand now why Hermes, as phallic herm, is god of fertility of flocks and herds, but also, as Psychopompos ["accompanier of souls"], god of ghosts and the underworld. He, a snake to begin with and carrying always the snake-staff, is the very *daimon* of reincarnation' (*Themis: A Study of the Social Origins of Greek Religion* (London, 1963), p. 295). As a necromancer, Hermes is also sometimes represented as bearing a magician's staff or wand; as such, he is Prospero's prototype. WE associates Hermes' staff with the thyrsus, a staff entwined with ivy and vine-leaves: the emblem of Dionysus (although Dionysus is not usually linked with snakes, any dead god readily turns into a snake). In the Garden of Eden, Hermes here has also become Satan as the snake.

61 into] in to *CP 1949*

62 *fertile thief, and journal to inquire*: *fertile* because of his associations with love and sex but also in the sense of ingenious: on the day of his birth, Hermes stole cattle in the care of Apollo. (See the fourth 'Homeric' hymn in Shelley's translation.) 'Journal' (the name Mercury has been the title of a journal or newspaper, and is also used generally for a newspaper) signifies that even on his birth day the precocious Hermes went looking for things to create: he made the first lyre, out of a tortoiseshell and the gut of a cow – and Apollo was so entranced by it that he bought it. As in l. 61, Hermes functions here as Satan too, stealing Eve from her first obedience.

63–4 *mortal Eden forming, and the fire. / A smash resounding*: picks up the suggestion in l. 60 that a mistake, attributable to a Hermes-mercury-thermometer-penis, has brought about the creation of the universe, Apocalypse (the fire that will end all), and the Fall of Adam.

65 *burst the planet Bacchus*: in 1956, WE remarked: 'The explosion of the planet **Bacchus has now been dated, by iron from asteroids, to between two and four hundred million years ago; the idea that it would be visible for the emerging amphibia, and probably bad for them, might have come into the poem'** (*CP*, second impression, *1956*). Yet, it remains a mystery how WE in the 1930s came by the information or the notion that there was a planet, or even an asteroid, named *Bacchus*: according to Brian Marsden (Harvard University), there is a minor planet called Bacchus – but it was discovered only in 1977, and so named in 1978.

65 Bacchus] bacchus *Poetry* 1942

67 *So soon*: ch. XV of *Mandeville's Travels* observes of Adam: 'the same daye that he was put into Paradyse, the same day he was driven out, for so soone he synned' (*The Travels of Sir John Mandeville* (1928), p. 72). Furthermore, in his notes on Wicksteed's translation of *Paradiso*, WE was incited by Canto XXIX, ll. 49–51 (p. 355) – 'Nor should one, counting, come so soon to twenty as did a part of the Angels disturb the substrate of your elements' – to protest:

Angels were created at the same instant as matter and the heavens (29–30) and fell within twenty seconds. Man fell within six hours (that comes in Mandevil too). This gives an impression of ludicrous brutality in the Deity: they wouldn't have fallen with such comical promptness if he hadn't put them in an intolerable situation. 'So soon he fell' is sublime about Adam, but one is not saved by humility from finding it absurd about Satan: he just gave one look round, as he started into existence, and set off for hell right away. When people say that Milton wilfully made his God repulsive, this alteration of his is a point on the other side.

See also note to l. 7 of 'Doctrinal Point'.

67 *amalgam with mercury*: mercury is a solvent for most metals, the products being called amalgams: i.e. the alloy of a metal with mercury; see also ll. 70–71.

68 *given with it free*: WE first used this joke (in a review of Philippe Mairet, *ABC of Adler's Psychology*) in *Granta* (8 June 1928):

Professor Freud elaborates theories to fit particular neuroses with which he has had to deal, and then says that though of course that is not the whole of the matter, these processes probably play a large part in the average mind. It is no use at all to say he must be wrong because his mind is saturated with sex; you might as well say a plumber must be wrong because his mind is saturated with lead piping; he may not know the price of the furniture, but he is certainly competent to find where the pipes go, even if he says a really modern house has pipes running all over, and some American houses are given away with the plumbing. (*E in G*, pp. 61–2)

68–9 *the house / Not built with hands*: 'God that made the world and all things therein, seeing that he is Lord of heaven and earth, dwelleth not in temples made with hands' (Acts 17: 24); 'For Christ is not entered into the holy places made with hands, which are the figures of the true; but into heaven itself, now to appear in the presence of God for us' (Hebrews 9: 24).

69 *silver crucible*: see note to l. 5 of 'I remember to have wept'.

70–71 *flaked . . . / Paste for the backs of mirrors*: amalgams with a high mercury content are liquid; otherwise they are crystalline in structure – and so serviceable (for example) for mirrors.

73–92 *She whom the god had snatched . . . dark arches*: there is an important (auto-)biographical dimension here. '**The end of the poem goes back to a personal situation about a lady who was feeling the entire background to this thing**' (*Contemporary Poets Reading Their Own Poems*). This was Phyllis Chroustchoff (*née* Vipond-Crocker), who killed herself at the age of thirty-eight on 17 March 1938, and to whose memory *GS* was dedicated. The closing twenty lines of the poem are a coded elegy for Phyllis, who had befriended Empson in the early 1930s – and became his confidante. Phyllis was a beauty, with black bobbed hair: the composer Philip Heseltine (Peter Warlock) fell in love with her, and the artist Laura Knight drew her portrait on several occasions. Her husband was Boris Chroustchoff, a clever and eccentric man of White Russian descent; the complete hedonist, he simply suited himself and behaved in an outrageous manner. A gifted linguist, he was fluent in Russian, Italian, French, German and English. He owned the Salamander Bookshop in Silver Street, London; and he collected African fetishes (it is said that D. H. Lawrence, who became friendly with Boris Chroustchoff, first saw such fetishes at his bookshop). After a period of married life, Phyllis left him and went off to live with Dr Gilbert Back, another highly cultivated man, who was WE's landlord during the mid-1930s (see 'Thanks for a Wedding Present'). Sociable and wonderfully spirited, Phyllis adored pubs and liked to drink herself silly, 'to roar': they would all have 'a roaring evening' – which meant having a tremendous time without taking thought for the morrow. She committed suicide on Back's birthday, at their home at 4 Henniker Mews in London, after a domestic row. 'I'll give you a present!' she is said to have shouted at him, before going to bed and turning on the gas poker in her room. The death certificate records tersely, 'Carbon monoxide (coal gas) poisoning', while extending the ritual note of exonerating grace: 'Did kill herself while balance of her mind was disturbed.'

The concluding lines of this poem might therefore be seen, in one aspect, as an attempt by WE to hymn a dithyramb for Phyllis, to absolve the ghastly manner of her death. However, the lines are not syntactically ordered, so they are extremely resistant to lucid interpretation. WE in his notes says that the woman experiences 'tragic exultation', which might suggest that her close encounter with the fiery god, Jupiter/Zeus, as also with Bacchus, leads to her death. Accordingly, one implication is that alcoholism was her doom. And yet the whole of this last section of the poem, including portions subsequently cut from the full work, was written, and published, before Phyllis Chroustchoff's suicide. To look at this problem from a different angle, then: it is strange that the one aspect of Bacchus/ Dionysus that is not brought out in WE's notes is the sexual one, especially since WE always claimed to be fascinated by '**Freud and Frazer, in traces of the primitive**', as he put it. In Frazerian terms, this god was a vegetation spirit, a fertility god, and his rites were certainly occasions for free (though holy) indulgence in sex as well as wine. Another way to regard the climax of the poem, therefore, is that the woman is enabled by drink to overcome her despair, cross the gulf it had created (l. 75), come up the 'stair' (l. 74), and initiate a successful sexual encounter, which the last line of the poem may celebrate. In terms of myth, Semele is snatched into a cloud by Jupiter, whereupon the god (perhaps it is now Bacchus, who is associated with fire from his birth as well as with sex and wine?) makes 'fire from her despair' (l. 79) and 'lit up her despair to fire' (l. 90).

But there is another aspect of the final section of the poem which complicates the picture in an extraordinary fashion. This fifth section of the poem (ll. 73–92) was first published – more than a year before Phyllis's suicide – as 'Bacchus Four' in *Poetry*. Another, virtually identical, typescript version of the closing section – though headed 'Bacchus III' – ('sailing' in l. 83 was typed as 'climbing', and WE himself made the handwritten emendation) – is now in the Poetry/Rare Books Collection of the University Libraries of the State University of New York at Buffalo. Both of those first versions originally included this additional passage immediately following l. 78:

> One cut as seizin from the turf the cross
> Whose arch of branches are the best for fire
> And made a fire enter their flue of cloud
> Who swallow into vaults a double cross
> And all the flounces of the trees made arches
> Whose offered branches were the first despair
> Whose rounded thought could hold a court for fire
> With which the raptured Adam could not cope
> And like a cow over the moon to fiddles
> We leapt in turn across the cope of fire.

This passage too is not susceptible to easy paraphrase, but certain points of information and interpretation may be available. For one matter, 'seizin' – WE's spelling is anomalous (*OED*) – refers to the symbolical act known as *livery of seisin*, 'the delivery of corporeal possession of a land or tenement' (Sir William

Blackstone, *Commentaries on the Laws of England* (1809), II. xx. p. 310): the handing over of an object such as a turf as a token of possession. By offering such *seisin*, 'One' (presumably Phyllis) allows possession. The following lines seem to refer to the perhaps quasi-religious construction and burning of a bonfire, a holocaust or burnt offering. Apart from the possible female sexual connotations of 'flue' and 'vaults', the fifth line borrows the final line of 'Sleeping out in a College Cloister': 'Drowned under flounces . . . of trees.' The fanciful accompaniment plays with the traditional idea that the form of Gothic architecture was suggested by trees, and also with the fact that 'groined vaulting' arises when two passages with Gothic ceilings meet, though the word 'groin/groyne' is probably off-stage here, but cf. l. 19. Perhaps most notably of all, the final lines appear to bring together hints of Adam's fall and a symbolical act of fertility. In 'Bacchus' as a whole, biblical imagery cuts across the classical (as in line 61, where the caduceus melds both with Dionysus' thyrsus and with Satan-as-snake bringing the knowledge of good and evil), and the same thing happens in the excised passage. Probably, the 'offered branches' are the forbidden tree in Eden, and the 'rounded thought' is the apple, the fruit of the tree of the knowledge of good and evil. (In *Pastoral*, WE wrote at length about the 'green thought' of Marvell's 'The Garden', l. 48; and 'rounded thought' may also be associated, since man's disobedience brought death into the world (with loss of Eden), with Prospero's calm reflection on death in *The Tempest*, IV.i.156–58: 'We are such stuff / As dreams are made on, and our little life / Is rounded with a sleep.') Accordingly, the phrase 'first despair' in l. 6 of this passage may derive from a conjunction of the first words of *PL* (I.1–2) – 'Of man's first disobedience, and the fruit / Of that forbidden tree' – and Belial's dread counsel to the rebel angels in II.142–3 – 'our final hope / Is flat despair' – which WE quoted in 'Rolling the Lawn', ll. 1–2. If such phrases are circumlocutions for Adam's yielding to temptation, then 'raptured Adam' in the following line may bring together Adam's access of passion at his first vision of Eve's pristine beauty – 'transported I behold, / Transported touch' (VIII.529–30) – and the sense that he 'could not cope' with the failure of obedience which issued in his Fall. Whatever the hermeneutic significance of the allusion, in the penultimate line of this passage, to the nursery (or nonsense) rhyme, 'Hey diddle diddle, / The Cat and the Fiddle, / The Cow jump'd over the Moon . . .', there is no question but that WE appeals to Sir James Frazer's concatenation of primitive rituals in his final image of leaping across a fire. As Frazer rehearses the topic, at many places in *The Golden Bough* (see, for example, Part I: *The Magic Art and The Evolution of Kings*, vol. II, and Part VI: *Balder the Beautiful*, vol. I), folk have been keen to jump over festive bonfires to promote generative and fertilizing effects; bonfire-hurdling is otherwise good for purification. In sum, the 10-line passage that Empson finally cut from 'Bacchus' convokes pagan bonfires, the temptation and fall of Adam in Eden (forbidden knowledge and sexual experience?), and an exuberant primitive activity that is believed to promote fertility.

The import of the passage may therefore be a celebration of 'pagan' sexuality; it is possible that Empson is celebrating in code his love for Phyllis Chroustchoff, or even a love-affair with her – it is, after all, the only point in the poem which speaks of an athletic activity being undertaken by the plural 'we'. But it is just as possible that it is in some sort a celebration of Phyllis's love for Dr Back (whose very surname may be subsumed in 'Bacchus'). Whether or not a personal reading of that sort is tenable, these lines assuredly link ecstatic love, sexual consummation, and a suprahuman passion which may eventuate in self-destruction. The key motifs of these final reverberant lines are despair and fire and divinity; the 'cope' or canopy of heaven is invoked alongside the 'arches' or 'vaults' of the tomb. We can only speculate as to why Empson cut those ten lines from the conclusion of the poem: maybe he felt simply that – in the face of Phyllis's actual fate, her awful (and possibly impulsive) suicide – their 'pagan' sexual exuberance was out of key.

80 from the] a *Poetry 1937*

81 An arch that cast his] Whose arch could cast a *Poetry 1937*

82 the other's] another's *Poetry 1937, The Poems of William Empson*

83 *Arachne sailing . . . rope of cloud*: Arachne's attempt (Ovid, *Met.* VI.5ff.) to hang herself when abused by Athena is assimilated to the cloud that did duty for a goddess (see note to ll. 1–4 of 'Invitation to Juno').

84 Tracer] tracer *Poetry 1937*

84 *photon*: a quantum of light or other electromagnetic radiation, a discrete 'particle' or packet of electromagnetic energy.

85–6 *purged his path with a thin fan of fire . . . lights of the god's car*: the biblical references are: 'The voice of him that crieth in the wilderness, Prepare ye the way of the Lord, make straight in the desert a highway for our God. Every valley shall be exalted, and every mountain and hill shall be made low' (Isaiah 40: 3–4); and John the Baptist, anticipating Jesus: 'he that cometh after me is mightier than I . . . Whose fan is in his hand, and he will thoroughly purge his floor' (Matthew 3: 11–12).

'Thin fan . . . lights of the god's car': a mirror is used as a reflector in a car's headlamp; its parabolic shape focuses the beam. (At Delphi, Dionysus was venerated with service of the winnowing-fan; see Harrison, *Prolegomena to the Study of Greek Religion*, p. 518.)

86 *Round steel . . . car*: 'The line . . . is meant to be isolated, with a line-gap before as well as after, since it acts as a bridge' (undated letter by WE, [?1977] to D. J. Enright).

87 *A wheel of fire*: King Lear cries out to Cordelia, 'Thou art a soul in bliss, but I am bound / Upon a wheel of fire, that mine own tears / Do scald like molten lead' (IV.vi.43–5). Jay L. Halio, in his edition of *King Lear* for the New Cambridge Shakespeare, provides a footnote which is just as germane – especially in linking Lear with Ixion – to a full understanding of WE's reference: 'This image is complex and syncretic, alluding to pagan, Christian and other symbols not only of torture and suffering, but also of energy (Elton [*King Lear and the Gods*, 1966], pp. 236–8). Lear thinks he is damned and Cordelia is an angel in heaven; in this context, Ixion's wheel, which was sometimes placed in the heavens . . ., is especially relevant' (*The Tragedy of King Lear* (Cambridge, 1992), p. 237).

88 crowd] cloud *Poetry* 1937

88 *crowd of cloud*: given 'arches' in ll. 76, 80 and 92, cf. Shelley, *Prometheus Unbound* (1820), Act I, ll. 710–13: 'the triumphant storm did flee, / . . . Between, with many a captive cloud, / A shapeless, dark and rapid crowd.' (Perhaps cf. too both Byron, 'The Vision of Judgment' (1821), LVIII.457–60: 'and then it grew a cloud; / And so it was – a cloud of witnesses. / But such a cloud! No land ere saw a crowd / Of locusts numerous as the heavens saw these', and Swinburne, 'The Armada 1588 : 1888', III.i.58: 'Lo, the cloud of his ships that crowd her channel's inlet with storm sublime'.)

89 *heaven's cope*: cf. *PL*, IV.992–3: 'the starry cope / Of heaven'.

92 *bells the vaults . . . dark arches*: cf. 'Song of the amateur psychologist', l. 17, and 'Doctrinal Point', l. 26. Perhaps cf. too James Russell Lowell, 'Fancy's Casuistry' (which opens with the apostrophe 'How struggles with the tempest's swells / That warning of tumultuous bells!'), ll. 37–40: 'The events in line of battle go; / In vain for me their trumpets blow / As unto him that lieth low / In death's dark arches'.

Your Teeth are Ivory Towers

Written by 1939 (see notes to ll. 8, 41–3), and first published in *GS*.

CP: There was a toothpaste advertisement saying your teeth are ivory castles and must be defended. Critics often say that modern poetry retires into an ivory tower, doesn't try to make contact with a reader, or escapes facing the problems of the time. I try to defend it by saying that there is a good deal of defence in ordinary life (talking or biting). A critic like Dr Leavis can speak with the same tone of moral outrage about an Escapist (sentimental) novel as a customs official would about *Lady Chatterley's Lover*, say; but this being over-simple, I was claiming, is itself a way of escaping the complexity of the critic's problem. The relation of the artist to his society may include acting as safety valve or keeping the fresh eye, etc., of the child, and therefore can't be blamed out of hand for escapism or infantilism. Then the poem drifts off onto the stock defence that poets have to be obscure because something has gone wrong with the public. Our civilization has been built up on two accepted but apparently irreconcilable ideals, worldly and Christian, and this gives a good deal of freedom – people with different views are still in contact because they are only finding different ways of resolving the same contradictions. It is not clear that in the new great machine or mass societies, which accept neither ideal, there is the same room for the artist. A star just too faint to be seen directly can still be seen out of the corners of your eyes; Max Beerbohm described some hero of the aesthetic movement as looking life straight in the face out of the very corners of his eyes. I suppose the reason I tried to defend my clotted kind of poetry was that I felt it was going a bit too far.

For *Listen* WE noted: ' "Your Teeth" defends this kind of poetry [i.e. the metaphysical or 'clotted kind of poetry' favoured by WE] against the objection of the 'thirties, that poetry should make contact with the public and current problems; however, I have always admired the poets who did.'

TITLE: 'Your Teeth are Ivory Castles – defend them with Gibbs Dentifrice' was one of the most successful advertising slogans of the years between the world wars; devised by the manufacturers D. & W. Gibbs Ltd, the 'Ivory Castle League and Crusade' lasted a full fifteen years, 1924–39, and enrolled some five million children in what turned into a national institution. Merchandise designed to highlight the delightful importance of dental hygiene featured the dauntless Gibbs Archer and his band of fairies in their unremitting combat with the Giant Decay and his Caries Imps. (See M. Bensley Thornhill, 'One Hundred Thousand Crusaders', *Progress* (January 1932), 21–5.) The craze for mocking artists who live in ivory towers was begun by Charles-Augustin Sainte-Beuve in *Pensées d'Août* (1837), with specific reference to Alfred de Vigny: '*Et Vigny, plus secret / Comme en sa tour d'ivoire, avant midi, rentrait*'. (Cf. Stephen Dedalus's enraptured musings on 'tower of ivory' in Joyce's *A Portrait of the Artist*.)

Ricks discusses 'the shape of the ending' of the poem, which is unique in WE (pp. 190–91). See also Morelli, pp. 137–9; *TGA*, pp. 157–63.

2–4 *Piaget's babies . . . to themselves*: the Swiss psychologist Jean Piaget discovered from extensive researches – what every adult always took to be common knowledge – that the very young child (one who has not yet reached the 'age of reason'), far from being in the least bit concerned to communicate with others, engages in a 'collective monologue'. The child operates at an intermediate stage between autism and a socially adapted intelligence, but he is none the worse for living in 'this bi-polar nature of reality'. If any of his so-called 'transductions' turn out to be 'valid', that is a matter of total luck. In sum, Piaget declared, children exist in a state of egocentrism: 'for the most part they are only talking to themselves' (*The Language and Thought of the Child*, trans. Marjorie Warden (London, 1926), p. 38). While Piaget's method in his first book consisted of non-interactive observation of two children, 'Lev' and 'Pie', its frightfully repetitious sequel, *Judgment and Reasoning in the Child* (1928), studied the ways and means of about forty children, and was based in large part on what Piaget termed 'personal interrogatory' – so his findings were, as WE puts it, 'Proved by interview' (l. 3).

2 *affection*: 'affectation' may be in view here, but WE's principal intent is to coin a variant of the psychological term 'affect', which is used variously to refer to transient states or changes of mood, ranging from the strongly positive to the strongly negative.

8 *Escape Verse has grown mortal sin*: see Olaf Stapledon's critical remarks on the 'ivory tower' attitude, in a symposium entitled 'Writers and Politics', *Scrutiny* 8:2 (September 1939), 151–6), followed by his outright denunciation, 'Escapism in Literature', *Scrutiny* 8:3 (December 1939), 298–308. See also next note. Compare 'Autumn on Nan-Yueh', ll. 79–80.

10–12 *Panoplied in / Virtuous indignation, gnawing his bone, / A man like Leavis*: the English literary critic F. R. Leavis (1895–1978). As noted in the Introduction, Leavis was an early and pro-active enthusiast for WE, both his verse and his prose. By 1934–5, however, he would refuse to print what he disparaged as WE's 'psycho-analytics about *Alice*' ('Alice: Child as Swain'). By Christmas 1934, when WE called on the Leavises after returning from Tokyo, Leavis privately recorded: 'He seems no less the clever young man than when he went out, and I'm less patient. I'm earnest, of course, and *Scrutiny*'s earnest (no, I don't mean Empson said so). And *Scrutiny* couldn't have been kept going on the clever young man's interesting ideas, etc.' (quoted in MacKillop, *F. R. Leavis*, pp. 205–6).

The big bust-up occurred when Leavis wrote a dismissive review of Richards's *Coleridge on Imagination* ('Dr Richards, Bentham and Coleridge', *Scrutiny* 3 (March 1935), 382–402), and WE leapt to defend his mentor. In a letter of April 1935 Leavis expressed his suspicion (for which there is no evidence) that WE's protest had been 'written in collusion with Richards, who doesn't propose to expose himself personally. We probably shan't print it. Then the story will go round that Empson wrote a devastating reply which we are afraid to print' (MacKillop, *F. R. Leavis*, p. 206). But Leavis had little option but to print the letter in *Scrutiny* (4:1 (June 1935):

Everybody must feel unwilling to enter the feverish atmosphere of Dr Leavis's quarrels, but someone ought to state the case against his review of Dr Richards' *Coleridge on Imagination*. We are told that the book does 'bluntly, nothing' towards the detailed linguistic analysis of poetry, and an answer must attempt a summary of the book.

There is a strictly literary point, supported by examples (nowhere referred to by Dr Leavis): that the mature poetry of Coleridge and Wordsworth depends on an interplay between, or a uniting of, two opposed views of Nature. Philosophy comes in because this process was partly cause of, partly caused by, the philosophical ideas Coleridge developed when he first revolted against Hartley; it is no use for the literary critic to ignore the connection. The process was also discussed by Coleridge in terms of psychology, and his ideas here, the book claims, are still valuable apart from his poetry. Many of the psychological ideas he developed and based his work upon after his revolt against the Hartleian dynasty of psychologists have now come to be accepted by that same dynasty; we are given examples. One of these is the Fancy–Imagination distinction, and there is a long defence of it; when

Dr Leavis complains of the triviality of the examples and the evasiveness of the results he does not know that these are Coleridge's results and Coleridge's examples, which Dr Richards is only trying to defend against the intervening attacks.

This seems enough to keep a small book from doing 'bluntly, nothing'. It may be true that the author fails in 'supporting, when they appear, some serious critical journals' (p. 392) and he may even be 'lighthearted', but these personal faults need not make his book quite empty. I should agree with Dr Leavis so far as he says that Dr Richards is too content to start hares and had better have worked out his material more fully; this does not account for so many pages of anathema. In saying that the 'poetic function' is of great importance to society Dr Richards is obviously not denying that the society must be such as can support it and be affected by it; he is merely talking about something else; and granted this point his 'preposterously extravagant' hope (p. 391) for a quasi-political salvation from literature is just that of Dr Leavis. The review is dimly aware of this, and then says it can't be true, or the man would fluff up his feathers and perpetually scream at the Book Society.

One or two minor points. Dr Richards is shown to be always insensitive as a prose writer because he calls the Old Coleridge the Highgate Spellbinder, not realizing that this implies something disagreeable (too comic to answer, but try Carlyle on the Old Coleridge). The slight on Mr Eliot seems imaginary; his work is referred to by implication in the context as 'the best criticism of today' and for that reason called in evidence. The motorbus (p. 390) is obviously not Science, whose intellectual constructs are not its brute facts. I am not even sure that Dr Richards disagrees with Dr Leavis about the Immortality Ode (p. 399), and he was not 'summing it up' but answering an attack by Coleridge on some of its lines; the suggestion that he is proved to have no taste in poetry by his failure to say that he agrees with Dr Leavis is ridiculous. On Dr Leavis's logical point it seems sufficient to read (p. 386) 'result in a Nature (iv) through which our power of control over part of Nature (i) is increasing by embarrassing leaps and bounds.' And there is a curious paragraph on page 385. Dr Richards is first blamed for introducing his pupils to things they probably did not know about before, such as the term 'nominalism'. Immediately after, as a destruction of his pretensions, 'one is left also with the impression of having been reminded of a number of commonplace philosophic considerations from which strict thinking might start'. This seems no bad ambition for a teacher.

Leavis's response was a curt footnote: 'No comment on the above seems necessary. Mr Empson is referred back to his texts.' However, years later, Leavis was to claim: 'In a subsequent private letter of apology [presumably to Leavis himself] Mr Empson expressed some regret for his public letter' (*Kenyon Review* 11 (Spring 1949), 315).

In June 1935 WE published in the *Criterion* (edited by T. S. Eliot) his own laudatory review of *Coleridge on Imagination*. Leavis reacted to WE's piece with a contempt expressed in a letter to Ronald Bottrall:

No intelligent man has any right to do such a review, however much he liked Richards.

Actually, I don't think Empson is very intelligent now, though he was once potentially. He was also dangerously clever, and I think that he's little else now: that terrible capacity for the intellectual game, for getting the ball back over the net, for never being at a loss – that's not thinking. For all its intelligent appearance, that review of Richards, if you know the book, is downright stupid. [*Coleridge on Imagination*] is as bogus a thing as I've read – and corrupt, through and through. I agree with you about [WE's] *Letter V*. I still admire very much the poems from *Cambridge Poetry 1929*: but I have never seen any of a later date I was convinced by.

(There is a slight puzzle here as to which of WE's pieces Leavis is actually referring to: he twice uses the word 'review', but it may be that he is adverting to WE's letter, reproduced above, and not to the later review. Although MacKillop gives the date of Leavis's letter as 26 March 1935, WE's review came out only in June.) WE dated the permanent emergence of Leavis's high moral tone – his 'Virtuous indignation', his trading in 'brickbats' – to this spat over Richards. (See also WE's anecdote about T. S. Eliot's apprehension *vis-à-vis* Leavis's spite, in 'The Hammer's Ring' (1973); A, p. 217.) Leavis reportedly once remarked, 'If you want a character study of Empson, go to Iago' (MacKillop, *F. R. Leavis*, p. 207). WE was not above casting his own aspersions; in notes (of uncertain later date) on the monograph by Leavis's associate L. C. Knights, *How Many Children had Lady Macbeth?* (1933), he would jot down: '**Interesting that the stupid title was supplied by Leavis, who never admits that anybody can be good unless he is an intellectual of lower middle class origin. Naturally the idea that it *mattered* whether the Macbeths had a male heir, because this was what Macbeth was selling his soul for, could not enter the mind of Leavis, who has always felt venomous against anybody who isn't a lower middle class intellectual, and even more venomous against the rest of them.**'

15–16 *The safety valve alone / Knows the worst truth about the engine*: cf. William James in *Varieties of Religious Experience* (1902): 'The difference between willing and merely wishing, between having ideals that are creative and ideals that are but pinings and regrets, thus depends solely either on the amount of steam-pressure chronically driving the character in the ideal direction, or on the amount of ideal excitement transiently acquired' (p. 266).

16–17 *only the child / Has not yet been misled*: see 'Alice: Child as Swain': '[Dodgson's heroine] is the free and independent mind . . . And it is the small observer, like the child, who does least to alter what he sees and therefore sees most truly . . . In this sort of child-cult the child, though a means of imaginative escape, becomes the critic . . .' (*Pastoral*, pp. 210, 213, 221).

18 *child? You may be wise or mild*: cf. Lancelot in *The Merchant of Venice*, II. ii.72: 'It is a wise father that knows his own child'; and Pope's 'Epitaph on John Gay', ll. 1–2: 'Of manners gentle, of affection mild, / In wit a man; simplicity a child.'

21–2 *anarchy . . . / We could once carry anarchy*: cf. Yeats's 'The Second Coming' (ll. 3–4): 'Things fall apart: the centre cannot hold; / Mere anarchy is loosed upon the world'.

23–4 *Christ and the magnificent milord / As rival pets*: cf. William James's reflections on the fundamental relation between Christian asceticism and sophisticated worldliness, in *Varieties of Religious Experience*: 'A certain kind of man, it is imagined, must be the best man absolutely and apart from the utility of his functions, apart from economical considerations. The saint's type and the knight's or gentleman's type, have always been rival claimants of this absolute ideality' (p. 374).

'Milord' derives from the sixteenth-century French *milour*, which was used exclusively to designate a snooty or foppish English lord. OED gives an example of the whole handy phrase from 1969 (though primarily as an illustration of 'milord' rather than as a fixed compound with 'magnificent').

25–6 *Faust . . . / 'All things that move between the quiet poles'*: Marlowe's Dr Faustus, anticipating his night of conjuring, hails the 'heavenly' merits of the 'metaphysics of magicians / And necromantic books': 'All things that move between the quiet poles / Shall be at my command' (I.i.58–9). For Faustus, the 'quiet poles' were the motionless poles of the universe.

35 *Look through the very corners of your eyes*: although WE's note attributes this mannerism to a '**hero of the aesthetic movement**', he slightly misapprehends his source: Beerbohm deploys the phrase in his characterization of Beau Brummell: 'All delicate spirits, to whatever art they turn, even if they turn to no art, assume an oblique attitude towards life. Of all dandies, Mr Brummell did most steadfastly maintain this attitude. Like the single-minded artist that he was he turned full and square towards his art and looked life straight in the face out of the corners of his eyes' ('Dandies and Dandies' (1896), *The Works of Max Beerbohm* (London, 1922), p. 10).

On a loose leaf of his papers (probably dating from the 1930s), Empson once noted: '**Some things are like stars which can only be seen when you are looking right away from them. Some, like sadism, dignity, Christianity, are like passing cars at night on the road: you have to aim almost right at the light and just pass it at the crucial moment, and it is very easy to get hypnotized by the light so that you smash right into it.**'

40 Or] But *1940*

41–3 *Assume what answers any wits have found / In evening dress on rafts upon the main / Not therefore uneventful or soon drowned*: even if one must settle in the modern era for doing without divine revelation or celestial response, life is not pointless or doom-laden: one can yet enjoy a full life with highly imaginative style. This 'moral' may have been indirectly triggered by a famous scene in the Marx Brothers' movie *At the Circus* (1939), to which WE would refer in a review (of *Conscience and the King* by Bertram Joseph) dating from 1953: '**The book takes twenty pages to show that the Elizabethans often said "things are not always what**

they seem"; it feels like the orchestra in one of the Marx brothers' films which is found to be disappearing out to sea on a raft while still playing at full blast' (*Strengths of Shakespeare's Shrew*, p. 40).
42 on] in *Listen*

Aubade

First published – with eight additional lines (a cinquain, a five-line stanza, succeeded by a tercet, a three-line stanza, in harmony with the established pattern of the poem) following line 32 (see below) – in *Life and Letters Today* 17:10 (Winter 1937), 68–9. The holograph fair copy, with some small variants (for example, 'wise' for 'strong' in the penultimate line), dates from a later period; penned in ink on notepaper with the printed heading 'Studio House, Hampstead Hill Gardens, London NW3', it may have been written out from memory (Empson Papers).

CP: **The same war in Tokyo then was the Manchurian Incident.**

WE wrote to Robert Herring, editor of *Life and Letters Today* (though it is possible the letter was not posted): '**The poem about a girl in Japan that you published left me entirely blank when I found it in the copy here. I feel only a vague embarrassment**' (14 July 1938).

On *The Poems of William Empson*, he commented:

I want now to take a poem called 'Aubade' – traditionally the song warning lovers to separate before dawn – and the difficulty here is in reading it aloud the right way rather than explaining it. There's a five-line verse followed each time by a three-line verse, each of them repeating their stock line at the end; and the stock lines ought to feel as if they were something different, as if they mean something different, each time they are repeated. I've sometimes been able to read it, but I'm not sure I can now. 'Standing', the main repeated idea in the stock lines, can be for instance getting out of bed, resisting an attack, or not going away. 'Flying' can mean going through the air or simply escaping; 'lying', of course, staying in bed or telling untruths. The poem is about a time in Japan during 1933 [1931] or so, when I was teaching there; and the Manchurian Incident [18–19 September 1931], as it was called, seemed an obvious part of the approach to world war. The conflict which my formula expects in a poem comes I suppose from this overhanging feeling that a separation between the lovers is somehow imposed. The meaning is supposed to be quite obvious, granting that you can put up with a few puns.

Listen gives this summary: ' "Aubade" was written in Tokyo during the Manchurian Incident, probably 1933. It was thought unwise for visiting Englishmen to marry Japanese ladies, because the two countries would clearly soon be at war.'

See Appendix 2 for WE's comments to Ricks in 1963.
On *Harvard*, WE remarked:

'Aubade' appears to be about the threat of an earthquake, which you often get in Tokyo; you then wait, wondering if you're going to get one of the big earthquakes afterwards. The doubt about whether you go into the garden arises because the Japanese have very heavy tiles on the roof, which usually hold the roof through the earthquake; if the house collapses they crush you, but if they come off sideways they may hit you in the garden. So whether you're safer in the house or in the garden has been greatly discussed. You may say, why does this rather casual love affair have anything to do with the prospect of a world war? Well, it really did: if you were a young Englishman coming to teach in Japan in the early 1930s, the wise old Englishman, leader of the colony, would at once tell you, 'Don't marry a Japanese lady, because the two countries will be at war within ten years.' If the poem seems obscure there, it is only because it is far away and long ago: the connection is meant to be obvious. The 'aubade' was a poem sung usually to the married couple after the wedding night; but anyway it's a poem sung at dawn.

The background is as follows. During Summer 1933, WE began an affair with a young Japanese woman, whose given name was Haru. It is possible that she lived with her parents, but more likely that she had come up from the country; she worked as a nursemaid. She is mentioned only a few times in WE's surviving papers, the first in a letter of 8 October 1933: ' **"Too much rice"** (the Chinese **rickshaw boys' name for illness in general – I don't know whether they would use it for starvation) has been grown in Japan this year, and the farmers are badly off. My young woman was expecting to have to sell herself to a German business man to support her parents, but a brother-in-law has rallied and we are all right. I made no offers but bought her some clothes'** (letter to John Hayward; King's College, Cambridge: WE/JDH/4). If that reference seems crude or super- cilious, it is almost certainly explained by the fact that in writing to the editor, bibliophile and wit John Hayward WE would invariably be flippant. But the relationship meant more to WE – and to Haru – than any easy or exploitative sexual encounter: it inspired this poem, one of only a handful he wrote while in Japan. 'Aubade' is also one of the few poems that is directly revealing about his private life.

WE had experienced his first earthquake, which killed thirteen people, just three weeks after his arrival, on 21 September 1931; and several minor tremors in the following two years. In the poem, as soon as the earth moves for the sleeping lovers, the woman's first imperative is not merely to seek safety by getting out of WE's villa but to rush home by taxi before the child in her charge cries out. Although the affair was not adulterous, it would still cause a scandal.

The key to the poem is its oscillation between the resonant and memorable refrains, 'It seemed the best thing to be up and go' and 'The heart of standing is you cannot fly', which point up the character of the conflict felt by the poet between duty and desire. Whether it would have been nobler for him to stand and marry the woman in Tokyo, or to heed the call of home and the deep honour of his political place: that question becomes the fulcrum of the remainder of the poem, and it closes by assenting to the large truth (reinforced by the generalization of the plural 'we' in the last line) that the new commitment has to be surrendered to the long inalienable obligation. Neither choice would be wholly satisfactory or less loaded with pain, but the principle of positive realism wins the contest. The poem, Empson said to Ricks, '**chiefly meant that you can't get away from this world war if it's going to happen**'; the keynote of the last five lines is '**passive endurance. We have to put up with it, we can't avoid this situation of history.**' Thus, with respect to the love-affair with the girl dramatized in the poem, it says starkly: '**we can't marry, we must expect to separate.**'

The next recorded reference to Haru occurs in January 1935, over a year after she and WE had separated, in a letter to his friend Lady Sansom (wife of the sinophile Sir George Sansom, commercial counsellor at the British Embassy in Tokyo): '**I had a Christmas card from Haru in Tokyo in which she said she was keeping the money I left and would send it back when I was seriously hard up, which she was sure I would be. She writes very cheerfully now. I wish there was some hopeful step that she could take.**' The phrasing suggests that he must have put a good deal of emotional distance between himself and her. Haru visited England for a while in 1935, working as a nursemaid for the future poet and academic David Wevill, who was to recall in 1988:

In autumn 1954 I had just started at Cambridge, coming from Canada. I wrote my parents a letter naming some of the poets I was reading, including Empson. My father, who knew nothing of writers or literature I think, wrote back asking if this was the William Empson he had confronted in our rented house in Croydon (I think) while we were on a visit to England [from Yokohama in 1935] ... My parents had brought the young woman across as a baby-*amah* for me, and by law my father was responsible for her safe return to Japan, as a Japanese national. Empson knocked on the door asking to see her, telling what story I don't know, but I believe Empson tried several times to see her, by various means. I seem to recall my father might have appealed to the police to restrain Empson ... (letter quoted in Sumie Okada, *Western Writers in Japan* (Basingstoke, Hants., 1999), p. 48)

While such tentative recollections suggest that Wevill's father believed that WE had been harassing the woman, or was at least over-importunate (it is certainly possible that WE might have treated himself to some Dutch courage before arriving at the house), further evidence indicates that WE did have a number of encounters with Haru – though it is not possible to determine who was the less willing. They even went out of town together and probably visited his friend Phyllis Chroustchoff (see notes to 'Bacchus' ll. 73–92) at her family home in

Devon. The evidence is an entry in a notebook he kept in 1942: 'I remember a Japanese girl walking into a Devonshire meadow with me, all roaring with its lush and careless summer; she looked at a hedge ten feet thick and fifteen feet high and said "In Japan we would eat all that" and otherwise was astounded and angry to find that everything hurt her legs: "Why do you let these things grow?" she could not understand, about the nettles and thistles. But I had thought of this as a form of the prettiness of Japan and the way farming there is gardening.' On 11 October 1935 he notified Sir George Sansom: 'Haru leaves England today, quite cheerful after wangling a last meeting yesterday.' His next bulletin to Sansom, on 13 November, carries an unmistakable tone of relief: 'Very cheerful letters from Haru in Canada, who has met friends there. The Wevilles [sic] mislaid their luggage and sent her on to fetch it back, and I do claim for Haru that she seems to have become a social figure as soon as let loose.'

However, there is a further piece of evidence that has to be taken into account. As first published in *Life and Letters Today*, the poem included eight lines, following line 32 (and immediately before the concluding couple of five-line stanzas), which suggest that the end of the affair was protracted, and probably very hurtful – more so for the woman than for himself:

> This is unjust to her without a prose book.
> A lyric from a fact is bound to cook.
> It was more grinding; it was much more slow.
> But still the point's not how much time it took.
> It seemed the best thing to be up and go.
>
> I do not know what forces made it die.
> With what black life it may yet work below.
> The heart of standing is you cannot fly.

Perhaps he found that the initially beguiling liaison had turned with terrible swiftness into an irritating blank mistake, or a big lie he could not face down. Perhaps he could not find it in himself to be firm enough to put an end to it. Or perhaps, when he begged to be released, she would not let him go. We cannot know for certain. All we do know is that he chose to cut out of future printings of the poem the lines last quoted, perhaps because the references to 'grinding' and 'black life' seemed to suggest that she had become bitter or even simply, self-humiliatingly clinging.

The unhappy truth is that she probably did try to keep their love alive too long after its natural term, for WE's last letter about the relationship was written to Ronald Bottrall on 23 July 1940 (he had been to China and returned home again since last seeing 'poor Haru', as he called her): 'I found a grindingly sad letter from her when I got back to England, and then lost the address; but maybe after all that was the best thing to do' (Harry Ransom Humanities Research Center, University of Texas at Austin).

See Ricks 1974, pp. 178–9; Wain 1977, pp. 315–16; Go, ' "Argufying" in Empson's "Aubade" '; Krautz, 'Imagery and Sexual Connotations in William Empson's *Aubade*'; Morelli, pp. 109–15; Willis, pp. 303–11; Havely, *William Empson and F. R. Leavis*, pp. 30–32; and *TGA*, pp. 163–8.

2 *on a cliff*: according to *TGA* (presumably on WE's authority), 'the "cliff" was an 8 ft. drop' (p. 165).

5 *It seemed . . . up and go*: cf. this 'anticipatory' reflection dating from 1929: 'Certainly all new acts are dangerous, but it is not necessarily less dangerous to avoid them. I may be run over if I go into the street, but the roof may fall on me if I stay indoors. Where nothing is known beforehand there is nothing for it but to be hopeful, and where there is no means of deciding between two courses of action it is more cheerful to choose the more active one' ('Obscurity and Annotation', *A*, pp. 86–7).

15 *Some solid ground for lying could she show*: *pace* Kenji Go's unqualified suggestion that the poet 'asks whether she knows "some solid ground" where they can keep on sleeping together' (p. 37), Krautz is clearly on more solid ground in arguing that the question 'can refer to her making up an excuse for her absence from home ("lying" semantically understood as "not telling the truth"), or to his asking her about some safe place for protection against the earthquake. But it can also refer to his asking her about some place to make love' (p. 238). Cf. 'China', l. 6.

17 *were*: the grammar may well be thought to require *was* – though WE rightly rejected the emendation when Hayward suggested it (letter of 21 May 1956).

18 *being woken he would bawl*: while internal evidence, and the cultural history of the 'aubade' (or 'alba'), might suggest that 'he' could be the woman's husband or father, S. F. Bolt revealed: 'This person . . . was a small boy in the charge of the nursemaid who was the poet's companion – as Empson explained when I wrote something which assumed a husband was involved' (letter to *London Review of Books* 15:16 (19 August 1993), 5). Dr Bolt further said: 'It occurred when I was poetry editor of *Delta*, and writing a series of articles on poetic devices. In the article on repetition I demonstrated how "The heart of standing etc." develops meaning, stanza by stanza. This involved interpretation, including taking "he" to be the husband. Ian MacKillop, another editor [and WE's colleague in the Department of English Literature at Sheffield University], showed it to WE prior to publication, and wrote to me that WE was indignant at the suggestion that the woman was another man's wife, affirming that she was a nursemaid employed by the German Ambassador' (letter to Haffenden, 26 August 1993).

20 **Half an Hour**] half an hour *1937*

23 *Till you have seen what a threat holds below*: Krautz, who is determined to hang a Freudian reading on every available part of the poem, thinks this line 'a very direct allusion to [the poet's] private parts – although excusable in lovers' parlance. The other interpretation is, of course, a reference to the gap created by the earthquake which has been already alluded to [in line 6]' (p. 238). One wonders whether Krautz, who seems to have been unaware of the original version of the line (see collation below), would have been so eager to pronounce that WE was referring to his own erection as 'a fright'.

23 threat holds below] fright has to show *1937*

27–8 *Glut me with floods where only the swine can row / Who cuts his throat and let him count his gains*: may be paraphrased: 'Satiate me with news of the outside world, where only the evil prosper, and that only in the short term.' Contrast Brabantio in *Othello* I.iii.54–8: 'nor doth the general care / Take hold on me; for my particular grief / Is of so flood-gate and o'erbearing nature / That it engluts and swallows other sorrows, / And it is still itself.' In the poem the speaker wishes for the reverse of this, i.e. that news of 'the general care' should 'englut and swallow' his 'particular grief'. *Glut* means fill or overfill, as in Keats, 'On the Sea' (1817), ll. 2–3, where the 'mighty swell / Gluts twice ten thousand Caverns'; mentally satiate or surfeit. The *floods* are not literal, like the drought and rains in l. 26, but metaphorical; the speaker asks that his mind be flooded with news. 'Flood' can also mean the sea, as in *Othello* (I.iii.135; II.i.17), and elsewhere in Shakespeare; and the sea can be a metaphor for the world's life. *Only the swine can row*: only the insensitive and unscrupulous man can survive, by 'rowing his own boat', i.e. looking after his own interests. As a morally disgusting person, especially through greed, the *swine* is connected to the sea through the Gadarene swine, who when possessed by devils 'ran violently down a steep place into the sea . . . and were choked' (Mark 5: 13). There may also be a recollection of the sailors in Homer, who after feasting with the sorceress Circe were changed into swine (*Odyssey* X.206–40). *Who cuts his throat*: there was a traditional belief that if a pig tried to swim it would cut its own throat with its trotters – a penalty for its fatness. To 'cut one's own throat' is a proverbial expression for bringing about one's own defeat. *Let him count his gains* is ironical; compare 'Success', l. 15. The 'swine' may mean in particular the ruthless businessman, making profits on the sea of commerce. WE may have in mind another sea-play by Shakespeare, *The Merchant of Venice*, where Antonio's doomed trading ships are likened to 'signiors and rich burghers of the flood' who 'overpeer the petty traffickers' (I.i.8–12). The man who becomes a swine in order to succeed will find his gains are illusory if his preoccupation with business has dehumanized him: Gratiano tells Antonio, 'You have too much respect upon the world: / They lose it that do buy it with much care' (I.i.74–75). Another sense in which the individualistic swine may be said to cut his own throat is that he is denying the social cooperation on which all human beings ultimately depend.

31 *Only the same war on a stronger toe*: while noting the poet's own account of the line as a reference to the '**Manchurian Incident**', Krautz ventures: 'With war being a favourite metaphor among poets, it can also be interpreted as sexual intercourse. ". . . on a stronger toe" in the same line would correspond to this interpretation, "toe" in that case being understood as a rude metaphor for the virile member' (p. 238). And yet nowadays, toe might just as well be toe.

35 *no die a god for a good throw*: appears to conflate two allusions to Shakespeare: the first the piquant moment when Bottom as Pyramus, fearing that his Thisbe has been devoured by a lion, kills himself with a sword ('Now die, die, die, die, die'), and earns for his pains this quip from Demetrius: 'No die, but an ace for him; for he is but one' (*A Midsummer Night's Dream*, V.i.301); the other, the terrible moment when Caliban abases himself to the drunken Stefano: 'I'll show thee every fertile inch o'th'island, / And I will kiss thy foot. I prithee, be my god' (*The Tempest*, II.ii.147–8). A 'die' may be taken for the singular of 'dice': but as a verb it also bears a sexual meaning, of which Elizabethan poets and dramatists never tired. Moreover, Krautz's remark (p. 238) that ' "a good throw" can connote sexual intercourse' is well founded: analogous usages exist in 'to have a tumble', for example, or in Flaubert's vulgar term for the act of sex: *tirer un coup* ('to fire a shot'). Empson discusses the pun on *die*, with the sense of copulation, in *Pastoral*, pp. 44–5. The poet asks to be told – since he and the woman have missed their chance – what those people are missing who do not elevate to divine status the dice (after one lucky throw) or sex (as perhaps after one satisfying climax – *TGA* notes the homophone 'throe').

38–42 *But as to risings . . . we cannot fly*: see Appendix 2, pp. 119–20.

42 we] you *Poems of William Empson, Harvard*

The Fool

First published in *GS*.

There is one surviving typescript version of the poem, though of unknown date (now owned by Theodore Hofmann). In it l. 9 is set off by itself, before the final, discrete stanza.

CP: 'The Fool', etc. I haven't been able to ask Miss Hatakeyama's permission to re-publish these 'translations' of her work. My part was only to polish up her own English version, and I do not think I added a metaphor or a thought. Maybe I ought to make clear that she has nothing to do with the Aubade poem.

Sadly, almost nothing can be discovered about 'C. Hatakeyama', whose work Empson took up with such warm interest. When WE was asked if she had been one of his pupils in Tokyo, he responded:

No, she was just a school teacher somewhere in the north of Japan who wrote and wanted

to have the English of her poems polished up. I thought they were very good. I did see her once – she turned up in Tokyo after she'd done all these things – I mean after she'd sent me all these poems and I'd sent them back – and I was sort of very keen to keep up the connection. But she was very sort of shrinking. I never saw her again and she didn't leave an address. But there was no quarrel – she was just shrinking . . . I thought they were good poems. I mean it's the same way I published 'The Fire Sermon' with no idea of saying I'd made it up. After all, it's a very small text, isn't it? I thought that any good poetry which came my way I'd much better print. But it's quite true I didn't make it up. (Unpublished interview by Christopher Norris and David Wilson; courtesy of Christopher Norris)

WE made himself available to promote decent, accessible translations into English, whether from Japanese or (later) from Chinese. From Tokyo on 28 December 1933, for example, he despatched to Parsons at Chatto & Windus a sample of a novel by a Miss Nanjo; this letter shows his robust attitude to the sensitive task of translating a literary work from one culture into the language of another:

This is one episode from a long Japanese novel – the rest apparently not so good. It would go by itself all right, if there was a note explaining that Sunaga is the son of one of his father's servants; what they are all hiding from him is that the old woman isn't his mother. The next and last episode, told I think by the uncle, simply makes Sunaga be told the truth: he then travels for some time and becomes manly in solitude. If you think a 7/6 novel size more hopeful than this short story size probably she had better do a couple of other short stories, one this length another shorter: a Proletarian story about country people seemed to me most hopeful. The others might be more recent, too: this one was written just before the war.

I have tinkered with the English a bit. It still feels Japaneasy but I daresay that's rather a good thing than not (the Japanese style is like a smell you can't wash out: I can't get it out of this) and she really writes quite well apart from that. I hope it may be thought decent in the office.

This is enough for a Dolphin, I think, if you felt like that. Otherwise it is sent as a sample: would you consider a longer book of short stories translated by her: do you think another London publisher would: do you think she had better just have it quietly and cheaply published in Tokyo[?]

It may well seem just rather out-of-date Russian, but it is actually very like the Japanese.

I come home next autumn and propose to offer you a smallish volume of essays [*Some Versions of Pastoral*]. Love, Bill E

(Still, Parsons turned down Miss Nanjo's work.)

Many years later, WE participated in a discussion with Arthur Waley (who, without ever visiting China or Japan, became the great interpreter for the modern age both of Chinese poetry and of classical Japanese literature) on the problems of translation. It was reported:

Mentioning the complexities of ancient languages, Mr Empson said that once he had found, on looking up a word, that a phrase could be translated:

'Thou shalt commit adultery – alas!' *or*
'Thou shalt commit adultery – hooray!'

He felt this helped to illustrate the great difficulties facing translators.

Asked if he thought 'the influence of poetry in translation was valuable to English poetry', WE 'replied that he thought Waley had already influenced English poetry a great deal; it seemed to him that when he was young poets were absorbing a great many different new influences' ('A Comparison between the British and Chinese Approach to Poetry', *P.E.N. News* (November 1957), 19–20).

11 *poison-flowers*: cf. Keats, 'Isabella; or The Pot of Basil', ll. 103–4: 'Even bees . . . / Know there is richest juice in poison-flowers'; and Tennyson, 'Maud', ll. 156–7: 'And most of all would I flee from the cruel madness of love, / The honey of poison-flowers and all the measureless ill.'

The Shadow

First published, with the title 'Echo' and without a space after l. 11, in *Contemporary Poetry and Prose* no. 7 (November 1936), 130. See headnote to 'The Fool'.

3 Clearly] No doubt *1936*

The Small Bird to the Big

First published in *Listener* (5 August 1936), 252. See headnote to 'The Fool'.
For *Listen* WE noted: ' "The Small Bird" is merely a re-phrasing of Miss Hatakeyama's own English translation of her Japanese poem.'

11 shall] will *1936*

Four Legs, Two Legs, Three Legs

First published, as 'Travel Note', *New Verse* no. 16 (August–September 1935), 9; this version did not include ll. 4–8; and l. 11 was positioned after l. 14.

CP: It struck me passing through Cairo that the Sphinx has a look of pathetic and devoted public spirit (like a good deal of Egyptian work) which makes the popular idea of her as a sinister mystery seem off the point. This made me think about Oedipus, who destroyed an ogre-like Sphinx by answering its riddle, and therefore had bad luck – at least they made him king out of gratitude for this feat, and that was how he came to marry his mother. He killed his father at a crossroad between the three towns of my first line; they seem meant to symbolize three ways of life, rather as the legs in the riddle do. A delta is a mathematical expression for the area of the triangle, here zero; he short-circuited life by keeping it all in the family. A metaphysician (somebody said) is like a blind man looking for a black cat in the dark which isn't there, and black cats are for luck. As Oedipus was wholly unconscious of his crimes it is uncertain whether he had an Oedipus complex, and he answered the riddle merely by saying Man, not by telling us anything about him. Napoleon's romantic paint can just be seen on her face; it is denied that her nose was broken by a deliberate cannon-shot of his. I have never seen anything in print about how dramatically she is placed between the desert and the sown; it seems that she always was, but at one time the river ran close under her paws.

For *Listen* WE wrote: ' "Four legs" mainly tries to convey the hint of some profound meaning often felt about the legend.'
On *Harvard*, he noted:

Of course the Egyptian sphinx has nothing to do with the mysterious demigod who put the question to Oedipus. But I don't know, why should you not say that this sphinx is still there? – and this sphinx was clearly not destroyed by Oedipus answering the riddle. It is a pure case of reflecting about the strangeness of life, and so much of metaphysical poetry is reflecting about the strangeness of life. I think this is slightly pointless, in a way, but I thought I could try it out.

WE first visited Egypt in Summer 1934 en route from Japan. It was between 1926 and 1938 that the Service des Antiquités, initially under the direction of Emile Baraize, undertook the first large-scale excavation of the Sphinx. Thus WE came to Giza at a good moment to see the monument – though there seem to have been no good guide-books available to him.
The following piece of his travel writing (previously unpublished), which was drafted soon after his visit, in addition to being of considerable intrinsic and historical interest, both expands upon the local background to the poem and affords a gloss on ll. 9–15:

I left the boat at Suez and crossed to Cairo by car, and was much moved by the great tins in which the tar for the road had been brought up. Filled with stones and painted white, three or four feet high, they are used to keep you on the road at night; perhaps it is because they are placed like the stones on the approach to Avebury [the site of massive sandstone boulders dating from about 2600 BC, in Wiltshire, England] that they are so impressive. But instead of rippling along the downs and keeping the holy goal out of sight they go slap to the horizon, with nothing else in view but occasional shrubs; it seemed at once Roman and primitive to get such a dramatic effect in such a sensible way. We passed near sand desert but did not cross any. Indeed I understand that about ten years ago the French produced cheap maps of the Sahara, and it was then found that the great caravan routes which for thousands of years had been crossing that intolerable sand, attended with terror, marked not with tins but with whitening bones, had always been entirely unnecessary; you could always have gone the thing in your Citroen car. Maybe it would have taken too long before the Citroen car had appeared, but the story is such a parable of the human race that it deserves to be believed. I was astonished to find that the bits of sand desert we would see were not yellow but white, either glittering or a salt and sinister pale grey, lighter than the North Sea; there was the same kind of shock in my first crevasse, which was a dirty fish-belly white, instead of the pale blues I had imagined, so that it looked alive like an octopus. We got a powerful mirage, a very beautiful thing from a car but not at all deceptive; the water is in movement, and you know at once it couldn't move like that; it is continually rippling or seeping into the next valley.

The Pyramids looked rather small after the fantastic stupas of Ceylon, but this made the shape more noticeable. It is easy to believe the theory that they mark some tremendous moral or mental failure of that Egypt which had invented half the arts of life, at fantastic speed with a splendid sense of freedom, and then stopped dead when the worship of death and the supreme authority got the upper hand. They are calculated to crush everything else down. We have heard this before, but nobody had told me where they put the Sphinx. It is right at the edge of the plateau, which behind it extends for thousands of miles of utter desert; at one time it had the Nile close in front, but it has always looked at cultivated land straight to the horizon. The pathetic eager patience of that great lifted head, like a dog hoping to be taken for a walk, has always waited on civilization as well as the sunrise. I am glad that I saw the Sphinx and some Pharaohs in the Cairo Museum when my head was full of Buddhas, because you only realize then how very Western they are, even how Christian. The weight on personal immortality makes it in some degree individualist, and the divine ruler is a hefty creature, labouring for his people, who keeps a touching sense that his powers are limited against heaven. He is never withdrawn into unity with the All, which so easily comes to mean into his own private world. Coming back from the pyramids and the Sphinx I fell into the greatest trap to which the traveller is exposed in the heartiest manner that I have yet achieved. I had no money, overcoat, tickets or passport, it had got dark and chilly, and I had entirely lost my hotel. This is fearfully easy to do; you feel quite safe and settled when you have got into the hotel, and you go out brightly to look at the town; it is an effort of the imagination to think of the difficulty of getting back. Most of the big hotels were shut, because the season was over. In the end I found an extremely kind hotel which telephoned to most of the inns in Cairo, and my place was about the twentieth. This was a sheer act of mercy, and also I had luckily been made to sign my name before I went out. Lacking those two accidents I suppose the only thing is to go to the police station and ask them to put you in the pound; you can hope for an inquiry from the hotel after a few days.

See Hedges, 'Empson Treatment'; *TGA*, pp. 169–72.

TITLE: **Four Legs, Two Legs, Three Legs**] Four legs, Three Legs, Two Legs *CP*. See note to ll. 16–18.

1 *Delphic and Theban and Corinthian*: Oedipus, in Sophocles' *Oedipus Rex*, is informed by the Delphic oracle that he will kill his own father; unaware that he is a Theban by birth, he regards himself as a Corinthian (because he had been taken into care there when abandoned as a hobbled child to die of exposure) and flees from Corinth towards Thebes – hastening to meet his destiny. WE later observed (*Harvard*): '**Oedipus killed his father, as he was fated to do, at a place where three roads met: one from Delphi – mysticism and prophecy and so on – one from Thebes, which was considered awfully rustic and countrified, the simple life, and one from Corinth, which was the glory of the world – where the Corinthian column came from . . . and so all human experience was, in a way, called in. Such is what the lead-in means.**'

2 *Three lines . . . met at a point*: while the initial meaning is geometrical – three lines intersecting (not enclosing a spatial area) – the phrase refers also to the idea of 'lines of descent' which Oedipus 'short-circuited' by slaughtering his father, marrying his mother and begetting offspring who were his siblings. Cf. 'Dissatisfaction with Metaphysics', l. 8, and 'Letter V', l. 22.

WE delighted in the connotations of the pun on 'line': see note to l. 22 of 'Letter V'. Furthermore, when reflecting upon Oedipus' fate, he would have recalled his thoughts on a couplet by Richard Crashaw – 'Hee'l have his teat e're long (a bloody one) / The Mother then must suck the Son' – '**The . . . couplet is "primitive" enough . . . The sacrificial idea is aligned with incest, the infantile pleasures, and cannibalism; we contemplate the god with a sort of savage chuckle; he is made to flower, a monstrous hermaphrodite deity, in the glare of a short-circuiting of the human order**' (*ST*, p. 257).

3 *delta*: the triangular tract of alluvial land at the mouth of the Nile (so named by Herodotus); it includes the site of the Great Sphinx of Giza, ll. 9–15, so the two sphinxes, Greek and Egyptian, are confused or conflated.

3 *zero*: signifies that the lines of descent (or the meeting-place of the roads from Delphi, Thebes and Corinth) of ll. 1–2 intersect in such a way that they describe not a triangular figure or geographical area but simply nought, nothingness, nullity: an end. Cf. 'The Scales', l. 14.

3 *trivial*: defined as 'commonplace, insignificant', and 'Of no consequence or interest, e.g. because equal to zero . . .', it appropriately derives from the Latin *trivium*: 'a place where three ways meet' (*OED*); see ll. 1–2.

4 *cross-road . . . shady*: Hedges comments (pp. 238–9): 'Christ enters the poem, at least negatively, by the "cross-road". Empson hyphenates here, whereas he spells it "crossroad" in the note . . . Oedipus in some ways parodies Christ or parries His implications. The Corinthian son seeking the Theban father is deceived by the spirit of the Delphic utterance that ought to have clarified the connection.' However, the hyphenation may have no special significance. (Cf. 'Rebuke for a dropped brick', l. 3: 'cross-roads'.)

Nevertheless, Hedges's main point may be taken from the combination of 'cross-road' and 'shady' – a word which may signify at once *darkly obscure* and *sinister* or *disreputable* as well as the shade trees provide, and links with 'in the dark' in line 5 – through a possible subliminal association on WE's part. The combination may have been generated by a memory of Joyce's coinage 'crosstree', as used by Stephen Dedalus in 'Proteus' when he notices a sailing ship with masts and arms that he perceives to resemble the Cross of Christ: 'He turned his face over a shoulder, rere regardant. Moving through the air high spars of a threemaster, her sails brailed up on the crosstrees, homing, upstream, silently moving, a silent ship' (*Ullysses*, p. 50). Likewise, in 'Scylla and Charybdis', Stephen's parody of the Apostles' Creed includes the phrase 'starved on crosstree' (p. 189).

5–6 *Killing a mistaken black cat . . . metaphysical trait*: it is not possible to locate the exact source of the aphorism; but Mencken has ascribed it to Baron Bowen of Colwood (1835–94) in the form: 'A metaphysician is a man who goes into a dark cellar at midnight without a light looking for a black cat that is not there' (*H. L. Mencken's Dictionary of Quotations* (1942), p. 782). Probably WE came across the saying in a chapter on 'Value as an Ultimate Idea', where Richards discusses what he calls the 'sensuous and supersensuous' kinds of metaphysical entity, and 'the subsistence of such a property' as 'goodness'; some people look on such concepts as a kind of 'abstractionism', he writes: 'A blind man in a dark room chasing a black cat which is not there would seem to them well employed in comparison with a philosopher apprehending such "Concepts" ' (*Principles of Literary Criticism*, p. 30).

7 *God walks in a mysterious way*: 'God moves in a mysterious way, / His wonders to perform, / . . . / God is his own Interpreter, / And he will make it plain' ('Light shining out of darkness' [*Olney Hymn 35*], *The Poems of William Cowper*, Vol. I: *1748–1782*, ed. John D. Baird and Charles Ryskamp (Oxford, 1980), p. 174).

8 *Neither delighteth he in any man's legs*: from Psalm 147: 10 – 'He delighteth not in the strength of the horse: he taketh not pleasure in the legs of a man' – though rephrased in the style of Robert Browning's 'Caliban upon Setebos'. Browning's Caliban, sour and cynical, postulates a God in accord with his own experience of the world: God does not make man in his own image, we make our gods in ours. WE's poem's parodic phrasing of the psalm works in dialogic contrast to the august idiom of the preceding line: it lampoons the pomposity of genuflections to the inscrutable mystery of divinity; line 7 is a patronizing clerical cliché, a piece of shushing evasion; line 8 takes the mickey out of mumbo-jumbo. Cf. too Hamlet's remark to Rosencrantz and Guildenstern: 'Man delights not me – no, nor woman neither' (*Hamlet*, II.ii.310–11).

9 *The wrecked girl . . . Napoleon's paint*: WE had the impression that the features of the Sphinx are meant to be female. (Cf. W. B. Yeats's 'The Double Vision of Michael Robartes', l. 18: 'A Sphinx with woman breast and lion paw'.) Herodotus had referred to it as the 'andro-sphinx'; and in modern times it has long been believed to represent the face of the 4th Dynasty king, Chephren (*Khafre* in Egyptian), who commissioned the huge monument, in the form of a seated lion with a human head dressed in a *nemes*-wig (with the distinctive flared lappets) – though notably without wings – to be carved in about 2500 BC from the outcrop of limestone at the base of the Giza plateau. (King Chephren's father, Cheops, had built the Great Pyramid.) In the travel writing quoted above, WE refers to this specific sphinx four times by the neuter pronoun 'it'; and in the sentences immediately following, he appears to speak at once of the Sphinx and of the pharaohs by the male gender (cf. his comment about '**a touching sense that his powers are limited**' with l. 15). Yet his own note to the poem makes it clear that he regarded the Great Sphinx as female.

This poem seeks to question all symbolic pretensions, religious or oracular, and WE (as he was to suggest on *Harvard*) deliberately conflates the Great Sphinx with the monster, the riddler-sphinx, the She-devil, whom Oedipus worsts. Thus WE can sardonically describe the Great Sphinx as a 'wrecked girl' (cf. 'Reflection from Anita Loos', l. 4) who perennially dogs the divine in unavailing hopes of a revelation (ll. 13–15). Yet more, he can also characterize her as 'raddled' (l. 9), and as a 'toy' (l. 13): a worn-out whore who might have succumbed to the ravages of venereal disease (l. 10). The primary meaning of 'raddled' here is 'painted with raddle; coarsely coloured with red or rouge' (cf. *OED* 'raddle' v^2). (WE knew also that English sheep are dabbed with raddle for purposes of identification; Thomas Hardy makes much of the mystery of the 'raddleman' in *The Return of the Native*.) But secondary implications are 'worn out' in both a literal and a figurative sense (*OED* 'raddled' *ppl. a.*^{2}) and 'woven or twisted together, inter-twined' ('raddle' v^1) – as WE raddles his riddles and his sphinxes.

WE relied too on the legend that Napoleon's occupying forces had painted the Sphinx red, e.g. in his reading at *Harvard*: '**You can dimly see the paint which Napoleon dressed it up in when he conquered Egypt as part of his campaigns. So you mustn't suppose it isn't true.**' But the evidence is that the paint predates the French invasion by thousands of years. Dr Mark Lehner, who has studied the construction of the Sphinx, reports: 'It is more likely than not that during its reconstruction in the 18th Dynasty the entire Sphinx was painted in bright colours . . . Traces of red paint still remain on the face, and red powder from ancient paint pours out of the seams of the masonry veneer' ('Reconstructing the Sphinx', *Cambridge Archaeological Journal* 2:1 [1992], p. 21). In fact, the scientists and engineers of the French expeditionary force who were marooned in Egypt for three years, 1798–1801, performed a major service to cultural history when they elected to describe the monuments.

10 *Nose eaten . . . conqueror*: there is no evidence for the tale that Napoleon's troops fired cannon at the Sphinx's nose; the phrase 'less clear conqueror', while admitting the doubt, works too to support the unpleasant figurative connotations of the epithets 'wrecked' and 'raddled' in the previous line.

11 Still] And *1935*

11 *orientated . . . average dawn*: the Sphinx looks east. WE made no mistake about the alignment of the monument – unlike W. H. Auden, who visited the Sphinx over three years after WE had padded round its plateau, and in January 1938 drafted an 80-line poem called 'The Sphinx' which described it as having 'A vast vacant accusing face / Peering out towards America, denying Progress'; when he trimmed his poem into a sonnet with the same title, Auden took care to reorientate the creature and depict it, though no less indecorously, as 'Turning / A vast behind on shrill America' (*The English Auden: Poems, Essays and Dramatic Writings, 1927–1939*, ed. Edward Mendelson (London, 1977), pp. 232, 425). In 'Escales' (1938) Auden and Christopher Isherwood wrote of their encounter with a Sphinx that is less (ambiguously) domesticated than in WE's poetic version: 'There it lies, in the utter stillness of its mortal injuries; the flat cruel face of a scarred and blinded baboon, face of a circus monstrosity, no longer a statue but a living, changing creature of stone . . . Once, no doubt, it was beautiful. Long ago, it could see. Now it lies there mutilated and sightless, its paws clumsily bandaged with bricks, its mane like an old actor's wig, asking no riddle, turning its back upon America – injured baboon with a lion's cruel mouth, in the middle of invaded Egypt' (in Isherwood, *Exhumations: Stories, Articles, Verses* (London, 1966), p. 145). WE's 'average dawn' is associated with 'the commonplace' (l. 18), for the poem constantly urges the value of ordinariness, this-worldliness.

12 *Behind, Sahara, before, Nile*: the Sphinx faces the Nile river valley, a narrow band of fertile cultivation; at its back, a carpet of sand unrolls for over 1,000 miles.

12–13 *Nile and man / A toy abandoned, sure*: although the syntax allows the construction that would require a comma after 'man', enabling the antecedent of the ablative clause 'A toy abandoned' to be the nominal group 'The wrecked girl' (l. 9), WE appears also to have intended the enjambment to invite the ambiguity whereby 'A toy abandoned' becomes a qualifier for 'man'; howsoever, 'sure' further qualifies the 'wrecked girl'. A toy is a diversion or plaything (perhaps educational): so was the sphinx to Chephren.

13–14 *after so many, / That the next sun . . . a walk*: the sense requires the meaning 'after so many suns have come and gone' or 'after so many suns have abandoned her, though her confidence is never dashed'. Some commentators have assimilated the face of the sphinx to that of the Sun-god Aton (cf. 'High Dive', l. 10 and note). However, Dr Lehner is more cautious, or cheerily indifferent: 'Whether the Great

Sphinx is more solar deity or pharaoh is a question which the Egyptians themselves who made it could probably not have answered' ('Reconstructing the Sphinx', p. 7). Nevertheless, as ll. 7–8 indicate, perhaps God is not like us at all; equally, the purpose of the Sphinx must remain a mystery.

15 *Still lifts . . . a sign*: see WE's travel piece quoted above. Sophocles sometimes calls the Theban sphinx a 'rhapsodic dog', as WE may have remembered; but it is more likely that WE is giving his personal impression of the Great Sphinx.

16–18 *Not one . . . the commonplace*: this sphinx was a savage ogre, a hybrid monster, with the face and bust of a woman, the body of a lion and the wings of a bird. Taking up her station on the 'Sphinx Mountain' (*Phikeion Oros*), she set out to tyrannize Thebes by challenging those who passed to solve a riddle: 'What being, with only one voice, has sometimes two feet, sometimes three, sometimes four, and is weakest when it has the most?' She devours everyone who fails to give the right answer. (An alternative version features in verses in Athenaeus X. 456b: 'A thing there is whose voice is one, / Whose feet are two & four & three. / So mutable a thing is now / That moves in earth or sky or sea. / When on most feet this thing doth go / Its strength is weakest and its pace most slow' (trans. J. T. Shepherd).) Oedipus offers the correct solution: 'Man, who in infancy crawls on all fours, who walks upright on two feet in maturity, and in his old age supports himself with a stick.' That response seals his fate. Thomas de Quincey suggested that the real answer to the sphinx's riddle is Oedipus himself. WE benignly mocks Oedipus' victory: Oedipus does not reflect on the meaning or implications of his answer: he is smart but not wise; impulsive, and no deep thinker; but yet Oedipus triumphs on behalf of 'the commonplace': common sense or ordinary human intelligence. The supernatural WE sees as beaten by the rational.

17 *Oedipus . . . a name*: the 'name' supplied by Oedipus was 'Man'.

19 *While too much . . . she fell and burst*: Diodorus Siculus IV.64 relates that when the sphinx was overcome by Oedipus' answer, she 'threw herself down a precipice' off Mount Phicium (*Diodorus of Sicily*, III, trans. C. H. Oldfather (London and Cambridge, Mass., 1939), p. 23), which is the consensus of other texts (see the convenient list of references prepared by Sir James Frazer in his edition of Apollodorus, *The Library* (London and New York, 1921), pp. 347–9). Yet why she should have committed suicide when the riddle was solved, remains a nice question. WE suggests that the sphinx over-reacted; but his primary emphasis is on the sickening literalness of her fall, her smash-up. Yet why does he stress her obliteration, with impacting verbal energy, when the nature of her fate seems otherwise so immaterial? He may be recollecting a tradition, descending from Asclepiades, which positions the sphinx on a pillar in the heart of the city, as a monstrous presiding icon (see Ingres' painting *Oedipus and the Sphinx*, in the National Gallery, London). Especially if she is figured as some sort of vessel, an amphora or a pelike (e.g. a famous red-figure vase of *c.* 470 BC, in the Vatican Museum, showing Oedipus and the Sphinx), she might be deemed to smash or 'burst' when toppled from her height. Tennyson, in 'Tiresias' (1885), describes 'that smooth rock / . . . altar-fashioned, where of late / The woman-breasted Sphinx, with wings drawn back, / . . . dashed herself / Dead in her rage' (141–48). However, what is most likely of all is that WE simultaneously but perhaps unconsciously recollected the very strange and scarcely explained fate of Judas Iscariot as Peter reports it: 'Now this man purchased a field with the reward of iniquity; and falling headlong, he burst asunder in the midst, and all his bowels gushed out' (Acts 1: 18). (According to Matt. 27: 5, Judas committed suicide by hanging himself, so exegetes invariably seek to reconcile those two accounts by suggesting that the rope must have broken over a cliff.)

19 to pretend] when he claims *1935*

20 *It is a comfort . . . an answer*: the dialogized heteroglossia of the poem culminates in the voice of the unflappable maiden aunt, suggesting that humanism prevails over supranaturalism; human wit wins over the signs and symbols of transcendence: forms of the absolute, terrible godheads. Indeed – given the earlier ironic reference to the Sphinx as 'eager for a sign' – God, as some theorists might say, is here the absent signified: the hidden villain.

Reflection from Rochester

First published in *Poetry* 49:2 (November 1936), 68–9; reprinted in *The Year's Poetry 1936*, ed. Denys Kilham Roberts and John Lehmann (London, 1936). A typescript that WE sent to Sylvia Townsend Warner (Reading) makes it clear that the prefatory quotation is meant to be an epigraph.

CP: The idea is that nationalist war is getting to a crisis because the machines make it too dangerous and expensive to be serviceable even in the queer marginal ways it used to be. However, actually, if you think of Jenghis, Tamburlane, and William harrowing the north of England, it is not clear that the new methods of destruction have yet proved themselves so much more effective than the old ones. The mind uses unconscious processes (mining underground) and an outpouring of loose words, sometimes poisonous (gas); the reasons that make the thought of a country succeed can be as queer as the reasons that sometimes make war good for it, and a mere change of proportion might make either fail to work any longer.

WE thought of this poem and the next one, 'Courage means Running', as essentially related, exploring the same theme from different angles. In 1953, in an untitled review of *Poems by John Wilmot, Earl of Rochester* (ed. V. de S. Pinto), he was to remark of 'The Satire on Man': **'The most powerful section is an argument as with hammer-blows that all human actions proceed from fear'** (*A*, p. 277). WE ruminates upon the traditional, even commonplace, contrast (deriving from Plutarch, Juvenal, Erasmus, Hobbes) between ruthless humankind and wild animals that forms the burden of Rochester's *A Satyr against Mankind* (1679). Taking his inspiration in a general way from Boileau's Satire VIII (which was itself based on Juvenal's Fifteenth Satire), Rochester argues that while animals kill only in order to eat – instinctively – Man's savagery is a function of treachery and caprice: our aggression is the product of vain self-interest or hypocritical self-protection. The lines that fire Empson's verses are the fulcrum of the poem (139–42):

> For hunger or for love they bite and tear,
> Whilst wretched man is still in arms for fear.
> For fear he arms and is of arms afraid,
> From fear to fear successively betrayed . . .
> (*The Complete Works*, ed. Frank H. Ellis (Harmondsworth, 1994), p. 75)

It is not known which edition of the poem WE made use of: H. J. C. Grierson and G. Bullough included it in *The Oxford Book of Seventeenth Century Verse* (Oxford, 1934), p. 940; and Vivian de Sola Pinto quoted the relevant verses in *Rochester: Portrait of a Restoration Poet* (London, 1935), p. 180 – except that both of those printings give the variant 'bite or tear' in l. 139, whereas Empson has the standard 'bite and tear' in line 25.

WE reflects upon the problem of war from a variety of perspectives: personal ambition, the arts of social coordination and political distraction, and sex and the paradoxes of sexual sublimation. For WE's reflections on varieties of sexual gratification, and on 'the good in action', see his essay 'The Ideal of the Good' (*c.* 1933) beginning: 'The theories to the effect that mankind is essentially a fighting creature, built up during the revolt against Christianity, have clearly done great harm during the last fifty years' (*A*, pp. 557–62; see also note to ll. 24–5 below).

For *Listen*, he noted: 'Rochester in the lines quoted from him was satirizing the duty of fighting duels; my poem uses them for the approach of the Second World War.'

Similarly, on *Contemporary Poets Reading Their Own Poems*: 'Rochester said that animals fight for good reasons, but men fight for absurd reasons . . . The poem is a reflection on how easily people approach these two world wars.'

On *Harvard*, WE remarked: 'I would like to do one of the direct war poems, "Reflection from Rochester". [Rochester] wrote a "Satire on Man", and was complaining about duelling: a grand man had to carry a sword and be willing to fight duels if he was offended or affronted, which no longer applies to individuals – but it does apply to the nation state. So what he said about the animals, who fight for quite sensible reasons . . . It expands this [Rochester's remarks] into modern terms.'

See Willis, pp. 319–26; *TGA*, pp. 172–6.

EPIGRAPH: slightly misquoted from Rochester: see headnote.

1 *'From fear ... betrayed'*: this opening quotation (see headnote) allows WE the opportunity to suggest a relentless – evolutionary? – progression from one manifestation of fear to the next; the syntax is naturally picked up in l. 8.

11 *Thought*: the syntax here is difficult, but WE almost certainly meant 'Thought' (past tense) and not 'Though' – though both Anne Ridler (*A Little Book of Modern Verse*, London, 1941) and Kenneth Allott (*The Penguin Book of Contemporary Verse*, Harmondsworth, 1950) have 'Though'.

14 *'attempted suicides'*: ' "Attempted suicides" is in quotes because it's remarkable how easy it is to kill the human body . . . It looks as though you are in two minds' (*Contemporary Poets Reading Their Own Poems*).

16 *'Virility from war'*: the quotation marks here look like those in l. 14, having the effect of 'so-called'; that is, they dissociate the speaker from the attitude or description implied without attributing it to anyone in particular, still less claiming an exact quotation. The idea that war is a manly activity and improves the virility of a race is traditional, but perhaps the 'Policies' to which WE refers as being based on this idea are Fascist and Nazi ones, influenced by Nietzsche and his successors. The middle of the poem says that with increased numbers and more powerful technology we cannot afford this traditional idea of war.

Derek Roper reports that WE privately commented, at the University of Sheffield, on John Wain's poem called 'When it Comes', and he agreed with Roper that the following lines were a poor description of nuclear holocaust

> when the knife
> Plunges at last into the world's sick heart
> And stills its pounding and its seething strife

– giving the reason that knives and daggers belonged to a time when we could still afford the luxury of war (letter to Haffenden, 18 February 1997).

17–20 *The mind ... irrelevant despair*: TGA (pp. 175–6) offers this gloss: 'As war spreads poison gas above ground and digs tunnels beneath it, so the mind operates both consciously ... and unconsciously ... It was once possible (as indicated in lines 2–3) for man consciously to channel his fears into self-selected risks (the first of these being the "root-confusion" from which the others grew), and build up as a result an increasing sense of "safety" from overcoming the despair created by those risks, an "irrelevant" despair because it was not the hereditary existential despair which drove him to his strange shifts in the first place.'

19 root-confusion] root confusion *Year's Poetry 1936*

22 *We now turn blank eyes*: possibly echoes Yeats's baleful intimation in 'The Second Coming' (1920) that some new 'revelation is at hand', grossly embodied

in a 'rough beast' – 'a vast image out of *Spiritus Mundi*' – with 'A gaze blank and pitiless as the sun' (l. 15). Cf. 'Ignorance of Death', l. 19, and 'Let it go', l. 1.
24-5 *involute compulsion played.* / *'For hunger or for love they bite and tear'*: 'involute' means 'entangled, intricate'. These lines look back to a less complicated world, a putatively more innocent age, when biting had two clear (and yet not unrelated) primitive purposes: for tearing up food in the big game of survival and for affectionate play – as the sign of love. For WE's quotation, see headnote. Cf. WE's reflections in 'The Ideal of the Good':

a great deal of cruelty is due to self-righteousness; a noble mind never wishes to make claims that its actions are truly generous, but is concerned to see all the possible sources of satisfaction in a given situation; and we under-rate our neighbours if we do not admit the painful complexity of their position . . .

A more scientific theory was provided by the Marquis de Sade, whose disciple Swinburne gives evidence about the effects of the theory when put into action as literature. This theory treats the lust to inflict pain on others as fundamental, as the idea in terms of which a complex affair should be analysed and understood. Swinburne cannot set out to describe passion felt between ordinary lovers (historical personages for instance) without dragging in the tortures that they inflicted on each other:

By the lips intertwisted and bitten
   Till the foam has a savour of blood ['Dolores', ll. 115–16]

is the centre of his invocation of the Queen of Passion. Of course it is not the perversion as such which one cocks one's eye at. If they both like it (and many couples do like a reasonable amount of biting) they are only giving each other a nice time. The question is rather what they think radically nice; whatever the means, what is the end[?] . . .

How do Swinburne's biters get to sleep? No doubt if they both enjoyed it they can go to sleep not only satisfied but proud; feeling, 'My word, I've given this girl a good time – she's almost bitten to rags' and so forth. The fundamental pleasure to which they sink back, in such an arrangement, is a feeling of pride in their own generosity, however grotesque the path by which it was achieved. Much fuss has been made about the idea that the primitive instincts of sex are fundamentally brutal; Aldous Huxley for instance in *After Many a Summer* made the undying earl become a sadist as a logical part of his return to the ape. But it is usual among the mammals for the male to woo the female; on this argument it is a deeply rooted element in human sex that the man is vain about his power to please, and the desire to please is not a brutal thing. Pure sadism, in the sense of only wanting the partner to suffer, is not an outbreak of the primitive but a very specialized form of disease. It should not therefore, it seems to me, be regarded as a fundamental thing in terms of which you interpret a more complex situation (as selfishness, for example, can be used) . . . (*A*, pp. 558, 561)

Courage means Running

First published in *Contemporary Poetry and Prose* no. 1 (May 1936), 6; reprinted in *The Year's Poetry 1936*, ed. Roberts and Lehmann. While linked, both formally and thematically, to the previous poem, this predates 'Reflection from Rochester' by some six months.

CP: **Fearful and Muchafraid of course are characters in Bunyan.** *Bard* **and** *hack* **I suppose come in a bit oddly, but the point is to join up the crisis-feeling to what can be felt all the time in normal life.**

Draft versions of some lines are pencilled on the back flyleaf of a copy of *The Progress of Poetry: An Anthology of Verse from Hardy to the Present Day*, ed. I. M. Parsons (London: Chatto & Windus, 1936), which WE left in China in 1939. His scarcely legible jottings, which must have been set down in the early part of 1936, include the following passages (the square brackets indicate an illegible passage):

> Not certain now, not certain yet
> A lot of other ones will get
>   This echo of a muddle now
> [. . .]
>   Yet most such moments
> (Folly to say all) when you escape emotion and reach clarity
> Escape by the rival emotion fear.
> It is a saner truth to say you learn by courage
> Which presumes fear; or pleasure, so does pleasure
> The woof of death lust in our Egyptian splendour
> A shot cloth, green and gold, Field of the Cloth
> of Gold, and no such shooting
> Muchafraid went over the river singing

(I am indebted to the late Professor Yang Zhouhan for giving me this treasured volume.)

On *The Poems of William Empson*, WE explained:

G. K. Chesterton had challenged anyone to deduce this meaning [i.e. that courage can sometimes necessitate running away] from the history of the word courage, so I did, but that isn't really part of the poem. The poem is so patriotic that I remember the editor of an advanced magazine who accepted it around 1936 expressing embarrassment; but I still think it sounds reasonable, though you could take it as a beforehand defence of the Munich

Agreement. Fearful and Muchafraid, when they come in the poem, are of course characters in Bunyan. The rhyme scheme is the Dante terza rima, but the rhythms are meant to go very casually.

For *Listen* he wrote: ' "Courage" is dull now but a magazine editor almost refused it in 1937 [1936] because to say anything for British policy was so shameful.' (According to *TGA*, p. 177, the editor in question was Roger Roughton, 'whose interest at the time was surrealism rather than politics'.)

'As for myself,' WE was to recall a good deal later, 'when I was a little boy I was very afraid I might not have the courage which I knew life to demand of me' (*Milton's God*, p. 89).

See Willis, pp. 326–35; *TGA*, pp. 176–81.

TITLE: it is not clear that Chesterton ever directly dismissed the possibility of deducing the paradoxical sense that 'courage means running' from the history of the meanings of *courage*; but WE may be recalling Chesterton's reflections on the paradox of courage in 'The Paradoxes of Christianity':

Paganism declared that virtue was in a balance; Christianity declared it was in a conflict: the collision of two passions apparently opposite. Of course they were not really inconsistent; but they were such that it was hard to hold simultaneously. Let us . . . takes the case of courage . . . Courage is almost a contradiction in terms. It means a strong desire to live taking the form of a readiness to die. 'He that will lose his life, the same shall save it', is not a piece of mysticism for saints and heroes . . . This paradox is the whole principle of courage; even of quite earthly or quite brutal courage . . . A soldier surrounded by enemies, if he is to cut his way out, needs to combine a strong desire for living with a strange carelessness about dying . . . He must seek his life in a spirit of furious indifference to it; he must desire life like water and yet drink death like wine. No philosopher, I fancy, has ever expressed this romantic riddle with adequate lucidity, and I certainly have not done so. But Christianity has done more: it has marked the limits of it in the awful graves of the suicide and the hero . . . And it has held up ever since above the European lances the banner of the mystery of chivalry: the Christian courage, which is a disdain of death; not the Chinese courage, which is a disdain of life. (*Orthodoxy* (London, 1909), pp. 168–9)

1 *Fearful 'had the root of the matter'*: WE got the name wrong: it is the 'Chickin-hearted' Mr *Fearing* who has 'the Root of the Matter in him' (John Bunyan, *The Pilgrim's Progress*, ed. James Blanton Wharey (1928); 2nd edn. by Roger Sharrock (Oxford, 1960, 1967), p. 249).

WE would later write about *The Pilgrim's Progress* in a congested paragraph of 'Honest Man' (first published in *Southern Review*, 1940). This sentence, on the subject of 'Honest', shows how WE links courage both to Bunyan and to Rochester (see 'Reflection from Rochester'):

He is old, brave and rugged, is called 'a Cock of the right kind', at first too modest to tell his name, at last says 'not Honesty in the abstract, but Honest is my name' (perhaps 'not the root idea but the mixed virtues that are so called'), comes from the town of Stupidity, which lies four degrees beyond the City of Destruction, for stupefied ones are worse than those merely carnal (we have seen the accuracy of this; it was Rochester who lived in the City of Destruction), though brave had much to do with Fearing, a man, he says, that had the root of the matter in him (Rochester never learned this about his friends), and has been acquainted with Self-Will. (*SCW*, pp. 194–5)

2 *he read well that ran*: in *The Pilgrim's Progress*, but it is not Mr Fearing who does it. In the First Part, Christian is discovered 'reading in his book', which tells him that he is 'condemned to die, and after that to come to judgement'; whereupon 'a man named Evangelist' directs him 'to fly from the wrath to come' towards the Celestial City – and so Christian immediately 'began to run' towards the light (*The Pilgrim's Progress*, pp. 9–10). As Willis (p. 329) noted, it would appear to be Empson who recognizes Bunyan's subtle allusion (which is not noted by Bunyan's editors), and who thus assimilates Christian's reading and running to Habakkuk 2:2: 'And the Lord answered me, and said, Write the vision, and make it plain upon tables, that he may run that readeth it.'

3–4 *Muchafraid . . . sang*: when the day comes for them to venture through the river to their 'Deliverance', Bunyan notes: 'The last Words of Mr *Dispondencie*, were, *Farewell Night, welcome Day*. His Daughter [*Much-afraid*] went thorow the River singing, but none could understand what she said' (*The Pilgrim's Progress*, p. 308).

4 *for a*] *for Year's Poetry 1936* (probably a typo)

7 *Get clap (the other is the eye)*: referring to certain symptoms of gonorrhoea – which is passed from infected mother to baby born blind. Cf. 'Villanelle', ll. 7–8.

10 *ballast*: given 'Steadily' (l. 7), *TGA* detects a recollection of Donne's 'Air and Angels', ll. 15–16: 'Whilst thus to ballast love, I thought, / And so more steadily to have gone'.

18 knits] knots 1936, Year's Poetry 1936; 'knots' may possibly have been a typo, though Willis makes this point: 'By changing "knots" to "knits" for the *Collected Poems*, Empson emphasizes the closer interweaving of pleasure with pain' (p. 331 note 1).

22 *urgent creed*: Richards remarks, in a footnote that presumably drew on conversation with WE: ' "The urgent creed" may be a puzzling phrase; a proof-reader queried it as a misprint for "urgent need". But if we think of the councils which drew creeds up, and what creeds are and do, and how urgently neces-sary it is for them ⌐to balance enough possibles⌐, and how thenceforward they work as such balances . . . reasons enough for the word will appear' (*How to Read a Page*, p. 79). (See note to ll. 23–4 for explanation of Richards's superscript system.)

23 *To balance enough possibles*: while 'possible' may certainly be used as a noun, it is just possible that WE was exploiting a private joke at the expense of Richards, who had recently written an equivocal review of *Poems* (1935), urging WE to eschew his poetical riddling in favour of deeper feeling: 'I hope he will reduce the compression, be content to score much less than a possible of puns, even when the feat is most tempting, and try a subject with more resistance to manipulation' ('Empson's "Poems" ', p. 253).

23 **possibles] possibilities** *Poems of William Empson*

23–4 *bard / And hack must blur or peg*: a *hack* is a jobbing journalist, unlike the poet; though working to supposedly opposite standards – the one creative, the other factual – both must occasionally turn out fudging approximations (*blur*), or be strait and categorical (*peg*) – though *peg* can also refer to the artificial stabilizing of a commodity price.

Richards, who sets out to expound stanza eight in *How to Read a Page*, ventures this explication:

The writer, whatever his rank, has two main devices by which to make you 'balance enough possibles' and thus support his meaning in your understanding. He may ʳblurʳ – ˢʷmake vague, general and unclearˢʷ – or he may ʳpegʳ – ˢʷfix, arbitrarily prevent from its natural movementsˢʷ. Both words have an unpleasing aura: ʷblurʷ suggests smudges and the effects of rain drops, or tears, on handwriting; ʷpegʷ suggests exchange control and the prevention of inflation, a step reluctantly taken to avoid worse loss of value. The bard we imagine regrets these necessary steps more than the hack. Which needs them most is another question. But ʷblurʷ at least reminds us that clarity can mislead: the precise, specific, concrete image offers us a thousand things to take up which are not to the author's purpose. The blurred or generalized meaning avoids that danger . . . ʷPegʷ, on the other hand, reminds us that our easiest way to control a meaning is to pin it (even if somewhat cruelly) to some other meaning that is in recognized currency (even though the two would not otherwise behave alike).

We 'blur' when – to avoid irrelevancies – we use a wider word that fits our thought. We 'peg' when we adopt a routine word in current use in place of the word which would better let our thought be itself. Pegging often blurs and blurring often pegs. But there is no point in technicalizing further these metaphoric descriptions. (pp. 80–81)

(Richards offers this 'Key' to his code-letters (pp. 68–9): 'ʳ . . . ʳ indicates that some special use of the word or phrase is being *referred to*'; 'ˢʷ . . . ˢʷ indicates that we are comparing what is *said with* the words and something *said with* other words. The marks are short for *said with*.')

24 **or] and** *Listen*

26–7 *economists raise / Bafflement to a boast we all take as guard*: almost certainly a reference to John Maynard Keynes's *The General Theory of Employment, Interest and Money* (New York, 1936), which appeared just two months before this poem. In his preface – as Willis (p. 333 note 2) points out – Keynes concedes that his work is essentially addressed to specialists, using 'a highly abstract argument' and 'much controversy', though he hopes it may be intelligible to non-economists. Compare this later incidental observation by WE on the political poetry of Auden and Spender: '**in England there was an obscure safety and bafflement in moving from the poem to consider what the country could possibly do**' ('A London Letter'). See also headnote to 'Just a Smack at Auden' below.

28 the wise patience of England] England's wise patience *1936*
28 wise] flat *Poems of William Empson, 1956*

In the first impression of *CP*, where the phrase appeared as 'the wise patience of England', WE noted in his *Corrigenda*: '**Thinking it over, I feel that the word *wise* in "The wise patience of England' merely spoils an otherwise decent poem; it seems bad taste now. I wrote this in 1937 [1936], and I remember how shocked the editor of the literary magazine was; he could only just bear to publish the thing. It was pretty near backing Munich; but still it was bold in a way, or it at least had a point. Now people have forgotten about that, so for *wise* please read "flat".**' The phrase was accordingly amended in *CP 1956*. However, since the poem was written by the early part of 1936 – two years before the Munich agreement (Prime Minister Neville Chamberlain's vain attempt to appease Hitler) – WE's afterthoughts, twenty years later, are anachronistic and unnecessarily self-exculpating. (WE never supported a policy of appeasing Germany, and no one would seriously have thought to accuse him of doing so: the thrust of a BBC talk, broadcast on 3 September 1936, on 'The Traps of Idealism' – quoted in part in the notes to 'Ignorance of Death', ll. 3–4, below – is against pacifism.) Willis observes, 'Reducing the wisdom to flatness in the later versions of the poem calls the patient policies of England into doubt . . . "Our final hope Is flat despair," says Empson in "Rolling the Lawn" [ll. 1–2], making flatness a doubtful quality' (pp. 327, 334). (Compare 'Success', l. 5.) Accordingly, there seems to be a good case for reinstating WE's first, bolder epithet in place of the retrospective, critical emendation.

29 '*high*' *policy*: cf. 'Sleeping out in a College Cloister', l. 29 and note.

Ignorance of Death

First published in *GS*, though probably drafted in 1936.

On *The Poems of William Empson*, WE commented: '**The next poem in the book is called "Ignorance of Death" and is printed in the same three-line verse form** [as the two preceding poems, "Reflection from Rochester" and "Courage means Running"] **but uses neither rhyme nor metre; it seems a good thing to have a break in these formalities, both in print and in broadcasting, so that one can feel they are only being used when needed.**'

For *Listen* he noted: ' "Ignorance" is printed as if in *terza rima* like the previous two but throws away form to feel like rock bottom.'

In his commentary for *Contemporary Poets Reading Their Own Poems*, WE said that this poem 'chucks away rhyme and metre . . . it's not meant to feel poetical. To write real *vers libre* is very much harder [than here in this poem].'

See Morelli, pp. 117–20; Willis, pp. 335–40; *TGA*, pp. 181–4; Jerome, *Poetry: Premeditated Art*, pp. 51–3.

3–4 *Buddhists and Christians . . . different ideals*: in 'Death and Its Desires' (1933), an essay published posthumously, WE remarked that the '**main effect**' of Buddhist doctrine, '**however profound it may be, is to remove** *all* **doctrinal props about immortality and still claim that death is somehow of the highest value. This rationalizing escape from the fear of death is carried so far that there is much less sense of tragedy and of the fascination of a sacrificial death than in Christianity with its certainly immortal individuals**' (*A*, p. 536).

In 'The Traps of Idealism', a talk broadcast by the BBC on 3 September 1936 (probably written at much the same time as the poem), WE included these pertinent observations:

G. K. Chesterton somewhere made an epigram to the effect that idealism means the ideals you do not live up to, and certainly this brings out the main point; that the traps of idealism are in the gulf between what you do and what you believe. But the trouble is rather that idealists do act on their ideals, choosing special cases and thinking at the wrong level, and then unfriendly people begin to discuss their real motives. That is how England got her reputation for hypocrisy. There is at least one case, I think, of a genuine ideal, which many people are the better for, and yet which you positively ought not to live up to: I mean the ideal of death. That is, the whole set of feelings that in the end death is the best. This is not what is ordinarily called idealism, and it is different in different cases. I shall try to make clear what I mean. As a rule people called idealists want to improve the conditions of life in the world, but the ideal of death is apt to be mystical and individualist. But it needs to come into this talk; it is the trump suit in most of literature and most of religion [cf. l. 14], and it raises the whole question I am talking about particularly sharply. The essential thing in understanding a tragedy, for instance, or in feeling rightly about it, is to realize just what levels of thought are in play. For instance, the ideal may be directly religious, a desire to leave the struggle of the world and enter the peace of heaven. It may seem wrong to call this an ideal of death, because Christianity has always tried to make heaven seem like real life; but the Christian ideal is very close to that of Buddhism, the other great religion of mankind, and Buddhism has always gone in for putting the final heaven further off from the ordinary worshipper (who will have rebirths in the world before he gets to it) and then insisting that this heaven is a kind of death. But in literature the use of this ideal is commonly not direct; the idea of death is continually used, instead, as a kind of frame or test for any conception of happiness. In effect the man says, 'I want to think about death here, because to do that makes me feel sure that I want what I am trying to get. It is worth trying for.' This is clearly very different, and there are a lot of things in between. Mr T. S. Eliot remarked the other day, answering someone who had said that the great thing was to have faith in life, that the only real thing was to have faith in death. I am not at all clear what he had most in mind there, but it is clearly a resounding saying in its way. And yet anyone who has had to deal with somebody threatening suicide must have felt the nuisance of all this background of splendour; you do not know how to stop the ideal from coming in too quick.

I came up against this difficulty of interpreting the idea of death in books when I first went to Japan as a teacher [in 1931], and thought that the poems of A. E. Housman would be a good thing for detailed reading. The sentiments were universal, the English easy, the edition cheap. Before the end of term several of the class were drafted to Shanghai, where there was a row at the time; one of them was killed, but I am thankful to say that he left early in the term, so that I cannot have pumped much of this poison into him, otherwise I might feel partly responsible for his death. Two or three students sent me in official essays later on, just before leaving for Shanghai, and as writing it was very good. 'I think Housman is quite right', one of them said – I am quoting from memory, but I know he said clearly what he meant – 'I will do no good to anyone by dying for my country, but I will be admired, and we all want to be admired, and anyway we are better dead.' I was very much shocked by this, and I thought that Housman himself would feel ashamed if he read the papers. It really is what Housman says, if you read him as a source of direct advice; a thing it had never occurred to me to do. What he meant, of course, is that this would be a fine thing for a man to feel under special circumstances; the man has gone to war thinking he had a good cause, and he dies disillusioned about the cause, but he still feels that his life was a fine one. For a man to *start* on a war in this spirit, not from patriotism but from the flat ideal of death, seemed to me painful and actually rather slavish. Even if you were to grant that at bottom death is the best, this was not the right way to bring in the ideal. Of course these cultivated young Japanese were drawing on Buddhism more than on Housman, and just what levels of thought are at work under the crucial desire for death in Buddhism is the last thing you would learn about that great religion. But I thought that this story ought to go in to any account of the traps of idealism.

5 Communists] communists CP *1949*
6–7 *people . . . rape them*: necrophiliacs. In 'Death and Its Desires' (1933), WE remarked upon

the obscure perversion of lusting after corpses, about which I know very little. Common sense agrees with Freud in connecting it with a regressive pleasure in dirt, and it may clearly be both sadistic and masochistic: corpses may be what you want to make of people who cannot stop you from ill-treating them; also you may want to hurt yourself by the unpleasantness of the pleasure or view yourself as similar to the corpses . . . The desire to return to the womb, conceived as a place of permanence and peace, is I believe much better in itself than the desire to rape corpses, and it is irritating to feel that when one is being humble before the first, in the poet Dante for example, one may if the truth were known only be being cheated by the second. It is reasonable to want to know which is which, and I think genuinely hard to find out. But it would be no use going on to say that all works of art based on corpse lusts are bad. (*A*, pp. 539–40)

8–9 *The Freudians . . . / Though 'the clamour of life' proceeds from its rival 'Eros'*: Freud formulated his dualistic classification in *Beyond the Pleasure Principle* (1920), positing a fundamental and endless conflict between 'Eros' (the libidinal, sexual or life instincts) and the death instincts, and again in chapter IV, 'The Two Classes of Instincts', of *The Ego and the Id* (1923), where he concludes – using the phrase quoted – 'we are driven to conclude that the death-instincts are by their nature mute and that the clamour of life proceeds for the most part from Eros' (trans. Joan Rivière (London, 1927), p. 66). See also the Editor's Note to 'Instincts and their Vicissitudes', in *Standard Edition*, vol. 14 (London, 1961), pp. 113–16. Cf. 'The Teasers', l. 3.

15 conceived] achieved *Listen*

16 *Heaven me, when a man is ready to die about*: On 5 March 1963 WE wrote to D. J. Enright (who had queried the eccentric idiom of the exclamation):

I can't say much more than that it isn't a misprint ('Heaven me, when a man is willing to die about . . .'). Of course these tricks of speech are rapidly variable, and might perhaps be objected to as 'private poetry', a thing I have often been accused of, but wrongly I thought. 'Heaven me' is meant to sound aunt-like, placid and in a way experienced; I am admitting to feeling respect for heroic behaviour, but do not want to present myself as heroic. 'Of course I don't deny that, but this is no occasion to get excited about it.' It still seems to me the right interjection for the occasion.

    I wonder if the difference is that your generation is determined to appear manly and sincere, with no hanky-panky, whereas mine thought it showed civilized awareness to make mild unfunny imitations of old ladies, pansies, Cockneys and so forth when expressing a view which the group imitated would especially sympathize with. Come to think of it, all you fiercely upright young men would die of shame rather than do that. (Courtesy of D. J. Enright)

Enright admired the poem and later included it in *The Oxford Book of Death* (1987).

Missing Dates

First published, as 'Villanelle', in *Criterion* 16:65 (July 1937), 618; written by 4 February 1937 – when WE wrote to John Hayward: **'I thought you seemed irritated lately by my drunken triviality, so wanted to do you a carbon of this thing while I did a clean copy. The name of the thing had better be Villanelle but it is called Missing Dates'*** (courtesy of Theodore Hofmann). In October 1939 Hayward, in London, was to write to Frank Morley (who was then working for the publishers Harcourt, Brace & Company in New York):

Ever since he sent me an extremely good poem by way of apology for being very drunk and uproarious and destructive in B. gardens [Bina Gardens, Kensington, London], I've pressed his claims on Tom [T. S. Eliot]. Now T. P. ['The Possum', Eliot's self-assumed nickname] writes to say that 'Richards has shown me a couple of unpublished poems of Bill's which impressed me; damned if I don't think Bill has more brain power, as well as more resistance to the ills that flesh is heir to (Shakespeare, as quoted by Mr. Sollory) than the rest of 'em poets'. He adds as a postscript: 'If Empson's poems have not been published in America, Harcourt B ought to get a lien on them, both published and unpublished. The new ones [they cannot be identified] are almost as good as the one about the poison in the bloodstream ["Missing Dates"]'. (Hayward Collection, King's College, Cambridge: JDH/FVM/15)

A typescript of the poem, headed 'Villanelle', was sent to John Hayward on 4 February 1937 (now owned by Theodore Hofmann).

CP: **It is true about the old dog, at least I saw it reported somewhere, but the legend that a fifth or some such part of the soil of China is given up to ancestral tombs is (by the way) not true.**

WE offered elucidatory comments on this poem on eight other occasions, as follows:

    (i) Friar and Brinnin, in *Modern Poetry*, pp. 498–9, print an expanded

---

*WE is echoing the White Knight's exchange with Alice in ch. 8 ('It's my own Invention') of *Through the Looking Glass, and What Alice Found There*:

'. . . The name of the song is called "*Haddocks' Eyes*".'
    'Oh, that's the name of the song, is it?' Alice said, trying to feel interested.
    'No, you don't understand,' the Knight said, looking a little vexed. 'That's what the name is *called*. The name really *is* "*The Aged Man*".'
    'Then I ought to have said, "That's what the *song* is called"?' Alice corrected herself.
    'No, you oughtn't: that's another thing. The *song* is called "*Ways and Means*": but that's only what it's *called*, you know!'

version of the *CP* note, which continues: 'Otherwise the poem, I think, consists of true statements, but I suppose what they add up to is a mood rather than an assertion, anyway not something you can feel all the time. The last verse is supposed to return with an effect of less pomp to the comparatively trivial, if not absurd, personal muddles which excited the general reflections. The point of the poem goes on, and ideally one should be able to emphasize a different word at each repetition. I think I got near that point in this use of the form.'

(ii) On *The Poems of William Empson*:

The next poem is in the very rigid form of a villanelle and called 'Missing Dates'. The only difficulty here is in reading it properly; the repeated lines ought to mean something different each time. The poem is meant to become increasingly serious until it generalizes itself in the last verse, so that the actual missing of dates seems almost comically trivial. I did read in some scientific periodical about changing an old dog's blood, and by the way I think poets ought to read science more than they do, and as older poets normally did. It is not true that ancestral tombs in China occupy a dangerous and increasing amount of farmland, but the legend is so familiar that I used it here.

(iii) WE's remarks, in conversation, are indirectly reported by Skelton: 'William Empson did not consciously decide upon writing a Villanelle when he began his poem, "Missing Dates". He was intent upon patterning a certain mood or attitude of mind. He wrote several lines before he realized that the poem was taking the form of a Villanelle, and then he deliberately allowed this tendency to develop, and within three hours, produced the completed version' (*Poetic Pattern*, pp. 52–3).

(iv) 'My poetry was written a long time ago, and looking back I realize it was meant to say "Life is strange and unexpected" but not to give any other awful warning. So I need to explain that this poem tells a lie. It says that we only get old because we are so untidy whereas of course the very tidiest people in their city offices get old too. How it can be a good poem if it is all wrong I cannot say. It is a villanelle' (undated notes for the launch of an anthology).

(v) *Contemporary Poets Reading Their Own Poems*: 'The difficulty of writing a villanelle is to stop it from dying as it goes on. It's very hard to read properly to justify the form. I was put on to it by Joyce's *A Portrait of the Artist* . . . I always thought "missing dates" was American slang; but it's not American slang, it means failing to come to an appointment.'

(vi) On *Harvard*, WE observed:

A villanelle called 'Missing Dates' is more widely accepted than anything else I've written, and I think probably is the best poem. James Joyce described himself in *A Portrait of the Artist* writing a villanelle, and this I think made all the poets of my generation try to write villanelles. It seemed a kind of test . . . It's a very rigid form, invented by the Italians, who apparently just thought it was musical: I don't think you'll find them struggling with the form – nor of course do the poets of the nineties like Dowson. They just regard the repetitions as musical. We felt that every time the line is repeated it has to mean something different; and treated like that, it becomes very hard to write. Anybody can push together the repetitions, only it's dead. Making it come to life is, I do think, hard. The best of them was written by W. H. Auden in *The Sea and the Mirror*, when all the characters in Shakespeare's *Tempest* come out and talk about themselves. Miranda comes out panting, completely astonished by the world – she has never seen a man before, except a monster and her father – and what she talks is a perfect villanelle, and this is an astounding piece of technical skill. I do think Auden is a wonderful technician. I remember pointing this out to Louis MacNeice when it first appeared, and he was rather cross and said, 'Of course it isn't a villanelle; it may remind you of villanelles, but it couldn't be one.' But it is literally a villanelle. However, my villanelles sound very stiff and rather like tombstones – but they are intended to, in a way. I wish to say that what this says is untrue. In writing it I thought this was a wonderful subject for a poem, but it never occurred to me to think whether it is true or not. It's a very odd thing that in poetry you can do that. I don't think it's bad because it's untrue. It says that if you lead an entirely tidy life – always arriving at the office at nine o'clock and picking up the pins from the carpet as you go to your desk – then you will never grow old; well, you will, as a matter of fact, just the same: it's rather a good thing, as a matter of fact. But what the poem says is that you won't. I think this is what I. A. Richards meant – long ago when it was new, and I sent him an early copy – by saying it was a joke: the last verse in a remote way is meant to sound facetious [said Richards]. Well, this is very mysterious. Max Brod, who was a close friend of Kafka, describes how in writing *The Trial* he had only written the first four verses [paragraphs], but one evening he read them to his young friends and they were all in fits of laughter: they thought *The Trial* was overwhelmingly funny. They were regarding it as satire on government officials, and in that political way it would seem funny. But if *The Trial* is funny, I'm very willing to believe that my little poem is funny too … but it's fairly remote, I should say. However, it's a very sympathetic comment [by Richards], I think: I wish it was funny.

(vii) A further comment is preserved in a letter (28 May 1976) to WE from David Pirie, who quoted back at WE his remark from a (now lost) letter: 'You say that in *Missing Dates* you are "**plainly writing about the process of aging in an individual man**"' (courtesy of David Pirie).

(viii) In a prefatory note, written in 1983, to the Hogarth Press edition of *CP* (1984), WE revealed:

When I. A. Richards saw the villanelle beginning 'Slowly the poison . . .' he said it was the best comic poem I had done so far; and I must have betrayed my surprise, because he added, not to hurt my feelings, that of course it was *deep* humour. I was not hurt but relieved; denouncing the universe has never seemed to me a sensible thing for a poem to do, and I had feared that my villanelle might be tainted with that pomposity. Much of the verse here [in CP] is about the strangeness of the world, in which we are often tripped up and made helpless, and the first thing to do in that situation is to understand it. In such a case, it is usual for some to laugh and others not.

This poem is recognized to have been the major influence upon other villanelles, including 'One Art' by Elizabeth Bishop and 'To Dumb Forgetfulness' by I. A. Richards.

See Brooks and Warren, *Understanding Poetry*, p. 258; Morelli, pp. 104–9; Spector, 'Form and Content in Empson's "Missing Dates" ', who tries to match the poem to the paradigm of courtly love poetry traditional for the villanelle; and Drew, *Poetry*, who draws attention to the wide metaphorical range in this short poem: 'toxins in the blood stream, the grinding of grain, blood transfusions, Chinese tombs, mining operations, land erosion, body metabolism and the double-edged title of missing dates'. Drew glosses further: 'active efforts do not exhaust us, even if they end in failure, nor does intellectual effort (system and clear sight) grind the life of the heart beneath the upper and the nether millstone. "The consequence a life requires" is, I suppose, the time-sequence ending in death. That must come finally, but the heart should not die before the body is consumed. No transfusions from outside can revive dwindling emotional vitality. Life gets cumbered with useless regrets for our dead past, waste products, when it could still be productive' (p. 140). See also Willis, pp. 340–47; Ricks, pp. 201–3; *TGA*, pp. 185–7; Lecercle, 'William Empson's Cosmicomics', pp. 280–81; and Fenton's discussion of the poem in 'Ars Poetica 36'.

See 'Villanelle' and 'Advice' for other instances of the conceit of disease.

2 *nor*: Hayward told WE in a letter (21 May 1956), 'orthodox grammar re-quires *or* as in l. 4' – but then the full impact of the sonorous negatives would be lost.
3,9,15,19 *The waste remains, the waste remains and kills*: as Richards noted ('William Empson'), the rhythm here – and, one might think, something of the deathly spirit – holds a memory of Tennyson's 'The woods decay, the woods decay and fall' ('Tithonus', l. 1); though Richards thought it only an 'unconscious echo'. In 1972 WE took part in a BBC radio programme, *Tennyson: Eighty Years On*, produced by Hallam Tennyson, in which he observed that 'Tithonus' is '**the best and deepest**' of Tennyson's poems and – in an astounding and memorable phrase – '**a poem in favour of the human practice of dying**' ('Empson on Tennyson', p. 108–9).

Cf. Shakespeare, Sonnet 129, l. 1: 'Th'expense of spirit in a waste of shame'.
4-5 *mills / Down*: ground in a mill, like flour; crushed or pounded down.
5 *the consequence a life requires*: 'If we are to take it as a truth that knows no exception that everything living dies for *internal* reasons – becomes inorganic once again – then we shall be compelled to say that "*the aim of all life is death*" ' (Freud,

Beyond the Pleasure Principle, trans. James Strachey; *Standard Edition*, vol. 18 (London, 1955), p. 38).

7 *rills*: small streams or brooks; possibly – given the refrain 'The waste remains, the waste remains and kills' – subsuming an allusion to Edward Young's *Love of Fame, The Universal Passion* (1752–8): 'Pure gurgling rills the lonely desart trace, / And waste their music on the savage race' (*Poetical Works*, ed. Mitford, vol. II (London, 1896), p. 103). WE cited a passage from *Love of Fame* in illustration of the third type of ambiguity (*ST*, p. 133).

7–8 *They bled an old dog . . . month's desires*: it is difficult to trace the precise experiment which WE claimed to have read about in a journal, but it is likely to have been something more drastic and nasty than a simple transfusion. C. H. Best and N. B. Taylor included in their standard text on physiology these comments on the state of blood-experimentation in 1937: 'Bayliss . . . reported that if an animal were bled to the extent of 40 per cent of its blood volume it usually succumbed, but that 70 per cent of the blood could be removed yet recovery occur if gum solution were used to restore the blood volume'; and again, 'In the treatment of certain conditions, e.g., severe toxemias, carbon monoxide poisoning, etc., the patient is first bled, his blood being then replaced by transfused blood (exsanguination transfusion)' (*The Physiological Basis of Medical Practice* (London, 1937), pp. 54–5).

However, it is most probable that the experiment to which WE refers, though not so precisely described in the poem, is the one carried out by Alexis Carrel and described by Lecomte de Noüy in *Biological Time* (London, 1936). Carrel was the originator of successful tissue culture following his demonstration that 'embryo tissue fluid' in the culture medium could prolong the survival of tissue cultures indefinitely, whereas the serum of older animals led to the death of the culture in a time which got shorter in proportion to the ageing of the donor animal:

There was at the Rockefeller Institute, before the war, a dog nearly eighteen years old. This poor animal never stirred from its corner and could hardly get up to eat . . .

This animal was anaesthetized, put on the operating table and treated as follows. Carrel bled him by the carotid artery and removed nearly two-thirds of his blood. This blood was collected aseptically and immediately centrifuged, so as to separate the red cells from the serum. The red cells were washed in Ringer solution, recentrifuged and mixed with fresh Ringer solution to re-establish the initial volume of the blood. This was then re-injected into the dog. The circulation was restored by massaging the heart, and the skin was sewn up . . . After several days he had regained strength and appetite. The same operation was repeated so as to eliminate practically all the serum of his blood and replace it by this artificial solution which, besides the blood cells, contained only salts such as chlorides of sodium, potassium, and calcium in the same proportion as those found in the blood. The animal lived. Not only did he live, but, once over the operative shock, he was a different dog. He ran and barked, a thing he had not done for years. His eyes were clear, his eyelids normal. His coat started to come in; he was gay, active, and most important of all, he was no longer indifferent to the charms of the other sex. He was rejuvenated. (p. 115)

(I am indebted to Professor Ivor Mills, Department of Surgery, University of Cambridge, for identifying that passage for me; see also the letter from Professor Mills on this subject: 'Empson's Missing Dates'.) In *Possible Worlds* Haldane had referred to Carrel's work on cultures (p. 151). WE took a positive interest in biological science, and reviewed the first volume of *The Eugenics Review*: 'Health, Wealth and Happiness' (*Granta*, 4 May 1928; *E in G*, p. 53); the variety of approaches to eugenics, he wrote, is **'a matter so pressing and so unfathomable'**.

It is possible too that WE's attention had been caught by Samuel Butler's scoff, in 'An Heroical Epistle of Hudibras to Sidrophel', ll. 59–62: 'As if the Art you have so long / Profest, of making old *Dogs* young, / In you had Virtue to renew / Not only Youth, but Childhood too.'

8 desires;] desires. *copy sent to John Hayward*; desires CP

10 *Chinese tombs*: refers to the shrines or small temples put up in innumerable Chinese fields. Harold B. Rattenbury, who lived in China during the 1930s, recorded: 'The simplest form of temple, and almost universal in my experience, is the little shrine that stands among the fields and is called by the Chinese "T'u-ti-Miao" – "local earth temple". Such shrines are perhaps ten feet high, roofed with tiles, and have only one little chamber in which stand two idol figures, about the size of a child's toy doll . . . It is evident they are the patrons of the field, the local deities, blessing the fertility of your fields and warding off pests from your crops' (*China, My China* (London, 1944), p. 132).

14 *The complete fire is death* may refer to the Buddha's 'Fire Sermon' (see pp. 139–52), or to the purgatorial fires of St Augustine and of Yeats (in 'Byzantium').

Success

First published, as 'Poem', in *Horizon* 1:5 (May 1940), 315; though probably written in 1937 (at about the same time as 'Missing Dates': see below).

The evidence of the reiterative rhyme scheme, and of two lines (2, 3) which are so repeated (19, 16) as to function as a refrain, suggests that WE may have tried to cast the poem as a villanelle, like 'Missing Dates' (it even has the necessary nineteen lines). *TGA* (p. 188) considers it 'a cross between villanelle and terza rima, with more refrains than the one and fewer rhymes than the other'.

CP: Dostoevsky had a kind of illumination while waiting to be shot but was brought back from it by a last-minute reprieve. I can't feel that the line about

'afterlight' comes off; the idea is that the glow after sunset with its peace is a kind of proof that the day was real or good, and the Will o' the Wisp is assumed to be like it. Doubting drugs is meant to be both doubting whether they have been used and doubting the value of what they have given.

On *Poems of William Empson*, the poet remarked:

After that ['Missing Dates'] in the book is a poem called 'Success' which rhymes at random and should have a feeling of coming out of all this solemnity; indeed a feeling of coming round from a drug; but the idea is that what you thought you learned under a drug may still be true. The novelist Dostoevsky, perhaps I ought to say, had a kind of illumination while waiting to be executed but was brought back from it by a last-minute reprieve; whether it only worked like a drug or not one can't know.

On *Poetry at the Mermaid*, he commented further: '**This isn't using an elaborate metre** . . . only throwing in various rhymes. It's recovering from a love affair and saying it did you good. I'm afraid I take . . . **this rather clinical view of love: it's saving you from madness. I'm not so enthusiastic as other poets have been.**'
   A letter to Maxwell-Mahon (6 November 1967) includes this simple (possibly 'Freudian') slip: ' **"Success" was another love-~~affair~~ poem**'.
   Thurley provocatively suggests, though without presenting any evidence for the claim: 'Some of the poems adjacent to "Missing Dates" in the *Collected Poems* – "Success", "Reflection from Anita Loos" – seem to turn, somewhat evasively, upon sexual impotence, either feared or disappointedly overcome' (' "Partial fires" ', p. 52). See also Willis, pp. 347–53; Wain, pp. 312–14; *TGA*, pp. 187–91.

3 that] who *1940. TGA* comments (p. 188): 'The alteration of the original "Those who doubt drugs" was presumably to allow the reading "People drugged by doubt", as well as the two other meanings mentioned by Empson in his note.'
5 *flatness*: cf. 'Rolling the Lawn', ll. 1–2, and 'Courage means Running', l. 28 (in its emended version in *CP 1956*; see note).
6 *Verse likes despair*: WE wrote in 'Foundations of Despair' (January 1937), on the posthumous verse of A. E. Housman:

It is true I think that all Despair Poetry needs a good deal of 'distance' (of the poet from the theme); you can only call despair a profound general truth when you are looking beyond all the practical particulars, which might well have been hopeful if the man had been stronger; and in a personal story, even a half-told one, you cannot do this easily . . . But there seems no decent ground for calling all Despair Poetry about love sentimental, and then all tragedy sentimental . . . And granting the stuff can be good, it has a technical condition, whatever the personal background. It wants as its apparent theme a case of love with great practical obstacles, such as those of class and sex, because the despair has to seem sensible before this curious jump is made, and it is called a universal truth. (*A*, p. 419)

8–9 *It was a reprieve / Made Dostoevsky . . . clear*: in 1849 Feodor Dostoevsky, at the age of 28, was charged by the General-Auditoriat with circulating literature against the government and the Orthodox Church, and condemned to death. His sentence was commuted by Tsar Nicholas I to eight years of penal servitude (which was in turn reduced to four years, to be followed by indefinite service in the Russian Army). He had been put through the hideous pantomime of a mock execution. A few hours after that supposedly last-minute reprieve, Dostoevsky wrote to his older brother Mikhail in a state of ecstatic deliverance: 'Life everywhere is life, life is in ourselves and not in the external . . . This is, after all, life. *On voit le soleil! . . .* Life is a gift, life is happiness, every minute can be an eternity of happiness. *Si jeunesse savait!*' His close encounter with death, at once ghastly and exhilarating, gave him access to a sense of the grace of life, he recorded. Years later, in *The Idiot*, Prince Myshkin speaks authoritatively of the last minutes of a man condemned to death, conveying a vision of pantheistic dissolution which would have greatly appealed to WE. WE's source may have been E. H. Carr, *Dostoevsky (1821–1881)* (London, 1931); or, more likely, Avrahm Yarmolinsky, *Dostoevsky: A Life* (New York, 1934); but in any case he must have been told all about Dostoevsky by his flatmate in London in the mid-1930s, Igor Vinogradoff, who was an expert on Russian culture.

9 talk] speak *1940*

9 *talk out queer and clear*: cf. Keats's 'On First Looking into Chapman's Homer', ll. 5–8: 'Oft of one wide expanse had I been told / That deep-brow'd Homer ruled as his demesne; / Yet did I never breathe its pure serene / Till I heard Chapman speak out loud and bold.' WE used the verb 'speak' in *1940* (see collation above), and changed it only a few weeks later for *GS*.

11 Zoo] zoo *1940*

15 *marsh lights*: suggests that the beloved was a will-o'-the-wisp or *ignis fatuus*: a snare and a delusion.

16 that] who *1940*

Just a Smack at Auden

First published in *Contemporary Poetry and Prose* (Autumn 1937), 24–6; reprinted in *The Year's Poetry 1938*, ed. Denys Kilham Roberts and Geoffrey Grigson (London, 1938), pp. 48–50.

    With the exception of both the five-line stanza which opens the poem and rhymes *abbba* and the culminating four-line stanza rhyming on '-end' (which were never subject to any modification), the remainder of the poem was initially printed in six-line stanzas, regularly rhyming on 'boys' and '-end' in the sequence *abbabb*. In the final version, with the exception of stanza 1, Empson sticks throughout the poem to the *epistrophe* on '-end'. (See also Randall Jarrell's 'discovery' below.) These first printings of the poem also included an additional stanza 5:

> Look at all the wise, boys,
> Can they stave or fend?
> Can they keep from cries, boys, waiting for the end?
> You can choose your ties, boys,
> Whether pecked or henned.
> All your wisdom dies, boys, waiting for the end.

It is not known why that stanza was removed from all later printings, from *GS* on, since it is not markedly more mocking or satirical than most of the other stanzas; it is possible that it was dropped because of a printing accident or oversight.

On 12 November 1932 WE had written from Tokyo to his friend Michael Roberts: '**What is "The Oxford Movement" I keep hearing about? Is it Hitler or Auden's Boy Scout attitude?**' (courtesy of Janet Adam Smith).

In 'A London Letter', he ventured, in a shrewd or whimsical way, to distinguish between British and American poetry:

The difference comes out for instance in the comparatively large (and well deserved) sales in England of poems by Auden and Spender, who were viewed as young communist uplift. The bulk of that new public of buyers, which was mainly interested in the political feelings expressed, were not I think idealists in the sense of enjoying sentiments they did not mean to act on, nor yet definite sympathizers who wanted to get something like that done. In America they would have been one or the other; in England there was an obscure safety and bafflement in moving from the poem to consider what the country could possibly do.

Some six months after publication, WE was passing through Hong Kong, when he ran into Auden and Christopher Isherwood on their way to write up the Japanese invasion of China: '**The great Auden was here**,' he wrote to his mother on 15 March 1938, '**who used to be a kind of rival poet to me and is now a prominent figure**' (Empson Papers).

WE always admired Auden's genius; his review of *Paid on Both Sides* offers this:

One reason the scheme [of the play] is so impressive is that it puts psychoanalysis and surrealism and all that, all the irrationalist tendencies which are so essential a part of the machinery of present-day thought, into their proper place; they are made part of the normal and rational tragic form, and indeed what constitutes the tragic situation. One feels as if at the crisis of many, perhaps better, tragedies, it is just this machinery which has been covertly employed. Within its scale (twenty-seven pages) there is the gamut of all the ways we have of thinking about the matter; it has the sort of completeness that makes a work seem to define the attitude of a generation. ('A Note on W. H. Auden's *Paid on Both Sides*' (1931); *A*, p. 371)

In an unpublished essay on pacifism drafted sometime after 1941, WE defended a famous line of Auden's poetry that would be subject to attack from various quarters, most notably by George Orwell:

Voigt was saying in a political book that the poets are all warmongers now, and illustrated this by a line from Auden's *Spain*: 'The conscious acceptance of guilt in the necessary murder'. Of course a paradox can always be read several ways: *murder* says this act of killing is wicked, and *necessary* (for the ends considered) says it is good, so you don't know what sorts of killing the poet has in view. But surely it comes from a conscience sensitive about war rather than brutalized. Cf. the song of Deborah, for real warmongering. But maybe there is a kind of German-philosophic quality in the line, which Voigt might feel more of a Nazi weapon than Auden did. The more striking thing about Auden is the horror of Power, e.g. The Ascent of F6. All power corrupts . . . It is remarkable to me that nobody has yet turned the epigram of Lord Acton backwards. All impotence corrupts; absolute impotence corrupts absolutely. This is quite as true as the other, but maybe they only recommend the same thing, a wide spreading of power through the country. It is always hard to translate the wisdom of the literary into political plans.

See also Appendix 3, pp. 126–8.

In a contribution in 1975 to a BBC TV *Bookstand* programme on Auden, WE insisted he had always kept faith with the Auden of the 1930s:

It is very hard, you see, to write what years later people called pylon poetry – to write about how you ought to have the socialist state and how you'd like it – without sounding phoney. And Auden somehow made it sound perfectly sincere by making it sound as if he was jeering at you for not being more sensible, but you didn't quite know what he was laughing at, but you could hear this, this mysterious tone of fun going on. It seemed to be immensely impressive. That was what was so striking about him. And he has moved away from it and so have all the pylon poets, who by the way were all Oxford when I was at Cambridge. That's why as a poet myself I was never able to imitate it properly. You had to be in on the movement from the start.

I have sometimes known later critics say, 'Oh, well, Empson wasn't so much of a mug as to be a pylon poet; he may have very little to say, but at least he didn't say that.' Well, of course, I agreed with the pylon poets entirely. I've always felt I ought to make that point plain whenever I had the opportunity: I think they were quite right, I just didn't know how to do this kind of poetry. And it does rather depend on the curl of the tongue.

You see, the pylon poets, beginning with the great slump of 1929 – you had tremendous numbers of people out of work, and the economic system was clearly badly out of order, and then you got Mussolini and Hitler coming up – what they were saying was that you ought to have more socialism at home, you want the Welfare State, and you ought to have the popular front against Hitler abroad, the line-up of the Allies. They went on saying that through the thirties, and by 1942 the whole country agreed with them. Well, it's a very lucky thing for a poet, I'm very sorry I wasn't in on it. ('Early Auden', *A*, pp. 375–6)

Furthermore, on *The Ambiguity of William Empson*, he commented:

The point about Auden's political poetry especially, and all his group, is their peculiar relation to [the] audience, you see, they're teasing the audience, they're telling them you're making fools of yourselves, you know perfectly well really what's going to happen and what you must do and you must face up to it, and this curious intimate relation to the audience is an extremely valuable one, of course. And when Leavis attacked it, saying that they're all talking like public schoolboys pretending to be workers, well, as a matter of fact it was all good propaganda; it wouldn't be now but it was then. The extent to which the country was prepared to resist Hitler in the end when the time [came] was very dependent on this immense amount of preparation. But, you see, it isn't a matter of opinions, it's a matter of having a certain relationship to your readers which I was not in . . . couldn't have done any of that, I don't think. But I thought that the work of Auden in preparing the public mind for the war to come, which was coming, had been extremely important. I didn't mean [in this poem] to blame him for doing it, still less to say that the war wasn't coming, I too thought it was. So an attack, it was more what they called trench humour in the First World War, in a way. We were all going through the same experience anyhow, I suppose, but it's . . . I feel I ought to explain that, and Auden when I next saw him said he thought it was very funny, it was not a quarrel scene – however, it has all the appearance of one. It's called 'Just a Smack at Auden' – who you understand had been writing for . . . since the beginning of the thirties saying you must expect this war to come.

Later still, on 14 August 1983, WE was to raise a small objection to the blurb that Andrew Motion had drafted for the reissue of *CP* (1984): he regretted that Motion appeared to have represented 'Just a Smack at Auden' as expressing a real quarrel with Auden's politics in the 1930s. '**Please take out . . . the phrase in brackets about Just a Smack at Auden**,' he wrote.

I entirely agreed with Auden, though I could not express the opinion nearly so well, that War II was coming, and that backing the People's Front was our only chance. I just thought that his hammering at it had become counter-productive, and by the time he read my joke he thought the hammering had become a boring duty. Later on I was praised for it by people who thought we ought to have chosen to lose the war, just as a snub for Stalin. So, as it would be too costly for me to explain myself [in the sense, he meant, that a fresh preface might put up the price of the volume], the subject had better be dropped. (Empson Papers)

For his part, Auden reciprocated WE's admiration, and later showed he had taken no offence at this incantatory lampoon (or 'gibing assault', as Valentine Cunningham has unfairly described it) by honouring Empson with 'A Toast', a piece of light verse written for the *festschrift William Empson*, ed. Gill – though it first appeared in Auden's *Epistle to a Godson* (London, 1972). Hailing WE ('dear Bill, dear fellow mandarin'), Auden begins by recalling, thirty-five years on: 'As *quid pro quo* for your enchanting verses, / when approached by Sheffield, at first I wondered / if I could manage *Just a Smack at Empson*, / but nothing occurred.' Nevertheless, it is possible that Auden had initially felt the force of Empson's baying at the 'boys', for he was to write in the 'Prologue' to *The Double Man* (1941), ll. 17–19: 'For we know we're not boys / And never will be: part of us all hates life, / And some are completely against it.' (Auden alludes too to a phrase in another WE poem, 'Who say after two aliens had one kiss' ('Aubade', l. 36), in *The Double Man*, l. 1069, 'If now, two aliens in New York'; I am grateful to Nicholas Jenkins for confirming this reference.)

Note also a letter from Randall Jarrell to Robert Lowell [November 1947]: 'You remember Empson's "Just a Smack at Auden" in which every line ends with *Boys*: I discovered he got this particular effect from a lovely early parody of Lewis Carroll's, quite worth reading' (*Randall Jarrell's Letters*, ed. Mary Jarrell (London, 1985), p. 185).

Kingsley Amis showed that he thoroughly appreciated the point of the refrain when he chose to extend the joke: in his copy of a 1939 edition of Auden's poems, Amis wrote: 'Waiting for the end, boys waiting for the end. May 1944' (see H. R. Woudhuysen, 'Sincere good wishes ... Mr Amis', *Times Literary Supplement*, 19 July 1996, p. 16).

See also Morelli, pp. 121–2; Neal Wood, *Communism and British Intellectuals*, p. 71; Harvey Gross, *Sound and Form*, p. 261; *TGA*, pp. 191–4. Willis (p. 354) remarks that Empson's ballad reflects 'the style of the songs in the Marxist verse plays (*The Dance of Death*, 1933, and *On the Frontier*, 1937), or the poem "Danse Macabre" ("It's farewell to the drawing-room's civilized cry"). It may even owe something to Auden's poem of 1934, " 'O where are you going?' said reader to rider".'

TITLE: 'smack' used in the colloquial sense of 'a slap or go *at* something' (*OED*[2] smack sb.[3] 3c). WE had used it while at Cambridge, in his capacity as editor of the new periodical *Experiment*, when on 14 September 1928 he wrote to E. E. Phare (later Elsie Duncan-Jones) at Newnham College: 'Do send along your Hopkins article, it would be rather a smack at Richards if we got somebody to say something quite different.' (Richards's essay 'Gerard Hopkins' had appeared in *Dial* 81 (1926); Phare's 'Valéry and Gerard Hopkins' – though she had not intended it to be a 'smack' – appeared in the first issue of *Experiment* in November 1928.)

15 that] who *1937*

27 Playing] Talking *1937*

31 *Playing at the child*: cf. WE's review (1940) of Auden's *Another Time* (1940):

you are afraid on every page that a horrid false note of infantilism will poke up its head. The poems here about famous men give striking cases of it. Voltaire, we are told, 'cleverest of them all, He'd led the other children in a holy war Against the infamous grown-ups' ['Voltaire at Ferney']. About Freud, on the other hand, and the voice of the poet breaks at the thought, we are told, 'He wasn't clever at all' ['In Memory of Sigmund Freud'] (he was just such a *good* boy, your heart aches to think of it). No doubt Freud himself is largely responsible for this idea that people are best understood by seeing them as children; and yet this curious line of sentiment about the word 'clever' would, I suppose, be as hard to translate into German as into French. It is something to do with the English system of education; it throws absolutely no light on Voltaire. At the end of 'Spain' the poet describes an ideal state . . . and it is a boys' school; there would be no room for Auden himself except as one of the masters. (*A*, p. 373)

33 *Each of us enisled*: cf. Matthew Arnold, 'To Marguerite – Continued' (1852), ll. 1–4: 'Yes! in the sea of life enisled, / With echoing straits between us thrown, / Dotting the shoreless watery wild, / We mortal millions live *alone*.'

34 *What was said by Marx, boys*: Auden seems to have studied, and assumed or borrowed, Marxist ideas at the latest by 1932, when he wrote the poems 'A Communist to Others' and 'I have a handsome profile'; see also Auden's 'Marxist' play *The Dance of Death*, written the following year. Even though he wrote to Rupert Doone in the autumn of 1932, 'No. I am a bourgeois. I shall not join the C. P.' (Humphrey Carpenter, *W. H. Auden: A Biography* (London, 1981), p. 153) – and he never did join the Communist Party – there is strong testimony to the fact that he was greatly drawn to a pro-Marxist position in the mid-1930s. Louis MacNeice, for example, was to write to Anthony Blunt in January 1933, 'Auden turned up and talked a good deal of communism' (Jon Stallworthy, *Louis Mac-Neice* (London, 1995), p. 153). See also Justin Replogle, 'Auden's Marxism', *PMLA* 80 (December 1965), 584–95.

36 *Treason of the clerks*: Julien Benda, in *La Trahison des Clercs* (Paris, 1928), castigated a number of writers – from Barrès and Péguy to D'Annunzio, Kipling and William James – for betraying their vocations as disinterested or 'pure' artists by involving themselves in the politics of their day. WE may have learnt about Benda's counter-campaign from reading a review by T. S. Eliot, 'The Idealism of Julien Benda', in the *Cambridge Review* 49 (6 June 1928), 485–8, printed directly alongside WE's 'Letter' (later 'Letter II').

The Beautiful Train

First published in G S.

CP: This was when I was going to a job in China a few weeks after the outbreak of the Chinese war. The thing is about a surprised pleasure in being among Japanese again, though the train itself was beautiful after the Russian one all right. What I abhorred or rightly felt I ought to abhor was Japanese imperialism. They have got themselves into a tragically false position, I think; the Chinese with their beautiful good humour were always patient when I told them I was more sorry for the Japanese than for China. Argentina was a famous Spanish dancer when I was young.

For *Listen* WE noted: ' "The Train" went south from Siberia to Peking in 1937 when the war had just begun there; though under contract to China I enjoyed being back among the Japanese.'
The occasion of this poem – the last stage of a Trans-Siberian journey to Peking in August 1937 – was so absorbing to Empson that he described it in a hitherto unpublished piece of travel writing:

We got very alarmed at the prospect of being stuck in Siberia; there was no news and we kept being held up for great troop trains going East; it seemed likely that Russia might come in at any time. Manchuria therefore gave a great feeling of release, odd to look back on. The frontier officials were positively welcoming, because they wanted us to give them information about troop movements, not that we had any. Little as dirt worries me, the cleanness of the new train went a long way; and then the roominess and elegance of it, the getting decent bread and beer again, the readiness and good temper and prettiness of the attendants – it all came as a great nervous relief. I lay awake because the rhythm of the train was so light and brilliant and reliable, after the long waits and hoots and enormous incompetent bumps that still don't make a Russian train move, and began writing fragments of verse about it, which may as well go in here as I cannot imagine using them any other way.

> So strong and proud, on such light gay feet

was the rather over-fond line that made me turn the light on, and this I thought became positively good as

> So firm, so burdened, on such light gay feet
> A magic train, just made of a cucumber
> As Argentina in one swing of the bell skirt

Without visible steps, shivering with her power,
Would take a call shunting from wing to wing.
Courting the last art to syncopate
Or counterpoint all dances in their turns
Within one lope for home.
Arbours and balconies and room and shade.

It must have been the next day or the day after that I had several hours wait on a platform extremely crowded with Japanese, and could again regard them with my usual very mixed feelings.

Related passages of this typescript enlarge upon the experience of journeying across the Russian frontier into Manchuria and so to Peking:

The blinds had to be pulled down at various stations over one part of the line, making one feel rather ridiculous in semi-darkness. It was done at stations only when generals or suchlike were being seen onto the train; probably because they mustn't be looked at from above rather than from any application of real spymania. Japanese children could not be prevented from looking at soldiers, but the rest of us observed the rule solemnly enough; it seemed rather like 'Don't look while nurse is washing.' I had to spend a night at Harbin, where the through service gave out, and from the German owner of an empty hotel got my first news of the universities. They had shut down even in Manchuria, because the Chinese teachers were under suspicion; he was sure I should find nothing in Peking, though he was all for anybody having a look. One of the remarkable things about that railway now is the number of White or refugee Russians that work for it, and they are thought not likely to help fight Russia. And the 'bandits' are still too bad, even round Harbin, for people to take trips out of the town; which they weren't before the occupation. He was not anti-Japanese, merely depressed about his hotel. The train to Tientsin, early next morning, was almost entirely a troop-train; my first-class seat was in a corner of a saloon employed as an office, with people coming and saluting and giving reports to superior officers all the time. The trying thing about most Japanese is the nervous embarrassment and the self-assertion that comes from it, and the officers are very free from all that. At least so I thought before, which may be why I found these ones rather agreeable people. The train went trickling on through floods, both sides of the frontier, sometimes covering the lines a foot deep, but I still blankly expected to get to Tientsin that night – normally it is about six hours' run. There turned out to be a restaurant, serving one elaborately shaped dish with fish and meat on different sections; it was being eaten by relays of soldiers looking younger and milder than the average university student. I tried to get Japanese *domburi*, which was accepted as a politeness, but it seemed the food for soldiers was European meat. By this time it was getting clear that we would spend the night sitting up, so I brought along my book of simple integrations to the restaurant and drank a solid amount of beer, to make sure of sleep, getting rather worse at my sums as time went on. By the time I got back there had been a magical transformation scene, which I am sorry to have missed. What they call Peter-ho, the wateringplace of the foreigners of Peking and Tientsin, had disgorged a platoon of European women and children, each woman determined to get a great deal of room for more than one child. Nearly all the generals had fled; where to I don't know. A few forlorn ones, still hanging to their seats, were being treated very badly to an eerie display of female bad manners; they at last gave place to the children and huddled together in one nook. I only woke to see the last of the sunrise over the flooded rice-fields, a lovely sight, and then there was just time for breakfast in Tientsin before the all-day train to Peking.

(Further passages from that unfinished memoir are quoted under 'Manchouli' below.)

See Willis, pp. 356–9; Breitkreuz, 'Empson's "The Beautiful Train"'; Breitkreuz, 'William Empsons *The Beautiful Train*'; *TGA*, pp. 184–96.

1 *Argentina*: La Argentina was the professional name of Antonia Mercé y Luque (1890–1936): a ballet dancer – première danseuse at the Madrid Opera – she resigned at fourteen to study the native dances of Spain; after 1927, when her solo performance was first acclaimed at the Théâtre des Champs-Elysées in Paris, she gained world-wide fame as originator and prime exponent of the Neoclassical style of Spanish dance.

8 *And I a twister love what I abhor*: in a footnote in the 1953 edition of *ST* (p. 119), WE observed: 'I remember how cross I was when a reviewer of my own verse used a poem in which I had addressed myself as a twister. He said that this was a surprising confession and exactly what was the matter with me. I thought that this showed an almost imbecile incompetence on the part of the critic.'

Charles Lumley, in John Wain's comic novel *Hurry On Down* (1953), works himself into a state of such frantic stimulation that he is driven to invent variants on this epigrammatic line: '*And I a lover twist what I abhor . . . And twister I, abhorring what I love . . . And I a whore, abtwisting what I love . . . Love eye and twist her and what I abhor*' (reprinted, Harmondsworth, 1979), pp. 29–30).

Manchouli

First published in *GS*.

CP: **Manchouli was as big a racial frontier as you see anywhere; I don't remember seeing any obvious 'Asiatics' in Siberia.**

TITLE: Manzhouli is the border town on the route of the Trans-Siberian railway between Siberia and Manchuria.

The background to this sane little poem is elaborated in the memoir, or piece of travel writing, that Empson began (but sadly never completed) in the spring of 1938, while journeying south by train from Changsha to Hong Kong, in company with others of the staff of the refugeeing National Peking University (see 'The Beautiful Train' above):

On this trip, though I felt that Germany when I was in it was an impoverished and painful place, 'the Europeans' became one as soon as we crossed the great frontier under the arch which I have not yet found a companion in travel to translate. I threw away, an unnecessary cowardice, my copy of the small depressions of the acute Gide. We began being herded about; time began to pass. Two German ladies produced jewel cases; a ludicrous man claimed to be pricing them, by a process of divination amusing to the owners. One gets petty about frontiers, but still counting and a rough description, let alone a seal on the case, are all a frontier can claim – who is the expert jeweller of the Soviet border? And then an Englishman with a lot of pears, every one pierced with wire for message or bomb, and at least my habitual incompetence has left me with large supplies of half-crowns, which happen to be peculiarly unintelligible; the jeweller is unable to understand or rather firmly and rationally disbelieves in the English money system. A Chinese at the far end makes an uproar, and apparently gets away with it; nobody knows what he is troubled by. 'Workers of the world, Unite' is written round the wall in most European languages, and I am pleased to see that only the English language can claim freedom from the fatuous term *Proletarian*, which if it meant anything in the ancient Roman from which they steal it meant cannon-fodder. I am just able to carry my luggage (I wish I had had the sense to bring the plump hamper of manuscript, mostly rubbish but now lost, with me that way) and eager not to involve myself in the infuriate rights of a Soviet porter, and this involves some apparently last-minute scrambling from one end of the train to the other, which yet leaves time for very last-minute money changing. I have been placed with an important young Englishman of ICI, one of the acquaintances of travel you always wish you had said more to, but how graceful we both felt it was to say so little to each other in so long a time . . .

My feelings about Russia when going through are no doubt largely due to ignorance of the language and of many other things; I say 'are', not 'were', because I have done it twice and expect to feel the same any other time; though to be sure I liked Russia better the first time, because then I had Russians in the carriage who spoke French to me. And the trip means Siberia rather than Russia. But still I think it sordid beyond the dreams of avarice; a thing that might catch you, safe as you are in your paid carriage. The absence of hens till you get east of Baikal seems an eerie detail, and the woman is the beast of burden as she is not in China. This time we had a wireless roaring political speeches at us, and the only cheerful thing about that was not understanding it – nobody dared sabotage the thing. The food I thought extremely good, though I was frightened of eating much caviare with vodka in so sedentary a life, and here as usual I wish I had the sense to remember names of dishes; but unless you had food tickets all through, as we had, the stuff was savagely expensive, and who were all these Russians, often delightful to look at (I think them a wonderful people) who were eating it too? If they get the food tickets with the transfer of job it is very civilized, but there are the beggars making monuments of the platforms; the great railway is the scene of as harsh a distinction of classes as ever, and the new gain is this queer weight of fear. I am not talking about the theory of Communism, an important thing that the civilized parts of the world need, and have to digest, but about that terrible country whose history has driven it downwards ever since the sixteenth century when Europe invented progress. Russia was built out of hopeless but triumphant war against the Golden Horde and the long strength of the Tartars; the movement to the rich river land about Moscow was a flight, and what agriculture could be done about the camps demanded a military order; the supremacy of Moscow was bought at the startling price of betraying its rivals to the hereditary enemy. The sudden conquests of the sixteenth century then opened an area of land comparable to America, and the two countries are still parallels or antitheses; but the only payment possible to the victorious armies was in land, and the peasants without whom the land was valueless were melting into the newly conquered steppes. Russia like America therefore required and imposed slavery. Another though an appalling mother of freedom in the West was the fanatic wars; this too turned backwards in Russia; the protestants there were devotees of the old Mumpsimus in her most dismal aspect, so far as that is known. Russia is one of the three great colonizing powers of Europe, with the Spaniards and the English (all of them speak of Europe as if they were outside it); but the conquest of Siberia and Alaska, achieved without hatred and long before the railway, was made by traders with no claims at home. The younger and eldest sons of the gentry were only allowed to split the estates that Peter had provided; enormous as they were, he might have calculated from them the three centuries to the revolution; as the estates shrank the pressure became heavier on the slaves, and the feeling of uselessness deeper on the owners. The obscure fear engendered by bureaucracy, a state of government in which everybody is helpless if they lose the papers at the top, joined to produce a habit of cruelty with the more sensible fears, that the abstract reformers might smash the only system still working, and that the oppressed might take a hideous revenge. People were accustomed, as they are now, to famine vaguely known but covering enormous areas among the peasants . . .

It is stupid to talk about fate, about a national habit of incompetence, about 'the Russians'; it may not be stupid to talk about racial characteristics, but we know the Russians are a great people. But if a man has a large burn a doctor is not talking about Fate if he says 'that will take three weeks or a month, and leave a scar'. It is a little harder to believe in history, but history is as real as a burn. Nobody with any sense of history is going to be surprised at the orgy of killing bureaucrats in modern Russia. I should fancy the country needs three centuries, and nobody could feel more excitement about a race than I did, trotting up and down the platforms and peeping at the cheekbones of the exhausted; I think them a tremendous people; and even this awful present-day despair I think is only a thing lanced and let to the surface. But goodness me, tell a Durham miner that Marx has something to tell him, and so he may, but don't pretend Stalin has . . .

The most attractive thing on the way through Russia was some kind of saints' day of the Machine Age – we never found out what, or I forget. The Russian engine-driver hoots a good deal, by way of asserting his public function (the motorhorns of Tokyo, on the other hand, squeal for ever in a glee of self-satisfaction). But, on this day, whenever we came to one of the great bare halts with a few huts and a statue of Stalin and ten tracks to shunt on, we would stay for some time, with steam full on, just going on hooting continually, among all the other engines. You would get five or six, not very near each other, in the first chill of winter, and I seem to remember a touch of fog, so that you peered at them along the bleak lines of rail, swathed in their own steam and baying in a continual triumph. It was like *Moby Dick* when they get drawn into the centre of the school of whales and see far down into the domestic pleasures of the leviathan. I felt like [Kipling's] little Toomai seeing the dance of the elephants . . .

For commentary on the way in which WE manipulates 'the implications of minor linguistic details' and the reader's presuppositions, see Forrest-Thomson, 'Rational Artifice', pp. 226–7. See also Morelli, pp. 64–5; Willis, pp. 360–61; *TGA*, pp. 196–7.

Reflection from Anita Loos

Written in 1937–8; first published in *GS*, though written in 1937–9 (see below).

CP: There is a strong paragraph in *Gentlemen Prefer Blondes* about Louie's spats. Dorothy told him to take them off, because 'Fun's fun, but a girl can't laugh all the time.' When she saw his socks she told him to put his spats back on. Unconsciously generalizing from the fine character of Dorothy, I seem to have taken a very feminist view here; actually no doubt women are about as ambitious as men. The *lime* is meant to be birdlime (also hanged criminals are buried in ordinary lime). I had better say some more about the line, as many readers may find it merely offensive. Anyway the religion of love produced appalling cruelties when made a governmental institution, but it seems arguable that the ideas of Jesus himself got fatally connected under the stress of persecution with the official and moneymaking cult of blood sacrifice, which he had tried to combat. That he drove out of the temple the doves being sold for sacrifice just before he became one is an awful irony in his story. The way earlier societies seem obviously absurd and cruel gives a kind of horror at the forces that must be at work in our own, but suggests that any society must have dramatically satisfying and dangerous conventions; and people can put up with almost any political conditions, either because they are lazy or because they are ambitious.

Seemingly inspired by Loos's quip, this villanelle brings together related reflections on the tyrannies of fashion, social convention and social climbing, the relativity of love, and the religion of love that is founded on a cruelty – 'the absurdities and cruelties at work in a society that calls itself Christian', as Deutsch put it (*Poetry in Our Time*, p. 213). Anita Loos was pleased by this poem, it is nice to know, though Gary Carey reports in his biography of her: 'In *Blondes* Dorothy Shaw comments, "Fun is fun, but no girl wants to go on laughing all the time." British poet William Empson paraphrased Dorothy's quip in a poem, "Reflections from Anita Loos", the final line of each stanza ending by saying "A girl can't go on laughing all the time." Anita was flattered, but the poem was just a bit pretentious, a little menacing. Prolonged study of Empson's reflections, she feared, might turn her into "a weeper".' (*Anita Loos: A Biography* (London, 1988), p. 316).

In a letter to Christopher Ricks (19 January 1975), WE remarked: '**My war started in 1937, when I refugeed with the Chinese universities, and I went on writing criticism there, also the Anita Loos poem, which I now think bad.**'

See Willis, pp. 361–7; Pfister, 'Die Villanelle', esp. pp. 303–8; and *TGA*, pp. 197–201.

1–2 *No man . . . safely placed*: Willis (p. 363) notes that WE seems here to be exploiting an ambiguity of the seventh type, the most ambiguous of all: 'The first two lines of the stanza assert, through two negatives, that ambition is all too human a characteristic. Insisting on the negative . . . as Empson explains in *Seven Types* (p. 205), suggests the opposite. Such a "disorder in the action of the negative" causes the reader to entertain the opposites defined by the content. Empson's negative lines in this poem might read, "All men are sure they need to climb", as well as "no man is sure whether or not he needs to climb".'

3 *A girl can't go on laughing all the time*: in Paris, the gold-digging duo Lorelei Lee and Dorothy Shaw meet up with a father and his son, Louis and Robert, both lawyers, who invite them out for a day trip to 'Fountainblo'. 'So Dorothy said we might as well go out to Fountainblo with Louie and Robber if Louie would take off his yellow spats that were made out of yellow shammy skin with pink pearl buttons. Because Dorothy said, "Fun is fun but no girl wants to laugh all of the time." So Louie is really always anxious to please, so he took off his spats but when he took off his spats, we saw his socks and when we saw his socks we saw that they were Scotch plaid with small size rainbows running through them. So Dorothy looked at them a little while and she really became quite discouraged and she said, "Well Louie, I think you had better put your spats back on"' (*Gentlemen Prefer Blondes: The Illuminating Diary of a Professional Lady* (1925); London, 1974, p. 87).

4 *Wrecked*: cf. 'Four Legs, Two Legs, Three Legs', l. 9.

5 *There are who*: the Latin phrase *sunt qui*, derived from Horace, gained currency in English poetry through Dryden's translations of Ovid and Juvenal as well as Pope's imitations of Horace; see, for example, Dryden's version of Juvenal's Sixth Satire, l. 483, 'There are, who in soft Eunuchs, place their Bliss', and Pope, 'Epistle to Dr Arbuthnot', l. 115, 'There are, who to my person pay their court'. Other poets who exploit the anonymity or distancing inherent in the phrase include Milton (in *Paradise Lost* VI.143), Wordsworth, Keats and Crabbe; and Kipling in his parodies of Horace. (I am indebted to Kenneth Haynes's scholarly research into the English history of the usage.) WE's grammar may be taken to imply, with a kind of airy disdain: 'there are some bad, vulgar or silly girls who can indeed go on laughing all the time'.

10 *Christ stinks of torture*: as early as 1928, WE had observed in a review of the movie *The King of Kings*, '**there seems little religion in a drawn-out sanctimonious gloating over tortures, whose theological interest is not once adumbrated**' (*Cambridge Review*, 19 October 1928, p. 34). Although he wrote about the subject guardedly as an undergraduate, then as later he felt it a repugnant conception of divinity that God the Father should have found it 'satisfying' to witness the appalling crucifixion of his Son. In later years, and especially in *Milton's God* (1961), he called Christianity the religion of the '**Torture-Monster**'; and he stressed in an undated letter to John Wain: '**a belief in a world-spirit is not belief in the Father who could be bought off torturing all mankind by the satisfaction of having his Son tortured to death.**' This verse also admits the sense that the incarnated Christ, being crucified, perished in the flesh.

Cf. the gloss that WE offered in *ST*, apropos what he considers '**the final contradiction**' in Herbert's 'The Sacrifice':

> Lo here I hang, charged with a world of sin
> The greater world of the two . . .

as the complete Christ; scapegoat and tragic hero; loved because hated; hated because godlike; freeing from torture because tortured; torturing his torturers because all-merciful; source of all strength to men because by accepting he exaggerates their weakness; and, because outcast, creating the possibility of society. (p. 269)

It is just such a totalizing ambiguity – wherein '**the two values**' are '**the two opposite meanings defined by the context, so that the total effect is to show a fundamental division in the writer's mind**' (*ST*, p. 225) – that Empson inscribes in l. 10: Christ as both stinking (obnoxious) torturer and as the victim of the torture (stinking because putrescent); as both criminal and scapegoat.

11 *No star . . . entirely waste*: see note to ll. 13–14 of 'Earth has Shrunk in the Wash'. In 1937–8, when WE was composing this poem, he wrote in a fable drafted in China, 'The Royal Beasts':

The justice of God was under a great strain anyway, because the vast majority of men hadn't been given a chance . . . But once there were any number of worlds that Christ hadn't died on and where people couldn't possibly hear the gospel the injustice of the thing would become intolerable. The only way out is to say that Christ does it on all the different worlds, probably does it all the time in several places at once, and that gives you quite a different idea of the historical Jesus. (*RB*, pp. 161–2)

Cf. Aldous Huxley, *The Perennial Philosophy* (1946; London, 1985), pp. 74–5, 78. This line may be construed satirically to mean: 'no star should be altogether written off, even if the news of Christ's redemptive sacrifice has not yet reached it'.

12 *No man is sure he does not need to climb*: cf. WE's controversial exposition, in *ST*, of this crucial passage from Herbert's 'The Sacrifice':

> Man stole the fruit, but I must climb the tree,
> The tree of life, to all but only me.

. . . He climbs the tree to repay what was stolen, as if he was putting the apple back; but the phrase in itself implies rather that he is doing the stealing, that so far from sinless he is Prometheus and the criminal. Either he stole on behalf of man (it is he who appeared to be sinful, and was caught up the tree) or he is climbing upwards, like Jack on the Beanstalk, and taking his people with him back to Heaven. The phrase has an odd humility which makes us see him as the son of the house . . . Jesus seems a child in this metaphor . . . (p. 269)

14 *Gentlemen prefer bound feet and the wasp waist*: WE put on record (in *Milton's God*, p. 111) that it was his own precocious curiosity, his greed for reading, that brought about his first – literal – 'gut reaction': 'When I was a little boy, about eight I think, I read a story in my sister's *Girl's Own Paper* about a catty girl who accused another of tightlacing, whereas the truth was, the story explained, that all these girls, including the catty one, were ill and in pain because they had to tightlace. I crept away sweating with horror, but feeling I had learned an important truth about the way people behave.'

Writing to his mother on 15 March 1938 – when he was likely to have been working on the poem – he would recall too, '**the only thing I heard about China as a child was descriptions of Chinese tortures from poor Miss St George** [presumably a mad or bad governess], **which always made me sick, and I never dared complain about it.**' It upset him just as much that his mother should suffer herself to wear stays at the bidding of her society as that the Christian God should be appeased by the sacrifice of his Son. It was a key article of Empson's rationalist-humanist faith that sadism is the chief evil of mankind.

WE brought together 'bound feet and the wasp waist' in an unpublished radio feature that he drafted while working for the Far Eastern Section of the BBC during World War II. As broadcast on the Home Service on 27 April 1942, this propaganda programme, 'China on the March', was a drastically (though necessarily) cut version of WE's original script and ran for just half an hour. The complete version, which fills 18 pages of single-spaced typescript, is more revealing of WE's personal attitudes, and I shall quote from it here. Drawing almost entirely on his own observations, it takes the form of a supposedly authentic round-table discussion about China's prospects, with contributions from five speakers: an announcer, 'A', who is described as 'romantic' and who 'hasn't been to China'; 'B', a businessman with socialist sympathies employed by a British firm in China; 'C', a good-tempered upperclass figure; 'D', an elderly Protestant missionary; and finally 'E', a 'Teacher from refugee Government university; pro-modern China but less Left-Wing than B' – who speaks more or less directly for WE himself. Even so, WE has the missionary rehearse his own feelings about bound feet; though obviously – given that this is pro-Chinese propaganda, produced in 1942 – he does what he can to put an indemnifying gloss on the horror:

It strikes me that people in England take a rather excessive tone of horror about bound feet in China. The footbinding in China was so bad that it was just about as bad as tightlacing was in England. To be sure there's a class difference; because only the rich women in Europe had the leisure to be tightlaced, whereas any farmer's wife in China could have bound feet. The reason for that is simply that the effects of tightlacing are very much more horrible than the effects of bound feet. If you go in China to any of these Buddhist pilgrimages where people walk up a sacred mountain [see stanza 3 of 'Autumn on Nan-Yüeh'] you'll see plenty of cheerful old women with bound feet carrying a child on their backs, and what they've undertaken is a fairly hearty piece of day-long climbing, and they're doing this for pleasure, it's a holiday. A smart Englishwoman in the nineties with a fifteen inch waist [i.e. Empson's own mother] could never have done that; she was too ill. And of course the purpose behind those two ways of mutilating women, so far as there was any purpose at all, and it wasn't just a crazy fashion, was exactly the same; it made the man feel more safe, because he knew the woman couldn't hit him back. So I don't think we've any call to take a sanctimonious tone about this, and think the Chinese are more cruel than anybody else . . .

That disquisition closes with a passage WE considered true to the 'character' of the unreconstructed old missionary: 'And there's just one last thing that I think it's only fair to say about footbinding. I can by this time well understand why Chinese men invented a rather technical trick for holding Chinese women down. Now that Chinese women have been let loose they do everything, they come everywhere, they shout [me] down whenever I open my mouth. When their feet were bound, you know, they were already handling all the money affairs of every household. I really don't know what more they want.'

See also note to ll. 31–6 of 'Autumn on Nan-Yüeh'.

The Teasers

First published, as 'Poem', without stanza 3, in *Furioso: A Magazine of Verse* 1:2 (New Year Issue, 1940), 13. Stanza 3 was included in *GS*.

WE commented, on *Poems of William Empson*:

I want now to give a poem called 'The Teasers', because I think it was nearly very good, above my level altogether, but I feel its final form is rather a cheat, with a solemn last verse giving a moral which the poem hasn't earned. I wrote a lot of other verses and cut them out, rightly I am sure, but I ought to have got better ones. It is a case where the poetry of conflict becomes rather too flat, just as Shelley's kind of poetry did when he thought it was sufficiently evocative to say 'O World, O Life, O Time' [the opening exclamation of Shelley's 'A Lament' (1821)]. I can't say what this poem means, partly because I don't remember, partly because I don't want to, and partly because it doesn't matter since the poem failed to say it. It is very tempting, in this kind of poetry, to put in a moral at the end in suitably ambiguous terms and hope it will sum up the conflict. Sometimes I think it would be better to cut out the last verse of this poem and sometimes I feel that would only make the poem sillier. But it is a wonderful form; I do not feel humble about that part, only about not filling it enough.

For *Listen* he remarked: 'I wrote more but felt later my grumbles were so trivial that only the general verses would do; it is not meant to be portentous.'

John Wain, in his pioneering essay 'Ambiguous Gifts' (1950), discusses this poem, beginning with mixed praise for the form: 'a blend of originality and imperfection. The first stanza suggests a real lyrical discovery – a metre one does not remember to have seen elsewhere, and a beautiful one.' Yet the rhyme-scheme is not sustained throughout the poem, Wain insists; likewise, the metre wavers between decasyllabics, octosyllabics and a 'shapeless nothing'. The meaning is more enticing, he finds: 'The teasers and dreams are our inward afflictions and aspirations – in Bacon's noble phrase, the "desires of the mind". These desires, though they die and are merged with the undiscriminating stream of existence ("the careful flood" – possibly with an underlying reference to Styx) are still so much more important than the "colder lunacies" – the disciplined and regulated actions – that it is useless to try to evade them (rendering l. 13 [10] as "do not, merely because they flash and die, seek to escape them"). Grouped about this hub of meanings is a riot of subsidiary meanings' (*Penguin New Writing* no. 40, pp. 123–4).

By way of answering and extending Wain's argument, G. S. Fraser, in a volume edited by Wain, devoted a number of pages to 'The Teasers' ('On the Interpretation of the Difficult Poem', pp. 225–34), including a celebration of WE's 'new kind of quatrain, made out of three iambic pentameter lines, by breaking the second line into two short lines at the caesura'; *pace* Wain's criticism of the formal failings of the poem, Fraser argues that its irregularity or inconsistency is a function of '*total* dramatic expressiveness'. With respect to the meaning of the poem, Fraser supports Wain's paraphrase with the suggestion, 'I think he should have emphasized the extent to which we find ourselves thinking at once . . . of dreams in a specifically erotic Freudian sense . . . So one might say that the phrase "the teasers and the dreams" covers the notion of love in the most carnal as well as the most spiritual sense.' Fraser's extended (though still tentative) analysis includes the suggestion: 'The careful flood is sleep, forgetfulness, the mechanism of repression, the death-wish. What they, the frustrated erotic impulses, clamour for is oblivion . . . Behind the mood of this stanza there is either a Buddhistic feeling about Karma, the endless inescapable chain of our desires . . . or Freudian insights built up, a little too speculatively, into Schopenhauerian pessimism.'

Happily, WE was given the chance to review Wain's volume, and he responded by appearing to endorse Fraser's well-meaning critique:

The epilogue by Mr G. S. Fraser 'On the Interpretation of the Difficult Poem' gives some sensible warnings, especially that even an analytical critic must always be prepared to say 'This is no good, but I don't know why.' He gives what he considers a parody-length analysis of four lines from Denham (the standard bit about the river 'without o'erflowing full' ['Cooper's Hill', l. 193]) to show that a great deal can always be said about good verse which doesn't need saying. He then uses a poem by myself called 'The Teasers', in which a metrical invention did not last long enough to make the argument definite (so that a lot of guessing about meaning could go on), to prove that one may need to know 'the cultural context' of an author, 'the kind of influences an author of his class and generation would have come under', but only need to expound it to an audience which does not know it already. The idea of my poem was to go on saying things which applied at once to the high and the low passions, the lusts and the ideals, but other impulses were at work which produced verses I later disliked, and the cut version is inadequate (may I agree with Mr Fraser that I see no point in making 'the flood' mean the act of sex [as Anthony Thwaite had urged in conversation with Fraser (*Interpretations*, p. 229)], above all if the poet is supposed to offer to administer it universally). I think Denham and I were fairly chosen by Mr Fraser as test cases, where the reading public is expected to know the kind of thing that is meant without any exegesis; for instance, bringing up Buddhism as rival to Christianity seemed to me sufficiently obvious there. ('The Calling Trumpets' (1955), in *A*, pp. 140–41)

See Appendix 2, pp. 117–18.

According to anonymous notes pencilled on the flyleaf of a copy of the second impression of *CP* (1956), WE remarked: '**I'm afraid it's rather sententious: would have been much worse if I hadn't cut it down**' (seen in *Ulysses* bookshop, London).

See also the next poem ('Not but they die, the terrors and the dreams'), which is evidently closely related to 'The Teasers' and may be the other '**grumbling**' verses that WE decided to delete from the poem (albeit they are in terza rima). Still, it is not certain that meaning in 'The Teasers' is impossibly opaque, even though the half-lines of each stanza stand for a breach of syntactical ordering which is so firmly marked that the poem seems to segue from one rhetorical gesture to the next. The effect is somewhat portentous (as WE feared), with its provisional intimations being abrupted or stifled in the utterance, until the final (and complete) declaration, which appears to stress the importance of being what Auden elsewhere styled the truly strong man.

W. D. Maxwell-Mahon notes (it is not clear with what authority): 'In its original form, it was an attack on the Christian preoccupation with pain and suffering in salvation and damnation. The "mud" that remained soluble [l. 8] seems to be the liquefaction of St Januarius's blood' ('William Empson: The Development of an Idiom', p. 25). (The relics of St Januarius (Gennaro), who was martyred c. 305, include a glass phial of blood which is alleged to liquefy from time to time, albeit erratically.)

See also Morelli, pp. 124–36; Ricks, pp. 203–4; *TGA*, pp. 201–3.

3 *clamour*: cf. 'Ignorance of Death', l. 9. Given 'dreams' (1), 'flood' (2) and 'rip to blood' (4), as well as WE's fascination with Bacchus (see 'Bacchus'), perhaps compare too Milton, *Paradise Lost*, VII.32–9: 'But drive far off the barbarous dissonance / Of Bacchus and his revellers, the race / Of that wild rout that tore the Thracian bard / In Rhodope, where woods and rocks had ears / To rapture, till the savage clamour drowned / Both harp and voice; nor could the Muse defend / Her son. So fail not thou, who thee implores: / For thou art heavenly, she an empty dream.'

'Not but they die'

First published in *RB*.

These lines are interesting because of their relation to the previous poem, 'The Teasers': they may be either a new poem altogether, though prompted by a fondness for the opening locution 'Not but they die', or a reconstitution of the verses that he cut out of 'The Teasers' (see headnote above). However, 'The Teasers' itself is in a form that WE invented – 'a new kind of quatrain, made out of three iambic pentameter lines, by breaking the second line into two short lines at the caesura', as George Fraser described it – whereas these verses are in terza rima. WE also said that although he wrote additional verses for 'The Teasers' he felt his '**grumbles were so trivial that only the general verses would do**' (*Listen*). It is therefore possible that 'Not but they die, the terrors and the dreams' does comprise those verses including '**other impulses**' which he came to dislike. It could also be the case that on the textual principle of *difficilior lectio* early drafts of 'The Teasers' itself may have opened with the phrase 'Not but they die, the terrors and the dreams' and that Empson introduced the more richly ambiguous term 'teasers' at a late stage, though before initial publication. In any event, these 'additional' verses have less to do with eroticism than with philosophical morality. In so far as they enter ambiguous caveats against self-preservation, for instance, they can be seen to reflect l. 2 of 'Reflection from Anita Loos'. To opt out of taking risks and into the sanity of playing safe may well be equivalent to dying; the healthy mind does not happily settle for ducking out of the action, since a sense of failure and remorse may result from electing the 'short view' (l. 5) which restricts emotional responsiveness. The verses are querulous and sardonic, so making an important comparison to the more firm-minded argument against 'madhouse' in the later 'Let it go'; and it may be that Empson rejected them simply because they appeared to endorse the idea of shrinking from life, whereas they actually incorporate grave misgivings about that policy. Although the rhythm of the verse breaks down by the end, the image of the magnifying glass as being 'able for the flame' affords a powerfully ambiguous conclusion: it suggests both that the man who has opted for short-sightedness (or non-involvement in life) could still start a fire with the burning point of his glasses and also that he reserves to himself the illusory ability to take a good look at the flames (or passions) generated in other people – to whom he stands in the relation of a spectator.

5 *short view*: cf. Pope's *Essay on Criticism*, l. 221–4: 'While from the bounded level of our mind, / Short views we take, nor see the lengths behind; / But, more advanc'd, behold with strange surprize / New distant scenes of endless science rise!' See also Pope, 'Epistle V: To Mr Addison', l. 33.

11–12 *short sight / Is the magnifying glass able for the flame*: apropos William Golding's *Lord of the Flies*, in which Piggy's glasses are famously used to start a fire, T. Hampton has written: 'This is impossible. The lenses used to correct myopia are diverging lenses and so will not bring the rays of the sun to a focus. Had Piggy been long-sighted then he would have been wearing converging lenses, which will focus light to a point' (*Notes and Queries*, July 1956). It seems that WE made the same mistake – many years before Golding.

Advice

First published in GS.

CP: 'Crash' is a pleasant coarse canvas-like material; the only point of the pun is the idea that what seems smashing may turn out quite healthy. It seems the discovery that general paralysis is a final result of syphilis was painful to many old gentlemen who till then had seen nothing scandalous in their complaint. 'We' who didn't do much better are supposed to be both people living now, when the disease is more curable, and politicians, etc., living now, who made a smash-up of international affairs though the issues and dangers were clearer than to the Victorians.

See *TGA*, pp. 204–7.

3 *the first of May*: May Day; Marxist Labour Day.

4-5 *greens. / The lovely grass is brown is dry*: cf. Marvell's 'The Garden', ll. 17–18: 'No white nor red was ever seen / So am'rous as this lovely green.' WE remarks that Marvell's various uses of *green* in his poetry make connections with '**grass, buds, children, an as yet virginal prospect of sexuality, and the peasant stock from which the great families emerge**'. On ll. 17–18 he notes: '**It is his grand attack on gardens which introduces both the connexion through wit between the love of woman and of nature, which is handled so firmly . . .**' Moreover, grass comes '**to be taken for granted as the symbol of pastoral humility**'; and: '**It seems also to be an obscure merit of grass that it produces "hay", which was the name of a country dance, so that the humility is gaiety**' (*Pastoral*, pp. 105–8). The phrase *all greens* (plural) may also imply that all green vegetables, boiled for the dining table (colloquially 'greens'), are regarded as poisonous.

7-8 *rushing on the green one if soon stabbed / Can then go munching on unburst*: if sheep graze lush pastures, especially clover-rich sward, they are in danger of suffering from 'bloat', an emergency condition which occurs when there is a blockage to the free escape (by 'belching') of the gases produced by the fermentation processes. In severe cases, the rumen, on the left flank, has to be punctured with a stylet or perforator called a trocar (or sharp pointed knife) to allow the gas to escape. The most famous case in literature takes place at the end of ch. XXI of Thomas Hardy's *Far from the Madding Crowd* (1874). The phrase *green one* may also have reference to Macbeth's riddling image of the ocean (II.ii.62): 'No, this my hand will rather / The multitudinous seas incarnadine, / Making the green one red.'

10 *The great and good*: 'But when the great and good depart / What is it more than this – / That Man, who is from God sent forth, / Doth yet again to God return? –' (Wordsworth, 'Lines Composed at Grasmere' (1806), ll. 19–22).

10-12 *murderously scabbed . . . spoil no game . . . not known to shame*: we have to rely on WE's note to communicate to us (as the poem fails to do) that these terms refer to the course of syphilitic infection. Only about one in four sufferers develop late symptomatic manifestations, often after many years. However, for the few who develop tertiary-stage symptoms, the disease can be incapacitating and even fatal. The sufferer who is not so severely crippled might yet incur benign late syphilis, which is characterized by ulcerated lesions: WE's phrase 'murderously scabbed' might be taken to refer to such symptoms – and yet, as a description of the symptoms of benign late syphilis (if that is what he really had in mind), it would appear to be a contradiction in terms, indicating a mistaken understanding on his part. Cf. 'Villanelle', ll. 7–8.

The degree to which this is a private (peculiarly private) poem may be indicated by the reference to 'G. P.' (l. 13), which for most readers would automatically mean 'General Practitioner' (the family doctor), and which Empson in his note refers to '**general paralysis**' – the tertiary stage of syphilis. However, 'G. P.' is a reference to the paterfamilias, WE's grandfather John William Empson (1817–93), who was always known as 'G. P.' (an abbreviation of 'Grandpapa'). That being the case, we are left to wonder if young WE had picked up a trace of family gossip to the effect that 'G. P.' had been afflicted in his declining years by syphilis. There are a variety of reasons why 'G. P.' should be thought 'not known to shame' (l. 12), the most obvious being that he neglected his inheritance as squire of Yokefleet Hall in Yorkshire after his marriage. It was only after the death of his wife in 1869 that he resolved to build a new manor house – the present Yokefleet Hall, where WE was to be born – but even then he found he could not bear to live on the dank lands by the River Ouse, so he tried to bully his son into presiding there in his stead. But John Henry, the eldest of five children, killed himself in 1881, and thereafter WE's father Arthur Reginald decided to meet the challenge of occupying the family home in Yorkshire. In 1890, Arthur's wife Laura discovered that her establishment was to be shared with her father-in-law, 'G. P.' This arrangement did not last long, for 'G. P.' was to die in 1893. Accordingly, 'G. P. came late' may refer to the fact that 'G. P.' took his own good time before deciding it would suit him to live off his son at Yokefleet Hall. The extensive lawns at Yokefleet would be made use of for games of bowls or croquet; for the Victorian 'G. P.' there would have been no need to spoil them with a 'dug-out' (l. 11), but the young WE would have known if dug-outs had desecrated the greens during the World War (he was twelve when the war ended).

15–16 *Now is Hell / Knowing worst not known to who can still say Worst*: this grammatically demanding closure conflates several allusions. Marlowe's Mephistopheles famously declares the Ubiquism of Hell (which is an heretical notion, since only God can be ubiquitous): 'Why, this is hell, nor am I out of it' (I.iii.77). Likewise, Milton's Satan speaks of his confounded condition: 'Which way I fly is hell; my self am hell' (*PL* IV. 75); and it is possible that WE's temporal comparatives echo a passage earlier in Book IV, where we learn that 'horror and doubt distract' Satan and 'stir / The hell within him, for within him hell / He brings', and moreover that his conscience 'wakes the bitter memory / Of what was, what is, and what must be / Worse' (18–26), which appears to imply that Satan can experience a sense of *déjà vu* – of going 'back to the future', as we might say. Finally, Edgar expostulates at the sight of his aged, tortured father, 'O gods! Who is't can say "I am at the worst"? / I am worse than e'er I was' (*King Lear*, IV.i.25–6) and later adds: 'And worse I may be yet: the worst is not / So long as we can say "This is the worst."' But WE's 'advice' seems only to add up to an old saw: we may wish to think that the world improves but it doesn't, and it is no use despising our forebears – they may have lived through the worst that we have yet to experience.

Anecdote from Talk

First published in *GS*.

See Willis, p. 380, and *TGA*, pp. 207–8.

China

First published in *GS*.

The second and fourth lines of the first six stanzas were not placed in parentheses in *GS*, so there was virtually no punctuation at line-ends – except for the dashes. This was amended in *CP*: WE wrote to Chatto & Windus: '**I would like to alter the typography of the not very good poem *China* . . . [in order] to make the intention, for what it is worth, much clearer to the eye of the reader.**'

CP: **The two main ideas put forward or buried in this poem now seem to me false, but the thing expresses a kind of ignorant glee which many visitors besides myself have felt about China (about the vitality which lets her keep the beauty of her life however cut up or disorganized, a vitality like a jellyfish, not needing a centre** [WE is actually thinking of the hydra, as described by H. G. Wells, Julian Huxley, G. P. Wells in *The Science of Life* (London, 1931), p. 245]), **and I hope that saves it from being offensive. The ideas are that Japanese and Chinese are extremely alike, since the Japanese are merely a branch of the same culture with a specialized political tradition, and that China can absorb the Japanese however completely they over-run her. This common forecast might work out, grindingly, after a few centuries, but does not make her need for victory now less urgent. However, I felt that while I was trying to help China I need not be solemn about her.**

The prolonged disorder of China made everything feel crumbling like cheese but with an effect of new growth trying to start as in inclement spring weather; 'Nature' is a repulsive deity, but you felt there might be something fertile in this struggle between her two allied fabulous creatures. The ideas of learning wisdom by not worrying and of getting your way by yielding, as in water, of course go a long way back into Chinese thought. The other nations perch about on rigid rules, not using laissez-faire and mutual accommodation. It is the Japanese rather than the Chinese who like being on hands and knees, but I was trying to

mix them up. The Chinese coolie still regards a chair as a not very pleasing luxury, and China like Japan has her boat population all right. The Japanese missed the chair, a late T'ang introduction, because they learned nearly all their customs in middle T'ang. You can trace a chair with crossed legs like a folding stool from Mohenjo-daro [a city on the Indus River in Pakistan] through sixth century Cambodian Buddhist sculpture to a copy of a late T'ang painting, and this probably shows the way the chair came, though not why it was adopted by the Chinese and dropped by the Indians.

The hills bleed in China because the trees have been cut down so that the red earth crumbles and washes away; it is an obvious symbol of disorder. (The re-afforestation plans seem to work as far as they go; I never saw new trees torn out again.) It seems pathetic that the classical literature of China should be interpreted as all about the principles of government, when governing is the one thing she doesn't seem to us good at. Confucius of course believed in ruling by music and by rites. The earliest surviving music is T'ang, preserved by the Japanese, but no doubt the older governmental music felt much as that does; concerned to make you keep your official seat and try hard, with a great deal of waiting for the snap, at the end of a rhythm slower than a heartbeat. Whereas the things the coolies sing to encourage their vast labours (both in Japan and China) are vaguely like Russian folk-music, very beautiful to us and with none of this complete strangeness. A bus is *under-roaded* when the road gives way under it and you spend hours digging in the mud and spreading branches (my friends don't seem to know this word, which I thought was a common one). The grammar is meant to run through alternate lines; I thought this teasing trick gave an effect of the completely disparate things going on side by side.

The next verse brings in again the idea of the separation of the beauty of the coolie life from the official arts (I cut out an intervening verse about Russia, who is an important influence on the country now, because it seemed no use pretending I had anything to say about proletarianism). The paddy fields in hill country, arranged of course to make level patches to hold water, are extremely beautiful, look like microscopic photographs of bees' wings, and seem never to have been treated by all the long and great tradition of Far Eastern landscape painters. And yet they have the same surprising jerking texture as the Great Wall making its way round precipitous hills, and the familiar dragon of the teacups (and by this identity the real line of military or magical defence is the country itself). The whole business of what a culture can become unconscious of and still use is an important and strange one. China from the air is a grand sight, but I meant to leave room in the word *flies* for us scholarly refugees, who were forced to look at the country because we were escaping.

As to the liverfluke, who comes in the *Outline of Life* by Wells, etc. [i.e. *The Science of Life*], its child does not kill the snail and cannot when fully inside be distinguished anywhere from the body of the snail; maybe it is not even cellular.

It only puts red patches containing its eggs on the horns of the snail so that these are seen and eaten by birds. The horns grow again. There is a third generation which gets from the bird to the sheep, and the child of that has to leave the sheep and dissolve itself in a snail. That the thing can play these tricks without having any structure at all is what is so frightening; it is like demoniacal possession. However, to do the Japanese justice, a normal Japanese is still rigidly Japanese after twenty years of living among Chinese in China; no man could be less like this eerie fluke. The idea that China unlike other nations can keep its peculiar life going without a central organization was the excuse for bringing it in.

Willis observes: 'Employing a long measure of iambic quatrains, Empson chooses the familiar heroic ballad measure, but he skilfully introduces variety to avoid a static quality. The first and last stanzas break the tetrameter metre with pentameter second and fourth lines . . . Empson also varies the customary rhyme scheme by maintaining the a-line throughout each stanza (abab, acac, etc.), thereby providing an interlinked effect unusual to the ballad' (pp. 381–2).

See also Morelli, pp. 122–4; *TGA*, pp. 208–12.

1 *The dragon hatched a cockatrice*: Isaiah 59: 5 (King James Version) reads: 'They hatch cockatrice' eggs, and weave the spider's web: he that eateth of their eggs dieth, and that which is crushed breaketh out into a viper' (all other translations refer not to the cockatrice but to a basilisk). The opening suggests Japan is the grim offspring of, or at least culturally derivative from, China – whose symbol is the dragon. Chang Monlin, Chancellor of the refugee National Peking University when WE taught there, observes: 'The offshoots of Chinese civilization in Japan were of the Tang era (618–905) . . . Dancing, music, the arts, ways of living, the pronunciation of Chinese words and China's martial spirit, all of Tang origin, found living embodiment in the Island Empire of the Rising – or hereafter the Setting – Sun. If you want to know something about the Tang civilization, go to Japan. Upon a foundation of Tang culture Japan made herself great by the absorption of Western science' (*Tides from the West: A Chinese autobiography* (New Haven, 1947), p. 230).

2 *Cheese . . . mites*: the cheese mite goes by the name *Acarus domesticus*.

6 *solid ground*: cf. 'Aubade', l. 15.

9 *Red hills bleed naked into screes*: cf. this observation by Hugh W. Farley, who toured China just two years before WE arrived there: 'Forbidding and unpleasant was the dark reddish brown, even brilliant red in parts, of the clay and wasteland where it showed naked on the hilltops far and wide' ('The Sacred Mountains of China: Nan Yu Shan, Hunan's sacred Taoist peak', *China Journal* 23 (1935), 217).

10–17 *The classics . . . teach the nations how to rule . . . They rule by music and by rites . . . / The serious music strains to squeeze*: in his feature programme 'China on the March', broadcast by the BBC Home Service on 27 April 1942 (see note to 'Reflection from Anita Loos', l. 14), WE remarked in the voice of the 'Teacher from refugee Government university' (i.e. himself):

You know Confucius said the empire was ruled by music and ceremonies. The kind of music he meant, that ruled the empire, was based on rhythms slower than a heartbeat. Oddly enough, the only people who still preserve it are the Japanese . . . You sit up straight in your official chair and try hard, waiting for the snap at the end of the beat. And the singing voice that goes with this music is a strained voice, outside its natural compass. It is not false, it is heroic; it's a very fine musical tradition, and works particularly well for ballet.

Those remarks rehearse the ideas he had already published in 'Ballet of the Far East' (*Listener*, 7 July 1937), in which he tied the differences between Western and Far Eastern music to a major difference in religious perspective:

In the West, the supreme God is a person, in the East he is not; their ideas about man follow from that . . . It is much the most fundamental line of division between the civilizations of the world, and we need to understand the people on the other side . . .
    The Noh theatre is fantastically slow . . . The music has a direct strain on the nerves. It is based on eight slow beats, taken separately by different percussive instruments. Now the scientists seem to agree that we feel differently about rhythm according as it is slower or faster than a heartbeat, and nearly all European music goes faster than a heartbeat. Our limit of slowness is the dead march, which goes about the pace of the heart. This music goes slower . . . All our instruments are meant to go bouncing along very frankly like a nice well-intentioned dog; in their music you sit still and strengthen yourself like a cat. There are long squalling noises that hold you up during the wait for the next beat, and at last the beat comes with a snap, as if you had stretched an elastic till it broke . . . The fundamental difference in all these things goes back to the view taken of God and of the individual man. A rhythm quicker than the heartbeat is one that you seem to control, or that seems controlled by some person; the apparently vast field of our music is always the frankness of the West, always the individual speaking up. Music based on rhythms slower than the heartbeat can carry a great weight of emotion and even of introspection, and of course incidental runs go quick, but it remains somehow impersonal. (*A*, pp. 577–8)

But perhaps WE's authentic response to the 'serious music' of China, the governing-class music that 'strains to squeeze', is recorded in a piece of journalism that he sketched while on the sacred mountain of 'Nan-Yueh' (see 'Autumn on Nan-Yueh'); this gives a more graphic sense of his visceral aversion to the official tunes, and it is echoed in the poem:

The man who sings Chinese music (surely quite badly) with an instrument made for the purpose gave me at first an idea that I loathed all that the Far East has put into music; the pleasure in extreme passive states of strain (anybody agrees with Arnold about the lyric of suffering once he gets outside them), the infantilism sustained with such eerie complacence, and the caterwauling that bullies and manhandles the hearer into sharing this condition of giant feebleness – I thought it all very dislikeable; but then a man began reciting what appeared to be English verse in a low tone and extremely sentimental voice, and there is no doubt that English poetry touches worse depths than the music of the East.

18 *The angel coolies sing like us*: in 'China on the March', 'E' observes:

Educated Chinese have always despised the coolie singing. The old official class's music was entirely different and to our ears much less beautiful . . . But all the time in China, underneath this very strained stuff, the coolie tradition of singing was going on, and that doesn't feel queer to us, like the official singing does, at all. It is moving on direct impulse, and the main reason for the singing is to make every man pull at the same time, and also to cheer him up when he's nearly dead beat. And the real problem for . . . the educated Chinese, is not joining on to Western culture but joining on to their own coolie culture. [The writer] Lin Yu Tang said a good thing there: he said that before the Chinese had suffered together they couldn't sing together.

However, not to leave any doubts in his listeners' minds as to the stalwart and progressive cohesiveness of the Chinese, 'E' is given the last word: '**But they're doing it in China. They are singing.**'

21–4 *The paddy-fields . . . contour of their walls*: in 1938, when the refugee National Southwest Associated University moved to a small town called Mengtzu in Yunnan province, WE would often venture out for country walks. In an undated draft letter to Hayward, he described one particularly delightful foray in terms which exactly match this stanza of the poem:

when I got just over this bare rocky series of fatuous rolling hills there turned out to be a little valley over the top, rich with trees, a whole village snug inside them, a lake or large pond with a sturdy temple at the far side . . . and coming down to the side into the lake the real hanging gardens of the mountain paddy fields, curved like the lines of bees' wings under the microscope, high thin standing rice at each stage that you could see down to the water through, a delicate pale acid green, and that strange effect of massive engineering or 'structural' palatial architecture (the terraces are very deep) – all in a little hollow just hidden from us that happens to have water, only a dimple if we could see it on our Siberian view of hills. It felt like coming home, I mean it gave me a nostalgia for the attractive parts of China and started me remembering my travels instead of daydreaming.

See also 'Chinese Bandits', *Strengths of Shakespeare's Shrew*, pp. 187–9.

As WE's *CP* note makes clear, however, at the back of the poem is a political proposition of a dual kind: the finale speaks for a devout hope that China might always be able to absorb those who invade it; but in this penultimate stanza it takes the form of a wish that high and low should come together, communicate with one another, comprehend one another and even sustain a new democracy. Once again, WE's spokesman in the radio programme 'China on the March' speaks (albeit with a fair deal of frustration) to this mystical-political aspiration: his Chinese colleagues and students, he laments,

will not feel the beauty of so many things in the coolie life. It's the foreigner who feels that. All their idea of beauty belongs to an ultraspecialized tradition handed down among the governing class who are literate, and it's got pretty tired. It's an extraordinary thing, but they've never even painted the rice fields. You know the Chinese started landscape painting about a thousand years before anybody else. What they painted was wild mountain country, where the gentleman wanted to be because he was sick of his government office. Now I've flown across various parts of China, and of course what you see is what anybody could see from hills before the aeroplane arrived . . . It looks like the dragon on our teacups and the willow-pattern on our plates . . . What you're seeing, chiefly, are the banks holding the water between one ricefield and the next; of course the water has to be saved very carefully and made to trickle through from one level to the next, and these banks are following the contours of the hills. They go jerking and coiling about exactly like the Great Wall of China . . . no Chinese painter has yet painted the ricefields. That's a fact about politics. You won't have a working democratic movement in China till they do paint the ricefields. Just the same thing comes up about the singing.

However, with respect to his gloss – the failure of the governing classes to appreciate the landscape of terraced rice-fields – and its political implications, he was too hasty to construct his thesis before he had looked fully into the subject. The terraced paddy fields would have been introduced into such a landscape only when the population outgrew flat arable lands; and moreover, as the late Professor Yang Zhouhan (one of WE's pupils) remarked: 'Even if they existed when painters of later dynasties were active, they would not have painted them because they were not part of Nature and smacked of "this-worldliness" ' (letter to Haffenden, 22 July 1985).

25–8 *A liver fluke . . . all histories*: the strong element of implied political mysticism may appear to be contradicted by the other main political argument put forward, derived from a selective interpretation of the classic treatise known as the *Lao Tzu* (which WE had studied in Arthur Waley's translation). Like many visitors to China, WE admitted to what he called an **'ignorant glee'** about the vitality of its people and accordingly persuaded himself that the pliancy of their temperament would readily allow China to **'absorb the Japanese however completely they over-run her'**. That fragile trust or supposition is underscored in this final stanza of the poem, which features a metaphor taken from the life-cycle of the liver-fluke. The suggestion is that however much the Japanese parasite might infest the host,

China could digest the intruder and reconstitute itself much as before. WE here misremembers both the source of his information and the specific kind of liver-fluke in question. *Distomum macrostomum* does not invade sheep but gets itself repulsively transferred from snail to bird and back again to snail, where it develops into 'a shapeless radiating web of living tissue . . . which becomes so mixed up with [the snail's] tissues that it is difficult or impossible for a dissector to separate it completely away' (H. G. Wells, Julian Huxley, G. P. Wells, *Science of Life*, p. 952). Still, WE's forgetfulness does no damage to the general point.

The argument 'buried' in the poem relies on the axiom that the meek gain all the more strength from their submissiveness: that in the longer term the Chinese people would be the ultimate victors even if conquered by the Japanese. But it needs to be recognized that such a notion can be attributed only to Taoism, whereas Confucianism had always been the dominant ideology in Chinese moral philosophy. WE was to debate his view of Taoism in a later year, in correspondence with Professor Chien Hsueh-hsi, who persuasively argued that Waley's mystical and quietistic version of the *Lao Tzu* had travestied the realism of its philosophy. The Taoistic teaching of peace or union with all 'is far from "mystical",' Professor Chien stressed; 'it can be reached by simple reasoning upon commonly-accessible experience.' Waley's version had grafted on to Taoism two inapplicable motifs: a yoga-quietism and a decided antagonism towards 'realists'. This poem, in appealing to such a questionable version of the *Lao Tzu*, borrowed its argumentative burden from Waley – but in doing so, WE relied more on his moral faith in the Chinese he knew personally than on any argument for quietism or pacifism, which he never credited. In any event, the fact that during the course of its long history the Chinese Empire had absorbed successive conquerors was due to a variety of causes other than merely yielding. As WE later acknowledged, his understanding of China at the time of writing the poem was faulty. The argument of the poem was put in question by the events of the summer of 1938, when WE witnessed China's unprecedented upsurge of nationalist feeling – its collective if uncoordinated determination not to yield but to fight back.

Autumn on Nan-Yüeh

First published in *GS*.

CP: **Nan-yueh is a sacred mountain about seventy miles southwest of Changsha; the Arts Departments of the Combined Universities were housed on it for a term in 1937, and then we moved further back to Yunnan. The 'two fates' are the opposed ideals of personal immortality and of extinguishing yourself or merging into a world soul; the mountain was a god before it became the cradle of what the Japanese call the Zen sect. Those of the beggars who are too deformed to walk** are carried up in baskets and placed along the pilgrims' route up the mountain. 'Flying' of course is being used here for escaping ordinary troubles as well as other things, and the pilgrimage is a holiday. The abbot of the monastery on the summit might quite naturally have passed Greats, though I don't know that he literally has done. *Like a gong* maybe reads as rather too easy a sentiment. The claim is that public opinion in England during this decade has been commonly right while independent of its political leaders and the machinery of propaganda; e.g. the outcry over the Hoare-Laval pact and the swing-round of the Trade Unions to rearmament then. Chinese wines aren't drunk except during meals; the point about Tiger Bone was that I found it made a good drink to sit over when drowned in hot water. The tiger bones in it are supposed to make you brave. I hope the gaiety of the thing comes through; I felt I was in very good company.

In a draft letter (14 July 1938) to Robert Herring (editor of *Life & Letters Today*), WE wrote, presumably with reference to this poem: 'The poem I sent you from Nanyueh I remember now as the kind of badtempered letter that makes people you are fond of quarrel with you. My attempts at getting out of the narrowness of my early verse are painfully halfbaked. The fact is my opinions are halfbaked; it seems to shine through.' Then he proceeded with this brilliantly double-edged observation: 'Your paper I think is extremely good. I used like other readers to think it was a valuable rag-bag, open to decent stuff of all sorts, but now that it is defining itself I feel less able to write for it. You want a more coherent politics than mine' (Empson Papers).

Why *Life & Letters* rejected the poem is not known; but in any event this poem is light verse, with a wonderful range from the silly to the sublime, and from alcohol to apotheosis, owing more to Byron than to the social bards of the 1930s. Yet WE took rejection as a rebuke for his failure as a political poet: he wrote to Michael Roberts on 4 December 1938: 'I am afraid I have cut myself off from Life and Letters by sending them a long poem on China which wasn't sufficiently Leftwing . . . Very proper to have politics important now but suggests England is a bit grim.' He wrote to Roberts again just two months later, expressing a sort of insouciance about his own work which would not serve to inspire much enthusiasm in the recipient: 'I enclose a long poem which they [*Life & Letters*] didn't want; seems to me now too glib, but Richards liked it. You might run across some paper that would care to publish it' (Empson Papers).

In a preface to GS he referred to it as 'a somewhat prattling long poem written under refugee conditions in Hunan'.

The historical background to the poem is as follows. Following the outbreak of the invasion of China on 7 July 1937, the Japanese worked with ferocious efficiency, encountering only a poorly organized resistance as their land forces attained their military objectives and won control of towns, railways and highways; and their aircraft held sway in the sky. Vast numbers of people from the Eastern seaboard hastily abandoned their occupied homelands and started to migrate inland. Wherever possible, factories and industrial plant were transported in what became one of the most astonishing evacuations of modern times.

The Japanese nurtured a particular loathing for the great universities of northern China, which had long denounced their territorial annexations and corrupt dominance. In the first fierce wave of the war the invaders took their revenge: 91 colleges and universities were either destroyed or forced to shut down by the end of the first year of the war. However, while the Japanese overran or smashed the fabric and facilities of the universities, they could not contain the movements of their personnel; considerable numbers of staff and students quickly joined the hegira out of the occupied territories. No fewer than fifty-two educational institutions fled to the Chinese interior; twenty-five others took refuge in the foreign concessions or in Hong Kong.

Peking National University and Tsing Hua University, together with Nan-kai University, reconvened in the city of Changsha, Hunan province, for the start of the autumn term on 1 November. There were about 1,500 students to begin with, but nearly 500 subsequently left, the majority to join the forces of Mao Tse-tung or to attend a course in war-time education and Marxist ideology at the Communist Resistance University in Yenan; the remainder to enlist in the war area service corps attached to the Nationalist Army. In Changsha, the universities were amalgamated under the title of the Temporary University (*Chang-sha lin-shih ta-hsueh*, or *Linta* for short). As WE reported, **'people got there across the vague Japanese lines with the clothes they stood up in and maybe some lecture notes; a fairly dangerous business, and you certainly couldn't take a library. It is curious to think of Oxford and Cambridge arriving together in Barrow under those conditions, and not quarrelling too much to combine'** ('A Chinese University', p. 239).

But a shortage of living space in the city necessitated a dispersal of the assembled body. Members of the School of Arts were taken by bus on a one-day journey to the village of Nan-Yüeh (Nanyu) – the Chinese characters for *Nan-Yüeh* mean 'South Mountain' – at the foot of the Heng Mountains, which make up an unbroken chain of 72 peaks. Just a few weeks earlier, in company with I. A. and Dorothea Richards, WE had clambered up the gentle and twisting path to the highest peak of the range, the most sacred of the southern holy summits, Tu Yun Feng: it takes only about four hours to get from village to summit. (See the account of that trip through southwest China by Victor Purcell, *Chinese Evergreen* (London, 1938), pp. 119–35, in which WE is inevitably 'Dudley': Empson thought it a 'good book'.)

Rosalie Chou – the writer Han Suyin – who joined another wave of refugees that lodged for a while at Nan-Yüeh just a year later, wrote in a letter (28 October 1938) that the countryside was 'wonderful'; and in *Birdless Summer*, the third book of her autobiography, she evoked the village in these terms: 'The great north-south Imperial highway paved with enormous blocks of limestone runs through it, for Nanyu was a fair centre on the road from Canton in the south to the Yangtze River cities – a road used by cavalrymen of the dynasties and the chariots of officials for centuries – and a place of pilgrimage. The beautiful Sung dynasty bridge which spanned the lovely river, with its tributary torrents leaping from the mountains, had seen the tribute of salt and grain pass over it, and silk for the Imperial Courts in Peking from the fertile provinces of central China, and fighting men and refugees had walked it many times. It had served the cohorts of the peasant uprisings in Taiping days, those peasant fighters marching up the road through Nanyu to Changsha and onwards to take Wuhan, a century ago' (London, 1968, 1982), p. 46).

In November 1937 the School of Arts of the Temporary University took up its temporary residence in the simple buildings of a missionary Bible Institute situated in a grove of pine trees. Empson aptly described the place as a kind of 'fundamentalist Simla' (draft of a 'Letter from China'). If the quarters were cramped and unsophisticated, the mountain scenery provided a spectacularly picturesque compensation. The Taoist temple at the summit of the sacred mountain could be reached over a distance of about twenty kilometres. The slopes are clothed with azaleas, and with groves of camphor trees, willow, pomegranate and pine; five rivers, including the Siang River, can be sighted from the summit. WE was to observe, in a draft of a 'Letter from China': 'The rule for a sacred mountain is that (first) it must be isolated so that people from all round can see the home town (second) that it must do the queer trick of seeming much bigger than it is . . . Sure enough, it gave me real delight, when I first trotted over this mountain, to find that I could get almost immediately over the shoulder into the next of the enormous gorges. The heart of magic is the sense of power; and any tolerable walker gets a sense of power here.' He found the landscape entrancing, 'airy and cosy, and the country . . . more beautiful every time you looked out of the window. The fog which envelops Hunan in the winter was to us merely a change in the view, and sometimes it was like the more improbable effects of Chinese painting, for instance the fog which is a mere flat white band with a round end, in the middle distance.' (See also Hugh W. Farley, 'The Sacred Mountains of China: Nan Yü Shan, Hunan's Sacred Taoist Peak', *China Journal* 23 (1935), 213–19; and Mary Augusta Mullikin and Anna M. Hotchkis, *The Nine Sacred Mountains of China: an illustrated record of pilgrimages made in the years 1935–1936* (Hong Kong, 1973), chapter IV, 'Heng-shan or Nan-yüeh', pp. 41–50.)

The sojourn at Nan-Yüeh was to last little over two months, from November 1937 till February the following year. Although some of the faculty found it too exacting to teach from memory, WE believed he gained enormously from the experience – his students felt stimulated by his professionalism, his mental alertness and his gift for treating them as intellectual equals – and he developed a deep sense of solidarity with his colleagues. Thenceforth he would always think of the mountain as his ideal of the academic community. Terribly isolated and poorly supplied with resources, the whole faculty of scholar-gypsies developed an extra-ordinary sense of purpose: though refugees in status, they were able to define their wartime role as maintaining an intellectual and civil leadership.

'A fashion has already got about of saying that no work was done on Nanyueh,' WE was to write in his notes in 1939. 'We just ticked over. I resent this very much.' Certainly he and his colleagues kept up their teaching to the best of their abilities; and somehow they were also able to produce a remarkable amount of scholarly and critical writing. WE himself continued to draft the essays that would eventually become *The Structure of Complex Words*; Jin Yue Lin (see note to ll. 41–2 below) completed his book *On the Tao*; Feng Youlan, China's most celebrated neo-Confucian scholar, finished the *New Li Xue*; Tang Yongtong completed the first part of his *History of Chinese Buddhism*. Other faculty members included the historian Wu Han; the poet Bian Zhilin; the legendary poet, artist, scholar and political activist Wen Yiduo (who was to be murdered by the Guomind-ang in 1946); and the logical positivist Hong Qian (1909–1992), who was to become China's most esteemed contemporary philosopher. (See also WE, 'A Chinese University' (1940), in *The Strengths of Shakespeare's Shrew*, pp. 190–94; and Pei-sung Tang, 'Chinese Universities on the March', *American Scholar* 10:1 (1940–41), 41–8.)

Willis (pp. 387–98) notes among many other matters: 'Empson seems to have invented the rhyme scheme as well as the stanzaic pattern . . . The metre is fairly regular iambic tetrameter rhymed carefully in repeating patterns of four lines: abcb / abcb / abcb. Extra a and b lines are added for the fourteen-line stanzas which superficially resemble sonnets. The seventeenth stanza alone rhymes ababab' (pp. 388–89). See also *TGA*, pp. 212–19.

EPIGRAPH: perhaps inevitably, given that the universities lacked a library, WE quotes from memory (though it has to be conceded that he would typically choose to quote from memory even when books were available). Taken from Yeats's poem 'The Phases of the Moon' (*The Wild Swans at Coole*, 1919); Michael Robartes is speaking:

> The soul remembering its loneliness
> Shudders in many cradles; all is changed.
> It would be the world's servant, and as it serves,
> Choosing whatever task's most difficult
> Among tasks not impossible, it takes
> Upon the body and upon the soul
> The coarseness of the drudge.

> OWEN AHERNE.   Before the full
> It sought itself and afterwards the world.

ROBARTES. Because you are forgotten, half out of life,
And never wrote a book, your thought is clear.
Reformer, merchant, statesman, learned man,
Dutiful husband, honest wife by turn,
Cradle upon cradle, and all in flight and all
Deformed, because there is no deformity
But saves us from a dream.   (ll. 88–102)

3–4 '*Turn but a stone*' . . . *Winged angels crawling that could sting*: Francis Thompson, in 'The Kingdom of God', ll. 13–16, averred that the kingdom of heaven is at hand – we are of its element, if only we are open to it – 'The angels keep their ancient places;– / Turn but a stone, and start a wing! / 'tis ye, 'tis your estrangèd faces, / That miss the many-splendoured thing' (*The Works of Francis Thompson: Poems*, vol. II (London, 1913), p. 226).

7 *Scorners eternal of the ground*: 'Better than all measures / Of delightful sound – / Better than all treasures / That in books are found – / Thy skill to poet were, thou Scorner of the ground!' (Shelley, 'To a Sky-Lark', ll. 96–100).

13 *I have flown here, part of the way*: since arriving in China at the end of August, WE had travelled with I. A. and Dorothea Richards on a journey from the heart of China down to Indo-China (see also John Paul Russo, *I. A. Richards: His Life and Work* (London, 1989), pp. 422–6). Then, at the beginning of October, he went with them back into China, specifically to visit Yunnan province – where he would return the following year when the refugee universities were thrust back. (See also 'Letter from China', in *Strengths of Shakespeare's Shrew*, pp. 183–6.) In mid-October, WE left the Richardses to make his way back to the central provinces. Dorothea Richards noted in her journal on 19 October 1937: 'Heard Bill's car leave at 5 am & saw at 6.10 his plane fly off to Chengtu – from there he goes by bus to Chunking & by river to Changsha' (Old Library, Magdalene College, Cambridge). Regrettably, Russo seriously misrepresents the situation: 'Realizing (well before Richards) the hopelessness of the political situation, Empson now decided to leave China[,] and Dorothea duly noted his plane taking off on 19 October' (*I. A. Richards*, pp. 425–6).

29–30 *Sacred to Buddha, and a god / Itself*: Nan-Yüeh is, properly speaking, sacred to Taoism; see Farley, 'The Sacred Mountains of China', p. 214:

While remembering that Nan Yü Shan is one of the five sacred Taoist peaks of China, it may be well to realize that here, as at most of the other sacred mountains, Taoist and Buddhist are closely intermingled. Indeed, this is well exemplified by the facts that Nan Yü Miao [the imposing temple in the village of Nan-Yüeh] is now completely Buddhist and that at most of the other temples and monasteries, too, Buddhism, rather paradoxically, predominates in this Taoist *sanctum sanctorum*.

31–6 *deformities to give ... in baskets or in crates*: every year, throughout the pilgrimage season of August–October, thousands of pilgrims climbed the path eleven hundred feet from the village to the summit of the Holy Mountain of Nan Yü Shan, at a height of 4,500 feet above sea level. Many were so distressingly deformed that they needed to be carried up in baskets. In a typescript draft of a 'Letter from China' WE candidly observed:

The main way up, which is all that most people take, has the most grisly collection of beggars I have yet seen. My own brand of charity would not dream of extending itself to anything so far removed from humanity. It is startling then, after you have passed these awful monstrosities carried up to their posts in baskets, or (if they see no hope in you) even as you pass, to hear them yelling and teasing at each other between baskets with the entire and indestructible gaiety of the Chinese people. It is not half so surprising to hear that they are for the moment happy as to hear that they are not mad. (Empson Papers)

(Cf. note to l. 14 of 'Reflection from Anita Loos'.) Purcell would find the same reason to remember the beggars on the mountain: 'Their diseases plumbed the utmost depths of pathology – or of invention. There were ulcers, bubos, skin eruptions, running sores, and every exaggeration of deformity ... To relieve this misery would require the resources of a government' (*Chinese Evergreen*, p. 132).

38 *The topmost abbot has passed Greats*: '**The other startling thing about the straight walk along the holy path is to find genuine civilization in the Buddhist monastery at the top,**' WE added to the draft of a 'Letter from China'. The monastery at the head of the mountain is called Shang Fêng Ssu: a Buddhist monastery on a mountain sacred to Taoism. It is WE's fancy that the cultivated abbot had passed 'Greats'; Purcell found him simply 'spruce' (*Chinese Evergreen*, p. 132).

41–2 *this room / Beds four and as I write holds two*: WE shared his room with one of China's foremost philosophers, Chin Yue Lin (Jin Yue Lin, or Y. L. Jin), who, like the majority of the faculty, had studied in the USA and England: they enjoyed swapping anecdotes about Wittgenstein. Professor Jin was perturbed only by WE's shameless but comfortable indifference to washing himself or his clothing. 'We had to force him to wash,' he recalled for me in April 1984. He thought WE otherwise a delightful companion, with 'very good spirit', but preoccupied to the point of eccentricity. WE was to write home in the summer of 1938: '**I am friends again with the professor of philosophy here (I was fool enough to say what I thought of his philosophy)**' (undated letter to his mother; Empson Papers).

43–4 *They shudder ... encourage 'flu*: autumn and winter brought on cold, wet weather for which the Bible School had not been designed: the buildings had no fireplaces or chimneys – '**a curious thing**', as WE remarked. Staff and students tried to keep warm by burning charcoal on iron plates, an activity so perilous that at least four students suffered from carbon monoxide poisoning – '**it turns the**

blood cherry pink,' WE observed with scientific detachment – and had to be revived with artificial respiration. At the very end of his stay WE acquired the luxury of a single room, but it made him all the more apprehensive about the real danger of asphyxiating himself with no one at hand. He adopted Chinese padded clothing but found that it made him sweat heavily during any sort of exercise, even typing or eager talking. The weight of clothing slowed him down, and the effect led him to think that he had discovered this partial if still puzzling insight into the Chinese mentality:

Life inside a bundle, cuddling the fingers, has to be conducted below what I consider par; you aim at keeping passive; the well-known inscrutable calm of the East begins to crop up. The wisdom of making few the desires becomes particularly obvious; you eat less, sleep less, and get less done. One might count it as one of the forces against individualism, because no man feels unique while he is just ticking over. The only thing that doesn't seem to fit this theory is the word 'bombast', which is easy here to explain on the blackboard; the Elizabethans called padded blank verse lines after their padded clothes, such as we all wear here, and the Elizabethans were about as rowdy, individualistic, and above par as any people you could name. (Empson Papers)

45–52 *The abandoned libraries . . . a poem as it grew*: 'The famine for books here is a remarkable spectacle,' WE recorded.

The universities of course had to leave their libraries, such of them as were not destroyed. For that matter most of the professors arrived with only the clothes they wore, and the students that get through are being lent money by their universities. I thought it was going to be a compound for professors, but there are too many students to handle with comfort. I can't help feeling that there had better be hardly any books, as long as they have to read after dark by nightlights and coastguard lanterns, or they would go blind. And it is a good joke, as far as it goes, to see the professors lecturing from memory. I know enough verse by heart, but I can't do prose.

The students were staggered by WE's ability to reproduce on his typewriter enormous quantities of poetry, and it is certainly true that he had an extraordinary facility for remembering lyric poetry in particular. His feats of memorial reconstruction are remembered to this day: they are a signal part of the folklore of the refugee universities. He modestly recalled in his Inaugural Lecture at Sheffield University in 1953:

It didn't upset the Chinese lecturers as much as it would most, because they have a long tradition of knowing a standard text by heart. I was well thought of because I could type out from memory a course of reading in English poetry, but this was praised more because it was good going for a foreigner than because it would have been remarkable for a Chinese.

Actually we did have an anthology of prose essays which could be typed out for them to do their Composition Class with [it included essays by Lytton Strachey, Aldous Huxley, Virginia Woolf and T. S. Eliot] . . . but apart from that there were really hardly any books.

And in the same lecture he graciously turned his own high capability into a tribute to his students and colleagues:

I thought the results we were getting by this method were strikingly good. No doubt the chief reason was that the standard of the students was very high; I was seeing the last of the great days of the effort of China to digest the achievements of Europe, when a well educated Chinese was about the best educated man in Europe. My colleagues habitually talked to each other in a jumble of three or four languages, without affectation, merely for convenience, using rather more English if they remembered I was listening; and of course a thorough grounding in Chinese literature would be taken for granted.

So much is true; but as so often the legend has tended to outrun even the remarkable facts, though it should also be said that nobody has been guilty of deliberate exaggeration. Some of his former students (many of whom were to become distinguished professors in their own right) recalled for instance that WE typed out the whole of *Othello* from memory (Professor Li Fu-ning, for example, in 'William Empson As I Remember Him – A Young Teacher of English in China' dated 26 January 1986; confirmed in interview with Li Fu-ning, 16 March 1984); whereas WE's own jottings disclose: '**A charitable man lent me a blinding 1850 complete Shakespeare, which makes me safe for one course. It turned out to have a loose flyleaf in it with autographs of both Swift and Pope, rather stirring on the sacred mountain**' (typescript draft of a 'Letter from China'). To cite such an admission is not to minimize his achievement, only to keep it in proportion.

Being obliged to reconstruct a work of literature from memory has '**a great effect,**' WE believed, '**in forcing you to consider what really matters, or what you already do know if you think, or what you want to get to know when you can.**' It is well known that he customarily quoted poetry from memory when writing his criticism, a procedure which might suggest either that he felt indifferent to details of phraseology and syntax or – what is much more likely – that he had taken the poetry to heart in every sense. On Christmas Eve, for example, when Professor Jin Yue Lin spontaneously sang a lovely German carol, WE felt genuinely annoyed with himself for not being able to reproduce all the words of 'Venite Adoremus'. '**We ought to be taught things by heart as children much more than we are,**' he wrote the very next day; '**the craving for quantity misleads all educators paid by result, and if you can select the right poem the other poems in the same style will be picked up as obvious; but then maybe nobody can do the selection**' (typescript notes, Christmas 1937).

In a draft fragment of this fourth stanza, WE dubs himself and his Chinese colleagues 'our forcedly pedantic crew'.

60–63 *Thank God I left . . . coolies beat their wives*: Peter Walsh, in Virginia Woolf's *Mrs Dalloway* (1925) – when reflecting with satisfaction that during his long years in the colonies he had escaped the snobbery, stuffiness and gossip of little England – 'thanked God he was out of that pernicious hubble-bubble if it were only to hear baboons chatter and coolies beat their wives'.

69–78 *As for the Tiger Bone . . . drink for getting near*: evidence for the fact that he found 'Tiger Bone' a good drink for 'getting near' his fellows is given in the notes he jotted after a feast at the erstwhile Hunan Bible Institute at Nan-Yüeh: 'The start was depressing to a hungry man, as would hors d'oeuvres if you had no security about what was coming; four dishes all fine and fantastic flavours, but none eatable in bulk; however as the food kept rolling in and [I] got down the Tiger Bone it became clear that this feast was all right. It was very fine indeed; I hope it goes on the messbill and isn't somebody's ruinous and unthanked gift.' On another occasion, however, he found that Tiger Bone was of little help in treating an appalling attack of nerves; these handwritten diary-notes date from Christmas 1937:

This evening I got an attack of neurotic fear, the first for some time, certainly the first since leaving England. I was reading Emerson about the English, which was in the library and might have been amusing, but the excessive praise of England and the feeling of inferiority about America, and the tiring quality of the Cultured style, all turned out very depressing . . . But the whole trouble with neurotic fear is that it isn't fear of anything you can tell yourself about. In myself it seems to appear in a reasonable manner, when I have a long prospect before me of a poor kind of life, but you can't make it into straightforward fear of that, as you would give yourself promises to take care about that, and feel better. I got a bad attack in my first year in Japan [1931–2] – so bad, that it was surprising, after I had got all right again, when some detail brought back the state of mind I was taking for granted. I drank a good deal of the unpleasant Tiger Bone, but alcohol is curiously bad at melting the firm stone in the heart – it doesn't even make you expansively dismal.

He goes on quickly to try to buck himself up with a version of 'thinking on the frosty Caucasus': 'But goodness me, there was a period in Japan when I had two houses and three rooms in different hotels, and spent my time going from one to another searching for a moment when I could escape fear with my hands shaking too much to handle my chopsticks. China doesn't give you [fear] on the same scale.'

In one of his draft 'Letters from China' he would admit too: 'now that we have been moved down [from mountain to village, towards the close of the period at Nan-Yüeh] I have a room to myself and can hear people talking Chinese all the time in all the other rooms, and that is a strain on the nerves. I write this after comforting the nerves with the brew called Tiger Bone, obtained from the village round the temples.' (A yellow-tiled temple built in the Ming period, Nan-Yüeh Miao, dominates the village.)

79–80 *Verse has been lectured . . . / Against Escape and being blah*: see 'Your Teeth are Ivory Towers', l. 8 and note. The onomatopoeic *blah* (originally US slang) means 'nonsense, humbug' (*OED*); perhaps WE has in mind the critical reception of his own early poetry; but more probably he is thinking of the 'blah' of the Surrealist movement (see l. 111).

83–6 *an aeronautic feat . . . where you are*: in *Through the Looking-Glass*, the Red Queen forces Alice to rush to stay on the spot:

'Now! Now!' cried the Queen. 'Faster! Faster!' And they went so fast that at last they seemed to skim through the air, hardly touching the ground with their feet, till suddenly, just as Alice was getting quite exhausted, they stopped, and she found herself sitting on the ground, breathless and giddy . . .

Alice looked round her in great surprise. 'Why, I do believe we've been under this tree the whole time! Everything's just as it was!'

'Of course it is,' said the Queen. 'What would you have it?'

'Well, in *our* country,' said Alice, still panting a little, 'you'd generally get to somewhere else – if you ran very fast for a long time as we've been doing.'

'A slow sort of country!' said the Queen. 'Now, *here*, you see, it takes all the running *you* can do, to keep in the same place . . .' (*The Complete Works of Lewis Carroll* (London, 1939), pp. 151–2)

99 *this Dream*: Yeats's *A Vision*, which was privately printed in 1925.

105–106 *Besides, I do not really like . . . 'Up the Boys'*: cf. WE's sentiments about Auden and his acolytes in 'Just a Smack at Auden'.

110–11 *other curly-headed toy's / The superrealistic comp.*: a reference to Dylan Thomas, whom he had met by Winter 1936. The curly-headed Thomas, in a letter to Vernon Watkins postmarked 20 April 1936, mentioned some recent 'Nights Out' with characters including 'old Bill Empson'; and he went on: 'Empson, by the way, has been very kind to me in print, in a review of the Faber anthology [*The Faber Book of Modern Verse*, ed. Michael Roberts (London, 1936)], saying, quite incorrectly, though than which etc. there could be nothing nicer for my momentary vanity, that little or nothing of importance, except for Owen and Eliot, comes between Eliot and ME. Ho! Ha' (*The Collected Letters of Dylan Thomas*, ed. Paul Ferris (London and Melbourne, 1985), p. 222). WE was to report his first personal impressions of the wildly entertaining young Thomas – whose work he admired a great deal – in 'A London Letter':

I was shocked recently by a Welsh poet who turned up in Kleinfeld's [Fitzroy Tavern, run by 'Papa' Kleinfeld] saying he needed money and had had an offer as checker-in at a Welsh mine; this was very absurd, and he had much more cozy plans to become a grocer. What with the Welsh nationalism, the vague and balanced but strong political interests of this man, the taste for violence in his writing, and the way he was already obviously exhausting his vein of poetry about events which involved the universe but happened inside his skin, it seemed to me that being a checker-in was just what he wanted; and I shouted at him for some time, against two talkers I should otherwise have been eager to hear, to tell him that he was wasting his opportunities as a Welshman and ought to make full use of a country in which he could nip across the classes. I still think that something like that ought to happen to him, but no doubt he was right in saying that the plan was no good.

(For WE's later, generously enthusiastic writings on Thomas, see *A*, pp. 382–412.) WE's critical characterization of Thomas's poetry as 'superrealistic' – a term occasionally used in the 1930s by Herbert Read and David Gascoyne, and by Wyndham Lewis (who observed in *The Diabolical Principle* (London, 1931), 'The *infantile* is the ink between the Super-realists and Miss Stein, as it is between Miss Stein and Miss Loos' (p. 65)) – may be understood in the light of WE's later comment: '**I wish I could write magical poetry like Dylan Thomas, some of which (though much less I think than people often say) probably couldn't be explained in notes**' (*Modern Poetry*, ed. Friar and Brinnin, p. 498). '*Comp.*' is a schoolboy abbreviation of 'composition' – an essay.

121–4 *Yeats is adroit . . . / For dreams in quite another shape, / And Freud*: see note to epigraph above.

Given 'superrealistic' (l. 111), see also WE in 'Alice: Child as Swain':

The purpose of a dream on the Freudian theory is simply to keep you in an undisturbed state so that you can go on sleeping; in the course of this practical work you may produce something of more general value, but not only of one sort. Alice has, I understand, become a patron saint of the Surrealists, but they do not go in for Comic Primness, a sort of reserve of force, which is her chief charm. Wyndham Lewis avoided putting her beside Proust and Lorelei to be danced on as a debilitating child-cult (though she is a bit of a pragmatist too) . . . (*Pastoral*, p. 221)

WE had written to Richards from Tokyo on 18 February 1933:

I am stopping trying to do literary work: it seems too hollow, for some reason [added in the margin: 'vapid remark. Time I went to China'.] It would be worth while doing some translation into Basic, but very little else. I have just lost all my lecture notes, with the pleasure which losing things I am irritated with always gives me. There was a point about the use of the word *dream* in Yeats which I should like to try and remember for you.

1 – vision from God telling absolute truth.
2 – conception of a way to live, write a poem, or solve a definite problem.
3 – conception of something valuable in terms of beliefs which one can no longer believe.
dream —— 4 – state of reverie in which one is protected so that such conceptions may be hoped from it.
5 – state of reverie useful as escape.
6 – daydream admitted to be debilitating.
7 – Freudian dream that sets to work unconscious forces admitted as lower, but claimed as a source of knowledge of oneself.

7 gets back to the 'mysterious forces' of 1 and 2. The 'romantic' Yeats manner always implies 'You've got to be high-toned if you're to read this: I don't write for the sort of man who thinks I mean a *nasty* dream – and if he does think that about *my* dreams he's probably wrong'. In his later use of *dream* he includes all the meanings –

> The soul remembering its loneliness
> Shudders in many cradles
>   – business man etc –
>   cradle within cradle, and all in flight and all
> Deformed because there is no deformity
> But saves us from a dream [Cf. note on epigraph]

1–4 saves us from a conception of value – which would involve powerful effort.
5–7 saves us from a conception of desire which would jolt us out of the order at present achieved.

Very tactful of him to keep his language and leave room for the Freudians in it: the dream is no longer necessarily admired. A sort of complacence in him makes him able to be a very intelligent poet, don't you think? (Richards Collection, Magdalene College, Cambridge)

138–40 *bombs. The railway . . . not / Take aim*: the final, unpublished 'Letter from China' that WE drafted at Nan-Yüeh begins: '**The Arts Departments are now leaving the Sacred Mountain, and the combined universities of Peking are going round to Yunnan-fu** [Kunming in Yunnan province] **via Hongkong, bag, baggage, and students; they will probably have to build a combined university when they get there. The whole thing is on a hearty scale, and comes just as the Japanese give one of their chivalrous announcements that they mean to give the railway a thorough bombing. I live very much out of the world here, and haven't seen the chancellor since his interview with Chiang Kai Shek about the move . . .**' As to the supposed inability of the Japanese bombers to hit their targets, he related in 'China on the March' an anecdote based on an authentic personal encounter – albeit through the 'character' of 'B', a businessman with 'socialist sympathies' who has been 'employed by one of the big British firms in China':

If you remember before the fall of Canton the Japanese went on for six months trying to break the railways from Canton, and all the Japanese had to do was to hit one of the bridges, but the plain truth was that they couldn't hit them. Month after month went by and still the Japanese airmen couldn't get a bomb on the bridges. Now I was sitting in Hongkong talking to some British Air Force men, and what these men said was 'It's disgusting. They're letting the whole show down.' What they meant by The Show was the profession of bombing, in which they were engaged. This was before the European war, but they'd go on talking like that whatever the war was . . . This little story isn't surprising to you, but it was to me. The striking thing if you have been living among Chinese before you heard these Englishmen talk is that no Chinese would ever possibly talk like that. There is no tradition in China of the salaried professional man proud of his profession. In the old days a man who passed the literary examinations was an administrator, good at any kind of Government work. But he wasn't anything like a professional doctor or a professional engineer.

144–6 *wrong . . . / And had I speeches they were song*: alludes to Yeats's 'The Phases of the Moon', l. 30: 'True song, though speech'. Furthermore, the rhymes here are likely to have been inspired by Shelley's 'Julian and Maddalo' (1818), ll. 544–6: 'Most wretched men / Are cradled into poetry by wrong; / They learn in suffering what they teach in song'. The association may have been triggered by the idea of *cradling* which links it with the epigraph from 'The Phases of the Moon'; see also WE's note 1 to 'Warning to undergraduates', and his allusion in a letter to Ronald Bottrall of 26 January 1937: 'I want to advise you strongly not to throw up the Singapore job unless you are quite sure of a better one in England, and I don't well know what it would be. It seemed to suit you very well . . . And Singapore is certainly better than e.g. Hull or Newcastle, as well as more paying. The only plausible reason for leaving it would be to learn in suffering what you might then teach in song, but this would be the sin of ambition' (Harry Ransom Humanities Research Center, University of Texas at Austin).

161–2 *Not nationalism nor yet race / Poisons the mind*: WE rated nationalism as 'an infectious and invincible disease' – 'a senseless thing' – 'but empirically,' he believed, 'it is the strongest thing in international politics' (draft letter to Robert Herring, 14 July 1938). But he saw it also as China's most potent weapon: it left him in no doubt that China would eventually win the war. 'If the Chinese can nurse up a nationalism they are all right,' he wrote in mid-1938; 'after all we [the British] can't rule Ireland or Palestine against nationalism' (undated letter to his mother). As to the vexed subject of race, he wrote at this time: 'race is a real thing, and the fantastic mixture of races in Japan is a very successful one; only it leaves them culturally part of China' (typescript draft of a 'Letter from China').

173–6 *Marx . . . Saul*: 'In the Hebraic triumvirate of Samuel, Saul, and David against the Philistines Empson may see the later group of Marx, Lenin, and Stalin against the bourgeoisie, or the communist trio of Lenin, Trotsky, and Stalin. No exact relationships seem to fit, however, for if Marx is Samuel or even Saul, Stalin is surely no David. Empson, perhaps siding with Trotsky against Stalin, may view Stalin as Saul persecuting David. (Trotsky had fled to Mexico in January 1937 . . .)' (Willis, p. 396).

178 saying that] saying *CP*; WE so instructed Parsons on 29 May 1956: 'insert *that*, "that they would not fall"' (Reading).

186 *dung a desert for a rose*: cf. Isaiah 35: 1: 'The wilderness and the solitary place shall be glad for them; and the desert shall rejoice, and blossom as the rose'; and George Herbert, 'Providence' (1633), l. 69: 'Sheep eat the grass, and dung the ground for more.'

189–94 *Economists . . . not disclose*: cf. WE's speculative remarks in a letter to Michael Roberts (8 August 1939), responding to a synopsis of a book Roberts was proposing to write on modern culture in crisis:

I have just read through the outline again . . . and think it's very good, though I seem to have no comments to make. Except that the economic muckup is surely more prominent than you make it. It looks quite likely that you won't get your war over there after all, but then what on earth is going to happen when the disarmament programs stop? It seems bound to mean the biggest slump yet recorded. If by chance or by being right the Russians are then able to keep up an air of prosperity they will have very strong claims. I suppose it's always possible that somebody might suddenly understand economics, sufficiently to hold the thing together, but at present I don't see how any one can get away from the economic antimonies as the fatal ones. After all the Totalitarians have done a very hearty mental change without getting away from them. Nor do I see how your completely industrialized state can ever happen or what it would be. It seems clear that some kind of communism would be the only working arrangement that could give hope of a stable state (if that is wanted) other than a simple agricultural one. People keep saying now that Russia is just like Germany, and morally it may be, but one claims to escape slumps and the other can't. I am not convinced of the claim anyhow, but it seems the main subject about the future of the world. (courtesy of Janet Adam Smith)

192 *The thread . . . the monster*: on the myth of Theseus and his penetration of the labyrinth, see 'Myth' and notes.

217 *Pandarus school of trout*: literally, a trout-pool near the college buildings; figuratively, as the reference to 'Pandarus' indicates, the trick of catching trout by tickling them is often used as a metaphor for seduction or pimping. Shakespeare in *Troilus and Cressida* has the scurrilous Thersites say, with reference to Troilus: 'He'll tickle it for his concupy' (V.ii.180). Cf. *Measure for Measure* (I.ii.91): 'Groping for trouts in a peculiar river', and Maria's relish at the prospect of entrapping Malvolio, in *Twelfth Night* (II.v.25): 'Here comes the trout that must be caught with tickling.'

219-20 *The Golden Bough ... crucifixions*: Sir James George Frazer discusses human sacrifice and crucifixion throughout *The Golden Bough* (12 vols., 1890–1915).

223 *tempest-tossed*: in view of the rhymes on '-ow' throughout this stanza, culminating in 'flow' (l. 234), the primary point of reference would seem to be *Romeo and Juliet*, wherein Capulet chides his desperate daughter for her weeping: 'The barque thy body is, / Sailing in this salt flood; the winds thy sighs, / Who, raging with thy tears and they with them, / Without a sudden calm will overset / Thy tempest-tossèd body' (III.v.133–7). However, given 'Scattering' in l. 224, WE's usage may also subsume a memory of Cowper, 'On the receipt of my mother's picture' (1790), ll. 102–5: 'Me howling winds drive devious, tempest toss'd, / Sails ript, seams op'ning wide, and compass lost, / And day by day some current's thwarting force / Sets me more distant from a prosp'rous course.' (When WE's great-grandfather, the Rev. John Empson (1787–1861) – best known as the 'Flying Parson', on account of his insatiable passion for hunting – set himself to place some verses on a memorial to his parents, he chose to make use of a scarcely modified version of four lines (108–11) from this Cowper poem. The tablet is in Scawby Church, Lincolnshire.)

226-33 *Man moves ... and train*: Shanghai fell in November 1938, and Nanjing in December, so that Chiang Kai-shek had to retreat deep inland. On the Sacred Mountain, the refugee universities awaited the progress of events in the major arena. But the Japanese forward line had encroached upon Hunan, and bombs started to fall on Changsha. The universities had to evacuate the area and move further south, to the province of Yunnan.

The Japanese seized Nan-Yüeh, the humble village that had become a towering symbol of Chinese intellectual resistance, in 1944.

234 *streams will chatter as they flow*: mountain streams, but also streams of refugees making their way to south-west China. Cf. WE's observations on a **'pantheistic quatrain'** from Henry Vaughan's 'The Bird', which he construes as **'at once wit and nature-study'**:

> So hills and valleys into singing break;
> And though poor stones have neither speech nor tongue,
> While active winds and streams both run and speak,
> Yet stones are deep in admiration.

Compared to *speech* and *speak*, *tongue* and *run* seem to be paired by sound rather than by sense; till one remembers that *tongues* may be said to 'run on', and that *streams* possess *tongues* in that they are *running*. It is by means of this verbal echo, which last-century critics would have regarded as a matter of Pure Sound, that the subdued puns are passed into the mind. (*ST*, p. 174)

Let it go

First published in *CP 1949*; written during the war.

For *Listen*, WE noted simply: ' "Let It Go" is about stopping writing poetry.'

On *Harvard*, he mused that the poem is 'perhaps too portentous . . . This little poem . . . is slightly self-important, perhaps, but there it is: I would not call it untrue. I think many poets had better have stopped writing.'

In *Ambiguity of William Empson*, WE commented: 'There was a poem about stopping writing which is very brief. I stopped writing because . . . I did write some more and then decided I didn't want to print them, and in a quite involuntary way I found that it no longer seemed to be working, but the reasons for that I don't know. So it was in a way discussing why I stopped writing verse – though I did write a little bit of it for a fair length of time really, I suppose. But it was about the stopping time.'

On *Contemporary Poets Reading Their Own Poems*, he remarked: 'It's been kindly praised by friends. It seems to me so slight.'

Similarly, late in 1981, when he was asked if the poem could be reprinted in the periodical *Spectacular Diseases* (no. 6), as an epigraph to 'Omaggio a William Empson, Il Miglior Fabbro' – a poem 'composed by systematic chance methods' by the American Jackson Mac Low – Empson curiously responded to the editor Robert Vas Dias on 1 December 1981 (though this letter was not actually sent):

Reading that poem feels like baby-watching an imbecile child, oozing at every hole and playing with itself incessantly, and trying to attract attention by untruthful cries of pain. A request from a hospital for such people, with photographs, arrived by the same post. My poem had said 'You don't want madhouse', and perhaps I deserve to get this eager reply 'O yes we do. Like mad.'

Still, the poem is already a success in America, from what you say, so if I say Yes I am not responsible for its appearance. I hope you won't imply, in a preface for instance, that I think it anything but hopelessly bad. With that understanding, it would seem fussy not to agree.

See also Morelli, pp. 142–3; *TGA*, pp. 219–21.

TITLE: Hawthorn, who explores the poem in 'Commitment in the Poetry of William Empson', pp. 27–9, adduces the example of Samuel Johnson's obsessive fear of madness, when describing his stroke, in a letter to Mrs Thrale (19 June 1783): 'I felt a confusion and indistinctness in my head which lasted, I suppose about half a minute; I was alarmed and prayed God, that however he might affect my body he would spare my understanding.' Johnson closed his letter with these words: 'I am almost ashamed of this querulous letter, but now it is written let it go.'

3,6 *were* / *there*: a perfect rhyme in WE pronunciation.

4 *contradictions cover such a range*: in a review (1939) of *Modern Poetry and the Tradition*, WE challenged Cleanth Brooks's reading of what he (WE) called

the frozen agony of *The Waste Land* . . . He denies that there is any 'despair' in the poem, and thinks critics who have said there was have misunderstood it. To be sure, it does not say that people can never be happy, but the poetry of flat contradiction is almost a clinical thing; it can only be done well as a way of treating yourself for a terrible state of mind. We had a lot of people in England trying to do that after Eliot . . . it seems to me that Mr Brooks's approach tends to treat the concentration of horror as no more than the balanced tone of good sense. (*A*, pp. 341–2)

6 *You don't want madhouse*: WE remarked, in *SCW*: 'A surprising number of the great writers went mad, and most of them feared to; indeed, the more you respect reason the more you must fear the irrational' (p. 169).

6 *whole thing*: cf. WE's comment in *Milton's God* (pp. 17–18), with reference to Blake's famous claim that Milton 'was of the Devil's party without knowing it': Recent studies have made it clear that Blake meant the whole thing by such utterances, not merely that Milton's Satan was good but that his God was bad.'

Thanks for a Wedding Present

First published in *CP 1949*.

The necklace and dedicatory poem were given to WE and Hetta Empson for their wedding in December 1941 by Dr Gilbert A. Back, who had been WE's landlord at 71 Marchmont Street, London, in the mid-1930s (see note to ll. 73–92 of 'Bacchus').

See Ricks, pp. 204–5, and *TGA*, pp. 221–2.

2 *de-Gauss*: a joke on the name of Karl Friedrich Gauss (1777–1855), German mathematician and natural philosopher, whose surname is used to designate the unit of magnetic induction; since the poem was written in 1941, *de-Gaussing* (signifying 'insulating from magnetic powers') could be regarded as analogous to de-lousing.

4 *Load of Hay*: the name of a public house almost opposite the Empsons' basement flat in Belsize Park, London.

Sonnet

First published, as 'Machine Age', in *Poetry* (Chicago) 59 (February 1942), 266; reprinted in *Tribune*, 17 December 1943, p. 19; reprinted, as 'Sonnet', in *The War Poets*, ed. Oscar Williams (New York, 1945), p. 337. In a letter (15 November 1944) to Oscar Williams, who had asked contributors for comments on the subject of poetry and war, WE responded: 'I . . . **can't think of any comments worth making about poetry and war**' (Kenyon College Archives).

CP: **This** *free* **I am afraid only sounds an offensively false use of the great emotive term, implying merely that the pygmies and the rest of us had better be 'left alone'. This may be true of pygmies, but I was trying to give the word the impact of a contradiction; as in** *Letter IV*, **where it probably doesn't come off either. The pygmy method of singing (on the sound-track of an excellent travel film) sounded spontaneous though it was a grotesque and extreme example of collectivism.**

'Machine Age', the original title, may have been meant as a reply to Michael Roberts's observation, in his introduction to the anthology *New Signatures* (1932): 'Rural poetry in recent years has been, in general, a cowardly escape into the past, whilst urban poetry, the poetry of the machine age, has seemed, even to intelligent and conscientious critics, abrupt, discordant, intellectual. It is hard to find words relating to city life which are such powerful emotive symbols as those which poets have used for centuries' (p. 8).

For *Listen* WE wrote: ' "Sonnet" leaves the paradox of freedom too much in the air, but the pygmies did sing well on this plan, in a travel film.'

See Morelli, pp. 85–6; *TGA*, pp. 222–4.

2 thinkers like the nations getting caught] thinkers, like the nations, getting caught, *1943*
4–5 machine. / It can be swung, is what these hopers mean,] machine: / It can be swung – is what these hopers mean – *1943*
7 ball. It] ball; it *1943*
9–10 *A more heartening fact . . . appalling stubbornness*: cf. WE's remark, in a review of W. H. Auden's *Another Time* (1940): '**What is heartening about people is their appalling stubbornness and the strong roots of their various cultures, rather than the ease with which you can convert them and make them happy and good. Probably a whole political outlook can turn on this**' (*A*, p. 373).
11 ten] three *1943*
11–13 *The gigan- / . . . all its booths*: cf. WE's observations in *Milton's God*:

When I first went to teach in Sheffield one of my colleagues kindly took me round a local museum, and we passed through a sheer hall containing nothing but Sheffield Plate. This caused intense depression; then we turned a corner and faced two huge ivory tusks, carved all over for the appalling and splendid court of Benin; not a surprising thing to find there, as Benin artworks were distributed widely after the sack of the capital (1897). They raised my spirits no end. I report this elementary reaction to point out that it is not an affectation or a perversion to feel so; we cannot help doing it; chiefly because we need to feel that, whatever we do with our small lives, the rest of the world is still going on and exercising the variety of its forces. (p. 276)

'The ages change, and they impose their rules'

Written (almost certainly) in 1949, not long before the accession to power of the Communists and the inauguration of the People's Republic of China on 1 October 1949; first published in *RB*.

Concerned with the new balance of power between the superstates, the USA and the USSR, this vatic villanelle may be glossed by means of the one surviving page of a letter that WE addressed to the American critic Stanley Edgar Hyman, who in 1948 had written of *Pastoral*, 'Empson draws heavily on sociology, chiefly of the Marxist variety'; and again, 'the book is implicitly Marxist throughout, something that only Kenneth Burke seems to have perceived' (*Armed Vision*, pp. 248–9).

... patently lunatic (one of them says that you mustn't get into a bath unless it is superheated steam and the other says you mustn't unless it is a solid block of ice); and the only hope for the world is to find an independently strong country which will be able to refuse to listen to the nonsense talked by either side. Such was my opinion before my return to China in 1947, and the later events have not altered it; of course Mao Tse Tung has to prevent petty gossip by taking his [Stalin's] side firmly in the present chatter, but he is still free to follow the interests of his own country. The reason is simply one of geography; China is not Bulgaria; in fact I suspect both America and Russia in a world war would be anxious *not* to have China as an ally into which they must sink troops and material as into a bog, whichever side the Government of China was backing. Of course if China induces Malaya to go Communist that bankrupts the British, but there are a number of natural stops against it, and the same for the Dutch in Java. Once you get international trade reopened from China on a firm basis you will no longer have a simple world war situation, please either tell lies for Russia or for China, and the whole assumption that we must have a world war depends on this simple opposition between two colonial European powers whose theories were both worked out in London. It is too silly to tell me that everybody who matters has got to be killed because these two colonial powers have made it a point of honour to destroy everything that knows better as well as each other ... Nobody has anything to gain from the muchtalkedof third world war, and if I, in my small way, can do anything to prevent the belief that it is inevitable I can do it better here than elsewhere. I will stay here if I am allowed. Earlier in this long paragraph I mentioned a possible censor, but I take it that this kind of talk is not too offensive in China. I am entirely in favour of the Chinese revolution, and think it less revolutionary than the British one; my deviation is merely that I suspect Stalin of nationalism, and I was saying so the other night to a Chinese communist who did not regard it as an unbearable point of view. From the other side, my deviation is that if Britain fights China I am a Conscientious Objector, solely on patriotic grounds, to try and improve my country's relations with China, and I think I would stick to that though I don't like to say what will happen; what I mean is that Britain and China want to survive, whereas the two lunatic colonials America and Russia haven't got anything worth keeping and only want to win, and both have the power to destroy everything worth keeping.

Such is the reason why I think I am right to stay here, and try to handle the Chinese set-up. It makes a tedious introduction but I want you to think me a decent man. The following paragraphs will discuss why I think you a decent man.

I did not think you one when I first read your book, at the Kenyon College Summer School last year. I am so old now that your praise seemed to me only a fact worth noticing for its public effects, good or bad. Your praise of me as a Marxist critic has (very falsely perhaps) given me a strong leg in the Peking area. You might regret what you did here.

Another piece of evidence figures in a letter that WE wrote to his wife on 13 July 1948, when he was in Gambier, Ohio (he would return to witness the Communist takeover of Peking at the end of the year):

Last Wednesday I had a public lecture in my turn on criticism and suchlike and started off by telling them how brave the [Chinese] students were against the secret police [of the Nationalist government of Chiang Kai-shek] the Americans sponsor, and would not take food from the Americans because they are so wicked, and so far as there was any military danger from the Chinese communists for the Americans in case of war with Russia it was entirely the result of American policy. I do not know how far you would approve of my remarks, because I said that the Russians were extremely like the Americans, both tending to be extremist out of raw national vanity, and both having a bad tradition of mob violence and police cruelty owing to their rapid growth. This was anti-Russian enough to make it go down fairly comfortably. But anyway it was all rather a flop, I thought, because though warmly supported by Matthiessen at question time to start off with, it was afterwards simply ignored, and the talk was mainly about the American educational system, oddly enough. They are highly professionalized people who regard politics as a separate business, and any attempt to make them feel responsible for American politics is likely to slide off them almost without being noticed. I had decided I was prepared to become uneligible for American jobs if necessary to make this kind of point, and feel now that my little effort was an anticlimax. There is a strong feeling of unreality in this whole fuss about criticism; but it ought to be a step towards educating the Americans as far as it goes, I think.

16 *There is world and time*: 'Had we but world enough and time' (Marvell, 'To His Coy Mistress', l. 1).

Chinese Ballad

First published, as 'Chinese Peasant Song', in *Nine* (Summer/Autumn 1952), p. 316; it appeared above a 'Note by translator in a letter' (WE had presumably written from Peking to G. S. Fraser, whose article on the criticism, 'Mr Empson and Poetic Truth', followed on pp. 317–25):

I am sending you a tiny bit of translation (the Chinese is a re-doing into modern peasant dialect of a classical theme, still a live superstition, but of course this linguistic angle can't appear in the English); it seemed to me to fall into English ballad style as world ballad style, and there is only one piece of fudging, the lines about dolls helping children, but the Chinese word here does mean toys for children, and carries the pathetic idea that they would rather have children, so I would claim it is word for word though it is two lines into four each time. The stream turns where he crosses because it is broader there hence shallower.

Reprinted, as 'Chinese Ballad', in *New Statesman and Nation* (6 December 1952).

CP: A bit from a long ballad by Li Chi, a Communist who collected country ballads during his other activities. It was written in 1945 in North Shensi, and has since been made into a much praised opera. This bit was considered technically interesting because the theme had been used in classical style, first, I am told, by the Yuan poet Chao Meng-fu, and was now transposed or restored into popular style. The translation is word for word, so far as I can know from simply being given the meanings of the characters; I added the bit about children, but I understand that is only like working a footnote into the text, because the term specifically means dolls for children. He crosses the stream where it turns because it is wider therefore shallower there. He is fighting the Japanese.

WE delighted in this poem:
(i) 'I want to give a bit of translation from Chinese ballad poetry, which has nothing to do with me except that I was delighted when it was pushed into my hands to find it falling straight into English ballad style . . . Perhaps I haven't been bothering enough about the criterion for metaphysical poetry in these remarks, but it seems to me a wider idea than critics usually make out. I think, in this ballad, it is very fine metaphysical poetry at the end, when the clumsy little doll is to wait, through all eternity, just for a few days' (*Poems of William Empson*).
(ii) 'The author [of the ballad] was moving around in the north under the Japanese Occupation, and collected peasant ballads . . . The translation is word for word except for the two lines about children, which seem to be part of the point as the word specifically means dolls for children – I do not know the language

but could ask about details' (*Poetry London–New York* 1:1 (March–April 1956), 11).

(iii) In *Poetry at the Mermaid*, he added: 'I was asked to translate it by a man who was doing a critique. I burst into tears when I found it just fell into international ballad metre. I was taught exactly what the characters mean.'

(iv) On *Harvard*, he remarked: 'It's not by me at all, you see, but I always feel it clears the palate after a reading of my stuff. It is the international ballad, and very surprisingly it really is metaphysical poetry.'

(v) 'I was in Peking for the Siege of Peking, teaching there, and after the Communist victory this ballad was printed, it's as long as a novel . . . and was very highly thought of, but it has very little to do with politics, you understand' (*Ambiguity of William Empson*).

The ballad is a translation of part of a narrative poem entitled *Wang Kuei and Li Hsiang-hsiang*, by Li Chi, who was born in a mountain village in Tangho District, Honan province, in 1921. In 1937, when Japan invaded China, Li Chi entered the Anti-Japanese Political and Military Academy at Yenan, which was then the political centre of the liberated areas. From 1939 to 1942 he worked as a political instructor in the People's Liberation Army, and from 1943 engaged in administrative work in local government. *Wang Kuei and Li Hsiang-hsiang* was written in 1945. His later writings include *Seventeen Short Poems*, a further long poem *The Chrysanthemum Stone*, and short stories and tales for children.

The complete poem is far more directly political than WE perhaps realized, since he presumably lacked a full translation: it covers the period from 1930 to the 1940s. After suffering years of oppression from Landlord Tsui, who mercilessly tortures Wang Kuei and who attempts to violate the beautiful and upright Li Hsiang-hsiang, the peasant lovers find common cause in their country's need to repel the Japanese invader; they reap their final reward when the Red Army liberates the rural communities, whereupon Landlord Tsui is taken away for punishment.

An authorized version of the section of the poem that WE renders so magically runs as follows:

> Ev'ry week or fortnight, when he was free,
> He would ask leave to go home Hsiang-hsiang to see.
> And she'd see him off to the end of the glen,
> When he went back to his corps again.
> Rich brown mud in the valley lay.
> 'Let's make two figures out of the clay.
> Make one of you and make one of me,
> Make them as lifelike as they can be.
> Break them and mix them and make them anew,
> A figure of me and a figure of you.

Then I'll have something of you in me,
And something of me in you there'll be.'
When the figures are finished, Hsiang-hsiang says,
'Come back, love, to see me in a few days.'
(*Wang Kuei and Li Hsiang-hsiang*, trans. Yang Hsien-yi and Gladys Yang (Peking:
  Foreign Languages Press, 1954), p. 24; courtesy of Yang Hsien-yi)

WE translated one further, shocking passage from the poem which survives
as a stanza typed at the head of a fair copy of his ballad (Empson Papers):

They dig the graveyards for the bones
  To grind to flour.
At last some mothers stew their children's flesh,
  Contented to devour.

Curiously, there is no exact equivalent for those lines in the official translation;
the passage that is closest in meaning comes at the beginning of the work – a
description of the effects of the famine of 1930:

When plants were gone, tree bark they found,
Into coarse flour the bark was ground.
Though March's dead in coffins lay,
No burial had those who died in May.
The grain in the barns was rotting away,
No end to the grain of Landlord Tsui.
Like homeless dogs were the starving poor,
But the landlord did not care a straw.

It is possible that WE himself chose to sensationalize that passage (especially if
he was supplied with a crude translation which implied the inescapable horror of
his version); it is equally possible that the censors of Communist China in the
early 1950s insisted upon a modification of the original to suppress the dread
revelation that Chinese peasants could ever have resorted to cannibalism – even
in conditions of insufferable famine.
  See Ricks, pp. 206–7.

5 mud is yellow, deep,] mud is yellow, broad, *1952;* **yellow mud is deep** *typescript*
in Columbia University Libraries, Rare Book and Manuscript Library: Ms Coll
PL-NY ('Poetry London-New York')
6 *where the stream turns:* in the Columbia typescript draft WE included a 'possible
footnote' which adds an interpretative detail: '**He crosses the stream at a bend**
because the swing of the current makes it broader and hence shallower there. But

of course the point of the detail is that she is turning like the stream as well as sticking like the mud.'

11–12 *Were there no magic . . . not thrive*: 'The term for *dolls* does specifically mean dolls for children; the young couple dare not have children until the war is over, while the guerrilla fighting is still going on, but they hope to have children later. That is almost like working a footnote into the text: I do fudge a little bit there' (*Harvard*). Cf. WE's observation in 'The Narrative Poems' (1968): 'A marriage does indeed require mutual accommodation, and love may genuinely receive "a mystical reinforcement" on the birth of a child' (*Essays on Shakespeare*, p. 21).

13 you have] you *1952*

14 shall] may *Harvard*

17 So] Then *1952*

17 shall] will *1952*

The Birth of Steel: A Light Masque

First published in *Sheffield University Gazette Jubilee Number* no. 21 (November 1954), 5–7. The fuller stage-directions of the original version (Department of Music, University of Sheffield) are more descriptive and helpfully expressive than WE's minimal stage-directions in *CP*.

On 27 October 1954 the Queen and the Duke of Edinburgh visited the University of Sheffield in order to inaugurate its Jubilee Session. No other reigning Sovereign had visited the principal university buildings since King Edward VII opened them in 1905. Six months before the Queen's visit, the Vice-Chancellor, Professor J. M. Whittaker, put to his recently appointed Professor of English Literature a 'general idea' with a much longer history – to celebrate the Queen's visit by reviving the masques with which Elizabeth I was greeted at Cambridge in 1564 and at Oxford in 1566 and 1592. Would WE assist in the creation of a new masque by 'writing such parts of it as would be spoken or sung'? The vocal part should be in English and not Latin, Whittaker suggested; it should have 'literary value' and be in modern idiom rather than a pastiche of Elizabethan poetry. 'At any rate,' he gentled WE, 'I hope you will turn the matter over in your mind and perhaps we could have a talk about it.'

As Roma Gill reported in *The Times Literary Supplement* (31 July 1987), WE advised the Vice-Chancellor that Elizabethan masquers would have told the Queen 'that she was God, and that she had invented steel'. According to WE himself (in an unpublished interview with Christopher Norris and David Wilson), the Vice-Chancellor responded without temerity: ' "Tell her she's God again" . . . And so I did. I thought this was magnificent Yorkshire behaviour.' WE forged ahead and sketched the outline of *The Birth of Steel* within a few days. The plot tells how a medieval alchemist – inevitably named Smith – is baffled in his attempts to fashion a steel sword; mocked by his minions, he appeals to Minerva, Goddess of Wisdom, who thereupon enters in majesty and introduces the instruments of modern science.

The open-air production took full shape during WE's summer absence at the School of Letters in Bloomington, Indiana. The student producer, Peter Cheeseman (now Director of the New Victoria Theatre, North Staffordshire), together with the stage manager Alan Curtis, bulked up WE's spare and insufficiently dramatic verse with 'alchemical mumbo-jumbo'; the composer Gilbert Kennedy ensured the grandness of the occasion with a score that incorporated blues and jazz rhythms, solemn chorales, and a triumphal tune to accompany Minerva's descent in a golden car; and the architect Alec Daykin designed a covered stage and backcloth. The volunteer orchestra numbered sixty-six, with a large brass section provided by the Sheffield Transport Band; and a huge chorus included university undergraduates, students from the City of Sheffield Training College and members of the Lydgate-Crosspool Choir. Such was the scale of the operation that the three groups – student orchestra, Transport Band, chorus – had to rehearse in separate venues, and they came together only just before the performance. The assembled company filled half the quadrangle, with the conductor's rostrum being sited directly above a central fountain. Pilkington Brothers produced a magnificent bullet-proof glass pavilion for the Queen, and so completed a setting – just as WE had prefigured – fit for her audience with a goddess (Pamela Brown, a statuesque student contralto, playing Minerva).

'I have just come back from my first hearing of the Masque for the Queen rehearsed with full orchestra,' WE wrote to his wife Hetta in an undated letter,

and I must say it sounds staggeringly magnificent; I feel rather like The Sorceror's Apprentice. A goddess (such is the text) descends from heaven, addresses the Queen personally, and says the Queen *is* the goddess, a spirit everywhere diffused, who created Sheffield and personally invented the entire technology of the steel industry. About two hundred people take part in the performance, counting orchestra and choir, and it is performed to the Queen sitting alone in front, high in a large glass cage. A certain number of spectators, of whom Hetta might be one, are allowed, but completely on the sides or peeping out of windows. I shouldn't think that any English royalty has received such extravagant flattery for three hundred years.

Of course you could look at it as a learned graceful memory of how they treated the old Elizabeth; but they are taking to it so very big and solemn; it seems another step towards reviving positive worship of the British monarchy. I have been shouting to get some of the little jokes back, and warning them that otherwise 'people may think it fulsome'. Not that that makes much difference.

The buildings alone for this fifteen minute performance are a pretty startling extravagance. I do feel it is rather a curiosity, which you might be sorry to have missed. I can't promise that we would both be presented to the Queen.

A month later, when requesting that the masque should be included in *Collected Poems*, Empson told Parsons:

It is I believe the first time English royalty has been given the real old flattery for three hundred years – Minerva descends and says she is identical with Elizabeth, addressing her personally, and creates the steel industry; in effect the Queen is told in person that, besides being a spirit universally diffused, she herself personally invented the entire technology of the steel industry. The Queen thought it funny and was sweet about it, to me and the composer (the music was terrific) and the two speaking parts. It isn't meant to be good poetry but it's somehow politically right (I mean, it combines queen-worship with pro-worker sentiment and fair claims for the university back-room boys) and it is really rather a curiosity . . . Now that it has gone off so very well (though unknown outside Sheffield) I don't see why it shouldn't be put in the book. (6 November 1954; Reading)

In truth, very few such masques had been attempted or achieved since Thomas Arne's *Alfred* (1740), produced for the Prince of Wales and chiefly memorable for including the first performance of 'Rule, Britannia'. (The only comparable undertaking in the modern era was a satirical *Masque of Hope* devised by Oxford University Dramatic Society for Princess Elizabeth's visit to the University in May 1948: produced by Glynne Wickham, it had notably starred Robert Hardy, John Schlesinger and Kenneth Tynan; see Graham Binns, 'Hope's Half Century', *Oxford Today* 10:3 (Trinity issue, 1998), 30–32.) Seven months later, when the music critic of *The Times* (unaware of Sheffield's brave enterprise) suggested that the masque must take a modest form if it is to survive in the modern world, WE fairly claimed in a letter to the editor (13 June 1955): 'We followed the old formula without inhibitions . . . The performance took just under fifteen minutes, and no doubt the old full length would have been thought too much. But, apart from that, we did not find that the modern world requires "modesty" in a masque. We actually puzzled our heads over this question, and the modern world turned out to think that the more knock-down the show could be the better.'

In 1955 – moved by the unique historical significance of the occasion and the awful implications of addressing the Queen as a goddess – he wrote a memoir which went unpublished during his lifetime: see 'The Queen and I', *Strengths of Shakespeare's Shrew*, pp. 220–31.

INDEX OF TITLES AND FIRST LINES